Lecture Notes in Computer Scie

Commenced Publication in 1973
Founding and Former Series Editors:
Gerhard Goos, Juris Hartmanis, and Jan van Leeuwen

Sihan Qing   Hideki Imai   Guilin Wang (Eds.)

Information and Communications Security

9th International Conference, ICICS 2007
Zhengzhou, China, December 12-15, 2007
Proceedings

 Springer

Volume Editors

Sihan Qing
Chinese Academy of Sciences
Institute of Software
Beijing 100080, China
E-mail: qsihan@ss.pku.edu.cn

Hideki Imai
Chuo University
Faculty of Science and Engineering
Tokyo 112-8551, Japan
E-mail: h-imai@aist.go.jp

Guilin Wang
University of Birmingham
School of Computer Science
Birmingham B15 2TT, UK
E-mail: G.Wang@cs.bham.ac.uk

Library of Congress Control Number: 2007940029

CR Subject Classification (1998): E.3, G.2.1, D.4.6, K.6.5, F.2.1, C.2, J.1

LNCS Sublibrary: SL 4 – Security and Cryptology

ISSN   0302-9743
ISBN-10   3-540-77047-X Springer Berlin Heidelberg New York
ISBN-13   978-3-540-77047-3 Springer Berlin Heidelberg New York

Springer is a part of Springer Science+Business Media

springer.com

© Springer-Verlag Berlin Heidelberg 2007
Printed in Germany

Typesetting: Camera-ready by author, data conversion by Scientific Publishing Services, Chennai, India
Printed on acid-free paper   SPIN: 12198054   06/3180   5 4 3 2 1 0

Preface

The ninth International Conference on Information and Communications Security, ICICS 2007, was held in Zhengzhou, Henan Province, China, December 12–15, 2007. The ICICS conference series is an established forum that brings together people working in different fields of information and communications security from universities, research institutes, industry and government institutions, and gives the attendees the opportunity to exchange new ideas and investigate state-of-the-art developments. Among the preceding conferences, ICICS 1997 took place in Beijing, China; ICICS 1999 in Sydney, Australia; ICICS 2001 in Xi'an, China; ICICS 2002 in Singapore; ICICS 2003 in Huhehaote city, China; ICICS 2004 in Malaga, Spain; ICICS 2005 in Beijing, China; and ICICS 2006 in Raleigh, NC, USA. The proceedings were released as Volumes 1334, 1726, 2229, 2513, 2836, 3269, 3783, and 4307 of the Springer LNCS series, respectively.

ICICS 2007 was sponsored by the Chinese Academy of Sciences (CAS), the Beijing Natural Science Foundation of China under Grant No. 4052016 and the National Natural Science Foundation of China under Grant No. 60573042. The conference was organized and hosted by the Institute of Software, Chinese Academy of Sciences, Institute of Software and Microelectronics, Peking University, and ZhongAn Scientific and Technological Group in co-operation with the Informatization Office of Provincial Government of Henan, China and the International Communications and Information Security Association (ICISA).

In total, 222 papers from 19 countries and districts were submitted to ICICS 2007, and 38 were accepted covering multiple disciplines of information security and applied cryptography. From those papers accepted, 13 were from China, five from USA, four from Australia, three from Singapore, two each from Hong Kong, Iran, Japan and Taiwan, and one each from Belgium, Canada, Germany, Korea, and UK.

All submissions to ICICS 2007 were anonymously reviewed by at least two PC members, while the majority were commented on by three or more reviewers. The reviewing process took six weeks. We are grateful to the Program Committee, which was composed of 56 members from 19 countries and districts; we thank them as well as all external referees for their precious time and valued contributions to the tough and time-consuming reviewing process.

We thank Guilin Wang for his great work in arranging the publishing of the proceedings, Jiayong Cai for his great contribution to the pre-conference arrangements, and Dadong Li, Jianbo He, Qi Guo and others from the Organizing Committee for helping with many local details.

Finally, we would like to thank all the authors who submitted their papers to ICICS 2007, and all the attendees from all over the world.

October 2007

Sihan Qing
Hideki Imai

ICICS 2007

Ninth International Conference
on Information and Communications Security

Zhengzhou, Henan Province, China
December 12–15, 2007

Organized by

ZhongAn Scientific and Technological Group, China
Institute of Software, Chinese Academy of Sciences (CAS)
Institute of Software and Microelectronics, Peking University, China

In co-operation with

Informatization Office of Provincial Government of Henan, China
International Communications and Information Security Association (ICISA)

Sponsored by

Chinese Academy of Sciences (CAS)
Beijing Natural Science Foundation of China
National Natural Science Foundation of China (NNSFC)

General Chair

Sihan Qing   Chinese Academy of Sciences, China

Program Chairs

Sihan Qing   Chinese Academy of Sciences, China
Hideki Imai   University of Tokyo, Japan

Program Committee

Mikhail Atallah   Purdue University, USA
Vijay Atluri   Rutgers University, USA
Tuomas Aura   Microsoft, UK
Michael Backes   Saarland University, Germany
Thomas Berson   Anagram Laboratories, USA
Elisa Bertino   Purdue University, USA

S. Felix Wu   University of California at Davis, USA
Yongdong Wu   Institute for Infocomm Research, Singapore
Alec Yasinsac   Florida State University, USA
Lisa Yiqun Yin   Independent Security Consultant, USA
Moti Yung   Columbia University & RSA Labs, USA
Jianying Zhou   Institute for Infocomm Research, Singapore
Sencun Zhu   Pennsylvania State University, USA

Publication Chair

Guilin Wang   I^{2}R, Singapore and University of Birmingham,
                               UK

Organizing Committee Chair

Dadong Li   Zhongan Technology Group Co., Ltd., China

External Reviewers

Andreas Albers	Man Ho Au	Jean-Philippe Aumasson
Joonsang Baek	Matthias Berg	Abhilasha Bhargav-Spantzel
Colin Boyd	Chiara Braghin	Sherman S.M. Chow
Cas Cremers	Marco Cremonini	S. Delaune
Yi Deng	André Deuker	Jintai Ding
Anh Dinh	Oscar Esparza	Chun-I Fan
Gerardo Fernandez	Carmen Fernandez-Gago	Annalisa Ferrara
Ernest Foo	Lothar Fritsch	Liang Gu
Keisuke Hakuta	Matt Henricksen	Juan Hernández-Serrano
Yoshiaki Hori	Lei Hu	Qiong Huang
Xinyi Huang	Kitae Jeong	Qingguang Ji
Jianchun Jiang	Haimin Jin	Audun Josang
Jorge Nakahara Jr	Christian Kahl	Ashish Kamra
Khoongming Khoo	Jongsung Kim	Tae Hyun Kim
Steve Kremer	Jin Kwak	Fagen Li
Tieyan Li	Zhuowei Li	Phen-Lan Lin
Joseph K. Liu	Liang Low	Luke McAven
Shiho Moriai	Aybek Mukhamedov	José L. Muñoz-Tapia
Toru Nakanishi	Juan Gonzalez Nieto	Stanley R. de Medeiros Oliveira
Josep Pegueroles	Kun Peng	Hasan Qunoo
Havard Raddum	Mike Radmacher	Sanjay Rawat
Rodrigo Roman	Denis Royer	Eve Schooler
Chang Shuang	Leonie Simpson	Chunhua Su
Christophe Tartary	Hayo Thielecke	Duc Liem Vo
Falk Wagner	Zhiguo Wan	Chih-Hung Wang

Chuen-Ching Wang	Peng Wang	Qihua Wang
Shuhong Wang	Ralf-Philipp Weinmann	Zhe Xia
Guomin Yang	Yanjiang Yang	Wentao Zhang
Zhengfeng Zhang	Yunlei Zhao	Yongbin Zhou
Bo Zhu	Jan Zibuschka	

Table of Contents

Watermarking

Fast Implementations

Applied Cryptography

Cryptanalysis

Formal Analysis

System Security I

System Security II

Network Security

Time and Space Efficient Algorithms for Two-Party Authenticated Data Structures*

Charalampos Papamanthou and Roberto Tamassia

Department of Computer Science, Brown University

Abstract. Authentication is increasingly relevant to data management. Data is being outsourced to untrusted servers and clients want to securely update and query their data. For example, in database outsourcing, a client's database is stored and maintained by an untrusted server. Also, in simple storage systems, clients can store very large amounts of data but at the same time, they want to assure their integrity when they retrieve them. In this paper, we present a model and protocol for two-party authentication of data structures. Namely, a client outsources its data structure and verifies that the answers to the queries have not been tampered with. We provide efficient algorithms to securely outsource a skip list with logarithmic time overhead at the server and client and logarithmic communication cost, thus providing an efficient authentication primitive for outsourced data, both structured (e.g., relational databases) and semi-structured (e.g., XML documents). In our technique, the client stores only a constant amount of space, which is optimal. Our two-party authentication framework can be deployed on top of existing storage applications, thus providing an efficient authentication service. Finally, we present experimental results that demonstrate the practical efficiency and scalability of our scheme.

1 Introduction

Data authentication has lately been very important due to the expansion of the Internet and the continuing use of it in daily transactions. Data authentication provides assurance for integrity of data, namely that data have not been corrupted (for example modified or deleted) by an adversary. Imagine for example the following scenario. There a lot of internet companies that provide cheap storage space. Clients that use this service are assigned a special account which they can use to store, query and update their data. They basically *outsource* their data in the storage servers provided by the companies. This is an amazing service but raises the following security issue. How can the client be assured that the data it is putting in the storage servers have not been tampered with? Each time the client issues a query, it would like to be assured that the data it receives is consistent with the previous state and nobody has changed something. Hence the server (the entity where data have been outsourced) and the client

---

* This work was supported in part by IAM Technology, Inc. and by the National Science Foundation under grants IIS–0713403 and OCI–0724806.

S. Qing, H. Imai, and G. Wang (Eds.): ICICS 2007, LNCS 4861, pp. 1–15, 2007.

(the entity that outsources the data) have to engage in an efficient two-party authentication protocol during which the client can send updates and queries to the server and be able to verify the answers it is receiving. Ideally, we would like this protocol not only to be secure (the security definition will be given later) but also to involve low computational overhead at the client's side, low communication cost between the server and the client and possible low computational overhead at the server's side.

One application of this model is database outsourcing [9]. In database outsourcing, a third party database service provider offers software, hardware and network resources to host its clients' data. Since the clients outsource their databases in an environment which is susceptible to attacks, the security of the hosted data is a big issue. These attacks can be caused by malicious outsiders or by the service provider itself. In any case, the client should be able to verify the *integrity* of its data. Yet another important problem in database outsourcing, orthogonal to what we investigate in this paper (data integrity), is ensuring data secrecy and privacy [8, 10]. Another application of this model is converting the widely known authenticated data structures model [12, 19], which is a three-party model, to a two-party model, where we want to maintain the efficiency of the corresponding authenticated data structure and have the client execute both updates and queries.

In this paper, we develop and analyze time- and space-efficient algorithms for outsourcing an authenticated skip list [5]. We aim at providing integrity checking of answers received from the data structure (privacy is orthogonal to our approach). Our technique is further applicable to other hash-based authenticated data structures [1, 7, 13] (for example, Merkle trees or dynamic trees), given that we can develop the respective algorithms for the operations defined on the specific data structure. We present algorithms for outsourcing a skip list [18] that run (both on the client and on the server side) in logarithmic time (in the size of the outsourced data) and incur logarithmic communication cost. Our method requires constant space (a single hash value) at the client side, which is optimal.

1.1   Related Work

There is considerable previous work on authenticated data structures in the three-party model, where a data owner outsources the data to a server, which answers queries issued by clients on behalf of the data owner. See [19] for a survey. In particular, the authentication of outsourced databases in the three-party model, using an authenticated B-tree for the indices, is presented in [11]. Client storage bounds in the three-party model are discussed in [21].

In [4], data integrity in the two-party model and solutions for multi-authored dictionaries are explored, where users can efficiently validate a sequence of updates. The authentication of outsourced databases using signature schemes appears in [15, 16], where it is mentioned that this approach is inefficient due to the high cost of the client's computation and the fact that the client has to engage in multi-round protocol in order the perform an update. In [2], a method for outsourcing a dictionary is presented, where a skip list is stored by the server into a table of a relational database management system (DBMS) and the client issues SQL queries to the DBMS to retrieve authentication information. A related solution is presented in [14]. This DBMS-based approach relies on external-memory storage of authentication information. Thus, it scales to large data sets but incurs a significant computational overhead.

1.2 Our Contributions

In this paper we provide a model and protocol for two-party authentication of data structures. Namely, a client outsources its data structure and verifies that the answers to queries are valid. Our framework is fairly general and can be extended to outsourcing a variety of authenticated data structures [1, 7, 13]. We focus on efficient algorithms to outsource a dictionary by using a skip list, which is a well known efficient randomized realization of a dictionary. Our authentication protocol is simple, and efficient. It is based on cryptographic hashing and requires the client to store only a single hash value. The computational overhead for the server and the client and the communication cost are logarithmic, which is optimal for hash-based authentication structures. We have fully implemented our scheme and we provide experimental results that confirm its efficiency and scalability in practice. Our protocol can be deployed on top of existing storage applications to provide a transparent authentication service.

1.3 Preliminaries

We briefly introduce some useful terminology for the authenticated skip list (the non-authenticated skip list was proposed by Pugh [18] and provides a dictionary functionality), since it will be the underlying data structure for our authentication protocol. In an authenticated skip list, every node of the skip list is associated with a hash value that is computed as a function of neighboring nodes according to a special DAG scheme [5]. The importance of the authenticated skip list comes in the verification of the result. When the client queries about the membership of an element x in the dictionary, the server returns a collection of hash values that allows the client to verify the result. For more details on authenticated data structures see [1, 5, 12].

2 Two-Party Authentication Model

In the two-party authentication model, there are two entities participating, an untrusted server S and a client C. The server stores a data collection, which is owned (and has been outsourced) by the client C, in a data structure (for example a dictionary) and the client issues updates (insertions, deletions) to its data. Also the client can issue queries (for example membership queries in a dictionary, connectivity queries in a graph) to the data structure. Since the server is untrusted, we want to make sure that if the server returns a wrong answer to a client's query (namely if the server tampers with the data of the client), then the client rejects the answer w.h.p.

An obvious solution to this, which has been adopted in practice (see for example [17]), is to have the client store and update hash values of the data objects it wants to outsource. In this way the client can always tell if the answers that it gets back from the untrusted server are correct or not. However, this solution is very space inefficient. Ideally, we would like the client to hold a constant size state (digest of the data) and to execute very simple algorithms in order to update this state, whenever it issues an update. We will assume that initially the server and the client share the same digest that correspond to the data. This digest (which later we will be calling s) can be computed and updated using any existing hashing scheme [21]. Then we are going to present protocols and algorithms that securely update this digest whenever updates occur, for the case of the skip list data structure.

2.1   The Protocol and Its Security

In the following we describe the protocol that ensures authentication of operations (insertions, deletions, queries) issued by the client. Then we give the definition of security and also prove that it is satisfied by the presented protocol. Before presenting the protocol, we give some necessary definitions:

Definition 1 (Sequential Hashing). *Given an ordered sequence of hash values $\Lambda = \lambda_1 \circ \lambda_2 \circ \ldots \circ \lambda_m$ and a collision-resistant hash function $h(.,.)$, then the sequential hashing $S(\Lambda)$ maps Λ to a hash value such that $S(\lambda_1 \circ \lambda_2 \circ \ldots \circ \lambda_m) = h(S(\lambda_1 \circ \lambda_2 \circ \ldots \circ \lambda_{m-1}) \circ \lambda_m)$ for $m \geq 2$. For $m = 1$, we define $S(\lambda_1) = \lambda_1$.*

The complexity of sequential cryptographic hashing $S(\Lambda)$ is a function of its input size, namely a function of $|\Lambda|$ (if we assume that λ_i is of fixed length, then $|\Lambda| = O(m)$). Moreover, it can be proved [20] that the time needed to perform a sequential hashing of Λ is $O(|\Lambda|)$. This means that the hashing complexity is proportional to the size of the data being hashed. Based now on the definition of collision resistance of the function h, we can prove the following:

Lemma 1. *Given an ordered sequence of hash values $\Lambda = \lambda_1 \circ \lambda_2 \circ \ldots \circ \lambda_m$, there is no probabilistic polynomial-time adversary than can compute another sequence of hash values $\Lambda' = \lambda_1' \circ \lambda_2' \circ \ldots \circ \lambda_m'$ such that $S(\Lambda) = S(\Lambda')$ with more than negligible probability.*

In the following we present one execution of the authentication protocol (for either an update or a query), which we call Auth2Party. The protocol uses three main procedures, namely certify, verify and update:

– Let s be the state (digest) that corresponds to the current data at the server's side. We assume that the client stores s (for the case of the skip list the digest is the hash of the top-left node with key $-\infty$).

- The client issues an operation $o \in \{I(x), D(x), Q(x)\}$ with respect to an element x that can be either an insertion (I), a deletion (D) or a query (Q).
- The server runs an algorithm $(\pi, a(o)) \leftarrow$ certify(o) that returns a proof π and an answer (with reference to the specific operation o) $a(o)$. Then it sends the proof and the answer to the client. If the operation is an update, the server executes afterward the update in its local data and $a(o) = $ null.
- The client runs an algorithm $(\{0, 1\}, s') \leftarrow$ verify$(o, a(o), \pi, s)$ and we have the following cases:
  1. If $o \in \{I(x), D(x)\}$ (if the operation issued by the client is either an insertion or a deletion) then we distinguish the following cases for the output of verify:
     a. If the sequential hashing (which is the main body of verify)[1] of the proof π hashes to s, i.e., if $S(\pi) = s$, then the output is $(1, s')$. In this case the client accepts the update, it runs an algorithm update on input π and computes the new digest s'.
     b. If the sequential hashing of the proof π does not hash to s, i.e., if $S(\pi) \neq s$, then the output is $(0, \perp)$. In this case the client rejects and the protocol terminates.
  2. If $o = Q(x)$ (if the operation issued by the client is a query) then if the sequential hashing of the proof π hashes to s, i.e., if $S(\pi) = s$, then verify outputs $(1, \perp)$ and the client accepts. Otherwise it outputs $(0, \perp)$ and the client rejects. Note that in this case the state of the client is maintained, since there are no structural changes in the data.

To distinguish between the proof returned when the client issues a query or when the client issues an update, we define as *verification* proof to be the proof returned to a query and as *consistency* proof to be the proof returned to an update. In the following we present the security definition for our protocol.

Definition 2 (Security of Two Party Authentication Protocol). *Suppose we have a two-party authentication protocol $\mathcal{D}$ with server $\mathcal{S}$, client $\mathcal{C}$ and security parameter k. We say that $\mathcal{D}$ is secure if no probabilistic polynomial-time adversary A with oracle access to algorithm* certify, *given any query $Q(x)$, can output an answer $a'(Q(x))$ and a verification proof π', such that $a'(Q(x))$ is an incorrect answer that passes the verification test. That is, there exists negligible[2] function $\nu(k)$, such that for every probabilistic polynomial-time adversary A and every query $Q(x)$*

$$\Pr\left[(\pi', a'(Q(x)))) \leftarrow A(Q(x)) \wedge (1, s') \leftarrow \text{verify}(Q(x), a'(Q(x)), \pi', s)\right] = \nu(k).$$

---

[1] In [5], it is described how one can use sequential hashing on a carefully constructed proof in order to compute the digest of the skip list. We use this scheme without loss of generality for the description of the protocol but we note that the computation of the digest depends on the data structure and the algorithms used.

[2] Formally, $\nu : N \rightarrow \Re$ is negligible if for any nonzero polynomial p, there exists m such that $\forall n > m \ |\nu(n)| < \frac{1}{p(n)}$.

We can now state the result for the security of our scheme (its proof is deferred to the full version of the paper):

Theorem 1. *If algorithm* update *correctly computes the new digest (i.e., the new digest is consistent with the issued update) and algorithm* verify *is correct, then protocol* Auth2Party *is secure.*

3   Operations

In this section, we describe our authentication protocol for a skip list. We describe how to use the proof returned by a contains() query in order to compute the digest of the skip list resulting from the insertion of a new element x. For more details on authenticated skip lists, see Section 1.3.

3.1   Search Path and Proof Path

For every node v of a skip list (if level$(v) > 0$ we consider as node every node that "makes" a difference in hashing, i.e., nodes with both right and down pointers not null) we denote with key(v) the key of the tower that this node belongs to, with level(v) the respective level of this node, with $f(v)$ the hash of the node of the skip list and with right(v) and down(v) the right and down pointers of the v. We finally write $u \leftarrow v^3$ if there is an actual link in the skip list from v to u (either a right or a down pointer). We also write $u \leftrightarrow v$ if there is no actual link between u and v but level$(v) =$ level$(u) = 0$ and u is a successor of v (this means that u belongs to a tower of height > 0).

Definition 3 (Search Path). *Given a skip list SL and an element x, then the search path $\Pi(x) = v_1 \leftrightarrow v_2 \leftarrow \dots \leftarrow v_{j-1} \leftarrow v_j \leftarrow v_{j+1} \leftarrow \dots \leftarrow v_m$ is an ordered sequence of nodes in SL satisfying the following properties:*

- v_m *is the top-leftmost node of the skip list.*
- $v_2 \leftarrow v_3 \leftarrow \dots \leftarrow v_m$ *is a path in the skip list consisting of the zero-level path $v_2 \leftarrow v_3 \leftarrow \dots \leftarrow v_j$ and the path $v_{j+1} \leftarrow v_{j+2} \leftarrow \dots \leftarrow v_m$ which contains nodes of level > 0.*
- *There is $2 \leq t \leq j$ such that* key$(v_t) <$ key$(x) \leq$ key(v_{t-1}).
- *Index j is defined as the "boundary" index.*
- *Index t is defined as the "insertion" index.*

Definition 4 (Proof Path). *Given an authenticated skip list SL, an element x and the respective search path $\Pi(x) = v_1 \leftrightarrow v_2 \leftarrow \dots \leftarrow v_m$ with boundary index j and insertion index t, we define the proof path $\Lambda(x) = \lambda(v_1) \circ \lambda(v_2) \circ \dots \circ \lambda(v_m)$ to be the following ordered sequence of values with the following properties:*

- *For all $i \leq j$ $\lambda(v_i) =$ key(v_i).*
- *For all $i > j$, $\lambda(v_i) = f(\text{right}(v_i))$ if* right$(v_i) \neq v_{i-1}$ *else* $\lambda(v_i) = f(\text{down}(v_i))$.

---

[3] Although it is more intuitive to write $v \to u$, we use this notation because the hashing proceeds from the last to the first element of the proof. This means that there are no actual pointers from v to u in the skip list and this notation is only used for indicating the hashing procedure.

Lemma 2. *Given an authenticated skip list SL and an element x (x ∈ SL or x ∉ SL), then there exist unique search and proof paths $\Pi(x)$ and $\Lambda(x)$ for x.*

Proof. By contradiction. Suppose there is another search or proof path for x. Then there would be a cycle of links in SL. This is a contradiction since pointers in SL define a tree structure.

Definition 5 (Node Removal). *Given a search path $\Pi(x) = v_1 \leftrightarrow v_2 \leftarrow \ldots \leftarrow v_m$ and the respective proof path $\Lambda(x) = \lambda(v_1) \circ \lambda(v_2) \circ \ldots \circ \lambda(v_m)$, then, for every $1 < i \le m$, we denote with $\mathsf{rem}(\Pi(x), v_i)$ and $\mathsf{rem}(\Lambda(x), \lambda(v_i))$ the search path $v_1 \leftrightarrow v_2 \leftarrow \ldots v_{i-1} \leftarrow v_{i+1} \leftarrow \ldots \leftarrow v_m$ and the proof path $\lambda(v_1) \circ \lambda(v_2) \circ \ldots \circ \lambda(v_{i-1}) \circ \lambda(v_{i+1}) \circ \ldots \circ \lambda(v_m)$ respectively.*

Theorem 2. *Given an authenticated skip list SL and an element x, then $S(\Lambda(x))$ (the sequential hashing of the proof path of x) is equal to the digest of SL.*

Suppose now we are given a search path $\Pi(x)$. For each element v_i of the search path we define $D_x(v_i)$ to be 1, if $\mathsf{key}(v_i) \ge x$, else 0. Also, we define $L_x(v_i)$ to be 0, if $i \le j$ (j is the boundary index) else it is defined as the level of v_i. An example of an authenticated skip list implemented with pointers is shown in Figure 1. In the following, we describe algorithms for the computation of the new digest from the client side after operations $\mathsf{insert}(x)$ and $\mathsf{delete}(x)$. From the definition now of the search path we have:

Lemma 3. *Every search path $\Pi(x)$ is sorted in increasing L_x order. Moreover, any elements u and v such that $L_x(v) = L_x(u)$ are sorted in decreasing key order.*

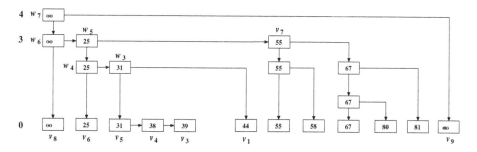

Fig. 1. An authenticated skip list implemented with pointers. For the non-existing element 41 (and also for the existing element 44), we have that the search paths are $\Pi(41) = \Pi(44) = v_1 \leftrightarrow v_3 \leftarrow v_4 \leftarrow v_5 \leftarrow w_3 \leftarrow w_4 \leftarrow w_5 \leftarrow w_6 \leftarrow w_7$ while the respective proof paths are $\Lambda(41) = 44 \circ 39 \circ 38 \circ 31 \circ f(v_1) \circ f(v_6) \circ f(v_7) \circ f(v_8) \circ f(v_9)$. Also note that $L_{41} = (0 \circ 0 \circ 0 \circ 0 \circ 2 \circ 2 \circ 3 \circ 3 \circ 4)$ and $D_{41} = (1 \circ 0 \circ 0 \circ 0 \circ 1 \circ 0 \circ 1 \circ 0 \circ 1)$. Note that the insertion index is 2 while the boundary index is 4.

3.2 Insertion and Deletion

Suppose now that $x \notin S$. The client wants to insert x in the skip list at level ℓ. The client gets the proof path $\Lambda(x)$ (non-membership proof) together with the vectors L_x and D_x. We show how it can compute the new proof path (the proof returned to a contains() query after the insertion of x). Suppose

$$\Pi(x) = v_1 \hookleftarrow v_2 \leftarrow \ldots \leftarrow v_{j-1} \leftarrow v_j \leftarrow v_{j+1} \leftarrow \ldots \leftarrow v_m$$

where j is the boundary index. Also

$$\Lambda(x) = \lambda(v_1) \circ \lambda(v_2) \circ \ldots \circ \lambda(v_{j-1}) \circ \lambda(v_j) \circ \lambda(v_{j+1}) \circ \ldots \circ \lambda(v_m)$$

is the initial proof path as defined in 4. Let $2 \leq t \leq j$ be the insertion index.

In the following we give an algorithm for the computation of the new search path $\Pi'(x)$ and the new proof path $\Lambda'(x)$ on input $\Pi(x)$, $\Lambda(x)$, D_x, L_x (and t). We have the following cases for insert(x, ℓ).

1. if $\ell = 0$ we *output* the final paths

$$\Pi'(x) = v_1 \hookleftarrow \ldots \leftarrow v_{t-1} \leftarrow x \leftarrow v_t \leftarrow \ldots \leftarrow v_m \qquad (1)$$
$$\Lambda'(x) = \lambda(v_1) \circ \ldots \circ \lambda(v_{t-1}) \circ \lambda(x) \circ \lambda(v_t) \circ \ldots \circ \lambda(v_m) \qquad (2)$$

2. if $\ell > 0$ we set

$$\Pi(x) = x \hookleftarrow v_t \leftarrow \ldots \leftarrow v_{j-1} \leftarrow v_j \leftarrow v_{j+1} \leftarrow \ldots \leftarrow v_m \qquad (3)$$
$$\Lambda(x) = \lambda(x) \circ \lambda(v_t) \circ \ldots \circ \lambda(v_{j-1}) \circ \lambda(v_j) \circ \lambda(v_{j+1}) \circ \ldots \lambda(v_m) \qquad (4)$$
$$\mathsf{temp} = S(\lambda(v_1) \circ \lambda(v_2) \circ \ldots \circ \lambda(v_{t-1}) \circ \lambda(x)) \qquad (5)$$

Then we sequentially process the hash values $\lambda(v_i)$ for $i = j+1, \ldots, m$ of the proof path and at each iteration we distinguish the following cases:
- If $\lambda(v_i)$ is such that $\ell < L_x(v_i)$ or ($\ell = L_x(v_i)$ and $D_x(v_i) = 0$) then we create a new node r at level ℓ and we *output* the final paths (nodes v_{i-1} and v_i are linked through the newly created node r in the search path)

$$\Pi'(x) = x \hookleftarrow v_t \leftarrow \ldots \leftarrow v_j \leftarrow \ldots \leftarrow v_{i-1} \leftarrow r \leftarrow v_i \leftarrow \ldots \leftarrow v_m \qquad (6)$$
$$\Lambda'(x) = \lambda(x) \circ \lambda(v_t) \circ \ldots \circ \lambda(v_j) \circ \ldots \circ \lambda(v_{i-1}) \circ \mathsf{temp} \circ \lambda(v_i) \circ \ldots \circ \lambda(v_m) \qquad (7)$$

- If $\lambda(v_i)$ is such that $\ell \geq L_x(v_i)$ and $D_x(v_i) = 1$ then we set

$$\Pi(x) = \mathsf{rem}(\Pi(x), v_i) \qquad (8)$$
$$\Lambda(x) = \mathsf{rem}(\Lambda(x), \lambda(v_i)) \qquad (9)$$
$$\mathsf{temp} = h(\mathsf{temp} \circ \lambda(v_i)) \qquad (10)$$

Definition 6. *Let x be any element in a skip list at height ℓ. We define as* guard(x) *the first tower on the left of x of height $\geq \ell$.*

We can now have the following main results (their proofs are deferred to the full version of the paper):

Lemma 4. *Let x be an element in a skip list at height ℓ. Then there is always a node $s(x)$ called spy of x that belongs to* guard(x) *such that* right$(s(x))$ *points to a node of the tower defined by x. Moreover, $s(x)$ always belongs to $\Pi(x)$.*

Lemma 5. *The sequence $\Pi'(x)$ is the correct search path after the insertion of element x at level ℓ and it can be computed in expected $O(\log n)$ time w.h.p..*

Lemma 6. *The sequence $\Lambda'(x)$ is the correct proof path after the insertion of element x at level ℓ and it can be computed in expected $O(\log n)$ time w.h.p., incurring expected $O(\log n)$ hashing complexity w.h.p..*

As we are going to show later, the proof path $\Lambda(x)$ should be extended to include information about the levels of the elements of the proof so that we could ensure security. Consider for example the following scenario. Suppose, the server in the beginning contains only the sentinel values $+\infty$ and $-\infty$. The client issues the command insert(x, ℓ). Suppose the server chooses another level ℓ' and inserts x at ℓ'. Obviously, the digest of the data structure will be exactly the same since the level of the element does not matter at all. However, the efficiency of the data structure is not assured, since the level was not chosen by flipping a coin. Therefore, the server could insert elements at arbitrary levels while the client would not notice anything.

Definition 7 (Extended Proof Path). *Let $\Lambda(x)$ be a proof path with respect to an element x. Let L_x and D_x be the vectors as defined before. We define as extended proof path $Q(x)$ the ordered sequence of triples $Q_i = (\lambda(v_i), L_x(v_i), D_x(v_i))$ for $i = 1, \ldots, |\Lambda(x)|$.*

The client, however, does not need to compute the new proof and search paths. All it needs to do is to update the digest. In the following we give a very simple algorithm that updates the digest. Algorithm update, shown in Figure 2, takes as input the *extended* proof path $Q = Q(x)$ as defined in 7 (in the case that the client wants to insert x in the data structure), the desired level of insertion ℓ and the element x the client wants to insert. Note that the levels of the nodes are also taken into consideration in the hash computations, since we use the extended proof path. In the following we outline the algorithm used for verification at the client's side, verify$(Q(x))$: On input $Q(x)$, it sequentially hashes $Q(x)$ to see if the computed digest matches the existing one. If not, it rejects, else it replaces the current digest by the one returned by calling update (if the operation is an update) and finally accepts. We now reduce an authenticated deletion to an authenticated insertion as follows. Suppose at some point the client and the server share the common digest s. The client then executes delete(x), where element x is at level ℓ in the skip list. The server deletes x and **then** constructs a proof π' by issuing a contains(x) query. Next, the server sends π' and the level ℓ to the client. The client runs the update algorithm on input π', x, ℓ. If the output digest is s, then the deletion is accepted and the new digest is $s' = S(\pi')$.

3.3   Analysis

In the data authentication model through hashing, where a three-party model is used, any hashing scheme with k digest nodes that implements an authenticated dictionary of size n has $\Omega(\log(\frac{n}{k}))$ update, verification and communication cost

10   C. Papamanthou and R. Tamassia

Algorithm update(Q, ℓ, x, t)

1: **if** $\ell == 0$
2:   **return** $S(Q_1 \circ \ldots \circ Q_{t-1} \circ (\text{key}(x), 0, 1) \circ Q_t \circ \ldots \circ Q_m)$;
3: **else**
4:   let r be the smallest index $\geq t$ such that $\ell < L_x(v_r)$ or $\ell = L_x(v_r)$ and $D_x(v_r) = 0$;
5:   **if** $\ell == L_x(v_r)$
6:     set $U = Q_{r+1} \circ \ldots \circ Q_m$;
7:   **else**
8:     set $U = Q_r \circ \ldots \circ Q_m$;
9:   $L = (\text{key}(x), \ell, 1)$;
10: $R = S(Q_1 \circ \ldots \circ Q_{t-1}) \circ (\text{key}(x), \ell, 1)$;
11: **for** $i = t, \ldots, r$
12:    **if** $\ell \geq L_x(v_i)$ and $D_x(v_i) = 1$
13:      $R = R \circ Q_i$;
14:    **else**
15:      $L = L \circ Q_i$;
16: **return** $S(L \circ S(R) \circ U)$;

Fig. 2. Algorithm executed by the client to update the digest after the insertion of an element x. The inputs to the algorithm are the extended proof path Q, the insertion level ℓ, the inserted element x, and the insertion index t. Variable m denotes the length of the extended proof sequence Q.

(see [21]). Using this result, we can prove that our protocol is optimal. To see this, suppose there exists a two-party authentication scheme that uses hashing and achieves better performance than $O(\log n)$ (update, verification, communication). Then we can use these algorithms and implement a three party protocol in the data authentication model through hashing with the same bounds, violating the existing lower bounds [21]. In addition, by using Theorem 1, the proof of correctness of the insertion algorithm and the results on the complexity of authenticated skip list operations [5], we obtain the main result of our paper:

Theorem 3. *Assume the existence of a collision-resistant hash function. Our two-party authentication protocol for outsourcing a dictionary of n elements supports authenticated updates* insert() *and* delete() *and authenticated query* contains() *and has the following properties:*

1. *The protocol is secure;*
2. *The expected running time of updates/queries is $O(\log n)$ at the server and at the client w.h.p.;*
3. *The expected communication complexity of updates/queries is $O(\log n)$ w.h.p.;*
4. *The expected hashing complexity of updates/queries is $O(\log n)$ w.h.p.;*
5. *The client uses space $O(1)$;*
6. *The server uses expected space $O(n)$ w.h.p.;*
7. *The protocol has optimal time, space, and communication complexity, up to a constant factor, over all hash-based authentication protocols.*

Taking into account constant factors (see the definitions in [21]), the communication and hashing complexity can be shown to be at most $1.5 \log n$ with high probability. Moreover, the client keeps a single hash value (e.g., a 128-bit or 256-bit digest, using standard hash functions).

4   Experimental Results

We have conducted experiments on the performance of the presented authentication protocol. The time needed for querying the server (construction of the proof) and for query verification have been reported extensively in [3]. Here we report times concerning the time needed for the client to securely update the digest (after doing a verification of the proof it receives) when it does an insertion or a deletion and also for the server to perform the respective update on the skip list. Concerning the client's side, insertion times include an initial verification of the proof and then the processing of the proof in order to update the digest. Also we give plots that indicate the size of the consistency and verification proof (bytes). From the plots we will see that the actual communication overhead of our protocol is very small; Only at most 1KB of information (for 1,000,000 elements) needs to be communicated from the server to the client so that the client can update the digest. For each operation, the average running time (or the average size in the case of proofs) was computed over 10,000 executions. The experiments were conducted on a 64-bit, 2.8GHz Intel based, dual-core, dual processor machine with 8GB main memory and 2MB cache, running Debian Linux 3.1 with Linux kernel 2.6.15 and using the Sun Java JDK 1.5. The Java Virtual Machine (JVM) was most of the times launched with a 7GB maximum heap size. Cryptographic hashing was performed using the standard Java implementation of the MD5 algorithm. We report the running times obtained in our experiments excluding the time consumed by the garbage collector. Our experimental results provide a measure of the computational and communication overhead. The results of the experiments concerning insertions and deletions are summarized in Figure 3. One can see that insertion/deletion at the client's side takes more than insertion/deletion at the server's side (Figures 3(a) and 3(b)). This is because for client insertions we count exactly the following time: The time needed for verifying that the consistency proof π hashes to the current digest and the time needed to run update on the current consistency proof in order to update the digest. For client-side deletions (see Figure 3(b)) we firstly have to run update and then do a verification. On the other hand, server side insertions and deletions do not have to do any verification at all. They are just a usual insertion/deletion in a skip list. This is enough to justify that difference in the execution times, since verification is a costly operation as it involves $O(\log n)$ hash computations. Finally, as we can see the times needed for insertion and deletion follow a logarithmic increase, verifying in this way our theoretical findings. Also, the actual time needed at the client's side is roughly $80\mu s$ which shows the efficiency of the method. The results of the experiments concerning the size of the proof are summarized in Figure 4. The size of the proof in bytes is computed as follows. First of all we compute the size of the structure Λ which is the input in update(). Let N be that size. It is easy to see that the maximum

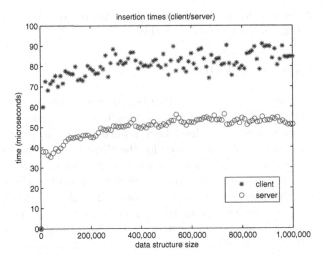

(a) Client/Server Insertion at the client's and server's side.

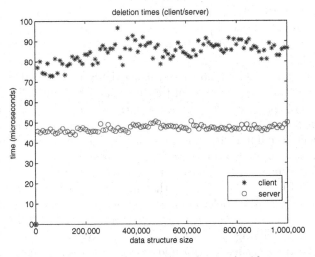

(b) Deletion at the client's and server's side.

Fig. 3. Insertion and deletion times. The times shown are the average of 10,000 executions on data structure sizes varying from 0 to 10^6 elements.

size (the size of vector Λ) of the proof in our experiments (for 10^6 elements) is 30 and it validates the theory since $1.5 \log(10^6) \simeq 30$. Since now for each element of Λ, Λ_i, it is $\Lambda_i = (\lambda(v_i), \ell_x(\lambda(v_i)), k_x(\lambda(v_i)))$, we have that each element of the extended proof needs exactly $(128 + \log(\mathsf{maxlevel}) + 1)$ bits. Here $\mathsf{maxlevel}$ is the maximum level of the skip list towers and for our experiments is 20. Hence for a consistency proof of size N we need exactly $\frac{N}{8} \times 134$ bytes. This holds for the case of the dictionary. If we want to use the map functionality (i.e., to bind a key with

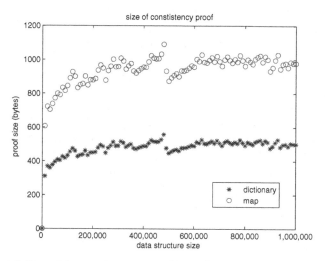

(a) Size of the consistency proof for a dictionary and a map.

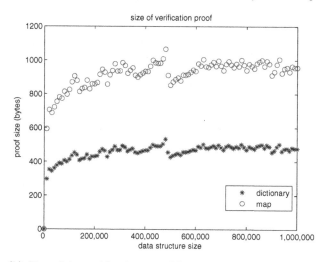

(b) Size of the verification proof for a dictionary and a map.

Fig. 4. Communication overhead (proof size). The sizes shown are the average of 10,000 executions on data structure sizes varying from 0 to 10^6 elements.

a value), which is something that has more applications, then the size of the proof is $\frac{N}{8}(2\times128+\log(\mathsf{maxlevel})+1)$ bytes, since we also need to hold a digest for the value. The plot for the size of the consistency proof is shown in Figure 4(a). One can observe the logarithmic increase. Also, for the case of the dictionary the average size of the proof is 0.5KB. The plot for the verification proof is shown in Figure 4(b). Finally the communication overhead of a consistency versus a verification proof is only a few bits (namely 6 per element).

5 Conclusions and Future Work

In this paper, we have presented an efficient protocol for two-party authentication based on cryptographic hash functions. Namely, we have given efficient, lightweight and provably secure algorithms that ensure the validity of the answers returned by an outsourced dictionary. We have implemented our protocol and we have provided experimental results that confirm the scalability of our approach. As future work, we envision developing a general authentication framework that can be applied to other data structures, such as dynamic trees [7]. Additionally, we could investigate realizations of two-party authenticated protocols based on other cryptographic primitives, (for example cryptographic accumulators [6]).

Acknowledgments

We thank Nikos Triandopoulos and Michael Goodrich for useful discussions.

References

[1] Anagnostopoulos, A., Goodrich, M.T., Tamassia, R.: Persistent authenticated dictionaries and their applications. In: Davida, G.I., Frankel, Y. (eds.) ISC 2001. LNCS, vol. 2200, pp. 379–393. Springer, Heidelberg (2001)

[2] Di Battista, G., Palazzi, B.: Authenticated relational tables and authenticated skip lists. In: Proc. Working Conference on Data and Applications Security (DBSEC), pp. 31–46 (2007)

[3] Goodrich, M.T., Papamanthou, C., Tamassia, R.: On the cost of persistence and authentication in skip lists. In: Proc. Int. Workshop on Experimental Algorithms (WEA), pp. 94–107 (2007)

[4] Goodrich, M.T., Shin, M., Tamassia, R., Winsborough, W.H.: Authenticated dictionaries for fresh attribute credentials. In: Nixon, P., Terzis, S. (eds.) iTrust 2003. LNCS, vol. 2692, pp. 332–347. Springer, Heidelberg (2003)

[5] Goodrich, M.T., Tamassia, R.: Implementation of an authenticated dictionary with skip lists and commutative hashing. In: Proc. DARPA Information Survivability Conference & Exposition II (DISCEX II), pp. 68–82. IEEE Computer Society Press, Los Alamitos (2001)

[6] Goodrich, M.T., Tamassia, R., Hasic, J.: An efficient dynamic and distributed cryptographic accumulator. In: Chan, A.H., Gligor, V.D. (eds.) ISC 2002. LNCS, vol. 2433, pp. 372–388. Springer, Heidelberg (2002)

[7] Goodrich, M.T., Tamassia, R., Triandopoulos, N., Cohen, R.: Authenticated data structures for graph and geometric searching. In: Joye, M. (ed.) CT-RSA 2003. LNCS, vol. 2612, pp. 295–313. Springer, Heidelberg (2003)

[8] Hacigümüş, H., Iyer, B., Li, C., Mehrotra, S.: Executing SQL over encrypted data in the database-service-provider model. In: Proc. Int. Conference on Management of Data (SIGMOD), pp. 216–227 (2002)

[9] Hacigümüş, H., Mehrotra, S., Iyer, B.: Providing database as a service. In: Proc. Int. Conference on Data Engineering (ICDE), p. 29 (2002)

[10] Hore, B., Mehrotra, S., Tsudik, G.: A privacy-preserving index for range queries. In: Proc. Int. Conference on Very Large Databases (VLDB), pp. 720–731 (2004)

[11] Li, F., Hadjieleftheriou, M., Kollios, G., Reyzin, L.: Dynamic authenticated index structures for outsourced databases. In: Proc. of ACM SIGMOD International Conference on Management of Data, pp. 121–132 (2006)

[12] Martel, C., Nuckolls, G., Devanbu, P., Gertz, M., Kwong, A., Stubblebine, S.G.: A general model for authenticated data structures. Algorithmica 39(1), 21–41 (2004)

[13] Merkle, R.C.: A certified digital signature. In: Brassard, G. (ed.) CRYPTO 1989. LNCS, vol. 435, pp. 218–238. Springer, Heidelberg (1990)

[14] Miklau, G., Suciu, D.: Implementing a tamper-evident database system. In: Grumbach, S., Sui, L., Vianu, V. (eds.) ASIAN 2005. LNCS, vol. 3818, pp. 28–48. Springer, Heidelberg (2005)

[15] Mykletun, E., Narasimha, M., Tsudik, G.: Authentication and integrity in outsourced databases. In: Proceeding of Network and Distributed System Security (NDSS) (2004)

[16] Narasimha, M., Tsudik, G.: Authentication of outsourced databases using signature aggregation and chaining. In: Proc. of 11th International Conference on Database Systems for Advanced Applications, pp. 420–436 (2006)

[17] Oprea, A., Reiter, M.K.: Integrity checking in cryprographic file systems with constant trusted storage. In: Proc. USENIX Security Symposium (USENIX), pp. 183–198 (2007)

[18] Pugh, W.: Skip lists: a probabilistic alternative to balanced trees. Commun. ACM 33(6), 668–676 (1990)

[19] Tamassia, R.: Authenticated data structures. In: Di Battista, G., Zwick, U. (eds.) ESA 2003. LNCS, vol. 2832, pp. 2–5. Springer, Heidelberg (2003)

[20] Tamassia, R., Triandopoulos, N.: On the cost of authenticated data structures. Technical report, Center for Geometric Computing, Brown University, Available (2003), from http://www.cs.brown.edu/cgc/stms/papers/costauth.pdf

[21] Tamassia, R., Triandopoulos, N.: Computational bounds on hierarchical data processing with applications to information security. In: Caires, L., Italiano, G.F., Monteiro, L., Palamidessi, C., Yung, M. (eds.) ICALP 2005. LNCS, vol. 3580, pp. 153–165. Springer, Heidelberg (2005)

New Construction of Group Secret Handshakes Based on Pairings

Lan Zhou, Willy Susilo, and Yi Mu

Centre for Computer and Information Security Research
School of Computer Science and Software Engineering
University of Wollongong, Wollongong, NSW 2522, Australia
lanz.cn@gmail.com, wsusilo@uow.edu.au, ymu@uow.edu.au

Abstract. In a secret handshake protocol, an honest member in the group will never reveal his group affiliation unless the other party is a valid member of the same group. However, most prior work of secret handshake are for 2-party secret handshakes. Tsudik and Xu extended the notion of secret handshake to a multi-party setting in 2005. Unfortunately, this seminal work is rather inefficient, since they consider a generic construction of such a scheme. Following this work, Jarecki et al. proposed an efficient solution to multi-party secret handshake. The aim of this paper is twofold. Firstly, we show that Jarecki et al.'s scheme has some drawbacks and therefore the scheme does *not* fulfill the security requirements of secret handshake. Secondly, we present a new construction of the group secret handshake scheme. In a group secret handshake protocol, a valid member in the group should never reveals his group affiliation unless *all* the other parties are valid members of the same group. In other words, if a handshake among this group of parties fails, the identities of every involved parties will not be disclosed. We then show that our scheme is secure under the bilinear Diffie-Hellman assumption and decisional bilinear Diffie-Hellman assumption in the random oracle model.

Keywords: Secret Handshake, Credential System, pairings, random oracle.

1 Introduction

The secret handshake (SH), introduced recently by Balfanz et al. [1], is a protocol whereby participants establish a secure, anonymous and unobservable communication channel only if they are valid members of the same group. In an SH protocol, two members of the same group can identify each other secretly. If one party does not belong to the group, he will learn nothing about the group affiliation of the other party. In other words, if the handshake protocol fails, the group affiliation of the participant will not be revealed. Another important property of the SH is that even if a third party observes the exchange in the protocol, he can learn nothing about the process including whether two participants belong to

S. Qing, H. Imai, and G. Wang (Eds.): ICICS 2007, LNCS 4861, pp. 16–30, 2007.

the same group or not. Nonetheless, the original motivation of SH only captures the two-party setting.

Recently, Tsudik and Xu extended the notion of SH to a multi-party setting, called Group Secret Handshake (GSH), which allows two or more members of the same group authenticate each other secretly. In a GSH protocol, an honest member in the group will never reveal his group affiliation unless *all* the other parties are valid members of the same group. If the handshake protocol fails, a valid party will never leak his group affiliation, even to other valid parties. The GSH also requires that it is indistinguishable to an invalid user who does not participate in a handshake protocol that a handshake is successful or unsuccessful. Jarecki, Kim and Tsudik [10] then proposed an efficient multi-party SH scheme based on an un-authenticated group key agreement protocol. However, we found a problem in their scheme. Following the definition of SH in [1], a valid party will never leak his group affiliation to other parties, if the group handshake protocol fails. In contrast to this requirement, in Jarecki et al.'s scheme, an invalid member has the ability to make other honest parties share a common group session key in a failed protocol. Hence he can learn that these parties belong to a same group, which violates the security requirements of SH defined in [1]. We shall show this problem in Appendix A. In addition to this drawback, their scheme does not include a key comparison stage. Therefore, before participants can decide whether the protocol is completed successfully or not, the scheme may need additional rounds to compare the common key among every participants.

Our Contributions

In this paper, we propose a two-round group secret handshake scheme by using pairing. We also prove that our scheme is secure under the bilinear Diffie-Hellman assumption and decisional bilinear Diffie-Hellman assumption in the Random Oracle Model (ROM). Our scheme is motivated by the multi-receiver identity-based encryption scheme in [12], which suits the situation that a single party encrypts messages and sends to multi-parties who cannot decrypt the messages unless they have the credential based on their identities. However, their scheme cannot ensure the validity of the senders.

2   Related Work

The seminal work on SH was proposed in [1] which uses pairings, and several SH schemes have been proposed following this work. These schemes use different digital signatures as credentials of the member in the group. Firstly, an SH scheme based on CA-Oblivious Encryption was introduced in [3], where it combines ElGamal encryption and Schnorr signature to construct a CA-oblivious PKI-enabled encryption scheme which is secure under the CDH assumption. Based on this primitive, they proposed a new SH scheme. The term "CA-Oblivious" implies that a credential which is not issued by a Certification Authority (CA) will not enable a user to guess whether another user he/she interacts with has the credential issued by the CA or not. Xu and Yung [14] also presented an SH scheme with reusable credentials, and the security does not rely on the random oracle model. Their scheme achieves unlinkability, and an invalid user can only infer that a participant is one out of a certain number k users in the worst case, so called k-anonymity. Another RSA-based SH scheme [5] was proposed by Vergnaud, which uses RSA signature as the credential and is proven secure against active impersonator and detector adversaries that rely on the difficulty of solving the RSA problem. Finally, two SH schemes based on ElGamal signature and DSA signature were proposed in [6].

We note that all the above solutions are only able to support 2-party secret handshakes. Recently, a framework of multi-party secret handshakes has been introduced by Tsudik and Xu [8], which is essentially a compiler that transforms three main ingredients, including a group signature scheme, a centralized group key distribution scheme, and a distributed group key agreement scheme, into a secure secret handshake scheme. They also constructed two instantiations based on the framework. However, the authors mentioned that they only aimed to construct a framework of multi-party secret handshake, and never optimize the efficiency of the framework. Subsequently, Jarecki, Kim and Tsudik [10] provided an efficient solution to multi-party SH, which is constructed based on an unauthenticated group key agreement protocol.

3   Background and Preliminaries

In this section, we first review some cryptographic assumptions that will be used throughout the paper.

3.1   The Bilinear Maps and Complexity Assumption

Let $\mathbb{G}_1$ be a cyclic additive group of prime order q. Let $\mathbb{G}_2$ be a cyclic multiplicative group of same order q. We assume that the discrete logarithm problem (DLP) in both $\mathbb{G}_1$ and $\mathbb{G}_2$ are hard to solve.

BDH Parameter Generator: Let Bilinear Diffie-Hellman (BDH) parameter generator $\mathcal{IG}_{DBH}$ be a probabilistic polynomial time (PPT) algorithm. When running in polynomial time, $\mathcal{IG}_{DBH}$ outputs two groups $\mathbb{G}_1$ and $\mathbb{G}_2$ of the same order q and a bilinear map $\hat{e} : \mathbb{G}_1 \times \mathbb{G}_1 \to \mathbb{G}_2$ which satisfies the following properties:

- *Bilinear:* for all $P, Q \in \mathbb{G}_1$ and $a, b \in \mathbb{Z}_q^*$ we have $\hat{e}(aP, bQ) = \hat{e}(P, Q)^{ab}$.
- *Non-degenerate:* if for $P \in \mathbb{G}_1$ we have $\hat{e}(P, Q) = 1$ for all $Q \in \mathbb{G}_1$, then $Q = \mathcal{O}$.
- *Computable:* for all $P, Q \in \mathbb{G}_1$, the pairing $\hat{e}(P, Q)$ is computable in polynomial time.

3.2   The Bilinear Assumptions

Bilinear Diffie – Hellman (BDH) Problem

The BDH problem is as follows: Given a cyclic group $\mathbb{G}_1, \mathbb{G}_2$ of the order q together with a bilinear map $\hat{e} : \mathbb{G}_1 \times \mathbb{G}_1 \to \mathbb{G}_2$, P is a generator of group $\mathbb{G}_1$, the Bilinear Diffie-Hellman problem is (t, ε)-hard if for all t-time adversaries $\mathcal{A}$ we have

$$\mathsf{Adv}_{\mathcal{A}}^{\mathsf{BDH}} = |\mathrm{Pr}[\mathcal{A}(\mathsf{P}, \mathsf{aP}, \mathsf{bP}, \mathsf{cP}) = \hat{\mathsf{e}}(\mathsf{P}, \mathsf{P})^{\mathsf{abc}}]| < \varepsilon$$

BDH Assumption: We say that if there exists a polynomial time algorithm which can solve BDH problem, the probability is negligible. In other words, no efficient algorithm can solve BDH problem with non-negligible advantage.

Decisional Bilinear Diffie – Hellman (DBDH) Problem
The decisional BDH problem is to distinguish between tuples of the form $(P, aP, bP, cP, \hat{e}(P, P)^{abc})$ and (P, aP, bP, cP, γ) for random $P \in \mathbb{G}_1$, and $a, b, c \in \mathbb{Z}_q^*$. the Decisional Bilinear Diffie-Hellman problem is (t, ε)-hard if for all t-time adversaries $\mathcal{A}$ we have

$$\mathsf{Adv}_{\mathcal{A}}^{\mathsf{DBDH}} = |\mathrm{Pr}[\mathcal{A}(\mathsf{P} \quad, \, aP, bP, cP, \hat{e}(P, P)^{abc}) = 1]$$
$$- Pr[\mathcal{A}(P, aP, bP, cP, \hat{e}(P, P)^{d}) = 1]| < \varepsilon$$

DBDH Assumption: We assume that the probability of a polynomial time algorithm to solve DBDH problem is negligible.

The above mentioned assumptions are widely believed to be computational hard. The BDH is used in [2,11], and the DBDH is needed for construction in [13,12].

4   Model and Security Requirements of GSH

4.1   Definition

The GSH model consists of a set $\mathcal{U}$ of possible users, and a set $\mathcal{G}$ of groups, where each group is a set of members managed by a group administrator GA. We define a *group secret handshake* scheme GSH by the following algorithms:

- GSH.CreateGroup: a key generation algorithm executed by the group administrator GA to establish a group G. It takes as input security parameters, and outputs the group public key p_G, the GA's private key s_G, and a revoked user list $\mathcal{RUL}$, which is originally set to empty. The $\mathcal{RUL}$ is made known only to current group members.
- GSH.AddUser: an algorithm executed between GA and a group member on GA's private key s_G and shared inputs: params, p_G, and the identity of the group member which is bit string ID of size regulated by params. After performing the algorithm, the group member will be issued a secret credential produced by GA for the member's identity ID.
- GSH.HandShake: an authentication protocol, executed by a set Δ of n users purporting to be members of a group G, where $\Delta = \{U_1, \ldots, U_n\}$ and $n \geq 2$. The protocol takes as public input the identities $\mathsf{ID}_{U_1}, \ldots, \mathsf{ID}_{U_n}$ of all the users in Δ, and params, and the private input is their secret credentials. The output of the protocol for each party is either *reject* or *accept*.
- GSH.RemoveUser: an algorithm executed by GA on input an identity of the user U and the $\mathcal{RUL}$, inserts U into the $\mathcal{RUL}$ and sends the updated $\mathcal{RUL}$ to the existing group members through the authenticated anonymous channel.

4.2   Security Properties

A GSH scheme must satisfy the properties of completeness, impersonation resistant, and detection resistant. In our security model, an adversary $\mathcal{A}$ is allowed to run the protocols several times and be able to make additional queries after each attempt, before he announces that he is ready for the true challenges. $\mathcal{A}$ can see all exchanged messages, delete, modify, inject and redirect messages, communicate with other party, and even reuse messages from past communications.

We denote the set of users involved in the GSH as Δ. $\{U_1, \ldots, U_n\}$ each denotes a user $U \in \Delta$. Consider that an adversary $\mathcal{A}$ may join the set Δ, and perform a GSH protocol with the valid users in G. G denotes the group of all the valid users.

Completeness. If all the participants $\{U_1, \ldots, U_n\}$ involved in the group secret handshakes are honest members of the same group with valid certificates from the group administrator. Then both parties output "accept", otherwise output "reject".

Impersonation Resistance. If an adversary $\mathcal{A} \notin G$ does not corrupt any member of its target group G, it has only a negligible probability in impersonating as an honest member of G.

Let $\mathcal{B}$ denote a challenger. Consider the following game in which $\mathcal{A}$ interacts with $\mathcal{B}$:

Phase 1: $\mathcal{A}$ outputs target multiple identities $\Delta = (\mathsf{ID}_1^*, \ldots, \mathsf{ID}_n^*)$, where $\mathsf{ID}_\mathcal{A} = \mathsf{ID}_i^*$ and $i \in [1, n]$.

Phase 2: $\mathcal{B}$ runs a key generation algorithm to generate the group public key p_G, the GA's private key s_G, and sends p_G to $\mathcal{A}$ while keeping s_G secret from $\mathcal{A}$.

Phase 3: $\mathcal{A}$ makes a number of credential extraction queries. To answer each query made by $\mathcal{A}$, $\mathcal{B}$ runs the GSH.AddUser algorithm, and outputs S_{ID} which is the group credential for identity ID, where $\mathsf{ID} \notin \Delta$.

Phase 4: $\mathcal{A}$ triggers a handshake protocol. $\mathcal{B}$ acts as honest parties in the protocol, who have valid credentials for their identities.

Phase 5: $\mathcal{B}$ answers $\mathcal{A}$'s credential extraction / random oracle queries as in Phase 2 and 3.

Phase 6: $\mathcal{A}$ returns the messages $\langle X_\mathcal{A}, Y_\mathcal{A} \rangle$, which can make other parties output "accept" after running the protocol.

We define the probability that attacker $\mathcal{A}$ impersonates successfully in the handshake protocol as $\mathsf{Adv}_\mathcal{A}^{Impersonate}$, which is identical to the probability that $\mathcal{A}$ outputs the valid pair $\langle X_\mathcal{A}, Y_\mathcal{A} \rangle$.

Detection Resistance. If an adversary $\mathcal{A} \notin G$, who does not corrupt any member of its target group G, is involved in the group secret handshakes, each participant in handshakes has only a negligible probability in distinguishing an interaction with an honest user $U_v \in G$ from the one with a simulator.

Let $\mathcal{A}$ denote an attacker, and $\mathcal{B}$ denote a challenger. Phases 2, 3, 5 of the attack game are identical to those for impersonation resistant. We only describe Phase 1, 4, 6 in the following:

Phase 1: $\mathcal{A}$ outputs two target multiple identities $\Delta = (\mathsf{ID}_1^*, \ldots, \mathsf{ID}_{i-1}^*,$ $\mathsf{ID}_{i+1}^*, \mathsf{ID}_n^*)$ and $\mathsf{ID}_i^0, \mathsf{ID}_i^1$, where $\mathsf{ID}_{\mathcal{A}} \neq \mathsf{ID}_i^*, i \in [1, n]$. $\mathsf{ID}_i^0 = \mathsf{ID}_v$ is a member, who holds an valid credential. ID_i^1 is a unqualified member, who does not have the valid group credential.

Phase 4: $\mathcal{A}$ triggers a handshake protocol. $\mathcal{B}$ randomly chooses a $\beta \in \{0, 1\}$, and set $\mathsf{ID}_i^* = \mathsf{ID}_i^\beta$. Then $\mathcal{B}$ simulates the handshake protocol with $\mathcal{A}$.

Phase 6: $\mathcal{A}$ outputs its guess β'.

We denote the probability that the attacker $\mathcal{A}$ can distinguish an interaction with an honest user $U_v \in G$ from the one with a simulator in the handshake protocol as $\mathsf{Adv}_{\mathcal{A}}^{Detect} = |Pr[\beta' = \beta] - \frac{1}{2}|$. In other words, an attacker involved in the handshake protocol has a probability of $\mathsf{Adv}_{\mathcal{A}}^{Detect}$ to know the group affiliation of other participants.

Indistinguishability to eavesdropper. An adversary $\mathcal{A}$, who does not participate in a handshake protocol, has only a negligible probability in learning any knowledge about whether the handshake is successful or not, even if $\mathcal{A} \in G$.

Let $\mathcal{A}$ denote an attacker, and $\mathcal{B}$ denote a challenger. Phases 2, 3, 5 of the attack game are identical to those for impersonation resistant. We only describe Phase 1, 4, 6 in the following:

Phase 1: $\mathcal{A}$ outputs two target multiple identities $\Delta_0 = (\mathsf{ID}_1^*, \ldots, \mathsf{ID}_n^*)$ and $\Delta_1 = (\mathsf{ID}_1, \ldots, \mathsf{ID}_n)$, where $\mathsf{ID}_{\mathcal{A}} \neq \mathsf{ID}_i^*$ and $\mathsf{ID}_{\mathcal{A}} \neq \mathsf{ID}_i, i \in [1, n]$. Δ_0 is a group, in which each user holds an valid credential. Δ_1 is a group, in which one or some users do not have the valid group credential.

Phase 4: $\mathcal{B}$ randomly chooses a $\beta \in \{0, 1\}$, and simulates a handshake protocol among the group Δ_β. An additional copy will be sent to $\mathcal{A}$ every time $\mathcal{B}$ simulates an interaction in GSH protocol.

Phase 6: $\mathcal{A}$ outputs its guess $\beta' \in \{0, 1\}$.

We denote the probability that the attacker $\mathcal{A}$ can distinguish an successful protocol from an unsuccessful one as $\mathsf{Adv}_{\mathcal{A}}^{Distinguish} = |Pr[\beta' = \beta] - \frac{1}{2}|$. If an attacker does not take part in a handshake protocol, he has a probability of $\mathsf{Adv}_{\mathcal{A}}^{Distinguish}$ to know whether the handshake protocol is successful or not.

Unlinkability. No adversary $\mathcal{A}$ is able to associate two handshakes involving a same honest user or a same set of honest users, even if $\mathcal{A} \in G$ and $\mathcal{A}$ participated in both executions.

5   Group Secret-Handshake Scheme from Pairings

In this section, we present our group secret handshake scheme called GSH. The protocol involves a group administrator GA. In the following description $H_1 : \{0, 1\}^* \to \mathbb{G}_1$ and $H_2 : \mathbb{G}_2 \to \{0, 1\}^n$ are cryptographic hash functions. H_1 and H_2 are considered as random oracles in the security analysis.

GSH.CreateGroup. GA runs BDH parameter generator to generate a prime q, two groups $\mathbb{G}_1, \mathbb{G}_2$ of order q, and an bilinear map $\hat{e} : \mathbb{G}_1 \times \mathbb{G}_1 \to \mathbb{G}_2$. Choose three random generators P, Q, $N \in \mathbb{G}_1$. Then GA picks a random $s \in \mathbb{Z}_q^*$, sets $P_{pub} = sP$ and $Q_{pub} = sQ$. GA keeps s secret as the *master secret key* and publishes system parameters

$$\mathsf{params} = \{\mathbb{G}_1, \mathbb{G}_2, \hat{e}, q, P_{pub}, P, Q_{pub}, Q, N, H_1, H_2\}$$

GSH.AddUser. When a user U_i with identity ID_i wishes to obtain a secret credential for his identity, GA computes the corresponding credential $S_{\mathsf{ID}_i} = sH_1(\mathsf{ID}_i)$, and returns S_{ID_i} to the user U_i.

GSH.HandShake Let $U_1, \ldots, U_n$ be the n users who want to conduct a group secret handshake. The protocol runs as follows:

- Each user U_i picks $k_i \overset{R}{\leftarrow} \mathbb{G}_2$ and $r_i \overset{R}{\leftarrow} \mathbb{Z}_q^*$. Then U_i computes $T_i^j = r_i H_1(\mathsf{ID}_j) + r_i N$, where $1 \le j \le n$ and $j \ne i$. U_i then computes

$$C_i = \langle r_i H_1(\mathsf{ID}_i), T_i^1, \ldots, T_i^n, r_i P, r_i Q, \mathcal{L} \rangle,$$

  where $\mathcal{L}$ is a label that contains information about how "T_i^j" is associated with each receiver. Then U_i broadcasts C_i to all others.
- Let $C_j = \langle R_j, T_j^1, \ldots, T_j^n, V_j, W_j, \mathcal{L} \rangle$. Upon receiving C_j, each responder U_i computes $K_i = k_i \cdot \hat{e}(S_{\mathsf{ID}_i}, -H_1(\mathsf{ID}_1) - \cdots - H_1(\mathsf{ID}_{i-1}) + H_1(\mathsf{ID}_{i+1}) + \cdots + H_1(\mathsf{ID}_n))$ and $K_i' = k_i \cdot \hat{e}(r_i S_{\mathsf{ID}_i}, -R_1 - \cdots - R_{i-1} + R_{i+1} + \cdots + R_n)$. U_i then computes

$$D_i = \langle \hat{e}(N, P_{pub})^{r_i} \cdot K_i, \ \hat{e}(N, Q_{pub})^{r_i} \cdot K_i' \rangle,$$

and broadcasts D_i to all others.

Let $D_j = \langle X_j, Y_j \rangle$. Now each user U_i, using $\mathcal{L}$, finds appropriate T_j^i and computes

$$K_1 K_2 \cdots K_n = \frac{\hat{e}(S_{\mathsf{ID}_i}, V_1 + \cdots + V_n)}{\hat{e}(T_1^i + \cdots + T_n^i, P_{pub})} \cdot (X_1 X_2 \cdots X_n)$$

$$K_1' K_2' \cdots K_n' = \frac{\hat{e}(S_{\mathsf{ID}_i}, W_1 + \cdots + W_n)}{\hat{e}(T_1^i + \cdots + T_n^i, Q_{pub})} \cdot (Y_1 Y_2 \cdots Y_n)$$

It is easy to see that the above equations are consistent. If C_i, D_i are valid messages,

$$\frac{\hat{e}(S_{\mathsf{ID}_i}, \sum_{j=1}^n V_j) \cdot \prod_{j=1}^n X_j}{\hat{e}(\sum_{j=1}^n T_j^i, P_{pub})} = \frac{\hat{e}(sH_1(\mathsf{ID}_i), \sum_{j=1}^n r_j P) \cdot \prod_{j=1}^n X_j}{\hat{e}(\sum_{j=1}^n (r_j H_1(\mathsf{ID}_i) + r_j N), sP)}$$

$$= \frac{\hat{e}(\sum_{j=1}^n r_j H_1(\mathsf{ID}_i), sP) \cdot \prod_{j=1}^n X_j}{\hat{e}(\sum_{j=1}^n (r_j H_1(\mathsf{ID}_i) + r_j N), sP)} = \frac{\prod_{i=1}^n \hat{e}(N, P_{pub})^{r_i} \cdot K_i}{\hat{e}(\sum_{i=1}^n r_i N, sP)} = \prod_{i=1}^n K_i$$

The same as above, we can also obtain

$$\frac{\hat{e}(S_{\mathsf{ID}_i}, \sum_{j=1}^n W_j) \cdot \prod_{j=1}^n Y_j}{\hat{e}(\sum_{j=1}^n T_j^i, Q_{pub})} = \prod_{i=1}^n K_i'$$

Then each user U_i verifies and accepts only if the following equation holds

$$K_1 K_2 \cdots K_n \overset{?}{=} K_1' K_2' \cdots K_n' \tag{1}$$

If the above verification succeed, then $U_1, \ldots, U_n$ finish all the steps of the GSH, and the handshake has been successful.

Each U_i can also create a shared secret key for future communication as follows:

$$K = H_2(K_1 K_2 \cdots K_n)$$

GSH.RemoveUser. To remove a user U from the group G, the administrator can simply add the identity of the user to the $\mathcal{RUL}$, and encrypts the update information by using an Identity-Based Encryption scheme. Then GA distributes the information to the members of the group, alerting them to abort any handshake should they find themselves performing the handshake with a user using any identity on the $\mathcal{RUL}$.

The correctness of the scheme is obvious and therefore it is omitted.

6   Security Proof

Theorem 1. *The above GSH scheme is impersonation resistant under the Bilinear Diffie-Hellman assumption in the Random Oracle Model.*

Proof. Assume that an adversary $\mathcal{A}$ violates the impersonation resistant property. Now we show how to construct an attacker $\mathcal{B}$ for solving the BDH problem. Suppose that $\mathcal{B}$ is given $(q, \mathbb{G}_1, \mathbb{G}_2, P, aP, bP, cP)$ as an instance of the BDH problem. Attacker $\mathcal{B}$ interacts with $\mathcal{A}$ as follows:

Phase 1: Suppose that $\mathcal{A}$ outputs target multiple identities $\Delta = (\mathsf{ID}_1^*, \ldots, \mathsf{ID}_n^*)$, where $\mathsf{ID}_A = \mathsf{ID}_i^*$ and $i \in [1, n]$.

Phase 2: $\mathcal{B}$ sets $P_{pub} = cP$, and gives $\{\mathbb{G}_1, \mathbb{G}_2, \hat{e}, q, P_{pub}, P, Q_{pub}, Q, N, H_1\}$ to $\mathcal{A}$ as the system parameters, where H_1 is a random oracle controlled by $\mathcal{B}$ as follows:

Upon receiving a random oracle query ID_j to H_1:

- If there exists $(\mathsf{ID}_j, l_j, L_j)$ in $H_1\mathsf{List}$, return L_j. Otherwise, do the following:
  * If $\mathsf{ID}_j = \mathsf{ID}_A$, where ID_A is the identity of the adversary $\mathcal{A}$, set $L_j = aP$.
  * Else if $\mathsf{ID}_j \neq \mathsf{ID}_n^*$, choose $l_j \in \mathbb{Z}_q^*$ uniformly at random and compute $L_j = l_j P$.
  * If $\mathsf{ID}_j = \mathsf{ID}_n^*$, search $H_1\mathsf{List}$ to get l_j that corresponds to ID_i^* for $i \in [1, n)$, and compute $L_j = (\sum_{j=1}^{i-1} l_j - \sum_{j=i+1}^{n-1} l_j)P + bP$.
  * Put $(\mathsf{ID}_j, l_j, L_j)$ in $H_1\mathsf{List}$ and return L_j as answer.

Phase 3: $\mathcal{B}$ answers $\mathcal{A}$'s private key extraction queries as follows: Upon receiving a private key extraction query on ID_j:
- If there exists $(\mathsf{ID}_j, l_j, L_j)$ in $\mathsf{H}_1\mathsf{List}$, compute $S_{\mathsf{ID}_j} = l_j P_{pub}$. Otherwise, do the following:
  * Choose $l_j \in \mathbb{Z}_q^*$ uniformly at random and compute $S_{\mathsf{ID}_j} = l_j P_{pub}$.
  * Put $(\mathsf{ID}_j, l_j, L_j)$ in $\mathsf{H}_1\mathsf{List}$ and return S_{ID_j} as answer.

Phase 4: $\mathcal{B}$ acts as honest parties and broadcasts messages as follows:
- Choose $r_j \in \mathbb{Z}_q^*$, where $j \in [1, n)$.
- Compute $R_j = r_j P$, and $R_n = (\sum_{j=1}^{i-1} r_j - \sum_{j=i+1}^{n-1} r_j)P$.
- Randomly choose $T_j^1, \ldots, T_j^n, V_j, W_j$ for $j \in [1, n]$ and $j \neq i$.
- Return $C_j = (R_j, T_j^1, \ldots, T_j^n, V_j, W_j)$ to $\mathcal{A}$.

Phase 5: $\mathcal{B}$ answers $\mathcal{A}$'s random oracle/private key extraction queries as in Phase 2 and 3.

Phase 6: $\mathcal{A}$ returns the messages $\langle X_{\mathcal{A}}, Y_{\mathcal{A}} \rangle$.

Analysis: Note that if $\langle X_{\mathcal{A}}, Y_{\mathcal{A}} \rangle$ is the valid response, ID_j^*, where $j \in [1, n)$, can extract the $(K_{\mathcal{A}}, K_{\mathcal{A}}')$. Then $K_{\mathcal{A}} \cdot K_{\mathcal{A}}'^{-1}$ should be identical to $(k_{\mathcal{A}} \cdot \hat{e}(S_{\mathsf{ID}_{\mathcal{A}}}, -\sum_{j=1}^{i-1} H_1(\mathsf{ID}_j^*) + \sum_{j=i+1}^{n-1} H_1(\mathsf{ID}_j^*) + H_1(\mathsf{ID}_n^*)) \cdot (k_{\mathcal{A}} \cdot \hat{e}(r_{\mathcal{A}} S_{\mathsf{ID}_{\mathcal{A}}}, -\sum_{j=1}^{i-1} R_j + \sum_{j=i+1}^{n-1} R_j + R_n))^{-1} = \hat{e}(S_{\mathsf{ID}_{\mathcal{A}}}, bP)$. Since $S_{\mathsf{ID}_{\mathcal{A}}} = caP$, $\mathcal{B}$ now gets $\hat{e}(P, P)^{abc} = \hat{e}(caP, bP)$. Consequently, we obtain

$$\mathsf{Adv}_{\mathcal{A}}^{Impersonate} < |Pr[\mathcal{B}(P, aP, bP, cP) = \hat{e}(P, P)^{abc}]| = \mathsf{Adv}_{\mathcal{A}}^{BDH} \qquad \square$$

Theorem 2. *The above GSH scheme is Detection Resistant under the Decisional Bilinear Diffie-Hellman assumption in the Random Oracle Model.*

Proof. Assume that one party U_v identified by ID_v is involved in a failure handshake protocol. An attacker $\mathcal{A}$, who also participates the handshake, can know whether U_v is an honest party or not.

Now we show how to construct an attacker $\mathcal{B}$ for solving the DBDH problem. Suppose that $\mathcal{B}$ is given $(q, \mathbb{G}_1, \mathbb{G}_2, P, aP, bP, cP, \gamma)$ as an instance of the DBDH problem. Attacker $\mathcal{B}$ interacts with $\mathcal{A}$ as follows:

Phase 1: Suppose that $\mathcal{A}$ outputs two target multiple identities $\Delta = (\mathsf{ID}_1^*, \ldots, \mathsf{ID}_{i-1}^*, \mathsf{ID}_{i+1}^*, \mathsf{ID}_n^*)$ and $\mathsf{ID}_i^0, \mathsf{ID}_i^1$, where $\mathsf{ID}_{\mathcal{A}} \neq \mathsf{ID}_i^*, i \in [1, n]$. ID_i^0 is a member, who holds an valid credential. ID_i^1 is a unqualified member, who does not have the valid group credential.

Phase 2: $\mathcal{B}$ sets $P_{pub} = cP$, and gives $\{\mathbb{G}_1, \mathbb{G}_2, \hat{e}, q, P_{pub}, P, Q_{pub}, Q, N, H_1\}$ to $\mathcal{A}$ as the system parameters, where H_1 is a random oracle controlled by $\mathcal{B}$ as follows:

Upon receiving a random oracle query ID_j to H_1:
- If there exists $(\mathsf{ID}_j, l_j, L_j)$ in $\mathsf{H}_1\mathsf{List}$, return L_j. Otherwise, do the following:
  * If $\mathsf{ID}_j = \mathsf{ID}_v$, set $L_j = aP$.
  * Else if $\mathsf{ID}_j \neq \mathsf{ID}_n^*$, choose $l_j \in \mathbb{Z}_q^*$ uniformly at random and compute $L_j = l_j P$.

* If $\mathsf{ID}_j = \mathsf{ID}_n^*$, search $\mathsf{H_1List}$ to get l_j that corresponds to ID_j^* for $j \in [1, n)$, and compute $L_j = (\sum_{j=1}^{i-1} l_j - \sum_{j=i+1}^{n-1} l_j)P + bP$.
* Put $(\mathsf{ID}_j, l_j, L_j)$ in $\mathsf{H_1List}$ and return L_j as answer.

Phase 3: $\mathcal{B}$ answers $\mathcal{A}$'s private key extraction queries as follows: Upon receiving a private key extraction query on ID_j:

- If there exists $(\mathsf{ID}_j, l_j, L_j)$ in $\mathsf{H_1List}$, compute $S_{\mathsf{ID}_j} = l_j P_{pub}$. Otherwise, do the following:
  * Choose $l_j \in \mathbb{Z}_q^*$ uniformly at random and compute $S_{\mathsf{ID}_j} = l_j P_{pub}$.
  * Put $(\mathsf{ID}_j, l_j, L_j)$ in $\mathsf{H_1List}$ and return S_{ID_j} as answer.

Phase 4: $\mathcal{B}$ now simulates the handshake protocol as follows: $\mathcal{B}$ choose (k_v^0, k_v^1, k_v), where $k_v^0 = k_v$ and $k_v^1 \neq k_v$.

- Choose $\beta \in \{0, 1\}$ at random.
- Choose t_j, $r_j \in \mathbb{Z}_q^*$, where $j \in [1, n), j \neq i$.
- Compute $R_j = t_j P$, and $R_n = (\sum_{j=1}^{i-1} t_j - \sum_{j=i+1}^{n-1} t_j)P$.
- Compute $T_j^k = r_j l_k P + r_j N, V_j = r_j P, W_j = r_j Q$, for $j, k \in [1, n]$.
- Return $C_j = (R_j, T_j^1, \ldots, T_j^n, V_j, W_j)$ to $\mathcal{A}$.
- Return D_j following the valid scheme for $j \neq i$.
- Return $D_i = (\hat{e}(N, P_{pub})^{r_v} \cdot \gamma k_v^\beta, \ \hat{e}(N, Q_{pub})^{r_v} \cdot k_v)$.

Phase 5: $\mathcal{B}$ answers $\mathcal{A}$'s random oracle/private key extraction queries as in Phase 2 and 3.

Phase 6: $\mathcal{A}$ outputs its guess β'. If $\beta' = \beta$, $\mathcal{B}$ outputs 1. Otherwise, it outputs 0.

Analysis: Let ϵ denote the probability $\mathsf{Adv}_{\mathcal{A}}^{Detect}$. We note that if $\gamma = \hat{e}(P, P)^{abc}$,

$$\gamma k_v^\beta = \hat{e}(acP, bP)k_v^\beta = \hat{e}(S_{\mathsf{ID}_v}, bP)k_v^\beta$$

$$= k_v^\beta \cdot \hat{e}(S_{\mathsf{ID}_v}, -\sum_{j=1}^{i-1} H_1(\mathsf{ID}_j^*) + \sum_{j=i+1}^{n} H_1(\mathsf{ID}_j^*)) \cdot$$

$$\hat{e}(r_v S_{\mathsf{ID}_v}, -\sum_{j=1}^{i-1} R_j + \sum_{j=i+1}^{n} R_j)^{-1}$$

It is clear that from the construction above, $\mathcal{B}$ simulates the random oracle H_1 and the private key extraction in Phase 3 and 5. Hence, we obtain $Pr[\mathcal{B}(P, aP, bP, cP, \hat{e}(P, P)^{abc}) = 1] = Pr[\beta = \beta']$, where $|Pr[\beta' = \beta] - \frac{1}{2}| > \epsilon$, and then $Pr[\mathcal{B}(P, aP, bP, cP, \gamma) = 1] = Pr[\beta = \beta'] = \frac{1}{2}$, where γ is uniform. Consequently, we get

$$\mathsf{Adv}_{\mathcal{A}}^{DBDH} = |Pr[\mathcal{B}(P, aP, bP, cP, \hat{e}(P, P)^{abc}) = 1] -$$
$$Pr[\mathcal{B}(P, aP, bP, cP, \gamma) = 1]|$$
$$> |(\frac{1}{2} \pm \epsilon) - \frac{1}{2}| = \mathsf{Adv}_{\mathcal{A}}^{Detect} \qquad \square$$

Theorem 3. *The above GSH scheme is Indistinguishable to eavesdropper under the Decisional Bilinear Diffie-Hellman assumption in the Random Oracle Model.*

Proof. Assume that if an adversary $\mathcal{A}$ is able to eavesdrop all the transcripts in a secret handshake protocol, $\mathcal{A}$ can distinguish between a successful handshake and an unsuccessful one.

Now we show how to construct an attacker $\mathcal{B}$ for solving the DBDH problem. Suppose that $\mathcal{B}$ is given $(q, \mathbb{G}_1, \mathbb{G}_2, P, aP, bP, cP, \gamma)$ as an instance of the DBDH problem. Attacker $\mathcal{B}$ interacts with $\mathcal{A}$ as follows:

Phase 1: Suppose that $\mathcal{A}$ outputs two target multiple identities $\Delta_0 = (\mathsf{ID}_1^*, \ldots, \mathsf{ID}_n^*)$ and $\Delta_1 = (\mathsf{ID}_1, \ldots, \mathsf{ID}_n)$, where $\mathsf{ID}_\mathcal{A} \neq \mathsf{ID}_i^*$ and $\mathsf{ID}_\mathcal{A} \neq \mathsf{ID}_i, i \in [1, n]$. Δ_0 is a group, in which each user holds an valid credential. Δ_1 is a group, in which one or some users does not have the valid group credential.

Phase 2: $\mathcal{B}$ sets $N = bP, P_{pub} = cP + Q_{pub}$, and gives $\{\mathbb{G}_1, \mathbb{G}_2, \hat{e}, q, P_{pub}, P, Q_{pub}, Q, N, H_1\}$ to $\mathcal{A}$ as the system parameters, where H_1 is a random oracle controlled by $\mathcal{B}$ as follows:

Upon receiving a random oracle query ID_j to H_1:
- If there exists $(\mathsf{ID}_j, l_j, r_j, L_j)$ in $H_1\mathsf{List}$, return L_j. Otherwise, do the following:
  * If $\mathsf{ID}_j = \mathsf{ID}_i^*$ for some $i \in [1, n]$, compute $L_j = l_j P - N$.
  * Else choose $l_j, r_j \in \mathbb{Z}_q^*$ uniformly at random and compute $L_j = l_j P$.
  * Put $(\mathsf{ID}_j, l_j, r_j, L_j)$ in $H_1\mathsf{List}$ and return L_j as answer.

Phase 3: $\mathcal{B}$ answers $\mathcal{A}$'s private key extraction queries as follows: Upon receiving a private key extraction query on ID_j:
- If there exists $(\mathsf{ID}_j, l_j, r_j, L_j)$ in $H_1\mathsf{List}$, compute $S_{\mathsf{ID}_j} = l_j P_{pub}$. Otherwise, do the following:
  * Choose $l_j, r_j \in \mathbb{Z}_q^*$ uniformly at random and compute $S_{\mathsf{ID}_j} = l_j P_{pub}$.
  * Put $(\mathsf{ID}_j, l_j, r_j, L_j)$ in $H_1\mathsf{List}$ and return S_{ID_j} as answer.

Phase 4: $\mathcal{B}$ now simulates the handshake protocol as follows: $\mathcal{B}$ constructs three sequences $(K_1^0, K_2^0, \ldots, K_n^0), (K_1^1, K_2^1, \ldots, K_n^1)$ and $(K_1, K_2, \ldots, K_n)$, where $K_1^0 K_2^0 \cdots K_n^0 = K_1 K_2 \cdots K_n, K_1^1 K_2^1 \cdots K_n^1 \neq K_1 K_2 \cdots K_n$ and $K_i^0 \neq K_i^1 \neq K_i$.
- Choose $\beta \in \{0, 1\}$ at random.
- Search $H_1\mathsf{List}$ to get l_j, r_j that corresponds to ID_j^* for $j \in [1, n]$.
- Compute $l_j r_i P$ for $i \in [1, n), j \in [1, n]$.
- Compute $l_j(aP - \sum_{i=1}^{n-1} r_i P), \gamma K_i^\beta$ for $i = n, j \in [1, n]$, and choose $e \in \mathbb{Z}_q^*$ at random.
- Return $C_i = (l_i r_i P, l_1 r_i P, \ldots, l_n r_i P, aP + eP, eP)$ and $D_i = (K_i^\beta, K_i)$ for $i \in [1, n)$ as transcripts in handshake protocol.
- Return $C_n = (l_n r_n P, l_1(aP - \sum_{i=1}^{n-1} r_i P), \ldots, l_n(aP - \sum_{i=1}^{n-1} r_i P), aP + eP, eP)$ and $D_n = (\gamma K_n^\beta, K_n)$ as transcripts in handshake protocol.

Phase 5: $\mathcal{B}$ answers $\mathcal{A}$'s random oracle/private key extraction queries as in Phase 2/3.

Phase 6: $\mathcal{A}$ outputs its guess β'. If $\beta' = \beta$, $\mathcal{B}$ outputs 1. Otherwise, it outputs 0.

Analysis: Let ϵ denote the probability $\mathsf{Adv}_\mathcal{A}^{Distinguish}$. We note that if $\gamma = \hat{e}(P, P)^{abc}$,

$$\gamma \prod_{i=1}^n K_i^\beta = \hat{e}(bP, cP)^a \prod_{i=1}^n K_i^\beta = \hat{e}(\sum_{i=1}^n r_i N, P_{pub} - Q_{pub}) \prod_{i=1}^n K_i^\beta$$

Note also that

$$l_i r_i P = l_i r_i P - r_i N + r_i N = r_i(l_i P - N) + r_i N = r_i H_1(\mathsf{ID}_i^*) + r_i N$$

for $i \in [1, n)$ and

$$l_n(aP - \sum_{i=1}^{n-1} r_i P)$$

$$= l_n(aP - \sum_{i=1}^{n-1} r_i P) - (aN - \sum_{i=1}^{n-1} r_i N) + (aN - \sum_{i=1}^{n-1} r_i N)$$

$$= (a - \sum_{i=1}^{n-1} r_i)(l_n P - N) + (a - \sum_{i=1}^{n-1} r_i)N$$

$$= (a - \sum_{i=1}^{n-1} r_i)H_1(\mathsf{ID}_n^*) + (a - \sum_{i=1}^{n-1} r_i)N$$

Hence C_i, D_i are valid messages. It is clear that from the construction above, $\mathcal{B}$ simulates the random oracle H_1 and the private key extraction in Phase 3 and 5. Hence, we get $Pr[\mathcal{B}(P, aP, bP, cP, \hat{e}(P, P)^{abc}) = 1] = Pr[\beta = \beta']$, where $|Pr[\beta' = \beta] - \frac{1}{2}| > \epsilon$, and $Pr[\mathcal{B}(P, aP, bP, cP, \gamma) = 1] = Pr[\beta = \beta'] = \frac{1}{2}$, where γ is uniform. Consequently, we obtain

$$\mathsf{Adv}_{\mathcal{A}}^{\mathsf{DBDH}} = |Pr[\mathcal{B}(P, aP, bP, cP, \hat{e}(P, P)^{abc}) = 1] - Pr[\mathcal{B}(P, aP, bP, cP, \gamma) = 1]|$$

$$> |(\frac{1}{2} \pm \epsilon) - \frac{1}{2}| = \mathsf{Adv}_{\mathcal{A}}^{Distinguish} \qquad \square$$

7 Conclusion

A group secret handshake is an extension of the secret handshake model which allows members of the same group to authenticate each other secretly, and the group affiliation of each member will never be disclosed if the handshake protocol fails. In this paper, we defined the security requirements of group secret handshake scheme, and proposed an efficient group secret handshake scheme. We also proved that our scheme is secure under the bilinear Diffie-Hellman and decisional bilinear Diffie-Hellman assumption in the Random Oracle Model.

References

1. Balfanz, D., Durfee, G., Shankar, N., Smetters, D., Staddon, J., Wong, H.: Secret Handshakes From Pairing-based Key Agreements. In: Proceedings of 2003 IEEE Symposium on Security and Privacy, pp. 180–196 (2003)
2. Boneh, D., Franklin, M.: Identity-based Encryption From the Weil Pairing. In: Kilian, J. (ed.) CRYPTO 2001. LNCS, vol. 2139, pp. 213–229. Springer, Heidelberg (2001)

3. Castelluccia, C., Jarecki, S., Tsudik, G.: Secret Handshakes From CA-Oblivious Encryption. In: Lee, P.J. (ed.) ASIACRYPT 2004. LNCS, vol. 3329, pp. 293–307. Springer, Heidelberg (2004)
4. Li, N., Du, W., Boneh, D.: Oblivious Signature-based Envelope. In: Proceedings of the 22nd ACM Symposium on Principles of Distributed Computing, pp. 182–189. ACM Press, New York (2003)
5. Vergnaud, D.: Rsa-based Secret Handshakes. In: Ytrehus, Ø. (ed.) WCC 2005. LNCS, vol. 3969, pp. 252–274. Springer, Heidelberg (2006)
6. Zhou, L., Susilo, W., Mu, Y.: Three-round Secret Handshakes Based on ElGamal and DSA. In: Chen, K., Deng, R., Lai, X., Zhou, J. (eds.) ISPEC 2006. LNCS, vol. 3903, pp. 332–342. Springer, Heidelberg (2006)
7. Nasserian, S., Tsudik, G.: Revisiting Oblivious Signature-based Envelopes. In: Di Crescenzo, G., Rubin, A. (eds.) FC 2006. LNCS, vol. 4107, pp. 221–235. Springer, Heidelberg (2006)
8. Tsudik, G., Xu, S.: A Flexible Framework for Secret Handshakes. In: PODC 2005: Proceedings of the twenty-fourth annual ACM symposium on Principles of distributed computing, pp. 39–39. ACM Press, New York (2005)
9. Tsudik, G., Xu, S.: Flexible Framework for Secret Handshakes (multi-party anonymous and un-observable authentication). Cryptology ePrint Archive, Report, /034, 2005 (2005), http://eprint.iacr.org/
10. Jarecki, S., Kim, J., Tsudik, G.: Authentication for paranoids: Multi-party secret handshakes. In: Zhou, J., Yung, M., Bao, F. (eds.) ACNS 2006. LNCS, vol. 3989, pp. 325–339. Springer, Heidelberg (2006)
11. Joux, A.: A one round protocol for tripartite diffie-hellman. In: Bosma, W. (ed.) Algorithmic Number Theory. LNCS, vol. 1838, pp. 385–394. Springer, Heidelberg (2000)
12. Baek, J., Safavi-Naini, R., Susilo, W.: Efficient Multi-Receiver Identity-based Encryption and Its Application to Broadcast Encryption. In: Vaudenay, S. (ed.) PKC 2005. LNCS, vol. 3386, pp. 380–397. Springer, Heidelberg (2005)
13. Boneh, D., Boyen, X.: Efficient selective-id secure identity based encryption without random oracles. In: Cramer, R.J.F. (ed.) EUROCRYPT 2005. LNCS, vol. 3494, pp. 223–238. Springer, Heidelberg (2004)
14. Xu, S., Yung, M.: k-anonymous secret handshakes with reusable credent. In: CCS 2004: Proceedings of the 11th ACM conference on Computer and communications security, pp. 158–167. ACM Press, New York (2004)

A   Security Drawbacks of Jarecki-Kim-Tsudik's Group Secret Handshakes Scheme

A construction of group secret handshake scheme was proposed by Jarecki, Kim and Tsudik [10], which extends the secret handshake protocol to a multi-party setting based on an un-authenticated group key agreement scheme. The definition of secret handshake requires that if a handshake among all participants fails, the group affiliation of each party will not be disclosed. In this section, we show an attack to the scheme in [10], which makes the honest parties involved in the protocol share a same session key, *even if* there is an adversary in the protocol.

Firstly, we review the group secret handshake scheme in [10].

CreateGroup. The administrator GA runs key generation algorithm, which takes as input a security parameter k, to generate the discrete logarithm parameters (p, q, g). g is a generator of a subgroup in $\mathbb{Z}_p$ of order q. Then GA picks a random $s \overset{R}{\leftarrow} \mathbb{Z}_q^*$, sets it the group secret, and computes the public key $y = g^s \bmod p$.

AddUser. To add a user U to the group, the administrator GA first allocates a list of random "pseudonyms" $\mathsf{ID}_{U_1}, \ldots, \mathsf{ID}_{U_t} \in \{0,1\}^*$ for U, where t is chosen to be larger than the number of handshakes U will execute before receiving new user secret. The GA then computes a corresponding list of Schnorr signature $(\alpha_1, \beta_1), \ldots, (\alpha_t, \beta_t)$, where $\alpha_k = g^{r_k} \pmod{p}$, and $\beta_k = r_k + sH(\alpha_k, \mathsf{ID}_{U_k})$ $\pmod{p}$, for random $r_k \overset{R}{\leftarrow} \mathbb{Z}_q$.

Handshake. Let $\Delta = \{U_1, \ldots, U_n\}$ be n users who would like to conduct an secret handshake. Each user U_i chooses an unused pseudonym $\mathsf{ID}_i \in \{ID_1, \ldots, ID_t\}$, together with the corresponding secret $\langle \alpha_i, \beta_i \rangle$. Then the group of users run the handshake protocol as follows:

Round 1: Each user U_i broadcasts $(\mathsf{ID}_i, \alpha_i)$
- When a user U_i finds a collision in the group of IDs, or finds a ID in the revoked user list, the protocol terminates.
- If there are no collision or revoked ID, U_i determines the order of each user based on their identities. Assume that the order of users in the group is $(U_1, U_2, \ldots, U_n)$, and $U_{n+1} = U_1$.

Round 2: U_i computes
$$z_{i+1} = \alpha_{i+1} y^{H(\alpha_{i+1},\, \mathsf{ID}_{i+1})} = g^{\beta_{i+1}} \pmod{p}$$
$$z_{i-1} = \alpha_{i-1} y^{H(\alpha_{i-1},\, \mathsf{ID}_{i-1})} = g^{\beta_{i-1}} \pmod{p}$$
$$X_i = H'(z_{i+1}^{\beta_i})/H'(z_{i-1}^{\beta_i}) \pmod{p}$$
Each U_i broadcasts X_i. U_i computes $K_i = H'(z_{i-1}^{\beta_i})^n \cdot X_i^{n-1} \cdot X_{i+1}^{n-2} \cdots X_{i-2}$ $\pmod{p}$.

Then each user U_i in the group outputs "accept" if they hold a common shared key. All the steps of the SH are finished, and the handshake has been successful.

To see that this scheme is sound, let:

$$C_{i-1} = H'(z_{i-1}^{\beta_i}) = H'(g^{\beta_{i-1}\beta_i}) \pmod{p}$$
$$C_i = H'(z_{i-1}^{\beta_i}) \cdot X_i = H'(g^{\beta_i\beta_{i+1}}) \pmod{p}$$
$$C_{i+1} = H'(z_{i-1}^{\beta_i}) \cdot X_i \cdot X_{i+1} = H'(g^{\beta_{i+1}\beta_{i+2}}) \pmod{p}$$
$$\cdots$$
$$C_{i-2} = H'(z_{i-1}^{\beta_i}) \cdot X_i \cdot X_{i+1} \cdots X_{i-2} = H'(g^{\beta_{i-2}\beta_{i-1}}) \pmod{p}$$

It is obvious that

$$K_i = C_{i-1}C_iC_{i+1} \cdots C_{i-2} = H'(z_{i-1}^{\beta_i})^n \cdot X_i^{n-1} \cdot X_{i+1}^{n-2} \cdots X_{i-2}$$
$$= H'(g^{\beta_1\beta_2}) \cdot H'(g^{\beta_2\beta_3}) \cdots H'(g^{\beta_n\beta_1}) \pmod{p}$$

Then if all the users involved in the protocol are valid, they will share the same symmetric key.

RemoveUser. To remove a user U from the group G, the administrator GA looks up the user pseudonyms $(\mathsf{ID}_{U_1}, \ldots, \mathsf{ID}_{U_t})$ it has issued to U and publishes them on the revoked user list.

Note that if U_i is not a valid member of the group, the group secret handshake will not succeed, because U_i cannot produce a valid X_i without having the knowledge of β_i, which corresponds to the α_i broadcasted at the beginning of the protocol.

However, we observe that U_i can wait till he receives all the X_j, where $j \neq i$, before he broadcasts X_i in Round 2. Then U_i computes

$$
X_i' = (\prod_{\substack{j \in [1,n] \\ j \neq i}} X_j)^{-1} = (\prod_{\substack{j \in [1,n] \\ j \neq i}} (H'(z_{j+1}^{\beta_j})/H'(z_{j-1}^{\beta_j})))^{-1}
$$

$$
= (\prod_{\substack{j \in [1,n] \\ j \neq i}} (H'(g^{\beta_{j+1}\beta_j})/H'(g^{\beta_{j-1}\beta_j})))^{-1} = (H'(g^{\beta_{i-1}\beta_i})/H'(g^{\beta_{i+1}\beta_i}))^{-1}
$$

$$
= H'(g^{\beta_{i+1}\beta_i})/H'(g^{\beta_{i-1}\beta_i}) = H'(z_{i+1}^{\beta_i})/H'(z_{i-1}^{\beta_i})
$$

From the discussion above, we can see that U_i computes the valid value X_i' and broadcasts it to other parties. Without knowing β_i, U_i *cannot* calculate the common group key K_i, but we note that other valid members still can share the same symmetric key. Then U_i may know that these parties belong to a same group, which makes the honest parties leak their group affiliation even if the handshake fails. □

nPAKE$^+$: A Hierarchical Group Password-Authenticated Key Exchange Protocol Using Different Passwords

Zhiguo Wan[1], Robert H. Deng[2], Feng Bao[3], and Bart Preneel[1]

[1] K.U.Leuven, ESAT/SCD, Kasteelpark Arenberg 10, Leuven, Belgium
[2] School of Information Systems, Singapore Management University, Singapore
[3] Institute for Infocomm Research, 21 Heng Mui Keng Terrace, Singapore

Abstract. Although two-party password-authenticated key exchange (PAKE) protocols have been intensively studied in recent years, group PAKE protocols have received little attention. In this paper, we propose a hierarchical group PAKE protocol nPAKE$^+$ protocol under the setting where each party shares an *independent* password with a trusted server. The nPAKE$^+$ protocol is a novel combination of the hierarchical key tree structure and the password-based Diffie-Hellman exchange, and hence it achieves substantial gain in computation efficiency. In particular, the computation cost for each client in our protocol is only $O(\log n)$. Additionally, the hierarchical feature of nPAKE$^+$ enables every subgroup obtains their own subgroup key in the end. We also prove the security of our protocol under the random oracle model and the ideal cipher model.

1 Introduction

Low-entropy and human-memorable passwords are widely used for user authentication and secure communications in real applications, e.g. internet banking and remote user access, due to their user friendliness and low deployment cost. The problem of strong authentication and key exchange between two parties sharing a password, referred to as the two-party *password-authenticated key exchange* (2PAKE) problem, has been well studied and many solutions have been proposed in the literature. With proliferation of group-oriented applications, e.g. teleconferencing, collaborative workspaces, there is an increasing need for group PAKE protocols to protect communications for a group of users.

In group-oriented communications, either the group shares a single password, or each client in the group shares an independent password with a trusted server. The single-password setting is not preferable in real applications for several reasons. First, if a client in the group leaves or the password of a client is compromised, the shared password has to be updated, which could be a very expensive process. Moreover, compromise of any client leads to breakdown of the entire system. Secondly, individual client identification is impossible in this setting. As a result, no one is able to distinguish one client from another, and it is impossible for a subset of the group to securely establish a session key and hence have secure communications. It is easy to see that the independent-password setting avoids the above problems and reflects more accurately what is happening in the real world.

S. Qing, H. Imai, and G. Wang (Eds.): ICICS 2007, LNCS 4861, pp. 31–43, 2007.
© Springer-Verlag Berlin Heidelberg 2007

Group PAKE protocols in the independent-password setting need more careful treatment since they suffer from attacks which are not present in the single password setting, such as attacks initiated by legitimate clients against other clients' passwords (e.g. [35]). Not only group PAKE protocols should be resistant to outsider attacks, but they should also be secure against insider attacks.

In this paper, we propose an efficient group PAKE protocol, referred to as nPAKE$^+$ protocol, for the independent-password setting. By employing a Diffie-Hellman key tree in group key establishment, the protocol achieves group key establishment and mutual authentication with only three message flows, and every client needs only to perform $5 + \lceil \log n \rceil$ exponentiations.

The remainder of the paper is organized as follows. In the next section, we discuss related work on PAKE protocols. Then we present our nPAKE$^+$ protocol, followed by the security proof. We analyze the performance of the proposed protocol and draw our concluding remarks at the end.

2   Related Work

Two-party PAKE (2PAKE) protocols were first studied by Bellovin and Merritt [5,6]. Since then, 2PAKE has been intensively investigated in the literature, see for examples [3,4,7,17,18,19,20,16,15,26,27,39]. Among them, the proposals in [4,7,16,19] are proven to be secure with formal treatment.

Some efforts were spent to extend 2PAKE protocols to the three party setting [31,25,13] where two clients each share an independent password with a trusted server. These protocols, referred to as the 2PAKE$^+$ protocols, establish a session key between two clients with the help of a trusted server. However, straightforward extension from 2PAKE protocols to 2PAKE$^+$ ones often leads to insecure designs since the latter are susceptible to more attacks, such as insider attacks. The 2PAKE$^+$ protocol presented in [31] was shown to suffer from a dictionary attack [24].

Though group PAKE protocols have important applications, they only received limited attention. Under the single-password setting, Asokan and Ginzboorg [2] proposed a group PAKE protocol for ad hoc networks, but its security is not formally proved. Bresson *et al.* [8] proposed a password-based group Diffie-Hellman PAKE protocol and proved its security formally. Schemes proposed in [23,36,14] are actually password-based version of the famous BD protocol [10]. By means of broadcast (or multicast), these protocols can achieve group key establishment in 3 rounds using a single password, just like the BD protocol.

As discussed earlier, group PAKE protocols in the single password setting are too restrictive and are expected to have limited applications in practice. To our best knowledge, there are only two schemes in the independent-password setting by Byun et al. [11,12]. However, the protocols EKE-U and EKE-M in [11] have been showed to be insecure against off-line dictionary attacks and undetectable on-line password guessing attacks [35]. The scheme in [12] is also insecure against undetectable on-line guessing attacks.

3 Model

In this section, we prove security of the proposed group password-authenticated key agreement protocol. We first define a model of nPAKE$^+$ based on the random oracle and ideal cipher model. and it is based on that of [8,9]. In this model, entities are modeled as oracles and attacks against the protocol is modeled as queries to these oracles. We prove that the protocol is secure under the random oracle model and ideal-cipher model, assuming intractability of the computational Diffie-Hellman problem.

3.1 Security Model

Players. Players in the model includes a server S and a set of clients $\mathbb{C}$ comprising clients $C_1, C_2, ..., C_n$. Each player participates in some distinct and possibly concurrent executions of the protocol, and each instance of their participation is modeled as an oracle. The j-th instance of the server is modeled as S^j, and the t_i-th instance of C_i is modeled as $C_i^{t_i}$, where $1 \leqslant i \leqslant n$ and $j, t_i \in \mathbb{N}$.

Each client obtains its distinct password p_i from a dictionary $\mathbb{D}$ containing N low-entropy passwords, and shares it with the server. The password is randomly chosen from the dictionary $\mathbb{D}$ with a uniform distribution.

The protocol nPAKE$^+$ comprises two algorithms:

- **PwdChoose**($\mathbb{D}$): a probabilistic password choosing algorithm which chooses a different password p_i uniformly distributed in the dictionary $\mathbb{D}$ for each client C_i.
- **GrpKeyAgrmt**($S, \mathbb{C}$): the group key agreement algorithm which involves the server S and clients from $\mathbb{C}$ produces a group session key for each client.

Queries. The adversary $\mathcal{A}$ can attack the protocol by making the following queries to the participants:

- **Execute**(S^j, $C_1^{t_1}, ..., C_n^{t_n}$): this query models passive attacks, in which the adversary $\mathcal{A}$ makes clients and the server to execute the protocol. The adversary can eavesdrop messages exchanged between all participants.
- **Send**($C_i^{t_i}$, m): this query models the adversary $\mathcal{A}$ sends a message m to the t_i-th instance of a client C_i. $\mathcal{A}$ then gets the output of oracle $C_i^{t_i}$ after it processes m according to the protocol nPAKE$^+$.
- **Send**(S^j, m): this query models the adversary $\mathcal{A}$ sends a message m to an instance of the server S. $\mathcal{A}$ then gets the output of oracle S^j after it processes m according to the protocol nPAKE$^+$.
- **Reveal**($C_i^{t_i}$), **Reveal**(S^j): These two queries model compromise of the session key derived by clients and the server. This query is only valid when the clients and the server hold a session key or are able to compute the session key.
- **Corrupt**($C_i^{t_i}$), **Corrupt**(S^j): These two queries model compromise of the long-term passwords p_i. The adversary $\mathcal{A}$ gets p_i by asking such a query, but he does not get any internal data of the instance being queried.

- **Test**($C_i^{t_i}$): This query models the semantic security of the group session key. This query can be asked only once and only if the queried oracle is fresh. This query is answered as follows: one flips a coin b and responses with **Reveal**($C_i^{t_i}$) if $b = 1$ or a random value if $b = 0$.

During the execution of the protocol, the adversary $\mathcal{A}$ tries to defeat the protocol nPAKE$^+$ by invoking the above queries. This execution is referred to as a game **Game**$^{\text{ake}}(nPAKE^+, \mathcal{A})$. The game runs as follows:

- **PwdChoose**($\mathbb{D}$) is run to choose a password p_i for the client C_i.
- Set each participant's group session key as null.
- Run the adversary $\mathcal{A}$ and answer queries made by $\mathcal{A}$.
- Adversary $\mathcal{A}$ outputs a guess b' for the bit b in the **Test** query.

Security Notion

- **Freshness.** An instance of the participant (i.e. an oracle) is said to be fresh if its session key is not corrupted, which means the oracle and its partners are not asked of a **Reveal** query.
- **AKE Security.** Depend on whether *Corrupt* query is available to the adversary, AKE security can be defined into two types, AKE security with (AKE-FS) and without (AKE) forward secrecy. The AKE(resp. AKE-FS) security is defined as the advantage of an adversary $\mathcal{A}$ winning the game **Game**$^{\text{ake}}(nPAKE, \mathcal{A})$(resp. **Game**$^{\text{ake-fs}}(nPAKE, \mathcal{A})$). We say that $\mathcal{A}$ wins if he correctly guess the bit b in the **Test** query in the game **Game**$^{\text{ake}}(nPAKE^+, \mathcal{A})$ (resp. **Game**$^{\text{ake-fs}}(nPAKE, \mathcal{A})$). The advantage of the adversary winning the game is $\text{Adv}_{nPAKE+}^{ake}(\mathcal{A}) = 2 \cdot Pr[b = b'] - 1$ (resp. $\text{Adv}_{nPAKE+}^{ake-fs}(\mathcal{A}) = 2 \cdot Pr[b = b'] - 1$), where the probability space is over all random coin tosses.
    The protocol nPAKE$^+$ is said to be **AKE-Secure**(resp. **AKE-FS-Secure**) if the adversary's advantage is negligible in the security parameter.
- **Authentication.** The probability of the adversary $\mathcal{A}$ successfully impersonating a client or a server is denoted as $\text{Succ}_{nPAKE+}^{auth}(\mathcal{A})$. The protocol nPAKE$^+$ is said to be **Auth-Secure** if $\text{Succ}_{nPAKE+}^{auth}(\mathcal{A})$ is negligible in the security parameter.

4   The nPAKE$^+$ Protocol

In this section, we present a group PAKE protocol, referred to as nPAKE$^+$ protocol, for the independent-password setting. They agree on two large primes p and q with $p = 2q+1$, a subgroup $\mathbb{G}$ of Z_p^*, a generator g of $\mathbb{G}$ and a cryptographic secure keyed hash function $\mathcal{H}(\cdot)$. Notations used in the description of the protocol are given in Table 1.

4.1   The Diffie-Hellman Key Tree

Key graphs are extensively used in non-password based group key agreement protocols to achieve great efficiency in both computation and communications.

Table 1. Notations

C_i	The i-th client, $i = 1, 2, ..., n$
S	The trusted server
p_i	The password shared between C_i and S
p, q	Two large primes with $p = 2q + 1$
$\mathbb{G}, g$	The subgroup of order q in Z_p^* and its generator, respectively
$\mathcal{H}(\cdot)$	A secure hash function mapping $\{0, 1\}^*$ to $\{0, 1\}^{len}$
K_i, BK_i [1]	The secret key and blinded key for client $C_i, i = 1, 2, ..., n$
$\langle l, v \rangle$	The v-th node at the l-th level on the binary key tree (Fig. 1)
$K_{\langle l,v \rangle}, BK_{\langle l,v \rangle}$	The secret key and blinded key for node $\langle l, v \rangle$
SK_i	The session key shared between C_i and $C_{i+1}, i = 1, 2, ..., n-1$

---

[1] They are interchangeable with $K_{\langle l,v \rangle}, BK_{\langle l,v \rangle}$ if C_i is located at $\langle l, v \rangle$ on the key tree.

Wong et al. [38] and Wallner et al. [37] are the first to introduce the concept of key graph, called the *Logical Key Hierarchy*(LKH), to improve efficiency in group key management. The *One-way Function Tree*(OFT) proposed by McGrew and Sherman [28] improves the hierarchical tree approach further. In OFT, the key of a parent is derived from the keys of its children, and hence it reduces the size of the rekeying messages to half of that of LKH. Based on the key tree, some group key agreement proposals [30,10,33,34,29,22] use the Diffie-Hellman exchange technique in group key establishment.

The Diffie-Hellman key tree used in our protocol is a binary tree in which each leaf represents a group member. Every interior node of the key tree has exactly two children and is not associated with any group member. An example of the key tree used in our protocol is shown in Fig. 1. The nodes are denoted $\langle l, v \rangle$, where $0 \leqslant v \leqslant 2^l - 1$ since each level l hosts at most 2^l nodes (the root is at the 0-th level). For any interior node $\langle l, v \rangle$, its left child and right child are denoted $\langle l + 1, 2v \rangle$ and $\langle l + 1, 2v + 1 \rangle$ respectively. Each node $\langle l, v \rangle$ on the key tree is associated with a secret key $K_{\langle l,v \rangle}$ and a corresponding blinded key $BK_{\langle l,v \rangle}$ computed as $g^{K_{\langle l,v \rangle}} \mod p$. The secret key $K_{\langle l,v \rangle}$ at a leaf node $\langle l, v \rangle$, which is associated with a client C_i, is constructed between the client C_i and the server S in our protocol. While the secret key of an interior node is derived from the keys of the interior node's two children by the Diffie-Hellman computation. The corresponding blinded key is then computed following the formula $BK_{\langle l,v \rangle} = g^{K_{\langle l,v \rangle}} \mod p$. Specifically, the secret key and the blinded key of an interior node $\langle l, v \rangle$ are computed recursively as follows:

$$
\begin{aligned}
K_{\langle l,v \rangle} &= \mathcal{H}(g^{K_{\langle l+1,2v \rangle} K_{\langle l+1,2v+1 \rangle}} \mod p) \\
&= \mathcal{H}((BK_{\langle l+1,2v \rangle})^{K_{\langle l+1,2v+1 \rangle}} \mod p) \\
&= \mathcal{H}((BK_{\langle l+1,2v+1 \rangle})^{K_{\langle l+1,2v \rangle}} \mod p), \\
BK_{\langle l,v \rangle} &= g^{K_{\langle l,v \rangle}} \mod p.
\end{aligned}
\tag{1}
$$

Note that if a client C_i is located at the leaf node $\langle l, v \rangle$ on the key tree, then its secret key and blinded key $K_{\langle l,v \rangle}, BK_{\langle l,v \rangle}$ are also denoted as K_i and BK_i

respectively. These two types of denotations (see Fig. 1) are interchangeable for a client C_i at a leaf node $\langle l, v \rangle$.

Therefore, computing a secret key at $\langle l, v \rangle$ requires the knowledge of the key of one child and the blinded key of the other child. The secret key $K_{\langle 0,0 \rangle}$ at the root node is the group key which is known only to the group members.

In order to compute the group key, a client C_i needs to know a set of blinded keys, which form a set called the co-path. With the blinded keys in the co-path, the client C_i can compute a set of keys from itself to the root of the key tree and these keys form another set called key-path. For the client C_i located at a leaf node $\langle l, v \rangle$, we denote its key-path as KP_i or $KP_{\langle l,v \rangle}$, its co-path as CP_i or $CP_{\langle l,v \rangle}$. On the key tree, the key path KP_i is a path from C_i itself to the root node ($\langle 0, 0 \rangle$) of the key tree. While the co-path CP_i is formed from all the nodes that are directly connected with the key-path KP_i on the key tree. The key-path KP_i splits the co-path CP_i into two halves: R_i on the right side and L_i on the left side.

For example, in Fig. 1 the client C_2's key-path is $KP_2 = KP_{\langle 3,1 \rangle} = \{K_{\langle 3,1 \rangle}, K_{\langle 2,0 \rangle}, K_{\langle 1,0 \rangle}, K_{\langle 0,0 \rangle}\}$, and its co-path is $CP_2 = CP_{\langle 3,1 \rangle} = \{BK_{\langle 3,0 \rangle}, BK_{\langle 2,1 \rangle}, BK_{\langle 1,1 \rangle}\}$. The key-path KP_2 is a path from C_2 (or $\langle 3, 1 \rangle$) to the root of the key tree. Each node from the co-path CP_2 is directly connected with the key-path KP_2 on the key tree. The co-path CP_2 is split into two halves by the key-path KP_2: $R_2 = \{BK_{\langle 2,1 \rangle}, BK_{\langle 1,1 \rangle}\}$, and $L_2 = \{BK_{\langle 3,0 \rangle}\}$.

The following two properties of the key tree are important for group key agreement in our protocol:

- For any binary Diffie-Hellman key tree with n leaves labeled from C_1 to C_n, client C_i can compute L_{i+1} using L_i, K_i, and $\{BK_j : 1 \leq j \leq n\}$. Similarly, C_i can compute R_{i-1} using R_i, K_i, and $\{BK_j : 1 \leq j \leq n\}$.
- For any binary Diffie-Hellman key tree with n leaves labeled from C_1 to C_n, client C_i can compute the group key using L_i, R_i, and K_i.

With all the blinded keys of its co-path, a client C_i can compute all the keys along the key-path, including the group secret $K_{\langle 0,0 \rangle}$. For the example in Fig. 1,

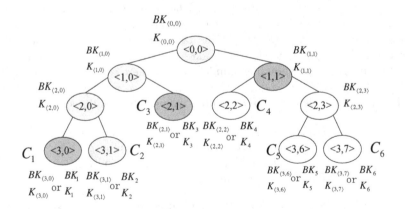

Fig. 1. An example of the key tree

with its own key $K_{\langle 3,1 \rangle}$, C_2 can compute $K_{\langle 2,0 \rangle}$, $K_{\langle 1,0 \rangle}$ and $K_{\langle 0,0 \rangle}$ using $BK_{\langle 3,0 \rangle}$, $BK_{\langle 2,1 \rangle}$ and $BK_{\langle 1,1 \rangle}$, respectively.

4.2 Description of the Protocol

After introducing the Diffie-Hellman key tree, we describe our nPAKE$^+$ protocol in this section. Our protocol achieves group key establishment and authentication with 3 message flows. The first flow starts from the client C_1, traverses through $C_2, C_3, ..., C_n$, and finally reaches the server S. The second flow initiated by the server propagates in the reverse direction from S until C_1. After the second flow terminates at C_1, C_1 starts the third flow towards C_n and terminates at S.

- **Flow 1:** As the initiator, client C_1 chooses $r_1 \in_R \mathbb{Z}_q^*$ and computes $X_1 = g^{r_1}$ and $X_1^* = \mathcal{E}_{p_1}(X_1)$. Then it initiates the protocol by sending the request $\{C_i\}_{i=1}^n | X_1^*$ to the next client. The request traverses all the clients from C_1 to C_n until it reaches the server. Upon receiving the request, each client C_i selects $r_i \in_R \mathbb{Z}_q^*$, computes $X_i = g^{r_i}$ and the encrypted exponential $X_i^* = \mathcal{E}_{p_i}(X_i) = \mathcal{E}_{p_i}(g^{r_i})$ and adds it to the request. When the request finally reaches the server S, it consists of n identities and n encrypted exponentials contributed by the n clients.

$$C_i \longrightarrow C_{i+1} : \quad \{C_j\}_{j=1}^n | \{X_j^*\}_{j=1}^i, \quad i = 1, 2, ..., n-1,$$
$$C_n \longrightarrow S : \quad \{C_j\}_{j=1}^n | \{X_j^*\}_{j=1}^n. \tag{2}$$

- **Flow 2:** The second message flow runs in the reverse direction, from the server S to C_1. After receiving the request in the first message flow, the server parses $\{C_i\}_{i=1}^n | \{X_i^*\}_{i=1}^n$, and uses the corresponding passwords to decrypt X_i^* to obtain $X_i = g^{r_i} (i = 1, 2, ..., n)$. Then for each client $C_i (i = 1, 2, ..., n)$, S chooses $s_i \in_R \mathbb{Z}_q^*$ and computes a session key $K_i = (X_i)^{s_i} = (g^{r_i})^{s_i}$. Then the server computes $Y_i = g^{s_i}$, $Y_i^* = \mathcal{E}_{p_i}(Y_i)$, $\pi = BK_1 | C_1 | \cdots | BK_n | C_n$ and $\tau_i = \mathcal{H}(\pi | X_i | Y_i | K_i)$, and sends $\pi | \{Y_j^* | \tau_j\}_{j=1}^n$ to C_n.
  The reply originated from the server S passes through C_n to C_1. Upon receiving the reply, $C_i (i = n, n-1, ..., 1)$ parses it as $\pi | \{Y_j^* | \tau_j\}_{j=1}^i | R_i | \xi_i$, (for $i = n$, $R_n | \xi_n = nil$). C_i decrypts Y_i^* to obtain $Y_i = g^{s_i}$ using its password. Then the client computes the session key $K_i = (Y_i)^{r_i} = (g^{s_i})^{r_i}$ and the blinded $BK_i = g^{K_i}$, and verifies whether the computed BK_i equals to BK_i in π. Then C_i verifies the validity of π by checking $\mathcal{H}(\pi | X_i | Y_i | K_i) \stackrel{?}{=} \tau_i$. In the case where $i \neq n$, C_i also computes $SK_i = (BK_{i+1})^{K_i}$ and verifies R_i by checking whether $\mathcal{H}(R_i | SK_i)$ equals ξ_i.
  If the reply passes all verifications, $C_i (i = n, n-1, ..., 2)$ prepares an outgoing message for the next client C_{i-1}. C_i computes R_{i-1} with R_i, K_i and π, and computes $SK_{i-1} = (BK_{i-1})^{K_i}$. Then he computes $\xi_{i-1} = \mathcal{H}(R_{i-1} | SK_{i-1})$ and sends $\pi | \{Y_j^* | \tau_j\}_{j=1}^{i-1} | R_{i-1} | \xi_{i-1}$ to C_{i-1}.

$$S \longrightarrow C_n : \quad \pi | \{Y_j^* | \tau_j\}_{j=1}^n,$$
$$C_i \longrightarrow C_{i-1} : \quad \pi | \{Y_j^* | \tau_j\}_{j=1}^{i-1} | R_{i-1} | \xi_{i-1}, \quad i = n, ..., 2. \tag{3}$$

where $\pi = BK_1 | C_1 | \cdots | BK_n | C_n$.

- **Flow 3:** When the reply in the second message flow finally reaches C_1, C_1 performs the verifications as specified in Flow 2. If the verifications are successful, C_1 computes the group key GK_1 with R_1 and K_1 as well as π. Then C_1 computes L_2, $\sigma_1 = \mathcal{H}(L_2|SK_1)$, $\eta_1 = \mathcal{H}(C_1|C_2|\cdots|C_n|K_1)$, and starts the last message flow by sending out $L_2|\sigma_1|\eta_1$ to C_2.

  Then each client $C_i(i = 2, 3, ..., n)$ receives the message $L_i|\sigma_{i-1}|\{\eta_j\}_{j=1}^{i-1}$, and verifies L_i by checking $\sigma_{i-1} \overset{?}{=} \mathcal{H}(L_i|SK_{i-1})$. If the verification is successful, the client computes the group key GK_i with K_i, L_i, R_i and π. If $i \neq n$, C_i computes $\sigma_i = \mathcal{H}(L_{i+1}|SK_i)$, computes L_{i+1} from L_i, K_i and π, computes $\eta_i = \mathcal{H}(C_1|C_2|\cdots|C_n|K_i)$, and sends the outgoing message $L_{i+1}|\sigma_i|\{\eta_j\}_{j=1}^{i}$ to C_{i+1}. Otherwise, C_n computes η_n and sends $\{\eta_j\}_{j=1}^{n}$ to the server S.

$$
\begin{aligned}
C_i \longrightarrow C_{i+1} &: \quad L_{i+1}|\sigma_i|\{\eta_j\}_{j=1}^{i}, \quad i = 1, ..., n-1. \\
C_n \longrightarrow S &: \quad \{\eta_j\}_{j=1}^{n}
\end{aligned}
\tag{4}
$$

After the third message flow finally reaches the server S, the server verifies each η_i from client C_i to authenticate each client. If any verification is failed, then the server can identify which client(s) is(are) invalid and not authenticated. This measure is intended to thwart on-line password guessing attacks.

After the last flow reaches the server, each client has already computed its L_i and R_i, so each client obtains its co-path $CP_i = L_i \cup R_i$, independently calculates the same group key $K_{\langle 0,0 \rangle}$ and uses it for secure group communications.

5 Security Results

To prove the security of the proposed protocol nPAKE$^+$, we incrementally define a series of games starting from the real protocol nPAKE$^+$ **G_0** until game **G_8**. The probability of the adversary $\mathcal{A}$ winning a game **G_m** is obtained according to a negligible probability difference from the winning probability in the next game **G_{m+1}**. Game **G_8** is a purely random game and the winning probability of $\mathcal{A}$ is $1/2$. Therefore, we prove security of the protocol by showing the advantage of $\mathcal{A}$ in **G_0**, i.e. the real protocol nPAKE$^+$, is negligible.

Theorem 1. *Let $nPAKE^+$ be the password-based group key agreement protocol with a password space $\mathbb{D}$ of size N. Let $\mathcal{A}$ be the adversary against* **AKE-Security** *of $nPAKE^+$ within a time bound t, with q_s interactions with the protocol participants and q_p passive eavesdroppings, q_h hash queries, and q_e encryption/decryption queries. Let $\mathsf{Succ}_{\mathbb{G}}^{\mathsf{CDH}}(T)$ be the success probability against the CDH problem of an adversary in time T. Then we have:*

$$
\mathsf{Adv}_{nPAKE+}^{ake}(\mathcal{A}) \leqslant 24n * q_h \mathsf{Succ}_{\mathbb{G}}^{\mathsf{CDH}}(t') + \frac{6q_s}{N} + \frac{4q_s + q_h^2}{2^{len}} + \frac{(2q_e + 3q_s + 6nq_p)^2}{q-1},
$$

where $t' = t + (q_s + (8n + n\log n) * q_p + q_e + n)\tau_{\mathbb{G}}$, with $\tau_{\mathbb{G}}$ being the computation time for an exponentiation in $\mathbb{G}$, n being the maximum number of clients in all protocol executions.

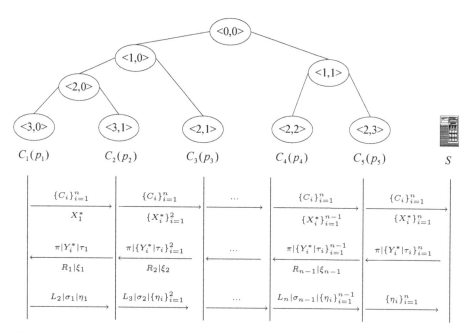

Fig. 2. The nPAKE$^+$ protocol with n clients and a server illustrated with a sample 5-leaf key tree: $X_i^* = \mathcal{E}_{p_i}(X_i) = \mathcal{E}_{p_i}(g^{r_i})$; $Y_i^* = \mathcal{E}_{p_i}(Y_i) = \mathcal{E}_{p_i}(g^{s_i})$; where $r_i, s_i \in_R \mathbb{Z}_q^*$. $\pi = BK_1|C_1|BK_2|C_2|...|BK_n|C_n$; $K_i = g^{r_i s_i}$. $\tau_i = \mathcal{H}(\pi|X_i|Y_i|K_i)$; $\xi_i = \mathcal{H}(R_i|SK_i)$; $\eta_i = \mathcal{H}(C_1|C_2|...|C_n|X_i|Y_i|K_i)$; $\sigma_i = \mathcal{H}(L_{i+1}|SK_i)$.

Proof. Due to lack of space, we can only sketch the proof process. We define a series of games in which a simulator simulates the protocol nPAKE$^+$ and provides oracle queries to the attacker. The first game is the real protocol nPAKE$^+$, while in the last game each client obtains a random group session key so that the attacker's advantage against the last game is 0. By embedding a CDH instance into the game and using random self-reducibility, we can calculate probability differences of the attacker winning different games. Finally, we can obtain the attacker's advantage against the real protocol nPAKE$^+$ under the random oracle and ideal cipher model, which is related to the attacker's advantage against the CDH problem.

The theorem essentially shows that the nPAKE$^+$ protocol is secure against the dictionary attacks as the adversary's advantage against the protocol is constrained by the number of **Send**-queries, which represents the number of interactions with a client or a server. Normally the number of online guessing failures is restricted in existing applications, which ensures security of the proposed protocol. On the other hand, the adversary's advantage with offline dictionary attacks is proportional to its capability in solving the CDH problem. Under the assumption of hardness of the CDH problem, the protocol is secure. It is worth to note that the security of nPAKE$^+$ relies only on the CDH hardness assumption, while other protocols requires also the TGCDH (Trigon Group CDH) assumption and the MDDH (Multi-DDH) assumption [8,11].

Theorem 2. *Let $\mathcal{A}$ be the adversary against* **Auth-Security** *of $nPAKE^+$ within a time bound t, with q_s interactions with the protocol participants and q_p passive eavesdroppings, q_h hash queries, and q_e encryption/decryption queries. Let $\mathsf{Succ}_{\mathbb{G}}^{\mathsf{CDH}}(T)$ be the success probability against the* CDH *problem of an adversary in time T. Then we have:*

$$\mathsf{Succ}_{nPAKE^+}^{auth}(\mathcal{A}) \leqslant 11n * q_h \mathsf{Succ}_{\mathbb{G}}^{\mathsf{CDH}}(t') + \frac{3q_s}{N} + \frac{4q_s + q_h^2}{2^{len+1}} + \frac{(2q_e + 3q_s + 6nq_p)^2}{2(q-1)},$$

where $t' = t + (q_s + (8n + n\log n) * q_p + q_e + n)\tau_{\mathbb{G}}$, with $\tau_{\mathbb{G}}$ being the computation time for an exponentiation in $\mathbb{G}$, n being the maximum number of clients in all protocol executions.

This theorem states that the adversary's advantage of breaking the authentication property is proportional to the number of **Send** queries, which is the number of online attacking attempts of the adversary. Same as in Theorem 1, the advantage of the adversary by offline dictionary attacks is negligible assuming hardness of the CDH problem.

Theorem 3. *Let $\mathcal{A}$ be the adversary against* **AKE-FS-Security** *of $nPAKE^+$ within a time bound t, with q_s interactions with the protocol participants and q_p passive eavesdroppings, q_h hash queries, and q_e encryption/decryption queries. Let $\mathsf{Succ}_{\mathbb{G}}^{\mathsf{CDH}}(T)$ be the success probability against the* CDH *problem of an adversary in time T. Then we have:*

$$\mathsf{Adv}_{nPAKE^+}^{ake-fs}(\mathcal{A}) \leqslant 2(10 + (q_s + q_p)^{(n+1)}) \cdot nq_h \mathsf{Succ}_{\mathbb{G}}^{\mathsf{CDH}}(t') + \frac{6q_s}{N}$$
$$+ \frac{4q_s + q_h^2}{2^{len}} + \frac{(2q_e + 3q_s + 6nq_p)^2}{q-1},$$

where $t' = t + (q_s + (8n + n\log n) * q_p + q_e + n)\tau_{\mathbb{G}}$, with $\tau_{\mathbb{G}}$ being the computation time for an exponentiation in $\mathbb{G}$, n being the maximum number of clients in all protocol executions.

With this theorem, we state that the protocol is secure with forward secrecy. In case of password compromise, *fresh* session keys are still secure against dictionary attacks. This makes the protocol secure against valid-but-curious clients interested in knowing other clients' passwords. A valid-but-curious client is prevented from knowing keys of a group of which he is not a member, and a compromised password cannot be used to gain non-negligible advantage in breaking *fresh* keys.

6   Discussion

Under the independent password setting, our protocol is both flexible and efficient in communications and computation. First, our protocol accommodates formations of secure subgroups. Any subgroup of the whole group can run the protocol to establish a group key for the subgroup. Secondly, the protocol employs key tree in group key construction to provide communication and computation efficiency.

In the nPAKE$^+$ protocol, the group key computation is closely related to tree structure. By default, the key tree is formed to be a balanced binary tree to reduce the computation cost to minimal. Alternatively, the first client (the initiator) or the server can decide the tree structure. This key structure information should be protected from manipulation. Either it is agreed upon via an out-of-band channel, or it is authenticated during the protocol.

The hierarchical structure of the protocol has a good feature that a subgroup of clients corresponding to a subtree of whole key tree. For each internal node of the key tree, its key can be used to secure communications among the clients that are its descendants. Therefore, a tree structure can be decided so that the clients requiring a separate key is allocated to the same subtree of the key tree.

The protocol needs only three message flows to establish the group key, and each client needs only $5 + \lceil \log n \rceil$ exponentiations while the server needs $3n$ exponentiations. A comparison on computation cost between the protocol by Bresson et al. [8], EKE-U [11] and our protocol is given in Table 2. Both Bresson's protocol and EKE-U require $O(n)$ exponentiations for each client on the average, while our protocol requires only $O(\log n)$ for each client. And the total number of exponentiations required in our protocol $O(n \log n)$ is also lower than $O(n^2)$ in Bresson's protocol and EKE-U.

Table 2. Computation Efficiency Comparison: Number of Exponentiations

	Client (Avg.)	Server	Total
Bresson's Protocol	$(n+5)/2$	-	$n(n+5)/2$
EKE-U Protocol	$(n+3)/2$	$(n+1)(n+2)/2$	$n^2 + 3n$
nPAKE$^+$ Protocol	$5 + \lceil \log n \rceil$	$3n$	$n(8 + \lceil \log n \rceil)$

7 Conclusion

In this paper, we proposed a hierarchical group password-authenticated key exchange protocol where each client shares an independent password with a trusted server. Under this independent-password setting, our protocol provides better flexibility than those protocols under the single-password setting. Moreover, the protocol employs a Diffie-Hellman key tree for group key agreement, and hence achieves great efficiency in both computation and communications. Finally, we prove its security under the random oracle and ideal cipher models, and compare its performance with existing protocols.

Acknowledgement

This work was supported in part by the Concerted Research Action (GOA) Ambiorics 2005/11 of the Flemish Government and by the IAP Programme P6/26 BCRYPT of the Belgian State (Belgian Science Policy). Zhiguo Wan is supported in part by a research grant of the IBBT (Interdisciplinary institute for BroadBand Technology) of the Flemish Government.

References

1. Abdalla, M., Pointcheval, D., Scalable, A.: A Scalable Password-Based Group Key Exchange Protocol in the Standard Model. In: Lai, X., Chen, K. (eds.) ASIACRYPT 2006. LNCS, vol. 4284, pp. 332–347. Springer, Heidelberg (2006)
2. Asokan, N., Ginzboorg, P.: Key Agreement in Ad-hoc Networks. Computer Communications 23(18), 1627–1637 (2000)
3. Bellare, M., Rogaway, P.: The AuthA Protocol for Password-Based Authenticated Key Exchange. In: Contribution to the IEEE P1363 study group (March 2000)
4. Bellare, M., Pointcheval, D., Rogaway, P.: Authenticated Key Exchange Secure Against Dictionary Attack. In: Preneel, B. (ed.) EUROCRYPT 2000. LNCS, vol. 1807, Springer, Heidelberg (2000)
5. Bellovin, S.M., Merritt, M.: Encrypted Key Exchange: Password Based Protocols Secure against Dictionary Attacks. In: Proceedings 1992 IEEE Symposium on Research in Security and Privacy, pp. 72–84. IEEE Computer Society Press, Los Alamitos (1992)
6. Bellovin, S.M., Merritt, M.: Augmented EncryptedKey Exchange: A Password-based Protocol Secure against Dictionary attacks and Password File Compromise. In: Proceedings of CCS 1993, pp. 244–250 (1993)
7. Boyko, V., MacKenzie, P.D., Patel, S.: Provably Secure Password-Authenticated Key Exchange Using Diffie-Hellman. In: Preneel, B. (ed.) EUROCRYPT 2000. LNCS, vol. 1807, pp. 156–171. Springer, Heidelberg (2000)
8. Bresson, E., Chevassut, O., Pointcheval, D.: Group Diffie-Hellman Key Exchange Secure against Dictionary Attacks. In: Zheng, Y. (ed.) ASIACRYPT 2002. LNCS, vol. 2501, Springer, Heidelberg (2002)
9. Bresson, E., Chevassut, O., Pointcheval, D.: Security Proofs for an Efficient Password-Based Key Exchange. In: Proceedings of the 10th ACM Conference on Computer and Communications Security 2003, pp. 241–250 (2003)
10. Burmester, M., Desmedt, Y., Secure, A.: Efficient Conference Key Distribution System (extended abstract). In: De Santis, A. (ed.) EUROCRYPT 1994. LNCS, vol. 950, Springer, Heidelberg (1995)
11. Byun, J.W., Lee, D.H.: N-Party Encrypted Diffie-Hellman Key Exchange Using Different Passwords. In: Ioannidis, J., Keromytis, A.D., Yung, M. (eds.) ACNS 2005. LNCS, vol. 3531, pp. 75–90. Springer, Heidelberg (2005)
12. Byun, J.W., Lee, S.-M., Lee, D.H., Hong, D.: Constant-Round Password-Based Group Key Generation for Multi-layer Ad-Hoc Networks. In: Clark, J.A., Paige, R.F., Polack, F.A.C., Brooke, P.J. (eds.) SPC 2006. LNCS, vol. 3934, pp. 3–17. Springer, Heidelberg (2006)
13. Byun, J.W., Jeong, I.R., Lee, D.H., Park, C.-S.: Password-Authenticated Key Exchange between Clients with Different Passwords. In: Deng, R.H., Qing, S., Bao, F., Zhou, J. (eds.) ICICS 2002. LNCS, vol. 2513, pp. 134–146. Springer, Heidelberg (2002)
14. Dutta, R., Barua, R.: Password-Based Encrypted Group Key Agreement. International Journal of Network Security 3(1), 23–34 (2006)
15. Gennaro, R., Lindell, Y.: A Framework for Password-Based Authenticated Key Exchange. In: Biham, E. (ed.) EUROCRPYT 2003. LNCS, vol. 2656, pp. 524–543. Springer, Heidelberg (2003)
16. Goldreich, O., Lindell, Y.: Session-Key Generation Using Human Passwords Only. In: Kilian, J. (ed.) CRYPTO 2001. LNCS, vol. 2139, pp. 408–432. Springer, Heidelberg (2001)
17. Jablon, D.: Strong Password-Only Authenticated Key Exchange. Computer Communication Review, ACM SIGCOMM 26(5), 5–26 (1996)

18. Jablon, D.P.: Extended Password Key Exchange Protocols Immune to Dictionary Attacks. In: WETICE 1997, pp. 248–255. IEEE Computer Society, Los Alamitos (June 1997)
19. Katz, J., Ostrovsky, R., Yung, M.: Efficient Password-Authenticated Key Exchange Using Human-Memorable Passwords. In: Pfitzmann, B. (ed.) EUROCRYPT 2001. LNCS, vol. 2045, pp. 475–494. Springer, Heidelberg (2001)
20. Katz, J., Ostrovsky, R., Yung, M.: Forward Security in Password-Only Key Exchange Protocols. In: Cimato, S., Galdi, C., Persiano, G. (eds.) SCN 2002. LNCS, vol. 2576, Springer, Heidelberg (2003)
21. Kim, Y., Perrig, A., Tsudik, G.: Simple and Fault-tolerant Key Agreement for Dynamic Collaborative Groups. In: Proceedings of CCS 2000 (2000)
22. Kim, Y., Perrig, A., Tsudik, G.: Communication-Efficient Group Key Agreement. In: Proceedings of IFIP SEC 2001 (2001)
23. Lee, S.-M., Hwang, J.Y., Lee, D.H.: Efficient Password-Based Group Key Exchange. In: Katsikas, S.K., Lopez, J., Pernul, G. (eds.) TrustBus 2004. LNCS, vol. 3184, pp. 191–199. Springer, Heidelberg (2004)
24. Lin, C.-L., Sun, H.-M., Hwang, T.: Three-party Encrypted Key Exchange: Attacks and A Solution. ACM Operating Systems Review 34(4), 12–20 (2000)
25. Lin, C.-L., Sun, H.-M., Hwang, T.: Three-party Encrypted Key Exchange Without Server Public-Keys. IEEE Communications Letters 5(12), 497–499 (2001)
26. Lucks, S.: Open Key Exchange: How to Defeat Dictionary Attacks Without Encrypting Public Keys. In: Security Protocols Workshop, pp. 79–90 (1997)
27. MacKenzie, P.: The PAK suite: Protocols for Password-Authenticated Key Exchange. Submission to IEEE P1363.2, (April 2002)
28. McGrew, D., Sherman, A.: Key Establishment in Large Dynamic Groups Using One-way Function Trees. Techinical Report 0755, Network Associates, Inc (1998)
29. Perrig, A., Song, D., Tygar, D.: ELK, A New Protocol for Efficient Large-Group Key Distribution. In: Proceedings of IEEE Syposium on Security and Privacy (2001)
30. Steer, D., Strawczynski, L., Diffie, W., Wiener, M.: A Secure Audio Teleconference System. In: Goldwasser, S. (ed.) CRYPTO 1988. LNCS, vol. 403, Springer, Heidelberg (1990)
31. Steiner, M., Tsudik, G., Waidner, M.: Refinement and Extension of Encrypted Key Exchange. ACM SIGOPS Operating Systems Review 29(3), 22–30 (1995)
32. Steiner, M., Tsudik, G., Waidner, M.: Diffie-Hellman Key Distribution Extended to Group Communication. In: Proceedings of CCS 1996 (March 1996)
33. Steiner, M., Tsudik, G., Waidner, M.: Cliques: A New Approach to Group Key Agreement. In: IEEE TPDS (August 2000)
34. Steiner, M., Tsudik, G., Waidner, M.: Key Agreement in Dynamic Peer Groups. In: IEEE Transactions on Parallel and Distributed Systems (August 2000)
35. Tang, Q., Chen, L.: Weaknesses in Two Group Diffie-Hellman Key Exchange Protocols. Cryptology ePrint Archive (2005)/197
36. Tang, Q., Choo, K.-K.: Secure Password-based Authenticated Group Key Agreement for Data-Sharing Peer-to-Peer Networks. In: Zhou, J., Yung, M., Bao, F. (eds.) ACNS 2006. LNCS, vol. 3989, Springer, Heidelberg (2006)
37. Wallner, D.M., Harder, E.J., Agee, R.C.: Key Management for Multicast: Issues and Architectures, Internet Request for Comments 2627, (June 1999)
38. Wong, C.K., Gouda, M., Lam, S.: Secure Group Communications Using Key Graphs. In: Proceedings of SIGCOMM 1998 (1998)
39. Wu, T.: The Secure Remote Password Protocol. In: 1998 Internet Society Symposium on Network and Distributed System Security, pp. 97–111 (1998)

An Efficient Password-Only Two-Server Authenticated Key Exchange System[*]

Haimin Jin[1,2], Duncan S. Wong[1], and Yinlong Xu[2]

[1] Department of Computer Science
City University of Hong Kong
Hong Kong, China
duncan@cityu.edu.hk
[2] Department of Computer Science
University of Science and Technology of China
China
jhm1213@mail.ustc.edu.cn, ylxu@ustc.edu.cn

Abstract. One of the prominent advantages of password-only two-server authenticated key exchange is that the user password will remain secure against offline dictionary attacks even after one of the servers has been compromised. The first system of this type was proposed by Yang, Deng and Bao in 2006. The system is efficient with a total of eight communication rounds in one protocol run. However, the security assumptions are strong. It assumes that one particular server cannot be compromised by an active adversary. It also assumes that there exists a secure communication channel between the two servers. Recently, a new protocol has been proposed by the same group of researchers. The new one removes these assumptions, but in return pays a very high price on the communication overhead. It takes altogether ten rounds to complete one protocol run and requires more computation. Therefore, the question remains is whether it is possible to build a protocol which can significantly reduce the number of communication rounds without introducing additional security assumptions or computational complexity. In this paper, we give an affirmative answer by proposing a very efficient protocol with no additional assumption introduced. The protocol requires only six communication rounds without increasing the computational complexity.

1 Introduction

Password-only authenticated key exchange is a scheme which allows a user who holds only a low-entropy password to conduct authentication and key exchange with a server. Comparing with related types of authenticated key exchange schemes, for example, schemes based on cryptographic keys, password-only authenticated key exchange is very practical with high usability, because users only need to memorize a short password which is already used commonly in existing authentication systems.

---

[*] The work was supported by CityU grants (Project Nos. 7001844, 7001959, 7002001).

S. Qing, H. Imai, and G. Wang (Eds.): ICICS 2007, LNCS 4861, pp. 44–56, 2007.

A **Password-only Two-Server Authenticated Key Exchange** (PTAKE) scheme [18,17] is an extension of the conventional single-server setting [13]. Besides a user and a server, PTAKE also has an additional server. The existing, front-end, server that the user is communicating with is called the *Service Server*, SS, and the additional, back-end, server which communicates only with SS is called the *Control Server*, CS. In a conventional single-server scheme, the server has a database of the users' passwords or some verification data of the passwords. If the server is compromised, an adversary can obtain the passwords of all the users directly from the database, or be able to launch offline dictionary attacks against all users' passwords as the database provides enough information about the passwords. This problem is generally referred to as *single point of failure*.

In a PTAKE scheme instead, the password of each user is split into two shares and each server is given only one share, so that the password cannot be obtained in an information theoretic sense if only one share is known. Currently, all the concrete PTAKE schemes [18,17] use the same splitting mechanism: two random shares π_1 and π_2 are generated such that the password $\pi \equiv \pi_1 + \pi_2 \pmod{q}$ for a large prime q. A secure PTAKE scheme is designed such that even if one of the two servers is compromised, the scheme should still be able to thwart offline dictionary attacks against π. This feature together with the architecture of PTAKE yields a very desirable and practical system. As we can see, users only interact with SS but will never interact directly with CS, while CS only interacts with SS. This creates two networks, one *external* and one *internal*, with SS acting as the bridge/firewall between these two. In practice, this makes an outsider very difficult to compromise the internal network. The internal network can also be totally hidden from the outsiders. It is even possible for us to make outsiders totally unaware of the existence of CS. In addition, since CS only interacts with SS, it is relatively easy to provide maximal security protection for CS and make it much more difficult to compromise. To defend against insider attacks, it is also much easier to do so than the conventional one-server scheme as the administrative and operational tasks of SS and CS are separated and can be carried out by two independent teams. They do not share any secret.

The first PTAKE was proposed by Yang, Deng and Bao [18] in 2006. In one protocol run of their scheme, the user carries out four rounds of communications with SS and the CS carries out another four rounds with SS. The total number of communications rounds is therefore eight. Following the notion of external and internal networks, they assume that the internal network is impossible for an active adversary[1] to compromise. This assumption makes certain sense for some systems, but not in general. An insider who has full access to CS but not to SS may collude with an outsider and launch a successful offline dictionary attack against their scheme. Another issue of the scheme is that the communication channel between the two servers needs to be secure against eavesdroppers in order to ensure the security of the session key. This also introduces some additional cost for actual implementation of the scheme.

---

[1] An active adversary is considered to be an adversary which can do both eavesdropping and hijacking of messages.

Recently, a new scheme has been proposed by the same group of researchers [17]. The new one solves both of the problems mentioned above. In addition, it further enhances the security with respect to the session key, namely, CS can no longer compute the session key established between the user and SS. This is a desirable feature in practice as SS (Service Server) is generally the one to provide actual services while CS is simply called in for authenticating the user. There is no need or it simply downgrades the user's privacy if we let CS know the session key. The tradeoff of this new scheme is that the number of communication rounds for completing one protocol run is increased to ten.

1.1   Our Results

For the latest conventional password-only single-server schemes [13], the number of communication rounds between the user and the server is usually only three. In the two-server setting, there are three parties. The question we are asking is whether we can build a secure PTAKE scheme which takes only three communication rounds for mutual authentication between the user and SS, another three rounds for mutual authentication between CS and SS, and piggybacks some additional messages along these rounds for mutual authentication between the user and CS. As a result, the scheme only requires six rounds of communications to complete one protocol run. It is also desirable if we can attain the same level of security as in [17], namely

1. the scheme remains secure against offline dictionary attacks after one of CS and SS has been compromised by an *active* adversary;
2. no secure channel is required between CS and SS;
3. at the end of a protocol run, for any of the three parties (the user, SS and CS), the party can ensure that the other two parties have been involved; and
4. an *honest-but-curious* CS cannot compute the session key.

In this paper, we give an affirmative answer to this question. We propose a very efficient protocol which requires only six communication rounds with no additional assumption introduced, and satisfies all the security requirements above.

1.2   Related Work

Passwords chosen by users generally have very low entropy. Dictionary attacks are feasible by efficiently enumerating all the possible passwords from a dictionary, if enough information is given to an attacker. Dictionary attacks can be launched *online* or *offline*. In an online attack, an attacker attempts to logon to a server by trying all possible passwords until a correct one is found. Usually, this can easily be defended against at the system level by designing a system such that an unsuccessful online attack is *detectable* and limiting the number of unsuccessful login attempts. In an offline attack, the attacker records several successful login sessions and then tries all the possible passwords against the login transcripts. This type of attacks is notoriously difficult to defend against and it is the main challenge for designing a secure password-based authenticated key exchange scheme.

On the design of password-based authenticated key exchange schemes, most of the schemes (e.g. most of the schemes in [13]) belong to the *single-server* category. As explained, single-server setting has a serious drawback which is called single point of failure. For enhancing the robustness, *two-server* and *multi-server* models have been proposed [12,14,15,16]. For multi-server schemes, although they alleviate the robustness problem, they usually require a user to communicate simultaneously with multiple servers or have the protocols become very expensive, especially when too many servers are getting involved.

The two-server setting seems to facilitate a very good balance between robustness and protocol complexity. Recently, a practical two-server architecture is proposed by Yang, Deng and Bao [18,17]. This architecture is a password-only variant of the one introduced by Brainard et al. [8]. As described in the Introduction section of this paper, the user communicates only with the Service Server (SS) while the Control Server (CS) communicates with SS only. In this paper, we propose a scheme which achieves the same security level as that of [17] (summarized in Sec. 1.1) but with much fewer number of communication rounds. Our scheme has even fewer rounds than the weaker scheme proposed in [18].

Organization. In the next section, we describe the basic tools that are used in our PTAKE scheme and then give the full details of the scheme. In Sec. 3, we analyze its security in terms of off-line dictionary attacks, pairwise mutual authentication and key privacy against Control Server. In Sec. 4, we provide the performance analysis and compare our protocol with Yang, Deng and Bao's in [17]. In Sec. 5, we conclude and mention some of our future work.

2   A New Efficient PTAKE

As introduced in Sec. 1, a protocol run of PTAKE involves a user U, a Service Server SS and a Control Server CS. There is a communication link between U and SS, another link between SS and CS, but no direct link between U and CS.

We consider two types of adversaries: passive adversaries and active adversaries. A passive adversary can eavesdrop any of the channels and try to derive user passwords from protocol transcripts. If a server is compromised by the passive adversary, all the internal states, which include the password share, of the server will be accessible by the adversary, but the server will still behave according to the protocol specification. An active adversary controls all the communication channels. If a server is compromised by an active adversary, all internal states of the server will be known to the adversary and the adversary has full control on how the server behaves.

Note that all literature [18,17] in this field assumes that the servers do not support multiple simultaneous sessions for one single user. We believe that this assumption is realistic as it usually indicates identity theft when multiple sessions from the same user are initiating from different places, for example, in the e-banking applications. We leave the study of simultaneous multiple session setting as our future work.

2.1 Registration and Initialization

To begin with, user U first needs to register to the servers through some out-of-band channels. In this paper, we assume that U has already generated random password shares π_1 and π_2 such that U's password π is congruent to $\pi_1 + \pi_2$ (mod q) for some large prime q. We refer readers to [18] for details on how this registration and initialization phase can be carried out.

In the following, we let g_1 and g_2 be distinct random generators of some multiplicative group G of large prime order q. Assume that the discrete logarithm problem in G is intractable, and also the discrete logarithm of g_2 to g_1 is intractable.

2.2 Basic Techniques

Before describing our proposed PTAKE, in this section, we propose several primitive techniques that we use repeatedly in our protocol. These techniques are mainly for defending against offline dictionary attacks while carrying out key exchange.

Since the password $\pi \equiv \pi_1 + \pi_2$ (mod q), our protocol has to prevent an active adversary from obtaining any information related to $\pi_1 + \pi_2$ even under the condition that the adversary has already known one of these two password shares. There are two basic building blocks in our design.

The first building block is applying a *blinding factor* to the password or a password share. This building block has the message form of $M_1 = g_1^r g_2^x$. Here x is the password or a password share (i.e. π, π_1 or π_2), and r is chosen uniformly at random from $\mathbb{Z}_q^*$. From M_1, the adversary cannot get anything useful for launching offline dictionary attacks for getting x (from g_2^x) as g_1^r is not known. Table 1 shows some examples of this building block being used in our protocol which will be described shortly.

Table 1. Examples of the First Building Block

U → SS: $B = g_1^a g_2^\pi$	g_1^a is the blinding factor
SS → CS: $B_1 = B/(g_1^{b_1} g_2^{\pi_1})$	$g_1^{b_1}$ is the blinding factor
CS → SS: $B_4 = g_1^{b_4} g_2^{\pi_2}$	$g_1^{b_4}$ is the blinding factor

The second building block is the *randomization* of the messages received which are in the form of $M_2 = (D/g_2^x)^r$, $M_3 = g_1^r$. Here $r \in_R \mathbb{Z}_q^*$, x is a password share (but not the password), D is the message received.

Note that D can be generated by the adversary. This implies that the adversary is able to compute $(g_2^x)^r$ from M_2 and M_3. To see this, suppose the adversary sets $D = g_1^d$ for some arbitrarily picked d. The adversary can compute

$(g_2^x)^r = M_3^d/M_2$. Since r is chosen uniformly at random from $\mathbb{Z}_q^*$ and is unknown to the adversary, knowing g_1^r and g_2^{rx} does not help the adversary compute x as the adversary cannot determine the value of g_2^r under the assumption that DDH problem is hard[2]. Table 2 lists some examples on how this building bock is used in our protocol.

Table 2. Examples of the Second Building Block

CS → SS: B_2, A_1
$B_2 = (B_1/g_2^{\pi_2})^{b_2}$, $A_1 = g_1^{b_2}$
SS → U: B_5, A_3
$B_5 = ((Bg_1^{b_6}/B_4)/g_2^{\pi_1})^{b_5}$, $A_3 = g_1^{b_5}$

2.3 The PTAKE Protocol

The protocol is described in Fig. 1.

To initiate a request for service, U selects a random $a \in_R \mathbb{Z}_q^*$ and computes $B = g_1^a g_2^{\pi}$, then sends request Req, identity U and B to SS in $M1$. Upon receiving $M1$, SS selects a random $b_1 \in_R \mathbb{Z}_q^*$, computes $B_1 = B/(g_1^{b_1}g_2^{\pi_1}) = g_1^{a-b_1}g_2^{\pi_2}$, then sends U, SS and B_1 to CS in $M2$. Upon receiving $M2$, CS selects $b_2, b_4 \in_R \mathbb{Z}_q^*$, computes $B_2 = (B_1/g_2^{\pi_2})^{b_2} = (g_1^{a-b_1})^{b_2}$, $A_1 = g_1^{b_2}$ and $B_4 = g_1^{b_4}g_2^{\pi_2}$, then sends A_1, B_2 and B_4 back to SS in $M3$. SS selects $b_3, b_5, b_6 \in_R \mathbb{Z}_q^*$ and computes $B_3 = (B_2 A^{b_1})^{b_3} = g_1^{ab_2b_3}$, $S_1 = h(B_3)$, $A_2 = A_1^{b_3}$, $B_5 = (B/(B_4 g_2^{\pi_1}))^{b_5}g_1^{b_6 b_5} = g_1^{(a-b_4+b_6)b_5}$ and $A_3 = g_1^{b_5}$, then sends S_1, A_2, B_5, A_3 to U in $M4$. Upon receiving $M4$, U checks if $S_1 \stackrel{?}{=} h(A_2^a)$: if true, U accepts and computes $S_2 = h(A_2^a, 0)$. It then selects a random $a^* \in_R \mathbb{Z}_q^*$, computes $A_4 = A_3^{a^*}$, $B_6 = (A_3^a/B_5)^{a^*}$ and sends S_2, B_6, A_4 to SS in $M5$. The session key $K_u = h(A_2^a, U, SS)$ is also computed. Otherwise, U aborts. Upon receiving $M5$, SS checks whether $S_2 \stackrel{?}{=} h(B_3, 0)$: if true, SS accepts, computes $S_3 = h(B_6 A_4^{b_6})$ and session key $K_{ss} = h(B_3, U, SS)$, and sends S_3, A_4 to CS in $M6$. Otherwise, SS aborts. Upon receiving $M6$, CS checks whether $S_3 \stackrel{?}{=} h(A_4^{b_4})$, if it does not hold, CS aborts. Otherwise, CS accepts. In all the steps above, when an element of G is received, the party should always check if the element is not equal to 1. If so, the protocol should be aborted.

3 Security Analysis

Recall that one of the main goals of our proposed scheme is to resist off-line dictionary attacks by an active adversary who has compromised one of the two servers. In the following, we first examine the proposed scheme against a compromised $\mathcal{CS}$ and then a compromised $\mathcal{SS}$. We do not need to consider the case

---

[2] DDH assumption: given (g, g^r, h, z) where $g, h \in_R G$, $r \in_R \mathbb{Z}_q$, determine if $z = h^r$ or just an element chosen uniformly at random from G.

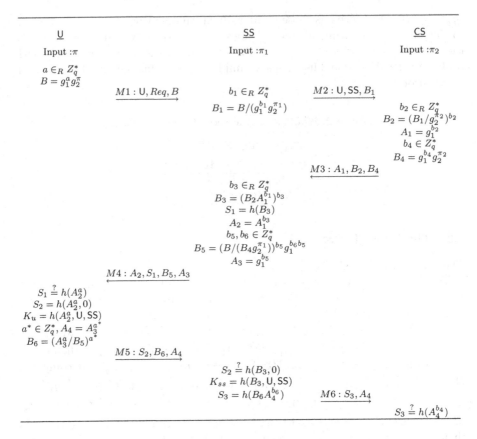

Fig. 1. Our Proposed Efficient PTAKE

that an active adversary does not have any server compromised, as this scenario has already been considered in the first two scenarios. After evaluating the security against off-line dictionary attacks, we will show that the scheme satisfies the authentication requirement as well as the desirable session key privacy, especially against the *Honest-but-Curious* CS.

3.1 Security Against Off-Line Dictionary Attacks

So far for PTAKE, there is no formal security model defined with comparable formality to [2,9] for conventional single-server password-based authenticated key exchange or [4,5,1,10] for cryptographic key based authenticated key exchange schemes. We believe that it is important to propose a formal security model for PTAKE and we consider this to be our next work. In this paper, our focus is on the performance optimization while providing the proposed scheme with some heuristic security evidence which is comparable to that in [17].

Also note that we follow the current literature [18,17] in this field by assuming that the servers do not support multiple simultaneous sessions from one single user. If a user is attempting to make simultaneous logins, the servers should consider this as some impersonation attacks. For conventional single-server password-based authenticated key exchange, multiple sessions are generally considered in the corresponding models [2,9]. For preventing various kinds of interleaving attacks [6,7], "binding" mechanisms of the identities of senders and receivers as well as the session IDs are generally required. Under the current single-session setting, the mechanisms may not be needed. Also because of this weaker security requirement, our scheme can achieve such a great efficiency. We believe that it is interesting to construct a provably secure PTAKE without sacrificing its efficiency when compared with our proposed scheme in this paper.

Proposition 1. *The proposed scheme can defend against offline dictionary attacks launched by an active adversary which has compromised* CS.

Through eavesdropping and hijacking the communication channels, we can see that the honest parties, U and SS, are actually providing the following oracles to the active adversary:

- Oracle1: It outputs $B = g_1^a g_2^\pi$, where a is chosen uniformly at random from $\mathbb{Z}_q^*$ and π is the password of U.
- Oracle2: On input $B, X, Y, Z \in G$, it outputs a quadruple: $B/(g_1^{b_1} g_2^{\pi_1})$, X^{b_3}, $h((YX^{b_1})^{b_3})$, $(B/(Zg_2^{\pi_1}))^{b_5} g_1^{b_5 b_6}$, where $b_1, b_3, b_5, b_6 \in_R \mathbb{Z}_q^*$ and π_1 is SS's password share.
- Oracle3: On input $U, V, W, B \in G$ and another finite binary string S_1, it outputs $O_1 = h(W^a, 0)$, $O_2 = U^{a^*}$, $O_3 = (U^a/V)^{a^*}$ only if $S_1 = h(W^a)$, where a is the random number chosen by Oracle1 when outputting B. If Oracle1 has never outputted B before, Oracle3 returns $\perp$. Note that a^* above is chosen uniformly at random by Oracle3.
- Oracle4: On input $S, T, S_2, U, V, O_1, O_2, O_3$, it outputs $h(ST^{b_6})$ only if $h((VU^{b_1})^{b_3}, 0) = S_2$, where U, V, b_1, b_3 and b_6 are corresponding to one query of Oracle3. Note that O_1, O_2, O_3 are needed to be in the query for identifying which query of Oracle3 it is associated with.

Oracle1 outputs B in the form of first building block described in Sec. 2.2. As explained, it gives no additional information about π. Oracle2's output has forms of both first and second building blocks described in Sec. 2.2. Again, as explained, they give no additional information about π or π_1 if DDH problem is hard. For Oracle3 and Oracle4, no particular password related information is involved and therefore do not provide additional information about π or π_1.

Proposition 2. *The proposed scheme can defend against offline dictionary attacks launched by an active adversary which has compromised* SS.

Similarly, we may consider the honest parties, U and CS, to provide the following oracles to the active adversary:

- Oracle1': It outputs $B = g_1^a g_2^\pi$, where a is chosen uniformly at random from $\mathbb{Z}_q^*$ and π is the password of U.

- Oracle2': On input $X \in G$, it outputs a triple: $g_1^{b_2}$, $(X/g_2^{\pi_2})^{b_2}$, $g_1^{b_4}g_2^{\pi_2}$, where $b_2, b_4 \in_R \mathbb{Z}_q^*$ and π_2 is CS's password share.
- Oracle3': On input $U, V, W, B \in G$ and S_1, it outputs $h(W^a, 0), U^{a^*}, (U^a/V)^{a^*}$ only if $S_1 = h(W^a)$, where a is the random number chosen by Oracle1' when outputting B. If Oracle1' has never outputted B before, Oracle3' returns $\perp$. Note that a^* above is chosen uniformly at random by Oracle3'.

Oracle1' outputs B in the form of first building block described in Sec. 2.2. It gives no additional information about π. The output of Oracle2' has forms of both first and second building blocks described in Sec. 2.2. As explained, they give no additional information about π or π_2 if DDH problem is hard. For Oracle3', no particular password related information is involved and therefore do not provide any additional information about π or π_2.

3.2   Authentication

Unlike one-way or mutual authentication in a two-party setting, a secure TPAKE should ensure that *for each* of the three parties (i.e. U, SS, CS), the party is given enough evidence of the involvement of the other two parties before the party can complete a protocol run without early abortion.

U *authenticates* CS *and* SS: The authentication idea is to have U send a 'masked' commitment of π, in the form of $B = g_1^a g_2^\pi$, to servers and require the servers to work jointly to remove the commitment g_2^π of π from B. If the returned value is g_1^a, the two servers are authenticated. However, it is not trivial to do so because all the communication channels are open and susceptible to both passive and active attacks. For making the authentication idea work, blinding factors and randomization techniques are introduced. We can see that SS computes $B_1 = g_1^{-b_1} B g_2^{-\pi_1}$ and CS computes $B_2 = (B_1 g_2^{-\pi_2})^{b_2}$, where the component $g_1^{-b_1}$ in the computation of B_1 is the blinding factor; and the power b_2 for computing B_2 is the randomization. The authentication idea remains the same, that is, $B g_2^{-\pi_1}$ when computing B_1 and $B_1 g_2^{-\pi_2}$ when computing B_2, in other words, having SS and CS remove g_2^π from B using their knowledge of π_1 and π_2. Note that after adding the blinding factor and randomization, the value received by U becomes $h(B_3) = h(g_1^{ab_2b_3})$ where b_3 is the randomization introduced by SS. This is to prevent a malicious CS from launching off-line dictionary attack against an honest SS.

Note that randomization is an important technique to defend against off-line dictionary attack while allowing an initiator (in this case, it is U) to authenticate. This can be seen by imagine that the two servers were one single party holding π. Upon receiving $B = g_1^a g_2^\pi$, the combined server computes $S_1 = h((B/g_2^\pi)^{b'})$ for a random $b' \in \mathbb{Z}_q^*$, and sends S_1 and $A_2 = g_1^{b'}$ back to U. U then checks if $S_1 \overset{?}{=} h(A_2^a)$. Suppose an adversary impersonates U and sets B as $g_1^{a'}$. The received response from the combined server will become $h(g_1^{a'b'} g_2^{-\pi b'})$. We can see that the adversary is not able to determine $g_2^{b'}$ from all the known values and therefore, is not able to launch off-line dictionary attack.

CS *authenticates* **SS** *and* **U:** The approach is similar to the above. The 'masked' commitment of π_2 is $B_4 = g_1^{b_4} g_2^{\pi_2}$. SS and U then work jointly to remove the commitment $g_2^{\pi_2}$ from B_4 using their knowledge of π_1 and π, respectively. After introducing blinding factors and randomization techniques, the value received by CS becomes $S_3 = h(g_1^{b_4 a^* b_5})$. With $A_4 = g_1^{a^* b_5}$, CS can check if $S_3 \overset{?}{=} h(A_4^{b_4})$.

As mentioned, the role of $\mathcal{CS}$ is to assist $\mathcal{SS}$ in authenticating $\mathcal{U}$. Therefore, it some security model, it may be fine if we remove the components corresponding to authenticating $\mathcal{SS}$ and $\mathcal{U}$ by $\mathcal{CS}$, that is, those related to B_4. However, in a more general security model, $\mathcal{SS}$ may make use of $\mathcal{CS}$ as an oracle for launching an *unlimited* and *undetectable* online dictionary attack for compromising $\mathcal{CS}$'s password share π_2. Specified in our protocol, $[B_4, B_5, B_6, A_3, A_4, S_3]$ are added to provide this authentication. If without checking $S_3 \overset{?}{=} h(A_4^{b_4})$ by $\mathcal{CS}$, $\mathcal{SS}$ can arbitrarily choose a trial password π_{guess} and send $B_1 = g_2^{\pi_{guess} - \pi_1}$ to $\mathcal{CS}$, then check if the received value B_2 from $\mathcal{CS}$, which should be of the form $(g_2^{\pi_{guess} - \pi_1} / g_2^{\pi_2})^{b_2}$ is equal to 1. Without S_3, we can see that $\mathcal{CS}$ has no way to find out if $\mathcal{SS}$ is launching this kind of online dictionary attacks. Therefore, $\mathcal{SS}$ can simply repeat the trial above until the value of π_2 is found. Without B_4 and the associated components for authenticating $\mathcal{SS}$ and $\mathcal{U}$, this type of online dictionary attacks is *undetectable* and therefore cannot be defended against using the conventional system-level method which is commonly applied to limit the number of unsuccessful login attempts (Sec. 1.2).

SS *authenticates* **CS** *and* **U:** The authentication idea is similar but with a different order. SS obtains a 'masked' commitment of π from U first. SS asks CS to work together for removing the commitment of π. If the 'masked' commitment received from the claimed U is properly formatted and CS also performs according to the protocol, the commitment of π will be removed, with the blinding factors and randomization remained as $S_2 = h(g_1^{ab_2 b_3}, 0)$. SS knows the value of b_3. From $B_2 = g_1^{(a-b_1)b_2}$, $A_1 = g_1^{b_2}$ and b_1, SS can compute $g_1^{ab_2}$. Hence SS can verify if $S_2 \overset{?}{=} h(g_1^{ab_2 b_3})$.

3.3 Key Privacy Against an Honest-But-Curious CS

In the following, we focus on discussing the key privacy against an honest-but-curious CS rather than an eavesdropper. This is because the key privacy against the honest-but-curious CS implies the key privacy against an eavesdropper.

Our idea is based on the Diffie-Hellman key exchange between U and SS. At the end of the protocol, we target to have each of U and SS generate a session key which is essentially computed from the Diffie-Hellman contributions of these two parties, while ensuring the CS is not able to get the discrete logarithm of any of the two contributions.

The session key established between U and SS is $h(g_1^{ab_2 b_3}, \mathsf{U}, \mathsf{SS})$, where b_2 is picked by CS. Due to the idealness assumption of h as a random oracle [3], CS has to know $g_1^{ab_2 b_3}$ in order to obtain the session key. This implies that CS has to know $g_1^{ab_3}$. However, the only available information related to $g_1^{ab_3}$ is g_1^a and

g^{b_3}. Hence CS has to solve the Computational Diffie-Hellman problem in order to obtain the session key.

4   Performance

We now compare the performance of our proposed scheme with the YDB scheme proposed by Yang, Deng and Bao [17] as their scheme is the only one currently known to also satisfy all the requirements stated in Sec. 1.1.

Let $|p|$ and $|h|$ denote the bit length of p and the output of hash function $h(.)$, respectively. The performance comparison is given in Table 3.

Table 3. Performance Comparison

		U	SS	CS
Computation	YDB scheme	5/2	6/1	3/1
(exponentiations)	our scheme	4/1	6/2	4/2
Communication	YDB scheme	$4|p| + 2|h|$	$8|p| + 3|h|$	$4|p| + |h|$
(bits)	our scheme	$6|p| + 2|h|$	$11|p| + 2|h|$	$5|p| + 1|h|$
Communication	YDB scheme	6	10	4
(rounds)	our scheme	3	6	3

Computational Complexity: Since the complexity of exponentiation dominates a party's computational overhead, we count the number of exponentiations required for each party. The digits before "/" in the table denote the total number of exponentiations performed by the party, the digits followed denote the number of exponentiations that can be pre-computed. Note that by leveraging on the techniques in [11], each of $g_1^a g_2^\pi$, $g_1^{b_1} g_2^{\pi_1}$, $(B_2 A^{b_1})^{b_3}$ and $(B_1/g_2^{\pi_2})^{b_2}$ can be computed by a single exponentiation operation. We can see that the computational complexity of our proposed scheme is comparable to that of YDB scheme.

Communication Performance in terms of Effective Bits: As $|Q|$ is only one bit longer than $|p|$, we do not distinguish them when evaluating the YDB scheme. The number of bits transmitted by each party is comparable to the YDB scheme. Note that this measures the total number of *effective* bits transmitted that are related to the protocol. It does not include the additional overhead of headers and trailers required for transferring the data packets in each communication round. We will see just in the next point that our proposed scheme has much fewer number of rounds than that of YDB scheme. Therefore, our scheme incurs much less communication overhead due to headers and trailers in actual implementation.

Communication Performance in terms of Rounds: One round is a one-way transmission of messages. Our proposed scheme has a total of six rounds while YDB scheme requires altogether 10 rounds to complete one protocol run. Also note that the number of rounds made by U is significantly reduced to half from the original number. This is desirable especially for low-power wireless users.

5   Conclusion and Future Work

We proposed a new PTAKE which outperforms all previously proposed ones in terms of the number of communications rounds, while maintaining almost the same extent of computational complexity.

This proposed scheme is particularly suitable for implementation on resource-constrained wireless devices. Transmitting radio signals on these devices usually consumes much more power than computation does. Furthermore, if we use appropriate elliptic curve groups in actual implementation, the computational requirement of our scheme can further be reduced. Therefore, our scheme which reduces the number of communication rounds by 40% helps reducing battery power consumption as well as improving the performance of actual implementation significantly.

While we examined the security of the proposed protocol, a formal treatment of the system is necessary. Currently, there is no formal security model proposed for PTAKE. Therefore, our future work is to formally define and validate the security of PTAKE and provide formal proofs with various desirable security features captured. Examples of desirable features are security against known-key attacks[3], forward secrecy[4], etc.

Acknowledgements

We would like to thank Yanjiang Yang for his valuable comments.

References

1. Bellare, M., Canetti, R., Krawczyk, H.: A modular approach to the design and analysis of authentication and key exchange protocols. In: Proc. 30th ACM Symp. on Theory of Computing, pp. 419–428. ACM, New York (1998)
2. Bellare, M., Pointcheval, D., Rogaway, P.: Authenticated key exchange secure against dictionary attacks. In: Preneel, B. (ed.) EUROCRYPT 2000. LNCS, vol. 1807, Springer, Heidelberg (2000)
3. Bellare, M., Rogaway, P.: Random oracles are practical: A paradigm for designing efficient protocols. In: First ACM Conference on Computer and Communications Security, Fairfax, pp. 62–73. ACM, New York (1993)
4. Bellare, M., Rogaway, P.: Entity authentication and key distribution. In: Stinson, D.R. (ed.) CRYPTO 1993. LNCS, vol. 773, pp. 232–249. Springer, Heidelberg (1994)
5. Bellare, M., Rogaway, P.: Provably secure session key distribution – the three party case. In: Proc. 27th ACM Symp. on Theory of Computing, Las Vegas, pp. 57–66. ACM, New York (1995)

---

[3] An adversary should not be able to compromise the long-term secret (e.g. password) after obtaining some session keys.

[4] Previously established session keys should remain secure after all long-term secrets have been compromised.

6. Bird, R., Gopal, I., Herzberg, A., Janson, P., Kutten, S., Molva, R., Yung, M.: Systematic design of two-party authentication protocols. In: Feigenbaum, J. (ed.) CRYPTO 1991. LNCS, vol. 576, pp. 44–61. Springer, Heidelberg (1992)
7. Boyd, C., Mathuria, A.: Protocols for Authentication and Key Establishment. Springer, Heidelberg (2003)
8. Brainard, J., Juels, A., Kaliski, B., Szydlo, M.: A new two-server approach for authentication with short secrets. In: USENIX Security Symposium, pp. 201–214 (2003)
9. Canetti, R., Halevi, S., Katz, J., Lindell, Y., MacKenzie, P.: Universally composable password-based key exchange. In: Cramer, R.J.F. (ed.) EUROCRYPT 2005. LNCS, vol. 3494, pp. 404–421. Springer, Heidelberg (2005), http://eprint.iacr.org/2005/196
10. Canetti, R., Krawczyk, H.: Analysis of key-exchange protocols and their use for building secure channels. In: Pfitzmann, B. (ed.) EUROCRYPT 2001. LNCS, vol. 2045, pp. 453–474. Springer, Heidelberg (2001), http://eprint.iacr.org/2001/040/
11. Dimitrov, V.S., Jullien, G., Miller, W.C.: Complexity and fast algorithms for multiexponentiations. IEEE Transactions on Computers 49(2), 141–147 (2000)
12. Ford, W., Kaliski, B.: Server-assisted generation of a strong secret from a password. In: WETICE 2000: IEEE 9th International Workshop on Enabling, pp. 176–180. IEEE, Los Alamitos (2000)
13. IEEE. P1363.2 / D26: Standard Specifications for Password-based Public Key Cryptographic Techniques, (September 2006)
14. Jablon, D.P.: Password authentication using multiple servers. In: Naccache, D. (ed.) CT-RSA 2001. LNCS, vol. 2020, pp. 344–360. Springer, Heidelberg (2001)
15. MacKenzie, P., Shrimpton, T., Jakobsson, M.: Threshold password-authenticated key exchange. Journal of Cryptology 19(1), 22–66 (2006)
16. Raimondo, M.D., Gennaro, R.: Provably secure threshold password-authenticated key exchange. In: Biham, E. (ed.) EUROCRPYT 2003. LNCS, vol. 2656, pp. 507–523. Springer, Heidelberg (2003)
17. Yang, Y., Deng, R.H., Bao, F.: Fortifying password authentication in integrated healthcare delivery systems. In: ASIACCS 2006: Proc. the 2006 ACM Symposium on Information, Computer and Communications Security, pp. 255–265. ACM Press, New York (2006)
18. Yang, Y., Deng, R.H., Bao, F.: A practical password-based two-server authentication and key exchange system. IEEE Trans. Dependable and Secure Computing 3(2), 105–114 (2006)

Formal Definition and Construction of Nominative Signature

Dennis Y.W. Liu[1], Duncan S. Wong[1], Xinyi Huang[2], Guilin Wang[3],
Qiong Huang[1], Yi Mu[2], and Willy Susilo[2]

[1] Department of Computer Science
City University of Hong Kong
Hong Kong, China
{dliu,duncan,csqhuang}@cs.cityu.edu.hk*
[2] Centre for Computer and Information Security Research
School of Computer Science and Software Engineering
University of Wollongong
Wollongong, NSW 2522, Australia
{xh068,ymu,wsusilo}@uow.edu.au
[3] Institute for Infocomm Research, Singapore and
School of Computer Science University of Birmingham, UK
G.Wang@cs.bham.ac.uk

Abstract. Since the introduction of nominative signature in 1996, there
are three problems that have still not been solved. First, there is no convincing application proposed; second, there is no formal security model
available; and third, there is no proven secure scheme constructed, given
that all the previous schemes have already been found flawed. In this
paper, we give positive answers to these problems. First, we illustrate
that nominative signature is a better tool for building user certification
systems which were originally implemented using universal designated-
verifier signature. Second, we propose a formal definition and adversarial
model for nominative signature. Third, we show that Chaum's undeniable signature can be transformed to an efficient nominative signature
by simply using a standard signature. The security of our transformation
can be proven under the standard number-theoretic assumption.

1 Introduction

A nominative signature (NS) involves three parties: *nominator A*, *nominee B*
and *verifier C*. The nominator A arbitrarily chooses a message m and works
jointly with the nominee B to produce a signature σ called nominative signature.
The validity of σ can only be verified by B and if σ is valid, B can convince
the verifier C the validity of σ using a *confirmation protocol*; otherwise, B can
convince C the invalidity of σ using a *disavowal protocol*. Based on the previous

---

* The authors were supported by CityU grants (Project nos. 7001844, 7001959,
7002001).

S. Qing, H. Imai, and G. Wang (Eds.): ICICS 2007, LNCS 4861, pp. 57–68, 2007.

literature [13,11,17,9], we consolidate the security requirements for a nominative signature as follows.

1. (*Joint Work of Nominator and Nominee*) A or B alone is not able to produce a valid σ;
2. (*Only Nominee Can Determine the Validity of Signature*) Only B can verify σ;
3. (*Can Only be Verified with Nominee's Consent*) The validity of σ is only verifiable with the aid of B, by running a confirmation/disavowal protocol with B;
4. (*Nominee Cannot Repudiate*) If σ is valid, B cannot mislead C to believe that σ is invalid using the disavowal protocol. If σ is invalid, B cannot mislead C to believe that σ is valid using the confirmation protocol;

Since the introduction of nominative signature (NS) [13], it has been considered as a dual scheme of undeniable signature (US) [4,2,5]. For an undeniable signature, its validity can only be verified with the aid of the signer, while for a nominative signature, its validity can only be verified with the aid of the nominee, rather than the nominator. Nominative signature is also related to designated verifier signature (DVS) [12], designated confirmer signature (DCS) [3] and universal designated-verifier signature (UDVS) [15]. We illustrate their similarities and differences below.

	Parties Involved	Creator(s) of Signature	Playing the Role of Prover		
			A	B	C
US	A, C	A	$\checkmark$	NA	$\times$
DCS	A, B, C	A	$\checkmark$	$\checkmark$	$\times$
DVS	A, C	A	$\checkmark$	NA	$\times$
UDVS	A, B, C	A and B[1]	$\checkmark$	$\checkmark$	$\times$
NS	A, B, C	A and B	$\times$	$\checkmark$	$\times$

Legend: A – Signer or Nominator (for NS); B – Confirmer (for DCS) or Signature Holder (for UDVS) or Nominee (for NS); C – Verifier or Designated Verifier (for DCS or UDVS); NA – not applicable.

As we can see, only NS does not allow the signer to prove the validity of a signature to a third party.

1.1 User Certification Systems

Since the introduction of NS in 1996 [13], there are only a few schemes [13,11] proposed. Unfortunately, all of them have already been found flawed [17,9]. Even worse, there is no convincing application described and NS still remains as of theoretical interest only. In the following, we show that NS is actually a much better tool for building *user certification systems* than UDVS [15] which was originally believed to be one of the most suitable ways of implementing this type of systems.

---

[1] A first creates a standard publicly verifiable signature and sends it securely to B; B then generates a UDVS signature based on the received standard signature.

UDVS, introduced by Steinfeld et al. [15] in 2003, allows a signature holder B to convince a designated verifier C that B holds a signer A's signature s on some message m, while C cannot further convince anybody of this fact. As illustrated in [15], UDVS is useful for constructing user certification systems, which concern about showing the validity of users' birth certificates, driving licences and academic transcripts, issued by an authority A. In such a system, a user B does not want a designated verifier C to disseminate B's certificate s (issued by A), while B needs to convince C that the certificate s is authentic, that is, signed by A.

NS can also be used for this purpose, but in a more natural way. For UDVS, A (the signer *or* the authority) should be trusted by B (the signature holder *or* the user of a certificate) in a very strong sense. If A is malicious, there are two attacks which will compromise B's interest on protecting his certificates. First, A may maliciously reveal the pair (s, m) to the public, and since s is a standard publicly verifiable signature, once s becomes public, everyone can verify its validity. B cannot show whether s is released by A because B himself can also make s public. Second, A can generate a UDVS signature all by himself because the UDVS signature can readily be generated from the public keys of A and C in addition to the pair (s, m). Hence, A can impersonate B arbitrarily. In contrast, NS does not have these weaknesses.

For NS, A cannot confirm or disavow a nominative signature σ (which is a user certificate in this type of applications) and σ is not publicly verifiable. Also, B does not have a publicly verifiable signature issued by A. Note that A can still issue standard signature on m or NS on m jointly with other nominees. But these events will just show that A is dishonest.

1.2   Related Work

The notion and construction of nominative signature (NS) were first proposed by Kim, Park and Won [13]. However, their construction was later found flawed [11] as the nominator in their construction can always determine the validity of a nominative signature, that is, violating Property 2 of NS described at the beginning of Sec. 1. In [11], Huang and Wang proposed the notion of convertible nominative signature, which allows the nominee to convert a nominative signature to a publicly verifiable one. They also proposed a new scheme. However, in [17,9], it was found that the nominator in their scheme can generate valid signatures on his own and show the validity of the signature to anyone without the consent of the nominee. That is, their scheme does not satisfy Properties 1 to 3.

In [11], a definition and some requirements for nominative signature were specified. However, their definition does not match with the scheme they proposed and the set of security requirements is incomplete and does not seem to be formal enough for provable security.

Our Results. We propose a formal definition and a rigorous set of adversarial models for nominative signature. We also propose a provably secure construction, which is based on Chaum's undeniable signature [2] and a strongly unforgeable signature scheme.

Paper Organization. The definition of nominative signature and its security models are specified in Sec. 2. The description and security analysis of our construction are given in Sec. 3. The paper is concluded in Sec. 4.

2   Definitions and Security Models

A nominative signature (NS) consists of three probabilistic polynomial-time (PPT) algorithms (SystemSetup, KeyGen, Ver^{nominee}) and three protocols (SigGen, Confirmation, Disavowal).

1. SystemSetup (System Setup): On input 1^k where $k \in \mathbb{N}$ is a security parameter, it generates a list of system parameters denoted by param.
2. KeyGen (User Key Generation): On input param, it generates a public/private key pair (pk, sk).
3. Ver^{nominee} (Nominee-only Verification): On input a message m, a nominative signature σ, a public key pk_A and a private key sk_B, it returns valid or invalid.

An NS proceeds as follows. Given a security parameter $k \in \mathbb{N}$, SystemSetup is invoked and param is generated. KeyGen is then executed to initialize each party that is to be involved in the subsequent part of the scheme. One party called nominator is denoted by A. Let (pk_A, sk_A) be the public/private key pair of A. Let B be the nominee that A nominates, and (pk_B, sk_B) be B's public/private key pair. In the rest of the paper, we assume that entities can be uniquely identified from their public keys. To generate a nominative signature σ, A chooses a message $m \in \{0,1\}^*$, and carries out SigGen protocol with B. The protocol is defined as follows.

SigGen Protocol: Common inputs of A and B are param and m. A's additional input is pk_B, indicating that A nominates B as the nominee; and B's additional input is pk_A indicating that A is the nominator. At the end, either A or B outputs σ. The party who outputs σ should be explicitly indicated in the actual scheme specification.

The validity of a nominative signature σ on message m (with respect to pk_A and pk_B) can be determined by B as Ver$^{nominee}(m, \sigma, pk_A, sk_B)$. To convince a third party C on the validity or invalidity of (m, σ, pk_A, pk_B), B as a prover and C as a verifier carry out the Confirmation or Disavowal protocol as follows.

Confirmation/Disavowal Protocol: On input (m, σ, pk_A, pk_B), B sets μ to 1 if valid $\leftarrow$ Ver$^{nominee}(m, \sigma, pk_A, sk_B)$; otherwise, μ is set to 0. B first sends μ to C. If $\mu = 1$, Confirmation protocol is carried out; otherwise, Disavowal protocol is carried out. At the end of the protocol, C outputs either accept or reject while B has no output.

Correctness. Suppose that all the algorithms and protocols of a nominative signature scheme are carried out accordingly by honest entities A, B and C, the scheme is said to satisfy the correctness requirement if

1. valid $\leftarrow$ Ver$^{nominee}(m, \sigma, pk_A, sk_B)$; and
2. C outputs accept at the end of the Confirmation protocol.

Validity of a Nominative Signature. A nominative signature σ on message m with respect to nominator A and nominee B is *valid* if $\mathsf{Ver}^{\mathsf{nominee}}(m, \sigma, pk_A, sk_B) =$ valid. In this case, we say that quadruple (m, σ, pk_A, pk_B) is *valid*. Note that only B can determine the validity of σ.

In the following, we propose and formalize a set of security notions for nominative signature. They are (1) unforgeability, (2) invisibility, (3) security against impersonation, and (4) non-repudiation.

2.1   Unforgeability

Intuitively, an adversary should not able to forge a valid nominative signature if any of the private keys of A and B is not known. Our game below is based on the notion of existential unforgeability against chosen message attack [8] with the extension of allowing access to confirmation/disavowal oracle based on passive attack or active/concurrent attack introduced by Kurosawa and Heng [14] in the undeniable signature setting.

We also allow the adversary to access an oracle called SignTranscript which simulates various interactions between the adversary and other honest entities. In addition, the adversary may collude with other parties or claim that some particular party is his nominee without the party's consent. Hence we also allow the adversary to adaptively access CreateUser oracle and Corrupt oracle as defined below.

Game Unforgeability: Let $\mathcal{S}$ be the simulator and $\mathcal{F}$ be a forger.

1. (*Initialization*) Let $k \in \mathbb{N}$ be a security parameter. First, param $\leftarrow$ SystemSetup(1^k) is executed and key pairs (pk_A, sk_A) and (pk_B, sk_B) for nominator A and nominee B, respectively, are generated using KeyGen. Then $\mathcal{F}$ is invoked with inputs 1^k, pk_A and pk_B.
2. (*Attacking Phase*) $\mathcal{F}$ can make queries to the following oracles:
   - CreateUser: On input an identity, say I, it generates a key pair (pk_I, sk_I) using KeyGen and returns pk_I.
   - Corrupt: On input a public key pk, if pk is generated by CreateUser or in $\{pk_A, pk_B\}$, the corresponding private key is returned; otherwise, $\perp$ is returned. pk is said to be *corrupted*.
   - SignTranscript: On input a message m, two distinct public keys, pk_1 (the nominator) and pk_2 (the nominee) such that at least one of them is uncorrupted, and one parameter called $role \in \{\mathsf{nil}, \mathsf{nominator}, \mathsf{nominee}\}$,
     - if $role = \mathsf{nil}$, $\mathcal{S}$ simulates a run of SigGen and returns a valid quadruple (m, σ, pk_1, pk_2) and $trans_\sigma$ which is the transcript of the execution of SigGen;
     - if $role = \mathsf{nominator}$, $\mathcal{S}$ (as nominee with public key pk_2) simulates a run of SigGen with $\mathcal{F}$ (as nominator with pk_1);
     - if $role = \mathsf{nominee}$, $\mathcal{S}$ (as nominator with pk_1) simulates a run of SigGen with $\mathcal{F}$ (as nominee with public key pk_2).

- Confirmation/disavowal: On input a message m, a nominative signature σ and two public keys pk_1 (the nominator), pk_2 (the nominee), let sk_2 be the corresponding private key of pk_2, the oracle responds based on whether a passive attack or an active/concurrent attack is mounted.
  - In a passive attack, if $\mathsf{Ver}^{\mathsf{nominee}}(m, \sigma, pk_1, sk_2) = $ valid, the oracle returns a bit $\mu = 1$ and a transcript of the Confirmation protocol. Otherwise, $\mu = 0$ and a transcript of the Disavowal protocol are returned.
  - In an active/concurrent attack, if $\mathsf{Ver}^{\mathsf{nominee}}(m, \sigma, pk_1, sk_2) = $ valid, the oracle returns $\mu = 1$ and then proceeds to execute the Confirmation protocol with $\mathcal{F}$ (acting as a verifier). Otherwise, the oracle returns $\mu = 0$ and executes the Disavowal protocol with $\mathcal{F}$. The difference between active and concurrent attack is that $\mathcal{F}$ interacts serially with the oracle in the active attack while $\mathcal{F}$ interacts with different instances of the oracle concurrently in the concurrent attack.
3. (*Output Phase*) $\mathcal{F}$ outputs a pair (m^*, σ^*) as a forgery of A's nominative signature on message m^* with B as the nominee.

The forger $\mathcal{F}$ *wins* the game if $\mathsf{Ver}^{\mathsf{nominee}}(m^*, \sigma^*, pk_A, sk_B) = $ valid and (1) $\mathcal{F}$ does not corrupt both sk_A and sk_B using oracle Corrupt; (2) $(m^*, pk_A, pk_B, role)$ has never been queried to SignTranscript for any valid value of $role$; (3) $(m^*, \sigma', pk_A, pk_B)$ has never been queried to Confirmation/disavowal for any nominative signature σ' with respect to pk_A and pk_B. $\mathcal{F}$'s advantage is defined to be the probability that $\mathcal{F}$ wins.

Definition 1. *A nominative signature scheme is said to be unforgeable if no PPT forger $\mathcal{F}$ has a non-negligible advantage in* Game Unforgeability.

Note that he second restriction above does not disallow $\mathcal{F}$ to query SignTranscript with $(m^*, pk_A, pk', role)$ provided that any $pk' \neq pk_B$.

2.2   Invisibility

We now formalize the requirement that only nominee B can determine whether a nominative signature is valid. We adopt the formalization idea given by Galbraith and Mao [7]. The formalization is indistinguishability based and is defined to distinguish between a valid signature σ on message m or just some value chosen uniformly at random from the corresponding signature space. Note that if the scheme is unforgeable in the sense of Def. 1, then it is negligible that a uniformly chosen value from the signature space is a valid signature on m.

Game Invisibility: The initialization phase is the same as that of Game Unforgeability and the distinguisher $\mathcal{D}$ is permitted to issue queries to all the oracles described in the attacking phase of Game Unforgeability.

1. At some point in the attacking phase, $\mathcal{D}$ outputs a message m^* and requests a challenge nominative signature σ^* on m^*. The challenge σ^* is generated based on the outcome of a hidden coin toss b.

- If $b = 1$, σ^* is generated by running SigGen.
- If $b = 0$, σ^* is chosen randomly from the signature space of the nominative signature scheme with respect to pk_A and pk_B.

2. At the end of the game, $\mathcal{D}$ outputs a guess b'.

$\mathcal{D}$ *wins* the game if $b' = b$ and (1) $\mathcal{D}$ does not corrupt sk_B; (2) the quadruple $(m^*, pk_A, pk_B, role)$, for any valid value of $role$, has never been queried to SignTranscript; (3) $(m^*, \sigma^*, pk_A, pk_B)$ has never been queried to Confirmation/disavowal.

$\mathcal{D}$'s advantage in this game is defined as $|\Pr[b' = b] - \frac{1}{2}|$.

Definition 2. *A nominative signature scheme is said to have the property of invisibility if no PPT distinguisher $\mathcal{D}$ has a non-negligible advantage in* Game Invisibility.

2.3 Security Against Impersonation

The notion of impersonation was first proposed by Kurosawa and Heng [14] in the context of undeniable signature. Instead of achieving zero-knowledgeness, it is noticed that the actual security requirement is to prevent the proving capability of the validity of a signature from being given away to any illegitimate party. This requirement is also commonly referred to as non-transferability. We consider the following game against an impersonator $\mathcal{I}$.

Game Impersonation: The initialization phase is the same as that of Game Unforgeability. The game has two phases as follows.

- *(Preparation Phase)* Impersonator $\mathcal{I}$ is invoked on input 1^k, pk_A, pk_B, sk_A. In this phase, $\mathcal{I}$ may query any of the oracles defined in Game Unforgeability. $\mathcal{I}$ prepares a triple (m^*, σ^*, μ) where m^* is some message, σ^* is a nominative signature (i.e. σ^* is in the signature space with respect to pk_A and pk_B) and μ is a bit.
- *(Impersonation Phase)* If $\mu = 1$, $\mathcal{I}$ (as nominee) executes Confirmation protocol with the simulator (as a verifier) on common inputs $(m^*, \sigma^*, pk_A, pk_B)$. If $\mu = 0$, $\mathcal{I}$ executes Disavowal protocol with the same set of inputs.

$\mathcal{I}$ *wins* if the simulator outputs accept at the Impersonation Phase while $\mathcal{I}$ has never corrupted sk_B in the game. $\mathcal{I}$'s advantage is defined to be the probability that $\mathcal{I}$ wins.

Definition 3. *A nominative signature scheme is said to be secure against impersonation if no PPT impersonator $\mathcal{I}$ has a non-negligible advantage in* Game Impersonation.

2.4 Non-repudiation

Due to the property of invisibility, no one except the nominee can determine the validity of a signature. In addition, even the nominator A and the nominee

B jointly generate a valid quadruple (m, σ, pk_A, pk_B), this only indicates that $\mathsf{Ver}^{\mathsf{nominee}}(m, \sigma, pk_A, sk_B)$ outputs valid. It does not imply that nominee B cannot cheat by executing Disavowal protocol successfully on (m, σ, pk_A, pk_B) with a verifier. Therefore, for ensuring that B cannot repudiate, we require this security notion. We consider the game below against a cheating nominee B.

Game Non-repudiation: The initialization phase is the same as that of Game Unforgeability and the cheating nominee B can query any of the oracles defined in Game Unforgeability. sk_B is also given to B.

- (*Preparation Phase*) B prepares (m^*, σ^*, μ) where m^* is some message and σ^* is a nominative signature. $\mu = 1$ if $\mathsf{Ver}^{\mathsf{nominee}}(m^*, \sigma^*, pk_A, sk_B) = $ valid; otherwise, $\mu = 0$.
- (*Repudiation Phase*) If $\mu = 1$, B executes Disavowal protocol with the simulator (acting as a verifier) on $(m^*, \sigma^*, pk_A, pk_B)$ but the first bit sent to the simulator is 0. If $\mu = 0$, B executes Confirmation protocol but the first bit sent to the simulator is 1.

B *wins* the game if the simulator acting as the verifier outputs accept. B's advantage is defined to be the probability that B wins.

Definition 4. *A nominative signature scheme is said to be secure against repudiation by nominee if no PPT cheating nominee B has a non-negligible advantage in Game Non-repudiation.*

3 Our Construction

In this section, we propose an efficient and provably secure construction of nominative signature. Our construction is based on Chaum's undeniable signature [2,14] and a strongly unforgeable signature scheme [1,16,10]. One desirable property of our construction is that one may generalize it to a generic scheme or instantiate it with some other undeniable signature schemes. We leave this as our further investigation. In the following, let σ^{undeni} be Chaum's undeniable signature and $\sigma^{standard}$ a strongly unforgeable standard signature. Also let $k \in \mathbb{N}$ be a system parameter.

SystemSetup: The algorithm generates a cyclic group G of prime order $q \geq 2^k$, a generator g, and a hash function $H : \{0,1\}^* \to G$. Let param $= (k, G, q, g, H)$. We say that (g, g^u, g^v, g^w) is a DH-tuple [14] if $w = uv \bmod q$; otherwise, it is a non-DH-tuple.

KeyGen: On input param, (pk, sk) is generated where $sk = (x, Sig)$ for some random $x \in_R \mathbb{Z}_q$ and standard signature generation algorithm Sig, and $pk = (y, Ver)$ for $y = g^x$ and standard signature verification algorithm Ver. We use $pk_A = (y_A, Ver_A)$ and $sk_A = (x_A, Sig_A)$ to denote nominator A's public and private key, respectively. Similarly, let (pk_B, sk_B) be nominee B's public/private key pair.

SigGen Protocol: Let $m \in \{0,1\}^*$ be a message. On input param and m, and specific input pk_B for A and pk_A for B, the protocol is carried out as follows.

1. B sends $\sigma^{undeni} = H(m\|pk_A)^{x_B}$ to A.
2. B then proves to A that $(g, y_B, H(m\|pk_A), \sigma^{undeni})$ is a DH-tuple using a Witness Indistinguishable (WI) protocol [6,14][2].
3. If A accepts, A outputs $\sigma = (\sigma^{undeni}, \sigma^{standard})$ where $\sigma^{standard} = Sig_A(\sigma^{undeni})$ which is A's standard signature on σ^{undeni}.

We say that $\sigma = (\sigma_1, \sigma_2)$ is a nominative signature (i.e. σ is in the signature space with respect to pk_A and pk_B) if $\sigma_1 \in G$ and σ_2 is in the set of A's signature on "message" σ_1, that is, $Ver_A(\sigma_1, \sigma_2) = 1$ meaning that σ_2 is a valid standard signature of "message" σ_1.

Ver^{nominee}: On input (m, σ, pk_A, sk_B), where $\sigma = (\sigma^{undeni}, \sigma^{standard})$ is a nominative signature (i.e. σ is in the signature space defined as above), if $\sigma^{undeni} = H(m\|pk_A)^{x_B}$, output valid; otherwise, output invalid.

Confirmation/Disavowal Protocol: On input (m, σ, pk_A, pk_B) where σ is a nominative signature, if Ver$^{\text{nominee}}(m, \sigma, pk_A, sk_B)$ = valid, B sends $\mu = 1$ to C; otherwise, $\mu = 0$ is sent to C. B then proves/disproves to C the DH-tuple/non-DH-tuple $(g, y_B, H(m\|pk_A), \sigma^{undeni})$ using WI protocols [6,14].

3.1 Discussions

Although each party's public or private key has two components, for nominator, only the component of standard signature (i.e. Sig_A, Ver_A) is used; while for nominee, only the component of undeniable signature (i.e. x_B, y_B) is used. In practice, the nominee of one message can be the nominator of another message. So we make the description above general enough for this practical scenario. Also, and more important, it abides by the definition (Sec. 2). In some settings, the two components of each key can be combined. For example, if both A and B are using discrete-log based keys for generating standard signatures, then one private key x is enough for each of them. Namely, each user can use the same private key for generating both standard signatures (e.g. Schnorr's signature scheme) and Chaum's undeniable signatures.

The standard signature $\sigma^{standard}$ generated by A only authenticates the "message" σ^{undeni} rather than the actual message m. There is still no proof on whether $(\sigma^{undeni}, \sigma^{standard})$ corresponds to m. Someone can replace m with another message, say m', and claim that $(\sigma^{undeni}, \sigma^{standard})$ corresponds to m'. No one can prove this claim, only nominee can.

Different from Chaum's original scheme [2] (precisely, we use the hash variant of Chaum's scheme [14]), the undeniable signature σ^{undeni} is computed as $H(m\|pk_A)^{x_B}$ rather than $H(m)^{x_B}$ as in the original scheme. It is important to

---

[2] First observed by Kurosawa and Heng [14], Chaum's undeniable signature (i.e. σ^{undeni}) can be confirmed/disavowed if the prover knows one of the two witnesses, that is, x_B or discrete logarithm of $H(m\|pk_A)$. This allows us to use the WI protocol.

include A's public key. Otherwise, the scheme will be insecure against unforgeability (Sec. 2.1) and invisibility (Sec. 2.2) due to the capture of multi-party environment in our security models. For example, under the model of unforgeability (Sec. 2.1), suppose pk_A is not included, forger $\mathcal{F}$ in the model can corrupt A's private key sk_A, then query SignTranscript on $(m, pk_I, pk_B, \text{nil})$ where pk_I is some public key returned by CreateUser. As defined, the game simulator will return a valid quadruple (m, σ, pk_I, pk_B) where pk_B indicates the nominee. Note that $\sigma = (H(m)^{x_B}, Sig_I(H(m)^{x_B}))$. Finally, $\mathcal{F}$ outputs $(m^*, \sigma^* = (\sigma^{undeni*}, \sigma^{standard*}), pk_A, pk_B)$ where $m^* = m$, $\sigma^{undeni*} = H(m)^{x_B}$ and $\sigma^{standard*} = Sign_A(H(m)^{x_B})$. This attack shows that a malicious party A can set a party B up and claim that B is A's nominee even B is not.

3.2   Security Analysis

We now analyze the security of the construction proposed above with respect to the security notions formalized in Sec. 2.

Lemma 1. *Let $k \in \mathbb{N}$ be a security parameter. For the nominative signature scheme proposed above, suppose a (t, ϵ, Q)-forger has obtained the nominee B's private key sk_B and is able to forge a valid nominative signature with probability at least ϵ, there exists a (t', ϵ')-adversary which can existentially forge a standard signature under the model of chosen message attack [8] with probability at least $\epsilon' = (1 - 2^{-k}Q)\epsilon$ after running at most time $t' = t + Qt_q + c$ where t_q is the maximum time for simulating one oracle query and c is some constant.*

Lemma 2. *Let $k \in \mathbb{N}$ be a security parameter. For the nominative signature scheme proposed above, suppose a (t, ϵ, Q)-forger has obtained the nominator A's private key sk_A and is able to forge a valid nominative signature, there exists a (t', ϵ')-adversary which can solve a CDH (Computational Diffie-Hellman) problem instance with probability at least $\epsilon' = (1 - 2^{-k})(1 - 2^{-k}Q)Q^{-1}\epsilon$ after running at most time $t' = t + Qt_q + c$ where t_q is the maximum time for simulating one oracle query and c is some constant.*

Theorem 1 (Unforgeability). *The nominative signature scheme proposed above is unforgeable (Def. 1) if there exists a standard signature scheme which is existentially unforgeable against chosen message attack [8] and CDH problem in G is hard.*

The theorem follows directly from Lemma 1 and 2.

Theorem 2 (Invisibility). *The nominative signature scheme proposed above has the property of invisibility (Def. 2) under the Decisional Diffie-Hellman (DDH) assumption, if the underlying standard signature scheme is strongly existentially unforgeable against chosen message attack (strong euf-cma [1,16,10]).*

Due to page limitation, we leave all the security proofs in the full version of this paper. We remark that our proof requires a stronger sense of secure signature scheme (namely, strong euf-cma secure) for invisibility, rather than a conventional euf-cma secure signature scheme as required for achieving unforgeability. It prevents the distinguisher in Game Invisibility from querying the Confirmation/disavowal oracle on an existentially forged value of the challenge signature σ^*. In practice, strong euf-cma secure signature schemes can be constructed efficiently. We refer readers to [1,16,10] for examples of efficient generic constructions of strong euf-cma secure signature schemes. Other methods in place of a strong euf-cma secure signature scheme may be feasible. For example, we may define an equivalence class of all valid signatures of σ^* and restrict the Confirmation/disavowal oracle from responding to any of the values in the class. We leave this as our further investigation.

Theorem 3 (Security Against Impersonation). *The nominative signature scheme proposed above is secure against impersonation (Def. 3) under the discrete logarithm (DLOG) assumption.*

Both confirmation and disavowal protocols use the WI protocols of [14], that have been proven to satisfy the requirement of security against impersonation in a similar model (Theorem 3 of [14]).

Theorem 4 (Non-repudiation). *The nominative signature scheme proposed above is secure against repudiation by nominee (Def. 4).*

This follows directly the soundness property of the WI proofs in [14].

4   Conclusion

In this paper, we proposed a rigorous set of security models for capturing the security notions of nominative signature. We also proposed a provably secure construction which efficiently converts Chaum's undeniable signature to a nominative signature using a strongly unforgeable signature scheme. We hope that with this formal security model, more provably secure nominative signature schemes can be proposed in the near future. We also believe that the security model is of independent interest and further enhancement of the security model is feasible. We consider this to be our future work.

References

1. Boneh, D., Shen, E., Waters, B.: Strongly unforgeable signatures based on computational Diffie-Hellman. In: Yung, M., Dodis, Y., Kiayias, A., Malkin, T.G. (eds.) PKC 2006. LNCS, vol. 3958, pp. 229–240. Springer, Heidelberg (2006)
2. Chaum, D.: Zero-knowledge undeniable signatures. In: Damgård, I.B. (ed.) EUROCRYPT 1990. LNCS, vol. 473, pp. 458–464. Springer, Heidelberg (1991)
3. Chaum, D.: Designated confirmer signatures. In: De Santis, A. (ed.) EUROCRYPT 1994. LNCS, vol. 950, pp. 86–91. Springer, Heidelberg (1995)
4. Chaum, D., van Antwerpen, H.: Undeniable signatures. In: Brassard, G. (ed.) CRYPTO 1989. LNCS, vol. 435, pp. 212–216. Springer, Heidelberg (1990)

5. Chaum, D., van Antwerpen, H.: Cryptographically strong undeniable signatures, unconditionally secure for the signer. In: Feigenbaum, J. (ed.) CRYPTO 1991. LNCS, vol. 576, pp. 470–484. Springer, Heidelberg (1992)
6. Feige, U., Shamir, A.: Witness indistinguishable and witness hiding protocols. In: Proc. 22nd ACM Symp. on Theory of Computing, pp. 416–426. ACM Press, New York (May 1990)
7. Galbraith, S., Mao, W.: Invisibility and anonymity of undeniable and confirmer signatures. In: Joye, M. (ed.) CT-RSA 2003. LNCS, vol. 2612, pp. 80–97. Springer, Heidelberg (2003)
8. Goldwasser, S., Micali, S., Rivest, R.: A digital signature scheme secure against adaptive chosen-message attack. SIAM J. Computing 17(2), 281–308 (1988)
9. Guo, L., Wang, G., Wong, D.: Further discussions on the security of a nominative signature scheme. Cryptology ePrint Archive, Report 2006/007 (2006)
10. Huang, Q., Wong, D.S., Zhao, Y.: Generic transformation to strongly unforgeable signatures. In: ACNS 2007, pp. 1–17. Springer, Heidelberg (2007), also available at: http://eprint.iacr.org/2006/346
11. Huang, Z., Wang, Y.: Convertible nominative signatures. In: Wang, H., Pieprzyk, J., Varadharajan, V. (eds.) ACISP 2004. LNCS, vol. 3108, pp. 348–357. Springer, Heidelberg (2004)
12. Jakobsson, M., Sako, K., Impagliazzo, R.: Designated verifier proofs and their applications. In: Maurer, U.M. (ed.) EUROCRYPT 1996. LNCS, vol. 1070, pp. 143–154. Springer, Heidelberg (1996)
13. Kim, S.J., Park, S.J., Won, D.H.: Zero-knowledge nominative signatures. In: PragoCrypt 1996, International Conference on the Theory and Applications of Cryptology, pp. 380–392 (1996)
14. Kurosawa, K., Heng, S.: 3-move undeniable signature scheme. In: Cramer, R.J.F. (ed.) EUROCRYPT 2005. LNCS, vol. 3494, pp. 181–197. Springer, Heidelberg (2005)
15. Steinfeld, R., Bull, L., Wang, H., Pieprzyk, J.: Universal designated-verifier signatures. In: Laih, C.-S. (ed.) ASIACRYPT 2003. LNCS, vol. 2894, pp. 523–542. Springer, Heidelberg (2003)
16. Steinfeld, R., Pieprzyk, J., Wang, H.: How to strengthen any weakly unforgeable signature into a strongly unforgeable signature. In: Abe, M. (ed.) CT-RSA 2007. LNCS, vol. 4377, pp. 357–371. Springer, Heidelberg (2006)
17. Susilo, W., Mu, Y.: On the security of nominative signatures. In: Boyd, C., González Nieto, J.M. (eds.) ACISP 2005. LNCS, vol. 3574, pp. 329–335. Springer, Heidelberg (2005)

Short Group Signature Without Random Oracles

Xiaohui Liang, Zhenfu Cao*, Jun Shao, and Huang Lin

Department of Computer Science and Engineering
Shanghai Jiao Tong University
200240, Shanghai, P.R. China
`liangxh127@sjtu.edu.cn, zfcao@cs.sjtu.edu.cn`

Abstract. We construct a short group signature which is proven secure without random oracles. By making certain reasonable assumptions and applying the technique of non-interactive proof system, we prove that our scheme is full anonymity and full traceability. Compared with other related works, such as BW06 [9], BW07 [10], ours is more practical due to the short size of both public key and group signature.

Keywords: Group signature, standard model, short signature, non-interactive proof system.

1 Introduction

Group signature is a useful cryptographical tool, which is widely discussed in the literature and also has many potential applications, such as network meeting, online business, and software trading. The similar requirement of these applications is to allow a member to sign a message on behalf of the group, and still remain anonymous within the group. Group signature schemes meet this requirement by providing anonymity and traceability at the same time, that is, a group signature can be related with its signer's identity only by a party who possesses an open authority. In such environment, there exists a group manager to distribute certificates, open authority and other group settings. If one group member generates a group signature, anyone can only verify the signature by using group public parameters. When some dissention happens, an opener finds out the real signer's identity. In this way, group members could protect their privacy.

In 1991, Chaum and van Heyst [13] firstly proposed group signature. Then, many papers on this subject proposed various of approaches to give a secure and practical group signature scheme. There exist a lot of practical schemes secure in the random oracle model [2,7,19,20,21]. However, Canetti, Goldreich and Halevi [11,12,14] have shown that security in the random oracle model does not imply the security in the real world in that a signature scheme can be secure in the random oracle model and yet be broken without violating any particular intractability assumption, and without breaking the underlying hash functions.

---

* Corresponding author.

S. Qing, H. Imai, and G. Wang (Eds.): ICICS 2007, LNCS 4861, pp. 69–82, 2007.
© Springer-Verlag Berlin Heidelberg 2007

Therefore, to design a secure group signature scheme in the standard model becomes an open and interesting research problem. Bellare et. al. introduced security definitions for group signatures and proposed a scheme based on trapdoor permutation in [6]. Furthermore, Bellare et. [8] strengthened the security model to include dynamic enrollment of members. After that, Groth [15] also gave a group signature scheme based on bilinear groups which is proven CCA secure in the standard model under the decisional-linear assumption. Their scheme was constructed in the BSZ-model [8], but still the size of group signature is enormous.

Ateniese, Camenisch, Hohenberger and de Medeiros [1] designed a practical group signature with high efficiency which is also secure in the standard model. The drawback of their scheme was that if the user's private key is exposed, it can be used to trace the identity of the user's past signatures. Unfortunately, this is not according with BSZ-models, and needs to be prevented.

Boyen and Waters [9] suggested group signature schemes that are secure in a restricted version of the BMW-model [6], where the anonymity of the members relies on the adversary can not make any query on the tracing of group signature. The size of both public parameter and group signature are both logarithm of identity and message. Afterwards, they [10] proposed a group signature scheme the signature of which is of constant size (only 6 group elements) of signature. However, the size of public parameter is still logarithm of identity. Groth also presented a group signature scheme [16] based on non-interactive witness indistinguishable proof of knowledge and other existing tools, which enhances the security notion of BW [9,10]. We will compare our scheme with theirs in Section 7, specifically.

Our Contribution

We propose a new group signature scheme secure in the standard model. We use short signature [3] and non-interactive proof system [17] as the foundation to construct ours. Then we prove our scheme is secure in a restricted BMW-model. Furthermore, the sizes of both public parameter and group signature are reduced to two constants, and are shorter than that of both schemes in [10,16]. To the best of our knowledge, our group signature is the shortest one secure in the standard model. Besides, the overall computational cost of our scheme is low. Therefore, our scheme is more practical compared with the others.

Roadmap

The rest of this paper is arranged as follows. In next section, we provide the preliminaries of our scheme including bilinear groups of composite order and complexity assumptions. In Section 3, we describe the formal model of group signature scheme. Then we propose the two-level signature and group signature schemes in Section 4 & 5, respectively. We give the details of security proofs in Section 6. Finally, we draw comparisons between ours and other related works in Section 7 and summarize our paper in Section 8.

2 Preliminaries

2.1 Bilinear Groups of Composite Order

Recently, a lot of cryptographical schemes are based on bilinear groups of composite order. We briefly review some notions about it from other related works [5,18,17,9,10].

Consider two finite cyclic groups G and G_T having the same order n, where $n = pq$, p, q are large primes and $p \neq q$. It is clear that the respective group operation is efficiently computable. Assume that there exists an efficiently computable mapping $e : G \times G \rightarrow G_T$, called a bilinear map or pairing, with the following properties.

- Bilinear: For any $g, h \in G$, and $a, b \in Z_n$, we have $e(g^a, h^b) = e(g, h)^{ab}$, where the product in the exponent is defined modulo n.
- Non-degenerate: $\exists\, g \in G$ such that $e(g, g)$ has order n in G_T. In other words, $e(g, g)$ is a generator of G_T, whereas g generates G.
- Computable: There is an efficient algorithm to compute $e(g, h)$ for all $g, h \in G$.

2.2 Complexity Assumptions

Before describing our new group signature, we firstly introduce the complexity assumptions from other related works [5,18,17] and then propose new ones.

Subgroup Decision Problem. The subgroup decision problem in G of composite order $n = pq$ is defined as follows: given a tuple (n, G, G_T, e) and an element h selected at random either from G or from G_q as input, output 1 if $h \in G_q$; else output 0.

Definition 1. *We say that the subgroup decision assumption holds for generator $\mathcal{G}_{BGN}$ if any non-uniform polynomial time adversary $\mathcal{A}$ we have*

$$\begin{aligned} \Pr[(p, q, G, G_T, e, g) &\leftarrow \mathcal{G}_{BGN}(1^k); n = pq; r \leftarrow Z_n^*; \\ h &= g^r : A(n, G, G_T, e, g, h) = 1] \\ = \Pr[(p, q, G, G_T, e, g) &\leftarrow \mathcal{G}_{BGN}(1^k); n = pq; r \leftarrow Z_n^*; \\ h &= g^{pr} : A(n, G, G_T, e, g, h) = 1] \end{aligned}$$

l-Strong Diffie-Hellman Problem. [3] The l-SDH problem in G is defined as follows: given a $(l+1)$-tuple $(g, g^x, g^{(x^2)}, ..., g^{(x^l)})$ as input, output a pair $(c, g^{\frac{1}{x+c}})$ where $c \in Z_p^*$. An algorithm $\mathcal{A}$ has advantage ϵ in solving l-SDH in G if

$$\Pr[\mathcal{A}(g, g^x, g^{(x^2)}, ..., g^{(x^l)}) = (c, g^{\frac{1}{x+c}})] \geq \epsilon$$

Definition 2. *We say that the (l, t, ϵ)-SDH assumption holds in G if no t-time algorithm has advantage at least ϵ in solving the l-SDH problem in G.*

Now, we give some new assumptions and observe the relationship between them.

l-One More Strong Diffie-Hellman Problem. (l-OMSDH) The l-one more strong Diffie-Hellman problem in the prime-order bilinear group G is defined as follows: on input three generator $g, g^x \in G$, and l distinct tuples $(c_i, g^{\frac{1}{x+c_i}})$, where $c_i \in \mathbb{Z}_n, i \in \{1, 2, ..., l\}$, outputs another tuple $(c, g^{\frac{1}{x+c}})$ distinct of all the others. An algorithm $\mathcal{A}$ has advantage ϵ in solving l-OMSDH in G if

$$\Pr[\mathcal{A}(g, c_1, g^{\frac{1}{x+c_1}}, c_2, g^{\frac{1}{x+c_2}}, ..., c_l, g^{\frac{1}{x+c_l}}) = (c, g^{\frac{1}{x+c}})] \geq \epsilon,$$

$$\text{where } c \neq c_i, \text{ for } i = 1, 2, ..., l$$

Definition 3. *We say that the (l, t, ϵ)-OMSDH assumption holds in G if no t-time algorithm has advantage at least ϵ in solving the l-OMSDH problem in G.*

l-Modified One More Strong Diffie-Hellman Problem. (l-MOMSDH) The l-modified one more strong Diffie-Hellman problem in the prime-order bilinear group G is defined as follows: on input three generator $g, g^x \in G$, and l distinct tuples $(c_i, g^{\frac{1}{x+c_i}})$, where $c_i \in \mathbb{Z}_n, i \in \{1, 2, ..., l\}$, outputs another tuple $(g^c, g^{\frac{1}{x+c}}, g^{\frac{1}{c+m}}, m)$ where $c \notin \{c_1, ..., c_i\}$ and $m \in_R \mathbb{Z}$. An algorithm $\mathcal{A}$ has advantage ϵ in solving l-SDH in G if

$$\Pr[\mathcal{A}(g, c_1, g^{\frac{1}{x+c_1}}, c_2, g^{\frac{1}{x+c_2}}, ..., c_l, g^{\frac{1}{x+c_l}}) = (g^c, g^{\frac{1}{x+c}}, g^{\frac{1}{c+m}}, m)] \geq \epsilon,$$

$$\text{where } c \neq c_i, \text{ for } i = 1, 2, ..., l$$

Definition 4. *We say that the (l, t, ϵ)-MOMSDH assumption holds in G if no t-time algorithm has advantage at least ϵ in solving the l-MOMSDH problem in G.*

It is easy to see that for any $l \geq 1$, hardness of the l-SDH problem implies hardness of the l-OMSDH problem in the same group. Meanwhile, hardness of the l-MOMSDH problem implies hardness of the l-OMSDH problem in the same group. To be more convincing, we claim all of these problems are hard to solve, and the proof of them will appear in the full paper.

3   Formal Model of Group Signatures

In this section, we introduce some basic models and security issues which have been defined in the papers [9,10]. A group signature scheme consists of the following algorithms: Setup, Join, Sign, Verify and Trace.

1. Setup: Taking as input the system security parameter λ, this algorithm outputs group's public parameter PP for verifying signatures, a master key MK for enrolling group members, and a tracing key TK for identifying signers.
2. Join: Taking as input the master key MK and an identity id, and outputs a unique identifier s_{id} and a private signing key K_{id} which is to be given to the user. That is: $K_{id} \leftarrow \text{Join}(\text{PP}, \text{MK}, id)$.

3. Sign: Taking as input a user's private key K_{id} and a message M, and outputs a group signature σ. That is $\sigma \leftarrow \text{Sign}(\text{PP}, K_{id}, M)$.
4. Verify: Taking as input a message M, a signature σ, and the group's public parameter PP, and outputs valid or invalid. That is "Valid" or "Invalid" $\leftarrow$ Verify(PP, σ, M).
5. Trace: Taking as input a group signature σ, and a tracing key TK, and outputs an identity s_{id} or $\perp$. That is s_{id} or $\perp \leftarrow \text{Trace}(\text{PP}, \sigma, \text{TK})$

Consistency. We require that the following equations hold.

$$\text{Verify}(\text{PP}, \text{Sign}(\text{PP}, K_{id}, M), M) = \text{Valid}$$

$$\text{Trace}(\text{PP}, \text{Sign}(\text{PP}, K_{id}, M), \text{TK}) = s_{id}$$

Security.

Bellare, Micciancio, and Warinschi [6] presented the fundamental properties of group signatures, which are considered to be restrictions in the following designs. The most two important properties are:

Full Anonymity which requires that no PPT adversary is able to find the identity of a group signature. The game could be described as follows: the adversary $\mathcal{A}$ could firstly query some private keys and some valid signatures from the simulator $\mathcal{B}$, then $\mathcal{A}$ outputs id_1, id_2, m and sends them to $\mathcal{B}$. $\mathcal{B}$ random choose $b \in \{0, 1\}$ and generate σ_b corresponding with (id_b, m). If $\mathcal{A}$ has negligible advantage to guess the correct b, our group signature scheme is full anonymity (CPA). We notice that if we give the trace oracle to the adversary, the full anonymity is enhanced, which is similar with the CCA-secure notion. In this paper, we following [10] and using non-interactive proof system to design a simple group signature in the CPA-full anonymity notion.

Full Traceability which requires that no forged signatures, even if there exists a coalition of users. The game could be described as follows: the adversary $\mathcal{A}$ is given group public parameters PP and the tracing key TK. Then $\mathcal{A}$ could query some private keys and some valid signatures from the simulator $\mathcal{B}$. The validity of signature and identity tracing could be checked by $\mathcal{A}$. At some point, $\mathcal{A}$ outputs a forged group signature σ^* with its tracing identity id^* and message m^*. The restrictions are that the private key of id^* and (id^*, m^*) should not be queried before. If $\mathcal{A}$ has only negligible advantage to forge a valid signature, our group signature scheme is full traceability.

We refer the reader to [6] for more details of these and related notion.

4 Hierarchical Signatures

We build a hierarchical signature scheme based on the short signature proposed by BB04 [3]. To implement a group signature scheme, we construct a short two-level hierarchical signature with existential unforgeability against adaptive chosen message attacks based on l-MOMSDH assumption. The first level can be seen as a certificate that signed by the group manage, while the second level is a short signature on message m.

4.1 Two-Level Signature Scheme

Let λ be the security parameter. Suppose the user's identity id and the message M are chosen from $\{0,1\}^\lambda$. We build a group G with order $n = pq$ and record g as a generator of G_p, where G_p is a subgroup of G with order p. There exists a bilinear map e from $G \times G$ to G_T.

Setup(1^λ): It firstly generates the master key $\mathsf{MK} = z \in \mathbb{Z}_p$ and calculates the public parameter $\mathsf{PP} = \{Z = g^z\} \in G_p$. Moreover, it generates the public collision-resistant hash function $H : \{0,1\}^\lambda \to \mathbb{Z}_p$.

Extract($\mathbf{PP}, \mathbf{MK}, id$): To create a private key for an user, it chooses a secret value $s_{id} \in \mathbb{Z}_p$ and return:

$$K_{id} = (K_1, K_2) = \left(s_{id}, g^{\frac{1}{z+s_{id}}}\right) \in \mathbb{Z}_p \times G_p$$

Note that the value $z + s_{id}$ must lie in $\mathbb{Z}_p^*$

Sign($\mathbf{PP}, K_{id}, M$): To sign a message $M \in \{0,1\}^\lambda$, the algorithm generates and outputs:

$$\sigma = (\sigma_1, \sigma_2, \sigma_3) = \left(g^{s_{id}}, g^{\frac{1}{z+s_{id}}}, g^{\frac{1}{s_{id}+H(M)}}\right)$$

Note that the probability of $s_{id} + H(M) \equiv 0 \pmod p$ is negligible.

Verify($\mathbf{PP}, M, \sigma$): To verify whether the signature σ is valid for a message M, the algorithm checks:

$$e(Z\sigma_1, \sigma_2) \overset{?}{=} e(g, g)$$

$$e(g^{H(M)}\sigma_1, \sigma_3) \overset{?}{=} e(g, g)$$

If the above two equations both hold, the verifier outputs valid; else outputs invalid.

Notice that this signature scheme doesn't reveal the user's identity, the private key generator could record the mapping from id to s_{id}. However, the signatures signed by one user can be easily linked with invariant values σ_1, σ_2. We modified two-level hierarchical signature scheme to group signature which achieves unlinkability and anonymity by using non-interactive proof system mentioned in G07 [16].

4.2 Existential Unforgeability

The two-level signature scheme proposed above is existential unforgeable against adaptive chosen message attacks. We review the short group signature in BB04, and prove the security issues based on the hardness of q-SDH and l-MOMSDH problems.

Theorem 1. *Our two-level signature scheme is (t, q_e, q_s, ϵ)-secure against existential forgery under a chosen message attack provided that $(t', q, \epsilon_{OMSDH})$-OMSDH assumption and $(t'', l, \epsilon_{MOMSDH})$-MOMSDH assumption hold in G_p, where*

$$\epsilon \le 2q_s\epsilon_{OMSDH} + 2\epsilon_{MOMSDH} \text{ and } t \approx max(t', t''), \ q \ge q_s + 1 \text{ and } l \ge q_e + q_s$$

The proofs are detailed in the full paper.

5   Proposed Group Signature

We now present the group signature scheme in details.

5.1   Schemes

The group signature scheme is described as the following algorithms. Figure 1. presents the scheme executed by three parties: group manager, user and verifier.

Setup(1^λ): The input is a security parameter 1^λ. Suppose the maximum group members 2^k and the signing message in $\{0,1\}^m$, where $k = O(\lambda), m = O(\lambda)$. It firstly chooses $n = pq$ where p, q are random primes of bit size $\lceil log_2p \rceil, \lceil log_2q \rceil = \Theta(\lambda) > k$. We builds a cyclic bilinear group G and its subgroup G_p and G_q of respective order p and q. Denote g a generator of G and h a generator of G_q. Next, The algorithm picks a random exponents $z \in \mathbb{Z}_n^*$, and defines $Z = g^z \in G$. Additionally, a public collision-resistant hash function H is from $\{0,1\}^m$ to $\mathbb{Z}_n$.
The public parameters consist,

$$\mathrm{PP} = (g, h, Z) \in G \times G_q \times G_p$$

The master key MK and the tracing key TK are

$$\mathrm{MK} = z \in \mathbb{Z}_n^*, \mathrm{TK} = q \in \mathbb{Z}$$

Join$(\mathrm{PP}, \mathrm{MK}, id)$: The input is a user's identity id. The algorithm assigns a secret unique value $s_{id} \in \mathbb{Z}_n$ for tracing purpose. Then the secret key is constructed as:

$$K_{id} = (K_1, K_2) = (s_{id}, g^{\frac{1}{z+s_{id}}})$$

The user may verify that the key is well formed by checking

$$e(Zg^{K_1}, K_2) \stackrel{?}{=} e(g,g)$$

Sign$(\mathrm{PP}, id, K_{id}, M)$: To sign a message $M \in \{0,1\}^m$, a user parse $K_{id} = (K_1, K_2)$ and computes a two-level signature:

$$\rho = (\rho_1, \rho_2, \rho_3) = (g^{K_1}, K_2, g^{\frac{1}{K_1 + H(M)}})$$

Notice that, ρ does not satisfy the anonymity and unlinkability to anyone, since ρ_1, ρ_2 are unchangeable for each signature. So, by adopting the same approach from BW07 [10] and G07 [16], we let the signers choose $t_1, t_2, t_3 \in \mathbb{Z}_n$ and computes:

$$\sigma_1 = \rho_1 \cdot h^{t_1}, \sigma_2 = \rho_2 \cdot h^{t_2}, \sigma_3 = \rho_3 \cdot h^{t_3}$$

Additionally, it computes a proof:

$$\pi_1 = \rho_2^{t_1}(Z\rho_1)^{t_2}h^{t_1t_2}, \quad \pi_2 = \rho_3^{t_1}(g^{H(M)}\rho_1)^{t_3}h^{t_1t_3}$$

The output signature is:

$$\sigma = (\sigma_1, \sigma_2, \sigma_3, \pi_1, \pi_2) \in G^5$$

Verify(PP, M, σ): To check the validity of signature σ, the verifier calculates:

$$T_1 = e(\sigma_1 Z, \sigma_2) \cdot e(g,g)^{-1}, \ T_2 = e(\sigma_1 g^{H(M)}, \sigma_3)e(g,g)^{-1}$$

Then verifies:

$$T_1 \overset{?}{=} e(h, \pi_1), \ T_2 \overset{?}{=} e(h, \pi_2)$$

If the above equations hold, the verifier outputs valid; else outputs invalid.

Trace(PP, TK, σ): Let σ be a valid signature, the opener parses it and finds the element σ_1. Then, to trace the identity of signer, it calculates σ_1^q and tests:

$$(\sigma_1)^q \overset{?}{=} (g^{s_{id}} \cdot h^{t_1})^q = (g^{s_{id}})^q$$

Since all the $(g^{s_{id}})^q$ can be pre-calculated firstly and recorded in a list by opener, the time to find the identity id is linearly dependent on the number of initial users.

Group Manager	User	Verifier
generate secret value $K_1 = s_{id}$ $K_2 = g^{\frac{1}{z+s_{id}}}$ $\xrightarrow{K_1, K_2}$	Verifies $e(Zg^{K_1}, K_2) \overset{?}{=} e(g,g)$ random chooses $t_1, t_2, t_3 \in Z_q^*$ $\sigma_1 = g^{K_1} \cdot h^{t_1}$ $\sigma_2 = K_2 \cdot h^{t_2}$ $\sigma_3 = g^{\frac{1}{K_1 + H(M)}} \cdot h^{t_3}$ $\pi_1 = K_2^{t_1}(Zg^{K_1})^{t_2}h^{t_1 t_2}$ $\pi_2 = g^{\frac{t_1}{K_1+H(M)}}g^{t_3(K_1+H(M))}h^{t_1 t_3}$ $\xrightarrow{\sigma_1, \sigma_2, \sigma_3, \pi_1, \pi_2}$	Verifies $T_1 = e(\sigma_1 Z, \sigma_2) \cdot e(g,g)^{-1}$ $T_2 = e(\sigma_1 g^{H(M)}, \sigma_3) \cdot e(g,g)^{-1}$ $T_1 \overset{?}{=} e(\pi_1, h)$ $T_2 \overset{?}{=} e(\pi_2, h)$ if all pass, the signature is valid

Fig. 1. Short Group Signature Scheme

6   Security Analysis

We now analyze the security of our group signature scheme.

6.1   Full Anonymity

Since our scheme adopts the same approach from BW06 [9] and BW07 [10], we only prove the security of our group signature scheme in the anonymity game against chosen plaintext attacks. The proof sketch borrows from G07 [16]. That is, if h is chosen from G, we achieve perfect hiding property. Meanwhile, if h is chosen from G_q, we achieve perfect biding property. However, the adversary

$\mathcal{A}$ can not distinguish these two different environment, since subgroup decision problem is unsolvable in polynomial time. Therefore, we give the following theorem.

Theorem 2. *Suppose no t-time adversary can solve the subgroup decision problem with advantage at least ϵ. Then for every t'-time adversary $\mathcal{A}$ to break the full anonymity, we have that $Adv_{\mathcal{A}} < 2\epsilon_{sub}$, where $t \approx t'$.*

To prove the above theorem, the two lemmas are necessary.

Lemma 1. *For all t'-time adversaries $\mathcal{A}$, the probability to distinguish the true environment and the simulated environment is negligible. That is $Adv_{\mathcal{A}} - Adv_{\mathcal{A},\mathcal{S}} < 2\epsilon_{sub}$*

Proof. Suppose there is a simulator $\mathcal{B}$ trying to solve subgroup problem. Upon receiving a tuple (e, G, G_T, n, h), he wants to find out whether $h \in G_q$ or not. Firstly, he setups the group signature scheme by choosing the public parameters exactly as in the group signature scheme. Then $\mathcal{B}$ publishes them to the adversary $\mathcal{A}$. Whether h is chosen from G_q or not, $\mathcal{B}$ can always answer all queries, since it knows the master key. If $h \in_R G_q$, then the simulated environment is identical to the actual one.

At some point, the adversary $\mathcal{A}$ chooses a message M and two identities id and id'. The constraints are the secret keys of id and id', and $(M, id), (M, id')$ should not be queried before. Then, B outputs the challenge signature with (M, id^*), where $id^* \in \{id, id'\}$. After that, $\mathcal{A}$ outputs its guess. If it is correct, B outputs 1; else outputs 0. Denote by $Adv_{\mathcal{B}}$ the advantage of the simulator $\mathcal{B}$ in the subgroup decision game. As we know that

$$\Pr[h \in G] = \Pr[h \in G_q] = \frac{1}{2}$$

we obtain that,

$$\begin{aligned}
Adv_{\mathcal{A}} - Adv_{\mathcal{A},\mathcal{S}} &= Pr[b=1|h \in G_q] - Pr[b=1|h \in G] \\
&= 2Pr[b=1, h \in G_q] - 2Pr[b=1, h \in G] \\
&= 2Adv_{\mathcal{B}} \\
&< 2\epsilon_{sub}
\end{aligned}$$

Thus, under our subgroup decision assumption in Section 2.2, the probability to distinguish the actual environment and the simulated one is negligible. ∎

Lemma 2. *For any adversary $\mathcal{A}$, we have $Adv_{\mathcal{A},\mathcal{S}} = 0$*

Proof. The proof sketch is similar to that of BW07 [10] and G07 [16]. We prove that when h is chosen uniformly from G at random, instead of G_q, the adversary $\mathcal{A}$ can not sense the identity from the challenge signature. Although the tracing value s_{id} may have been used to answer previous signing queries on (id, M) and (id', M), the challenge signature is statistically independent of the real identity.

To proceed, we write the challenge ciphertext is $\sigma = (\sigma_1, \sigma_2, \sigma_3, \pi_1, \pi_2)$.

Since the signature $\sigma_1, \sigma_2, \sigma_3$ is blinded with random number $h_1, h_2, h_3 \in G$, respectively, they reveal nothing about the identity. Then, we give two signatures:

σ with (id, M) and σ' with (id', M) and analyze two tuples $\pi = (\pi_1, \pi_2)$, $\pi' = (\pi'_1, \pi'_2)$.

If $\sigma_1 = \sigma'_1, \sigma_2 = \sigma'_2$ and $\sigma_3 = \sigma'_3$, we show that π and π' do not reveal the identity either.

$$
\begin{aligned}
g^{s_{id}} h^{t_1} &= g^{s_{id'}} h^{t'_1} \\
g^{\frac{1}{z+s_{id}}} h^{t_2} &= g^{\frac{1}{z+s_{id'}}} h^{t'_2} \\
g^{\frac{1}{s_{id}+H(M)}} h^{t_3} &= g^{\frac{1}{s_{id'}+H(M)}} h^{t'_3}
\end{aligned}
$$

Suppose $h = g^\eta, \varepsilon = \frac{z+s_{id}}{z+s_{id'}}, \tau = \frac{s_{id}+H(M)}{s_{id'}+H(M)}$, we obtain that

$$
\begin{aligned}
t'_1 &= t_1 + \frac{s_{id}-s_{id'}}{\eta} \\
t'_2 &= t_2 + \frac{1}{\eta}\left(\frac{1}{z+s_{id}} - \frac{1}{z+s_{id'}}\right) = t_2 + \frac{1-\varepsilon}{\eta(z+s_{id})} \\
t'_3 &= t_3 + \frac{1}{\eta}\left(\frac{1}{s_{id}+H(M)} - \frac{1}{s_{id'}+H(M)}\right) = t_3 + \frac{1-\tau}{\eta(s_{id}+H(M))}
\end{aligned}
$$

Now, we need to show that π_1, π_2 do not reveal any information about the user's identity. Taking the adversary's view, we see that $\pi_1, \pi_2, \pi'_1, \pi'_2$ satisfy,

$$
\begin{aligned}
\pi'_1 &= g^{\frac{t'_1}{z+s_{id'}}} g^{(z+s_{id'})t'_2} h^{t'_1 t'_2} \\
\log_g \pi'_1 &= \frac{t_1 + \frac{s_{id}-s_{id'}}{\eta}}{z+s_{id'}} + (z+s_{id'})\left(t_2 + \frac{1-\varepsilon}{\eta(z+s_{id})}\right) + \eta\left(t_1 + \frac{s_{id}-s_{id'}}{\eta}\right)\left(t_2 + \frac{1-\varepsilon}{\eta(z+s_{id})}\right) \\
&= \frac{t_1}{z+s_{id'}} + \frac{s_{id}-s_{id'}}{\eta(z+s_{id'})} + zt_2 + s_{id'}t_2 + \frac{(1-\varepsilon)(z+s_{id'})}{\eta(z+s_{id})} + \eta t_1 t_2 + s_{id}t_2 - s_{id'}t_2 + \\
& \quad \frac{t_1(1-\varepsilon)}{z+s_{id}} + \frac{(1-\varepsilon)(s_{id}-s_{id'})}{\eta(z+s_{id})} \\
&= \frac{t_1}{z+s_{id}} + (z+s_{id})t_2 + \eta t_1 t_2 \\
\pi'_1 &= g^{\frac{t_1}{z+s_{id}} + (z+s_{id})t_2 + \eta t_1 t_2} \\
&= g^{\frac{t_1}{z+s_{id}}} g^{(z+s_{id})t_2} h^{t_1 t_2} \\
&= \pi_1
\end{aligned}
$$

$$
\begin{aligned}
\pi'_2 &= g^{\frac{t'_1}{s_{id'}+H(M)}} g^{(s_{id'}+H(M))t'_3} h^{t'_1 t'_3} \\
\log_g \pi'_2 &= \frac{t_1 + \frac{s_{id}-s_{id'}}{\eta}}{s_{id'}+H(M)} + (s_{id'}+H(M))\left(t_3 + \frac{1-\tau}{\eta(s_{id}+H(M))}\right) \\
& \quad + \eta\left(t_1 + \frac{s_{id}-s_{id'}}{\eta}\right)\left(t_3 + \frac{1-\tau}{\eta(s_{id}+H(M))}\right) \\
&= \frac{t_1}{s_{id'}+H(M)} + \frac{s_{id}-s_{id'}}{\eta(s_{id'}+H(M))} + H(M)t_3 + s_{id'}t_3 + \frac{(1-\tau)(s_{id'}+H(M))}{\eta(s_{id}+H(M))} \\
& \quad + \eta t_1 t_3 + s_{id}t_3 - s_{id'}t_3 + \frac{t_1(1-\tau)}{s_{id}+H(M)} + \frac{(1-\tau)(s_{id}-s_{id'})}{\eta(s_{id}+H(M))} \\
&= \frac{t_1}{s_{id}+H(M)} + (s_{id}+H(M))t_3 + \eta t_1 t_3 \\
\pi'_2 &= g^{\frac{t_1}{s_{id}+H(M)} + (s_{id}+H(M))t_3 + \eta t_1 t_3} \\
&= g^{\frac{t_1}{s_{id}+H(M)}} g^{(s_{id}+H(M))t_3} h^{t_1 t_3} \\
&= \pi_2
\end{aligned}
$$

Therefore, π_1, π_2 is identical to π'_1, π'_2. The challenge signature σ does not reveal the identity id, though the simulator uses s_{id} to generate it. Hence, we claim that the adversary $\mathcal{A}$ in the anonymity game under the simulated environment has negligible advantage to guess the correct identity. ∎

6.2   Full Traceability

We prove that our group signature is existential unforgeability based on the security of two-level signature scheme proposed in Section 4.1.

Theorem 3. *If there exists a (t, ϵ) adversary for the full traceability game against the group signature scheme, then there exists a (t', ϵ) adaptive chosen message existential unforgeability adversary against the two-level signature scheme, where $t \approx t'$.*

Proof. We note that our group signature scheme is an extension form of our two-level signature scheme by adding some random number on the signing and verifying equations. Intuitively, we prove that our group signature is secure against adaptive chosen message attack by using two-level signature's unforgeability.

Suppose there exists a simulator $\mathcal{B}$, who interacts with the adversary $\mathcal{A}$ and wants to break two-level signature scheme. Then, $\mathcal{B}$ executes the following algorithms and plays a game with $\mathcal{A}$.

In Setup algorithm, $\mathcal{B}$ runs two-level signature Setup, generates public parameters and publishes them. Furthermore, $\mathcal{B}$ deliveries TK $= q$ to $\mathcal{A}$, and $\mathcal{A}$ is entitled the authority to tracing authority.

$\mathcal{A}$ queries a secret key on id to $\mathcal{B}$. To answer this request, $\mathcal{B}$ queries the key extract oracle of two-level signature scheme and obtains the user's secret key K_{id}. Then $\mathcal{B}$ sends K_{id} to $\mathcal{A}$.

$\mathcal{A}$ queries a signature on (id, M) to $\mathcal{B}$. $\mathcal{B}$ directly queries the signing oracle of two-level signature scheme and obtains $\sigma = (\sigma_1^\star, \sigma_2^\star, \sigma_3^\star)$ corresponding with (id, M). Then, $\mathcal{B}$ randomly choose t_1, t_2, t_3, and generates the group signature,

$$\sigma = (\sigma_1^\star \cdot h^{t_1}, \sigma_2^\star \cdot h^{t_2}, \sigma_3^\star \cdot h^{t_3}, (\sigma_2^\star)^{t_1} (Z\sigma_1^\star)^{t_2} h^{t_1 t_2}, (\sigma_3^\star)^{t_1} (g^{H(M)} \sigma_1^\star)^{t_3} h^{t_1 t_3}) \quad (1)$$

We could see that this is a valid group signature. After receiving the responding signature. $\mathcal{A}$ could check its validity by using PP and trace its identity by using TK $= q$. These verification equations are correct.

At some point, $\mathcal{A}$ outputs its forgery signature $\sigma^* = (\sigma_1^*, \sigma_2^*, \sigma_3^*, \pi_1^*, \pi_2^*)$ with (id^*, M^*). According to the game's constraints, id^* should be excluded from key extract queries and (id^*, M^*) should not be queried from signing oracle before.

Then, $\mathcal{B}$ generates λ which satisfies $\lambda \equiv 1 \pmod{p}$ and $\lambda \equiv 0 \pmod{q}$. Then, from π_1^*, π_2^* and the verification equations, we obtain:

$$e(\sigma_1^* Z, \sigma_2^*) \cdot e(g,g)^{-1} = e(\pi_1^*, h)$$
$$e(\sigma_1^* g^{H(M^*)}, \sigma_3^*) e(g,g)^{-1} = e(\pi_2^*, h)$$

And we use λ to obtain:

$$e(\sigma_1^{*\lambda} Z, \sigma_2^{*\lambda}) = e(g,g)$$
$$e(\sigma_1^{*\lambda} g^{H(M^*)}, \sigma_3^{*\lambda}) = e(g,g)$$

Since $(\sigma_1^{*\lambda}, \sigma_2^{*\lambda}, \sigma_3^{*\lambda})$ pass the verification equations of two-level signature scheme in Section 4.1, they are a forged two-level signature, which means $\mathcal{B}$ successfully breaks the unforgeability of two-level signature scheme. Thus, Theorem 3 has been proved. ∎

By combining with Theorem 2 and Theorem 3, we prove our scheme to have full anonymity and full traceability in the standard model.

7   Comparison

In this section, we compare our group signature with others. Boyen and Waters [9] proposed a nice group signature based on the Waters's identity-based signature [22]. However, the hierachical identity-based signature in that scheme leads logarithmic size of both group public key and group signature. Then, Boyen and Waters [10] improved the signature to be constant size. Furthermore, we propose a new group signature to achieve constant size of both public key and signature. We could see the details in table 1. ($M \in \{0,1\}^m$, $id \in \{0,1\}^k$):

Table 1. Comparisons on size in Group Signatures

	BW06 [9]	BW07 [10]	Our Scheme
Public Key	$(k+m+3)\|G\|$ $+\|G_q\|+\|G_T\|$	$(m+4)\|G\|$ $+\|G_q\|+\|G_T\|$	$2\|G\|+\|G_q\|$
Master Key	$\|G\|$	$\|G\|+\|\mathbb{Z}_n\|$	$\|\mathbb{Z}_n\|$
User Key	$3\|G\|$	$3\|G\|$	$\|G\|+\|\mathbb{Z}_n\|$
Signature	$(2k+3)\|G\|$	$6\|G\|$	$5\|G\|$

More than that, we continue to compare the computational cost on every participant in these group signature schemes. In Table 2, we note that $\mathbf{T_{Exp}}, \mathbf{T_{Pair}}, \mathbf{T_{Mul}}$ to represent the time for one modular exponentiation, one bilinear pairing computation, and one group multiplication, respectively. Certainly, our approach largely reduces the computational cost and enhances the whole efficiency, that means, our scheme is more applicable in real environment.

Recently, Groth [16] proposed a group signature scheme with full anonymity (CCA) in the standard model. His scheme adopts the existing tools, including certisignature scheme, strong one-time signature scheme, non-interactive proofs

Table 2. Comparisons on computational cost in Group Signatures

	BW06 [9]	BW07 [10]	Our Scheme
Join	$3\mathbf{T_{Exp}}+(k+2)\mathbf{T_{Mul}}$	$3\mathbf{T_{Exp}}$	$\mathbf{T_{Exp}}$
Sign	$(2k+5)\mathbf{T_{Exp}}+(3k+m+6)\mathbf{T_{Mul}}$	$12\mathbf{T_{Exp}} + (m+10)\mathbf{T_{Mul}}$	$11\mathbf{T_{Exp}}+8\mathbf{T_{Mul}}$
Verify	$(2k+3)\mathbf{T_{Pair}}+(2k+m+4)\mathbf{T_{Mul}}$	$6\mathbf{T_{Pair}}+3\mathbf{T_{Exp}}+(m+5)\mathbf{T_{Mul}}$	$6\mathbf{T_{Pair}}+3\mathbf{T_{Exp}}+4\mathbf{T_{Mul}}$
Open	$k\mathbf{T_{Exp}}$	$\mathbf{T_{Exp}}$	$\mathbf{T_{Exp}}$
Exhaustively Search	No	Yes	Yes

system for bilinear groups, selective-tag weakly CCA-secure encryption, but it increases the size and computational cost. The total size of a group signature is 50 group elements in G. In case full anonymity (CPA) is sufficient, the signature is reduced to 30 group elements. Thus, taking efficiency into consideration, our scheme is better.

8   Conclusion

In this paper, we proposed a practical group signature scheme, which has shorter sizes of both public key and signature than that of the other existing schemes. Since we adopted the approach of short signature proposed by BB04 [3] and non-interactive proof system [17], we proved the security of ours without random oracles, including full anonymity and full traceability. Furthermore, our scheme reduces the computational cost on both user and verifier sides. In the future work, we should improve ours on the full anonymity security in the CCA notion without random oracles and develop other practical group signature schemes based on weaker assumptions.

Acknowledgement

The authors would like to thank anonymous referees and Rongxing Lu for their suggestions to improve this paper. Besides, this research is supported by National Nature Science Foundation of China, No. 60673079 and No. 60773086, National 863 Program of China, No. 2006AA01Z424.

References

1. Ateniese, G., Camenisch, J., Hohenberger, S., de Medeiros, B.: Practical group signatures without random oracles. Cryptology ePrint Archieve, Report, /385 (2005) (2005), http://eprint.iacr.org/
2. Ateniese, G., Camenisch, J., Joye, M., Tsudik, G.: A practical and provably secure coalition-resistant group signature scheme. In: Bellare, M. (ed.) CRYPTO 2000. LNCS, vol. 1880, pp. 255–270. Springer, Heidelberg (2000)
3. Boneh, D., Boyen, X.: Short Signatures Without Random Oracles. In: Cachin, C., Camenisch, J.L. (eds.) EUROCRYPT 2004. LNCS, vol. 3027, pp. 56–73. Springer, Heidelberg (2004)
4. Blaze, M., Bleumer, G., Strauss, M.: Divertible protocols and atomic proxy cryptography. In: Blaze, M., Bleumer, G., Strauss, M. (eds.) EUROCRYPT 1998. LNCS, vol. 1403, pp. 127–144. Springer, Heidelberg (1998)
5. Boneh, D., Goh, E.-J., Nissim, K.: Evaluating 2-dnf formulas on ciphertexts. In: Kilian, J. (ed.) TCC 2005. LNCS, vol. 3378, pp. 325–341. Springer, Heidelberg (2005)
6. Bellare, M., Micciancio, D., Warinschi, B.: Foundations of group signatures: Formal definitions, simplified requirements, and a construction based on general assumptions. In: Biham, E. (ed.) EUROCRPYT 2003. LNCS, vol. 2656, pp. 614–629. Springer, Heidelberg (2003)

82   X. Liang et al.

7. Boneh, D., Shacham, H.: Group signatures with verifier-local revocation. In: Proceedings of ACM CCS 2004, pp. 168–177. ACM Press, New York (2004)
8. Bellare, M., Shi, H., Zhang, C.: Foundations of group signatures: The case of dynamic groups. In: Menezes, A.J. (ed.) CT-RSA 2005. LNCS, vol. 3376, pp. 136–153. Springer, Heidelberg (2005)
9. Boyen, X., Waters, B.: Compact Group Signatures Without Random Oracles. In: Vaudenay, S. (ed.) EUROCRYPT 2006. LNCS, vol. 4004, pp. 427–444. Springer, Heidelberg (2006)
10. Boyen, X., Waters, B.: Full-Domain Subgroup Hiding and Constant-Size Group Signatures. In: PKC 2007. LNCS, vol. 4450, pp. 1–15. Springer, Heidelberg (2007)
11. Canetti, R., Goldreich, O., Halevi, S.: The random oracle methodology, revisited. In: Proceedings of STOC 1998, pp. 209–218 (1998)
12. Canetti, R., Goldreich, O., Halevi, S.: On the random-oracle methodology as applied to length-restricted signature schemes. In: Naor, M. (ed.) TCC 2004. LNCS, vol. 2951, pp. 40–57. Springer, Heidelberg (2004)
13. Chaum, D., van Heyst, E.: Group signatures. In: Davies, D.W. (ed.) EUROCRYPT 1991. LNCS, vol. 547, pp. 257–265. Springer, Heidelberg (1991)
14. Furukawa, J., Imai, H.: An efficient group signature scheme from bilinear maps. In: Boyd, C., González Nieto, J.M. (eds.) ACISP 2005. LNCS, vol. 3574, pp. 455–467. Springer, Heidelberg (2005)
15. Groth, J.: Simulation-sound nizk proofs for a practical language and constant size group signatures. In: Lai, X., Chen, K. (eds.) ASIACRYPT 2006. LNCS, vol. 4284, pp. 444–459. Springer, Heidelberg (2006)
16. Groth, J.: Fully Anonymous Group Signatures without Random Oracles. Cryptology ePrint Archieve, Report 2007/186 (2004), http://eprint.iacr.org/
17. Groth, J., Sahai, A.: Efficient Non-interactive Proof Systems for Bilinear Groups. Cryptology ePrint Archieve, Report, 2007/155 (2005), http://eprint.iacr.org/
18. Groth, J., Ostrovsky, R., Sahai, A.: New Techniques for Non-interactive Zero-Knowledge. In: Dwork, C. (ed.) CRYPTO 2006. LNCS, vol. 4117, pp. 97–111. Springer, Heidelberg (2006)
19. Kiayias, A., Yung, M.: Extracting group signatures from traitor tracing schemes. In: Biham, E. (ed.) EUROCRPYT 2003. LNCS, vol. 2656, pp. 630–648. Springer, Heidelberg (2003)
20. Kiayias, A., Yung, M.: Group signatures: Provable security, efficient constructions and anonymity from trapdoor-holders. Cryptology ePrint Archieve, Report 2004/076, (2004), http://eprint.iacr.org/
21. Kiayias, A., Yung, M.: Group signatures with efficient concurrent join. In: Cramer, R.J.F. (ed.) EUROCRYPT 2005. LNCS, vol. 3494, pp. 198–214. Springer, Heidelberg (2005)
22. Waters, B.: Efficient Identity-Based Encryption Without Random Oracles. In: Cramer, R.J.F. (ed.) EUROCRYPT 2005. LNCS, vol. 3494, pp. 114–127. Springer, Heidelberg (2005)

(Convertible) Undeniable Signatures Without Random Oracles

Tsz Hon Yuen[1], Man Ho Au[1], Joseph K. Liu[2], and Willy Susilo[1]

[1] Centre for Computer and Information Security Research
School of Computer Science and Software Engineering
University of Wollongong
Wollongong, Australia
{thy738,mhaa456,wsusilo}@uow.edu.au
[2] Department of Computer Science
University of Bristol
Bristol, UK
liu@cs.bris.ac.uk

Abstract. We propose a convertible undeniable signature scheme without random oracles. Our construction is based on Waters' and Kurosawa and Heng's schemes that were proposed in Eurocrypt 2005. The security of our scheme is based on the CDH and the decision linear assumption. Comparing only the part of undeniable signatures, our scheme uses more standard assumptions than the existing undeniable signatures without random oracles due to Laguillamie and Vergnaud.

Keywords: Convertible undeniable signature, random oracle model, pairings.

1 Introduction

Standard digital signatures allow universal verification. However in some real world scenarios, privacy is an important issue. In this situation, we may require that the verification of signatures is restricted by the signer. Then, the verification of a signature requires an interaction with the signer. A signer can deny generating a signature that he never signs, but cannot deny one that he signs. The proof by the signer cannot be transferred to convince other verifiers. This concept is known as the "Undeniable Signatures" that was proposed by Chaum and van Antwerpen [11]. Later, Boyar, Chaum, Damgård and Pedersen [6] proposed an extension called "Convertible Undeniable Signatures", that allows the possibility to transform an undeniable signature into a self-authenticating signature. This transformation can be restricted to a particular signature only, or can be applied to all signatures of a signer.

There are many different undeniable signatures with variable features and security levels. These features include convertibility [6,13,23,24], designated verifier technique [16], designated confirmer technique [10,25], identity based scheme

S. Qing, H. Imai, and G. Wang (Eds.): ICICS 2007, LNCS 4861, pp. 83–97, 2007.
© Springer-Verlag Berlin Heidelberg 2007

[22], time-selective scheme [21], etc. The security for undeniable signatures is said to be *secure* if it is unforgeable, invisible and the confirmation and disavowal protocols are zero-knowledge. It is believed that the zero-knowledgeness is required to make undeniable signatures non-transferable. However, Kurosawa and Heng [18] suggested that zero-knowledgeness and non-transferability can be separated; and the concept of witness indistinguishability can be incorporated. They proposed another security notion called impersonation attack.

The random oracle model [3] is a popular technique in provable security. However several papers proved that some cryptosystems secure in the random oracle were actually provably insecure when the random oracle was instantiated by any real-world hashing functions [9,2]. As a result, recently there are many new signature schemes which prove their security without random oracles, such as group signatures [1,8], ring signatures [12,4], blind signatures [17], group-oriented signatures [26], undeniable signatures [20], universal designated verifier signatures [28], etc. Nonetheless, some of them introduce new security assumptions that are not well studied, which are the main drawback of some schemes.

Our Contribution. We propose the *first* convertible undeniable signatures without random oracles in pairings. Most of the existing convertible undeniable signatures are proven secure in the random oracle model only [6,23,24,21][1], except the recent construction in RSA [19].

Most efficient undeniable signatures are proven secure in the random oracle model only. [14] is secure in the random oracle model currently.[2] Recently, Languillaumie and Vergnaud proposed the first efficient undeniable signatures without random oracles [20]. However, their anonymity relies on their *new assumption* DSDH, while their unforgeability relies on the GSDH assumption with the access of a DSDH oracle, which seems to be contradictory. Our proposed variant of undeniable signature is proven unforgeable by the CDH assumption and anonymous by the decision linear assumption. Therefore by removing the protocol for convertible parts, our undeniable signature scheme is the *first* proven secure scheme *without using random oracles* and *without using a new assumption* in discrete logarithm settings.

We extend the security model of [18] to convertible undeniable signatures. We also use the 3-move witness indistinguishable (WI) protocol in [18]. Therefore we incorporate the concept of WI into the convertible undeniable signatures and propose the first 3-move convertible undeniable signatures.

Organization. The next section briefly explains the pairings and some related intractability problems. Section 3 gives the security model and some basic building blocks are given in Section 4. Section 5 gives our construction and security proofs. The paper ends with some concluding remarks.

---

[1] [13] does not prove the invisibility property. The authors only conjecture the security in section 5.1 and 5.2.
[2] Refer to section 1.1 in [19] for details.

2 Preliminaries

2.1 Pairings and Intractability Problem

Our scheme uses bilinear pairings on elliptic curves. We now give a brief revision on the property of pairings and candidate hard problem from pairings that will be used later.

Let $\mathbb{G}, \mathbb{G}_T$ be cyclic groups of prime order p, writing the group action multiplicatively. Let g be a generator of $\mathbb{G}$.

Definition 1. *A map $\hat{e} : \mathbb{G} \times \mathbb{G} \to \mathbb{G}_T$ is called a bilinear pairing if, for all $x, y \in \mathbb{G}$ and $a, b \in \mathbb{Z}_p$, we have $\hat{e}(x^a, y^b) = \hat{e}(x, y)^{ab}$, and $\hat{e}(g, g) \neq 1$.*

Definition 2 (CDH). *The Computational Diffie-Hellman (CDH) problem is that, given $g, g^x, g^y \in \mathbb{G}$ for unknown $x, y \in \mathbb{Z}_p^*$, to compute g^{xy}.*

We say that the (ϵ, t)-CDH assumption holds in $\mathbb{G}$ if no t-time algorithm has the non-negligible probability ϵ in solving the CDH problem.

Definition 3 (Decision Linear [5]). *The Decision Linear problem is that, given $u, u^a, v, v^b, h, h^c \in \mathbb{G}$ for unknown $a, b, c \in \mathbb{Z}_p^*$, to output 1 if $c = a + b$ and output 0 otherwise.*

We say that the (ϵ, t)-Decision Linear assumption holds in $\mathbb{G}$ if no t-time algorithm has probability over half ϵ in solving the Decision Linear problem in $\mathbb{G}$. The decision linear assumption is proposed in [5] to prove the security of short group signatures. It is also used in [7] and [15] for proving the security of anonymous hierarchical identity-based encryption and obfuscating re-encryption respectively.

3 Undeniable Signature Security Models

In this section we review the security notions and model of (convertible) undeniable signatures. Unforgeability and invisibility are popular security requirement for undeniable signatures. Kurosawa and Heng [18] proposed another security notion called impersonation. We will use the security model of [18], and extend it to convertible undeniable signatures. The changes for convertible undeniable signatures will be given in brackets.

3.1 Security Notions

An (convertible) undeniable signature scheme has the following algorithms:

- **Setup.** On input security parameter 1^λ, outputs public parameters param.
- **Key Generation.** On input public parameters param, outputs a public key pk and a secret key sk.
- **Sign.** On input public parameters param, a secret key sk and a message m, outputs an undeniable signature σ.

- **Confirm/Deny.** This is an interactive protocol between a prover and a verifier. Their common inputs are public parameters param, a public key pk, a message m and a signature σ. The prover's private input is a secret key sk. At the end of the protocol, the verifier outputs 1 if σ is a valid signature of m and outputs 0 otherwise.

(The following algorithms are for convertible schemes only.)

- **Individual Conversion.** On input public parameters param, a secret key sk, a message m and a signature σ, outputs an individual receipt r which makes it possible to universally verify σ.
- **Individual Verification.** On input public parameters param, a public key pk, a message m, a signature σ and an individual receipt r, outputs $\perp$ if r is an invalid receipt. Otherwise, outputs 1 if σ is a valid signature of m and outputs 0 otherwise.
- **Universal Conversion** On input public parameters param and a secret key sk, outputs an universal receipt R which makes it possible to universally verify all signatures for pk.
- **Universal Verification.** On input public parameters param, a public key pk, a message m, a signature σ and an universal receipt R, outputs $\perp$ if R is an invalid receipt. Otherwise, outputs 1 if σ is a valid signature of m and outputs 0 otherwise.

3.2 Unforgeability

Existential unforgeability against chosen message attack is defined as in the following game involving an adversary $\mathcal{A}$ and a simulator $\mathcal{S}$.

1. $\mathcal{S}$ gives the public keys and parameters to $\mathcal{A}$. (For convertible schemes, $\mathcal{S}$ also gives $\mathcal{A}$ the universal receipt R.)
2. $\mathcal{A}$ can query the following oracles:
   - Signing queries: $\mathcal{A}$ adaptively queries q_s times with input message m_i, and obtains a signature σ_i.
   - Confirmation/disavowal queries: $\mathcal{A}$ adaptively queries q_c times with input message-signature pair (m_i, σ_i). If it is a valid pair, the oracle returns a bit $\mu = 1$ and proceeds with the execution of the confirmation protocol with $\mathcal{A}$. Otherwise, the oracle returns a bit $\mu = 0$ and proceeds with the execution of the disavowal protocol with $\mathcal{A}$.
     (For convertible scheme, this oracle is not necessary as the universal receipt is given.)
3. Finally $\mathcal{A}$ outputs a message-signature pair (m^*, σ^*) where m^* has never been queried to the signing oracle.

$\mathcal{A}$ wins the game if σ^* is a valid signature for m^*.

Definition 4. *An (convertible) undeniable signature scheme is* (ϵ, t, q_c, q_s)- *unforgeable against chosen message attack if there is no t time adversary winning the above game with probability greater than ϵ.*

3.3   Invisibility

Invisibility against chosen message attack is defined as in the following game involving an adversary $\mathcal{A}$ and a simulator $\mathcal{S}$.

1. $\mathcal{S}$ gives the public keys and parameters to $\mathcal{A}$.
2. $\mathcal{A}$ can query the following oracles:
   - Signing queries, Confirmation/disavowal queries: same as unforgeability.
   - (For convertible schemes only.) Receipt generating oracle: $\mathcal{A}$ adaptively queries q_r times with input message-signature pair (m_i, σ_i), and obtains an individual receipt r.
3. $\mathcal{A}$ outputs a message m^* which has never been queried to the signing oracle, and requests a challenge signature σ^* on m^*. σ^* is generated based on a hidden bit b. If $b = 1$, then σ^* is generated as usual using the signing oracle, otherwise σ^* is chosen uniformly at random from the signature space.
4. $\mathcal{A}$ can adaptively query the signing oracle and confirmation/disavowal oracle, where no signing query (and receipt generating query) for m^* and no confirmation/disavowal query for (m^*, σ^*) is allowed.
5. Finally $\mathcal{A}$ outputs a guessing bit b'

$\mathcal{A}$ wins the game if $b = b'$. $\mathcal{A}$'s advantage is $Adv(\mathcal{A}) = |\Pr[b' = b] - \frac{1}{2}|$.

Definition 5. *An (convertible) undeniable signature scheme is $(\epsilon, t, q_c, q_r, q_s)$-invisible if there is no t time adversary winning the above game with advantage greater than ϵ.*

3.4   Impersonation

Impersonation against chosen message attack is defined as in the following game involving an adversary $\mathcal{A}$ and a simulator $\mathcal{S}$.

1. $\mathcal{S}$ gives the public keys and parameters to $\mathcal{A}$.
2. $\mathcal{A}$ can query the Signing oracle and Confirmation/disavowal oracle, which are the same as the one in unforgeability.
3. Finally $\mathcal{A}$ outputs a message-signature pair (m^*, σ^*) and a bit b. If $b = 1$, $\mathcal{A}$ executes the confirmation protocol with $\mathcal{S}$. Otherwise $\mathcal{A}$ executes the disavowal protocol with $\mathcal{S}$.

$\mathcal{A}$ wins the game if $\mathcal{S}$ is convinced that σ^* is a valid signature for m^* if $b = 1$, or is an invalid signature for m^* if $b = 0$.

Definition 6. *An (convertible) undeniable signature scheme is (ϵ, t, q_c, q_s)-secure against impersonation if there is no t time adversary winning the above game with probability at least ϵ.*

Remark: For convertible schemes, if an adversary can forge an individual or universal receipt, he can always convince a verifier in the interactive protocol, by directly giving the receipt to him. Therefore the model of impersonation attack already includes the security notion regarding receipts in convertible schemes.

4   Basic Building Blocks

4.1   Waters Signature Scheme

Waters [27] presented a secure signature scheme based on CDH problem without random oracles. The scheme is summarized as follows:

1. **Gen.** Randomly choose $\alpha \in \mathbb{Z}_p$ and let $g_1 = g^\alpha$. Additionally, choose two random values $g_2, u' \in \mathbb{G}$ and a random n-length vector $\mathsf{U} = (u_i)$, whose elements are chosen at random from $\mathbb{G}$. The public key is $pk = (g_1, g_2, u', \mathsf{U})$ and the secret key is g_2^α.
2. **Sign.** To generate a signature on message $M = (\mu_1, \ldots, \mu_n) \in \{0,1\}^n$, pick $s \in_R \mathbb{Z}_p^*$ and output the signature as $\sigma = (g_2^\alpha \cdot (u' \prod_{j=1}^n u_j^{\mu_j})^s,\ g^s)$ with his secret key g_2^α.
3. **Verify.** Given a signature $\sigma = (\sigma_1, \sigma_2)$ on message $M = (\mu_1, \ldots, \mu_n) \in \{0,1\}^n$, it outputs 1 if $\hat{e}(g, \sigma_1) = \hat{e}(g_1, g_2) \cdot \hat{e}(u' \prod_{i=1}^n u_i^{\mu_i}, \sigma_2)$. Otherwise, it outputs 0.

4.2   WI Protocol

We review the witness indistinguishable (WI) protocol for Diffie-Hellman (DH) tuple and non-DH tuple from [18]. Let $\mathbb{G}$ be an Abelian group with prime order p. Let L be a generator of $\mathbb{G}$. We say that $(L, L^\alpha, L^\beta, L^\gamma)$ is a DH tuple if $\gamma = \alpha\beta \mod p$. Kurosawa and Heng [18] proposed a WI protocol to prove if (L, M, N, O) is a DH tuple or non-DH tuple using the knowledge of α $(= \log_L M)$. For the details of the definition and security model of WI protocol, please refer to [18] for details. We summarize the protocols in table 1 and 2.

Table 1. WI protocol for DH tuple (L, M, N, O)

Prover		Verifier
$c_2, d_2, r \xleftarrow{R} \mathbb{Z}_p$ $z_1' = L^{d_2}/N^{c_2}$ $z_2' = M^{d_2}/O^{c_2}$ $z_1 = L^r$ 1 $\quad z_2 = N^r$	$\xrightarrow{z_1, z_2, z_1', z_2'}$	
2	$\xleftarrow{\quad c \quad}$	$c \xleftarrow{R} \mathbb{Z}_p$
$c_1 = c - c_2 \mod p$ 3 $\quad d_1 = r + c_1\alpha \mod p$	$\xrightarrow{c_1, c_2, d_1, d_2}$	
		$c \stackrel{?}{=} c_1 + c_2 \mod p$ $L^{d_1} \stackrel{?}{=} z_1 M^{c_1}$ $L^{d_2} \stackrel{?}{=} z_1' N^{c_2}$ $N^{d_1} \stackrel{?}{=} z_2 O^{c_1}$ $M^{d_2} \stackrel{?}{=} z_2' O^{c_2}$

Table 2. WI protocol for non-DH tuple (L, M, N, O)

Prover		Verifier
$c_2, d_1', d_2', r, a, b \xleftarrow{R} \mathbb{Z}_p$		
$A' \xleftarrow{R} \mathbb{G}$ with $A' \neq 1$		
$z_1' = M^{d_1'}/(O^{d_2'} A'^{c_2})$		
$z_2' = L^{d_1'}/N^{d_2'}$		
$A = (N^\alpha/O)^r$		
$z_1 = N^a/O^b$		
1 $z_2 = L^a/M^b$	$\xrightarrow{A, A', z_1, z_2, z_1', z_2'}$	$A \overset{?}{\neq} 1, \ A' \overset{?}{\neq} 1$
2	$\xleftarrow{c}$	$c \xleftarrow{R} \mathbb{Z}_p$
$c_1 = c - c_2 \bmod p$		
$d_1 = a + c_1\alpha r \bmod p$		
3 $d_2 = b + c_1 r \bmod p$	$\xrightarrow{c_1, c_2, d_1, d_2, d_1', d_2'}$	
		$c \overset{?}{=} c_1 + c_2 \bmod p$
		$N^{d_1}/O^{d_2} \overset{?}{=} z_1 A^{c_1}$
		$M^{d_1'}/O^{d_2'} \overset{?}{=} z_1' A'^{c_2}$
		$L^{d_1}/M^{d_2} \overset{?}{=} z_2$
		$L^{d_1'}/N^{d_2'} \overset{?}{=} z_2'$

5 Convertible Undeniable Signature Scheme

5.1 Scheme Construction

In this section, we present our convertible undeniable signature scheme. The scheme consists of the following algorithms.

Setup. Let $\mathbb{G}, \mathbb{G}_T$ be groups of prime order p. Given a pairing: $\hat{e} : \mathbb{G} \times \mathbb{G} \to \mathbb{G}_T$. Select generators $g, g_2 \in \mathbb{G}$. Generator $u' \in \mathbb{G}$ is selected in random, and a random n-length vector $\mathsf{U} = (u_i)$, whose elements are chosen at random from $\mathbb{G}$.

Select an integer d as a system parameter. Denote $\ell = 2^d$ and $k = n/d$. Let $H_j : \{0,1\}^n \to \mathbb{Z}_\ell^*$ be collision resistant hash functions, where $1 \leq j \leq k$.

Key Generation. Randomly select $\alpha, \beta', \beta_i \in \mathbb{Z}_p^*$ for $1 \leq i \leq \ell$. Set $g_1 = g^\alpha$, $v' = g^{\beta'}$ and $v_i = g^{\beta_i}$. The public keys are $(g_1, v', v_1, \ldots, v_\ell)$. The secret keys are $(\alpha, \beta', \beta_1, \ldots, \beta_\ell)$.

Sign. To sign a message $m = (m_1, \ldots, m_n) \in \{0,1\}^n$, denote $\bar{m}_j = H_j(m)$ for $1 \leq j \leq k$. The signer picks $r \in_R \mathbb{Z}_p^*$ and computes the signature:

$$S_1 = g_2^\alpha \left(u' \prod_{i=1}^n u_i^{m_i}\right)^r \qquad S_{2,j} = \left(v' \prod_{i=1}^\ell v_i^{\bar{m}_j^i}\right)^r$$

The output signature is $(S_1, S_{2,1}, \ldots, S_{2,k})$.

Confirm/Deny. On input $(S_1, S_{2,1}, \ldots, S_{2,k})$, the signer computes for $1 \leq j \leq k$

$$L = \hat{e}(g, g_2)$$

$$M = \hat{e}(g_1, g_2)$$

$$N_j = \hat{e}(v' \prod_{i=1}^{\ell} v_i^{\bar{m}_j^i}, g_2)$$

$$O_j = \hat{e}(v' \prod_{i=1}^{\ell} v_i^{\bar{m}_j^i}, S_1)/\hat{e}(S_{2,j}, u' \prod_{i=1}^{n} u_i^{m_i}). \tag{1}$$

We have the 3-move WI protocols of the equality or the inequality of discrete logarithm $\alpha = log_L M$ and $log_{N_j} O_j$ in $\mathbb{G}_T$ shown in table 1 and 2.

Individual Conversion. Upon input the signature $(S_1, S_{2,1}, \ldots, S_{2,k})$ on the message m, the signer computes $\bar{m}_1 = H_1(m)$ and:

$$S_2' = S_{2,1}^{1/(\beta' + \sum_{i=1}^{\ell} \beta_i \bar{m}_1^i)}$$

Output the individual receipt S_2' for message m.

Individual Verification. Upon input the signature $(S_1, S_{2,1}, \ldots, S_{2,k})$ for the message m and the individual receipt S_2', compute $\bar{m}_j = H_j(m)$ for $1 \leq j \leq k$ and check if:

$$\hat{e}(g, S_{2,j}) \overset{?}{=} \hat{e}(S_2', v' \prod_{i=1}^{\ell} v_i^{\bar{m}_j^i})$$

If they are not equal, output $\perp$. Otherwise compare if:

$$\hat{e}(g, S_1) \overset{?}{=} \hat{e}(g_1, g_2) \cdot \hat{e}(S_2', u' \prod_{i=1}^{n} u_i^{m_i})$$

Output 1 if the above holds. Otherwise output 0.

Universal Conversion. The signer publishes his universal receipt $(\beta', \beta_1, \ldots, \beta_\ell)$.

Universal Verification. Upon input the signature $(S_1, S_{2,1}, \ldots, S_{2,k})$ on the message m and the universal receipt $(\beta', \beta_1, \ldots, \beta_\ell)$, check if:

$$v' \overset{?}{=} g^{\beta'} \qquad v_i \overset{?}{=} g^{\beta_i} \qquad \text{for } 1 \leq i \leq \ell$$

If they are not equal, output $\perp$. Otherwise compute $\bar{m}_j = H_j(m)$ for $1 \leq j \leq k$ and compare if:

$$\hat{e}(g, S_1) \overset{?}{=} \hat{e}(g_1, g_2) \cdot \hat{e}(S_{2,j}^{1/(\beta' + \sum_{i=1}^{\ell} \beta_i \bar{m}_j^i)}, u' \prod_{i=1}^{n} u_i^{m_i})$$

Output 1 if the above holds. Otherwise output 0.

5.2 Security Result

Theorem 1. *The scheme is (ϵ, t, q_s)-unforgeable if the (ϵ', t')-CDH assumption holds in $\mathbb{G}$, where*

$$\epsilon' \geq \frac{\epsilon}{4 q_s (n+1)}$$

$$t' = t + O\left(q_s \rho + (n+\ell) q_s \omega\right)$$

and $H_j : \{0,1\}^n \rightarrow \mathbb{Z}_\ell^*$, where $1 \leq j \leq k$, are some collision resistant hash functions and ρ, ω are the time for an exponentiation in $\mathbb{G}$ and an addition in $\mathbb{Z}_p$ respectively.

Proof. Assume there is a (ϵ, t, q_s)-adversary $\mathcal{A}$. We are going to construct another PPT $\mathcal{B}$ that makes use of $\mathcal{A}$ to solve the CDH problem with probability at least ϵ' and in time at most t'.

$\mathcal{B}$ is given a CDH problem instance (g, g^a, g^b). In order to use $\mathcal{A}$ to solve for the problem, $\mathcal{B}$ needs to simulates a challenger and the oracles for $\mathcal{A}$. $\mathcal{B}$ does it in the following way.

Setup. Let $l_p = 2q_s$. $\mathcal{B}$ randomly selects integer κ such that $0 \leq \kappa \leq n$. Also assume that $l_p(n+1) < p$ for the given values of q_s, and n. It randomly selects the following integers:

- $x' \in_R \mathbb{Z}_{l_p}$; $y' \in_R \mathbb{Z}_p$
- $x_i \in_R \mathbb{Z}_{l_p}$, for $i = 1, \ldots, n$. Let $\hat{X} = \{x_i\}$.
- $y_i \in_R \mathbb{Z}_p$, for $i = 1, \ldots, n$. Let $\hat{Y} = \{y_i\}$.

We further define the following functions for binary strings $\mathfrak{m} = (m_1, \ldots, m_n)$ as follow:

$$F(\mathfrak{m}) = x' + \sum_{i=1}^{n} x_i m_i - l_p \kappa \qquad \text{and} \qquad J(\mathfrak{m}) = y' + \sum_{i=1}^{n} y_i m_i$$

$\mathcal{B}$ randomly picks $\beta', \beta_i \in \mathbb{Z}_p^*$ for $1 \leq i \leq \ell$. Set $v' = g^{\beta'}$ and $v_i = g^{\beta_i}$. $\mathcal{B}$ constructs a set of public parameters as follow:

$$g, \qquad g_2 = g^b, \qquad u' = g_2^{-l_p \kappa + x'} g^{y'}, \qquad u_i = g_2^{x_i} g^{y_i} \text{ for } 1 \leq i \leq n$$

The signer's public key is $(g_1 = g^a, v', v_1, \ldots, v_\ell)$.

Denote $G(\mathfrak{m}) = \beta' + \sum_{i=1}^{\ell} \beta_i \mathfrak{m}^i$. Note that we have the following equation:

$$u' \prod_{i=1}^{n} u_i^{m_i} = g_2^{F(\mathfrak{m})} g^{J(\mathfrak{m})}, \qquad v' \prod_{i=1}^{\ell} v_i^{\bar{\mathfrak{m}}_j^i} = g^{G(\bar{\mathfrak{m}}_j)} \qquad \text{for } 1 \leq j \leq k$$

where $\bar{\mathfrak{m}}_j = H_j(\mathfrak{m})$ for $1 \leq j \leq k$. All public parameters and universal receipt $(\beta', \beta_1, \ldots, \beta_\ell)$ are passed to $\mathcal{A}$.

Oracles Simulation. $\mathcal{B}$ simulates the oracles as follow:

(*Signing oracle.*) Upon receiving query for message $\mathsf{m}_i = \{m_1, \ldots, m_n\}$, although $\mathcal{B}$ does not know the secret key, it still can construct the signature by assuming $F(\mathsf{m}_i) \neq 0 \bmod p$. It randomly chooses $r_i \in_R \mathbb{Z}_p$ and computes the signature as

$$S_1 = g_1^{-\frac{J(\mathsf{m}_i)}{F(\mathsf{m}_i)}} \left(g_2^{F(\mathsf{m}_i)} g^{J(\mathsf{m}_i)}\right)^{r_i}, \quad S_{2,j} = \left(g_1^{-\frac{1}{F(\mathsf{m}_i)}} g^{r_i}\right)^{G(\bar{\mathsf{m}}_{i,j})}$$

where $\bar{\mathsf{m}}_{i,j} = H_j(\mathsf{m}_i)$ for $1 \leq j \leq k$.

By letting $\tilde{r}_i = r_i - \frac{a}{F(\mathsf{m}_i)}$, it can be verified that $(S_1, S_{2,1}, \ldots, S_{2,k})$ is a signature, shown as follow:

$$
\begin{aligned}
S_1 &= g_1^{-\frac{J(\mathsf{m}_i)}{F(\mathsf{m}_i)}} \left(g_2^{F(\mathsf{m}_i)} g^{J(\mathsf{m}_i)}\right)^{r_i} \\
&= g^{-\frac{aJ(\mathsf{m}_i)}{F(\mathsf{m}_i)}} \left(g_2^{F(\mathsf{m}_i)} g^{J(\mathsf{m}_i)}\right)^{\frac{a}{F(\mathsf{m}_i)}} \left(g_2^{F(\mathsf{m}_i)} g^{J(\mathsf{m}_i)}\right)^{-\frac{a}{F(\mathsf{m}_i)}} \left(g_2^{F(\mathsf{m}_i)} g^{J(\mathsf{m}_i)}\right)^{r_i} \\
&= g^{-\frac{aJ(\mathsf{m}_i)}{F(\mathsf{m}_i)}} g_2^a g^{\frac{aJ(\mathsf{m}_i)}{F(\mathsf{m}_i)}} \left(g_2^{F(\mathsf{m}_i)} g^{J(\mathsf{m}_i)}\right)^{\tilde{r}_i} \\
&= g_2^a \left(u' \prod_{j=1}^{n} u_j^{m_j}\right)^{\tilde{r}_i} \\
S_{2,j} &= \left(g_1^{-\frac{1}{F(\mathsf{m}_i)}} g^{r_i}\right)^{G(\bar{\mathsf{m}}_{i,j})} = \left(g^{r_i - \frac{a}{F(\mathsf{m}_i)}}\right)^{G(\bar{\mathsf{m}}_{i,j})} = g^{G(\bar{\mathsf{m}}_i)\tilde{r}_i} = \left(v' \prod_{w=1}^{\ell} v_w^{\bar{\mathsf{m}}_{i,j}^w}\right)^{\tilde{r}_i}
\end{aligned}
$$

$\mathcal{B}$ outputs the signature $(S_1, S_{2,1}, \ldots, S_{2,k})$. To the adversary, all signatures given by $\mathcal{B}$ are indistinguishable from the signatures generated by the signer.

If $F(\mathsf{m}_i) = 0 \bmod p$, since the above computation cannot be performed (division by 0), the simulator aborts. To make it simple, the simulator will abort if $F(\mathsf{m}_i) = 0 \bmod l_p$. The equivalence can be observed as follow. From the assumption $l_p(n+1) < p$, it implies $0 \leq l_p\kappa < p$ and $0 \leq x' + \sum_{i=1}^{n} x_i m_i < p$ ($\because x', x_i < l_p$). We have $-p < F(\mathsf{m}_i) < p$ which implies if $F(\mathsf{m}_i) = 0 \bmod p$ then $F(\mathsf{m}_i) = 0 \bmod l_p$. Hence, $F(\mathsf{m}_i) \neq 0 \bmod l_p$ implies $F(\mathsf{m}_i) \neq 0 \bmod p$. Thus the former condition will be sufficient to ensure that a signature can be computed without abort.

Output. Finally $\mathcal{A}$ outputs a signature $(S_1^*, S_{2,1}^*, \ldots, S_{2,k}^*)$ for message m^*. $\mathcal{B}$ checks if $F(\mathsf{m}^*) = 0 \bmod p$. If not, $\mathcal{B}$ aborts. Otherwise $\mathcal{B}$ computes $\bar{\mathsf{m}}_1^* = H_1(\mathsf{m}^*)$ and outputs

$$\frac{S_1^*}{S_{2,1}^{*\, J(\mathsf{m}^*)/G(\bar{\mathsf{m}}_1^*)}} = \frac{g_2^a \left(u' \prod_{i=1}^{n} u_i^{\mathsf{m}_i^*}\right)^r}{\left(v' \prod_{i=1}^{\ell} v_i^{\bar{\mathsf{m}}_1^{*\,i}}\right)^{r J(\mathsf{m}^*)/G(\bar{\mathsf{m}}_1^*)}} = \frac{g_2^a \left(g^{J(\mathsf{m}^*)}\right)^r}{g^{r J(\mathsf{m}^*)}} = g^{ab}$$

which is the solution to the CDH problem instance.

Probability Analysis and Time Complexity Analysis. They are given in the full version of the paper.   □

Theorem 2. *The scheme is $(\epsilon, t, q_c, q_r, q_s)$-invisible if the (ϵ', t')-decision linear assumption holds in $\mathbb{G}$, where*

$$\epsilon' \geq \epsilon \cdot \frac{1}{4(q_s + 1)(n + 1)(q_s + q_r)^k} \cdot \left(1 - \frac{1}{q_s + q_r}\right)^{(q_s + q_r)k}$$

$$t' = t + O\left((q_s + q_r)\rho + q_c\tau + \left(nq_s + \ell\right)\omega\right)$$

where $H_j : \{0,1\}^n \rightarrow \mathbb{Z}_\ell^*$, where $1 \leq j \leq k$, are some collision resistant hash functions and ρ, τ, ω are the time for an exponentiation in $\mathbb{G}$, an exponentiation in $\mathbb{G}_T$ and an addition in $\mathbb{Z}_p$ respectively, under the assumption that $\ell > q_s + q_r$.

Proof. Assume there is a $(\epsilon, t, q_c, q_r, q_s)$-adversary $\mathcal{A}$. We are going to construct another PPT $\mathcal{B}$ that makes use of $\mathcal{A}$ to solve the decisional linear problem with probability at least ϵ' and in time at most t'.

$\mathcal{B}$ is given a decisional linear problem instance (u, v, h, u^a, v^b, h^c). In order to use $\mathcal{A}$ to solve for the problem, $\mathcal{B}$ needs to simulates the oracles for $\mathcal{A}$. $\mathcal{B}$ does it in the following way.

Setup. Let $l_p = 2(q_s+1)$. $\mathcal{B}$ randomly selects integer κ such that $0 \leq \kappa \leq n$. Also assume that $l_p(n + 1) < p$ for the given values of q_c, q_r, q_s, and n. It randomly selects the following integers:

- $x' \in_R \mathbb{Z}_{l_p}$; $y' \in_R \mathbb{Z}_p$
- $x_i \in_R \mathbb{Z}_{l_p}$, for $i = 1, \ldots, n$. Let $\hat{X} = \{x_i\}$.
- $y_i \in_R \mathbb{Z}_p$, for $i = 1, \ldots, n$. Let $\hat{Y} = \{y_i\}$.

We further define the following functions for binary strings $\mathfrak{m} = (m_1, \ldots, m_n)$ as follow:

$$F(\mathfrak{m}) = x' + \sum_{i=1}^n x_i m_i - l_p\kappa \quad \text{and} \quad J(\mathfrak{m}) = y' + \sum_{i=1}^n y_i m_i - l_p\kappa$$

Then $\mathcal{B}$ randomly picks a set of distinct numbers $\mathcal{S} = \{c_1^*, \ldots, c_s^*\} \in (\mathbb{Z}_\ell^*)^s$. We further define the following functions for any integer $\bar{m} \in \mathbb{Z}_\ell^*$

$$G(\bar{m}) = \prod_{i \in \mathcal{S}} (\bar{m} - i) = \sum_{i=0}^s \gamma_i \bar{m}^i \quad \text{and} \quad K(\bar{m}) = \prod_{i=1, i \notin \mathcal{S}}^\ell (\bar{m} - i) = \sum_{i=0}^{\ell-s} \alpha_i \bar{m}^i$$

for some $\gamma_i, \alpha_i \in \mathbb{Z}_p^*$.

$\mathcal{B}$ constructs a set of public parameters as follow:

$$g = u, \quad g_2 = h, \quad u' = g_2^{-lk+x'} g^{-lk+y'}, \quad u_i = g_2^{x_i} g^{y_i} \text{ for } 1 \leq i \leq n$$

The signer's public key is:

$$g_1 = u^a, \quad v' = v^{\alpha_0} g^{\gamma_0}, \quad v_i = v^{\alpha_i} g^{\gamma_i} \text{ for } 1 \leq i \leq s, \quad v_j = v^{\alpha_i}$$

for $s + 1 \leq i \leq \ell$. Note that we have the following equation:

$$u' \prod_{i=1}^{n} u_i^{m_i} = g_2^{F(\mathfrak{m})} g^{J(\mathfrak{m})}, \qquad v' \prod_{i=1}^{\ell-1} v_i^{\bar{\mathfrak{m}}_j^i} = g^{G(\bar{\mathfrak{m}}_j)} v^{K(\bar{\mathfrak{m}}_j)} \qquad \text{for } 1 \leq j \leq k$$

where $\bar{\mathfrak{m}}_j = H_j(\mathfrak{m})$ for $1 \leq j \leq k$. All public parameters are passed to $\mathcal{A}$. $\mathcal{B}$ also maintains an empty list $\mathcal{L}$.

Oracles Simulation. $\mathcal{B}$ simulates the oracles as follow:

(*Signing oracle.*) Upon receiving query for message $\mathfrak{m}_i = \{m_1, \ldots, m_n\}$, although $\mathcal{B}$ does not know the secret key, it still can construct the signature by assuming $F(\mathfrak{m}_i) \neq 0 \bmod p$ and $K(\bar{\mathfrak{m}}_{i,j}) = 0 \bmod p$, where $\bar{\mathfrak{m}}_{i,j} = H_j(\mathfrak{m}_i)$ for all $1 \leq j \leq k$. It randomly chooses $r_i \in_R \mathbb{Z}_p$ and computes the signature as

$$S_1 = g_1^{-\frac{J(\mathfrak{m}_i)}{F(\mathfrak{m}_i)}} \left(g_2^{F(\mathfrak{m}_i)} g^{J(\mathfrak{m}_i)} \right)^{r_i}, \quad S_{2,j} = \left(g_1^{-\frac{1}{F(\mathfrak{m}_i)}} g^{r_i} \right)^{G(\bar{\mathfrak{m}}_{i,j})} \qquad \text{for } 1 \leq j \leq k$$

Same as the above proof, $(S_1, S_{2,1}, \ldots, S_{2,k})$ is a valid signature. $\mathcal{B}$ puts $(\mathfrak{m}_i, S_1, S_{2,1}, \ldots, S_{2,k})$ into the list $\mathcal{L}$ and then outputs the signature $(S_1, S_{2,1}, \ldots, S_{2,k})$. To the adversary, all signatures given by $\mathcal{B}$ are indistinguishable from the signatures generated by the signer.

(*Confirmation/Disavowal oracle.*) Upon receiving a signature $(S_1, S_{2,1}, \ldots, S_{2,k})$ for message $\mathfrak{m}$, $\mathcal{B}$ checks whether $(\mathfrak{m}, S_1, S_{2,1}, \ldots, S_{2,k})$ is in $\mathcal{L}$. If so, $\mathcal{B}$ outputs Valid and runs the confirmation protocol with $\mathcal{A}$, to show that (L, M, N_j, O_j) in equation (1) are DH tuples, for $1 \leq j \leq k$. Notice that since $\mathcal{B}$ knows discrete logarithm of N_j with base L ($= 1/G(\bar{\mathfrak{m}}_{i,j})$), it can simulate the interactive proof perfectly.

If the signature is not in $\mathcal{L}$, $\mathcal{B}$ outputs Invalid and runs the disavowal protocol with $\mathcal{A}$. By theorem 1, the signature is unforgeable if the CDH assumption holds. $\mathcal{B}$ runs the oracle incorrectly only if $\mathcal{A}$ can forge a signature. However if one can solve the CDH problem, he can also solve the decision linear problem.

(*Receipt generating oracle.*) Upon receive a signature $(S_1, S_{2,1}, \ldots, S_{2,k})$ for message $\mathfrak{m}$, $\mathcal{B}$ computes $\bar{\mathfrak{m}}_j = H_j(\mathfrak{m})$ for $1 \leq j \leq k$. If $K(\bar{\mathfrak{m}}_j) \neq 0 \bmod p$ for any j, $\mathcal{B}$ aborts. Otherwise $\mathcal{B}$ outputs $S_2' = S_{2,1}^{1/G(\bar{\mathfrak{m}}_1)}$, which is a valid individual receipt for the signature.

Challenge. $\mathcal{A}$ gives $\mathfrak{m}^* = (\mathfrak{m}_1^*, \ldots, \mathfrak{m}_n^*)$ to $\mathcal{B}$ as the challenge message. Denote $\bar{\mathfrak{m}}_j^* = H_j(\mathfrak{m}^*)$ for $1 \leq j \leq k$. If $F(\mathfrak{m}_i^*) = 0 \bmod p$, $J(\mathfrak{m}_i^*) \neq 0 \bmod p$ or $G(\bar{\mathfrak{m}}_j^*) \neq 0 \bmod p$ for any j, $\mathcal{B}$ aborts.

Otherwise, $\mathcal{B}$ computes:

$$S_1^* = h^c, \qquad S_{2,j}^* = v^{bK(\bar{\mathfrak{m}}_j^*)/F(\mathfrak{m}_i^*)} \qquad \text{for } 1 \leq j \leq k$$

and returns $(S_1^*, S_{2,1}^*, \ldots, S_{2,k}^*)$ to $\mathcal{A}$.

Output. Finally $\mathcal{A}$ outputs a bit b'. $\mathcal{B}$ returns b' as the solution to the decision linear problem. Notice that if $c = a + b$, then:

$$S_1^* = g_2^{a+b} = g_2^a (g_2^{F(\bar{m}_i^*)})^{b/F(\bar{m}_i^*)} = g_2^a (u' \prod_{i=1}^{n} u_i^{m_i^*})^{b/F(\bar{m}_i^*)},$$

$$S_{2,j}^* = v^{bK(\bar{m}_j^*)/F(\bar{m}_i^*)} = (v' \prod_{i=1}^{\ell} v_i^{\bar{m}_j{}^i})^{b/F(\bar{m}_i^*)} \qquad \text{for } 1 \le j \le k$$

Probability Analysis and Time Complexity Analysis. They are given in the full version of the paper. □

Theorem 3. *The scheme is (ϵ, t, q_c, q_s)-secure against impersonation if the (ϵ', t')-discrete logarithm assumption holds in $\mathbb{G}$, where*

$$\epsilon' \ge \frac{1}{2}(1 - \frac{q_s}{2p})(\epsilon - \frac{1}{p})^2$$

$$t' = t + O\left(q_s\rho + q_c\tau + (n+\ell)q_s\omega\right)$$

where $H_j : \{0,1\}^n \rightarrow \mathbb{Z}_\ell^*$, for $1 \le j \le k$, are some collision resistant hash functions and ρ, ω are the time for an exponentiation in $\mathbb{G}$ and an addition in $\mathbb{Z}_p$ respectively.

Proof. (Sketch) Assume there is a (ϵ, t, q_c, q_s)-adversary $\mathcal{A}$. We are going to construct another PPT $\mathcal{B}$ that makes use of $\mathcal{A}$ to solve the discrete logarithm problem with probability at least ϵ' and in time at most t'. $\mathcal{B}$ is given a discrete logarithm problem instance (g, g^a). The remaining proof is very similar to the proof of theorem 1 and also the proof in [18], so we sketch the proof here.

With $1/2$ probability, $\mathcal{B}$ sets $g_1 = g^a$ and hence the user secret key is a. The oracle simulation is the same as the proof in theorem 1, except that $\mathcal{B}$ now knows $b = \log_g g_2$. At the end of the game, $\mathcal{A}$ outputs a message-signature pair (m^*, σ^*) and a bit b. For either $b = 0/1$, $\mathcal{B}$ can extract a with probability $1/2$, as shown in [18].

With $1/2$ probability, $\mathcal{B}$ sets $v' = g^a$ and hence $\mathcal{B}$ knows the signing key α. $\mathcal{B}$ can simulate the oracles perfectly with α. At the end of the game, $\mathcal{A}$ outputs a message-signature pair (m^*, σ^*) and a bit b. For either $b = 0/1$, $\mathcal{B}$ can extract $a + \sum_{i=1}^{\ell} \beta_i \bar{m}_1^{*i}$ with probability $1/2$, as shown in [18]. Hence $\mathcal{B}$ can find a.

Probability Analysis and Time Complexity Analysis. They are given in the full version of the paper. □

Remarks. The security of our scheme is related to the length of our signature, as shown in the security theorem. For example, the number of $q_s + q_r$ query and the value of k (the number of blocks) cannot be very large, in order to claim an acceptable security. The number of $q_s + q_r$ query allowed maybe set to 128 and the suitable value of k maybe set to be around 7, to gain a balance between efficiency and security.

6   Conclusion

In this paper, we propose the first convertible undeniable signatures without random oracles in pairings. Comparing with the part of undeniable signatures, our scheme is better than the existing undeniable signatures without random oracles [20] by using more standard assumption in the security proofs. Furthermore, our scheme is particularly suitable for applications that do not require a large number of signing queries.

References

1. Ateniese, G., Camenisch, J., Hohenberger, S., de Medeiros, B.: Practical Group Signatures without Random Oracles. Cryptology ePrint Archive, Report, 2005/385 (2005), http://eprint.iacr.org/
2. Bellare, M., Boldyreva, A., Palacio, A.: An Uninstantiable Random-Oracle-Model Scheme for a Hybrid-Encryption Problem. In: Cachin, C., Camenisch, J.L. (eds.) EUROCRYPT 2004. LNCS, vol. 3027, pp. 171–188. Springer, Heidelberg (2004)
3. Bellare, M., Rogaway, P.: Random Oracles are Practical: A Paradigm for Designing Efficient Protocols. In: ACM Conference on Computer and Communications Security, pp. 62–73. ACM Press, New York (1993)
4. Bender, A., Katz, J., Morselli, R.: Ring Signatures: Stronger Definitions, and Constructions without Random Oracles. In: Halevi, S., Rabin, T. (eds.) TCC 2006. LNCS, vol. 3876, pp. 60–79. Springer, Heidelberg (2006)
5. Boneh, D., Boyen, X., Shacham, H.: Short Group Signatures. In: Franklin, M. (ed.) CRYPTO 2004. LNCS, vol. 3152, pp. 41–55. Springer, Heidelberg (2004)
6. Boyar, J., Chaum, D., Damgård, I., Pedersen, T.P.: Convertible Undeniable Signatures. In: Menezes, A.J., Vanstone, S.A. (eds.) CRYPTO 1990. LNCS, vol. 537, pp. 189–205. Springer, Heidelberg (1991)
7. Boyen, X., Waters, B.: Anonymous Hierarchical Identity-Based Encryption (Without Random Oracles). In: Dwork, C. (ed.) CRYPTO 2006. LNCS, vol. 4117, pp. 290–307. Springer, Heidelberg (2006)
8. Boyen, X., Waters, B.: Compact Group Signatures Without Random Oracles. In: Vaudenay, S. (ed.) EUROCRYPT 2006. LNCS, vol. 4004, pp. 427–444. Springer, Heidelberg (2006)
9. Canetti, R., Goldreich, O., Halevi, S.: The Random Oracle Methodology, Revisited. In: Proc. 13th ACM Symp. on Theory of Computing, pp. 128–209. ACM Press, New York (1998)
10. Chaum, D.: Designated Confirmer Signatures. In: De Santis, A. (ed.) EUROCRYPT 1994. LNCS, vol. 950, pp. 86–91. Springer, Heidelberg (1995)
11. Chaum, D., van Antwerpen, H.: Undeniable Signatures. In: Brassard, G. (ed.) CRYPTO 1989. LNCS, vol. 435, pp. 212–216. Springer, Heidelberg (1990)
12. Chow, S.S., Liu, J.K., Wei, V.K., Yuen, T.H.: Ring Signatures without Random Oracles. In: ASIACCS 2006, pp. 297–302. ACM Press, New York (2006)
13. Damgård, I., Pedersen, T.P.: New Convertible Undeniable Signature Schemes. In: Maurer, U.M. (ed.) EUROCRYPT 1996. LNCS, vol. 1070, pp. 372–386. Springer, Heidelberg (1996)
14. Gennaro, R., Rabin, T., Krawczyk, H.: RSA-Based Undeniable Signatures. Journal of Cryptology 13(4), 397–416 (2000)

15. Hohenberger, S., Rothblum, G., Shelat, A., Vaikuntanathan, V.: Securely Obfuscating Re-Encryption. In: Vadhan, S.P. (ed.) TCC 2007. LNCS, vol. 4392, pp. 233–252. Springer, Heidelberg (2007)
16. Jakobsson, M., Sako, K., Impagliazzo, R.: Designated Verifier Proofs and Their Applications. In: Maurer, U.M. (ed.) EUROCRYPT 1996. LNCS, vol. 1070, pp. 143–154. Springer, Heidelberg (1996)
17. Kiayias, A., Zhou, H.-S.: Concurrent Blind Signatures without Random Oracles. In: De Prisco, R., Yung, M. (eds.) SCN 2006. LNCS, vol. 4116, pp. 49–62. Springer, Heidelberg (2006)
18. Kurosawa, K., Heng, S.-H.: 3-Move Undeniable Signature Scheme. In: Cramer, R.J.F. (ed.) EUROCRYPT 2005. LNCS, vol. 3494, pp. 181–197. Springer, Heidelberg (2005)
19. Kurosawa, K., Takagi, T.: New Approach for Selectively Convertible Undeniable Signature Schemes. In: Lai, X., Chen, K. (eds.) ASIACRYPT 2006. LNCS, vol. 4284, pp. 428–443. Springer, Heidelberg (2006)
20. Laguillaumie, F., Vergnaud, D.: Short Undeniable Signatures Without Random Oracles: The Missing Link. In: Maitra, S., Madhavan, C.E.V., Venkatesan, R. (eds.) INDOCRYPT 2005. LNCS, vol. 3797, pp. 283–296. Springer, Heidelberg (2005)
21. Laguillaumie, F., Vergnaud, D.: Time-Selective Convertible Undeniable Signatures. In: Menezes, A.J. (ed.) CT-RSA 2005. LNCS, vol. 3376, pp. 154–171. Springer, Heidelberg (2005)
22. Libert, B., Quisquater, J.-J.: Identity Based Undeniable Signatures. In: Okamoto, T. (ed.) CT-RSA 2004. LNCS, vol. 2964, pp. 112–125. Springer, Heidelberg (2004)
23. Michels, M., Petersen, H., Horster, P.: Breaking and Repairing a Convertible Undeniable Signature Scheme. In: CCS 1996. Proceedings of the 3rd ACM conference on Computer and Communications Security, pp. 148–152. ACM Press, New York (1996)
24. Michels, M., Stadler, M.: Efficient Convertible Undeniable Signature Schemes. In: Proc. SAC 1997, pp. 231–244 (1997)
25. Okamoto, T.: Designated Confirmer Signatures and Public Key Encryption are Equivalent. In: Wolper, P. (ed.) CAV 1995. LNCS, vol. 939, pp. 61–74. Springer, Heidelberg (1995)
26. Wang, H., Zhang, Y., Feng, D.: Short Threshold Signature Schemes Without Random Oracles. In: Maitra, S., Madhavan, C.E.V., Venkatesan, R. (eds.) INDOCRYPT 2005. LNCS, vol. 3797, pp. 297–310. Springer, Heidelberg (2005)
27. Waters, B.: Efficient Identity-Based Encryption Without Random Oracles. In: Cramer, R.J.F. (ed.) EUROCRYPT 2005. LNCS, vol. 3494, pp. 114–127. Springer, Heidelberg (2005)
28. Zhang, R., Furukawa, J., Imai, H.: Short Signature and Universal Designated Verifier Signature Without Random Oracles. In: Ioannidis, J., Keromytis, A.D., Yung, M. (eds.) ACNS 2005. LNCS, vol. 3531, pp. 483–498. Springer, Heidelberg (2005)

A New Dynamic Accumulator for Batch Updates

Peishun Wang[1], Huaxiong Wang[1,2], and Josef Pieprzyk[1]

[1] Centre for Advanced Computing – Algorithms and Cryptography
Department of Computing, Macquarie University, Australia
{pwang,hwang,josef}@ics.mq.edu.au
[2] Division of Mathematical Sciences
School of Physical and Mathematical Sciences
Nanyang Technological University, Singapore
hxwang@ntu.edu.sg

Abstract. A dynamic accumulator is an algorithm, which gathers together a large set of elements into a constant-size value such that for a given element accumulated, there is a witness confirming that the element was indeed included into the value, with a property that accumulated elements can be dynamically added and deleted into/from the original set such that the cost of an addition or deletion operation is independent of the number of accumulated elements. Although the first accumulator was presented ten years ago, there is still no standard formal definition of accumulators. In this paper, we generalize formal definitions for accumulators, formulate a security game for dynamic accumulators so-called Chosen Element Attack (CEA), and propose a new dynamic accumulator for batch updates based on the Paillier cryptosystem. Our construction makes a batch of update operations at unit cost. We prove its security under the extended strong RSA (es-RSA) assumption.

Keywords: Dynamic accumulator, Paillier cryptosystem.

1 Introduction

An accumulator is an algorithm that merges a large set of elements into a constant-size value such that for a given element there is a witness confirming that the element was indeed accumulated into the value. It was originated by Benaloh and de Mare [3] as a decentralized alternative for digital signatures and was used in the design of secure distributed protocols. Baric and Pfitzmann [2] refined the concept of accumulators asking from them to be collision-free. The collision freeness requires that it is computationally hard to compute a witness for an element that is not accumulated. However, in many practical applications, the set of elements changes with the time. A naive way of handling such situations would be to re-run the accumulator. Obviously, this is highly impractical, especially when the element set is very large. To solve this problem, Camenisch and Lysyanskaya [4] developed more practical schemes – accumulators with dynamic addition and deletion of elements to or from the original set of accumulated elements. The cost of adding or deleting elements and updating individual witnesses is independent from the number of elements accumulated.

S. Qing, H. Imai, and G. Wang (Eds.): ICICS 2007, LNCS 4861, pp. 98–112, 2007.
© Springer-Verlag Berlin Heidelberg 2007

Accumulators are useful in a number of privacy-enhancing applications, such as time-stamping [3], fail-stop signatures [2], identity escrow and group signature schemes with membership revocation [4], authenticated dictionary [9], ad-hoc anonymous identification and ring signatures [6], and broadcast encryption [8]. However, they are still a relatively new tool in Cryptography, and there are only a handful of papers on the topic and they do not constitute a systematic and organized effort. In particular, there is still no standard formal definition for them, and the definitions used so far are driven by specific applications rather than a systematic study of underlying properties of the accumulator.

In the existing dynamic accumulators, usually the witnesses must be updated immediately whenever old elements leave or new elements join. In some applications, the updates of the witnesses for some elements cannot be done immediately after the changes. When the witnesses of elements need to be updated after a batch of N addition and deletion operations occurred, they have to be computed N times – one by one in the time sequence, that means, the time to bring a witness up-to-date after a batch of N operations is proportional to N. Clearly, these schemes are inefficient for batch update. In these circumstances, it is reasonable to cluster the updates into one single operation. In this paper we address an open question formulated by Fazio and Nicolosi in [7]. The question asks about how to design an efficient dynamic accumulator whose witnesses can be updated in one go independently from the number of changes. We answer this question by proposing a new dynamic accumulator that allows batch updates.

Related Work. In general, there exist two different types of accumulators, namely RSA-based [2,3,4,9,14,15] and combinatorial hash-based accumulators [11].

The basic RSA accumulator [3] is constructed as follows. Given a set of elements $X = \{x_1, \ldots, x_m\}$ that can be accumulated, the accumulator function is $y_i = f(y_{i-1}, x_i)$, where f is a one-way function defined as $f(u, x) = u^x \bmod n$ for suitably-chosen values of the seed u and RSA modulus n. The accumulated value is $v = u^{x_1 \cdots x_m} \bmod n$ and the witness for the element x_i is $w_i = u^{x_1 \cdots x_{i-1} x_{i+1} \cdots x_m} \bmod n$. This basic RSA accumulator has many different variants depending on the intended application. Baric and Pfitzmann [2] used the accumulator for elements that must be primes and they proved that it is collision-resistant provided factoring is intractable. Camenisch and Lysyanskaya studied in [4] dynamic RSA accumulators for which the domain of accumulated elements consists of primes in a particular range. The seed u is a random quadratic residue and the modulus is a safe number. Tsudik and Xu [15] relaxed the constraint and allowed the accumulated elements to be composite numbers that are products of two primes chosen from a specific interval. Goodrich et al. in [9] constructed dynamic RSA accumulators in which the seed u needs to be coprime to the modulus n only. This constraint is very easy to satisfy.

The collision resistance of RSA accumulators relies on the secrecy of factorization of the modulus n. Normally, the designers of accumulators are going to know the factors of n and therefore able to forge membership proofs and break the collision resistance. A solution to this problem has been provided by Sander [14] who constructed accumulators whose designers do not know the factors of the modulus. Security of all existing RSA accumulators is based on the strong RSA assumption.

In order to remove need for trapdoor information, Nyberg [11] came up with a combinatorial accumulator based on hashing. In the scheme, a one-way hash function is used to map bit strings of arbitrary length to bit strings of fixed length, and then each resulting output string is divided into small blocks of a fixed length. Next every block is replaced by 0 if it consists of all 0 bits, otherwise by 1. In such way, each accumulated element is mapped to a bit string of a fixed short length. Finally, the accumulated value is computed as a bitwise product of the bit strings of all elements. To verify whether an element has been accumulated, one first hashes the element, partitions the hash output into blocks and then converts the blocks into bits (as discussed above). The element is accumulated with a high probability if the 0 bits of the element coincide with the 0 bits of the accumulated value. The accumulator does not need witnesses and is provably secure in the random oracle model. However, it is not dynamic, and not space and time efficient.

Nguyen [10] constructed a dynamic accumulator from bilinear pairings, which, however, gives away the secret of the accumulator on a particular input. It has been proved that the scheme is not secure [16]. To make Nguyen scheme secure, Au *et al.* [1] constrained the number of accumulated elements and introduced a notion of bounded accumulator.

Our Contributions. Our technical contributions can be divided into the following:

Formal Definitions. We generalize formal definitions for dynamic accumulators, provide a definition of their security. Despite the fact that first accumulators were introduced more than 10 years ago, there is no standard definition of them. The definitions used so far are all application specific. In this paper we are going to rectify this by proposing generic definitions.

Security Game. We formulate a security game for dynamic accumulators that is based on the so-called Chosen Element Attack (CEA). The security game provides an environment for interaction between an accumulator algorithm and an adversary. The adversary can access the accumulator via an oracle, *i.e.* he provides inputs to the oracle and is able to collect outputs generated by the oracle. The game consists of two stages. In the first stage, the adversary chooses adaptively a set of elements L and then queries the accumulator oracle. Each time the oracle is queried, it provides the accumulated value and the witnesses to the adversary. Clearly, the next query depends on the reply obtained from the oracle. In the second stage, the adversary adaptively adds/deletes some elements and queries the oracle for the corresponding accumulated values and witnesses. In both stages, the adversary is allowed to issue a polynomial number of queries. The adversary wins the game if the adversary can forge another legitimate element and its witness such that the witness proves that the forged element is also included in the accumulated value corresponding to the set.

New Dynamic Accumulator. We construct a new dynamic accumulator from the Paillier cryptosystem, and prove its security under a new complexity assumption – extended strong RSA (es-RSA) assumption. Existing accumulators apply elements that are either primes or products of primes. We remove the restrictions on the selection of elements and allow them to be chosen from $Z_{n^2}^*$. Our scheme permits also for an efficient batch update of witnesses independently from the number of changes.

Affirmative Answer to an Open Problem. Existing accumulators have to update witnesses after each single addition/deletion operation. Fazio and Nicolosi posed the following question [7]: is it possible to construct dynamic accumulators in which the time to update a witness can be made independent from the number of changes that need to be done to the accumulated value? We answer this question in the affirmative, and have constructed a scheme in which, the time necessary to bring a witness up-to-date for a batch with an arbitrary number of additions and deletions is done at the unit cost.

Organization. Section 2 introduces notation and provides a cryptographic background necessary to understand our presentation. In Section 3 we give a few related definitions for accumulators. In Section 4 we construct a new dynamic accumulator. Section 5 describes a batch update. Section 6 shows the correctness of the construction. In Section 7 the security of the proposed scheme is proved. Finally Section 8 concludes our paper and discusses a possible future research.

2   Preliminaries

2.1   Notation

Throughout this paper, we use the following notation.

PPT denotes *probabilistic polynomial time.* For any positive integer m, $[m]$ denotes the set of integers $\{1, \ldots, m\}$. Let $a \xleftarrow{R} A$ denote that an element a is chosen uniformly at random from the set A. Let M be the upper bound on the number of elements that can be securely accumulated and $\mathcal{C}$ be an efficiently-samplable domain where all accumulated elements are coming from.

2.2   Complexity Assumption

Let us state without proof some basic number-theoretic facts, and make a complexity assumption that will be used in our work.

Fact 1: For a safe number $n = pq$, *i.e.* $p, q, \frac{p-1}{2}, \frac{q-1}{2}$ are prime, Euler's Totient function $\phi(n) = (p-1)(q-1)$, $\phi(n^2) = n\phi(n)$, and Carmichael's function $\lambda(n) = lcm(p-1, q-1)$, $\lambda(n^2) = lcm((p-1)p, (q-1)q)$.

Catalano *et al* in [5] introduced a variant of the RSA problem in $Z_{n^2}^*$ – Computational Small s-Roots (CSR) problem.

Definition 1 (CSR Problem). *Given a safe number n, an integer $s \in Z_{n^2}^* \setminus \{2\}$ and a random number $x \in Z_{n^2}^*$, the s-th roots problem is the task of finding $y \in Z_{n^2}^*$ such that $x = y^s \bmod n^2$.*

Catalano *et al* [5] gave evidence to that the CSR problem is intractable, even for every $s > 2$ such that $gcd(s, \lambda(n^2)) = 1$, when the factorization of n is unknown. However, they recommended $s = 2^{16} + 1$ for practical applications.

Fact 2: There exists a PPT algorithm that, given integers x, s, n, and the factorization of n, outputs x's s-th roots mod n^2.

We describe a variant of the Discrete Logarithm (DL) problem in $Z_{n^2}^*$, which we call the extended Discrete Logarithm (e-DL) problem.

Definition 2 (e-DL Problem). *Given a safe number n without integer factorization and two random numbers $x, y \in Z_{n^2}^*$, the discrete logarithm of x under the base y is an integer s such that $x = y^s$ mod n^2.*

The general DL problem is defined as follows. Let g be a generator of a finite cyclic group $G = \langle g \rangle$ of order N. For a random number $x \in G$, we wish to find an integer s ($0 \le s < N$) such that $g^s = x$. If N is composite, *i.e.*, $N = p_1^{k_1} p_2^{k_2} \cdots p_j^{k_j}$, one first computes $s \bmod p_i^{k_i}$ ($1 \le i \le j$) in the subgroup of order $p_i^{k_i}$ for each prime power $p_i^{k_i}$, and then, one applies the Chinese Remainder Theorem to compute s. According to [13], calculating the discrete logarithm in the subgroup of order $p_i^{k_i}$ can be reduced to finding the discrete logarithm in the group of prime order p_i. Therefore, the e-DL problem is related to the DL problem in the subgroup of prime order $max(p_1, \cdots, p_j)$. If the DL problem is hard, then the e-DL problem is also intractable.

Now we introduce a new complexity assumption called the extended strong RSA (es-RSA) assumption, which is a variant of the strong RSA problem [2] in $Z_{n^2}^*$.

Assumption 1 (es-RSA). *There exists no PPT algorithm that, given a safe number n whose factors are secret and a number $x \in Z_{n^2}^*$, outputs a pair of integers (s, y) such that $x = y^s$ mod n^2, $n^2 > s > 2$ and $y \in Z_{n^2}^*$.*

We are neither aware of any corroboration that it should be hard, nor can we break it. However, we can design an algorithm for solving the es-RSA problem if we know algorithms that solve the CSR or e-DL problems.

1. The first algorithm selects at random the exponent s and then calls, as a subroutine, the algorithm for solving the CSR problem.
2. The second algorithm chooses at random the value of y and then calls, as a subroutine, the algorithm for solving the e-DL problem.

This also means that the complexity of es-RSA has to be lower bounded by the complexities of CSR and e-DL problems. Note that the algorithm solving es-RSA is able to manipulate the pair (y, s) by using variants of the baby-step giant-step algorithms or the birthday paradox. Although the es-RSA assumption appears to be valid even for $s = 3$, we still recommend that one uses $s \ge 2^{16} + 1$ in practice.

2.3   Paillier Cryptosystem

We now briefly review the Paillier cryptosystem. For the detail, refer to [12]. Let n be a safe number. $\mathcal{B}_\alpha \subset Z_{n^2}^*$ denotes the set of elements of order $n\alpha$, and

$\mathcal{B}$ denotes their disjoint union for $\alpha = 1, \ldots, \lambda$, where λ is adopted instead of $\lambda(n)$ for visual comfort. Randomly select a base g from $\mathcal{B}$, and define a function $F(x) = \frac{x-1}{n}$.

The Paillier cryptosystem defines an integer-valued bijective function:

$$E_g\colon Z_n \times Z_n^* \to Z_{n^2}^*, \ (x, r) \to g^x \cdot r^n \bmod n^2,$$

where (n, g) are public parameters whilst the pair (p, q) (or equivalently λ) remains private. The encryption and decryption algorithms are as follows:

Encryption:

plaintext $x < n$, randomly select $r < n$, ciphertext $y = g^x \cdot r^n \bmod n^2$.

Decryption:

ciphertext $y < n^2$, plaintext $x = D(y) = \frac{F(y^\lambda \bmod n^2)}{F(g^\lambda \bmod n^2)} \bmod n$.

The cryptosystem has the following additive homomorphic properties:

$$\forall \sigma \in Z^+, \ D(y^\sigma \bmod n^2) = \sigma x \bmod n, \qquad \text{and}$$
$$\forall y_1, y_2 \in Z_{n^2}, \ D(y_1 y_2 \bmod n^2) = x_1 + x_2 \bmod n$$

3   Accumulator and Security Definitions

In this section we give a few related definitions for accumulators. Firstly we generalize definitions of accumulators given in [2,3,4,7], and then we describe the security definition for dynamic accumulators and our security game.

Definition 3 (Accumulator)
An accumulator consists of the following four algorithms:

KeyGen(k, M)**:** *is a probabilistic algorithm that is executed in order to instantiate the scheme. It takes as input a security parameter 1^k and the upper bound M on the number of accumulated elements, and returns an accumulator parameter $\mathcal{P} = (P_u, P_r)$ where P_u is a public key and P_r is a private key.*

AccVal$(L, \mathcal{P})$**:** *is a probabilistic algorithm that computes an accumulated value. It takes as input a set of elements $L = \{c_1, \ldots, c_m\}$ $(1 < m \le M)$ from a domain $\mathcal{C}$ and the parameter $\mathcal{P}$, and returns an accumulated value v, along with some auxiliary information a_c and A_l that will be used by other algorithms.*

WitGen$(a_c, A_l, \mathcal{P})$**:** *is a probabilistic algorithm that creates the witness for every element. It takes as input the auxiliary information a_c and A_l, and the parameter $\mathcal{P}$, and returns a witness W_i for c_i $(i = 1, \ldots, m)$.*

Verify(c, W, v, P_u)**:** *is a deterministic algorithm that checks if a given element is accumulated in the value v or is not. It takes as input an element c, its witness W, the accumulated value v and the public key P_u, and returns Yes if the witness W constitutes a valid proof that c has been accumulated in v, or No otherwise.*

Definition 4 (Dynamic Accumulator). *A dynamic accumulator consists of the following seven algorithms:*

KeyGen, AccVal, WitGen, Verify *are the same as in the Definition 3.*
AddEle$(L^\oplus, a_c, v, \mathcal{P})$**:** *is a probabilistic algorithm that adds some new elements to the accumulated value. It takes as input a set of new elements $L^\oplus =$*

$\{c_1^{\oplus}, \ldots, c_k^{\oplus}\}$ ($L^{\oplus} \subset C, 1 \leq k \leq M - m$) *that are to be added, the auxiliary information* a_c, *the accumulated value* v *and the parameter* $\mathcal{P}$, *and returns a new accumulated value* v' *corresponding to the set* $L^{\oplus} \cup L$, *witnesses* $\{W_1^{\oplus}, \ldots, W_k^{\oplus}\}$ *for the newly inserted elements* $\{c_1^{\oplus}, \ldots, c_k^{\oplus}\}$, *along with new auxiliary information* a_c *and* a_u *that will be used for future update operations.*

DelEle($L^{\ominus}, a_c, v, \mathcal{P}$): *is a probabilistic algorithm that deletes some elements from the accumulated value. It takes as input a set of elements* $L^{\ominus} = \{c_1^{\ominus}, \ldots, c_k^{\ominus}\}$ ($L^{\ominus} \subset L, 1 \leq k < m$) *that are to be deleted, the auxiliary information* a_c, *the accumulated value* v *and the parameter* $\mathcal{P}$, *and returns a new accumulated value* v' *corresponding to the set* $L \setminus L^{\ominus}$, *along with new auxiliary information* a_c *and* a_u *that will be used for future update operations.*

UpdWit(W_i, a_u, P_u): *is a deterministic algorithm that updates witnesses for the elements that have been accumulated in* v *and also are accumulated in* v'. *It takes as input the witness* W_i, *the auxiliary information* a_u *and the public key* P_u, *and returns an updated witness* W_i' *proving that the element* c_i *is accumulated in the new value* v'.

Definition 5 (Security for Dynamic Accumulator). *An dynamic accumulator is secure if the adversary has only a negligible probability of finding a set of elements* $L = \{c_1, \ldots, c_m\} \subseteq C$ ($1 < m \leq M$), *an element* $c' \in C \setminus L$ *and a witness* w' *which can prove that* c' *has been accumulated in the accumulated value corresponding to the set* L, *where the probability is taken over the random strings generated by the adversary and the accumulator.*

There exist other two weak security definitions used in the literature as follows.

Definition 6 (Security for Accumulator [3]). *Given a set of elements* $L = \{c_1, \ldots, c_m\}$ ($1 < m \leq M$), *their accumulated value* v *and an element* $c' \in C \setminus L$. *Then an accumulator is weakly secure if an adversary has a negligible probability of finding a witness* w' *which can prove that* c' *has been accumulated in* v, *where the probability is taken over the random coins of the adversary and of the accumulator.*

Definition 7 (Security for Accumulator [2]). *Given a set of elements* $L = \{c_1, \ldots, c_m\}$ ($1 < m \leq M$), *their accumulated value* v. *Then an accumulator is weakly secure if an adversary has a negligible probability of finding an element* $c' \in C \setminus L$ *and a witness* w' *which can prove that* c' *has been accumulated in* v, *where the probability is taken over the random coins of the adversary and of the accumulator.*

Note that the difference among these two security definitions and our definition is that, in the definition 6 the adversary tries to forge a witness for a given element c', in the definition 7 the adversary can choose a forged element c' himself, and in the definition 5 the adversary might be able to choose both a set of elements L that are to be accumulated and a forged element c' himself.

To capture the notion of security for a dynamic accumulator, we define a security model – Chosen Element Attack (CEA) against Dynamic Accumulator:

Definition 8 (CEA Game). *CEA is a security game between a PPT adversary $\mathcal{ADV}$ and a challenger $\mathcal{CHA}$:*

Setup. $\mathcal{CHA}$ *runs the* **KeyGen** *algorithm to set up the parameters of the accumulator.* $\mathcal{ADV}$ *chooses a family of sets $L^* \subset \mathcal{C}$ and returns them to $\mathcal{CHA}$. $\mathcal{CHA}$ runs the algorithm* **AccVal** *to compute their corresponding accumulated values and* **WitGen** *to make witnesses for the elements in each set, and sends them to $\mathcal{ADV}$.*

Queries. $\mathcal{ADV}$ *is allowed to adaptively modify the sets L^* and ask $\mathcal{CHA}$ to add a set of elements $L^\oplus$ ($L^\oplus \subset \mathcal{C}$) to some accumulated values and/or remove a set of elements $L^\ominus$ ($L^\ominus \subset L^*$) from some accumulated values as he wishes. $\mathcal{CHA}$ runs the* **AddEle** *and/or* **DelEle** *algorithm, and sends back the new accumulated values, the auxiliary information for updating witnesses, along with witnesses for the newly inserted elements in the case of an* **AddEle** *operation. Then $\mathcal{ADV}$ runs the* **UpdWit** *algorithm to update the witness for each element, which has been accumulated in the old accumulated value and is currently accumulated in the new value, in the corresponding set.*

Challenge. *After making a number of queries, $\mathcal{ADV}$ decides on challenge by picking a set of elements $L = \{c_1, \ldots, c_m\}$ ($1 < m \leq M$) from $\mathcal{C}$ and sends L to $\mathcal{CHA}$ who invokes* **AccVal** *to obtain the corresponding accumulated value v and* **WitGen** *to make witnesses $\{W_1, \ldots, W_m\}$ for the m elements and returns them to $\mathcal{ADV}$. On receiving v and $\{W_1, \ldots, W_m\}$, $\mathcal{ADV}$ produces an element c' ($c' \in \mathcal{C} \setminus L$) with a witness W', and sends them to $\mathcal{CHA}$. Then $\mathcal{CHA}$ runs the* **Verify** *algorithm to test if c' with W' is accumulated in v.*

Response. *Eventually the* **Verify** *algorithm outputs a result. We say $\mathcal{ADV}$ wins in this game, if it, with non-negligible advantage, manages to produce the legitimate pair (W', c') such that the output of* **Verify** *is* Yes.

4   New Dynamic Accumulator

We construct a new dynamic accumulator as follows.

KeyGen(k, M): Given a security parameter 1^k and the upper bound M on the number of accumulated elements, generate a suitable safe modulus n that is k-bit long and an empty set V. Let $\mathcal{C} = Z_{n^2}^* \setminus \{1\}$ and $T' = \{3, \cdots, n^2\}$. Select adaptively a number $\sigma \in Z_{n^2}$ and compute $\beta = \sigma \lambda \bmod \phi(n^2)$ such that $\beta \in T'$. Choose $\gamma \xleftarrow{R} Z_{\phi(n^2)}$ such that $\gamma \notin \{\beta, \sigma\}$. Set the public key $P_u = (n, \beta)$ and the private key $P_r = (\sigma, \lambda, \gamma)$, then output the parameter $\mathcal{P} = (P_u, P_r)$.

AccVal$(L, \mathcal{P})$: Given a set of m distinct elements $L = \{c_1, \ldots, c_m\}$ ($L \subset \mathcal{C}$, $1 < m \leq M$) and the parameter $\mathcal{P}$, choose $c_{m+1} \xleftarrow{R} \mathcal{C}$, and compute

$$x_i = F(c_i^{\gamma \sigma^{-1}} \bmod n^2) \bmod n \ (i = 1, \ldots, m+1),$$

$$v = \sigma \sum_{i=1}^{m+1} x_i \bmod n,$$

$$y_i = c_i^{\gamma \beta^{-1}} \bmod n^2 \ (i = 1, \ldots, m+1), \text{ and}$$

$$a_c = \prod_{i=1}^{m+1} y_i \bmod n^2.$$

Then output the accumulated value v and the auxiliary information a_c and $A_l = \{y_1, \ldots, y_m\}$.

WitGen$(a_c, A_l, \mathcal{P})$: Given the auxiliary information a_c and A_l, and the parameter $\mathcal{P}$, choose randomly a set of m numbers $T = \{t_1, \ldots, t_m\} \subset T' \setminus \{\beta, \gamma\}$ $(i = 1, \ldots, m)$, and compute

$$w_i = a_c y_i^{\frac{-t_i}{\gamma}} \bmod n^2 \ (i = 1, \ldots, m).$$

Then output the witness $W_i = (w_i, t_i)$ for c_i $(i = 1, \ldots, m)$.

Verify(c, W, v, P_u): Given an element c, its witness $W = (w, t)$, the accumulated value v and the public key P_u, test whether $\{c, w\} \subset \mathcal{C}$, $t \in T'$ and $F(w^\beta c^t \bmod n^2) \equiv v \pmod n$. If so, output Yes; otherwise, output No.

AddEle$(L^\oplus, a_c, v, \mathcal{P})$: Given a set of elements $L^\oplus = \{c_1^\oplus, \ldots, c_k^\oplus\}$ $(L^\oplus \subset \mathcal{C} \setminus L, 1 \leq k \leq M - m)$ to be inserted, the auxiliary information a_c, the accumulated value v and the parameter $\mathcal{P}$, choose $c_{k+1}^\oplus \xleftarrow{R} \mathcal{C}$ and a set of k numbers $T^\oplus = \{t_1^\oplus, \ldots, t_k^\oplus\} \xleftarrow{R} T' \setminus \{T \cup \{\beta, \gamma\}\}$, and compute

$$x_i^\oplus = F((c_i^\oplus)^{\gamma \sigma^{-1}} \bmod n^2) \bmod n \ (i = 1, \ldots, k+1),$$

$$v' = v + \sigma \sum_{i=1}^{k+1} x_i^\oplus \bmod n,$$

$$y_i^\oplus = (c_i^\oplus)^{\gamma \beta^{-1}} \bmod n^2, \ (i = 1, \ldots, k+1),$$

$$a_u = \prod_{i=1}^{k+1} y_i^\oplus \bmod n^2, \text{ and}$$

$$w_i^\oplus = a_c a_u (y_i^\oplus)^{\frac{-t_i^\oplus}{\gamma}} \bmod n^2 \ (i = 1, \ldots, k).$$

Set $a_c = a_c a_u \bmod n^2$, $T = T \cup T^\oplus$ and $V = V \cup \{a_u\}$.

Then output the new accumulated value v' corresponding to the set $L \cup L^\oplus$, the witnesses $W_i^\oplus = (w_i^\oplus, t_i^\oplus)$ for the new added elements $c_i^\oplus$ $(i = 1, \ldots, k)$ and the auxiliary information a_u and a_c.

DelEle$(L^\ominus, a_c, v, \mathcal{P})$: Given a set of elements $L^\ominus = \{c_1^\ominus, \ldots, c_k^\ominus\}$ $(L^\ominus \subset L, 1 \leq k < m)$ to be deleted, the auxiliary information a_c, the accumulated value v and the parameter $\mathcal{P}$, choose $c_{k+1}^\ominus \xleftarrow{R} \mathcal{C}$, and compute

$$x_i^\ominus = F((c_i^\ominus)^{\gamma \sigma^{-1}} \bmod n^2) \bmod n \ (i = 1, \ldots, k+1),$$

$$v' = v - \sigma \sum_{i=1}^{k} x_i^\ominus + \sigma x_{k+1}^\ominus \bmod n,$$

$$y_i^\ominus = (c_i^\ominus)^{\gamma \beta^{-1}} \bmod n^2 \ (i = 1, \ldots, k+1), \text{ and}$$

$$a_u = y_{k+1}^{\ominus} \prod_{j=1}^{k} (y_j^{\ominus})^{-1} \bmod n^2.$$

Set $a_c = a_c a_u \bmod n^2$ and $V = V \cup \{a_u\}$.

Then output the new accumulated value v' corresponding to the set $L \backslash L^{\ominus}$ and the auxiliary information a_u and a_c.

UpdWit(W_i, a_u, P_u): Given the witness W_i, the auxiliary information a_u and the public key P_u, compute $w_i' = w_i a_u \bmod n^2$, then output the new witness $W_i' = (w_i', t_i)$ for the element c_i.

Notice that the second part t_i of the element c_i's witness W_i is generated in the first execution of the algorithm **WitGen** or **AddEle**, after that, no matter how many times the algorithms **AddEle** and **DelEle** are run, the value of t_i never changes, only the first part w_i does. So, t_i can also be treated as an alternative identifier of c_i in the accumulator. In addition, as we mentioned in Section 2.2, it is recommended for practical applications that $T' = \{2^{16} + 1, \cdots, n^2\}$.

5   Batch Update

Each element in the set V created by the algorithm **KeyGen** and updated by the algorithms **AddEle** and **DelEle** is related to a time when the element was added to V, and all element are arranged chronologically. When an element wants to use the accumulator after he missed N times update of witness, he can contact the accumulator and tell her the time of his last update, then the accumulator checks the set V, collects all data items $\{v_{i_1}, \ldots, v_{i_N}\} \subset V$ that the element did not use, computes the update information $a_u = v_{i_1} \ldots v_{i_N} \bmod n^2$, and returns a_u to the element. On receiving a_u, the element computes $w_i' = w_i a_u \bmod n^2$ to obtain the new witness $W' = (w_i', t_i)$.

Observe that, the element does not know the number of changes and the types of the changes, and makes batch update at unit cost (1 multiplication) without requiring knowledge of any sensitive information, and the accumulator takes N modular multiplications for the batch update. As mentioned above, the existing accumulators do not allow for batch updates so any collection of updates must be done sequentially. The sequential update is very inefficient if it is compared with our batch update. Consider the update operations for the dynamic accumulator from [4]. If one addition operation happens, then the witness w_i is updated as follows: $w_i' = (w_i)^{v_{i_j}} \bmod n$, where v_{i_j} $(j \in [N])$ is the update information for the addition. If one deletion operation happens, on receiving the update information v_{i_j} for the deletion, an element computes a pair (a, b) of integers such that $ac_i + bv_{i_j} = 1$, and then updates her witness $w_i' = (w_i)^b (v')^a \bmod n$, where v' is the new accumulated value. Therefore, to make a batch update, an element first needs to know the type of every change (addition or deletion), chooses different algorithms for different types of the change, and then, updates her witness one change by one change in the time sequence. In particular, for a deleting operation, an element must use the new accumulated value to update her witness.

To the best of our knowledge, our scheme is the first one to do batch update efficiently and give an answer in the affirmative to Fazio and Nicolosi's open problem [7].

6   Correctness

First we show the output of the algorithm **Verify** is correct for a regular accumulator. According to the properties of the Paillier cryptosystem, for ciphertexts $\{c_1^{\gamma\beta^{-1}}, \ldots, c_{m+1}^{\gamma\beta^{-1}}\}$ and their plaintexts $\{z_1, \ldots, z_{m+1}\}$, we have

$$\sigma(z_1 + \ldots + z_{m+1}) \equiv \frac{F((c_1^{\gamma\beta^{-1}} \ldots c_{m+1}^{\gamma\beta^{-1}})^{\sigma\lambda} \bmod n^2)}{F(g^\lambda \bmod n^2)} \pmod{n}.$$

It follows that,

$$\sigma \sum_{j=1}^{m+1} z_j F(g^\lambda \bmod n^2) \equiv F(\prod_{j=1}^{m+1}(c_j^{\gamma\beta^{-1}})^\beta \bmod n^2) \pmod{n}.$$

Since $z_j F(g^\lambda \bmod n^2) \equiv F((c_j^{\gamma\beta^{-1}})^\lambda \bmod n^2) \pmod{n}$, i.e.,

$$z_j F(g^\lambda \bmod n^2) \equiv F(c_j^{\gamma\sigma^{-1}} \bmod n^2) \pmod{n},$$

and $y_j = c_j^{\gamma\beta^{-1}} \bmod n^2$, i.e., $c_j^\gamma = (y_j^{\frac{\gamma - t_j}{\gamma}})^\beta (y_j^{\frac{t_j}{\gamma}})^\beta \bmod n^2$, for any $i \in [m]$, we have

$$\sigma \sum_{j=1}^{m+1} F(c_j^{\gamma\sigma^{-1}} \bmod n^2) \equiv F((y_i^{\frac{\gamma - t_i}{\gamma}} \prod_{j\in[m+1]\setminus\{i\}} y_j)^\beta (y_i^{\frac{t_i}{\gamma}})^\beta \bmod n^2) \pmod{n}.$$

From the construction of accumulator, we know that

$$x_j = F(c_j^{\gamma\sigma^{-1}} \bmod n^2) \bmod n, \quad (y_i^{\frac{t_i}{\gamma}})^\beta = c_i^{t_i} \bmod n^2 \text{ and}$$
$$w_i = y_i^{\frac{\gamma - t_i}{\gamma}} \prod_{j\in[m+1]\setminus\{i\}} y_j \bmod n^2.$$

Therefore,

$$\sigma \sum_{j=1}^{m+1} x_j \equiv F(w_i^\beta c_i^{t_i} \bmod n^2) \pmod{n}.$$

That is,

$$F(w_i^\beta c_i^{t_i} \bmod n^2) \equiv v \pmod{n}.$$

The congruence shows that, in a regular accumulator, if an element c_i ($i \in [m]$) is accumulated in the value v, the witness $W_i = (w_i, t_i)$ can give c_i a valid proof.

When some elements are added, for the new added elements $c_i^\oplus$ ($i = 1, \ldots, k$), it is easy to verify the correctness in the same way; for the old elements (previously accumulated) c_i $(i = 1, \ldots, m)$ whose witness $W_i = (w_i, t_i)$ is updated to be $W'_i = (w'_i, t_i)$, we show the correctness as follows.

$$F((w'_i)^\beta c_i^{t_i} \bmod n^2)$$

$$\equiv F((w_i a_u)^\beta c_i^{t_i} \bmod n^2) \pmod{n}$$

$$\equiv F(((y_j^{\frac{\gamma - t_j}{\gamma}})^\beta \prod_{j \in [m+1] \setminus \{i\}} y_j^\beta)(\prod_{i \in [k+1]} (y_i^\oplus)^\beta (y^{\frac{t_i}{\gamma}})^\beta) \bmod n^2) \pmod{n}$$

$$\equiv F((\prod_{j \in [m+1] \setminus \{i\}} c_i^\gamma) c_i^\gamma (\prod_{i \in [k+1]} ((c_i^\oplus)^{\gamma \beta^{-1}})^\beta) \bmod n^2) \pmod{n}$$

$$\equiv F((\prod_{j \in [m+1]} c_i^{\gamma \beta^{-1}})^{\sigma \lambda} (\prod_{i \in [k+1]} ((c_i^\oplus)^{\gamma \beta^{-1}})^{\sigma \lambda}) \bmod n^2) \pmod{n}$$

$$\equiv \sigma(\sum_{i=1}^{m+1} F(c_i^{\gamma \sigma^{-1}} \bmod n^2) + \sum_{i=1}^{k+1} F((c_i^\oplus)^{\gamma \sigma^{-1}} \bmod n^2)) \pmod{n}$$

$$\equiv \sigma(\sum_{i=1}^{m+1} x_i + \sum_{i=1}^{k+1} x_i^\oplus) \pmod{n}$$

$$\equiv v + \sigma \sum_{i=1}^{k+1} x_i^\oplus \pmod{n}$$

$$\equiv v' \pmod{n}$$

When some elements are deleted, for the left elements (which has been accumulated and is still accumulated currently) c_i with updated witnesses $W'_i = (w'_i, t_i)$, the correctness can be verified in the same way.

It is also easy to verify the correctness for batch update in the same way.

7   Security

The following theorem states that any PPT adversary can not find membership proofs for those elements that are not in the accumulated set.

Theorem 1. *If the es-RSA Assumption holds, then the proposed dynamic accumulator is secure under CEA.*

Proof. Suppose that there exists a PPT adversary $\mathcal{ADV}$ who wins in the CEA game with non-negligible advantage, that means, on input (n, β), $\mathcal{ADV}$ finds with non-negligible advantage m elements $\{c_1, \ldots, c_m\} \subset \mathcal{C}$ with their witnesses $\{W_1, \ldots, W_m\}$ and an element $c' \in \mathcal{C} \setminus \{c_1, \ldots, c_m\}$ with $W' = (w', t')$ such that $F(w'^\beta c'^{t'} \bmod n^2) \equiv v \pmod{n}$, where v is the accumulation value of $(c_1, \ldots, c_m)$. We construct an algorithm $\mathcal{B}$ that breaks es-RSA Assumption with non-negligible advantage. $\mathcal{B}$ simulates $\mathcal{CHA}$ as follows:

Setup. $\mathcal{B}$ runs the algorithm **KeyGen**(k, M) to get the element domain $\mathcal{C} = Z_{n^2}^* \setminus \{1\}$ and setup the system parameters. $\mathcal{ADV}$ requests the accumulated values and corresponding witnesses for a polynomial number of sets $L^* \subset \mathcal{C}$ from $\mathcal{B}$.

Queries. $\mathcal{ADV}$ adaptively modifies the sets L^* and asks $\mathcal{B}$ to add a set of elements $L^\oplus$ $(L^\oplus \subset \mathcal{C})$ to some accumulated values and/or remove a set of elements $L^\ominus$ $(L^\ominus \subset L^*)$ from some accumulated values as he wishes; $\mathcal{B}$ runs the algorithm **AddEle**$(L^\oplus, a_c, v, \mathcal{P})$ and/or **DelEle**$(L^\ominus, a_c, v, \mathcal{P})$ to reply $\mathcal{ADV}$. Then $\mathcal{ADV}$ runs the algorithm **UpdWit**(W_i, a_u, P_u) to update the witness for related elements.

Challenge. After making a polynomial number of queries, $\mathcal{ADV}$ decides on challenge by picking a set of elements $L = \{c_1, \ldots, c_m\}$ $(1 < m \leq M)$ from $\mathcal{C}$ and querying $\mathcal{B}$ for the corresponding accumulated values v and witnesses $\{W_1, \ldots, W_m\}$. On receiving them, $\mathcal{ADV}$ produces an element c' $(c' \in \mathcal{C} \setminus L)$ with a witness $W' = (w', t')$, and sends them to $\mathcal{B}$.

Response. $\mathcal{B}$ runs the **Verify** algorithm to test if c' is accumulated in v. If **Verify** outputs Yes with non-negligible advantage, then we say $\mathcal{B}$, without n's integer factorization, has non-negligible advantage to breaks the es-RSA assumption; otherwise, nothing.

Let's analyze that how $\mathcal{B}$ breaks the es-RSA assumption.

Because the scheme appends a random element to compute the accumulated value v every time in running the algorithm **AccVal**, **AddEle** and **DelEle**, and t_i is chosen at random, the probability distributions of v, w_i, t_i and a_u are uniform. Observing the outputs of queries for the keyword lists in the stage of **Queries** and their changes cannot help $\mathcal{ADV}$ to forge anything. So, let's only consider the challenge set $L = \{c_1, \ldots, c_m\}$.

With n's integer factorization, $\mathcal{B}$ computes the v and $\{W_1, \ldots, W_m\}$ for the set $L = \{c_1, \ldots, c_m\}$, so $\mathcal{B}$ has m congruences $F(w_i^{\beta} c_i^{t_i} \bmod n^2) \equiv v \pmod{n}$ $(i = 1, \ldots, m)$, which means that $\exists k \in Z$ such that

$$\frac{w_i^{\beta} c_i^{t_i} \bmod n^2 - 1}{n} = kn + v.$$

It follows that,

$$w_i^{\beta} c_i^{t_i} \equiv vn + 1 \pmod{n^2}.$$

This congruence can also be expressed in the following two ways:

$$w_i^{\beta} \equiv (vn + 1) c_i^{-t_i} \pmod{n^2}.$$

$$c_i^{t_i} \equiv (vn + 1) w_i^{-\beta} \pmod{n^2}.$$

Therefore, $\mathcal{B}$ has m triples (c_i, w_i, t_i) such that c_i, w_i and t_i are the t_i-th root of $(vn + 1) w_i^{-\beta} \pmod{n^2}$, the β-th root of $(vn + 1) c_i^{-t_i} \pmod{n^2}$ and the logarithmic value of $(vn + 1) w_i^{-\beta} \pmod{n^2}$ based on c_i, respectively.

If $\mathcal{ADV}$ wins in the CEA game with non-negligible advantage, the **Verify** outputs Yes with non-negligible advantage. That means, without n's integer factorization, $\mathcal{B}$ has non-negligible advantage to get a congruence

$$F(w'^{\beta} c'^{t'} \bmod n^2) \equiv v \pmod{n},$$

thus, $\mathcal{B}$ has non-negligible advantage to get a distinct triple (c', w', t') such that c', w' and t' are the t'-th root of $(vn + 1) w'^{-\beta} \pmod{n^2}$, the β-th root of $(vn + 1) c'^{-t'} \pmod{n^2}$ and the logarithmic value of $(vn + 1) w'^{-\beta} \pmod{n^2}$ based on c', respectively.

We know that $c' \notin L$, that means $c' \neq c_i$ for any $i \in 1, \ldots, m$, so let's identify four cases, depending on whether $w' = w_i$ or $t' = t_i$ (or not) for some $i \in [m]$.

Case 1: $w' \neq w_i$ for any $i \in [m]$.

We have $w'^{\beta} \neq w_i^{\beta} \pmod{n^2}$, so $(vn + 1)w'^{-\beta} \neq (vn + 1)w_i^{-\beta} \pmod{n^2}$. That means, $(vn + 1)w'^{-\beta} \pmod{n^2}$ is a distinct number from $\{(vn + 1)w_i^{-\beta} \pmod{n^2}\}_{i=1,\ldots,m}$, and $\mathcal{B}$ has its t'-th root c' or the logarithmic value t' based on c'. Thus, $\mathcal{B}$ breaks the es-RSA assumption.

Case 2: $w' = w_i$ for some $i \in [m]$.

We have $c'^{t'} = (vn + 1)w'^{-\beta} = (vn + 1)w_i^{-\beta} = c_i^{t_i} \pmod{n^2}$, so $t' \neq t_i$. That means, $\mathcal{B}$ has c' as the t'-th root of $(vn + 1)w'^{-\beta} \pmod{n^2}$ and t' as the logarithmic value of $(vn + 1)w'^{-\beta} \pmod{n^2}$ based on c'. Thus, $\mathcal{B}$ breaks the es-RSA assumption.

Case 3: $t' = t_i$ for some $i \in [m]$.

We have $c'^{t'} \neq c_i^{t_i} \pmod{n^2}$. It is convenient to split this case into two subcases:

Case 3a: $c'^{t'} = c_j^{t_j} \pmod{n^2}$ for some $j \in [m] \setminus \{i\}$. This case is the same as in **Case 2**.

Case 3b: $c'^{t'} \neq c_j^{t_j} \pmod{n^2}$ for any $j \in [m] \setminus \{i\}$. So, $(vn+1)c'^{-t'} \pmod{n^2}$ is a distinct number from $\{(vn+1)c_i^{-t_i} \pmod{n^2}\}_{i=1,\ldots,m}$, and $\mathcal{B}$ has its β-th root w'. This means, $\mathcal{B}$ breaks the es-RSA assumption.

Case 4: When $t' \neq t_i$ for any $i \in [m]$.

We also split this case into two subcases:

Case 4a: $c'^{t'} = c_j^{t_j} \pmod{n^2}$ for some $j \in [m]$. This case is the same as in **Case 2**.

Case 4b: $c'^{t'} \neq c_j^{t_j} \pmod{n^2}$ for any $j \in [m]$. This case is the same as in **Case 3b**.

Consequently, the theorem is proved.

8   Conclusions and Future Direction

We have considered the problem of design of the dynamic accumulators, and introduced formal generic definitions of accumulators and a new security model called CEA. We constructed a new dynamic accumulator that allows an efficient batch update. The scheme is based on the Paillier public-key cryptosystem, and is sound and secure under the es-RSA assumption.

The computation complexity of our approach is reasonable, but the length of witnesses is $4 \log n$ bits and the scheme needs to compute at least $(2^{16} + 1)$-th roots. So designing more space-efficient and time-efficient accumulators remains a challenging open problem.

Acknowledgments

The work was in part supported by Australian Research Council Discovery grants DP0663452, DP0558773 and DP0665035. Huaxiong Wang's research was in part supported by Singapore Ministry of Education grant T206B2204.

References

1. Au, M.H., Wu, Q., Susilo, W., Mu, Y.: Compact E-Cash from Bounded Accumulator. In: Abe, M. (ed.) CT-RSA 2007. LNCS, vol. 4377, pp. 178–195. Springer, Heidelberg (2006)
2. Baric, N., Pfitzmann, B.: Collision-free accumulators and fail-stop signature schemes without trees. In: Fumy, W. (ed.) EUROCRYPT 1997. LNCS, vol. 1233, pp. 480–494. Springer, Heidelberg (1997)
3. Benaloh, J., Mare, M.: One-way accumulators: a decentralized alternative to digital signatures. In: Helleseth, T. (ed.) EUROCRYPT 1993. LNCS, vol. 765, pp. 274–285. Springer, Heidelberg (1994)
4. Camenisch, J., Lysyanskaya, A.: Dynamic Accumulators and Application to Efficient Revocation of Anonymous Credentials. In: Yung, M. (ed.) CRYPTO 2002. LNCS, vol. 2442, pp. 61–76. Springer, Heidelberg (2002)
5. Catalano, D., Gennaro, R., Howgrave-Graham, N., Nguyen, P.: Paillier's Cryptosystem Revisited. In: ACM CCS 2001, pp. 206–214 (2001)
6. Dodis, Y., Kiayias, A., Nicolosi, A., Shoup, V.: Anonymous Identification in Ad Hoc Groups. In: Cachin, C., Camenisch, J.L. (eds.) EUROCRYPT 2004. LNCS, vol. 3027, pp. 609–626. Springer, Heidelberg (2004)
7. Fazio, N., Nicolosi, A.: Cryptographic Accumulators: Definitions, Constructions and Applications. Available (2003), at http://www.cs.nyu.edu/fazio/papers/
8. Gentry, C., Ramzan, Z.: RSA Accumulator Based Broadcast Encryption. In: Zhang, K., Zheng, Y. (eds.) ISC 2004. LNCS, vol. 3225, pp. 73–86. Springer, Heidelberg (2004)
9. Goodrich, M., Tamassia, R., Hasić, J.: An efficient dynamic and distributed cryptographic accumulator. In: Chan, A.H., Gligor, V.D. (eds.) ISC 2002. LNCS, vol. 2433, pp. 372–388. Springer, Heidelberg (2002)
10. Nguyen, L.: Accumulators from Bilinear Pairings and Applications. In: Menezes, A.J. (ed.) CT-RSA 2005. LNCS, vol. 3376, pp. 275–292. Springer, Heidelberg (2005)
11. Nyberg, K.: Fast accumulated hashing. In: Gollmann, D. (ed.) 3rd Fast Software Encryption Workshop. LNCS, vol. 1039, pp. 83–87. Springer, Heidelberg (1996)
12. Paillier, P.: Public-Key Cryptosystems based on Composite Degree Residue Classes. In: Stern, J. (ed.) EUROCRYPT 1999. LNCS, vol. 1592, pp. 223–238. Springer, Heidelberg (1999)
13. Pohlig, S., Hellman, M.: An Improved Algorithm for Computing Logarithms in $GF(p)$ and its Cryptographic Significance. IEEE Trans. Inform. Theory IT-24, 106–111 (1978)
14. Sander, T.: Efficient accumulators without trapdoor. In: Varadharajan, V., Mu, Y. (eds.) Information and Communication Security. LNCS, vol. 1726, pp. 252–262. Springer, Heidelberg (1999)
15. Tsudik, G., Xu, S.: Accumulating Composites and Improved Group Signing. In: Laih, C.-S. (ed.) ASIACRYPT 2003. LNCS, vol. 2894, pp. 269–286. Springer, Heidelberg (2003)
16. Zhang, F., Che, X.: Cryptanalysis and improvement of an ID-based ad-hoc anonymous identification scheme at CT-RSA 2005, Cryptology ePrint Archive, Report 2005/103

Preventing Unofficial Information Propagation

Zhengyi Le[1], Yi Ouyang[1], Yurong Xu[1], James Ford[2], and Fillia Makedon[2]

[1] Computer Science Department, Dartmouth College, Hanover, NH, 03755
[2] Heracleia Lab, Computer Science and Engineering Department
University of Texas at Arlington, Arlington, TX, 76019
{zyle,ouyang,yurong}@cs.dartmouth.edu, {jcford,makedon}@uta.edu

Abstract. Digital copies are susceptible to theft and vulnerable to leakage, copying, or manipulation. When someone (or some group), who has stolen, leaked, copied, or manipulated digital documents propagates the documents over the Internet and/or distributes those through physical distribution channels many challenges arise which document holders must overcome in order to mitigate the impact to their privacy or business. This paper focuses on the propagation problem of digital credentials, which may contain sensitive information about a credential holder. Existing work such as access control policies and the Platform for Privacy Preferences (P3P) assumes that qualified or certified credential viewers are honest and reliable. The proposed approach in this paper uses short-lived credentials based on reverse forward secure signatures to remove this assumption and mitigate the damage caused by a dishonest or honest but compromised viewer.

1 Introduction

Digital credentials are widely used in the Internet, and the issue of privacy related to release of credentials is attracting increasing attention. Digital credentials may be used with various security services, including access control, data origin authentication, and trust negotiation. They are issued and signed by Certificate Authorities (CAs) or Attribute Authorities (AAs) and often contain sensitive information about credential holders, since like the drivers licenses and other multi-purpose documents they may replace, they often bundle private information of different types together. Whether in the real world or online, it is preferable that private information should only be accessible by authorized parties: for example, a bar patron providing a drivers license as an age verification document may reasonably object to having their address and other details recorded, and a newly admitted graduate student may only want to show her history of previous grades to the graduate advisor of the department, and not all department staff and faculty. However, after you reveal your credential to other parties, your information is exposed to potential leakage.

There are two specific situations of information leakage we wish to prevent from happening: first, that others get more information from credentials than they are intended to, and second, that after others view and verify the information in credentials, they pass them to others (or their computers are compromised) and information is exposed to attackers. Existing work, such as on

S. Qing, H. Imai, and G. Wang (Eds.): ICICS 2007, LNCS 4861, pp. 113–125, 2007.
© Springer-Verlag Berlin Heidelberg 2007

privacy preserving credentials [6], has addressed the first problem by altering an original certificate to cover private information and still maintain its usage. However, as soon as sensitive information is revealed, neither the credential holder nor the issuer can prevent others from propagating this information. This paper focuses on this problem. The current solutions are access policies and the Platform for Privacy Preferences (P3P). Access policies can prevent unqualified parties from viewing protected credentials; they cannot help with information leakage intentionally or unintentionally by qualified parties, as for example in the cases described in [21]. P3P provides a technical mechanism for ensuring that users can be informed about privacy policies before they release sensitive information [2]. It does not provide a technical mechanism for making sure sites act according to their policies.

This paper addresses this problem from another angle. We clearly cannot prevent the propagation of information that others have already obtained. However, we can take steps to make credential contents they propagate unofficial, in the sense that they lose the credential's basic ability to prove the correctness of its contents. For example, suppose A knows B's annual income because B showed A a credential with this information in it. If A wants to leak the information of B's annual income and prove to C she does have the correct information, A can show C the credential of B or send C a copy of the credential; once C verifies the credential, C knows B's annual income for sure. We can prevent this sequence of events by revoking the credential; in other words, if the credential is time-limited, then after an interval A cannot prove to C that her copy of B's credential is authentic. If the interval is dependent on the action of B, and B can, after using the credential once, invalidate it, then B's information liability will be more limited than before. Thus, whether A distributes B's actual or past salary information or any arbitrary made-up figure, A will be unable to prove that whatever number she has is or ever was valid.

However, if traditional public/private key pairs are used to implement the time-limited credential, a CA could be overwhelmed with generating key pairs, issuing public keys, signing credentials, and revoking. This paper approaches this problem with two schemes—interactive and non-interactive. The basis of our schemes is *Forward Secure Signature (FSS)* crytosystems. In FSS, there are a series of private keys with consecutive indexes and a single, fixed public key. Private keys evolve with a one-way function. Once the current private key is exposed, future private keys are exposed too. In the context of our problem, the FSS fixed public key can improve efficiency considerably since it avoids repeatedly issuing public/private key pairs, but forward private key updating will invalidate future credentials when private key exposure happens. Thus, in our schemes, a CA signs credentials with FSS private keys and invalidates each in reverse order when requested (interactive) or at regular intervals of time (non-interactive) so that even though the past private keys and corresponding signatures are invalid, its public key does not need to be re-signed and its future signatures are still valid. Moreover, since these credentials are time-limited, this eliminates the need for a revocation mechanismt, such as OCSP and CRLs, which is typically costly in PKI systems. This idea, while simple, does not seem to have appeared previously. Yet, the result is a direct improvement in both the overall computational complexity, as well as the revocation efficiency, over previous traditional approaches.

A variety of electronic transactions, such as online pharmacy prescriptions, medicaid/medicare applications, and digital library browsing, run a risk of information propagation. Our schemes can establish credentials to help with this problem. Users can assure friends, business associates, and online services that the electronic information they receive is authentic and after a short system-defined time, the information is not official any longer.

The rest of the paper is organised as follows. Section 2 surveys related work. Section 3 describes two approaches that follow the outline given above. Section 4 discusses practical issues related to underlying cryptosystems and revocation. Some applications are suggested in Section 5. Section 6 compares performance against RSA. Section 7 presents conclusions and describes future work.

2   Related Work

2.1   Credentials

Trust negotiation is an important application of digital credentials. Winsborough *et al.* first introduced the notion of Automated Trust Negotiation (ATN) and an architecture for managing the exchange of credentials between two strangers for the purpose of determining bilateral trustworthiness [21]. As an example, suppose an AIDS patient is interested in a free online service and treatment. He sends a request to the server. The server checks its access policies and sends a counter request for required credentials, such as a signed prescription and citizenship. The patient reads the counter request and checks his local credential release policies, which say his citizenship is not sensitive but the disease information is and his diagnosis can be released only to HIPAA[1]certified hospitals. Then, he sents his citizen credential and a request for a HIPAA certificate to the server. If the server's policy says its HIPAA certificate is publicly accessble, the server will send it to the patient. After the patient successfully verified the certificate, he will send the diagnosis to the server and the trust negotiation succeeds. In this way, ATN involves digital credentials and uses access policies to allow only qualified parties to view sensitive credentials in a step-wise manner to build trust.

However, how to prevent the illegal propagation of released credentials has been one of the open problems in the ATN research. Researchers have designed ATN systems [7,22,23] and addressed related privacy and security issues in [6,19,20,24]. In order to work against unnecessary information leakage in trust negotiation, the authors proposed privacy preserving credentials to release minimal information [6]. The idea is that sensitive attributes in protected credentials are selectively disclosed. A sensitive attribute "A" is replaced with "$H(A|R)$",

---

[1] The Health Insurance Portability and Accountability Act (HIPAA) was enacted by the U.S. Congress in 1996. Its Privacy Rule took effect on April 14, 2003. http://www.HIPAA.org

in which R is a random number, "H" is a hash function, and "|" means concatenation. The new credential is signed by a CA. To verify it, "R" and "H" should be disclosed to the other party. This can prevent credential viewers from obtaining additional information. However, once the "R" and "H" are revealed to aother party, he can show them to someone else to prove the authenticity of the information he obtained.

Another approach, the Platform for Privacy Preferences Project (P3P) [2], defines the syntax and semantics of privacy policies, and the mechanisms for associating policies with Web resources. So, the privacy terms and conditions of web sites can be expressed in a standard format and users can retrieve and interpret this information automatically and then make a decision to release their personal information or not. However, whether and how the sites comply with the policies is outside the scope of the P3P specification.

2.2 Forward Security

The first Forward Secure Signature (FSS) scheme was designed by Bellare and Miner [4]. Their idea is based on dividing time into periods: $0, 1, 2, \ldots, T$. The public key PK is fixed, and the corresponding private key evolves every period through a one-way function: SK_0, SK_1, SK_2,..., SK_T. In period i, $(0 \leq i \leq T)$, a message M is signed by the current private key SK_i and the current time period index i. To verify the signature SIG of M, a receiver needs to use the fixed PK and the time period index i in which the message was signed. In case a private key, SK_i, is compromised, the previous signatures signed by $SK_j (0 \leq j < i)$ are still valid (see Figure 1) though the future signatures are disabled. This is because the key evolving algorithm is one-way and public, so that once an attacker successfully compromises SK_i he can easily derive the future keys but it is computationally hard to reverse the process to obtain the previous keys. So, this scheme mitigates the damage caused by the private key exposure. Following that work, many improvements and similar forward secure schemes have been published (e.g., [3,13,15,16,8,5]).

Here we give an overview of a general FSS that is the basis of our proposed schemes. FSS is a 4-tuple of poly-time algorithms (Gen, Upd, Sgn, Vrf):

- Gen: the key generation algorithm.

$$Gen(k, l) \rightarrow (PK, SK_0),$$

  where k and l are two security parameters, PK is the fixed public key, and SK_0 is the initial private key.
- Upd: the user private key update algorithm.

$$Upd(SK_i) \rightarrow SK_{i+1}.$$

  The user uses his current private key for period i to generate a new private key for the next period.
- Sgn: the signing algorithm.

$$Sgn(M, i, SK_i) \rightarrow \langle i, SIG \rangle,$$

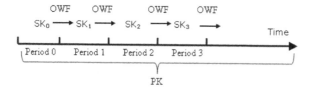

Fig. 1. Forward Secure Signature Scheme

where SIG is the signature, and i indicates the time period in which M is signed.

– Vrf: the verification algorithm.

$$Vrf(PK, M, \langle i, SIG \rangle) \rightarrow true/false.$$

If verification succeeds, Vrf outputs $true$. Otherwise, $false$.

In addition, key-insulated cryptosystems, such as [9] and [14], can provide both forward and backward security. The idea is similar to FSS, but it uses a physically secure device to store a master key to help with evolving the private key. When a user sends a request to the device to update his private key, the device generates a partial secret from its master key and then sends the partial secret to the user. The user generates the next private key from the partial secret and his current private key. Thus, the key update cannot be performed without the interaction of the secure device. However, this technology is not ready for practical use because of its efficiency.

3   Preventing Unofficial Information Propagation

Even though access policies and P3P can prevent unqualified or uncertified parties from viewing sensitive credentials, qualified or certified parties might become corrupt or be compromised by attackers so that the sensitive credentials they have viewed are at risk of being exposed. The challenge is how to disallow credential propagation by viewers. However, digital documents are well-known for being susceptible to copying, so our approach is to make credentials invalid shortly after being viewed. This mitigates the impact caused by corrupted parties or attackers. If a viewer becomes corrupt or attackers succeed after an invalidation, they will have an authentic but invalid copy of a credential. They cannot prove to other parties that the content in that credential is true since the signing key has been disabled and the signature can be forged by anyone.

There are two naïve ways to prevent this kind of unofficial information propagation: CAs can make credential expiration dates occur very soon, or credential holders can request the revocation of a credential after each usage. However, when we step further into these naïve solutions, problems arise. In the first method, if the credential owner wants to show a credential to someone else after the expiration date, he needs to ask the CA to issue a new credential. In the second method, the CA needs to put the credential on the revocation list (or list it through OCSP responders) on request and issue a new credential for each usage. In addition, in either method, as long as the CA's signing key is still valid after the expiration date or the revocation, the invalid credential cannot be forged. This is a problem because it creates a special status for obsolete credentials that makes them distinguishable from arbitrary information. So, the problem of information leakage still occurs. In order to avoid this, the CA must change its signing key frequently. If so, either its parent CA needs to be involved in signing new public keys for the CA or the CA needs to adopt a primary key pair which is used to sign a series ephemeral key pairs for itself. When the CA uses a new key to sign a credential, PKI clients will search for a new certificate for that key pair in known repositories such as LDAP directories. This introduces a tremendous cost.

This paper gives two schemes to achieve the same goal but avoid the problems caused by these two methods. The first is an interactive approach. Credential holders request of a CA that it invalidate the credentials after each usage. The second is a non-interactive one designed for credential holders who prefer to invalidate the credentials at regular intervals of time. In this approach, the CA invalidates credentials periodically on its own. Both of them use FSS in reverse order as the cryptosystem for the CA to sign the credentials. In this way, the

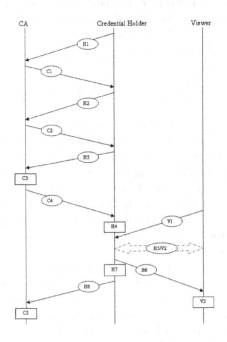

Fig. 2. Interactive Scheme

CA only has its FSS public key issued once, and each private key is invalidated before a revocation becomes necessary, so there is no need to revoke and re-issue its key pairs frequently. Further details about revocation are in Section 4.2.

The interactive scheme is given in Figure 2 and Table 1. In Figure 2, the timeline of each entity is represented by a vertical line. The communication responses and messages between each entity are represented by arrows and ellipses. Each action is defined by a rectangle. It works as follows. A user sends a request to a CA for a credential. After they agree to the type of the service, the user sends the CA the document to be signed. Then the CA verifies the contents through some online or offline methods. If they are correct, the CA signs it with multiple FSS private keys and sends the multiple FSS signatures back to the user. When the user wants to show his credential to someone else, he presents his document and the signature signed with the last FSS private key of the CA. After a grace period, he notifies the CA to disable the last FSS private key. When the CA receives the notification, it just posts the last FSS private key in a public repository. Then the key and the released signature is disabled and nobody is liable to visit or download anything from that public repository. When the user want to show his credential to another party, he sends the document and the next to last signature. Afterwards the CA disables the next to last private key.

Table 1. Interactive Scheme

CA:
$C1$: Answer the request for credential issuance with "YES" or "NO".
$C2$: If the on-request service is available and T is acceptable, send back "OK" to the credential holder. Otherwise send "DENY".
$C3$: Verify the content sent by the credential requester by on-line or off-line methods. If successful, use $SK_1, \ldots, SK_T$ to generate $SIG_1, \ldots, SIG_T$ on the document M.
$C4$: Send $SIG_1, \ldots, SIG_T$ to the credential requester.
$C5$: Release SK_{T-i} when requested for i times.

Credential Holder:
$H1$: Send the request for credential insurance to CA.
$H2$: Check with CA whether the on-request service with T is available.
$H3$: If accepted, send M, the content to be signed, to CA.
$H4$: Receive the credentials and review them.
$H5$: If there are local policies to protect its credentials, ask the viewer to provide documents to satisfy the policies.
$H6$: Send the credential and SIG_{T-i} to a viewer when he is qualified.
$H7$: Wait for a grace period of time.
$H8$: Send invalidation request to CA.

Viewer:
$V1$: Ask for the credential before providing some services or releasing sensitive credentials.
$V2$: If required, send a qualification proof.
$V3$: Receive the credential, check its validity and verify it.

Table 2. Non-Interactive Scheme

$C2'$: If the on-period service is available and $\langle t,T \rangle$ is available, send back "OK" to the credential holder. Otherwise send "DENY".
$C5'$: Release the signing keys at regular intervals of time.
$H2'$: Check with CA whether the on-period service with $\langle t,T \rangle$ is available.

In this way, the user consumes the FSS signatures in reverse order. For example, in $C3$, the CA runs $Gen(k,l) \to (PK, SK_0)$ to generate the fixed public key and the initial private key, and $Upd(SK_{j-1}) \to SK_j$ n times to generate $SK_1, \ldots, SK_n$. Then the CA runs $Sign(M, i, SK_i) \to \langle i, SIG_i \rangle$ to generate n signatures, $SIG_1, \ldots, SIG_n$, for M, the contents to be certified. T is a mutually agreed on total number of FSS signatures when the user requests this kind of service from the CA.

In the non-interactive scheme, the CA automatically releases a private key periodically as agreed. So, there is no step $H7$ or $H8$ to notify the CA, and $H2$, $C2$, and $C5$ are replaced by $H2'$, $C2'$ and $C5'$ in Table 2. T becomes the total number of time periods and t is the interval length.

Note that in either scheme, when the CA is ready to release a private key, it just posts it in a public repository and no seperate revocation mechanisms are needed. The private key is disabled even though nobody is required to visit or download that public repository. This is because making past private keys publicly accessible already invalidates the proof of its creator. Thus, verifiers do not need to be involved with any credential status checking procedures. So, this rules out the bandwidth and scability issue of PKI revocation.

4   Practical Issues

Here, we discuss practical issues that arise when applying our schemes. We will explain why we chose FSS instead of other new public key algorithms (see also Section 6, where we show that FSS is more practical than an RSA-based solution with respect to performance). Then the benefits of the time-limited certificates over traditional CRLs and OCSP will follow.

4.1   Underlying Cryptosystems

FSS was motivated by the key exposure problem, and they addressed this problem by mitigating the damage caused by key exposure. The first practical FSS scheme was constructed by Bellare and Miner and it is based on the ideas underlying the Fiat-Shamir [11] and Ong-Schnorr [18] identification and signature schemes. In order to solve our problem, frequently changing the CA's public key is not desired. So, directly applying the Fiat-Shamir scheme or the related GQ scheme [12] does not help ease the CA of its burden. However, FSS has a fixed public key, which meets our requirement. In our schemes, a CA releases FSS private keys in reverse order on purpose to make past credentials unofficial. Our experiments in Section 6 also show that FSS with reasonable T is practical and efficient with regard to solving our problem.

Generally speaking, most FSS algorithms require the input of the total time periods, T, during the key generation phase. So, once the T is fixed, the credential holder cannot ask for more than T credentials without changing the public key when needs increase (changing the public key necessarily involves the CA). In contrast to typical FSS algorithms, KIS has no such limitation — it supports an unbounded number of periods. We therefore considered KIS as the basis for our approach. However, its computational time for a single signature is more than hours when k is greater than 16 on a representative Intel® Pentium® 4 machine with CPU 2.00GHz and 512KB cache, where 1024-bit RSA takes microseconds.

In addition, since there are variants of FSS, such as [3,13,15], we limit ourselves to general methods based on FSS so as to make our work independent of FSS progress. This should ensure that any improvement to the underlying FSS cryptography will benefit our scheme.

4.2   Revocation and Expiration

In PKI, certificate revocation is one of the hardest problems and consequently one of the major costs. Muñoz et al. evaluated the main revocation policies: OCSP and Overissued-CRL in their paper [17]. In general, for a high request rate, a high bandwidth is needed. Certificate Revocation Lists (CRL) ask users to download the entire list but almost 99% of revoked certificates may be irrelevant to users. In practice, many applications do not use CRLs at all since downloading a large CRL takes too much time and makes users uncomfortable when opening a file. In addition, in order to conserve bandwidth, it is common that CRLs have a validity period of one week. Such a delay can be critical.

In contrast, the Online Certificate Status Protocol (OCSP) requires verifiers to request an online responder certificate status only for specific certificates. This solves the scalability problem of CRLs. However, the responses provided by many OCSP responders are based on CRLs. OCSP itself does not provide a timely update so that the OCSP responses is as outdated as the underlying CRLs.

Short-lived certificates are proposed in order to avoid revocation issues [1,10]. In the former paper, the idea is to make certificates expire, in weeks to hours, before a revocation becomes necessary, thereby ruling out the need for a seperate revocation mechanism. The resulting increased cost of renewing certificates by a CA is not negligible. In the latter paper, in order to decrease the expense of updating short-lived certificates, the idea is that a batch of certificates can be stored in a Certificate Verification Tree (CVT) and signed ahead of time with a single CA signature. However, it is problematic when the CA uses one signing key for all subsequent short-lived certificates in the scenario of unofficial propagation. Assuming that a previous certificate was signed by the same and currently valid signing key, this certificate will remain unforgeable even when it is expired. In order to work against this unintended information leaking, the CA has to change its signing key very frequently. This requires the involvement of its parent CA or that it adopt a long-term key pair and use them to issue ephemeral key pairs (sign public keys) for the CA itself. In contrast, in our schemes both credentials and the CA's signing keys are short-lived but there is one fixed public key for the CA and it needs to be signed only once. This releases the CA completely from the burden of signing ephemeral public keys frequently. So it solves the problem when short-lived certificates are introduced to work against unofficial information propagation. In addition, according to the results of our experiments in Section 6, our approach can also benefit the CVT-based micropayment scheme in [10] with improved efficiency.

5   Applications

Our schemes can be applied wherever digital credentials are used. As an example from the research domain, digital credentials play a key role in Automated Trust Negotiation (ATN) and the issue of how to protect privacy and deal with sensitive credentials has called for technical solutions since ATN was introduced. In industry, on-line prescription and drug purchasing systems may have stronger requirements for privacy issues. As mentioned in the previous section, a qualified credential viewer may leak the information by saving a copy of the credential he viewed and showing it to others — the viewer becomes malicious later in this case, or he remains honest but is compromised by an attacker. In either case, the effect is that locally stored copies of credentials are no longer secret. If our schemes are adapted, this kind of information leakage can be prevented: the corrupted viewer cannot prove the authenticity of the copy to others after a specified amount of time has passed; and the attacker cannot get a valid copy of the credential unless he hacks the viewer's system in time. The trade-off is that CAs and credential holders need to pay extra computational and communication costs for it. The following section will compare the performance between our schemes and the traditional approach.

6   Experiments and Performance

From Section 3 and 4, we have shown that using traditional public/private key pairs need more CA involvement to issue and invalidate short-lived certificates. This section focuses on the comparison of the computational cost: the run time

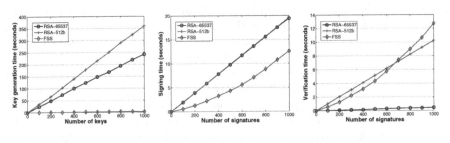

Fig. 3. Key Generation   **Fig. 4.** Signature   **Fig. 5.** Verification

of generating keys, signing documents, and verifying signatures (Figures 3 – 5). The first practical forward secure signature algorithm [4] is used for comparison. Other FSS improvements, such as [3,13,15,16], may have better performance.

The experiments are running on the same Pentium 4 platform described in Section 4.1. We set $k = 1024$ in both RSA and FSS. The performance of RSA depends not only on the length of its module but also on it length of its public key. So, we test two settings of RSA with 1024-bit module: the first is that the public key is always set to 65537, which is the default setting in OpenSSL since a common public key greater than 3 is generally considered safe; the second is that the public key is a 512-bit random prime (in the legend these cases are referred to as RSA-65537 and RSA-512b). Assuming one private key for one day, in the largest case of our experiments, the life time of FSS public key is around 3 years.

The data show RSA-65537 takes 241.84 seconds to generate 1000 public/private key pairs and RSA-512b takes 359.77 seconds while FSS takes only 2.47 seconds to generate a fixed public key and 1000 private keys. So, FSS is around 100 times faster in key generation. Figure 4 shows FSS is 1.54 times faster than RSA when signing a document. Note that RSA-65535 and RSA-512b merge together in this figure. This is because even though their public keys have different lengh, their private keys remain 1024 bits long. In Figure 5, FSS is 28.93 times slower than RSA-55537 when verifying a signature, but is not significantly different from RSA-512b. This is because verification involves a public exponent, and 65537 ($=2^{16} + 1$, 17 bits) and a 512-bit prime as an exponent have a significant impact. Another effect of this is that RSA verification is much faster than its signature. If we manually set public keys longer than 512 bits, the RSA key generation and verification will be slower.

In addition, FSS takes 12.58 seconds to sign 1000 documents on a Pentium 4 machine. Thus, signing is practical for a CA (who may have a faster machine than the Pentium 4 used in our experiments). One thousand FSS verifications take 12.73 seconds, but they are calculated by different verifiers. A single FSS verification takes only 12.73 microseconds on a Pentium 4 on average. This is also practical for common users.

7   Conclusion and Future Work

Unofficial information propagation has been a prominent concern with the growing use of digital credentials. This paper presents two schemes to address this problem: an interactive scheme and a non-interactive one. In our schemes, forward secure signature cryptosystems are used in reverse order for the purpose of validating signatures so that a credential will lose its ability to prove its authenticity in a short time after it is viewed. This new approach to short-lived certificates avoids significant costs caused by traditional pair-wise signature algorithms, which are not practical because of their performance and public key issuance considerations. In order to compare, we use the first FSS algorithm for experiments and note that further performance improvements benefit our schemes when using newer FSS versions. Our experiments show that this version of FSS is practical with a reasonable number of keys and comparable security parameters.

However, even though the proposed schemes can help with unofficial information propagation, the cooperation of the CA is required to generate multiple signatures as needed and send them to users. We are interested in the possibility of a better solution, ideally one where the CA is only required to sign once, and users can evolve a signature by themselves but cannot change the signed content. In this way, users could disable signatures as needed exclusively by themselves.

Acknowledgments

The authors would like to thank the anonymous reviewers for their valuable comments and suggestions. This work is supported in part by the National Science Foundation under award number ITR 0312629/0733673 and IDM 0308229. Any opinions, findings, and conclusions or recommendations expressed in this publication are those of the author(s) and do not necessarily reflect the views of the National Science Foundation.

References

1. Revocation Made Simpler (January 2006),
   http://www.pgp.com/downloads/whitepapers
2. The Platform for Privacy Preferences 1.1 (P3P1.1) Specification (November 2006),
   http://www.w3.org/TR/P3P11/
3. Abdalla, M., Reyzin, L.: A New Forward-Secure Digital Signature Scheme. In: Okamoto, T. (ed.) ASIACRYPT 2000. LNCS, vol. 1976, pp. 116–129. Springer, Heidelberg (2000)
4. Bellare, M., Miner, S.K.: A Forward-Secure Digital Signature Scheme. In: Wiener, M.J. (ed.) CRYPTO 1999. LNCS, vol. 1666, pp. 431–448. Springer, Heidelberg (1999)
5. Bellare, M., Yee, B.: Forward-Security in Private-Key Cryptography. In: Joye, M. (ed.) CT-RSA 2003. LNCS, vol. 2612, pp. 1–18. Springer, Heidelberg (2003)
6. Bertino, E., Ferrari, E., Squicciarini, A.C.: Privacy-Preserving Trust Negotiation. In: Proc. of the 4th Workshop on Privacy Enhancing Technologies, pp. 283–301 (2004)
7. Bertino, E., Ferrari, E., Squicciarini, A.C.: Trust-X: A Peer-to-Peer Framework for Trust Establishment. IEEE Trans. Knowl. Data Eng. 16(7), 827–842 (2004)
8. Canetti, R., Halevi, S., Katz, J.: A Forward-Secure Public-Key Encryption Scheme. In: Biham, E. (ed.) EUROCRPYT 2003. LNCS, vol. 2656, pp. 255–271. Springer, Heidelberg (2003)
9. Dodis, Y., Katz, J., Xu, S., Yung, M.: Strong Key-Insulated Signature Schemes. In: Desmedt, Y.G. (ed.) PKC 2003. LNCS, vol. 2567, pp. 130–144. Springer, Heidelberg (2002)
10. Domingo-Ferrer, J.: On the Synergy Between Certificate Verification Trees and PayTree-like Micropayments. In: Katsikas, S.K., Gritzalis, S., Lopez, J. (eds.) EuroPKI 2004. LNCS, vol. 3093, pp. 180–190. Springer, Heidelberg (2004)

11. Fiat, A., Shamir, A.: How to Prove Yourself: Practical Solutions to Identification and Signature Problems. In: Odlyzko, A.M. (ed.) CRYPTO 1986. LNCS, vol. 263, pp. 186–194. Springer, Heidelberg (1986)
12. Guillou, L.C., Quisquater, J.-J.: A "Paradoxical" Indentity-Based Signature Scheme Resulting from Zero-Knowledge. In: Proc. of Advances in Cryptology - Advances in Cryptology - CRYPTO 88, 8th Annual International Cryptology Conference, pp. 216–231 (1988)
13. Itkis, G., Reyzin, L.: Forward-Secure Signatures with Optimal Signing and Verifying. In: Kilian, J. (ed.) CRYPTO 2001. LNCS, vol. 2139, pp. 332–354. Springer, Heidelberg (2001)
14. Itkis, G., Reyzin, L.: SiBIR: Signer-Base Intrusion-Resilient Signatures. In: Yung, M. (ed.) CRYPTO 2002. LNCS, vol. 2442, pp. 499–514. Springer, Heidelberg (2002)
15. Kozlov, A., Reyzin, L.: Forward-Secure Signatures with Fast Key Update. In: Cimato, S., Galdi, C., Persiano, G. (eds.) SCN 2002. LNCS, vol. 2576, pp. 241–256. Springer, Heidelberg (2003)
16. Krawczyk, H.: Simple Forward-Secure Signatures From Any Signature Scheme. In: Proc. of the 7th ACM Conference on Computer and Communication Security, CCS 2000, pp. 108–115 (2000)
17. Muñoz, J.L., Forné, J., Castro, J.C.: Evaluation of Certificate Revocation Policies: OCSP vs. Overissued-CRL. In: Hameurlain, A., Cicchetti, R., Traunmüller, R. (eds.) DEXA 2002, pp. 511–518. IEEE Computer Society, Los Alamitos (2002)
18. Ong, H., Schnorr, C.: Fast Signature Generation with a Fiat Shamir—Like Scheme. In: Damgård, I.B. (ed.) EUROCRYPT 1990. LNCS, vol. 473, pp. 432–440. Springer, Heidelberg (1991)
19. Seamons, K.E., Winslett, M., Yu, T., Yu, L., Jarvis, R.: Protecting Privacy during On-Line Trust Negotiation. In: Proceedings of the 4th Workshop on Privacy Enhancing Technologies, pp. 129–143 (2002)
20. Winsborough, W.H., Li, N.: Protecting sensitive attributes in automated trust negotiation. In: WPES 2002. Proc. of the 2002 ACM Workshop on Privacy in the Electronic Society, pp. 41–51 (2002)
21. Winsborough, W.H., Seamons, K., Jones, V.: Automated Trust Negotiation. In: DARPA Information Survivability Conference and Exposition (DISCEX 2000), 1st edn, pp. 64–73 (2000)
22. Yu, T., Winslett, M.: A Unified Scheme for Resource Protection in Automated Trust Negotiation. In: IEEE Symposium on Security and Privacy, pp. 110–122 (2003)
23. Yu, T., Winslett, M., Seamons, K.E.: Interoperable strategies in automated trust negotiation. In: Proc. of the 8th ACM Conference on Computer and Communications Security, CCS 2001, pp. 146–155 (2001)
24. Yu, T., Winslett, M., Seamons, K.E.: Supporting structured credentials and sensitive policies through interoperable strategies for automated trust negotiation. ACM Trans. Inf. Syst. Secur. 6(1), 1–42 (2003)

A Novel Method for Micro-Aggregation in Secure Statistical Databases Using Association and Interaction

B. John Oommen[1] and Ebaa Fayyoumi[2]

[1] *Chancellor's Professor*; *Fellow: IEEE* and *Fellow: IAPR*.
School of Computer Science, Carleton University, Ottawa, Canada: K1S 5B6
oommen@scs.carleton.ca
[2] School of Computer Science, Carleton University, Ottawa, Canada: K1S 5B6
efayyoum@scs.carleton.ca

Abstract. We[1] consider the problem of micro-aggregation in secure statistical databases, by enhancing the primitive Micro-Aggregation Technique (MAT), which incorporates proximity information. The state-of-the-art MAT recursively reduces the size of the data set by excluding points which are farthest from the centroid, and those which are closest to these farthest points, while it ignores the mutual Interaction between the records. In this paper, we argue that inter-record relationships can be quantified in terms of two entities, namely their "Association" and "Interaction". Based on the theoretically sound principles of the neural networks (NN), we believe that the proximity information can be quantified using the mutual Association, and their mutual Interaction can be quantified by invoking transitive-closure like operations on the latter. By repeatedly invoking the inter-record Associations and Interactions, the records are grouped into sizes of cardinality "k", where k is the security parameter in the algorithm. Our experimental results, which are done on artificial data and on the benchmark data sets for real-life data, demonstrate that the newly proposed method is superior to the state-of-the-art by as much as 13%.

Keywords: Information loss (IL), Micro-Aggregation Technique (MAT), Inter-record association, Interaction between micro-units.

1 Introduction

A lot of attention has recently been dedicated to the problem of maintaining the confidentiality of statistical databases through the application of statistical tools, so as to limit the identification of information on individuals and enterprises. Statistical Disclosure Control (SDC) seeks to balance between the confidentiality and the data utility criteria. For example, federal agencies and their contractors

---

[1] The first author is also an Adjunct Professor with the University of Agder, in Grimstad, Norway. This work was partially funded by NSERC, the Natural Sciences and Engineering Research Council of Canada.

S. Qing, H. Imai, and G. Wang (Eds.): ICICS 2007, LNCS 4861, pp. 126–140, 2007.

who release statistical tables or micro-data files are often required by law or by established policies to protect the confidentiality of released information. However, this restriction should not affect public policy decisions which are made by only accessing non-confidential summary statistics [1]. SDC can be applied to information in several formats: Tables, responses to dynamic database queries and micro-data [2,3]. The protection provided by SDC results from either generating a set of synthetic data from a model fitted to the real data, or modifying the original data in a special way [3].

Micro-aggregation is one of the most recent techniques that has been used to mask micro-individuals in view of protecting them against the re-identification in secure statistical databases [2,4,5]. Moreover, it is modeled as a clustering mechanism with group size constraints, where the primitive goal is to group a set of records into clusters of size at least k, based on a proximity measure involving the variables of interest [6,7,8,9,10].

The Micro-Aggregation Problem (MAP), as formulated in [4,5,8,9], can be stated as follows: A micro-data set $\mathcal{U} = \{U_1, U_2, \ldots, U_n\}$ is specified in terms of the n "micro-records", namely the $U_i's$, each representing a data vector whose components are d continuous variables. Each data vector can be viewed as $U_i = [u_{i1}, u_{i2}, \ldots, u_{id}]^T$, where u_{ij} specifies the value of the jth variable in the ith data vector. Micro-aggregation involves partitioning the n data vectors into m mutually exclusive and exhaustive groups so as to obtain a k-partition $\mathbb{P}_k = \{G_i \mid 1 \leq i \leq m\}$, such that each group, G_i, of size, n_i, contains either k data vectors, or between k and $2k - 1$ data vectors.

The optimal k-partition, $\mathbb{P}_k^*$, is defined to be the one that maximizes the within-group similarity, which is defined as the *Sum of Squares Error*, $SSE = \sum_{i=1}^{m} \sum_{j=1}^{n_i} (X_{ij} - \bar{X}_i)^T (X_{ij} - \bar{X}_i)$. This quantity is computed on the basis of the Euclidean distance of each data vector X_{ij} to the centroid $\bar{X}_i$ of the group to which it belongs. The *Information Loss* is measured as $IL = \frac{SSE}{SST}$, where SST is the squared error that would result if all records were included in a single group and is given $SST = \sum_{i=1}^{m} \sum_{j=1}^{n_i} (X_{ij} - \bar{X})^T (X_{ij} - \bar{X})$, where $\bar{X} = \frac{1}{n} \sum_{i=1}^{n} X_i$.

As mentioned in the literature, this problem in its multi-variate setting is known to be NP-hard [11], and has been tackled using different approaches such as hierarchical clustering [4,5], genetic algorithms [4,5,12], graph theory [8,9], fuzzy clustering [13,14] and machine learning [15]. All the heuristic Micro-aggregation Techniques ($MATs$), seek to minimize the value of the IL. However, minimizing the loss in the data utility is an important issue that is difficult to enforce, primarily because this strategy was intended to enhance the security in an SDC technique. Indeed, the definition of optimality for an SDC is defined in the literature as being equivalent to offer the best trade-off between the IL and disclosure risk [16,17]. In spite of this, the recent development of $MATs$ [18] leaves the researcher no excuse to circumvent the problem of trying to reduce the value of the IL as much as possible [19].

In general, minimizing the IL directly follows maximizing the similarity between records in each group. The state-of-art $MATs$ depend on utilizing the "Euclidean" distance, which serves as the criterion playing a central role in estimating the similarity between the records. However, this distance function does not completely capture the appropriate notion of similarity for any data set. Our position is that the notion of similarity should be measured by using a metric that also unravels the relationship between the inter-records. We believe that this can be quantified in terms of two quantities, namely the mutual "Association" between the individual records and their mutual "Interaction". We propose to measure these quantities using Association Similarity Rules[2] ($ASRs$). In this context, we mention that the concepts of Association and Interaction are derived from the Associative Cluster Neural Network ($ACNN$) [26].

The main contribution of this paper is to integrate the foundational concepts of $ASRs$ with $MATs$ so as to devise a new strategy for estimating the similarity. This new method demonstrates that the IL can be reduced taking two measurements into consideration. First of all, we consider the mutual Association between the records. Secondly, and more importantly, we also consider the mutual Interaction between the records by using a transitive-closure like operation when $k \geq 3$. This, in turn, is achieved by invoking our newly proposed Interactive-Associative Micro-Aggregation Technique ($IAMAT$). The effect of these considerations can be seen to minimize the IL by up to 13% when compared to the state-of-the-art.

The structure of this paper is as follows: In the following section 2 we start with a concise survey about the reported $MATs$. Subsequently, we summarize the Associative Cluster Neural Network algorithm. In Section 3, the Interactive-Associative Micro-Aggregation Technique is presented informally and algorithmically. Then, in Section 4, we present the results of experiments we have carried out for synthetic and real data sets. The paper finishes in Section 5 with some conclusions.

2   Micro-Aggregation

As mentioned in Section 1, the MAP has been tackled using different techniques. Basically, a MAT relies on a clustering technique and an aggregation technique. $MATs$ were originally used for numerical data [10], and they can be further classified as below.

- *Uni-variate vs. Multi-variate*
  The difference between the uni-variate and the multi-variate $MATs$ depends on the number of random variables used in the micro-aggregation process. Uni-variate $MATs$ deal with multi-variate data sets by micro-aggregating one variable at a time, such as Individual ranking [27, 28]). Multi-variate $MATs$ either rank multi-variate data by projecting them onto a single axis[3], or dealing directly with the unprojected data. Working on unprojected multi-variate data allows simultaneous micro-aggregation of several variables so

---

[2] Association Similarity Rules are well-known data mining techniques used to discover the relationships between patterns in different application domains [20,21,22,23,24,25].

[3] The multi-variate data is projected onto a single axis by using either a particular variable, the sum-z-scores or a principle component analysis prior to micro-aggregation [5].

that a single k-partition for the entire data set is obtained. Since there is no straightforward formal algorithm to sort multi-variate data without projection [4, 29, 30], many heuristic methods have been proposed such as the Maximum Distance to Average Vector ($MDAV$) [4,18], the Minimum Spanning Tree (MST) [9] and the Object Migrating Micro-aggregated Automaton ($OMMA$) [15].

– *Fixed-size vs. Data-oriented*

The difference between the fixed-size and the data-oriented $MATs$ depends on the number of records in each group. Fixed-size $MATs$ require all groups to be of size k except for a single group whose cardinality is greater than k when the total number of records, n, is not a multiple of k. The last group is used to contain more than k records [30], but as pointed out in [4], assigning the additional records to the group containing the modal value of the data, reduces the value of the IL [29]. Data-oriented $MATs$ allow groups to be of size greater than k and less than $2k - 1$ depending on the structure of the data. These methods yield more homogenous groups, which help to further minimize the IL [2, 4, 5]. Although these methods are marginally more complex than those involving fixed-size $MATs$, they are less likely to compromise the *"privacy"* of the micro-file as shown in [31]. Examples of data-oriented $MATs$ are those which use a genetic algorithm [4,5], the k-Ward MAT [4,32,5] and the Variable-size Maximum Distance to Average Vector scheme ($V - MDAV$) [33].

– *Optimal vs. Heuristic*

The first reported optimal uni-variate MAT with a polynomial complexity is given in [8], which solves the MAP as a shortest path problem on a graph. Unfortunately, the optimal MAP for multi-variate micro-aggregation is an NP-hard problem [11]. Therefore, researchers seek heuristic $MATs$ that provide a good solution - close to the optimal.

2.1   Associative Clustering Neural Network ($ACNN$)

The Associative Cluster Neural Network ($ACNN$), was proposed [26] as a recurrent NN model that dynamically evaluates the Association of any pair of patterns through the Interaction between them and the group of patterns. The $ACNN$ possesses many attractive features, such as its simple structure, its respective learning mechanism, and its efficient clustering strategy, which uses the Association as a new similarity measure. Its superiority in clustering and analyzing gene expression data has also been demonstrated [34]. The rationale behind this superiority probably lies in the inherent advantages of $ASRs$, which possess the potential to ensure that the similarities between patterns within the same cluster increase, whereas the similarities between different clusters decrease.

  The $ACNN$ initializes the Association between any two neurons by evaluating the relationship between them and by setting the learning ratio, α, to the most suitable value. The learning ratio should guarantee that the initial Association is large when the distance between the patterns is small. The $ACNN$ studies the Interaction level of each pair of patterns based on the Association made by the other patterns, and defines the similarity threshold which ensures a robust performance.

The association value between any two patterns has to be updated based on the result of the Interaction level, and this is, in turn, scaled by using the well-known sigmoidal function. This procedure has to be iteratively executed until there is no noticeable change in the successive associations. Subsequently, the $ACNN$ constructs the cluster characteristic matrix to describe the cluster property at the end of the learning phase, after which it determines the number of clusters and labels the patterns with the index of the cluster that they belong to. We refer the interested reader to [26] for a complete explanation of this clustering strategy.

3   Interactive-Associative Micro-Aggregation Technique ($IAMAT$)

The state-of-the-art $MATs$ use a proximity function, and in particular, the Euclidean distance, to measure the similarity between records. To the best of our knowledge, the combination of the Association *and* the Interaction between individual records has not been taken into consideration while micro-aggregating the data file. We now discuss how these two criteria are applicable to micro-aggregate the data file so as to further minimize the IL.

3.1   Inadequacy of Using the $ACNN$ Directly

Although the basic $ACNN$ dynamically evaluates the Association and the Interaction between the patterns, it is not directly applicable to the MAP in its virgin form for the following reasons:

- **Feature Values**
  In a neural setting, the weights of the neurons are updated based on the relative relationship between them. These weights are usually updated by gradient-like considerations, so that a change in the weights leads to a better classifications. Consequently, in the $ACNN$ the weights could be both positive or negative, quite simply because increasing the values of certain features may have a negative impact on the optimization problem.
  As opposed to this, it is meaningless to have weights that are negative in the MAP. This is because the fundamental reason for tackling the problem is to determine how the records are associated with each other, and clearly, the concept of the records being negatively associated is irrelevant. Thus, if we are to use the principles of the $ACNN$ to solve the MAP, it is imperative that the weights are never allowed to become negative. Rather, we would prefer that they stay within the interval $[0, 1]$.
- **Ineffectiveness of Sigmoidal Mappings**
  When Minsky suggested the weakness of the Perceptron, he showed that it was incapable of resolving the basic XOR problem. However, the field of NNs received a huge "boost" when it was discovered that if these primitive neural units were cascaded and interconnected, the discriminant could be arbitrarily complex. To effectively model the switching and clipping effects in such complex domains, researchers introduced functions such as the

sigmoidal function whose purpose was to transform the input space using highly non-linear mappings.

It is our position that such switching and clipping effects are not pertinent to the study of the MAP. The reason for this is: The Associations and the Interactions between the records are, in one sense, related to their relative proximity, and we have no reason to believe that these quantities fall off or change *abruptly*. Rather, our experience is that these quantities vary smoothly with the relative proximity of the records.

– **Transitive-Closure-like Properties**
Obtaining the set of shortest paths on a graph can be achieved by using a transitive-closure algorithm that traverses all the edges of the graph. In this case, the shortest paths are obtained by using the operation of "Addition" on the weights of the edges along any given path, and invoking the "Minimum" operation over all the possible paths. However, the underlying algorithm has been proven to be more powerful if it is mapped using the properties of a semi-ring $(S, \oplus, \otimes)$, where (i) S is the set of weights associated with an edge, (ii) $\oplus$ represents an abstract "Addition" operation over the elements of S, and (iii) $\otimes$ represents an abstract "Multiplication" operation over the elements of S. In particular, if S is the set of reals, and $\oplus$ and $\otimes$ represent the arithmetic addition and product operations respectively, the transitive-closure algorithm would lead to a matrix multiplication scheme, which is central in determining the multi-step Markov matrix for a Markov chain.

The basic $ACNN$ computes the Interaction between the neurons using the product involving a_{ip} and a_{pj}. The total two-step Interaction is thus, effectively, the contribution of the transitive-closure operation of the path from X_i to X_j via all the possible intermediate nodes, X_p. In our case, the issue of interest is *not* the total Interaction between the relevant nodes, but rather the node X^* which contributes to the maximal Interaction between X_i and X_j. Thus, unlike the $ACNN$, in our solution, we do not compute the sum of all the Interactions between the nodes. Rather, we report the one which is maximally interacting with the nodes already in the same cluster, say X_i and X_j. This is a fundamental difference between our present scheme and the $ACNN$, because it renders the computations both easier and faster, and is yet able to coalesce the nodes based on the inferred interactions.

– **One-shot Training**
The final difference between our present scheme and the $ACNN$ is the fact that we have resorted to a one-shot "training" mechanism. This is *atypical* for most NNs. Indeed, most NNs repeatedly run the NN over the data set till their respective weights converge. Some families of NNs (for example, the Adachi's network [35]) have been reported, which actually yield the final weights using a single pass over the data set.

In our case, we argue that repeatedly running the updating algorithm over the data set is superfluous. Rather, by initially computing the Associations, we are able to arrive at the best Interactions. The $ACNN$ requires that the set of associations are then re-computed. But, since these associations are computed based on the relative proximities of the records, and since the Interactions are computed based on the latter, it is meaningless, in the case of the MAP, to re-compute the Associations. Indeed, if we resorted to doing this, it would lead to weights that are negative and which again, as argued above, is unacceptable. It would also lead to the "rejection" of many records- which is inappropriate for the MAP. Thus, in the $IAMAT$, the corresponding matrices are computed in a one-shot manner. Subsequent computations are required only after the learned groups of size k are removed in each learning cycle.

Based on the above principles, we now present the design of our newly-proposed scheme, the Interactive-Associative Micro-Aggregation Technique ($IAMAT$).

3.2   Design of the $IAMAT$

We propose $IAMAT$ to micro-aggregate the records in the data set by using a new methodology to evaluate the similarity between them. This similarity is intuitively expressed by their inter-record relationships, and is estimated by measuring the "Association" and "Interaction" as *modeled* in the $ACNN$. The resulting measurements are similar to the ones that cluster the records based on the distance between them. Consequently, instead of merely assigning relatively "close" records to be in the same group, we choose to "estimate" the Association *and* the Interaction between them, and if the combination of these indexes is relatively high, we assign them to be in the same group. Otherwise, we determine that they should be in two different groups. We believe that using this pair of measurements will help to achieve a more robust performance than other existing measures, which is a claim that we have verified. From a top level, we can describe it as below.

The $IAMAT$ is a consequence of incorporating the above considerations into the elegant $MDAV$ strategy. Consider the $IAMAT$ for any specific value of k. The $IAMAT$ uses the centroid of the data set to relatively determine the farthest record, say X_r. Subsequently, we achieve a quick search to obtain the record that is most associated to X_r, say X_s. After this, we propose to choose $k-2$ records based on the mutual *Interaction* between each record inside the group and the remaining unassigned records. Consequently, the next step consists of creating a cluster that comprises the associated pair $\langle X_r, X_s \rangle$ and the most interactive $k-2$ records. At the end of this stage, the cluster is micro-aggregated and removed from the original data set. The above steps are iteratively repeated until no more that $k-1$ records remain in the original data set. The $IAMAT$ terminates by assigning the remaining unassigned records to the last group. The scheme is algorithmically described below in Algorithm 1, after which each step is explained in greater detail.

Unlike the $MDAV$, instead of measuring the distance between the records, the $IAMAT$ utilizes the Association as per the $ACNN$. The $ACNN$ classifies the records as being associated if the value of the association index, a_{ij}, is positive. Otherwise the neurons will be classified as being unrelated, leading to its "rejection". Clearly, rejecting records will not comply with the spirit and goal of the MAP whose aim is to minimize the IL. We believe that an Association

Algorithm 1. Interactive-Associative Micro-Aggregation Technique ($IAMAT$)

Input: The original micro-data file, $\mathcal{D}$, that contians n unassigned records, and the parameter, k.

Output: The micro-aggregated micro-data file, $\mathcal{D}'$.

Method:

1: Compute the centroid of $\mathcal{D}$ as $\mu = \frac{1}{n}\sum_{i=1}^{n} X_i$.

2: Compute the scaling factor α as related to the mean square distance as $\alpha = \frac{\sqrt{n}}{\frac{1}{n}(\sum_{i=1}^{n}||X_i - \mu||^2)}$.

3: Compute the association values between μ and each record, X_i, in $\mathcal{D}$ as $a_{\mu i} = e^{-\frac{||X_i - \mu||^2}{\alpha}}$.

4: Initialize the number of groups to zero.

5: **while** there are more than $(k-1)$ *Unassigned* records in $\mathcal{D}$ **do**

6:     Increment the number of groups by unity.

7:     Initialize the number of records inside the group to zero.

8:     Select the least associated *Unassigned* record, X_r, to the centroid μ as follows $X_r = Min \ a_{\mu i}$.

9:     Mark X_r as *Assigned* record.

10:     Compute the association values between X_r and each *Unassigned* record, X_i, in $\mathcal{D}$.

11:     Select the most associated *Unassigned* record, X_s, to X_r as follows $X_s = Max \ a_{ri}$.

12:     Mark X_s as an *Assigned* record.

13:     Compute the association values between X_s and each *Unassigned* record, X_i, in $\mathcal{D}$.

14:     Add X_r and X_s to the group and increment the number of records inside the group by two units.

15:     **while** the number of records inside the group is less than k **do**

16:         **for all** *Unassigned* records, X_p, in $\mathcal{D}$ **do**

17:             Initialize the Interaction of X_p, η_p, to 1.

18:             **for all** *Assigned* records inside the group, X_i **do**

19:                 Update the value of Interaction as follows $\eta_p = \eta_p * a_{ip}$.

20:             **end for**

21:         **end for**

22:         Let X^* be the record which has the highest value for η_p.

23:         Mark X^* as an *Assigned* record.

24:         Add X^* into this group and increment the number of records inside the group by unity.

25:         Compute the association values between the most interactive record, X^* and each *Unassigned* record, X_i, in $\mathcal{D}$.

26:     **end while**

27:     Remove the present cluster from the set $\mathcal{D}$.

28: **end while**

29: Assign the remaining *Unassigned* records to the last group.

30: Build the micro-aggregated data file, $\mathcal{D}'$.

31: **return** $\mathcal{D}'$.

32: **End Algorithm** Interactive-Associative Micro-Aggregation Technique ($IAMAT$)

between any pair of records exists regardless of its value, and this could be very small when it is close to zero, or very large when is close to unity. Therefore, the $IAMAT$ quantifies the value of the Association between two records, say X_i and X_j, to belong to the interval $[0, 1]$, and this is computed as follows:

$$a_{ij} = a_{ji} = r(X_i, X_j) = e^{-\frac{||X_i - X_j||^2}{\alpha}}.$$

where $r()$ is the identical function used in the definition of the $ACNN$, which evaluates the relationship between any two records, and which also involves α. The value of α is assigned so as to guarantee that the initial Association is large when the distance between X_i and X_j is small and vice versa. It is given as:

$$\alpha = \frac{\sqrt{n}}{\frac{1}{n}(\sum_{i=1}^{n} ||X_i - \frac{1}{n}(\sum_{i=1}^{n} X_i)||^2)}.$$

The rationale for incorporating the Association with the Interaction between the records inside a group, is that it leads to more homogeneous groups. The concept of the *Interaction* turns out to be crucial in forming the cluster, because we believe that merely being close to the farthest records is not a reason that is sufficiently important for any record to be grouped with the most distant one. Rather, we propose that the Interaction with respect to all the records inside the group has to be taken into consideration while clustering the records. As mentioned earlier, the latter is computed by invoking transitive-closure like operations. Finding the most interactive record with the associated pair is achieved by searching for the maximum product of the Association between the unassigned records, say X_p, and each record in the associated pair, $\langle X_i, X_j \rangle$, as follows:

$$\eta_{ij} = \begin{cases} a_{ip}(t-1) \times a_{pj}(t-1) & p \neq i, j \text{ and } i \neq j \\ 0 & i = j. \end{cases}$$

The equation above is valid when $k = 3$. By increasing the value of k, the transitive-closure is applied by adding one unassigned record at a time. The decision of grouping the unassigned record with other records in the group depends on the Interaction of that record with respect to other records inside the group. Logically, the most interactive unassigned record has been chosen as follows:

$$Index\ Maximum_{1 \leq p \leq n}\ \eta_p,$$

where η is computed as follows:

$$\eta_p = \prod_{i=1}^{n_i} a_{ip}$$

where X_i represents the record inside the group, G_j, of size n_j and X_p represents the unassigned record.

4   Experimental Result

4.1   Data Sets

The $IAMAT$ has been rigorously tested and the results obtained seem to be very good, where the "goodness" of a scheme refers to the combination of its being efficiently computed, and its leading to a minimum value for the IL. We have tested it using the two real-life benchmark reference data sets used in previous studies: (i) The *Tarragona* data set which contains 834 records with 13 variables [4]. (ii) The *Census* data set which contains 1080 records with 13 variables [36].

To further investigate the performance of the new scheme, many experiments have been carried out using various simulated data sets involving vectors with dimensions ranging from 10 up to 80, and sets of cardinality from 10,000 up to 100,000. The simulated multi-variate data sets were generated using *Matlab's* built-in-functions: (i) Uniform distribution (min=0; max=1000). (ii) Normal distribution (μ=0;σ=0.05).

The experiments were also used to investigate the scalability of the $IAMAT$ with respect to the size of the data, its dimensionality, and the group size.

4.2   Results

For a given value of the security parameter k, which represents the minimum number of records per group, we compared the percentage value of the $IL = (SSE/SST)$ times 100 (as defined in Section 1) resulting from the $IAMAT$ and the $MDAV$ strategies. It is important to mention that the $MDAV$ was implemented based on the centroid concept and not a diameter concept.[4] All the programs were written in the $C++$ language, and the tests were performed on an Intel(R) Pentium (R)M. Processor 1.73 GHz., with 512 MB of RAM.

Table 1 shows the improvement of the solution obtained by using the $IAMAT$ as opposed to the $MDAV$ on the multi-variate real data sets, where all the 13 variables are used simultaneously during the micro-aggregation process. The reduction in the value of the IL attains up to 8% on the Tarragona data set, and 5.12% on the Census data set when the group size is equal to 3. It is clearly evident that the impact of the group size on the solution is minimized by increasing the number of records per group. To be fair, we also mention that computational time required to execute the $IAMAT$ is almost double the computational time required for the $MDAV$, although, in every case, the time was less than 0.5 second. In term of comparison, we believe that minimizing the loss in the data utility is more important than minimizing the extremely small computational time, especially because the micro-aggregation is usually performed off-line where the additional time requirement is less crucial. However, the question of how the decrease of IL is related to the increase in the computational time is still open.

We undertook a comprehensive evaluation of the performance of the $IAMAT$ scheme so as to investigate the it scalability with respect to the size of the data set, its dimensionality and the group size as shown in Table 2 in Appendix A.

- **The scalability of the $IAMAT$ with respect to the data set size**
  We tested both the $IAMAT$ and the $MDAV$ schemes using data based on the uniform and the normal distributions with cardinalities ranging from

---

[4] We did not program the $MDAV$ scheme. We are extremely thankful to Dr.Francesc Sebé for giving us his source code.

Table 1. Comparison of the percentage of the IL and the computational time between the $MDAV$ and the $IAMAT$ on the Tarragona and Census data sets

Data Set	k value	$MDAV$		$IAMAT$		Improv. (%)
		IL	Time	IL	Time	
	3	16.9593	0.17	15.6023	0.31	8.00
Tarragona	4	19.7482	0.12	19.2872	0.22	2.33
	5	22.8850	0.12	22.7164	0.23	0.74
	3	5.6535	0.22	5.3639	0.41	5.12
	4	7.4414	0.19	7.2170	0.44	3.02
Census	5	8.8840	0.17	8.8428	0.42	0.46
	6	10.1941	0.17	9.9871	0.42	2.03

10,000 records up to 100,000 with 10 variables. The percentage of the improvement achieved by invoking the $IAMAT$ in the IL, (when $k = 4$) reached as high as 13.73% for the normal distribution and 13.67% for the uniform distribution. It is fair to state that the $IAMAT$ requires almost triple the computational time needed to execute the $MDAV$ scheme. In general, increasing the size of the data set tends to minimize the IL value.

- **The scalability of the $IAMAT$ with respect to dimensionality**
  We also tested the $IAMAT$ and the $MDAV$ on the uniform and the normal distributions for various dimensions ranging from 10 to 80, when the data size was set to 10,000 records, and the value of k was set to 3. The highest percentage of the improvement in the IL was about 10% for both the uniform and normal distributions. The computational time required to micro-aggregate all the individual records was directly proportional to the dimensionality in both schemes, and the required computational time in the $IAMAT$ was almost double the required time for the $MDAV$. As expected, increasing the dimensionality implies increasing the IL. This is intuitively appealing because increasing the dimensionality tends to minimize the similarity between the individual records and, at the same time, reduce the Association and the Interaction between the different multi-variate records.

- **The scalability of the $IAMAT$ with respect to the group size**
  The scalability of the $IAMAT$ and the $MDAV$ with regard to the group size was studied for both the uniform and the normal distributions, where the group size ranged from 3 to 10, and for the cardinality of the data set being 10,000 records, with a dimensionality of 10 variables. The percentage of improvement in reducing the value of the IL. This reduction reached 12.74% for the normal distribution when the group size was 5, and reached 12.31% for the uniform distribution when the group size was 4. This is, again, a fair observation, because having many records in the group tends to minimize the within-group similarity, and to simultaneously maximize the similarity between the groups. This also tends to increase the IL value.

5   Conclusions

In this paper, we have considered the problem of achieving micro-aggregation in secure statistical databases. The novelty of our method involves enhancing the primitive MAT that merely incorporates proximity information. The state-of-the-art MAT recursively reduced the size of the data set by excluding points which were farthest from the centroid and those which were closest to these farthest points. Thus, although the state-of-the-art method was extremely effective, we have argued that it uses only the proximity information, and ignores the mutual Interaction between the records. In this paper, we have proved that inter-record relationships can be quantified in terms of two entities, namely their "Association" and "Interaction" that can be measured by invoking transitive-closure like operations, and by mapping the problem into a neural setting using the $ACNN$. By repeatedly invoking the inter-record Associations and Interactions, we have shown that the records can be grouped into sizes of cardinality "k". Our experimental results, which were done on artificial data and on the benchmark data sets for real life data, demonstrate that the newly proposed method is superior to the state-of-the-art by as much as 13%. Thus, we believe that our strategy leads to a very promising tool for solving the MAP.

We foresee two avenues for future work. The first avenue is to extend the $IAMAT$ towards data-oriented micro-aggregation, where the group size, n_i, satisfies $k \leq n_i < 2k$. The second involves investigating the effect of having a dynamic α^5 on the compactness of each group and on the value of the IL.

Acknowledgements

The authors would like to thank Dr. Josep Domingo-Ferrer for all his support and advice, and for providing us with the data sets. We are also thankful to him, Dr. Josep Mateo-Sanz, and Dr. Francesc Sebé for answering our queries, and for providing the code for the $MDAV$ scheme. Without their help, we would not have been able to produce these results.

References

1. Adam, N., Wortmann, J.: Security-Control Methods for Statistical Databases: A Comparative Study. ACM Computing Surveys 21(4), 515–556 (1989)
2. Cuppen, M.: Secure Data Perturbation in Statistical Disclosure Control. PhD thesis, Statistics Netherlands (2000)
3. Willenborg, L., Waal, T.: Elements of Statistical Disclosure Control (ILL Number: 2132712). Springer, Heidelberg (2001)

---

[5] We believe that we can compute the dynamic value of α in any iteration based on the remaining *Unassigned* records at the end of every iteration in the clustering phase. As opposed to this the fixed value is computed once before invoking the clustering phase, and is based on the entire data set.

4. Domingo-Ferrer, J., Mateo-Sanz, J.: Practical Data-Oriented Microaggregation for Statistical Disclosure Control. IEEE Transactions on Knowledge and Data Engineering 14(1), 189–201 (2002)
5. Mateo-Sanz, J., Domingo-Ferrer, J.: A Method for Data-Oriented Multivariate Microaggregation. In: Proceedings of Statistical Data Protection98, Luxembourg: Office for Official Publications of the European Communities, pp. 89–99 (1999)
6. Domingo-Ferrer, J.: Statistical Disclosure Control in Catalonia and the CRISES Group. Technical report (1999)
7. Domingo-Ferrer, J., Torra, V.: Aggregation Techniques for Statistical confidentiality. In: Aggregation operators: new trends and applications, Germany: Heidelberg, Physica-Verlag GmbH, pp. 260–271 (2002)
8. Hansen, S., Mukherjee, S.: A Polynomial Algorithm for Univariate Optimal Microaggregation. IEEE Transactions on Knowledge and Data Engineering 15(4), 1043–1044 (2003)
9. Laszlo, M., Mukherjee, S.: Minimum Spanning Tree Partitioning Algorithm for Microaggregation. IEEE Transactions on Knowledge and Data Engineering 17(7), 902–911 (2005)
10. Torra, V.: Microaggregation for Categorical Variables: A Median Based Approach. In: Domingo-Ferrer, J., Torra, V. (eds.) PSD 2004. LNCS, vol. 3050, pp. 162–174. Springer, Heidelberg (2004)
11. Oganian, A., Domingo-Ferrer, J.: On The Complexity of Optimal Microaggregation for Statistical Disclosure Control. Statistical Journal of the United Nations Economic Comission for Europe 18(4), 345–354 (2001)
12. Solanas, A., Martinez-Balleste, A., Mateo-Sanz, J., Domingo-Ferrer, J.: Multivariate Microaggregation Based Genetic Algorithms. In: 3rd International IEEE Conference on Intelligent Systems, pp. 65–70 (2006)
13. Domingo-Ferrer, J., Torra, V.: Fuzzy Microaggregation for Microdata Protection. Journal of Advanced Computational Intelligence and Intelligent Informatics (JACIII) 7(2), 153–159 (2003)
14. Torra, V., Domingo-Ferrer, J.: Towards Fuzzy C-Means Based Microaggregation. In: Grzegorzewski, P., Hryniewicz, O., Gil, M. (eds.) Advances in Soft Computing: Soft Methods in Probability, Statistics and Data Analysis, Germany: Heidelberg, Physica-Verlag, pp. 289–294 (2002)
15. Fayyoumi, E., Oommen, B.: A Fixed Structure Learning Automaton Micro-Aggregation Technique for Secure Statistical Databases. In: Privacy Statistical Databases, Italy: Rome, pp. 114–128 (2006)
16. Crises, G.: Trading off Information Loss and Disclosure Risk in Database Privacy Protection. Technical report (2004)
17. Mateo-Sanz, J., Domingo-Ferrer, J., Sebé, F.: Probabilistic Information Loss Measures in Confidentiality Protection of Continuous Microdata. Data Mining and Knowledge Discovery 11(2), 181–193 (2005)
18. Domingo-Ferrer, J., Torra, V.: Ordinal, Continuous and Heterogeneous k-Anonymity Through Microaggregation. Data Mining and Knowledge Discovery 11(2), 195–212 (2005)
19. Domingo-Ferrer, J., Sebé, F.: Optimal multivariate 2-microaggregation for microdata protection: a 2-approximation. In: Privacy Statistical Databases, Italy: Rome, pp. 129–138 (2006)
20. Agrawal, R., Imielinski, T., Swami, A.: Mining Association Rules Between Sets of Items in Large Databases. In: Proceedings of ACM SIGMOD, USA: Washington DC, pp. 207–216 (1993)

21. Agrawal, R., Mannila, H., Srikant, H., Toivonen, R., Verkamo, I.: Fast Discovery of Association Rules. In: Advances in Knowledge Discovery and Data Mining, pp. 307–328 (1996)
22. Bacao, F., Lobo, V., Painho, M.: Self-organizing Maps as Substitutes for K-Means Clustering. In: International Conference on Computational Science, pp. 476–483 (2005)
23. Feng, L., Dillon, T., Weigana, H., Chang, E.: An XML-Enabled Association Rule Framework. In: Mařík, V., Štěpánková, O., Retschitzegger, W. (eds.) DEXA 2003. LNCS, vol. 2736, pp. 88–97. Springer, Heidelberg (2003)
24. Markey, M., Lo, J., Tourassi, G.: Self-Organizing Map for Cluster Analysis of A Breast Cancer Database. Artificial Intelligence in Medicine 27, 113–127 (2003)
25. Park, J., Chen, S., Yu, P.: Using A Hash-Based Method with Transaction Trimming for Mining Association Rules. IEEE Transactions on Knowledge and Data Engineering 9, 813–826 (1997)
26. Yao, Y., Chen, L., Chen, Y.: Associative Clustering for Clusters of Arbitrary Distribution Shapes. Neural Processing Letters 14, 169–177 (2001)
27. Defays, D., Anwar, M.: Masking Micro-data Using Micro-Aggregation. Journal of Official Statistics 14(4), 449–461 (1998)
28. Defays, D., Anwar, N.: Micro-Aggregation: A Generic Method. In: Proceedings of the 2nd International Symposium on Statistical Confidentiality, Luxembourg: Office for Official Publications of the European Communities, pp. 69–78 (1995)
29. Domingo-Ferrer, J., Mateo-Sanz, J., Oganian, A., Torra, V., Torres, A.: On The Security of Microaggregation with Individual Ranking: Analytical Attacks. International Journal of Uncertainty, Fuzziness and Knowledge-Based Systems 10(5), 477–491 (2002)
30. Mas, M.: Statistical Data Protection Techniques. Technical report, Eustat: Euskal Estatistika Erakundea,Instituto Vasco De Estadistica (2006)
31. Li, Y., Zhu, S., Wang, L., Jajodia, S.: A privacy-enhanced microaggregation method. In: Eiter, T., Schewe, K.-D. (eds.) FoIKS 2002. LNCS, vol. 2284, pp. 148–159. Springer, Heidelberg (2002)
32. Fayyoumi, E., Oommen, B.: On Optimizing the k-Ward Micro-Aggregation Technique for Secure Statistical Databases. In: 11th Austratasian Conference on Information Security and Privacy Proceeding, Australia: Melbourne, pp. 324–335 (2006)
33. Solanas, A., Martínez-Ballesté, A.: V-MDAV: A Multivariate Microaggregation With Variable Group Size. In: 17th COMPSTAT Symposium of the IASC, Rome (2006)
34. Yao, Y., Chen, L., Goh, A., Wong, A.: Clustering Gene Data via Associative Clustering Neural Network. The 9th International Conference on Neural Information Processing (ICONIP 2002) 5, 2228–2232 (2002)
35. Adachi, M., Aihara, K.: Associative Dynamics in a Chaotic Neural Network. Neural Networks 10(1), 83–98 (1997)
36. Domingo-Ferrer, J., Torra, V.: A Quantitative Comparison of Disclosure Control Methods for Microdata. In: Doyle, P., Lane, J., Theeuwes, J., Zayatz, L. (eds.) Confidentiality, Disclosure and Data Access: Theory and Practical Applications for Statistical Agencies, Amesterdam: North-Holland, Berlin, pp. 113–134. Springer, Heidelberg (2002)

Appendix A

Table 2. Comparison of the percentage of the IL and the computation time between the $MDAV$ and the $IAMAT$ on simulated data. The results demonstrate the scalability of the $IAMAT$ with respect to the size of the data set, dimensionality and the group size.

Investigate scalability with respect to the size of the data set									
	Normal Distribution					Uniform Distribution			
Data	$MDAV$		$IAMAT$		improv.	$MDAV$		$IAMAT$		improv.
size	IL	Time	IL	Time	(%)	IL	Time	IL	Time	(%)
10	13.9376	12.05	12.2106	29.37	12.39	13.9202	12.24	12.2069	29.96	12.31
20	11.9354	48.90	10.3653	120.37	13.15	11.9617	63.15	10.4275	145.09	12.83
30	10.8849	111.84	9.4488	277.20	13.19	10.9228	143.17	9.4976	328.02	13.05
40	10.2238	200.42	8.8732	494.94	13.21	10.2733	222.74	8.9063	526.37	13.31
50	9.7234	315.04	8.4382	773.92	13.22	9.7694	389.45	8.4574	903.39	13.43
60	9.3513	457.50	8.1119	1,115.69	13.25	9.3707	644.32	8.1338	1386.01	13.20
70	9.0358	623.89	7.8243	1,520.94	13.41	9.0776	629.73	7.8523	1500.12	13.50
80	8.7898	809.397	7.6063	1,981.06	13.46	8.8183	1002.77	7.6247	1959.25	13.54
90	8.5584	1,044.77	7.4010	2,505.86	13.52	8.5885	1252.61	7.4140	2485.42	13.68
100	8.3799	1,512.68	7.2293	3,413.98	13.73	8.3933	1656.90	7.2456	3546.72	13.67

Investigate scalability with respect to the dimensionality of the data set									
Number	Normal Distribution					Uniform Distribution			
of	$MDAV$		$IAMAT$		improv.	$MDAV$		$IAMAT$		improv.
variables	IL	Time	IL	Time	(%)	IL	Time	IL	Time	(%)
10	10.5383	13.53	9.4821	30.14	10.02	10.5437	13.75	9.4400	33.87	10.47
20	24.3766	24.30	22.3577	41.26	8.28	24.4692	25.03	22.2454	46.40	9.09
30	32.6044	35.50	29.9938	69.79	8.01	32.5113	36.67	29.9711	60.00	7.81
40	37.5679	47.00	34.8732	64.98	7.17	37.4627	47.18	34.8052	72.68	7.09
50	40.8705	40.87	38.2173	67.87	6.49	40.8427	58.78	38.2470	85.98	6.36
60	43.3104	70.01	40.7761	89.88	5.85	43.3912	69.48	40.8478	98.81	5.86
70	45.3212	82.78	42.7483	104.6	5.68	45.3778	81.45	42.8263	112.48	5.62
80	46.8119	93.78	44.3459	113.17	5.27	46.8533	97.10	44.4367	132.42	5.16

Investigate scalability with respect to the group size									
	Normal Distribution					Uniform Distribution			
k	$MDAV$		$IAMAT$		improv.	$MDAV$		$IAMAT$		improv.
value	IL	Time	IL	Time	(%)	IL	Time	IL	Time	(%)
3	10.5383	13.53	9.4821	32.96	10.02	10.5437	13.75	9.4400	33.87	10.47
4	13.9376	11.93	12.2106	28.79	12.39	13.9202	12.24	12.2069	29.96	12.31
5	16.5221	11.17	14.4167	26.67	12.74	16.4020	11.45	14.4091	29.32	12.15
6	18.7797	10.68	16.4650	26.86	12.33	18.5484	10.96	16.4152	28.78	11.50
7	20.3782	10.32	18.0344	25.48	11.50	20.2887	10.56	18.0431	28.28	11.07
8	21.6869	10.12	19.1562	26.67	11.67	21.5464	10.31	19.1668	26.32	11.04
9	22.8931	9.87	20.4255	24.92	10.78	22.7587	10.07	20.3952	26.02	10.39
10	23.8439	9.07	21.4969	26.06	9.84	23.6922	9.92	21.4520	25.92	9.46

Privacy Protection on Multiple Sensitive Attributes

Zhen Li and Xiaojun Ye

Key Laboratory for Information System Security, Ministry of Education
School of Software, Tsinghua University, 100084 Beijing, China
li-zhen05@mails.tsinghua.edu.cn, yexj@tsinghua.edu.cn

Abstract. In recent years, a privacy model called *k-anonymity* has gained popularity in the microdata releasing. As the microdata may contain multiple sensitive attributes about an individual, the protection of multiple sensitive attributes has become an important problem. Different from the existing models of single sensitive attribute, extra associations among multiple sensitive attributes should be invested. Two kinds of disclosure scenarios may happen because of *logical associations*. The *Q&S Diversity* is checked to prevent the foregoing disclosure risks, with an *α Requirement* definition used to ensure the diversity requirement. At last, a two-step greedy generalization algorithm is used to carry out the multiple sensitive attributes processing which deal with quasi-identifiers and sensitive attributes respectively. We reduce the overall distortion by the measure of *Masking SA*.

1 Introduction

In this information growing society, there has been a tremendous growth in the amount of personal data that will be collected and analyzed. In many scenarios, access to large amounts of personal data is essential for accurate inferences to be drawn. As a original form of information, microdata is a valuable source of data for the allocation of public funds, medical research, and trend analysis. For example, a hospital may release patient's diagnosis records so that researchers can analyze the characteristics of various diseases or use them to produce various statistical reports. The data providers must be careful when providing outside users access to such data, because they have obligations towards the individuals to which the data refer to make sure that it is (almost) impossible for a user to use the data to disclose confidential information about these individuals[11,14]. In order to use personal data without disclose confidential information, efficient anonymization techniques should be adopted. First, some uniquely identifying attributes like *names* and *social security numbers* are removed from the table. However, sets of other attributes (like *age*, *gender*, and *zipcode*) can be linked with external data to uniquely identify individuals. These attributes are called *quasi-identifier*[1]. To prevent linking attacks using quasi-identifiers, Samarati and Sweeney proposed a model of privacy called *k-anonymity*[9]. A release of microdata is said to adhere to *k*-anonymity if each

S. Qing, H. Imai, and G. Wang (Eds.): ICICS 2007, LNCS 4861, pp. 141–152, 2007.

record in the released dataset has at least $(k$-$1)$ other records with respect to the set of quasi-identifier attributes[2,7,12]. However, the k-anonymity model has drawbacks itself, because lack of diversity in sensitive attributes and adversaries' background knowledge may lead to additional disclosure risks. Two improved k-anonymity model *l-diversity*[8] and *(α, k)-anonymity*[16] are proposed to solve this problem. However, both models only focus on dealing with microdata with single sensitive attribute (single-SA). When there comes the situation that attackers can do some inference disclosures based on multiple sensitive attributes, data providers should consider all the possible conditions that may happen before releasing the microdata with multiple sensitive attributes (multi-SA).

The existing methods concerning about multi-SA microdata publishing are discussed on[8]. The idea is described as follows: Suppose S and V are two sensitive attributes of one microdata set. Only if we treated S as part of the quasi-identifier when checking for diversity in V (and vice versa), we can ensure the diversity principle held for the entire dataset. Effectively protect the privacy of microdata with multi-SA, and at the same time with considerable utilities of the data. This is the original intention of this paper. The main contributions of this paper include:

(1) We set out by analyzing the problems of multiple sensitive publishing and the disclosure scenarios which may happen because of *logical associations* existing between multiple sensitive attributes. Then a *Q&S Diversity* requirement is proposed to prevent attacks in the foregoing disclosure scenarios. And finally, an α *Requirement* definition is given to ensure the diversity requirement.

(2) We propose an effective multiple sensitive attributes processing framework integrating different generalization algorithms on quasi-identifiers and sensitive attributes respectively. In order to evaluate the performance of our framework, the corresponding information loss metrics are subsequently defined. And we experimentally show the effectness of overall distortion reduction based on our proposed measure implemented in the framework.

The rest of the paper is organized as follows. We start by discussing related work (Section 2). Section 3 analyzes the problems existing in the multiple sensitive attributes publishing, and takes measures to prevent the disclosure risk caused by logical associations. Section 4 explains the whole generalization framework for the multiple sensitive attributes processing. Section 5 experimentally evaluates the effectiveness of our solutions, and we conclude finally in Section 6 our future work.

2   Related Work

At present, many k-anonymity models have been proposed in the literature to prevent re-identification risks caused by external information linking with quasi-identifiers [3,6]. However, these k-anonymity models have drawbacks themselves, because they do not consider problems existing in the diversity of sensitive attributes. Two improved k-anonymity model *l-diversity*[8] and $(α,k)$-anonymity[16] are proposed to solve this problem. The parameter l should be "well-represented". We should ensure the l-diversity requirement on sensitive attribute at the same time with k-anonymity requirement on quasi-identifiers. A more practical approach is not to consider every value in the sensitive attribute as sensitive. If we only have a small number of sensitive vales, a reasonable protection is that the inference confidence from a group of k-anonymous records to a sensitive value is below a threshold. This is the basic idea of the (α,k)-anonymity model. Most of the existing k-anonymity methods focus only on dealing with single sensitive attribute. However, as inference disclosure may be deduced on multiple attributes, the multiple sensitive attributes privacy protection should be supported in k-anonymity. This is the motivation of this work.

3   Multiple Sensitive Attributes

3.1   Basic Definitions

Definition 1(Equivalence Class). *Let T be a dataset with quasi-identifier attributes $Q_1, \dots, Q_d$. An equivalence class for T is the set of all tuples in T containing identical values $(q_1, \dots, q_d)$ for the quasi-identifiers.*

Definition 2(K-Anonymity Property). *T is said to satisfy the k-anonymity property with respect to the quasi-identifiers if each tuple $(q_1, \dots, q_d)$ on $Q_1, \dots, Q_d$ occurs at least k times.*

To prevent the re-identification risk, if we make sure that each record is in an *equivalence class* containing at least k members, we can guarantee that each record relates to at least k individuals even if the released records are linked to external information. This is the basic idea of k-anonymity.

Definition 3(α Requirement). *Given an equivalence class E and a value s in the domain of sensitive attribute S from dataset T. Let (E, s) be the set of tuples in equivalence class E containing s for S and α be a user-specified threshold, where $0<\alpha<1$. T satisfies α Requirement if for each sensitive value s in S, the relative frequency of s in every equivalence class is less than or equal to α.*

This definition presents another way to ensure diversity of sensitive values. The basic idea is similar with[16]. If this α Requirement is satisfied, we would have at least $1/\alpha$ diversity ensured, because if each frequency of s does not exceed the threshold $1/\alpha$, there will be at least $1/\alpha$ different values in an *equivalence class*. Beacause frequency of s in every *equivalence class* is less than or equal to α, by setting α,individuals can control the frequency of s. This is heavily needed beacause if one sensitive value s appears too frequently, intruders may disclose s with high confidence.

3.2   Disclosure Risks on Multi-SA

If the microdata is treated only as one sensitive attribute, we just need to consider this attribute's diversity in each *equivalence class*. This is called single diversity

(SD). But for the microdata with multi-SA consideration, associations among sensitive attributes should also be considered. Because these associations can lead to additional disclosure scenarios. Most of the time, one sensitive attribute do play a part in the statistical analyzing as the identifiers of other ones. For example,*Disease* and *Household Disease* are two sensitive attributes of Medical microdata. As shown in Table1, if users want to stat. *"the probability of Disease coming from Household Disease"*, data providers have to publish multi-SA at the same time. In this situation, in addition to satisfy the requirement of single sensitive attribute disclosure controlled, associations existing between multiple sensitive attributes should also be considered. Otherwise, some disclosure scenarios may happen because of these associations. There are two types of association. One can be regarded as the semantic association, the other one the logical association. The semantic association is just another say of dependency. Dependencies in the microdata can be of a logical nature or of a statistical nature[13]. Ignoring such dependencies may lead to underestimation of the disclosure risk. However, current disclosure risk measures we adopt do not take into account them which might exist between variables or records, because they might complicate the analysis considerably. A proper treatment of such data may require tailor-made models[13], which can be time-consuming and complicated. Therefore, they are not taken into account when assessing the disclosure risk or when modifying the data in an attempt to increase their safety. By now, we just come across one work which considers hiding strong associations between some attributes and sensitive classes and combines k-anonymity with association hiding. This model is called the template-based model [13]. This model is good for users who know exactly what inferences are damaging, but is not suitable for users who do not know. So it can not gain most of the popularity. Another type of association is the logical association which will be mostly considered in the following.

Definition 4(Logical Association). *Suppose $S_1, \ldots, S_m$ are m sensitive attributes of dataset T, t denoted a tuple of T. For the publishing of microdata with multi-SA, in each tuple t, the values $t.S_1, \ldots, t.S_m$ should not be disordered in order to keep statistics property. Each time a disclosure or elimination of $t.S_i$ $(1 \leq i \leq m)$ means the disclosure or elimination of the other $t.S_j (1 \leq j \leq m, i \neq j)$. This is caused by the logical association among multi-SA.*

As the above definition shows, the logical association happens because of the position corresponding, i.e. all the sensitive values of each record are in the same line and the sensitive values of each column should not be disordered in order to keep the original statistical characteristic.

If the logical association exists among multi-SA and disclosure happens on one attribute, the other ones will be disclosed correspondingly. Two kinds of disclosure risks will happen on each single attribute, *positive disclosure* and *negative disclosure*. After ensuring the single l-diversity of each sensitive attribute, intruders need to eliminate at least l-1 possible values of S in order to infer a positive disclosure. If the positive disclosure of one attribute successes, the corresponding values of other sensitive attributes will be disclosed at the same time. Another kind of disclosure is the negative disclosure. If intruders can eliminate one sensitive value with high confidence, the logical corresponding values of the other sensitive attributes can also be eliminated. If the left values in each sensitive attribute lack diversity, disclosure risk happens. This disclosure risk happens on one sensitive attribute because of negative disclosure on another attribute. For example, as Table 1 shows, *Disease* and *Household Disease* are two sensitive attributes, and consider the set of quasi-identifier attributes in the first *equivalence class*. This *equivalence class* is 3-diverse for attribute *Disease*, and also the same with attribute *Household Disease*. However, if intruders have the background knowledge that the value for *Disease* is not *Albinism*, they can make sure that the value for attribute *Household Disease* cannot be *Albinism* or *No*, and therefore must be *Asthma*. Thus we see that an equivalence class with diversity in each sensitive attribute separately in a multi-SA microdata may still violate the principle of diversity.

For multiple sensitive attributes, besides the requirement of single *l*-diversity on each attribute, additional measures should be taken in order to prevent the attacks happened by the lack of diversity between sensitive attributes.

Table 1. Medical database with sensitive attribute Disease &Household Disease

Age	Sex	Zipcode	Disease	Household Disease
[10,30]	M	[15001,20000]	Albinism	Albinism
[10,30]	M	[15001,20000]	Albinism	No
[10,30]	M	[15001,20000]	Albinism	No
[10,30]	M	[15001,20000]	Asthma	Asthma
[10,30]	M	[15001,20000]	Pneumonia	Asthma
[10,30]	M	[15001,20000]	Pneumonia	Asthma
[30,60]	F	[30000,60000]	Haemophilia	Hepatitis
[30,60]	F	[30000,60000]	Cold	No
[30,60]	F	[30000,60000]	Liver cancer	Pneumonia
[30,60]	F	[30000,60000]	Liver cancer	Hepatitis
[30,60]	F	[30000,60000]	Liver cancer	Hepatitis
[30,60]	F	[30000,60000]	Cold	No

Definition 5 (Q&S Diversity). *Let T be a dataset with non-sensitive attributes $Q_1, \ldots, Q_d$ and sensitive attributes $S_1, \ldots, S_m$. S_i is treated as the sole sensitive attribute and $Q_1, \ldots, Q_d$, $S_1, \ldots, S_{i-1}$, $S_{i+1}, \ldots, S_m$ is treated as the quasi-identifier. If the value of S_i is diverse according to $Q_1, \ldots, Q_d$, $S_1, \ldots, S_{i-1}$, $S_{i+1}, \ldots, S_m$, We say S_i is Q&S Diverse.*

Definition 6 (Multi-Diversity (MD)). *Let T be a dataset with non-sensitive attributes $Q_1, \ldots, Q_d$ and sensitive attributes $S_1, \ldots, S_m$. If for each sensitive attribute S_i ($i = 1, \ldots, m$), the Q&S Diversity is satisfied, we say T is satisfied Multi-Diversity.*

Only the released dataset which satisfies *MD* requirement can be regarded as the proper result of multiple sensitive attribute processing. See the example in

Table 1 again, the *MD* is satisfied only if the *Q&S Diversity* are satisfied in both following situations: regarding *Age,Sex,Zipcode,Disease* as quasi-identifiers with *Household Disease* sensitive and regarding *Age,Sex,Zipcode,Household Disease* as quasi-identifiers with *Disease* sensitive. However, this requirement is a little too strict which may lead to over-distortion of quasi-identifiers and correspondingly cause too much information loss. The masking of sensitive attribute values with more general patterns may help to alleviate this problem.

Definition 7 (Masking SA). *Suppose s_{child} is one sensitive value in relation T, s_{parent} is the parent node of s_{child} in the more general domain with N leaf nodes in the sensitive attribute tree. If we replace s_{child} with s_{parent}, the possibility of disclosing s_{child} is reduced to $1/N$. This measure which can reduce disclosure risks is called Masking SA.*

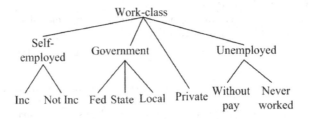

Fig. 1. Taxonomy tree for the attribute Education

For example, as in Fig. 1 shows, *Local Government* is one leaf node of *Government*. If we mask *Local Government* with *Government*, the possibility of disclosing *Local Government* is reduced to 1/3. The implementing of *Masking SA* and an effective generalization algorithm framework will be proposed in the following.

4   The Generalization Framework

4.1   Two-Step Generalization Algorithm

As the number of sensitive attributes grows, it is not hard to see that we will inevitably need larger and larger *equivalence class* to ensure the diversity of sensitive attributes[10,17]. To avoid over-distortion of quasi-identifiers, we implement *Masking SA* on sensitive attributes in company with the quasi-identifiers generalization. Although making sensitive values more general may result in less accurate values on sensitive attributes, it retains more information on the quasi-identifiers. Generally, the diversity requirement of sensitive attribute according to each quasi-identifier *equivalence class* and each sensitive *equivalence class* should not be the same. This can be proved by the experiments in the next section. We define α-*QI* and α-*SA* with respect to QI and SA to show this different diversity requirement.

Our generalization scheme is composed by a *two-step generalization* [18] as shown in Fig.2. The first phase applies quasi-identifiers generalization on microdata, and we choose the *top-down specialization greedy algorithm* for it [5]. Then, the second step produces the final microdata by performing *Masking SA* on the foregoing result quasi-identifiers *equivalence class*, employing a *bottom-up local recoding algorithm* for each equivalence class [13]. The execution proceeds in rounds. In each iteration,

- The top-down specialization greedy algorithm slightly refines one of $f_1, \ldots, f_d$ and lead to a new T^* with lower information loss. We choose the "best" attribute for the refining function. The "best" attribute means that the refine of that can involve the largest number's tuples. The core of the greedy algorithm is to make the largest extent specialization in each round, so as to find the anonymity result with the least information loss quickly.
- For each *equivalence class*, the bottom-up local recoding algorithm finds the corresponding value of sensitive *equivalence class*, in which the α-*SA requirement* is not satisfied. Then, we carry on the local recoding which also adopt the greedy algorithm, i.e. finding the value with the least number's tuples from the same generalization hierarchy with the former value. Afterwards, we impose the generalization function on the tuples which contains these two values. The generalization is only done in this special *equivalence class*, therefore, this is a local recoding algorithm.

The current round finishes after executing the two-step generalization algorithm. As our generalization framework is devoting itself into finding the optimum result with the least information loss, we should measure the amount of information gain by implying the top-down specialization on quasi-identifiers and the information loss by implying the bottom-up local recoding on sensitive attributes. If we get more information gain than the information loss, we will carry on the next iteration. Or else, the current result is regarded as the optimum one and we finish the iteration.

4.2   Information Loss Metrics

In order to evaluate the effectiveness of our two-generalization algorithm, the corresponding information loss metrics are subsequently defined. Based on the general loss metric (LM)[6], information in all the potentially identifying attributes will be assumed to be described equally important in LM. So the total information loss due to generalizations will be computed by summing up a normalization information loss for each of these attributes.

Definition 8 (Distortion Ratio). *Given a microdata set T, after the processing of generalization, a T^* is obtained. We compute all the tuple's information loss of T^*, compared with the overall tuple's absolute information loss by making all the attribute values to the most generalized domain. The result is called Distortion Ratio.*

The Greedy Two-step Generalization Algorithm

Input: microdata T, generalization hierarchies of all attributes, value of
        α-QI and α-SA
Output: publishable relation T^*
Body:
    for each QI attribute $Q_i (1 \leq i \leq d)$
        initialize a generalization function f_i with a single
        partition covering the entire domain of Q_i
    $T^*=$ the relation after applying QI-generalization on T
        according to $F=f_1,\ldots,f_d$
    While(true)
        $T^*_{best}= T^*$
        for each QI-group
            check whether the α-QI and α-SA are satisfied;
        if(true)
            finding the best $F'=f'_1,\ldots,f'_d$ obtain from F with "single
            partition"(specialization)
            $T^{*'}=$the relation after applying F' on the
                quasi-identifiers *equivalence class* of T^*
        else if(α-QI is not satisfied)
            withdraw the last "single partition" on quasi-identifiers
        else if(α-SA is not satisfied)
            s= the value of corresponding sensitive *equivalence class*
            s-company= the value with the least number tuples in the same
                generalization hierarchy with s
            do the *Masking SA* on s and s-Company of this quasi-identifiers
            equivalence class
        end if
        if (Distortion Ratio($T^{*'}$)< Distortion Ratio (T^*_{best}))
            $T^*_{best}= T^*$
        else
            return T^*_{best}
    End While

Fig. 2. Algorithm for the Greedy Two-step Generalization

Let v be a value in the domain of attribute A. We use $InfoLoss(v^*)$ to capture the amount of information loss in generalizing v to v^*. The number of values in v^* is expressed by *value.number(v^*)* and the number of values in the domain of A by *value.number(domain A)*. Formally,

$$InfoLoss(v^*) = \frac{value.number(v^*) - 1}{value.number(domain A)} \qquad (1)$$

For instance, in Fig. 1, the taxonomy of *Work-class* has 8 leaves, generalizing *Local Government* to *Government* results in *InfoLoss(Government)*=(3-1)/8=1/4, where 3 is the number of leaves under *Government*. Obviously, if v is not generalized, $InfoLoss(v^*)$ equals 0, i.e., no information is lost. The overall information loss $InfoLoss_{tuple}(t_{qi}^*)$ and $InfoLoss_{tuple}(t_{sa}^*)$ of a generalized tuple t^* respectively equals the follows,

$$InfoLoss_{tuple}(t_{qi}^*) = \sum_{i=1}^{d} InfoLoss(t^*.A_i^{qi}) \qquad (2)$$

$$InfoLoss_{tuple}(t_{sa}^*) = \sum_{i=1}^{m} InfoLoss(t^*.A_i^{sa}) \qquad (3)$$

The total information loss of the entire relation T^* is computed following the definition 3, given out respectively for quasi-identifiers and sensitive attributes as the *QI Distortion Ratio* and *SA Distortion Ratio*,

$$QI.DistortionRatio(T^*) = \frac{\sum_{\forall t^* in T^*} InfoLoss_{tuple}(t_{qi}^*)}{\sum_{\forall t^* in T^*} \sum_{i=1}^{d} 1} \qquad (4)$$

$$SA.DistortionRatio(T^*) = \frac{\sum_{\forall t^* in T^*} InfoLoss_{tuple}(t_{sa}^*)}{\sum_{\forall t^* in T^*} \sum_{i=1}^{m} 1} \qquad (5)$$

The overall Distortion Ratio is the sum of *QI Distortion Ratio* and *SA Distortion Ratio*.

5   Experiments

This section experimentally evaluates the effectiveness of our approach using the Adult Database from the UCI Machine Learning Repository[4]. We select about 48000 tuples from the Adult Database. The microdata has 8 attributes: *Salary, Marital-status, Family-status, Race, Gender, Education, Occupation and Employment*. All the columns are categorical. In our experiments, we used *Occupation* and *Employment* as two sensitive attributes, *Education, Occupation* and *Employment* for three-sensitive attributes, *Family-status, Education, Occupation* and *Employment* for four-sensitive attributes. The left columns are quasi-identifiers. All experiments were run on a Celeron(R) PC with CPU 2.40GHz and RAM 512MB.

Intuitively, the dataset *Distortion Ratio* with *MD* is higher than that with *SD*, because the *MD* requirement is much stricter than the *SD* requirement. In fact, as illustrated in Fig. 3, the contrast is not so far. We regard the sensitive attribute *Education* as quasi-identifier, obtaining the curse "1-attribute", and ensure the *MD* on both *Education* and *Occupation*, obtaining the curse "2-attribute", showing in Fig. 3(a). This result perfectly proves the good performance of *Masking SA*. The conclusion is same with Fig. 3(b). It is this *Masking SA* which prevents quasi-identifiers from over-distortion.

Fig. 4 shows the *QI Distortion Ratio* and *SA Distortion Ratio* and Execution Time. As we see, in Fig. 4(a), the *QI Distortion Ratio* decreases when α increases, opposite for the curse of *SA Distortion Ratio*. We can also see that the extent of *SA Distortion Ratio* is not large, however, decreasing the *QI Distortion Ratio* all the

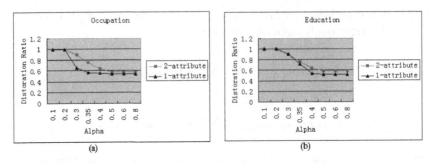

Fig. 3. Distortion Ratio Comparison between SD and MD

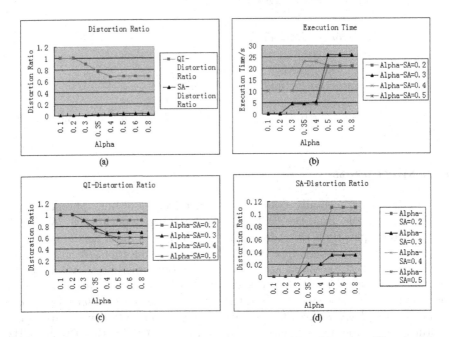

Fig. 4. QI and SA Distortion Ratio and Execution Time Versus α-QI and α-SA

same. The higher diversity requirement, the more information loss. Therefore, we should choose α between 0.3 and 0.5. The execution time in Fig. 4(b) displays the computation cost of different α-SA parameter. Fig. 4(c) and Fig. 4(d) respectively shows the *QI Distortion Ratio* and *SA Distortion Ratio* according to different diversity requirement of (α-SA). As we see, the requirement should not be too strict. Otherwise, we would get the terrible result with both *QI Distortion Ratio* and *SA Distortion Ratio* so high, e.g., when α-SA =0.2.

Fig. 5 shows the performance of different number's sensitive attributes. As the number increases, both the *QI Distortion Ratio* and *SA Distortion Ratio* become higher. This result illustrates that the more sensitive attributes, the

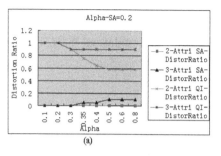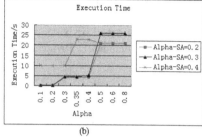

Fig. 5. Distortion Ratio and Execution Time of Different Number Sensitive Attributes

heavier information loss we get and the more Execution time it costs. We should reduce the diversity requirement of *MD* as the number of sensitive attributes increases, otherwise, the released dataset will be useless. Moreover, in the view of statistics analysis, if the number of sensitive attributes is large enough, we should not impose *MD* on them again, because attackers impossibly has so much background knowledge as to reduce identifying possibility by detecting association between sensitive attributes. In conclusion, experiments have proved the feasibility and advantage of our processing method for microdata anonymity with multiple sensitive attributes and illustrated the effectiveness of *Masking SA*. Through these experiments, we also obtain the principle of how to set proper parameters so as to make good performance. Moreover, we have discovered one important principle that whether imposing *MD* requirement on a dataset should be according to the number of sensitive attributes of the releasing microdata.

6   Conclusion

Most of the existing k-anonymity methods focus only on dealing with single-SA. For microdata with multi-SA publishing, the disclosure scenarios may happen because of *logical associations* existing between multi-SA. A *Q&S Diversity* requirement is proposed to prevent inference attacks in the foregoing disclosure scenarios. The *MD definition* is proposed to ensure the diversity among multi-SA. We make sure the diversity by ensuring the frequency of each sensitive value below the threshold α in each *equivalence class*. Additionally, we reduce the overall distortion by the measure of *Masking SA*. We propose a multiple sensitive attributes processing framework implementing top-down specialization on quasi-identifiers and local recoding bottom-up generalization on sensitive attributes. The experiment proves the feasibility and advantage of our method, and we also get additional knowledge from the experiment results. For future work, in order to retain more information of a released dataset, we will consider the local suppression as the supplement of our generalization techniques to integrate with this framework and validate our solution by more real experiments.

Acknowledgements

This work is supported by National Natural Science Foundation(60673140) and National High-Tech R&D Program(2007AA01Z156).

References

1. Bettini, C., Wang, X.S., Jajodia, S.: The role of quasi-identifiers in k-anonymity revisited. Technical Report N. RT-11-06 DICo - University of Milan, Italy (2006)
2. Bayardo, R., Agrawal, R.: Data privacy through optimal k-anonymity. In: Proc of the ICDE (2005)
3. Ciriani, V., De Capitani di Vimercati, S., Foresti, S., Samarati, P.: Samarati. k-Anonymity. In: Secure Data Management in Decentralized Systems (2007)
4. ftp://ftp.ics.uci.edu/pub/machine-learning-databases/adult
5. Fung, B., Wang, K., Yu, P.: Top-down specialization for information and privacy preservation. In: Proc of ICDE (April 2005)
6. Iyengar, V.: Transforming data to satisfy privacy constraints. In: Proc of SIGKDD (2002)
7. LeFevre, K., DeWitt, D.J., Ramakrishnan, R.: Mondrian multidimensional k-anonymit. In: Proc of ICDE (2006)
8. Machanavajjhala, A., Gehrke, J., Kifer, D., Venkitasubramaniam, M.: l-diversity: Privacy beyond k-anonymity. In: Proc of ICDE (2006)
9. Sweeney, L.: K-anonymity: A model for protecting privacy. International Journal on Uncertainty, Fuzziness, and Knowledge-based Systems (2002)
10. Sweeney, L.: Achieving k-anonymity privacy protection using generalization and suppression. Int'l Journal on Uncertainty, Fuzziness, and Knowledge-based Systems (2002)
11. Samarati, P.: Protecting respondents' identities in microdata release. IEEE Trans. on Knowledge and Data Engineering (2001)
12. Samarati, P., Sweeney, L.: Protecting privacy when disclosing information: k-anonymity and its enforcement through generalization and suppression. Technical report, CMU, SRI (1998)
13. Wang, K., Yu, P., Chakraborty, S.: Bottom-up generalization: A data mining solution to privacy protection. In: Perner, P. (ed.) ICDM 2004. LNCS (LNAI), vol. 3275, Springer, Heidelberg (2004)
14. Willenborg, L., deWaal, T.: Elements of Statistical Disclosure Control. Lecture Notes in Statistics. Springer, Heidelberg (2000)
15. Wang, K., Fung, B.C.M, Yu, P.S.: Template-based privacy preservation in classifica-tion problems. In: Proc of ICDM 2005 (2005)
16. Wong, R.C.-W., Li, J., Fu, A.W.-C., Wang, K.: α,k-Anonymity: An Enhanced k-Anonymity Model for Privacy-Preserving Data Publishing. In: Proc of KDD 2006 (2006)
17. Xu, J., Wang, W., Pei, J., Wang, X., Shi, B., Fu, A.W.-C.: Utility-Based Anonymization Using Local Recoding. In: Proc of KDD 2006 (2006)
18. Xiao, X., Tao, Y.: Personalized Privacy Preservation. In: Proc of the SIGMOD (2006)

Audio Watermarking Algorithm Based on Centroid and Statistical Features*

Xiaoming Zhang[1] and Xiong Yin[1,2,**]

[1] College of Information Engineering, Beijing Institute of Petrochemical Technology,
Beijing 102617, China
[2] College of Information Science and Technology, Beijing University of Chemical Technology,
Beijing 100029, China
{zhangxiaoming,yinxiong}@bipt.edu.cn

Abstract. Experimental testing shows that the relative relation in the number of samples among the neighboring bins and the audio frequency centroid are two robust features to the Time Scale Modification (TSM) attacks. Accordingly, an audio watermark algorithm based on frequency centroid and histogram is proposed by modifying the frequency coefficients. The audio histogram with equal-sized bins is extracted from a selected frequency coefficient range referred to the audio centroid. The watermarked audio signal is perceptibly similar to the original one. The experimental results show that the algorithm is very robust to resample TSM and a variety of common attacks. Subjective quality evaluation of the algorithm shows that embedded watermark introduces low, inaudible distortion of host audio signal.

Keywords: Audio watermarking, FFT, Centroid, Histogram, TSM.

1 Introduction

Audio watermarking plays an important role in ownership protection. According to IFPI (International Federation of the Phonographic Industry), audio watermarking should be robust to temporal scaling of $\pm 10\%$ and be able to resist most of common signal processing manipulations and attacks, such as cropping, re-sampling and etc [1].

The algorithms for audio watermarking can be classified into two categories: algorithms in time domain and algorithms in transform domain, including those in compressed domain. Data hiding in the least significant bits of audio samples in the time domain is one of the simplest algorithms with very high data rate of additional information. In [2], the authors presented an audio watermarking algorithm in discrete wavelet transform domain. The watermark is embedded in the frequency point of discrete wavelet transform by replacing least significant bit. The capacity of algorithm is high and is robust to resample and cropping. In [3], a blind audio information bit hiding algorithm with effective synchronization is proposed. The algorithm embedded

---

* This work is supported by the Funding Project for Academic Human Resources Development in Institutions of Higher Learning Under the Jurisdiction of Beijing Municipality.
** Corresponding author.

S. Qing, H. Imai, and G. Wang (Eds.): ICICS 2007, LNCS 4861, pp. 153–163, 2007.

synchronization signals in the time domain to resist the attacks such as cropping while keeping the computation for resynchronization being lower. The watermark is placed in block DCT coefficients of the original audio exploiting the human auditory system (HAS) features.

The algorithm in [4] is very robust against de-synchronization attacks such as time scale modification (TSM), cropping. However, this watermarking algorithm is sensitive somewhat to additive noise attacks such as MP3 audio compression and low-pass filter. Of course, many audio watermarking algorithms (algorithm in literature [5]) are robust against additive noise attacks, but these algorithms cannot effectively resist TSM attacks.

In the existing literature, several algorithms have been proposed aiming at solving this problem by using exhaustive search, synchronization pattern, invariant watermark, and implicit synchronization. In [6], an audio watermarking method is presented by using music content analysis. The watermark is embedded into the edges of audio signal by viewing pitch-invariant TSM as a special form of random cropping, removing and adding some portions of audio signal while preserving the pitch. The watermark is robust to $\pm 9\%$ pitch-invariant TSM but vulnerable to other stretching modes such as solving playback speed modifications, which change the edges in the signal. In [7], side information is exploited to improve the searching of the watermark aiming at solving playback speed modifications. One weakness of this scheme is that the detection procedure is not blind. The histogram specification is first introduced for image watermarking in [8]. By using the robustness of image color histogram to rotations and geometric transformations, the authors in [9] proposed a general method is very robust to image geometric distortions. In [10], a watermarking algorithm to geometric distortion in DWT domain is proposed. In the algorithm, a watermark was embedded adaptively in low band of DWT domain, according to the conceal quality of Human Visual System; Especially, the geometric transformation could be corrected before the watermarking detection, owing to embedding a template in a circle of middle frequency in DFT and extracting a invariant centroid from a restricted area inside the image. Moreover, an improvement on centroid detection method was presented in [11]. The improved method constructs a centroid series which were convergent in probability to centroid of initial text line using both initial profile and reproduced profile of text line, and the watermark capacity is increased.

In this paper, the invariance of histogram and centroid in the frequency domain to TSM is presented. This is followed by a description of our proposed watermark method. Then, analyze the watermark performance and test the watermark robustness on resynchronization distortions, as well as some common signal processing and some attacks in Stirmark Benchmark for Audio. Finally, the conclusion is drawn.

2   Invariant Features in Frequency Domain

Since the bits embedded in the frequency domain can provide a stronger robustness against additional noises than in the time domain, in this section, we investigate the invariance of the histogram and centroid in the frequency domain by experimental testing as follows.

2.1 Centroid in Frequency Domain

For audio signal sequence (W_s bits/sample f_s/sample frequency), we first consider 20ms audio signal as a frame (80ms audio signal before compression). Then, a frame is divided into 32 sub-bands. Each sub-band contains K ($K = f_s * S_d * W_d * 20/(8000*32)$) samples, each frame contains K*32 samples, $s_i(j)(j \in [1...32])$ denotes the audio samples in j sub-band of i frame. $fft(s_i(j))(j \in [1...32])$ Denotes the audio samples in j sub-band of i frame is FFT transformed. The centroid in the frequency domain is calculated by formula (1) and formula (2):

$$M_j = \sqrt{\frac{\sum_{i=1}^{K}(20*\log 10(fft(s_i(j))))^2}{K}} \tag{1}$$

$$C = \frac{\sum_{j=1}^{32} j * M_j}{\sum_{j=1}^{32} M_j} \tag{2}$$

2.2 Histogram

A histogram is often used to describe the data distribution. The style of histogram may be described by:

$$H_M = \{h_M(i) \,|\, i = 1,...,L\}, \tag{3}$$

where H_M is vector, and denotes the volume-level a histogram of audio signal F, and $h_M(i)$ denotes the number of samples in the 'th bin. Suppose that the resolution the audio signal is R bits, for a signed signal, the number of bins are calculated as:

$$L = \begin{cases} 2^R / M & if \ Mod(2^R / M) = 0 \\ \lfloor 2^R / M \rfloor + 1 & other \end{cases} \tag{4}$$

where M is the size of bins, $h_M(i)$ includes all samples the range of sample value from $-2^{R-1} + (i-1)*M$ to $-2^{R-1} + i*M - 1$, and $\lfloor . \rfloor$ is the floor function.

2.3 Experimental Testing

We choose an audio signal (16-bit signed mono audio file sampled at 44.1 kHz with the length of 20s) to test the effects of the TSM on the histogram and centroid in the FFT domain. As to other kinds of audio signals, such as pop music, piano music and speech, etc, the simulation results are almost similar.

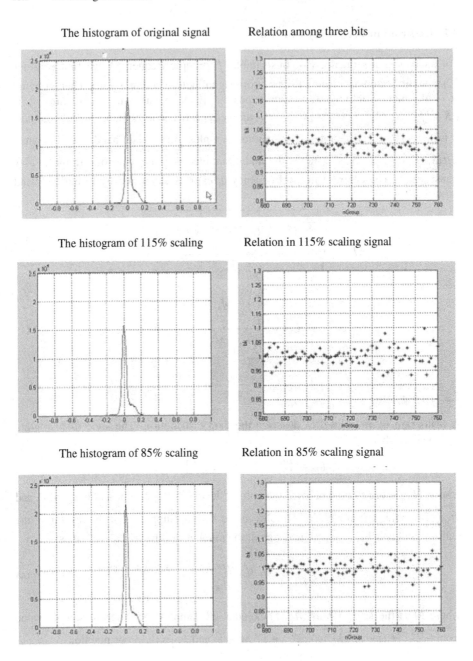

Fig. 1. The invariance of histogram to the pitch-invariant TSM: the sub-plots in left side is the histogram of original audio and scaled one with 85% and 115%, while the sub-plots in right side demonstrate the relative relation among three neighboring bins

The histogram of original signal   Relation among three bits

The histogram of 85% scaling   Relation in 85% scaling signal

The histogram of 115% scaling   Relation in 115% scaling signal

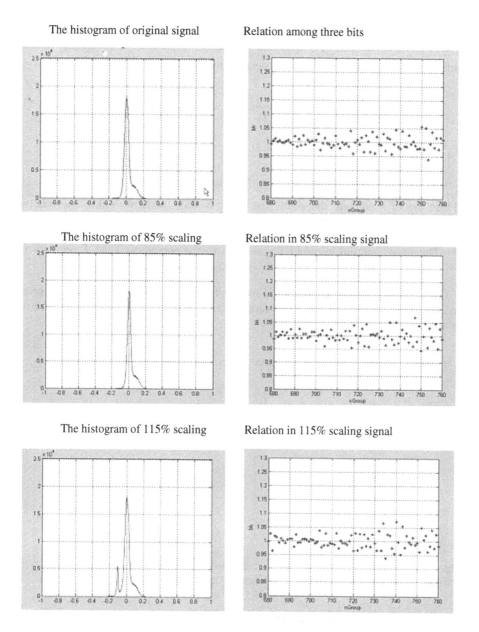

Fig. 2. The invariance of histogram to the resample TSM. The sub-plots in left side is the histogram of original audio and scaled one with 85% and 115%, while the sub-plots in right side demonstrate the relative relation among three neighboring bins.

The histograms are extracted from audio file after FFT transformed. The size of the bins M=0.5. Fig.1 and Fig.2 show the effects of the TSM attacks with the two different modes, respectively. Fig.3 plots the centroid values of the original and its scaled versions under 85%~115% TSM (pitch-invariant and resample) with the step size of 1%. Referenced to [4], the relative relations in the number of samples among three neighboring bins calculated and denoted by β_k :

$$\beta_k = \frac{2 * h_M(k)}{h_M(k-1) + h_M(k+1)} \qquad for \quad h_M(k) \gg L \qquad (5)$$

2.4 Comments

Based on the extensive testing, we have the following observations:

(1) In the FFT domain, the audio histogram is very robust to TSM. The relative relation among three neighboring bins is from 0.9 to 1.1. Refer to Figure.1 and Figure.2.
(2) The audio centroid in the FFT domain is robust enough to TSM. From 85% to 115% TSM, the error ratio of centroid is limited in $\pm 3\%$ (see Figure.3).

Overall, in the watermark design, if we incorporate the invariance of the histogram and centroid to TSM and the watermark in the FFT domain, the watermark will be robust.

Invariant centroid in pitch-invariant mode   Invariant centroid in resample mode

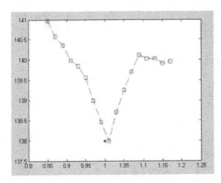
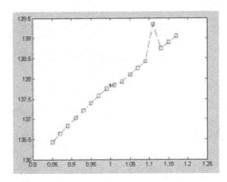

Fig. 3. The centroid of the example audio and scaled ones under the TSM of 85%~115% with resample (right) and pitch-invariant (left) stretching modes, respectively

3 Watermark Algorithm Design

The watermark embedding and extracting are described by the histogram specification. The robustness of the audio centroid and relative relation in the number of sample among different bins to the TSM attacks presented in the previous section are used in the design. First, the FFT transform is applied. And, the watermark is embedded into the coefficients of FFT instead of into the time domain signal itself.

3.1 Watermark Embedding Approach

The basic idea of the proposed embedding is to extract the histogram from a selected coefficient of FFT. Divide the bins into many groups, each group including three consecutive bins. For each group, one bit watermark is embedded by reassigning the number of samples in the three bins. The watermarked audio is obtained by modifying the coefficient of FFT according to the watermarking rule. The embedding approach is shown in Figure 4.

The detail embedding process is described as follows.

Suppose that there is a binary sequence $W = \{w_i \mid i = 1,...,L_w\}$ to be hidden into a digital audio $F = \{f(i) \mid i = 1,...,N\}$. The centroid of audio, denoted by A, is calculated as formula (1) and (2).

Then, select the amplitude range $B = [\lambda A, 1/\lambda A]$ from audio coefficient of FFT to extract the histogram $H = \{h(i) \mid i = 1,...,L\}$, where $L = 3 * L_w$. $\lambda \in [0.6, 0.9]$, is a suggested range in which the bins extracted from B often hold enough samples.

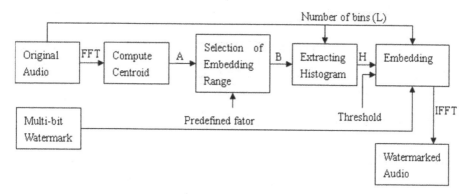

Fig. 4. Watermark embedding framework

After extracting the histogram, suppose that three consecutive bins, Bin_1, Bin_2 and Bin_3, their samples in the number are denoted as a, b and c. apply the follow equation to embed one bit of information, described as [4]:

$$\begin{array}{ll} 2b/(a+c) \geq T & if \quad w(i) = 1 \\ (a+c)/2b \geq T & if \quad w(i) = 0 \end{array}, \qquad (6)$$

where T is a selected threshold used to control the watermark robustness performance and the embedding distortion. T should be not less than 1.1, in order to resist TSM.

If the embedded bit $w(i)$ is '1' and $2b/(a+c) \geq T$, no operation is needed. Otherwise, the number of samples in three different bins, a, b, c, will be adjusted until satisfying $2b/(a+c) \geq T$. Some selected samples from Bin_1 and Bin_3 in the number denoted by I1 and I3, will be modified to fall into Bin_2. The modification rule is described as Equation (7):

$$\begin{cases} ff_1'(i) = ff_1(i) + M & 1 \le i \le I1 \\ ff_3'(i) = ff_3(i) - M & 1 \le i \le I3 \end{cases}, \tag{7}$$

where $ff_1(i)$ and $ff_3(i)$ denote the ^{i}th modified sample in Bin_1 and Bin_3, $ff_1'(i)$ and $ff_3'(i)$ are the modified samples belong to Bin_2.

If the embedded bit $w(i)$ is '0' and $(a+c)/2b < T$, I1 and I3, some selected samples from Bin_2 will be modified to fall into Bin_1 and Bin_3, respectively. The rule is described as Equation (8):

$$\begin{cases} ff_2'(i) = ff_2(i) - M & 1 \le i \le I1 \\ ff_2'(i) = ff_2(i) + M & 1 \le i \le I3 \end{cases}, \tag{8}$$

where $ff_2(i)$ denotes the ith modified sample in Bin_2, $ff_2'(i)$ are the corresponding modified.

This process is repeated to embed all watermark bits. In our proposed embedding, the watermark is embedded by modifying the values of some selected coefficients of FFT samples from the audio. Hence, the re-construction of the watermarked audio will be formed by the IFFToperation.

3.2 Watermark Extracting Approach

In the extracting, a predefined searching space, B is designed to de-scale the effects of various attacks on the centroid.

$$B = [A'(1 - \Delta 1), A'(1 - \Delta 2)] \tag{9}$$

Where A' denotes the centroid of watermarked audio signal. $\Delta 1$ And $\Delta 2$ denote the down and up error ratios of centroid in the FFT domain caused by various attacks. The hidden message is synchronization bits, followed by the hidden multi-bit watermark.

The histogram is extracted with L bins as in the process of watermark embedding. The hidden bit is extracted by comparing the number of coefficients in three consecutive bins, denoted by a'', b'' and c'', formulated as:

$$w_i' = \begin{cases} 1 & if \quad 2b''/(a'' + c'') \ge 1 \\ 0 & other \end{cases} \tag{10}$$

The process is repeated until all hidden bits are extracted. Once synchronization sequence is matched with extracted synchronization bits or the searching process is finished, according to the best matching, extract the hidden watermark following the synchronization. In the extraction phase, the parameters, L_w, λ and synchronization sequence are known, so the detection process is blind.

4 Experimental Results

The parameter values are given as follows: $\lambda = 0.8$ and $T = 1.5$. And, 183 bins extracted from a 20s light music is watermarked with 61bits of information composed of a 31-bit m sequence and the 30-bit watermark. In the embedding, the probability of the watermarked samples their values added or reduced is approximately equivalent, hence the watermark hardly make any affection on the audio centroid, 137.9813 and 137.9517 before and after embedding respectively. The relative relation in the number of samples among three neighboring bins is calculated by Equation (5) and plot in Figure 5.

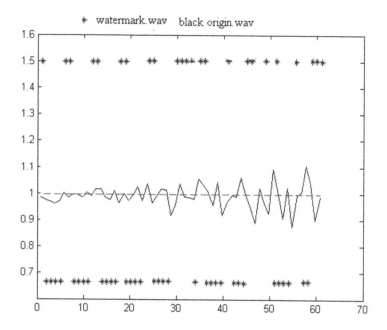

Fig. 5. The relative relation in the number of samples before and after watermarking

The SNR is 40.83dB. The higher SNR is that only a small part of samples is modified for watermarking. We test the robustness of the proposed algorithm according to IFPI with BER. The audio editing and attacking tools adopted in our experiments are Cool EditPro v2.1 and Stirmark Benchmark for Audio v0.2. The test results under common audio signal processing, time-scale modification and Stirmark for Audio are listed in Tables 1-3.

Table 1. Robustness performance to common attacks

Attack Type	Error Number of Bits	Attack Type	Error Number of Bits
Normalize	3	Low Pass (11025Hz)	0
Resample (kHz) 44.1->16->44.1	0	Low Pass (7kHz)	6
Re-quantization (bit) 16->32->16	0	Low Pass (4kHz)	10
Re-quantization (bit) 16->8->16	0		

Table 2. Robustness Performance to TSM with two different stretching modes

Pitch-Invariant TSM	Error Number of Bits	Resample TSM	Error Number of Bits
TSM −10%	Failed	TSM −10%	3
TSM −8%	15	TSM −8%	2
TSM −6%	12	TSM −6%	2
TSM −4%	8	TSM −4%	0
TSM −2%	6	TSM −2%	0
TSM +2%	6	TSM +2%	0
TSM +4%	8	TSM +4%	0
TSM +6%	11	TSM +6%	0
TSM +8%	14	TSM +8%	0
TSM +10%	Failed	TSM +10%	1

Table 3. Robustness Performance to some common attacks in Stirmark Benchmark for Audio

Attack Type	Error Number of Bits	Attack Type	Error Number of Bits
Addbrumm_100	0	Addnoise_100.wav	3
Addbrumm_1100	0	Addnoise_300.wav	5
Addbrumm_10100	0	Addnoise_500.wav	9
Addsinus	0	Compressor	0
Invert	0	Original	0
Stat2	3	Rc_lowpass	3
Zerocross	10	Zeroremove	Failed
Cutsamples	10	FFT_RealReverse	0

From Table 1, we can see that our algorithm is robust enough to some common audio signal processing manipulations such as resample, re-quantization and low pass of 11025Hz.

The test results of a light music under TSM form -10% to +10% with two different stretching modes are tabulated in Table 2. The algorithm shows strong robustness to this kind of attacks up to 10% for resample TSM.

Stirmark Benchmark for Audio is a common robustness evaluation tool for audio watermarking techniques. From Table 3, it is found that the watermark shows stronger resistance to those common attacks. In the cases of failure ('Failed' mean the number of error bits is over 20), the audio centroid is changed severely or audio quality is distorted largely.

5 Conclusions

A multi-bit audio watermarking method based on the centroid and statistical features in FFT domain is proposed and implemented by histogram specifications.

Extensive experiments shows that the superiority of statistical features, the relative relations in the number of samples among different bins and the frequency centroid of audio signal. The two features are very robust to the TSM. Accordingly, by applying the two features, audio watermarking scheme is designed.

The extensive experimental have shown that the watermark scheme is robust against some common signal processing, attack in Stirmark Benchmark for Audio and attack in resample TSM. However, it is still weak to resist pitch-invariant TSM attack.

References

1. International Federation of the Phonographic Industry, http://www.ifpi.org
2. Yin, X., Zhang, X.: Covert Communication Audio Watermarking Algorithm Based on LSB. 2006 10th International Conference on Communication Technology, pp. 308–311.
3. Huang, J., Wang, Y., Shi, Y.Q.: A Blind Audio Watermarking Algorithm with Self-Synchronization. In: Proceedings of IEEE International Symposium on Circuits and Systems, Arizona, USA, vol. 3, pp. 627–630 (2002)
4. Xiang, S., Huang, J., Yang, R.: Time-scale Invariant Audio Watermarking Based on the Statistical Features in time Domain. In: Proc. Of the 8th Information Hiding workshop (2006)
5. Yeo, I.K., Kim, H.J.: Modified Patchwork Algorithm: The Novel Audio Watermarking Scheme. IEEE Transactions on Speech and Audio Processing 11, 381–386 (2003)
6. Li, W., Xue, X.Y., Zh, P., Zh, P.L.: Robust audio watermarking based on rhythm region Detection. IEEE Electronics Letters 41(4), 218–219 (2005)
7. Sylvain, B., Michiel, V.D.V., Aweke, L.: Informed detection of audio watermark for resolving playback speed modifications. In: Proc.of the Multimedia and Security Workshop, pp. 117–123 (2004)
8. Coltuc, D., Bolon, P.: Watermarking by Histogram Specification. In: Proc. of SPIE International Conference on Security and Watermarking of Multimedia Contents II, vol. 3657, pp. 252–263 (1999)
9. Roy, S., Chang, E.C.: Watermarking Color Histograms. In: Proc. of International Conference of Image Processing, vol. 4, pp. 2191–2194 (2005)
10. Hu, Y.P., Han, D.Z., Yang, S.Q.: Image-adaptive Watermarking Algorithm Robust to Geometric Distortion in DWT Domain. Journal of System Simulation 17(10), 2470–2475 (2005)
11. Dai, Z.X, Hong, F., Li, X.G., Dong, J.: Improvement on centroid detection method for text document watermarking. Computer Applications 27(5), 1064–1066 (2007)

A Semi-blind Watermarking Based on Discrete Wavelet Transform

Chin-Chen Chang, Yung-Chen Chou, and Tzu-Chuen Lu

Department of Information Engineering and Computer Science, Feng Chia University,
Taichung 40724, Taiwan
ccc@cs.ccu.edu.tw
Department of Computer Science and Information Engineering, National Chung
Cheng University, Chiayi 62102, Taiwan
jackjow@cs.ccu.edu.tw
Department of Information Management, Chaoyang University of Technology,
Taichung41349, Taiwan
tclu@cyut.edu.tw

Abstract. This paper proposed a robust watermarking scheme based on discrete wavelet transform to hide a grayscale watermark in a digital image for image authentication. The proposed scheme employed toral automorphism to scramble the host image and the watermark so as to enhance the security and fidelity of the embedded watermark. Later, the permuted watermark and the permuted host image were transformed by discrete wavelet transform. Next, the transformed watermark was concealed in the low frequency coefficient of the transformed image by using the concept of codebook matching. Simulation results showed that the required extra storage of the proposed scheme for extracting the watermark was lower than that of Lu et al.'s scheme. In addition, the extracted watermark image quality of the proposed methods was better than that of Shieh et al.'s scheme. According to the experimental results, the proposed scheme indeed outperformed Shieh et al.'s and Lu et al.'s schemes. Moreover, the proposed scheme was robust to various attacks, such as JPEG compression, Gaussian blurred, sharpening, cropping, brightness, contrast enhancement, rotation, and so on.

Keywords: Digital Watermark, discrete wavelet transformation, semi-blind watermarking, toral automorphism.

1 Introduction

With the recent growth of the information techniques, digital images are easy to create, edit, adjust, and share. The digital image can be accurately copied and arbitrarily distributed via the Internet, Intranet or other types of networks within seconds. However, these convenient techniques also bring forth several challenging problems that need to be resolved, such as illegal copying, non-authenticated invasion or tampering. For this reason, many image protection mechanisms such

S. Qing, H. Imai, and G. Wang (Eds.): ICICS 2007, LNCS 4861, pp. 164–176, 2007.

as cryptography, watermarking, or data hiding have been proposed to establish the authenticity and integrity of a digital image. Watermarking is one of the popular digital image protection mechanisms that have been widely used in various applications such as intellectual property right, copyright protection, forgery detection, authorship inference, content identification, or image authentication and so on. In a watermarking scheme, a digital signal, called watermark, is embedded in a host image to generate a watermarked image. The watermark is extracted from the watermarked image to prove the ownership of the image when necessary.

Cox et al. [4] classified watermarking techniques as robust watermarking, fragile watermarking [1, 3], and semi-fragile watermarking. In a robust watermarking scheme [5], the watermark is invisibly embedded in the host image. The embedded watermark must be robust enough to resist any regular image processing or malicious attacks [2]. A robust watermarking scheme must satisfy the following requirements: imperceptibility, robustness, unambiguousness, capacity, security, and multiple watermarks. The robust watermarking schemes are used to protect copyright or to verify the ownership.

Different from the robust watermarking, a fragile watermarking scheme concerns the completeness of image content. Any slightest alternation may destroy the embedded watermark. The fragile watermarking schemes are used to ensure the received image is exactly the authorized one, and to verify the image content is selfsame to the original. The semi-fragile watermarking schemes, like fragile watermarking schemes, concern the integrity of the image content. Moreover, the semi-fragile watermarking schemes allow regular image processing such as transmission error, image compression, noise, and so on.

The watermarking schemes can also be divided into three categories: non-blind watermarking scheme, semi-blind watermarking, and blind watermarking. If the original host image is required to reliably extract the embedded watermark, the scheme is non-blind. The practicality of the non-blind watermarking scheme is limited, since it needs extra storage to maintain the source image. Semi-blind watermarking scheme uses the watermark or side information instead of the host image to extract the embedded watermark. In contrast, the blind watermark scheme does not need the host image or extra information.

In this paper, we shall propose a robustness semi-blind watermark scheme for image authentication and copyright protection. The proposed scheme is based on discrete wavelet transformation. In order to increase the security of the watermarked image, the proposed scheme adopts toral automorphism to permute the host image and the digital watermark. Further, the permuted host image and the permuted watermark are transformed by using discrete wavelet transformation. The lower coefficients of the transformed host image are used to train a codebook. The transformed watermark is concealed into the lower coefficients of the transformed host image by using the concept of codebook matching. In order to reliably extract the embedded watermark, the proposed scheme needs some extra information. However, the amount of the required extra information is less than that required by other semi-blind schemes.

The rest of this paper is organized as follows. In Section 2, we briefly review related literatures. Section 3 details the proposed scheme, and Section 4 presents the experimental results. Finally, the conclusions are proposed in Section 5.

2   Literature Review

In the past decade, many semi-blind watermarking techniques have been proposed in various literatures. For example, Voyatzis and Pitas [14] proposed a watermarking scheme in 1996, in which toral automorphisms was applied to scramble the digital watermark. Then, the permuted watermark was inserted into the host image. The toral automorphism was a permutation function that transformed two dimensional data into irregular data. Let us consider an image of size $h \times w$. The value of the coordinates (x, y) of the image is denoted as $P = \begin{bmatrix} x \\ y \end{bmatrix}$. Then, the image is iteratively transformed by toral automorphism t times. Let $P_t = \begin{bmatrix} x_t \\ y_t \end{bmatrix}$ be the value of coordinates (x, y) in t period, where $P_t = \begin{bmatrix} x_t \\ y_t \end{bmatrix} = \begin{bmatrix} 1 & 1 \\ K & K+1 \end{bmatrix} \begin{bmatrix} x_{t-1} \\ y_{t-1} \end{bmatrix} mod \begin{bmatrix} h \\ w \end{bmatrix}$. The image after K iterations, each pixel will be back to its original position.

Lu et al. [9] proposed a cocktail watermarking scheme in 2000. Two complementary watermarks, positively modulated watermark and negatively modulated watermark, were embedded in the wavelet coefficients of the host image. In their scheme, the positions of the watermarks were needed for watermarking extraction. A random mapping function was used to distinguish the positions of the watermarks. Then, the extracted watermark was compared with the original embedded watermark for image authentication. Afterwards, Lu et al. [8] proposed a semi-blind watermarking scheme based on the human visual system for image protection. In their scheme, the host image and a grayscale watermark were transformed by discrete wavelet transform. Next, the host image and the watermark were permuted by using toral automorphism. Then, they used one-to-one mapping function to embed the watermark into larger coefficients of the host image. The mapping function was used to indicate the location of the embedded watermark.

In 2001, Solachidis et al. [11] embedded a circularly symmetric watermark in a host image by using discrete Fourier transformation. In 2001, Lin et al. [6] concealed the watermark in the frequency domain by using Fourier-Mellin transformation. Stankovic et al. [12] embedded a two dimensions watermark with a variable spatial frequency in the host image. The watermark was extracted by using 2-D space/spatial-frequency Radon-Wigner distributions. All these schemes required the original watermark for watermark detection.

In 2005, Shieh et al. [10] proposed a semi-blind watermarking scheme based on singular value decomposition. In their scheme, a grayscale watermark was concealed into a digital image. The first step of their scheme was to divide the watermark and the host image into several blocks. In the second step, each block was transformed by using singular value decomposition (SVD). Next, they found a similar block for each block of the watermark from the host image. The singular value of the block was used to replace that of the similar block of the host image.

However, the image quality of the extracted watermark image of Shieh et al.'s scheme was low. In addition, the computation complexity of their scheme was too heavy, since the scheme used SVD to compute the singular value for each block. In order to solve these problems, this paper will propose a low computation watermarking scheme based on discrete wavelet transformation (DWT). The image quality of the extracted watermark of the proposed scheme is better than that of Shieh et al.'s scheme.

3   Proposed Method

The main idea of our proposed method is to generate the relationship between the host image and watermark to be the right ownership information. Thus, the proposed method uses DWT to transform the host image and watermark from the spatial domain into frequency domain, respectively. After the relationship is constructed, we register the information to a trustworthy third party for further usage. Briefly, this watermarking method can be divided to watermark embedding phase and watermark extraction phase. The details of the proposed method are described as follows.

3.1   Watermark Embedding

Fig. 1 shows the watermark embedding procedure of the proposed scheme. In the figure, the symbol H is a host image and W is a watermark. Both of H and W contain $H \times W$ pixels. The scheme first uses toral automorphism with a secret key [13] to permute H and W into two noise-like images H' and W', respectively. The permutation operation makes the embedded watermark robust for malicious cropping operations.

After that, the scheme applies DWT to transform H' and W' from the spatial domain into frequency domain. DWT decomposes an image into high and low frequency components. The low frequency components compose the base of an image, and the high frequency components refine the outline of the image. The human eye is relatively insensitive to the high-frequency components. Hence, many researchers conceal information in the high-frequency components. However, most perceptual coding techniques, such as JPEG, affect the high-frequency components during image compression. In order to avoid the embedded information from being filtered out, the scheme conceals the information in low-frequency components.

In DWT, each level of decomposition creates four sub-bands of an image, $LL, LH, HL,$ and HH. The LL sub-band can be continually decomposed to obtain another level of decomposition. The scheme performs the DWT twice to obtain two levels of decomposition. The obtained sub-bands are LL_2, HL_2, LH_2, HH_2, HL_1, LH_1, and HH_1. Let H^* and W^* be the transformed images of H' and W', respectively. Next, the scheme consults the sub-band LL_2 of H^* to generate a codebook for embedding the watermark. In the embedding process, the sub-band LL_2 of W^* is divided into several non-overlapping blocks. For each

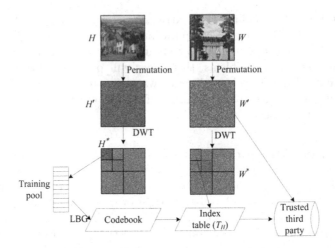

Fig. 1. The diagram of the watermark embedding procedure

block, the scheme searches a similar pattern from the codebook by using the concept of vector quantization. Next, the indices of the patterns are stored for further verification. In the following subsection, we will describe how to generate the codebook as well as how to construct the indices for image authentication.

3.2   Codebook Generation

Before generating a codebook, the scheme uses a normalization function to normalize the coefficients of the sub-band LL_2 of H^* and W^* to ensure that the coefficients are ranging in the same scale. In the other words, all coefficients in LL_2 are ranging from 0 to 255. The normalization function is defined as follows:

$$c' = (c - \min(LL2)) \times r, \tag{1}$$

where c is the coefficient, c' is the normalized coefficient, and r is the normalized ratio computed by

$$r = \frac{255}{\max(LL_2) - \min(LL_2)}. \tag{2}$$

The symbols $\max(LL_2)$ and $\min(LL_2)$ are the maximum function and the minimum function used to find the maximum and minimum values from sub-band LL_2.

Next, the scheme uses a sliding window to move over the normalized LL_2 of H^* one coefficient at a time and generate a set of patterns. The size of the sliding window is $k \times k$, and the set of patterns is called a training pool (denoted as TP). Let $TP = \{tp_i | i = 1, 2, ..., N_{TP}\}$ be the training pool, where tp_i is the i-th pattern and N_{TP} is the number of patterns in TP.

Fig. 2 illustrates an example for constructing a training pool. Fig. 2(a) shows a part of the normalized LL_2 coefficients of an image, and Fig. 2(b) is a diagram

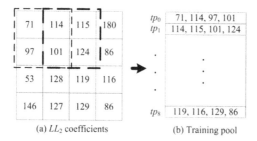

(a) LL_2 coefficients   (b) Training pool

Fig. 2. An example for constructing a training pool

for the training pool. In Fig. 2(a), the sliding window is sized two by two. For instance, first pattern is $tp_0 = \{71, 114, 97, 101\}$, and the second pattern is $tp_1 = \{114, 115, 101, 124\}$.

After the training pool is constructed, we employ the LBG algorithm [7] to train a coefficient codebook. The first step of the LBG algorithm is to randomly choose N_B patterns from the training pool and set them as the initial coefficient codebook. Further, the classification operation classifies the patterns into N_B classes according to the initial coefficient codebook. After the classification, a new coefficient codebook will be constructed by computing the central value of each class. The training of the codebook is terminated when the change between the newly trained codebook and previous iteratively trained codebook is smaller than a pre-defined threshold.

Next, the scheme constructs an indices table to indicate the relationship between H^* and W^*'s LL_2 coefficients. In this stage, the scheme divides the subband LL_2 of W^* into several blocks, and matches a most similar pattern from the codebook for each block. The indices of the most similar pattern are collected to form an indices table. The indices table and the permuted watermark W' are stored for further watermark verification.

3.3   Watermark Extracting

The watermark extracting procedure is used to prove the ownership of an image. Fig. 3 shows the diagram of the watermarking extracting procedure. In the figure, the symbol V denotes a controversial image. The scheme permutes V by using toral automorphism with the secret key, and uses the DWT to transform the permuted image from the spatial domain into frequency domain. The normalized coefficients are used to generate a codebook. Further, the corresponding indices table of V and the permuted watermark W' are retrieved from the trustworthy third party to reconstruct the watermark. The inverse DWT (IDWT) is used to transform the watermark from the frequency domain into spatial domain. Then, the scheme de-permutes the transformed watermark to construct an extracted watermark image.

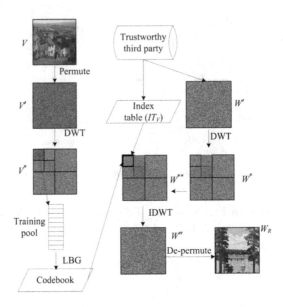

Fig. 3. A diagram of the watermark extracting procedure

4 Experiments and Experimental Results

This section demonstrates the performance of the proposed scheme. In addition, Shieh et al.'s method [10] and Lu et al.'s method [8] are employed to be the benchmarks. Fig. 4 shows six commonly used test images. The size of each image is 256 × 256 pixels. We use the test images to be watermarks and the host images for our experiments.

This paper adopts the peak-signal-to-noise ratio (PSNR) to measure the image quality of the extracted watermark. The PSNR in decibels (dB) is computed by

$$PSNR = 10 \log \frac{255^2}{MSE}(dB), \text{where} \quad MSE = \frac{1}{H \times W} \sum_{i=1}^{H} \sum_{i=1}^{W} (I_{ij} - I'_{ij})^2, \quad (3)$$

where MSE is the mean square error between the extracted watermark and the original watermark.

The PSNR is not meaningful, but it is a useful measurement for comparing the differences between the extracted watermark and the original one. The high PSNR value means that the extracted watermark has less distortion from original watermark. On the contrary, low PSNR means that the extracted watermark has more distortion from the original watermark.

4.1 Experimental Results

Tables 1 and 2 show the PSNR of the extracted watermark. The size of the sliding window is a critical factor that influences the performance of image quality.

(a) Baboon   (b) Barbara   (c) Goldhill

(d) Lena   (e) Sailboat   (f) Zelda

Fig. 4. The testing images of size 256×256

Table 1. The visual quality of the extracted watermark by using the proposed method (size of sliding window = 4×4)

Watermarks	Host images					
	Baboon	Barbara	Goldhill	Lena	Sailboat	Zelda
Baboon	-	26.3294	27.4068	27.6417	24.7498	29.6612
Barbara	29.7243	-	27.47	27.6137	24.7539	29.6618
Goldhill	26.158	29.6332	-	27.437	24.637	29.5769
Lena	26.3497	29.7531	27.3282	-	24.7412	29.6427
Sailboat	26.3081	29.7163	27.4058	27.6096	-	29.6241
Zelda	26.3391	29.7603	27.4717	27.6377	24.7578	-

According to the experimental results shown in Table 1 and Table 2, we can see that larger sliding window size has lower visual quality results. For example, the sliding window in Table 1 is sized four by four, and that in Table 2 is two by two. The average PSNR in Table 1 is 27.5633 dB while that in Table 2 is 29.6022 dB. The different sliding window sizes have different benefits. We will discuss the effects of different sliding window size in next sub-section. In this paper, the sliding window is sized four by four to test the performance of the proposed method.

Table 2. The visual quality of the extracted watermark by using the proposed method (size of sliding window = 2 × 2)

Watermarks	Host images					
	Baboon	Barbara	Goldhill	Lena	Sailboat	Zelda
Baboon	-	28.3201	29.5233	29.7928	26.6956	31.5927
Barbara	31.7595	-	29.5151	29.7909	26.6945	31.594
Goldhill	31.7169	28.2465	-	29.7161	26.6629	31.5657
Lena	31.7539	28.3174	29.4524	-	26.6894	31.581
Sailboat	31.7612	28.3178	29.5197	29.791	-	31.5928
Zelda	31.7696	28.319	29.5265	29.7922	26.696	-

(a) Original watermark   (b) Extracted watermark

Fig. 5. The original watermark and the extracted watermark

In the experimental results, the worst case is to embed the watermark "Sailboat" into the host image "Goldhill". In Table 1, the PSNR value of the extracted watermark is 24.637 dB. The original watermark is shown in Fig. 5(a) and the extracted watermark is shown in Fig. 5(b). Obviously, Fig. 5(b) is meaningful and recognizable.

For the robustness evaluation, we apply the lossy image compression and commonly used image processing to evaluate the integrity and recognizability of the extracted watermark. In this experiment, JPEG and JPEG2000 are used to compress the host image "Goldhill" with compression ratios of 41:1 and 62:1, respectively. The extracted watermarks are shown in Figs. 7(a) and Fig. 7 (b).

Figs. 6(c)-(i) are the modified images which use the Gaussian blurring with 5 as the radius, sharpening, Gaussian noise with 10%, cropping, brightness adjustment with 50%, contrast enhancement with 50%, and rotating the image with degree = 40°. The extracted watermarks corresponding to the modified images are shown in Figs. 7(c)-(i). All the extracted watermarks are meaningful and recognizable. Even though the watermarked image had been cropped into a quarter of original image, the PSNR value of the extracted watermark is 20.6521 dB.

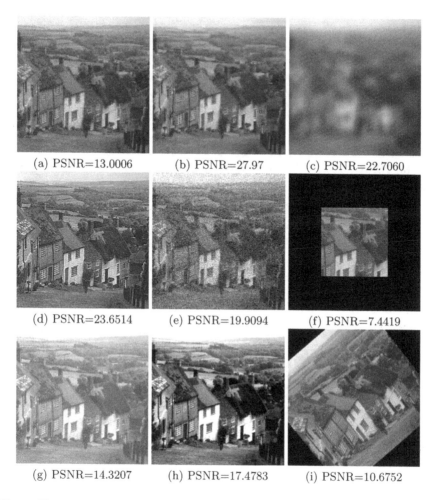

(a) PSNR=13.0006   (b) PSNR=27.97   (c) PSNR=22.7060

(d) PSNR=23.6514   (e) PSNR=19.9094   (f) PSNR=7.4419

(g) PSNR=14.3207   (h) PSNR=17.4783   (i) PSNR=10.6752

Fig. 6. The attacked images; (a) JPEG compression, (b) JPEG2000 compression, (c) Gaussian blurred (radius=5), (d) Sharpening, (e) Gaussian noise (10%), (f) Cropping, (g) Brightness, (h) Contrast enhancement, (i) Rotation

Table 3 shows the comparing results of the extracted watermark between the proposed method and Shieh et al.'s method. Generally speaking, the visual quality of the watermark extracted by using the proposed method is higher than that by Shieh et al.'s method. Lu et al. proposed a semi-blind water-marking method in 2001 [8]. Lu et al.'s method transforms both host image and watermark into the frequency domain by DWT. They applied the just noticeable distortion (JND) to decide how watermark's coefficients are embed-ded to host image's coefficients. The comparisons are summarized in Table 4.

174   C.-C. Chang, Y.-C. Chou, and T.-C. Lu

(a) PSNR=21.5204 (b) PSNR=21.475 (c) PSNR=20.7827

(d) PSNR=20.5033 (e) PSNR=20.4593 (f) PSNR=20.6521

(g) PSNR=21.1743 (h) PSNR=21.4077 (i) PSNR=21.2435

Fig. 7. Extracted watermark from modified images; (a) JPEG compression, (b) JPEG2000 compression, (c) Gaussian blurred (radius=5), (d) Sharpening, (e) Gaussian noise (10%), (f) Cropping, (g) Brightness, (h) Contrast enhancement, (i) Rotation

Table 3. The results (PSNR) for comparing to Shieh et al.'s method (watermark = "Sailboat")

Methods	Host images				
	Baboon	Barbara	Goldhill	Lena	Zelda
Proposed method	29.7163	26.3081	27.4058	27.6096	29.6241
Shieh et al.'s method	19.3061	28.3829	22.5033	23.7203	15.4935

Table 4. The comparison of the proposed method and existing method

Items	Lu et al. [5]	Shieh et al. [7]	Proposed
Original image size (byte)	256×256	256×256	256×256
Watermark size (byte)	256×256	256×256	256×256
Required extra storage (byte)	524,288	65,792	65,792
Retrieval strategy	Semi-blind	Semi-blind	Semi-blind
Domain (host/watermark)	DWT/DWT	SVD/SVD	DWT/DWT
Multiple watermarking	No	Yes	Yes

4.2 Discussions

The size of the sliding window is corresponding to that of a pattern used to train a codebook. Different size of pattern will affect the visual quality of the extracted watermark and the extra storage of extracting information. The pattern with large size leads worse visual quality of extracted watermark and little storage needed for storing the extra information. On the contrary, the pattern with small size can obtain better visual quality of the extracted watermark. However, it requires more storage to keep the extra information. This is a trade-off problem.

In the proposed method, two-level DWT transform was performed to embed and extract watermarks. In level one DWT transform, the number of lower frequency coefficients is a quarter of the number of pixels of the host image so that it will result in a large number of patterns in the training pool. A large training pool affects the computation cost of training a suitable codebook. On the other hand, more than two levels of DWT transform can not provide enough patterns for constructing the training pool. Thus, based on our experimental experiences, it is suggested that the two-level DWT transform be suitable for the proposed method. However, the number of transformation level is not fixed because it corresponds to the size of images. In other words, an image can be transformed by more than two levels when the particular coefficients of the transformed image produce enough training patterns.

A user may bring up an un-registered image and apply the watermark retrieving procedure to exploit an image that belongs to a certain company. In our proposed watermark retrieving procedure, a verifier will request the corresponding secret watermark W^* and index table data from the trusted unit. Thus, only the righteous owner of the image can ask to verify the watermark.

5   Conclusions

In this paper, we have demonstrated a semi-blind watermark technology based on discrete wavelet transformation. In the embedding process, the host image and the watermark were permuted by toral automorphism to increase the security, and fidelity of the embedded watermark and to resist the counterfeiting attack. The proposed scheme embedded the watermark in the frequency domain that could provide a greater control in terms of the robustness and fragility of the watermark. The benefits have been demonstrated in our experiments which indicated that our proposed scheme outperformed Lu et al.'s and Shieh et al.'s schemes in terms of the quality of extracted watermarks and the amount of the required storage.

References

1. Chang, C.C., Hu, Y.S., Lu, T.C.: A Watermarking-Based Image Ownership and Tampering Authentication Scheme. Pattern Recognition Letters 27, 439–446 (2006)
2. Chang, C.C., Tsai, P.Y., Lin, M.H.: SVD-based Digital Image Watermarking Scheme. Pattern Recognition Letters 26(10), 1577–1586 (2005)
3. Chang, C.C., Wu, W.C., Hu, Y.C.: Public-Key Inter-Block Dependence Fragile Watermarking for Image Authentication Using Continued Fraction. Informatica 28, 147–152 (2004)
4. Cox, I.J., Kilian, J., Leighton, F.T., Shamoon, T.: Secure Spread Spectrum Watermarking for Multimedia, IEEE Transactions on Image Processing, Vol. IEEE Transactions on Image Processing 6(12), 1673–1687 (1997)
5. Licks, V., Jordan, R.: On Digital Image Watermarking Robust to Geometric Transformation. In: Proceedings of IEEE International Conference on Image Processing, vol. 3, pp. 690–693 (2000)
6. Lin, C.Y., Wu, M., Bloom, J.A., Cox, I.J., Miller, M.L., Lui, Y.M.: Rotation, Scale, and Translation Resilient Watermarking for Images. IEEE Transactions on Image Processing 10, 767–782 (2001)
7. Linde, Y., Buzo, A., Gray, R.M.: An Algorithm for Vector Quantizer Design. IEEE Transactions on Communications 28, 84–95 (1980)
8. Lu, C.S., Huang, S.K., Sze, C.J., Liao, H.Y.: A New Watermarking Technique for Multimedia Protection, Multimedia Image and Video Processing, Chap. 18, pp. 507–530. CRC Press, Boca Raton, USA (2001)
9. Lu, C.S., Huang, S.K., Sze, C.J., Liao, H.Y.: Cocktail Watermarking for Digital Image Protection. IEEE Transactions on Multimedia 2(4), 209–224 (2000)
10. Shieh, J.M., Lou, D.C., Chang, M.C.: A Semi-blind Digital Watermarking Scheme Based on Singular Value Decomposition. Computer Standards & Interfaces 28(4), 428–440 (2006)
11. Solachidis, V., Pitas, I.: Circularly Symmetric Watermark Embedding in 2-D DFT Domain. IEEE Transactions on Image Processing 10, 1741–1753 (2001)
12. Stankovic, S., Djurovic, I., Pitas, I.: Watermarking in the Space/Spatial-Frequency Domain Using Two-Dimensional Radon-Wigner Distribution. IEEE Transactions on Image Processing 10, 650–658 (2001)
13. Voyatzis, G., Pitas, I.: Digital Image Watermarking Using Mixing Systems. Computers & Graphics 22(4), 405–416 (1998)
14. Voyatzis, G., Pitas, I.: Applications of Toral Automorphisms in Image Watermarking. In: IEEE Conference on Image Processing, pp. 237–240 (1996)

On the Design of Fast Prefix-Preserving IP Address Anonymization Scheme

Qianli Zhang, Jilong Wang, and Xing Li

CERNET Center, Tsinghua University
zhang@cernet.edu.cn

Abstract. Traffic traces are generally anonymized before used in analysis. Prefix-preserving anonymization is often used to avoid privacy issues as well as preserve prefix relationship after anonymization. To facilitate research on real time high speed network traffic, address anonymization algorithm should be fast and consistent. In this paper, the bit string based algorithm and the embedded bit string algorithm will be introduced. Bit string based algorithm uses precomputed bit string to improve the anonymization performance. Instead of only using the LSB of each Rijndael output, the embedded bit string algorithm will take advantage of the full size Rijndael output to anonymize several bits at the same time. The implementation can be downloaded from https://sourceforge.net/projects/ipanon.

1 Introduction

There has been a growing interest in internet traffic research. However, real-world internet traffic traces are still very rare, only a few organizations would share their traffic traces (NLANR/MOAT Network Analysis Infrastructure (NAI) project [2], WIDE project [9], and ACM ITA project [3]). Even with these traces, there still lack of the most recent traces of high speed network. To make the research on most recent traffic traces possible, DragonLab (Distributed Research Academic Gigabit Optical Network Lab) [1] began to establish the real-time traffic analysis environment.

In DragonLab, network traffic is collected from Tsinghua university campus network border router. Tsinghua University campus network is the first and the largest campus network in China, it is connected to China Education and Research Network with two gigabit links. Experimenters can assign incoming or outgoing traffic from one of these two links, and then this traffic will be replayed to the experimenter's measurement point.

To avoid the leak of users' privacy information, traffic traces are subject to an anonymization process [4] [5] [6] before being studied: payload will be erased, the source IP address and destination IP address of packets will be anonymized. IP address anonymization is one of the major steps in this process.

There have been many anonymization schemes available. A straightforward approach is to map each distinct IP address appearing in the trace to a random 32-bit address. The only requirement is that this mapping be one-to-one.

S. Qing, H. Imai, and G. Wang (Eds.): ICICS 2007, LNCS 4861, pp. 177–188, 2007.

However, the loss of the prefix relationships among the IP addresses renders the trace unusable in situations where such relationship is important (e.g., routing performance analysis, or clustering of end systems [7]). It is, therefore, highly desirable for the address anonymization to be prefix-preserving. That is, if two original IP addresses share a k-bit prefix, their anonymized mappings will also share a k-bit prefix.

Inconsistent mapping is also undesirable. For inconsistent mappings, same original address may be mapped into different anonymized addresses when applied independently on more than one traces. Consistent mapping is important because of the following reasons. First, if the traffic anonymization process stops and restarts after a while, the previous and current anonymized traffic traces will take different mappings, thus make the consistent research impossible; secondly, there is a real need for simultaneous (yet consistent) anonymization of traffic traces in different sites, e.g., for taking a snapshot of the Internet. It would be very cumbersome if hundreds of traces have to be gathered first and then anonymized in sequence.

Speed of IP address anonymization is also worth a serious consideration in research on real time traffic. Even for off-line anonymization, speed is important since slow anonymization algorithm may require traffic to be stored to disk beforehand, which is time consuming and inconvenient.

In this paper, we will propose a group of novel prefix-preserving IP address anonymization algorithms; they are all based on the precomputation of random bits. The rest of this paper is organized as follows. In section 2 we briefly introduce related works, including the operation of TCPdpriv and Crypto-pan. In section 3 we describe our schemes in details, section 4 will discuss some concerns in implementation and its performance. The paper is concluded in section 5.

2   Related Works

2.1   TCPdpriv

One possible prefix-preserving approach is adopted in TCPdpriv developed by Greg Minshall [8] and further modified by K. Cho [9]. TCPdpriv can be viewed as a table based approach. It stores a set of $< raw, anonymized >$ binding pairs of IP addresses to maintain the consistency of the anonymization. When a new raw IP address a needs to be anonymized, it will try to find the longest prefix match and anonymize the rest in random. The new generated pair will be added to the binding table. Since only the memory lookup and random generation are required in this algorithm, it may operate very fast.

However, this algorithm is not consistent: the mappings are determined by the raw IP addresses and the relative order in which they appear in a trace. Therefore, a raw address appearing in different traces may be mapped into different anonymized addresses by TCPdpriv, hence the inconsistency. Also, to store all the binding pairs a large amount of memory will be consumed.

2.2 Crypto-pan

Crypto-pan [10] [11] is a deterministic mapping function from raw addresses to anonymized addresses based on the Canonical Form Theorem [11]. With the same key, it can anonymize traffic traces consistently. In this algorithm, $f_i, i = 1 \ldots n$ are defined as follows: $f_i(a_1 a_2 \ldots a_i) := L(R(P(a_1 a_2 \ldots a_i); K)), i = 0, 1, \ldots, n-1$, where L returns the least significant bit, R is a pseudo-random function or a pseudo-random permutation (i.e., a block cipher) such as Rijndael [12], and P is a padding function that expands $a_1 a_2 \ldots a_i$ into a longer string that matches the block size of R. K is the cryptographic key used in the pseudo-random function R. Since the cryptography based anonymization function is uniquely determined by K, same address appearing in two different traces will be mapped to the same anonymized address if the same key is used.

However, to anonymize an IP address, Crypto-pan needs 32 rounds of Rijndael encryption, thus makes it unsuitable for real time anonymization without special hardware. It can only anonymize 10000 IP addresses per second with a PIII machine [11]. Consider the overhead of packet capture, the Crypto-pan is not practical for anonymization in wire speed. Thus, unlike Tcpdpriv, Crypto-pan can only be used off-line.

3 Bit String Based Schemes

3.1 Methodology

Assume S is a random bit string of length L_S, and P_i is a function from $\{0, 1\}^i$ to $\{0, L_S - 1\}$, for $i = 1, 2, \ldots, n-1$ and $P_0 \equiv 0$. Let $B(S, n)$ be the n'th bit of S, define $f_i(a_1 a_2 \ldots a_i) = B(S, P_i(a_1 a_2 \ldots a_i))$, The anonymization process would be:

Given an IP address $a = a_1 a_2 \ldots a_n$, let $F(a) = a'_1 a'_2 \ldots a'_n$ where $a'_i = a_i \bigoplus f_{i-1}(a_1, a_2, \ldots, a_{i-1})$, and $\bigoplus$ stand for the exclusive-or operation, for $i = 1, 2, \ldots n$.

According to Canonical Form Theorem [11], the map is prefix-preserving. This is also straightforward since given $a = a_1 a_2 \ldots a_n$, the anonymized IP address $a'_1 a'_2 \ldots a'_n$ is generated with $a'_i = a_i \bigoplus B(S, P_{i-1}(a_1 a_2 \ldots a_{i-1}))$, which only depends on $a_1 a_2 \ldots a_{i-1}$.

The length of bit string S is crucial for the security of anonymization. We have the following results:

Lemma 1. *If for any $a_1 a_2 \ldots a_i \neq b_1 b_2 \ldots b_j$, $P_i(a_1 a_2 \ldots a_i) \neq P_j(b_1 b_2 \ldots b_j)$, $0 \leq i, j \leq n-1$, string S is at least $2^n - 1$ bits size.*

Proof. For any $a_1 a_2 \ldots a_i \neq b_1 b_2 \ldots b_j$, $P_i(a_1 a_2 \ldots a_i) \neq P_j(b_1 b_2 \ldots b_j)$, imply:

1. If $i \neq j$, $1 \leq i, j \leq n-1$, $P_i(a_1 a_2 \ldots a_i) \neq P_j(b_1 b_2 \ldots b_j)$.
2. If $i = j$, $a_1 a_2 \ldots a_i \neq b_1 b_2 \ldots b_i$, $1 \leq i \leq n-1$, $P_i(a_1 a_2 \ldots a_i) \neq P_i(b_1 b_2 \ldots b_i)$

Consider 2, since the number of all possible i bits prefix is 2^i, $P_i(a_1a_2\ldots a_i)$ has at least 2^i different return values. Now consider 1 and $P_0 = 0$, string S has at least $1 + 2 + 4 + \ldots + 2^{n-1} = 2^n - 1$ different positions, thus the length of S is at least $2^n - 1$ bits.

To prefix-preserving anonymize the complete 32 bits IPv4 address, a string of $2^{32} - 1$ bits (or about 512M bytes) long is required for the maximum security level. The bit string S could be precomputed and preloaded to accelerate the anonymization process. Since memory is rather cheap now, this algorithm can operate very fast with commodity hardware. In situations where anonymizing the first 24 bits is enough, a shorter string with $2^{24} - 1$ bits (or about 2M bytes) long is required.

3.2 Construction of P_i Function

Now the problem is how to construct bit string S and find the proper position mapping function P_i. An ideal group of $P_i, i = 1, 2, \ldots, n-1$ should be easy to present and fast to calculate. We propose the binary tree traversal based method to find such mapping functions. The tree is formed as:

- the root node of the tree is $P_0 = 0$;
- the left child node of $P_i(a_1a_2\ldots a_i)$ is $P_{i+1}(a_1a_2\ldots a_i0)$ and the right child node is $P_{i+1}(a_1a_2\ldots a_i1)$.

Thus the problem becomes to assign values of 1 to $L_S - 1$ to all nodes (except the root node) of this binary tree. We can think of this problem to assign a traversal sequence number to each node. Though the assignment scheme may be arbitrary, to be simple in implementation, we only consider two typical schemes in this paper: the breadth first scheme and the depth first scheme(Fig. 1).

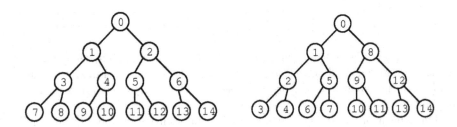

Fig. 1. Breadth first (left) scheme and depth first (right) scheme

For the breadth first scheme, the P_i function is: $P_i(a_1a_2\ldots a_i) = 2^i - 1 + VAL(a_1a_2\ldots a_i)$, $i = 1, 2, \ldots, n-1$. $VAL(a_1a_2\ldots a_i)$ is the value of $a_1a_2\ldots a_i$. Consider

$$\begin{aligned}
P_i(a_1a_2\ldots a_i) &= 2^i - 1 + VAL(a_1a_2\ldots a_i) \\
&= 2(2^{i-1} - 1 + VAL(a_1a_2\ldots a_{i-1})) \\
&\quad + 1 + a_i \\
&= 2P_{i-1}(a_1a_2\ldots a_{i-1}) + a_i + 1
\end{aligned} \tag{1}$$

Thus, P_i function can also be presented as:

$$P_i(a_1 a_2 \ldots a_i) = 2 P_{i-1}(a_1 a_2 \ldots a_{i-1}) + 1$$
$$\text{if } a_i = 0$$
$$P_i(a_1 a_2 \ldots a_i) = 2 P_{i-1}(a_1 a_2 \ldots a_{i-1}) + 2 \tag{2}$$
$$\text{if } a_i = 1$$
$$i = 1, 2, \ldots, n-1$$

For the depth first scheme, the P_i function is:

$$P_i(a_1 a_2 \ldots a_i) = P_{i-1}(a_1 a_2 \ldots a_{i-1}) + 1$$
$$\text{if } a_i = 0$$
$$P_i(a_1 a_2 \ldots a_i) = P_{i-1}(a_1 a_2 \ldots a_{i-1}) + 2^{n-i} \tag{3}$$
$$\text{if } a_i = 1$$
$$i = 1, 2, \ldots, n-1$$

In both schemes $P_0 = 0$.

3.3   Reuse Distance Based Data Locality Analysis

Access to large memory often incurs many cache misses and thus seriously affects the performance. Since the cache policy is often complicated and highly dependent on the specific CPU's architecture, we will use the reuse distance [13] to measure the cache behavior. The reuse distance of a reference is defined as the number of distinct memory references between itself and its reuse. For bit string base algorithms, to anonymize the first k bits prefix, a total of k memory accesses (the address of each access is $S[0], \ldots, S[P_{i-1}(a_0 a_1 \ldots a_{k-1})/8]$) are required. Since each anonymization round starts from the access to $S[0]$, we will evaluate the reuse distance to anonymize one IP address. Note the fact that $P_i(a_1 a_2 \ldots a_i a_{i+1}) > P_i(a_1 a_2 \ldots a_i)$ always holds for depth first and breadth first schemes, only consecutive accesses may result in accesses to the same cache line. We have the following results.

Lemma 2. *For a cache line size of $c = 2^m$ bits, $L_S = 2^k - 1$ bits and $k \le c \ll L_S$, To anonymize k bits, for breadth first scheme, the reuse distance N for each address' anonymization satisfy*

$$k - 1 - m \le N \le k - m \tag{4}$$

For depth first scheme, N satisfy

$$1 \le N \le k - m \tag{5}$$

Proof. Defined $Diff(i) = P_{i+1}(a_1 a_2 \ldots a_{i+1}) - P_i(a_1 a_2 \ldots a_i)$. For breadth first scheme, since

$$Diff(i) = P_{i+1}(a_1 a_2 \ldots a_{i+1}) - P_i(a_1 a_2 \ldots a_i)$$
$$= P_i(a_1 a_2 \ldots a_i) + 1 + a_{i+1} \tag{6}$$

For $i \geq m, Diff(i) \geq 2^m$, and $Diff(i) = 2^m$ only when $i = m, a_1 = a_2 = \ldots = a_{i+1} = 0$. Thus if $i > m + 1$, each access is in a different cache line. Since $i \leq k - 1$, it is easy to see $N \geq k - 1 - (m + 1) + 1 = k - 1 - m$ and $N \leq k - 1 - (m + 1) + 2 = k - m$.

For depth first scheme, since $Diff(i) = 1$ if $a_{i+1} = 0$, and $Diff(i) = 2^{k-1-i}$ if $a_{i+1} = 1$. For $i \leq k - 1 - m$, if and only if $a_i = 1$, $Diff(i) \geq 2^m$, an access is in a different cache line. When IP address is 0, only one memory read is required ($k \leq c$). The worst case happens when all bits are 1, in which case $k - m$ cache misses. If for each bit 1 and 0 have the same possibility, the expectation of reuse distance is $(k - m)/2$.

It looks like that depth first algorithm will be faster than breadth first algorithm in average for single IP address anonymization given that the cache miss number is the only affecting factor. When anonymizing a number of IP addresses, the scenario will be a little different. For breadth first algorithm, the most frequently used bits are all located in the beginning of the bit string S. It is generally easier to cache the most frequently used memory. In contrast, the most frequently used bits in depth first algorithm are relatively sparsely located in the bit string. For random generated IP addresses, suppose the size of cache is C bits and the size of of cache line is C_L bits, in situation where half of the cache size is used to cache the most frequently used $C/2$ bit string, for breadth first algorithm, the first $log_2(C/2)$ bits' anonymization will not incur a cache miss, while for depth first algorithm, since half of the most frequently used bit (the 1 branch) are sparsely located across the bit string, thus only the first $log_2(C/2/C_L) + 1$ bits will be anonymized without cache miss. In experiment, we find that depth first algorithm is generally slower when $k < 31$. This indicates that to anonymize single IP address and to anonymize a large number IP address consecutively are quite different.

3.4   Block Tree Based Prefix Preserving Algorithms

From the above analysis, it can be inferred that if the bit string can be completely loaded into cache, the algorithm would be greatly accelerated. Thus a group of block tree based algorithms are designed. Block tree algorithm is constructed based on the depth first or breadth first bit string algorithms. The basic idea behind this is to divide one IP address into several parts, for each part, there is a correspondent bit string block. These blocks are also organized as a tree. The algorithm is defined by each part's bit number, the position mapping function among blocks and the position mapping function inside each block.

Assume to anonymize the first k bits of IP address, there are n parts and the i'th part has $L_i, i = 0, \ldots n - 1$ bits, $\sum_{i=0}^{n-1} L_i = k$, the part i of IP address IP is $part(i, ip)$, and the bit string is S_i, the algorithm is:

$$for\ i = 0 : n - 1$$
$$anonymize(part(i, ip), L_i, S(P_i(ip))) \qquad (7)$$
$$end\ for$$

$P_i(ip)$ determines which block of the string S should be used to anonymize the i'th part of IP address ip. P can be breadth first position function or depth first position function. The anonymization function can also be depth first or breadth first algorithms. About the length of bit string S, it can be proved that string S also requires at lease $2^k - 1$ bits long.

It is because, to anonymize the L_i bits of IP address, about $2^{L_i} - 1$ bits are required. Assume there are B_i blocks for the i'th part of the IP address. For the $part(i, ip)$ anonymization, the total number of bits required is $B_i(2^{L_i} - 1)$ bits. After anonymization, each block has 2^{L_i} branches. Thus:

$$B_0 = 1$$
$$B_i = B_{i-1}2^{L_{i-1}} \tag{8}$$

Thus the total number of bits required is

$$
\begin{aligned}
N &= \sum_{i=0}^{n-1} B_i(2^{L_i} - 1) \\
&= \sum_{i=0}^{n-1} (B_i 2^{L_i} - B_i) \\
&= \sum_{i=0}^{n-1} (B_{i+1} - B_i) \\
&= B_n - B_0 \\
&= \prod_{i=0}^{n-1} 2^{L_i} - B_0 \\
&= 2^k - 1
\end{aligned}
\tag{9}
$$

If $L_i = 1, i = 0, \ldots, n-1$, it becomes the depth first or breadth first algorithm.

Comparing to the simple depth first or breadth first algorithms, with proper parameters, block tree based algorithms may further minimize cache misses. For example, for CPU with $512K$ cache and 128 bytes size cache line, to anonymize 29 bits prefix,split the 29 bits into two parts: $21, 8$, in the optimal situation, the first bit string ($256K$ bytes) is loaded into cache and only one cache miss will be incurred to anonymize one address.

3.5   Embedded Bit String Based Prefix Preserving Algorithms

Embedded bit string based approach is another variant that aims to reduce the memory required. As described before, to anonymize 32 bits IPv4 addresses, about 512M bytes memory is required. It makes the algorithm infeasible for memory-limited devices like network processors. Also, it is impossible to anonymize IPv6 addresses with this algorithm, even if only anonymize the first 64 bits prefix (subnet prefix). Embedded bit string based algorithm can be thought as to divide one IP address into several parts, for each part, there is a correspondent bit string block. Unlike block tree based approach, these blocks are generated dynamically with cryptographical secure method.

Assume to anonymize the first k bits of IP address, there are n parts and the i'th part has $L_i, i = 0, \ldots n-1$ bits, $\sum_{i=0}^{n-1} L_i = k$, the part i of IP address IP is $part(i, ip)$, and the bit string is S_i, off_i is the first bit offset of the i'th parts' in IP address, the algorithm is:

$$
\begin{aligned}
&for\ i = 0 : n - 1 \\
&\quad S_i = encrypt((ip >> (32 - off_i)) << (32 - off_i)) \\
&\quad anonymize(part(i, ip), L_i, S_i) \\
&end\ for
\end{aligned}
\tag{10}
$$

For example, if the encrypt function is 128 bits block cipher, each time 7 bits can be anonymized. For an IPv4 address, about 5 rounds are needed. To anonymize the first 64 bits prefix of IPv6 addresses, about 10 rounds are necessary, comparing to 64 rounds of Rijindael encryption of Crypto-Pan. Obviously, in this algorithm, cache misses are not the deciding factor for performance. It is welcome since a widening gap between processor and memory speeds has been witnessed in recent years.

4   Implementation and Experiment Results

4.1   Implementation

The bit string S is generated with some pseudo-random number generator. The selection of such PRNG is arbitrary, in this paper, we use the ISAAC [14] algorithm. ISAAC (Indirection, Shift, Accumulate, Add, and Count) generates 32-bit random numbers. Averaged out, it requires 18.75 machine cycles to generate each 32-bit value. The results are uniformly distributed, unbiased, and unpredictable. ISAAC is a secure pseudo random number generator for practical applications and hasn't been broken since it was published 5 years ago. No bias has been detected either. Recent research indicates an estimated known plain text attack on ISAAC may require a time of 4.67×10^{1240} [15]. The initial seed of ISAAC is generated from secret key K via a cryptographic secure pseudo-random number generator. For example, HMAC [16] algorithm or some block cipher.

The anonymization process will load the large bit string S in advance, then for each input IP address, calculate the $f_i(a_1 a_2 \ldots a_i) = B(S, P_i(a_1 a_2 \ldots a_i)), i = 1, 2, \ldots, n, f_0 = B(S, 0)$

Now consider the B and P function. $B(S, bit)$ function is defined as:

```
((S[bit >> 3]&(0x80>>(bit & 0x07)))!= 0)
```

We implement two $P(ip, i)$ functions corresponding to the breadth first scheme and the depth first scheme. $P(ip, i)$ for breadth first scheme and depth first are:

```
(ip&(0x80000000>>i))?
                ((P(ip,i-1)<<1)+1)
                :((P(ip,i-1)<<1)+2)
(ip&(0x80000000>>i))?
                (P(ip,i-1)+(1<<(32-i))
                :(P(ip,i-1)+1)
```

For block tree based algorithm, we use the breadth-breadth approach, that is, the construction inside the blocks or among blocks are all breadth first based. The selection of number of parts and each part's bit number often depend on the specific CPU's cache size. In this paper, we use the two level approach: the first bit string is $64K$ bytes and will anonymize the first 19 bits, the rest bits will be anonymized by another bit string.

For embedded bit string algorithm, we use Rijindael/128 algorithm, thus each round will anonymize 7 bits.

The implementation can be downloaded from https://sourceforge.net/ projects/ipanon.

4.2   Experiment Results

We evaluate the these implementations in two systems: one is PIV 2.8G intel CPU with 1G memory(machine A) and the other is PIV 1.8G intel CPU with 1G memory (machine B). Both of them have a L2 cache size of $512K$ bytes and a cache line size of 128 bytes. We also modify Crypto-pan for a comparison. For each scheme, we generate 16,777,216 (16M) sequential or random IP addresses, and measure the elapsed time in anonymization. The input IP addresses are in 32 bits integer format. We measure the elapsed time after the initialization (for bit string based scheme, after the bit string is generated and loaded). The results are shown in table 1 and table 2. The first row is from machine A and the second row is from machine B.

Table 1. Experiment results for anonymization(random input)

	depth	breadth	cpan	block tree	embedded bit string
Time(us)	1.91	1.98	7.75	1.12	1.45
Time(us)	2.32	2.77	11.34	1.60	2.26

Table 2. Experiment results for anonymization (sequential input)

	depth	breadth	cpan	block tree	embedded bit string
Time(us)	0.24	0.24	7.24	0.37	1.20
Time(us)	0.37	0.37	11.05	0.58	1.84

Experiment result shows that bit string based schemes(depth first, breadth first, block tree, embedded bit string) are 3 to 6 times faster than Crypto-pan in the worst case. For 32 bits random input anonymization, depth first scheme is a little faster than breadth first scheme, while embedded bit string algorithm is faster than both. Block tree algorithm is considerably faster than all the other schemes. A comparison of the machine A and machine B is also interesting. For CPU sensitive algorithms like crypto-pan and embedded bit string, a performance increase of 40% is gained from slower machine B to A; while for memory access sensitive algorithms like breadth first or depth first algorithm, only about 20% is gained. Although the performance of CPU has increased a lot, the speed of memory access is roughly the same. Previous experiments in a PIV 1.4G machine indicate that depth first algorithm is more than 10 times faster than Crypto-pan. For 1.8G machine this ratio is 4.89 and for 2.8G machine this ratio is 4.06.

We evaluate the time required vs. number of bits to be processed, the results are shown in Fig.2. For algorithms like depth first algorithm, breadth first algorithm and block tree algorithm, the property of input can affect the performance dramatically. For example, sequential input may be more than 6 times faster than random input for depth first algorithm. The reason is that 16,777,216 sequential IP addresses share a common 8 bits prefix, thus has far less cache misses and the deciding factor is the computation overhead. For schemes that are not cache miss sensitive like Crypto pan and embedded bit string algorithm, there is little difference between sequential and random scenarios.

For random input, the computation time of breadth first and depth first anonymization algorithms are roughly linear before 22 bits with a fixed slope of computation overhead per bit. The time is roughly linear after 22 bits with the increasing cache misses, though the slope is a lot steeper. The embedded bit string based algorithm, is a staircase function since there is little overhead inside each 7 bits block. For block tree based approach, it can be separated into 3 lines, for the first line (1-22), since the complete bit string can be loaded into cache, there is little cache misses. Because Intel CPU's cache line size is 128 bytes, from 22 to 29, there is only one cache misses. From 30 to 32 bits, there will be one cache misses added per bit increased.

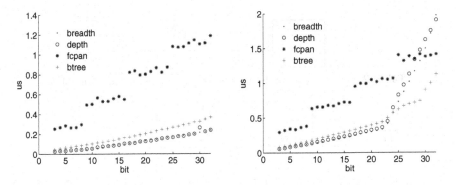

Fig. 2. Processing time per address (averaged from 16,777,216 IP addresses anonymization), sequential input (left) and random input (right). Depth first algorithm is shortened as depth, breadth first algorithm as breadth, Crypto-pan as cpan, block tree algorithm as btree and the embedded bit string algorithm as fcpan.

The IP addresses in real traces are often more complex: addresses inside ISP are heavily clustered while addresses outside ISP may be very random. To evaluate the performance of these anonymization scheme in real environment, we anonymize a public 24 hours traffic trace provided by WIDE [9]. The trace is captured on Feb 27, 2003 and is stored in pcap format. It contains a total of 364,483,718 packets. After gzip compression, the traffic trace occupies about 10G disk space. The proposed schemes are applied on it. Traces after anonymization are also stored in disk in pcap format. As shown in table 3, bit string based schemes are much faster than Crypto-pan.

Table 3. Experiment results for anonymization of real traces

	Time	PPS
Depth first	3437.3447s	105,566
Breadth first	3544.4881s	102,357
Crypto-pan	20338.0471	17,841
Depth first 24	2607.2846s	139,175
Breadth first 24	2570.0872s	141,189
Crypto-pan 24	15757.2146s	23,028
Block tree	3195.3225s	113,562
No anonymization	1923.2942s	188, 670

5   Conclusion

In this paper, we propose a group of novel prefix-preserving IP address anonymization algorithms which all base on the bit string based algorithm. Experiment results indicate that these algorithms are all much faster than Crypto-pan.

More research is still going on to accelerate the anonymization speed so that anonymization of IPv6 addresses in gigabit wire speed is possible.

Acknowledgment

This research was supported by the research Program of China (863) under contract number 2005AA112130 and research Program of China (973) under contract number 2003CB314807.

References

1. DragonLab, http://www.dragonlab.org/
2. McGregor, T., Braun, H., Brown, J.: The NLANR network analysis infrastructure. IEEE Communications Magazine 38(5), 122–128 (2000)
3. The Internet traffic archive (April 2000), http://ita.ee.lbl.gov/
4. Patarin, S., Makpangou, M., Pandora, M.: A flexible network monitoring platform. In: Proceedings of the 2000 USENIX Annual Technical Conference (June 2000)
5. Peuhkuri, M.: A Method to Compress and Anonymize Packet Traces. SIGCOMM IMW (2001)
6. Pang, R., Paxson, V.: A high-level programming environment for packet trace anonymization and transformation. SIGCOMM (2003)
7. Krishnamurthy, B., Wang, J.: On network-ware clustering of web clients. In: SIG-COMM (2000)
8. Minshall, G.: TCPdpriv Command Manual (1996)
9. Cho, K., Mitsuya, K., Kato, A.: Traffic data repository at the wide project. In: Proceedings of USENIX 2000 Annual Technical Conference: FREENIX Track, San Diego, CA (June 2000)
10. Xu, J., Fan, J., Ammar, M.H., Moon, S.B.: On the design and performance of prefix-preserving IP traffic trace anonymization. In: SIGCOMM IMW (2001)

11. Xu, J., Fan, J., Ammar, M.H., Moon, S.B.: Prefix-preserving IP address anonymiza-tion: measurement based security evaluation and a new cryptography-based scheme. In: ICNP (2002)
12. Daemen, J., Rijmen, V.: AES proposal: Rijndael, Tech. Rep., Computer Security Resource Center, National Institute of Standards and Technology (February 2001), http://csrc.nist.gov/encryption/aes/rijndael/Rijndael.pdf
13. Beyls, K., D'Hollander, E.: Reuse distance-based cache hint selection. In: Procced-ings of the 8th International Euro-Par Conference (August 2002)
14. Jenkins, B.: ISAAC: a fast cryptographic random number generator, http://burtleburtle.net/bob/rand/isaac.html
15. Pudovkina, M.: A known plaintext attack on the ISAAC keystream generator, http://eprint.iacr.org/2001/049.pdf
16. Krawczyk, H., Bellare, M., Canetti, R.: RFC 2104: HMAC: Keyed-Hashing for Message Authentication (February 1997)
17. Ylonen, T.: Thoughts on how to mount an attack on tpcpdriv's "-50" option, in TCPpdpriv source distribution (1996)

High Speed Modular Divider Based on GCD Algorithm

Abdulah Abdulah Zadeh

Shahid Beheshti University, Tehran, Iran
A.Zadeh@mail.sbu.ac.ir

Abstract. GCD algorithm is a well known algorithm for computing modular division and inversion which is widely used in Elliptic Curve Cryptography (ECC). Also division is the most time-consuming operation in Elliptic and Hyperelliptic Curve Cryptography. The conventional radix-2 GCD algorithm, is performed modular division over $GF(2^m)$ in approximately $2m$ iterations (or clock cycles). These algorithms consist of at least four comparisons at each iteration. In this paper the conventional algorithm is extended to radix-4. To increase the efficiency of algorithm the number of comparisons is reduced. So the algorithm enables very fast computation of division over $GF(2^m)$. The proposed algorithm described in such a way that its hardware realization is straightforward. The implemented results show reducing the division time to m clock cycles. Also the proposed architecture is compared with other reported dividers and it has been shown that the proposed architecture only occupies %14 more LUT (over $GF(2^{163})$) while the computation time is decreased to half.

Keywords: GCD algorithm, Radix four, ECC, Finite Field.

1 Introduction

Arithmetic operations (i.e. addition, multiplication and inversion or division) over finite fields are widely used in data communication systems, coding and particularly in cryptography. By developing Elliptic Curve Cryptography, which requires division, many attempts have been made to increase the efficiency of this operation [1-18].

Different approaches and architectures have been proposed for division. These approaches are usually listed as three categories. 1) Dividers which are based on Fermat's theorem; 2) Divider which are based on binary GCD (greatest common divisor) algorithm and 3) Dividers which include solving a system of linear equations and the almost inverse algorithm. Among them, GCD based dividers offer most efficient approaches in terms of time and area [19]. In this paper we propose a new high speed algorithm and architecture for division which is based on GCD algorithm. We called the proposed algorithm as extended radix-4 GCD algorithm. The Extended radix-4 GCD algorithm is twice faster than conventional GCD algorithms.

The rest of this paper is organized as follow: in section 2 a brief introduction to GCD algorithm and a review to previous works are presented. In section 3 the extended radix 4 GCD algorithm is proposed. In section 4 the proposed architecture and its implementation is presented and compared with the former reported implementations. Section 5 concludes the paper.

S. Qing, H. Imai, and G. Wang (Eds.): ICICS 2007, LNCS 4861, pp. 189–200, 2007.
© Springer-Verlag Berlin Heidelberg 2007

2 Preliminaries

2.1 GCD Algorithm

The GCD algorithm is an efficient way of calculating modular division and inversion which can be used over both GF(P) and GF(2^m). Consider the residue class field of integers with an odd prime modules $P(x)$. Let A and $B(\neq 0)$ be elements of the field and $S(x)=P(x)$.

$$A(x) = a_{m-1}x^{m-1} + a_{m-2}x^{m-2} + ... + a_1x^1 + a_0 \qquad (1)$$

$$B(x) = b_{m-1}x^{m-1} + b_{m-2}x^{m-2} + ... + b_1x^1 + b_0 \qquad (2)$$

$$S(x) = x^m + s_{m-1}x^{m-1} + ... + s_1x^1 + s_0 \qquad (3)$$

$$V(x) = v_{m-1}x^{m-1} + v_{m-2}x^{m-2} + ... + v_1x^1 + v_0 \qquad (4)$$

The coefficients of each polynomial are binary digits 0 or 1.

The algorithm calculates V, where $V=A/B$ mod $P(x)$. The algorithm performs modular division by intertwining the procedure for finding the modular quotient with that for calculating GCD(S,A). The following properties are applied iteratively to calculate GCD(A,S).

1- if A and S both are even then $GCD(A,S) = 2 \times GCD\left(\frac{A}{2}, \frac{S}{2}\right)$

2- if A is even and P is odd then $GCD(A,S) = GCD\left(\frac{A}{2}, S\right)$

3- if A and P both are odd then $GCD(A,S) = GCD\left(\frac{(A+S)}{2}, S\right)$

Let a_0 and s_0 be the least significant bit (LSB) of A and S respectively then these properties could be listed as table1.

The GCD divider algorithm reduces the problem of finding the greatest common divisor (GCD) by repeatedly applying these identities.

Table 1. Assumptions of Radix 2 GCD algorithm

a_0	s_0	GCD(A,S) is equal to
0	0	$2 \times GCD\left(\frac{A}{2}, \frac{S}{2}\right)$
1	0	$GCD\left(\frac{A}{2}, S\right)$
1	1	$GCD\left(\frac{(A+S)}{2}, S\right)$

2.2 Previous Works

The classical algorithm which is based on GCD algorithm, computes inversion i.e. $B^{-1}(x)$ mod $P(x)$ where $P(x)$ is the irreducible polynomial of polynomial representation over $GF(2^m)$. Thus to do division i.e. $A(x)/B(x) \bmod P(x)$, an extra multiplication was required. Based on classical GCD algorithm N.Takagi proposed an algorithm to compute division $A(x)/B(x) \bmod P(x)$ [14-15]. The proposed algorithm in [14-15] employed a *while* loop where *while* loop is not appropriate for hardware realization [4,5,7]. Also unfixed (and unknown) number of iterations or computation time makes the use of this algorithm difficult in crypto-processors.

To solve this problem a new algorithm has been proposed in [4,5] which was based on extended Euclid's algorithm. Replacing *while* loop by *for* loop, lets the algorithm to be more efficient for hardware implementing. This algorithm needs exactly $2m$ iterations to perform the division [5]. Wu et.al [17] and Brunner et.al [18] proposed similar serial binary shift-right algorithms exploring the counter idea for division [7].

A faster algorithm has been proposed in [7] to compute division. The proposed algorithm in [7] was extended of N.Takagi algorithm which performs division with *while* loop. This algorithm performs division serially in radix-4. Although it had a higher speed but it still suffered from a *while* loop and unfixed number of iterations.

Another high speed algorithm has been used and implemented for inversion which executes in m clock cycles in [20]. The implemented algorithm in [20] is based on serial implementation exist which is based on conventional GCD algorithm. The drawback of this implementation is that this architecture required an extra multiplication time and unit to convert inversion results to division.

3 High Speed Rdix-4 GCD Algorithm

The proposed algorithm in [5] to compute modular division, using *for* loop, is shown

```
input : A(x), B(x), P(x)
output : A(x)/B(x)  mod  P(x)
R = B(x); S = P(x); U = A(x); V = 0;
for  i = 1 to 2m
    if (state = 0) then
        cnt = cnt + 1;
        if (r₀ = 0) then
            (R,S) = (S + R,R); (U,V) = (V + U,U);
            state = 1;
    else
        cnt = cnt - 1;
        if (r₀ = 0) then
            (R,S) = (S + R,S); (U,V) = (V + U,V);
    if (cnt = 0)then
        state = 0;
R = R/x;
U = U/x  mod P(x);
return (V);
```

Algorithm 1. GCD based algorithm proposed in [5] in which replacing *while* with *for* in algorithm1. As shown in Eq.3 S is $m+1$ bit length and other variables are m bit length.

In algorithm1, by keeping S odd, some comparisons of classical N.Takagi algorithm has been omitted. To accelerate the proposed GCD algorithm two iterations of this algorithm should be performed in one clock cycle. This method has been used in [21].

Table 2. Assumptions of GCD algorithm in radix 4

$S_1 S_0$	$a_1 a_0$	$GCD(A,S)$ is equal to
00	00	$GCD(A,S) \rightarrow 4GCD(\frac{A}{4}, \frac{S}{4})$
01 or 11	00	$GCD(A,S) \rightarrow GCD(\frac{A}{4}, S)$
10	00	$GCD(A,S) \rightarrow 2GCD(\frac{A}{4}, \frac{S}{2})$
10	10	$GCD(A,S) \rightarrow 2GCD(\frac{A+S}{2}, \frac{S}{2})$ $GCD(A,S) \rightarrow 2GCD(\frac{A+S}{2}, \frac{A}{2})$
01	01	$GCD(A,S) \rightarrow GCD(\frac{A+S}{4}, S)$ $GCD(A,S) \rightarrow GCD(\frac{A+S}{4}, A)$
11	01	$GCD(A,S) \rightarrow GCD(\frac{A+S}{4} + \frac{R}{2}, S)$ $GCD(A,S) \rightarrow GCD(\frac{A+S}{4} + \frac{S}{2}, S)$ $GCD(A,S) \rightarrow GCD(\frac{A+S}{4} + \frac{R}{2}, R)$ $GCD(A,S) \rightarrow GCD(\frac{A+S}{4} + \frac{S}{2}, R)$
10	01	$GCD(A,S) \rightarrow GCD(\frac{S}{4} + \frac{A}{2}, R)$ $GCD(A,S) \rightarrow GCD(\frac{S}{4} + \frac{A}{2}, \frac{S}{2})$
11	10	$GCD(A,S) \rightarrow GCD(\frac{A}{4} + \frac{S}{2}, \frac{R}{2})$ $GCD(A,S) \rightarrow GCD(\frac{A}{4} + \frac{S}{2}, S)$
11	11	$GCD(A,S) \rightarrow GCD(\frac{A+S}{4}, R)$ $GCD(A,S) \rightarrow GCD(\frac{A+S}{4}, S)$

Since each iteration of algorithm1 includes 4 comparisons, employed algorithm in [21] has 16 comparisons at each iteration. The great number of comparisons makes implement difficult. To decrease the number of comparisons algorithm2 is presented in this paper. This algorithm is extended of GCD algorithm proposed in [5], in which the

```
input : A(x), B(x), S(x)
output : A(x)/B(x) mod  S(x)
R = B(x); S = S(x); U = A(x); V = 0;
1. for  i = 1  to  m
2.  if( state = 0 )
3.       if( r_1 r_0 = 00 )              cnt = cnt + 1;
4.       elsif( r_1 r_0 = 10 )           (R,S) = (R + 2S, R/2 );
5.                                       (U,V) = (U + 2V, U/X);
6.                                       state = 1;  cnt = cnt + 1;
7.          elsif( r_1 r_0 = 01 )
8.                   state  = 1;
9.                   if( s_1 = 0 )  (R,S)    = (R + S, R) ;
10.                                 (U,V)    = (U + V, U) ;
11.                  else           (R,S)    = ( 3S + R, R) ;
12.                                 (U,V)    = ( 3V + U, U) ;
13.         else        // { r_1 r_0 = 11 }
14.                 state = 1;
15.                 if( s_1 = 1)  (R,S) = (R + S, R);
16.                               (U,V) = (U + V, U);
17.                 else          (R,S) = ( 3R + S, R);
18.                               (U,V) = ( 3U + V, U);
19.    else                // { state = 1 }
20.        if( r_1 r_0 = 00 )             cnt = cnt − 1;
21.        elsif( r_1 r_0 = 10 )          (R,S) = (R + 2S, S);
22.                                       (U,V) = (U + 2V, V );
23.                                       cnt = cnt − 1;
24.       elsif( r_1 r_0 = 01)       cnt = cnt − 1;
25.                   if( s_1 = 0)  (R, S) = (R + S, S);
                                    (U,V) = (U + V, V);
26 − 1.               else         (R, S) = (3S + R, S);
                                   (U,V) = (3V + U, V);
27.        else          // { r_1 r_0 = 11 }
                     cnt = cnt − 1;
28.                  if( s_1 = 1)  (R, S) = (R + S, S);
                                   (U,V) = (U + V, V)
29 − 1               else   (R, S) = (R + 3S, S);
                            (U,V) = (U + 3V, V);
30.          if (cnt = 0)      state = 0;
31.  U = U/x^2  mod P(x);
32.  R = R/x^2  mod P(x);
33. end loop;
33. return(V);
```

Algorithm 2. Radix 4 GCD algorithm with 12 comparisons

comparisons and operations performed in radix-4. To extend the GCD algorithm to radix 4, the applied properties should be extended to radix 4. The extended properties are listed in table2. In table2 $a_1 a_0$ and $s_1 s_0$ are denoted as two LSB bits of $A(x)$ and $S(x)$.

In algorithm2 the required iterations to execute division are m (for GF(2^m)) while each iteration includes 12 comparisons. As it can be seen, the number of iterations has break to half in compare to algorithm1 and the number of comparisons are also reduced from 16 to 12 compare to employed algorithm in [21].

Similar to algorithm1 in algorithm2, two variables $state$ and cnt are provided. The variable cnt is used for tracking the difference of degree between R and S, and the variable $state$ is used for identifying which one has the larger degree. Due to the values of $state$, R and S, 12 different conditions may be applied to find the GCD(R,S). Since the initial value of S is equaled to $P(x)$ (irreducible polynomial), the LSB of S is always remained at 1. Hence we have just to check the two last bits of R and s_1 (i.e. second LSB bit of S).

Increasing the value of cnt, decreases the degree of S and R by two in algorithm2 and by one in algorithm1. At the end of algorithm, $state$ and cnt will be zero and R and S will be equal to 1. The final value of V will be as the division's result.

In algorithm2 U, V, R and S are variables which are initialized at the beginning of the algorithm by $A(x)$, zero, $B(x)$ and $P(x)$ respectively; where $P(x)$ is the irreducible polynomial used to generate the field.

In the algorithm2 at each iteration (before U and R divided 4 or x^2), the variable R is replaced by one of the R, S, $R+S$, $R+2S$, $R+3S$ or $3R+S$ terms (i.e. one of these terms should be stored back into the R). The corresponding U which is another internal variable of the algorithm2 is replaced by one of the U, V, $U+V$, $U+3V$, $U+2V$ or $V+3U$ terms. Table3 lists the extension of R, S and U, V in the algorithm2.

Table 3. Replacements table for R, S and U, V

variable	Possible conversions	variable	Possible conversions
	R		U
	S		V
R, S	$R/2$	U, V	$U/2$
	$R+S$		$U+V$
	$R+3S$		$U+3V$
	$3R+S$		$3U+V$
	$R+2S$		$U+2V$

The valid term to store back into the R, among the possible terms (shown in table3 as *possible conversions*), depends on the last two bits of the terms. Two LSB of the term which should be stored back into R is always zero.

Using table3 a new algorithm is proposed to compute modular division in m clock cycles. In the new algorithm which is shown in algorithm3, the number of comparisons is reduced to 10. In proposed algorithm the structure and format of input : $A(x), B(x), P(x)$

output : $A(x)/B(x)$ mod $P(x)$

$R = B(x); S = P(x); U = A(x); V = 0;$

1. *for* $i = 1$ *to* m

2-1. $(R,U) \leftarrow (R,U) when (r_1 r_0 = 00)$

　　　　else $(R + S, U + V)$ when $((r_1 r_0 + s_1 s_0) = 00)$ $\{(r_1 r_0 = 01$ & $s_1 = 0)$or $(r_1 r_0 = 11$ & $s_1 = 1)\}$

　　　　else $(3R + S, 3U + V)$ when $(((r_1 r_0 + r_0 0 + s_1 s_0) = 00)$ & state $= 0)$

　　　　　　　　　　　　　　　$\{(r_1 r_0 = 11$ & $s_1 = 0)$or $(r_1 r_0 = 01$ & $s_1 = 1$ & state=0)\}$

　　　　else $(R + 3S, U + 3V)$ when $(((r_1 r_0 + 10 + s_1 s_0) = 00)$ & state $= 1)$ $\{(r_1 r_0 = 01$ & $s_1 = 1$ & state=1)\}$

　　　　else $(R + 2S, U + 2V);$

2-2. $(S,V) \leftarrow (S, V)$ when (state=1 *or* $r_1 r_0 = 00)$

　　　　else $(R/2, U/x)$ when $(r_1 r_0 = 10$ & $s_1 = 0$ & state=0)

　　　　else $(R,U);$

3.   if (state $= 1$) then

　　　　　　cnt $=$ cnt - 1;

　　　elsif (state $= 0$ & $r_0 = 0$)

　　　　　　cnt $=$ cnt + 1;

　　　end if;

4.   if (cnt $= 0$) then

　　　　　　state $= 0;$

　　　elsif ((r0 $= 1$ & st $= 0$) or (r $= 10$ & st $= 0$))

　　　　　　state $= 1;$

　　　end if;

5. $U = U/x^2$ mod $P(x);$ $R = R/x^2$ mod $P(x);$

6. *end loop*;

7. *return* $(V);$

Algorithm 3. The proposed Extended GCD   radix 4 algorithm whit 10 conditions at each iteration

comparisons are changed in such a way that its hardware realization is more straightforward. Fewer comparisons make the algorithm more efficient and simple for hardware implementation while the great number of comparisons makes the algorithm complex for hardware implementation.

In algorithm3 the LSB of possible terms to assign R and U (which are mentioned in table3) are considered to choose the valid term for replacing them. The role of *cnt*, *state*, and other variables in algorithm3 are same as algorithm2 and algorithm1.

As seen in algorithm3 (*line* 2-1), the new value for R is selected according to the values of R (current value) , S, $R+S$, $R+S+2S$, or $R+S+2R$ which were mentioned in table3. The value which has two zero LSB is candidate to assign R. The last bit of S is always one. So among all cases of S and R which were mentioned in table3, at least one term in has two zero bit in LSB. In one case, two specific terms of table3 have two zero in LSB, at the same time. When $r_1 r_0 = 01$ and $s_1 s_0 = 11$ both $U+3V$

and $3U+V$ are zero in two LSB. To identify the valid one to assign to R, state bit should be used. $U+3V$ should be assigned if state is equal to1 and $3U+V$ should be assigned if state is equal to 0. So in algorithm3, *state* and *cn*t should be considered as variables which are contributed in comparisons.

Furthermore the denoted lines in algorithm3 by 2-1 and 2-2 are completely independent; so they could be executed simultaneously and in parallel.

The novelty of the proposed algorithm (i.e. algorithm3) is in fewer number of comparisons which leads to implement division more efficiently in less area. Table4 is presented to compare the number of conditions and comparisons for each iterations in different algorithms.

Table 4. Number of conditions for different GCD algorithms

Algorithm	Number of iterations	Number of conditions in each iteration
Radix-2 GCD algorithm in [5] (Algorithm1)	$2m$	4
Algorithm[21]	m	16
Algorithm2	m	12
Algorithm3	m	10

4   Implementation of Extended Radix-4 GCD Algorithm

In this section an architecture is presented to implement algorithm3. In algorithm3, R and S should be filled by the values of R, S, $R/2$, $R+3S$, $3R+S$ or $R+2S$. Also U and V should be filled by U, V, $U/2$, $U+V$, $U+3V$, $3U+V$ or $U+2V$, depends on the algorithms conditions. To fill R and S registers with their new values (at the end of each iteration or clock) a component which called as RS_adder is implemented. Another similar component is implemented to compute the possible values of U and V which is called as UV_adder. The inputs of RS_adder component are old values of R and S and UV_adder is U and V and their outputs are possible values for R, S, U and V respectively.

The two last bits of RS_adder that should be assigned to R, are always zero. Thus division of the valid output of RS_adder to x or 2 can be performed by one bit shift to right so implementing the other term $R/2$ can be ignored and approached by wiring.

But because the last bit of the valid output of UV_adder component that should be assigned to U is not always zero then $U/2$ can not be approached from U by wiring and should be computed.

Then implementation of U/x is not so costly (as shown in [5]) and depends on irreducible polynomial of the finite field. The whole proposed architecture for extended radix-4 GCD is shown in figure1.

RR, SS, UU, and VV registers are temporary registers to store the final values at the end of each iteration for R, S, U and V respectively. In the proposed architecture, four multiplexers are implemented to choose the valid output for RR, SS, UU and VV

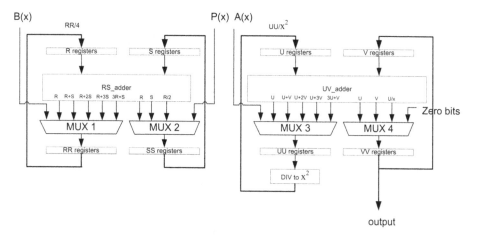

Fig. 1. Full architecture for Extended radix 4 GCD algorithm

registers (MUX1, MUX2, MUX3 and MUX4). By each iteration the values of RR and UU registers (after dividing to 4 and x^2) are stored in R and U registers. Also the values of SS and VV registers are stored in S and V registers.

Because last two bits (LSB) of RR are always equal to zero, the division of RR to x^2 can be performed by shifting two bits to the right (equal to $R/4$). Since the last two bits of UU are not always zero this technique can not be used for U and UU. Then a simple component to divide to x^2 is required before UU register connected to U register.

By first clock cycle initialization will be done. During the initialization, VV should be filled with zero and SS filled with $S(x)$. But RR and UU should be filled with $4 \times B(x)$ and $4 \times A(x)$. Because at the first iteration they are divided to x^2, thus they should be multiplied by four. To avoid losing the data, 2 extra bits should be implemented for all registers so after the division by x^2 at the first iteration, the R, S, V and U registers filled with exact values of B, S, A and zero. So for the GCD divider over GF(2^m), registers should be implemented with the length of $m+2$ bits.

A counter as *cnt* and a register for the *state* bit are required which is not shown in figure1. Also a clock counter which called *clkcounter* is employed to determine the finishing time (or last clock) of division. When the *clkcounter* is set to zero, RR, SS, UU and VV will be initialized by primary values ($B(x)$, $S(x)$, $A(x)$ and zero).

The above architecture is implemented on FPGA Xilinx series Vertex2 XC2V250-5 using Xilinx ISE software. The chosen fields for implementation are which recommended by NIST for Elliptic Curve Cryptography (ECC). Table5 summarized implementation in terms of slices, 4 input LUTs and flip flops to evaluate the required area on chip besides the maximum allowed frequency for comparing the required time of computation.

A GCD radix-2 divider over GF(2^{163}) for an ECC core has been implemented in [22,23]. Other inversion architectures has been proposed in [11,13]; It notes that in order to divide two operands, after inversion a multiplication should be performed so the multiplication time should be added to the time of inversion to find comparable

Table 5. Number of conditions for different GCD algorithms

	Slice	Flip Flop	4 input LUT	Max frequency (MHz)
$GF(2^{163})$	2240	684	3039	171
$GF(2^{233})$	3206	962	4337	165

values for division based on inversion of [11,13]. The results of proposed architectures are summarized in table6. As it can be seen the proposed architecture when implemented over $GF(2^{163})$ reduces computation time by half but requires %14 more LUT implementation compare to the radix-2 architecture which employed in [22,23].

Table 6. Implementation result for GCD radix -2 divider implemented

	Device	Area	Cycles	GF	
Division [22,23]	XCV2000E	1316 FF 2678 LUT	$2m$	$GF(2^{163})$	Employed the algorithm proposed in [5]
Inversion [13]	XCV3200E	10065 CLB 12 BRAMs	27(1.33us)	$GF(2^{193})$	(Multiplicative inversion)
Inversion [11]	XC2VP125	14800 CLB	586	256 bit	Classical and Montgomery

5 Conclusion

In this paper a new algorithm, based on GCD algorithm for modular division over finite fields was proposed. This algorithm executes modular division in radix-4. It is two times faster than the conventional radix-2 GCD dividers. In the proposed algorithm the number of conditions has been reduced so it has lower implementation complexity. For the proposed algorithm an architecture has been suggested. The proposed architecture has been implemented on FPGA over $GF(2^{163})$, $GF(2^{233})$. The frequency and required resources has been reported for the implementations. It was shown that the time performance is improved by %50 while its occupied area increased just %14, compare to the former reported algorithm in radix-2. So it can be used to accelerate the cryptography particularly in high speed ECC crypto-processors. Future work can be concentrated on extending the algorithm to radix 2^n and discussing about speed and area according to n. The other area for future study could be employing the proposed divider in an ECC crypto-processor and evaluating its performance.

References

1. Guajardo, J., Paar, C.: Itoh-Tsuji inversion in Standard Basis and Its Application in Cryptography and Codes, Design, Codes and Cryptography, pp. 207–216 (February 2002)
2. Rodríguez-Henríquez, F., Morales-Luna, G., Saqib, N.A., Cruz-Cortés, N.: Parallel Itoh-Tsujii Multiplicative Inversion Algorithm for a Special Class of Trinomials Cryptology, Report 2006/035.

3. Wei, S.-W.: VLSI architectures for computing exponentiations, multiplicative inverses, and divisions in GF(2m). IEEE Transactions on Circuits and SystemsII: Analog and Digital Signal Processing 44, 847–855 (1997)
4. Hoon Kim, C., Kwon, S., Pyo Hong, C.: Efficient bit-serial systolic array for division over GF(2/sup m/) [elliptic curve cryptosystem applications. In: Nam, G. (ed.) ISCAS 2003. Proceedings of the 2003 International Symposium on Circuits and Systems, vol. 2, pp. 252–255. IEEE, Los Alamitos (2003)
5. Hoon Kim, C., Pyo Hong, C.: High-speed division architecture for $GF(2^m)$. Electronics Letters 38, 835–836 (2002)
6. Daly, A., Marnane, W., Kerinsy, T., Popovici, E.: Fast Modular Division for Application in ECC on Reconfigurable Logic. In: Cheung, P.Y.K., Constantinides, G.A. (eds.) FPL 2003. LNCS, vol. 2778, Springer, Heidelberg (2003)
7. de Dormale, G.M., Quisquater, J.-J.: Novel iterative digit-serial modular division over GF(2m). In: Cryptographic Advances in Secure Hardware CRASH 2005 (January 2005)
8. Kaihara, M.E., Takagi, N.: A VLSI algorithm for modular multiplication/division. In: Proceedings of the 16th IEEE Symposium on Computer Arithmetic, pp. 220–227 (June 2003)
9. Weber, K.: The Accelerated Integer GCD Algorithm. ACM Transactions on Mathematical Software 21, 111–122 (1995)
10. Kaihara, M.E., Takagi, N.: A VLSI algorithm for modular multiplication/division. In: Proceedings of the 16th IEEE Symposium on Computer Arithmetic, pp. 220–227 (June 2003)
11. McIvor, C., McLoone, M., McCanny, J.V.: Improved Montgomery modular inverse algorithm. 2nd IEEE Electronicks Letters 40 (September 2004)
12. Savas, E.: A carry-free architecture for Montgomery inversion. IEEE Transactions on Computers 54, 1508–1519 (2005)
13. Rodr'iguez-Henr'iquez, F., Saqib1, N.A., Cruz-Cortés, N.: A Fast Implementation of Multiplicative Inversion over GF(2m). In: Proceedings of the International Conference on Information Technology: Coding and Computing (ITCC 2005)
14. Takagi, N.: A VLSI Algorithm for Modular Division Based on the Binary GCD Algorithm. IEICE Trans. Fundamentals E81-A, 724–728 (1998)
15. Weber, K.: The Accelerated Integer GCD Algorithm. ACM Transactions on Mathematical Software 21, 111–122 (1995)
16. de Dormale, G.M., Quisquater, J.-J.: Novel iterative digit-serial modular division over GF(2m). In: Ecrypt Workshop 2005, Cryptographic Advances in Secure Hardware-Crash (September 2005)
17. Wu, C.-H., Wu, C.-M., Shieh, M.-D., Hwang, Y.-T.: High-Speed, Low-Complexity Systolic Designs of Novel Iterative Division Algorithms in GF(2m). IEEE Transactions on Computers 53, 375–380 (2004)
18. Brunner, H., Curiger, A., Hofstetter, M.: On Computing Multiplicative Inverses in GF(2m). IEEE Transactions on computers 42, 1010–1015 (1993)
19. Cohen, A.E., Parhi, K.K.: Implementation of Scalable Elliptic Curve Cryptosystem Crypto-Accelerators for GF(2m). Conference Record of the Thirty-Eighth Asilomar Conference on Signals, Systems and Computers 1, 471–477 (2004)
20. Schmalisch, M., Timmermann, D.: A Reconfigurable Arithmetic Logic Unit for Elliptic Curve Cryptosystems over GF(2m). In: MWSCAS 2003. Proceedings of the 46th IEEE International Midwest Symposium on Circuits and Systems, vol. 2, pp. 831–834 (December 2003)

21. Park, J., Hwang, J.-T., Kim, Y.-C.: FPGA and ASIC Implementation of ECC Processor for Security on Medical Embedded System. In: ICITA 2005. Third International Conference on Information Technology and Applications, vol. 2, pp. 547–551 (July 2005)
22. Gura, N.H., et al.: An end–to-end systems approach to elliptic curve cryptography. In: Kaliski Jr., B.S., Koç, Ç.K., Paar, C. (eds.) CHES 2002. LNCS, vol. 2523, Springer, Heidelberg (2003)
23. Eberle, H., Gura, N., Chang-Shantz, S.: A cryptographic processor for arbitrary elliptic curves over GF(2m). In: Proceedings of IEEE International Conference on Application-Specific Systems, Architectures, and Processors, pp. 444–454 (June 2003)
24. Morales-Sandoval, M., Feregrino-Uribe, C.: On the Hardware Design of an Elliptic Curve Cryptosystem. In: ENC 2004. Proceedings of the Fifth Mexican International Conference in Computer Science, pp. 64–70. IEEE, Los Alamitos (2004)
25. Zadeh, A.A.: Design and simulation of a modular reconfigurable architecture for elliptic curve cryptography, Master thesis of Shahid Beheshti University (February 2007)

MDH: A High Speed Multi-phase Dynamic Hash String Matching Algorithm for Large-Scale Pattern Set

Zongwei Zhou[1,2], Yibo Xue[2,3], Junda Liu[1,2], Wei Zhang[1,2], and Jun Li[2,3]

[1] Department of Computer Science and Technology, Tsinghua University, Beijing, China
[2] Research Institute of Information Technology, Tsinghua University, Beijing, China
[3] Tsinghua National Laboratory for Information Science and Technology, Beijing, China
`zhou-zw02@mails.tsinghua.edu.cn`

Abstract. String matching algorithm is one of the key technologies in numerous network security applications and systems. Nowadays, the increasing network bandwidth and pattern set size both calls for high speed string matching algorithm for large-scale pattern set. This paper proposes a novel algorithm called Multi-phase Dynamic Hash (MDH), which cut down the memory requirement by *multi-phase hash* and explore valuable pattern set information to speed up searching procedure by *dynamic-cut heuristics*. The experimental results demonstrate that MDH can improve matching performance by 100% to 300% comparing with other popular algorithms, whereas the memory requirement stays in a comparatively low level.

Keywords: Network Security, String Matching Algorithm, Multi-Phases Hash, Dynamic-Cut Heuristics.

1 Introduction

Along with the rapid development of modern network technology, demands for anti-attack and security protection are now facing a drastic increase in almost all network applications and systems. String matching is one of the key technologies of them. For example, widely deployed network intrusion detection and prevention systems (NIDS/IPS) often use signature-based method to detect possible malicious attacks, so string matching algorithm is their basic operation. It has been demonstrated that string matching takes about 31% of the total processing time in Snort[1][5], the most famous open source NIDS system[8]. The other remarkable instance is content inspection network security systems. More and more such applications, including, but not limited to, anti-virus, anti-spam, instant message filtering, and information leakage prevention require payload inspection as a critical functionality. And, string matching is also the most widely used technology in payload scanning.

However, string matching technology now encounters new challenges from two important facts, both of which indicate that more efficient and practical high speed string matching algorithms for large-scale pattern set are urgently needed.

The first challenge is that large-scale pattern sets are becoming increasingly pervasive. In this paper, we define pattern set that has more than 10, 000 patterns as large-scale pattern set, in contrast to small or middle size pattern sets in typical

S. Qing, H. Imai, and G. Wang (Eds.): ICICS 2007, LNCS 4861, pp. 201–215, 2007.

network security systems. As more types of virus, worm, trojan and malware spread on the Internet, pattern set size in anti-virus applications keeps increasing. For example, the famous open source anti-virus software—Clam AntiVirus[2] now has more than 100,000 patterns, and daily update is still quickly enlarging it. From February 14th to March 18th, 2007, the pattern set size increase by about 10, 000. However, most existing string matching algorithms are designed and tested under small and moderate pattern set. They cannot be efficiently used in large-scale scenario.

Secondly, network edge bandwidth is increasing from 100Mbps to 1Gbps or even more. Such development demands for high throughput of current inline network security applications. In newly emerging UTM (Unified Threat Management) systems, turning on real-time security functionalities like intrusion prevention, anti-virus, and content filtering will greatly reduce the system overall throughput, because such functionalities all need extensive string matching operation. However, string matching algorithms now are still far from efficient enough to meet the needs driven by bandwidth upgrade.

This paper proposes a novel high-speed string matching algorithm, Multi-Phase Dynamic Hash (MDH), for large-scale pattern sets. We introduce *multi-phase hash* to cut down the memory requirement and to deal with high hash collision rate under large-scale pattern set. And we also propose a novel idea, *dynamic-cut heuristics*, which can explore the independence and discriminability of the patterns to speed up the string matching procedure. Experimental results of both random pattern sets and some real-life pattern sets show that MDH increases the matching throughput by about 100% to 300%, compared with some other popular string matching algorithms, whereas, maintain its memory requirement at a low level.

The rest of this paper is structured as follows: Section 2 overviews pervious work on string matching algorithms. Section 3 describes in detail our MDH algorithm. The experimental results are given out in Section 4 to demonstrate high matching performance and low memory requirement of our algorithm. Conclusions and future work are in the last section.

2   Related Work

There are basically two categories of string matching algorithms—*forward algorithm* and *backward algorithm*. They both use a window in the text, which is of the same length as the pattern (the shortest pattern if there are multiple patterns). The window will slide from leftmost of the text to the rightmost. *Forward algorithm* examines the characters in the text window from left to right, while *backward algorithm* starts at the rightmost position of the window and read the characters backward.

Among the *forward algorithms*, Aho-Corasick algorithm[6] is the most famous one. This algorithm preprocesses multiple patterns into a deterministic finite state automaton. AC examines the text one character at a time, so its searching time complexity is $O(n)$ when n is the total length of the text. This means that AC algorithm is theoretically regardless of pattern numbers. However, in practical usage, automaton size increases quickly when the pattern set size goes up, which would require too much memory. This limits the scalability of AC to large-scale string matching.

It has been demonstrated that *backward algorithm* have higher average search speed than *forward algorithm* in practical usage, because it can skip unnecessary character comparisons in the text by certain heuristics[3]. Boyer-Moore algorithm [7] is the most well-known *backward algorithm* used in single pattern matching. There are two important heuristics in BM algorithm, *bad character* and *good suffix*, which is shown in Fig.1. BM calculates both of the shift values according to these two heuristics and then shifts the window according to the bigger one.

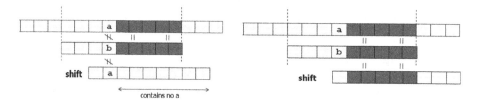

Fig. 1. Bad character (left) and good suffix (right) heuristic, y denotes the text and x is the pattern. u is the match suffix of the text window.

Wu-Manber algorithm[4] extended BM to concurrently search multiple strings. Instead of using *bad character* heuristic to compute the shift value, WM uses a character block including 2 or 3 characters. WM stores the shift values of these blocks in SHIFT table and builds HASH table to link the blocks and the related patterns. The SHIFT table and the HASH table are both hash tables which enable efficient search. Moreover, in order to further speed up the algorithm, WM also builds another hash table, the PREFIX table, with the two-byte prefixes of the patterns. This algorithm has excellent average time performance in practical usage. But, its performance is limited by minimum pattern length m since the maximum shift value in SHIFT table equals to m-1.

However, when pattern set is comparatively large, the average shift value in WM algorithm will decrease and thus the searching performance will be compromised. B. Xu and J. Li proposed the Recursive Shift Indexing (RSI)[10] algorithm for this problem. RSI engages a heuristic with a combination of the two neighboring suffix character blocks in the window. It also uses bitmaps and recursive tables to enhance matching efficiency. These ideas are enlightening for large-scale string matching algorithms.

J. Kytojoki, L. Salmela, and J. Tarhioin also presented a q-Grams based Boyer-Moore-Horspool algorithm[11]. This algorithm cuts a pattern into several q-length blocks and builds q-Grams tables to calculate the shift value of the text window. This algorithm shows excellent performance on moderate size of pattern set. However, when coming into large-scale scope, it is not good enough both in searching time and memory requirement.

C. Allauzen and M. Raffinot introduced Set Backward Oracle Matching Algorithm (SBOM)[12]. Its basic idea is to construct a more lightweight data structure called factor oracle, which is built only on all reverse suffixes of minimum pattern length m window in every pattern. It consumes reasonable memory when pattern set is comparatively large.

There are also some other popular *Backward algorithms* which combine the BM heuristic idea and AC automaton idea. C. Coit, S. Staniford, and J. McAlerney proposed AC_BM algorithm[8]. This algorithm constructs a prefix tree of all patterns in preprocessing stage, and then takes both BM bad character and good suffix heuristics in shift value computation. A similar algorithm called Setwise Boyer Moore Horspool (SBMH)[9] is proposed by M. Fisk and G. Varghese. It utilizes a trie structure according to suffixes of all patterns and compute shift value only using the bad character heuristic. However, these two algorithms are also limited by the memory consumption when the pattern set is large.

3   MDH Algorithm

We have reviewed some popular multiple string matching algorithms. They are the best algorithms under different circumstances. But, for large-scale pattern sets, all of them suffer drastic matching performance decline. Some of them, such as AC, AC_BM and SBMH, also face memory explosion. Moreover, as we have considered, there are few algorithms now solve the large-scale pattern set problem well. In this context, MDH is designed to both improve the matching performance and maintain moderate memory consumption. Based on WM algorithm, our new algorithm has two main improvements:

First, when pattern sets become larger, WM algorithm has to increase the size of the SHIFT table and the HASH table to improve matching performance. This would consume lots of memory. MDH introduces *multi-phase hash* to cut down the high memory requirement.

Second, WM algorithm considers only the first m characters of the patterns. It is simple and efficient, but overlooks helpful information in other characters. Therefore, MDH introduces *dynamic-cut heuristics* to select the optimum m consecutive characters for preprocessing. This mechanism will bring in higher matching performance.

3.1   Key Ideas of MDH

In the following description, we let B to be the block size used in WM and MDH, m to minimum pattern length, Σ to be the alphebet set of both pattern and text, $|\Sigma|$ to be the alphebet set size, k to be the total pattern number, l to be the average length of all the patterns.

3.1.1   Multi-phase Hash
In WM algorithm, a certain SHIFT table entry stores the minimum shift value of all the character blocks hashed to it. As the pattern number increases, high hash collision

will reduce the average shift value $E(shift)$ in SHIFT table and thus compromise the matching performance.

Therefore, a better algorithm for large-scale pattern set always increases character block size B to deal with the high hash collision rate. But larger B will result in bigger SHIFT and HASH table, and thereby greatly increases the memory requirement. Considering the limited cache in modern computers, high memory consumption will decline the cache targeting rate and increase average memory access time. It will in turn decrease the matching performance. On the other hand, it is also difficult to load such large data structures into SRAM when the algorithm is implemented on current high speed appliance such as network processor, multi-thread processing chips and FPGA. This will limit its scalability to hardware implementations.

Under such observations, we propose a novel technique called *multi-phase hash*. In WM algorithm, general hash function is used to build SHIFT table and HASH table, the character blocks and the hash table entries are one-to-one correspondent. But in MDH, we use two compressed hash table, the SHIFT table and the PMT table, to replace them. They are of the similar functionality, but consume less memory. MDH first choose a compressed hash function h_1, to reduce SHIFT table from $|\Sigma|^B$ entries to $|\Sigma|^{a/8}$ ($a < 8B$), which means that h_1 only uses a bits of the B-length character block. However, compressing the SHIFT table entries together will also reduce the average shift value, similar with increasing pattern set size. Some entries with non-zero shift value would be hashed into zero shift value entry. This will bring in more character comparison time in matching procedure. So we then introduce another compressed hash table, PMT table, to separate the non-zero shift value entries away from zero shift value entry. When a certain character block with non-zero shift value is hashed into a zero shift value entry, MDH uses another hash function h_2 to rehash it and store their shift value as *skip* value in the PMT table. PMT table is of the size $|\Sigma|^{b/8}$ ($b < a < 8B$). Moreover, PMT table also linked by some possible matching patterns, similar with HASH table in WM. The number of these pattern linked to a certain PMT table entry is recorded as its *num* value.

3.1.2 Dynamic-Cut Heuristics

Following the common practice of some previous work[3], the average character comparison times $E(comparison)$ is important for the matching performance of WM algorithm. Large-scale pattern set can increase $E(comparison)$ and compromise the matching performance. We handle it by introduce *dynamic-cut heuristics*. Mathematical analysis of $E(comparison)$ decides the detail mechanisms used in dynamic-cut heuristics.

Let **ZR** to be the ratio of the number of *zero entries* (entries with zero shift value) SHIFT entry to the total number of SHIFT table entries. Let T_0 to be the number of *non-zero entries* (entries linked with possible matching patterns) in PMT table, therefore k / T_0 is the *average number of possible matching patterns* (**APM**) in PMT table.

In the searching stage, MDH first checks the shift value in SHIFT table. If it is zero, the algorithm then checks the *skip* value in PMT table. Only if the *skip* value is also zero should the algorithm verify the possible matching patterns. So the probability of comparison times equals to x ($\Pr(comparison = x)$) is calculated as follows:

$$\begin{cases} \Pr(comparison = 1) = 1 - ZR \\ \Pr(comparison = 2) = ZR * (1 - T_0 / |\Sigma|^{b/8}) \\ \Pr(comparison > 2) = ZR * T_0 / |\Sigma|^{b/8} \end{cases} \qquad (1)$$

Thus, under average condition, $E(comparison)$ could be estimated as follows:

$$E(comparison) = 1 * \Pr(comparison = 1) + 2 * \Pr(comparison = 2) \\ + (2 + l * APM) * \Pr(comparison > 2) \qquad (2)$$

From (1) and (2), we get:

$$E(comparison) = 1 + ZR + l * k * ZR / |\Sigma|^{b/8} \qquad (3)$$

Moreover, the above analysis is only under the normal condition of network security application, when the pattern matches in the text are comparatively sparse. However, new denial-of-service attacks, such as sending text of extremely high matches and jamming the pattern matching modules, have emerge to compromise the network security application with BM-family string matching algorithms. Thus it is very necessary to consider the condition of heavy-load case or even worst-case, when there are lots of matches in the text. Under such circumstance, $E(comparison)$ will be calculated as follows:

$$E_w(comparison) \approx 2 + l * APM \qquad (4)$$

Therefore, after setting the SHIFT table size and PMT table size in *multi-phase hash*, there still remains two probabilities for improving the searching performance. First, from equation (3), smaller **ZR** results in smaller $E(comparison)$ under normal condition and thereby brings in higher average searching performance. Secondly, as in equation (4), smaller **APM** results in smaller $E_w(comparison)$ and thus ensures high searching performance for worse-case condition.

According to the above analysis, MDH uses *dynamic-cut heuristics* to *cut* every pattern into the optimum consecutive *m* characters and to reduce the **ZR** and **APM** in SHIFT table and PMT table. Theoretically, MDH could compute all the **ZR** and **APM** values under all the cutting conditions and then choose the optimum one. Apparently, such heuristic mechanism demands for high time and memory consumption in preprocessing when the pattern number k and average pattern length l are large. Note that in most network security application and systems with large-scale string matching, such as anti-virus and content inspection, pattern sets are changing very fast. It is improper to choose such complex preprocessing mechanism.

Thus we implement the heuristics in a comparatively simple way, which is described detail in the following section.

3.2 Algorithmic Details of MDH

3.2.1 Preprocessing Stage

In the following description, we let the block length $B=4$, SHIFT table size $a=20$, PMT table size $b=17$. The pattern set is {opionrate, torrential, extension, cooperation}. So the minimum pattern length $m=9$. << denotes for the bit operator of left shift. Hash function h_1 and h_2 are as follows:

$$h_1(block)=(*(block))\&0x000FFFFF \tag{5}$$

$$h_2(block)=((*(block)<<12)+(*(block+1)<<8) \\ +(*(block+2)<<4)+*(block+3))\&0x0001FFFF \tag{6}$$

There are three steps in preprocessing stage:

Step1: Initialize SHIFT table and PMT table, set all *shift* value and *skip* value to be $m-B+1$, all *num* value to be zero. Each pattern has its *offset* value, that is, the offset of optimum m window in the pattern. All *offset* value is initiated to zero.

Step2: Process the patterns one by one, set their optimum m window position according to the *dynamic-cut heuristics* and note down the *offset* value. Meantime, all the suffix character blocks of these windows are added into the SHIFT table and the PMT table. Related *shift* value and *num* value are set.

Step3: Process the patterns one by one again, add the other blocks (except the suffix block) in all the optimum m windows into the SHIFT table and the PMT table. Related *shift* value and *skip* value are set.

3.2.1.1 Step2—Optimum m Window Position Setting. In this step, the algorithm processes the patterns one pattern by another and calculates their optimum m window position.

"opionrate" is the one of the shortest patterns in the pattern set. So its optimum m window is "opionrate" itself. Its suffix block "rate" is added into SHIFT table and PMT table. The algorithm sets *Shift* value in the $h_1(rate)$ SHIFT entry to 0, set *num* value in the $h_2(rate)$ PMT entry to 1, and link the pattern after $h_2(rate)$ PMT entry.

For pattern "torrential", it has two possible m window positions—"torrentia" and "orrential". The algorithm check the $h_1(ntia)$ SHIFT entry, the shift value is 4. Then we check the $h_1(tial)$ SHIFT entry, this shift value is still 4. So optimum m window is not found, the algorithm will manually set "torrentia" as the optimum m window and set related *shift* and *num* value. The procedure of adding the pattern "extension" is similar with that of adding "opionrate" because they are both the shortest patterns. Then here comes the last pattern "cooperation". The procedure of adding this pattern reveals the effect of *dynamic-cut heuristics*. There are three possible m window positions—"cooperati", "ooperatio" and "operation". The algorithm first checks the $h_1(rati)$ SHIFT entry and found its shift value is 4, then checks the $h_1(atio)$ SHIFT entry and gets the same result. So, the algorithm moves the window again and checks the $h_1(tion)$ SHIFT entry. Since $h_1(tion)=h_1(sion)$, its shift value will be zero. Note

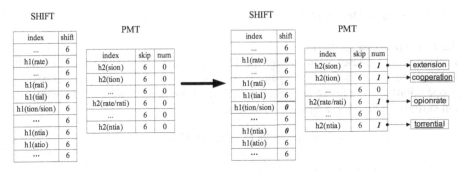

Fig. 2. SHIFT table and PMT table before and after setting optimum minimum m window position for pattern set {opionrate, torrential, extension, cooperation}

that the h_2(tion) PMT entry has a zero *num* value. According to our heuristics, "operation" will be the optimum m window of pattern "cooperation" and the related *offset* value is 2.

Figure 2 illustrates that, without *dynamic-cut heuristics*, the *shift* value of h_1(rati) SHIFT entry will be zero, there would be four SHIFT entries with zero *shift* value and therefore the **ZR** becomes bigger. And also "cooperation" and "opionrate" will both be linked to h_2(rate) PMT entry and **APM** becomes larger, since h_2(rate)=h_2(rati). Thus, it is demonstrated that *Dynamic-cut heuristics* helps to make both **ZR** and **APM** smaller, which will contribute to bring in higher searching performance. Comparison experiments between MDH without *dynamic-cut heuristics* and MDH full implementation will appear in Section 4 to further prove its effect.

3.2.1.2 Step3—Adding Characters Blocks in the optimum m windows. In this step, we take processing pattern "opionrate" for example. The algorithm put a B-length block window (B window) at the leftmost position of the pattern and slide. Let j to be the offset of B window, the shift value of the character block in B window can be calculated by m-B-j. First compute the hash value of "opio" by hash function

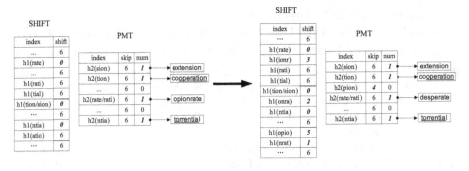

Fig. 3. SHIFT table and PMT table before and after filling shift value and skip value of all B-length character blocks in pattern "opionrate"

h_1. The *shift* value in h_1(opio) SHIFT entry is 6, and the shift value of "opio" is 5. So the algorithm will note down the smaller value 5 as the new *shift* value of this entry. Then we will compute the hash value of "pion", which is the same as h_1(tion/sion). The shift value of h_1(tion/sion) entry is zero. Under this condition, the algorithm will compute h_2(pion) and index to the related PMT entry. The *skip* value of h_2(pion) PMT entry is 6 and the shift value of "pion" is 4. So the algorithm will note down the smaller value 4 as the new *skip* value of this entry. Following this way, the algorithm then processes character block "ionr", "onra", "nrat".

Figure 3 shows the SHIFT table and the PMT table before and after the whole procedure above. Apparently, without *multi-phase hash* idea, character block "pion" will be hashed into h_1(tion/sion) SHIFT entry with zero *shift* value. It will cause unnecessary pattern verification of "cooperation" with a suffix block "tion". However, the algorithm will get its real shift value by checking the *skip* value of h_2(pion) PMT entry and unnecessary character comparison can be avoided.

3.2.2 Scanning Stage

The scanning procedure is comparatively simple and explicit. *B*-length text window slides from leftmost position of the text to right. Each time we examine *B* characters in the text window, calculates its hash value according to hash function h_1, check the relevant SHIFT table entry. If the shift value in this entry is not zero, move the text rightwards by the shift value and restart this procedure. Otherwise, hash this text block again using hash function h_2, use the new hash value to index to the corresponding PMT table entry. Verify every possible matching pattern linked in this entry using naïve comparison method. After that, move the text rightwards by the skip value of this entry and restart the whole procedure.

4   Experimental Results

This section gives out a serial of experiments to demonstrate the performance of MDH algorithm. The test platform is a personal computer with one dual-core Intel Centrino Duo™ 1.83GHz processor and 1.5GB DDR2 667MHz memory. The CPU has 32KB L1 instruction cache and 32KB L1 data cache. The shared L2 cache is 2048KB.

The text and patterns are both randomly generated on alphabet set $|\Sigma| = 256$. And we then insert all the patterns into random position of the text for three times to guarantee a number of matches between random text and patterns. In the first experiment of searching time comparison, we also use a recent antivirus pattern set from Clam AntiVirus to demonstrate the practical performance of MDH algorithm. The text size in the following tests is 32MB. The pattern length of our large-scale pattern sets extends from 4 to 100 and 80% of patterns are of the length between 8 and 16, which is comparatively close to content inspection based network security application such as instant message filtering and content inspection, recommend by CNCERT/CC [13].

4.1 Searching Time and Memory Requirement Comparison

To better evaluate the performance of MDH, we choose five typical multiple string matching algorithms which are widely deployed in recent practical applications. The source codes of AC, AC_BM, WM algorithms are adopted from Snort. Unnecessary codes about case sensitive related operations are eliminated to take off extra time and memory consuming. In WM algorithm, we set the block length $B=2$. The source codes of SBMH and SBOM are from [14].

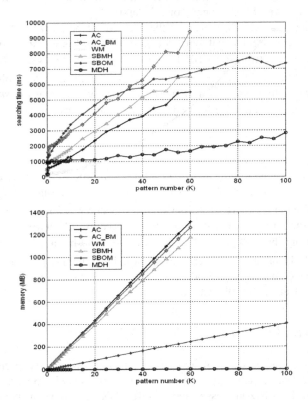

Fig. 4. The upper graph is the searching time comparison between MDH and some typical algorithms. Under the pattern sets larger than 30k, MDH is much better than any other algorithms in this experiment. And the scalability of MDH to even larger patter sets more than 100k is promising since its performance decline is not so rapid as other algorithms when pattern set size increases from 10k to 100k. The lower graph is the memory comparison. Table-based algorithm like MDH and WM algorithm consume much less memory than other algorithms in the experiment.

Figure 4 illustrates that the performance of all the five typical algorithms suffer drastic declines when pattern set size exceeds 30k. Their matching throughput is fewer than 96Mbps with 50k patterns. Algorithms like AC, AC_BM and SBMH can not support pattern sets larger than 60k under our test condition because of their high memory consumption. When there are 100k patterns, the matching throughput of

MDH algorithm is still more than 100Mbps. It exceeds SBOM by 169% and WM by 231%. In addition, MDH algorithm possesses high stability as pattern set size increases and also excellent scalability to small and moderate pattern set size. The stable performance also indicates that it has better scalability to supper-large-scale pattern sets. In our further test, the matching throughput of MDH is abut 48.8 Mbps when pattern set size is 200k, still better than that of WM and SBOM under 100k pattern set.

MDH algorithm is also superior in memory requirement. When pattern set size increases up to 50k, memory requirement of all algorithms except WM and MDH are more than 200MB. Table-based algorithms like WM and our solution only consume less than 20 MB memory even in 100k pattern sets.

4.2 Experiments on Real-Life Pattern Set

To demonstrate the practical performance of MDH algorithm, we choose the real-life pattern set used in Clam AntiVirus in this experiment. The total number of the current virus data base has 102, 540 patterns. We removed all the patterns that is either represented by regular expressions or of the length shorter than 4. After that, the pattern set size is 77, 607. We also form three different subset of the size 20k, 40k and 60k. The minimum pattern length of all these four pattern sets is 4. SBOM and WM are chosen to be compared with MDH, because these two algorithms also have reasonable searching time performance and memory consumption in Section 4.1.

Table 1. In this table, Mem represents the total memory consumption and Thr denotes the matching throughput, that is, size of the text that have been processed in a second Under large-scale pattern sets. Under Clam AntiVirus pattern set, MDH possesses both higher searching performance and lower memory consumption when comparing with WM and SBOM algorithm.

Algorithm	20k		40k		60k		77k	
	Thr (Mbps)	Mem (MB)	Thr (Mbps)	Mem (MB)	Thr (Mbps)	Mem (MB)	Thr (Mbps)	Mem (MB)
MDH	250.56	3.82	203.28	5.2	174.24	8.08	150.16	10.41
WM	329.52	3.33	126	5.2	66.88	8.53	43.36	11.27
SBOM	69.68	81.87	56.16	162.5	43.76	244.7	36.48	316.84

From Table 1, we can see, from 20k to 77k patterns, the searching throughput of MDH algorithm does not suffer drastic decline as WM and SBOM algorithm. This stable performance indicates that MDH has better scalability to even supper-large-scale pattern sets in real-life applications. When there are 77k patterns, the matching throughput of MDH algorithm is more than 150Mbps, which exceeds SBOM by 311% and WM by 246%. Meanwhile, MDH only consumes about 3 to 11 MB memory to process these pattern sets, no more than WM algorithm and much fewer than SBOM algorithm. It is fair to assert that MDH algorithm possesses excellent time and space performance under the large-scale pattern sets from real-life security applications.

4.3 Experiments on Multi-phase Hash

Table 2 is the result of comparison test between WM algorithm ($B=2$), WM algorithm ($B=3$) and MDH with *multi-phase hash*. In this table, **MEM** stands for the total memory used in WM or MDH algorithm. When pattern number is more than 10k, **ZR** becomes very high in WM algorithm ($B=2$). According to equation (3) in Section 3.1.2, higher **ZR** would bring in bigger $E(comparison)$ and greatly compromise the searching performance. If $B=3$, **ZR** becomes comparatively low to ensure good searching performance. However, under this condition, SHIFT table and HASH table will become bigger since these tables are both of the size $|\Sigma|^B$. So **MEM** in WM ($B=3$) increase to more than 80MB. With *multi-phase hash*, MDH is able to maintain moderate **ZR**. Its **MEM** is nearly in the same level with WM ($B=2$) and only about 2%~7% of WM ($B=3$).

Table 2. This table is a comparison of **ZR** and **MEM** between WM algorithm ($B=2$), WM algorithm ($B=3$) and MDH algorithm with *multi-phase hash*. **ZR** is high in WM algorithm ($B=2$) under large-scale pattern set. If $B=3$, WM algorithm possesses low **ZR**, but another problem is that it consumes too much **MEM**. MDH is both good in maintaining low **ZR** and resonable **MEM**.

Pattern number	WM($B=2$)		WM($B=3$)		MDH	
	ZR (%)	MEM (MB)	ZR (%)	MEM (MB)	ZR (%)	MEM (MB)
10k	14.2	0.95	0.059	80.64	0.85	2.42
25k	31.7	1.91	0.149	81.59	1.91	2.98
50k	53.3	3.5	0.297	83.19	3.46	3.93
75k	68.0	5.09	0.446	84.78	4.32	4.87
100k	78.3	6.69	0.594	86.38	6.25	5.81

4.4 Experiments on Dynamic-Cut Heuristics

From Table 3, we can see that **ZR** has a drastic decline when dynamic-cut heuristics are applied. In 10k pattern set, dynamic-cut heuristics reduce the zero entry number by about 10%, and in 100k patter set, this number increases up to nearly 30%. The heuristics' influence on **ZR** becomes more significant when pattern set size is larger. It also has been demonstrated that **APM** value becomes comparatively smaller owing to dynamic-cut heuristics.

As for time performance, dynamic-cut heuristics save about 7.6% to 14% searching time when pattern number ranges from 10k to 100k. Noticeably, the bigger the pattern set is, the more significant the time-saving effect will be. It strongly testifies the excellent scalability of the dynamic-cut heuristics to even larger pattern set. However, the overhead in processing time is still reasonable since most of the network security applications do not have high frequency of pattern set changing and more attentions are focused on improving the searching time.

Table 3. ZR is the zero SHIFT entry radio, the same as in Table 2. APM indicates the average number of possible matching patterns in PMT table. MP denotes of the MDH implementation without dynamic-cut heuristics. We can see that dynamic-cut herurisitcs have greatly reduce the Znum and AN in PMT, which contributes to the searching time decrease.

Pattern Number	ZR		APM		Preprocessing Time(ms)		Searching Time (ms)	
	MP	MDH	MP	MDH	MP	MDH	MP	MDH
10k	9940	8878	1.04	1.03	18.8	20.1	1112	1028
30k	29458	23391	1.12	1.08	26.4	37.4	1459	1312
50k	48461	36262	1.2	1.12	36	62.8	1668	1512
70k	67005	48198	1.29	1.16	49.9	84.4	2118	1877
100k	93842	65494	1.43	1.22	68.3	105.9	3117	2680

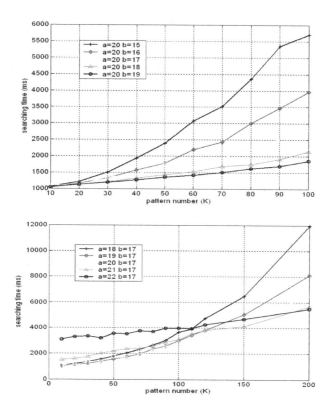

Fig. 5. In the upper graph, SHIFT table size is set to 2^{20} (a=20) and the PMT table size is ranging from 2^{15} (b=15) to 2^{19} (b=19). MDH has less run time (or better performance) when using larger PMT table size. The experiment related with the lower graph is done under same PMT table size as 2^{17} (b=17). SHIFT table size is ranging from 2^{18} (a=18) to 2^{22} (a=22). The optimum SHIFT table size is different under different pattern sets.

214   Z. Zhou et al.

4.5 SHIFT and PMT Table Size Selection

The selection of SHIFT and PMT table size is the critical part of MDH implementation. In the upper graph of Fig 5, we can conclude that bigger PMT table is more helpful in improving searching performance. It matches our previous analysis. When PMT table is larger, we are able to partition all character blocks with zero SHIFT value into more entries. So **APM** value could be smaller. This would highly reduce unnecessary verification time and benefit for final performance. Thus, within the memory limitation, it is better to choose as larger PMT table as possible. In MDH algorithm, we choose a moderate and acceptable PMT table size as 2^{17} (b=17).

In the lower graph of Fig 5, we test the selection of SHIFT table size under the same PMT table size of 2^{17} (b=17). The optimum SHIFT table size is related to the pattern set size. From 10k to about 110k patters, MDH with SHIFT table size of 2^{19} and 2^{20} are of higher searching speed than other ones. And for pattern set between 110k and 190k, a=21 becomes the best choice. When pattern number increases to 200k or even more, a=22 will perform better than others. Moreover, we can also conclude that the run times curve of larger SHIFT table size always possess smaller average slope. The reason is that in large SHIFT table, **ZR** is comparatively small. The pattern set increment can not significantly raise this ratio and compromise the matching performance.

Thus, we may conclude that the selection of SHIFT table size depends on the pattern set size. The algorithm should choose larger SHIFT table size to meet the needs of larger patter set. In this paper, we focus on pattern sets ranging from 10k to 100k and thus set the SHIFT table size to be 2^{20} (a=20).

5 Conclusion and Future Works

This paper proposes a novel string matching algorithm named Multi-Phases Dynamic Hash algorithm (MDH) for large-scale pattern set. Owing to *multi-phase hash* and *Dynamic-cut heuristics*, MDH can improve matching performance under large-scale pattern set by about 100% to 300% compared with other typical algorithms, whereas the memory requirement remains at a comparatively low level. Low memory requirement will help to raise the cache targeting rate in practical usage and thereby improve the matching performance. It would also contribute to support accelerating hardware architectures based on MDH, like FPGA and new multi-core chips.

However, several works will be considered in the future. We are in the progress of finding the relationships between character block B, SHIFT table size a, PMT table size b and pattern sets size k through more experimental and mathematic analysis. We can also study more complex and efficient alternatives for *dynamic-cut heuristics*. In addition, architecture design of network content filtering systems based on MDH and multi-thread models will also be within our scope.

Acknowledgement. The authors thank CNCERT/CC for their support of this work. CNCERT/CC is the abbreviation of National Computer Network Emergency Response Technical Team/Coordination Center of China. The authors would also like to thank Mr. Kai Li, Mrs. Xue Li, Mr. Bo Xu, Mr. Xin Zhou and Mr. Yaxuan Qi for enlightened suggestions and helps. Last but not least, the authors would like to thank numerous volunteers who contributed to the open source projects like Snort and Clam AntiVirus.

References

1. Roesch, M.: Snort: lightweight intrusion detection for networks. In: Proc. of the 1999 USENIX LISA Systems Administration Conference (1999)
2. Clam AntiVirus^{TM} http://www.clamav.net/
3. Navarro, G., Raffinot, M.: Flexible pattern matching in strings. Cambridge University Press, Cambridge (2002)
4. Wu, S., Manber, U.: A fast algorithm for multi-pattern searching, Technical Report TR-94-17, Department of Computer Science, University of Arizona (1994)
5. Snort, http://www.snort.org/
6. Aho, A., Corasick, M.: Fast pattern matching: an aid to bibliographic search. Journal on Communication ACM 18(6), 333–340 (1975)
7. Boyer, R., Moore, J.: A fast string searching algorithm. Journal on Communication. ACM 20(10), 762–772 (1977)
8. Coit, C., Staniford, S., McAlerney, J.: Towards faster string matching for intrusion detection or exceeding the speed of snort, DARPA Information Survivability Conference and Exposition, pp. 367–373 (2001)
9. Fisk, M., Varghese, G.: An analysis of fast string matching applied to content-based forwarding and intrusion detection. Technical Report CS2001-0607 (updated version), University of California-San Diego (2002)
10. Xu, B., Zhou, X., Li, J.: Recursive shift indexing: a fast multi-pattern string matching Algorithm. In: Zhou, J., Yung, M., Bao, F. (eds.) ACNS 2006. LNCS, vol. 3989, Springer, Heidelberg (2006)
11. Kytojoki, J., Salmela, L., Tarhio, J.: Tuning string matching for huge pattern sets? In: Baeza-Yates, R.A., Chávez, E., Crochemore, M. (eds.) CPM 2003. LNCS, vol. 2676, pp. 211–224. Springer, Heidelberg (2003)
12. Allauzen, C., Raffinot, M.: Factor oracle of a set of words, Technical report 99-11, Institut Gaspard-Monge, Universite de Marne-la-Vallee (1999)
13. National Computer Network Emergency Response Technical Team/Coordination Center of China, http://www.cert.org.cn/
14. Network Security Lab: Research Institute of Information Technology, Tsinghua University, Beijing, http://security.riit.tsinghua.edu.cn/share/pattern.html

Compact and Secure Design of
Masked AES S-Box*

Babak Zakeri[1], Mahmoud Salmasizadeh[1,2], Amir Moradi[3],
Mahmoud Tabandeh[1], and Mohammad T. Manzuri Shalmani[3]

[1] School of Electrical Engineering,
[2] Electronic Research Center,
[3] Department of Computer Engineering,
Sharif University of Technology
Azadi St., Tehran, Iran
babak_zakeri@ee.sharif.edu, salmasi@sharif.edu, a_moradi@ce.sharif.edu,
tabandeh@sharif.edu, manzuri@sharif.edu

Abstract. Composite field arithmetic is known as an alternative method
for lookup tables in implementation of S-box block of AES algorithm. The
idea is to breakdown the computations to lower order fields and compute
the inverse there. Recently this idea have been used both for reducing the
area in implementation of S-boxes and masking implementations of AES
algorithm. The most compact design using this technique is presented by
Canright using only 92 gates for an S-box block. In another approach,
IAIK laboratory has presented a masked implementation of AES algorithm with higher security comparing common masking methods using
Composite field arithmetic. Our work in this paper is to use basic ideas
of the two approaches above to get a compact masked S-box. We shall use
the idea of masking inversion of IAIK's masked S-box but we will rewrite
the equations using normal basis. We arrange the terms in these equations
in a way that the optimized functions in Canright's compact S-box can be
used for our design. An implementation of IAIK's masked S-box is also
presented using Canright's polynomial functions to have a fair comparison between our design and IAIK's design. Moreover, we show that this
design which uses two special normal basis for $GF(16)$ and $GF(4)$ is the
smallest. We shall also prove the security of this design using some lemmas.

Keywords: Composite field arithmetic, AES, Masking, Side-Channel
Attack.

1   Introduction

Although some of encryption algorithms are proven to be computationally secure, but implementation of these algorithms may cause some deficiencies. Information leakage which exists in various forms (power leakage, electro-magnetic
leakage, etc.) opens the way to access the secret values of the algorithm. Among

---

* This project is partially supported by Iran National Science Foundation and Iran
Telecommunication Research Center.

S. Qing, H. Imai, and G. Wang (Eds.): ICICS 2007, LNCS 4861, pp. 216–229, 2007.

them, power-analysis attacks are of great interest since they are proven to be able to break any implementation [5]. Different approaches are made to solve the vulnerability problem. Noise addition and toggle generators are examples of such efforts but they are area consuming and not secure [16].

Masking is another approach in which the input data and all other computations are to be masked with a random number. The masking should be in a way that the output data can be recovered easily and mask can be removed. Different ways of masking are proposed until now. For example of previously masked S-box designs see [1]. Multiplicative and additive masks are two main techniques of masking. Though multiplicative masks are easier for computations but they are vulnerable to attacks called zero-value attacks [3]. On the other hand additive masks are harder to implement mostly because of the inversion block of the S-box algorithm. In [11] a new way of implementation is presented base on some previous approaches. Composite field arithmetic is the main idea of this design, namely IAIK's design, in which computation of inverse is broken into computation of inverse in lower order fields. All computations are done securely so that no where in the design an unmasked data is generated.

Another parallel work is to minimize the implementation of the AES [10] algorithm. [9] is an example of such efforts. In [2] Canright has presented a very compact S-box using composite field arithmetic. The author there, has shown that the design is the most compact one using field arithmetic. One might think of mixing these two ideas to get the most compact masked S-box.

Our work in this paper is to use basic ideas of [2,11] to get the smallest masked S-box. We shall use the idea of masking inversion of IAIK's masked S-box but we will rewrite the equations using normal basis. We arrange the terms in these equations in a way that the optimized functions in Canright's compact S-box can be used for our design. An implementation of IAIK's masked S-box is also presented using Canright's polynomial functions to have a fair comparison between these two designs and we show that our design is better. Moreover, we show that this design which uses two special normal basis for $GF(16)$ and $GF(4)$ is the smallest using composite field arithmetic. We shall also prove the security of this design using lemmas presented in [11].

The rest of the paper is as follows: in Section 2 the Canright's design will be described in detail. The mathematical background needed for the rest of the paper will be presented in this section too. Section 3 illustrates the IAIK's design. In Section 4, our design is presented in detail. We prove that this design is the smallest. The security is also discussed in this part and the synthesis result is presented in the end comparing with the IAIK's design. Section 5 is the conclusions and future work discussion.

2 Compact S-Box Implementation Using Composite Field Arithmetic

In [2] Canright has presented a compact S-box implementation using composite field arithmetic. This is done using different strategies and tricks which will be discussed later in this section, but first we will have an overview of the steps made for computing S-box using composite fields. The author has completely described the mathematical background needed for understanding the paper. It is best for reader to refer to that paper whenever needed. But due to new approaches made in this paper, some new mathematical topics are introduced and some topics which were discussed earlier in Canright's paper are discussed from another point of view.

2.1   Mapping from $GF(2^8)$ to $GF(2^2) \times GF(2^2) \times GF(2^2) \times GF(2^2)$

For mapping an element a from $GF(2^8)$ to a pair of $GF(2^4)$ elements such as (a_1, a_2) there are different solutions. But the mapping should satisfy some characteristics. For better description and understand of these characteristics we first take a look to some field theory basics [4]. Some parts may seems hard to understand or irrelevant to the reader but the authors thought they would be necessary for a better underhand of the concept specially for those who want to continue this work.

Any finite field $GF(p^n)$ has some subfields of the form $GF(p^m)$ for any $m < n$. we say of the form, because the subfield does not exactly has the same elements with same labels (the element $\{10101011\}$ may represent an element of the subfield of $GF(2^8)$ of the form $GF(2^4)$ which can not be considered directly as an element of $GF(2^4)$). Thus, one has to find a way to show the equivalency of two fields. In Algebra this is done by a function called isomorphism. Isomorphism, regardless of the structure it is defined for, is a one to one and onto mapping from one structure to another which keeps the characteristics of the operators; most of the time this means that the mapping is a liner mapping but sometimes more conditions are applied. The conditions for a field isomorphism are as follows:

$$\varphi(x + y) = \varphi(x) + \varphi(y) \quad (1) \qquad \varphi(x.y) = \varphi(x).\varphi(y) \quad (2) \qquad \varphi(1) = 1 \quad (3)$$

On the other hand, it is proven in finite field theory that the multiplicative group of the $GF(p^n)$ is a cyclic one, which means that it is generated by a single element. Such an element, namely g, is of order of $m = p^n - 1$ (The order of an element g in a finite field is an integer m for which $g^m = 1$). We also know that the order of an element $x = g^k$ is equal to $m/(m, k)$ in which (m, k) is the greatest common divisor of k and m. Thus we can easily find some elements which are generators of such subfields. Any element of the order $p^k - 1$ is a generator for a subfield of order p^k. For example, if we find g as an element in $GF(2^8)$ which is a generator of its cyclic group, then g^{17} and all other powers of g have 17 as their gcd (great common devisor) with 255 can be assumed as generators of subfields of the form $GF(2^4)$.

The next step would be easy then; we find an element in $GF(2^8)$ which is a generator of its multiplicative group; we use its $17th$ power as a new generator and we write down all elements generated by this new element; we add 0 to them and the new set is a field of the form $GF(2^4)$ with multiplication and addition defined for $GF(2^8)$ (the elements of subfield are also elements of the main field).

This subfield is a starting point for us to define the mapping between elements of $GF(2^8)$ and pairs of elements of $GF(2^4)$. Finding the element g can be done by try and error but it is needed to be found once.

We call this subfield S and we use F for $GF(2^8)$ for simplicity; also $GF(2^4)$ is denoted by F'. We indicate the elements of F (and obviously S) by lower case bold fonts and the elements of F' by lower case normal fonts. Up to now we have S as a subfield of F which we know that S is isomorphic to F'. The next step is defining addition and multiplication on $F' \times F'$. Since any element in $F' \times F'$ is defined by a (a_1, a_2) then addition is defined in the natural way; any element of the pair is added to the same in the other pair. Defining multiplication is somehow different though and this is where S comes to use. Although F and S are fields over $GF(2)$ themselves, but F can be assumed as a vector space on S and thus any element of F can be written in the form of $xa + yb$ where x and y are various elements of S and a and b are two fixed elements of F which are called a basis for F. Obviously not every two elements can be used as basis (for example $\mathbf{a}$ and $\mathbf{b}$ can not be elements of S itself, otherwise the generated elements are all in S and do not cover the whole F). Having this basis means any element of F can be written in the form of $\mathbf{xa} + \mathbf{yb}$ and knowing that $\mathbf{a}$ and $\mathbf{b}$ are fixed elements gives the $(\mathbf{x}, \mathbf{y})$ representation of all elements of F. From vector space mathematics we also know that this representation is unique. Now, having any element of F in the form $(\mathbf{x}, \mathbf{y})$, multiplication is defined very easily.

$$(\mathbf{ax_1} + \mathbf{by_1})(\mathbf{ax_2} + \mathbf{by_2}) = \mathbf{a}^2\mathbf{x_1x_2} + \mathbf{b}^2\mathbf{y_1y_2} + \mathbf{ab}(\mathbf{x_2y_1} + \mathbf{x_1y_2}) \quad (4)$$

It is easy now to show that all the conditions for an isomorphism between F and $S \times S$ hold. We omit these further computations for not loosing the main concept.

Next, if there exists a polynomial in the form of $\mathbf{x}^2 + \mathbf{x} + \nu$ for which $\mathbf{a}$ and $\mathbf{b}$ are roots of the polynomial, then we have $\mathbf{ab} = \nu$ and $\mathbf{a} + \mathbf{b} = 1$ which means $\mathbf{a}^2 + \mathbf{b}^2 = 1$ then this multiplication can be written again of the form $\mathbf{x'a} + \mathbf{y'b}$. Note that the assumption of the coefficient of x to be 1 does not have any effect on the choices we have for the roots. In fact if the coefficient is not equal to 1 the mapping can be changed in a way that a different polynomial with the coefficient 1 has the same roots. The reason we insist on $\mathbf{a} + \mathbf{b} = 1$ is that it helps so much in the next computations.

It can be shown that the multiplication defined above is "good" enough as a field multiplication; which means it satisfies the characteristics needed for field multiplication. More, It can be shown that polynomial $\mathbf{x}^2 + \mathbf{x} + \nu$ which is irreducible in S (and thus its roots are in F) can be used for making a new basis. The new basis is then can be defined in different ways. Three choices are available; $(\mathbf{a}, 1)$, $(\mathbf{b}, 1)$ and $(\mathbf{a}, \mathbf{b})$ can all be considered as bases. The first two are named polynomial basis for the fact that computations can be done in this case easily considering any element of F in the form $\mathbf{s_1x} + \mathbf{s_2}$ and $\mathbf{s_1x}^2 + \mathbf{s_2}$, and computing addition and multiplication by polynomial addition and multiplication modula the irreducible polynomial defined above. The last one is called normal basis for the summation of the basis is equal to one.

As for now, the following steps are made:

1. Find the generator element of the multiplicative group of F
2. Consider some special powers of that element and generate S
3. Find some irreducible polynomial of the form $\mathbf{x^2 + x} + \nu$ with ν in S and find its roots $\mathbf{a}$ and $\mathbf{b}$.
4. Choose either of the bases possible and write down all elements with the new basis, all $\mathbf{xa + yb}$ for $\mathbf{x}$ and $\mathbf{y}$ elements of S for normal basis as an example, and get the mapping of F to pairs of S elements.

What is remained is the mapping of the elements of S to the elements of $GF(2^4)$ for getting rid of the elements of the form of $GF(2^8)$. After that we have any element of F represented in the form of $(\mathbf{a}, \mathbf{b})$ and the computations can be done choosing either basis type.

The element chosen as the generator of subfield and the irreducible polynomial are the degrees of freedom for finding the mapping. One may think of the mapping of S and $GF(2^4)$ as another option, but normally this does not affect the whole result and changing this gives one of the other existing mappings using another S.

The same process can be done for $GF(2^4)$ and $GF(2^2)$. Altogether these mappings can be considered as an $8*8$ matrix applied to any 8 bit element which gives another 8 bit, which in fact in four 2-bit numbers. After computations done in lower fields the inverse mapping should be applied to get back to $GF(2^8)$. This inverse mapping matrix can be mixed with the S-box affine transform matrix for optimization. There exist 432 cases considering all possible cases for the generator, polynomial and basis chosen and the one which gives the smallest matrix is selected between them as the explained in [2].

2.2 Inverse Computation Using Composite Fields

For any element of the form (x, y) with x and y in $GF(2^4)$ the inverse can be computed using some computations in $GF(2^4)$. What will be seen next shows that the computation of such an element leads to a computation of inverse of a $GF(2^4)$ element and some additions and multiplications in $GF(2^4)$ and this is the idea of using composite fields for computation of the inverse. In [2] the author has discussed this in detail. The general concept of such computations is given below.

For normal basis we have:

$$(a_1, a_0)^{-1} = (d^{-1}a_0, d^{-1}a_1) \tag{5}$$

in which

$$d = (a_1^2 + a_0^2)\nu + a_1 a_0 \tag{6}$$

And for polynomial basis:

$$(a_1, a_0)^{-1} = (d^{-1}a_1, d^{-1}(a_1 + a_0)) \tag{7}$$

in which
$$d = a_1^2 \nu + a_1 a_0 + a_0^2 \tag{8}$$

The author then has broken the computations in different parts and has used some alternative computations for some blocks. The gates needed for each case considering the basis and field ($GF(2^4)$ or $GF(2^2)$) is discussed and some further optimizations are applied at last. What is finally concluded is that, using normal basis gives a better result. It is worth to mention that the final design is presented using only 2 or 3 input AND, OR, XOR and XNOR gates.

3   Masked Inversion Using Composite Field Arithmetic

Masking methods are of great interest of cryptologists who work on Power Analysis attacks. The idea of masking is combining the input A with a random number M and do all the followed computations in a way that no part of unmasked data is available anywhere in the process. The result should be the S-box of A mixed with a function of M such that A can be obtained easily and the mask can be removed.

Although S-box computation of a multiplicative masked data (AM) is easy (the inverse which is the most difficult part of S-box to implement is easy to compute for a multiplication) but these masks are vulnerable to attacks which is so called zero-value attacks [3] as described before. The most natural way of defining the mask is addition masks which are somehow difficult to compute. The $A + M$ input is given to the inverse and the $A^{-1} + F(A, M)$ should be the result. In [11] a new way for doing this using composite field arithmetic have been presented. We now take a short look at what they have done.

First it is assumed that the mapping from $GF(2^8)$ to $GF(2^4)$ is done and the input 8-bit value $\mathbf{a_m} = \mathbf{a} + \mathbf{m}$ is mapped to some $a_{hm}x + a_{lm}$ and the mask m is mapped to $m_h x + m_l$. We are to find the a_h^{-1} and a_l^{-1} (the inverses of a_h and a_l having only a_{hm}, a_{lm}, m_h and m_l). the computations comes as follows:

$$a_h^{-1} = d^{-1} a_h = d^{-1}(a_{hm} + m_h) \tag{9}$$

$$
\begin{aligned}
d_{mh} = d + m_h &= a_h^2 \nu + a_h a_l + a_l^2 \\
&= (a_{hm} + m_h)^2 \nu + (a_{hm} + m_h)(a_{lm} + m_l) + (a_{lm} + m_l)^2 \\
&= a_{hm}^2 \nu + m_h^2 \nu + a_{hm}a_{lm} + a_{hm}m_l + a_{lm}m_h + m_h m_l + a_{lm}^2 + m_l^2
\end{aligned} \tag{10}
$$

$d_{mh} = d + m_h$ can be given to the next part and $d^{-1} + m_h$ is obtained using $GF(2^2)$ arithmetic. having $d^{-1} + m_h$ we have:

$$
\begin{aligned}
a_h^{-1} + m_h &= d^{-1}(a_{hm} + m_h) + m_h \\
&= (d^{-1} + m_h)(a_{hm} + m_h) + m_h + m_h a_{hm} + m_h^2
\end{aligned} \tag{11}
$$

Some points are noticeable in these computations. First, as an optimization point, some computations can be done more easily. For example there is no need to compute a_{hm}^2 first and then scaling it by ν. Next point is security of these computations. Authors of the paper have presented some lemmas which show

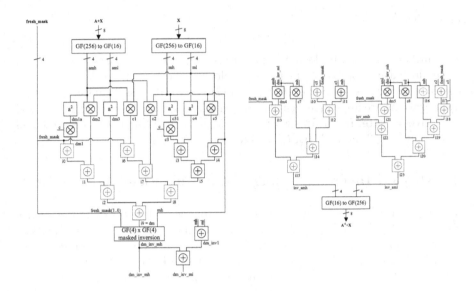

Fig. 1. IAIK's design for masked AES S-box block diagram [12] (i16 is corrected comparing to the original figure)

that each term computed above is secure. The problem shows where summation of some terms leads to omission of the additive mask. For example $a_{lm}m_h + a_{hm}m_l = a_l m_h + m_l m_h + a_h m_l + m_h m_l$. If this term is added by the $m_h m_l$ then what is remained has no additive mask and the terms remained are vulnerable to zero-value attack. One may think of adding two other terms but this happens in at least two additions regardless of the way terms are added. Thus authors have suggested the addition of a 4 bit fresh mask which to be applied at the beginning of these computations and to be removed before going to the next step. The block diagram of their design is shown in Figure 1. In [12] an implementation of their design added together with some other designs are presented. The comparison of the results show that this design is the smallest secure design among the others.

4   Compact Masked S-Box

4.1   Design Idea

We first take a look to the weaknesses of the design presented in [11]. First of all it uses polynomial basis which probably is not the best case for small area designs. Although area usage is almost the same for most of the blocks in a $GF(2^8)$ inverter including multiplication and $GF(2^4)$ inversion due to [2], but there are some differences when different basis are used. In a simple design without any masking as Canright has established in [2] the total amount of gate used without mappings and inverse mappings is nearly the same for normal basis and polynomial basis. But this is not necessarily true for our design because different equations are used and number of scalings and square-scalings are different comparing with Canright's design. Next the mapping used in [11] is not the most efficient mapping which probably would be. Considering the facts that area usage varies a lot when mappings and inverse mappings are changed, and the mappings presented in [2] are well optimized, this can play a great role in the area usage reduction. As a next point to notice, the affine matrix is not mixed with the inverse mapping matrix in the design of [11]. These two separate matrixes surely waste area while in Canright's design the two matrixes are mixed and optimized. As another important point to mention, the mappings in [11] is done in two steps: one from $GF(2^8)$ to $GF(2^4)$ at the beginning of the process, and the other one from $GF(2^4)$ to $GF(2^2)$ at the beginning of every $GF(2^4)$ block and its inverse mapping. However the design idea on [2] is done in a way that just one mapping and one inverse mapping is needed. Finally no more optimizations in area have been done in [11].

The weaknesses discussed above, all gives the idea of implementing the masked IAIK's S-box by the strategies used in Canright's compact S-box in hope of getting a noticeable reduction in area. The first part of this section will explore this idea. We shall rewrite the equations needed for computing the masked inversion of a $GF(2^8)$ element in normal basis. We try to do this in a way that there be no need to have new functions defined for normal basis. This helps us in conclusion part which we claim that our design is the smallest.

The main part of the design which should be replaced is the composite field arithmetic which is done in polynomial basis in IAIK's design. We shall change the computation of masked inverse to normal basis in a way that the security of calculations do not damage while using Canright's normal basis optimized functions. At very first, as described before, we have:

$$(a_h, a_l) = (d^{-1}a_l, d^{-1}a_h) \tag{12}$$

where

$$d = (a_h^2 + a_l^2)v + a_h a_l \tag{13}$$

For a masked input we have:

$$\begin{aligned} a_{hm} &= a_h + m_h \\ a_{lm} &= a_l + m_l \end{aligned} \tag{14}$$

The next equations comes as follows:

$$\begin{aligned} a_h^{-1} + m_h &= (d^{-1}a_l) + m_h \\ &= (d^{-1} + m_h)(a_l + m_l) + d^{-1}m_l + a_l m_h + m_h m_l + m_h \\ &= d_{imh}a_{lm} + (d^{-1} + m_h)m_l + m_l m_h + (a_l + m_l)m_h + m_l m_h \\ &+ m_h m_l + m_h = d_{pmh}a_{lm} + d_{pmh}m_l + a_{lm}m_h + m_h m_l + m_h \end{aligned} \tag{15}$$

where

$$d_{pmh} = d^{-1} + m_h \tag{16}$$

also for d we have:

$$d_{mh} = d + m_h = (a_h^2 + a_l^2)v + a_h a_l + m_h$$
$$= (a_{hm}^2 + m_h^2 + a_{lm}^2 + m_l^2)v + a_{hm}a_{lm} + m_h m_l + a_{hm}m_l + a_{lm}m_h + m_h$$
$$= SQSC(a_{hm}, a_{lm}) + a_{hm}a_{lm} + SQSC(m_h, m_l) + m_h m_l + a_{hm}m_l + a_{lm}m_h + m_h \qquad (17)$$

where $SQSC(x, y)$ is the square-scale of x and y.

Thus all equations is written by a_{hm}, a_{lm}, m_h and m_l. also the function $SQSC(x, y) + xy$ is easily optimized in [2]. Since there are shared parts in multiplication the shared factors can be computed and save the area for other multiplications.

For a_l we have:

$$a_l^{-1} + m_l = d^{-1}a_h + m_l \qquad (18)$$

So some changes should be made for computation of $a_l^{-1} + m_l$

Defining

$$d_{iml} = d_{imh} + m_h + m_l = d^{-1} + m_l \qquad (19)$$

we have

$$a_l^{-1} + m_l = d_{iml}a_{hm} + d_{iml}m_h + a_{hm}m_l + m_h m_l + m_l \qquad (20)$$

As described above a fresh mask is here needed too. Combining the above results with the fresh mask leads to the following equations:

$$f = a_{hm}m_l \qquad (21)$$

$$g = a_{lm}m_h \qquad (22)$$

$$c = SQSC(a_{hm}, a_{lm}) + a_{lm}a_{hm} + fm \qquad (23)$$

$$e = SQSC(m_h, m_l) + m_l m_h d_{mh} \qquad (24)$$

$$d_{mh} = (c + e) + (f + g + m_h + fm) \qquad (25)$$

And

$$i = m_h m_l \qquad (26)$$

$$i_2 = a_{hm}d_{ml} \qquad (27)$$

$$i_3 = m_h d_{ml} \qquad (28)$$

$$i_4 = a_{lm}d_{mh} \qquad (29)$$

$$i_5 = m_l d_{mh} \qquad (30)$$

Which gives the final result as:

$$a_l^{-1} + m_l = (i_2 + i_3 + fm) + (f + i + m_l + fm) \qquad (31)$$

$$a_h^{-1} + m_h = (i_4 + i_5 + fm) + (g + i + m_h + fm) \qquad (32)$$

Similar equations exist for computing the masked inverse in $GF(2^2)$ and their reputation is not necessary anymore.

Next we go through the mapping and inverse mapping functions. If we assume the mapping function as the matrix X and the affine transformation as $\alpha A + \beta$ then as suggested in [2], X^{-1} is combined with the matrix for optimization. For a non-masked input we have:

(1) AX
(2) $AX \rightarrow (AX)^{-1} \rightarrow X^{-1}A^{-1}$
(3) $\alpha X(X^{-1}A^{-1}) + \beta = \alpha A^{-1} + \beta = Sbox(A)$

The calculations for a masked-data are changed as follows:

(1) $(A + M)X = AX + MX$
(2) $AX + MX \rightarrow (AX)^{-1} + MX \rightarrow X^{-1}A^{-1} + MX$
(3) $\alpha X(X^{-1}A^{-1} + MX) + \beta = \alpha XX^{-1}A^{-1} + \beta + \alpha XMX = Sbox(A) + \alpha XMX$

As it can be seen, the final result consists of the S-box of input added by a function of the random mask. This part can be removed by a separate mask removal generator part which generates the XMX. Thus our method does not disturb the process of computing the rest of the AES algorithm and our goal is achieved.

4.2 Security Discussion

For security discussion we use the lemmas presented in [11]. These lemmas ensures that the design is resistant to simple DPA attacks without any need for real world implementation of the design. The lemmas are listed below. For a proof of each lemma one can refer to the main paper.

Lemma 1. Let a an element of $GF(2^n)$ be arbitrary. Let m uniformly be distributed in $GF(2^n)$ and independent of a. Then the distribution of $a + m$ is independent of a.

Lemma 2. Let a, b elements of $GF(2^n)$ be arbitraries. Let m_a, m_b be independently and uniformly distributed in $GF(2^n)$. Then the distribution of $(a + m_a)(b + m_b)$ is independent of a and b.

Lemma 3. Let a be an element of $GF(2^n)$ be arbitrary. Let m_a, m_b be independently and uniformly distributed in $GF(2^n)$. Then the distribution of $(a + m_a)m_b$ is independent of a.

Lemma 4. Let a an element of $GF(2^n)$ be arbitrary and p a constant. Let m_a be independently and uniformly distributed in $GF(2^n)$. Then, the distribution of $(a + m_a)^2$ and $(a + m_a)^2 p$ is independent of a.

Lemma 5. Let a_i elements of $GF(2^n)$ be arbitraries and M be independent of all a_i and uniformly distributed in $GF(2^n)$. Then the distribution of $\sum a_i + M$ is (pairwise) independent of a_i.

Lemmas 1, 2 and 3 ensure the security of equations 21,22 and 26-30. 23 is secure due to lemma 5. 25, 31 and 32 are secure due to their final result which is the masked output. Equation 24 is of no question because it combines some masks with each other.

4.3 Comparing the Results

Figure 2 gives a block diagram of our design. The additions and multiplications are all implemented in $GF(4)$ as given in [2]. The big gray boxes are optimized more as Canright has suggested in [2]. But at very first, as a comparison between polynomial basis and normal basis we ignore these optimizations. Thus the $m_h m_l$ computation needs not to be computed in the second part of the figure since $SQSC(m_h, m_l) + m_h m_l$ box is omitted and thus $m_h m_l$ is available. We will use Canright optimized polynomial functions in block diagram of IAIK's design to show that using normal basis leads to a better result and compactness of our design in not just a result of good mapping and some further optimizations.

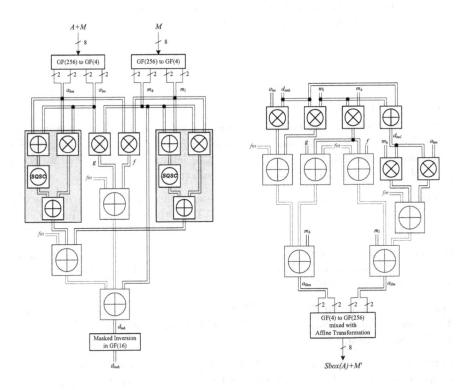

Fig. 2. Our compact masked AES S-box block diagram

As it is clear of the figures, 5 two-input addition, 9 three-input additions, 8 multiplications and 2 square-scaling blocks are used in normal basis block diagram. On the other hand it consumes 24 two-input additions, 8 two-input multiplications, 2 square-scaling and 2 scaling blocks. For polynomial basis, assuming any three-input addition as two 2-input additions, we have 23 additions,

8 multiplications and 2 square-scalings in normal basis while it is 24 additions, 8 multiplications, 2 square-scalings and 2 scalings for the polynomial basis. We shall prove shortly that our design based on normal basis is better; moreover we show this can be the most compact one using this technique. We use results of gate counting of Canright to do so. One can study [2] for detailed discussion.

Multiplications in $GF(16)$ use same amount of gates for either basis chosen in $GF(4)$; Square-scalings in $GF(16)$ differ in at most 3 2XOR gates due to what it is chosen for basis; Scalings in $GF(16)$ use same amount of gates ($2 + 2 = 4$ 2XOR gates) for either type of basis; Squaring is free in $GF(4)$ for normal basis while square-scaling is free for polynomial basis in the same field.

Thus if polynomial basis is chosen for $GF(16)$ we have a minimum of $4+4-3 = 5$ more gates (4 for addition, 4 for scalings and 3 for possible gate reduction using normal basis for $GF(16)$ SQSC box). Choosing polynomial basis in $GF(4)$ also causes $2 + 2 = 4$ more gates at least ensuring us that normal basis in better for masked inversion computation (note that this is not surely true if we were to compute inversion itself without any mask computations). On the other hand choosing different normal basis does not affect the number of gates so much. Square-scaling is the most differing part which gives little variance (3 XOR gates) in the number of the gates. So what can be seen is using different basis doesn't affect number of gates so much (However the little difference exist is good for us!). So the mapping chosen can play a great role in the area used for the total design. As it is illustrated in [2] the mapping presented is the best mapping can be. From the above discussion we can say that our design is the most compact one using this technique for masked s-box computation.

Table 1. Synthesis results of the design presented in [11]

Cell	Library	References		Total Area
IV1N0	scl05u	8	× 3	25 gates
IV1N1	scl05u	1	× 3	3 gates
ND2N0	scl05u	9	× 5	41 gates
NR2R0	scl05u	140	× 5	630 gates
NR2R1	scl05u	11	× 5	52 gates
XN2R0	scl05u	68	× 5	333 gates
XN2R1	scl05u	9	× 5	46 gates
XN2R2	scl05u	5	× 5	27 gates
XN3R0	scl05u	54	× 7	367 gates
XN3R1	scl05u	3	× 7	21 gates
XR2T0	scl05u	25	× 5	123 gates
XR2T1	scl05u	2	× 5	10 gates
XR2T2	scl05u	1	× 5	5 gates
XR3T0	scl05u	57	× 7	388 gates
XR3T1	scl05u	8	× 7	56 gates
XR3T2	scl05u	2	× 7	14 gates
Total no. of gates				2140
Total no. of instances				403

Table 2. Synthesis results of our compact masked design

Cell	Library	References		Total Area
IV1N0	scl05u	16	× 3	50 gates
ND2N0	scl05u	23	× 5	104 gates
NR2R0	scl05u	78	× 5	351 gates
NR2R1	scl05u	5	× 5	24 gates
XN2R0	scl05u	76	× 5	372 gates
XN2R1	scl05u	4	× 5	20 gates
XN3R0	scl05u	30	× 7	204 gates
XN3R1	scl05u	2	× 7	14 gates
XR2T0	scl05u	22	× 5	108 gates
XR2T1	scl05u	2	× 5	10 gates
XR3T0	scl05u	44	× 7	299 gates
XR3T1	scl05u	3	× 7	21 gates
Total no. of gates				1577
Total no. of instances				305

Overall, we applied the further optimizations in [2] on our design and we checked our design with the IAIK's design using Leonardo Spectrum Synthesis tool. The following two tables present the synthesis results of our design and IAIK's design using Leonardo Spectrum 2004's ASIC library.

The better result is obvious. More the result is even comparable with the one in [9] which is designed for non-masked s-box.

5 Conclusions and Future Works

In this paper we presented a masked S-box based on the composite field arithmetic. We mixed the ideas of [11] which has presented a masked S-box with composite field arithmetic and the design of [2] which is the smallest unmasked S-box using composite fields. We rewrote the equations of [11] with the basis and mapping presented in [2]. We checked this design with the one presented in [11] and we showed our design is smaller. We also showed that this design is smaller of any design using composite field arithmetic technique for masking. Finally we proved our design to be secure against simple side channel attacks using mathematical statements presented in [11].

There are some previous works done in designing compact masked S-box. In [15] the authors have presented an ASIC implementation of AES algorithm. They have used a method similar to Canright's method with polynomial basis. Though the design presented is smaller than our design (1556 gates comparing to 1577 in our design), but they have used gate level masking as one of their major techniques. As shown in [6] if the input arrival times of the gates of a masked gate be different, then there would be information leakage and masking would be useless. Since there is always delay between the input arrival times in real world implementation, thus gate masking appears to be insecure. However, our design is only based on masking at algorithm level and thus is safe. In fact, if our technique where used for the [15] a very better result would be archived due to the basis used.

In [7] it has been shown that there is a correlation between the number of transitions in the circuit and the unmasked input data for a chip designed using the IAIK's masking technique. They also have pinpointed the location of circuit which causes this correlation and they have claimed that the XOR gates of the masked multipliers produce the problem [8]. As a future work, we are to implement this design and see how good it is against the toggle count attack mentioned above. A new solution for implementing the design in a way that the correlation does not exist anymore is needed.

References

1. Akkar, M.-L., Giraud, C.: An Implementation of DES and AES, Secure against Some Attacks. In: Koç, Ç.K., Naccache, D., Paar, C. (eds.) CHES 2001. LNCS, vol. 2162, pp. 309–318. Springer, Heidelberg (2001)
2. Canright, D.: A Very Compact Rijndael S-box.Technical Report NPS-MA-04- 001, Naval Postgraduate School (September 2004),
   http://web.nps.navy.mil/~dcanrig/pub/NPS-MA-05-001.pdf

3. Golić, J.D., Tymen, C.: Multiplicative Masking and Power Analysis of AES. In: Kaliski Jr., B.S., Koç, Ç.K., Paar, C. (eds.) CHES 2002. LNCS, vol. 2523, pp. 198–212. Springer, Heidelberg (2003)
4. Conway, J.H.: On Numbers and Games. 2nd edn., AK Peters (2001)
5. Kocher, P.C., Jaffe, J., Jun, B.: Differential Power Analysis. In: Wiener, M.J. (ed.) CRYPTO 1999. LNCS, vol. 1666, pp. 388–397. Springer, Heidelberg (1999)
6. Mangard, S., Popp, T., Gammel, B.M.: Side-Channel Leakage of Masked CMOS Gates. In: Menezes, A. (ed.) CT-RSA 2005. LNCS, vol. 3376, pp. 351–365. Springer, Heidelberg (2005)
7. Mangard, S., Pramstaller, N., Oswald, E.: Successfully Attacking Masked AES Hardware Implementations. In: Rao, J.R., Sunar, B. (eds.) CHES 2005. LNCS, vol. 3659, pp. 157–171. Springer, Heidelberg (2005)
8. Mangard, S., Schramm, K.: Pinpointing the Side-Channel Leakage of Masked AES Hardware Implementations. In: Goubin, L., Matsui, M. (eds.) CHES 2006. LNCS, vol. 4249, pp. 76–90. Springer, Heidelberg (2006)
9. Mentens, N., Batina, L., Preneel, B., Verbauwhede, I.: A Systematic Evaluation of Compact Hardware Implementations for the Rijndael S-box. In: Menezes, A.J. (ed.) CT-RSA 2005. LNCS, vol. 3376, pp. 323–333. Springer, Heidelberg (2005)
10. National Institute of Standards and Technology (NIST). FIPS-197: Advanced Encryption Standard (November 2001), available online at: http://www.itl.nist.gov/fipspubs/
11. Oswald, E., Mangard, S., Pramstaller, N., Rijmen, V.: A Side-Channel Analysis Resistant Description of the AES S-box. In: Gilbert, H., Handschuh, H. (eds.) FSE 2005. LNCS, vol. 3557, pp. 21–23. Springer, Heidelberg (2005)
12. Pramstaller, N., Oswald, E., Mangard, S., Gürkaynak, F.K., Haene, S.: A Masked AES ASIC Implementation. In: Austrochip 2004, Villach, Austria, October 8th, 2004, pp. 77–82 (2004)
13. Rudra, A., Dubey, P., Julta, C., Kumar, V., Rao, J., Rohatgi, P.: Efficient Rijndael implementation with composite field arithmetic. In: Koç, Ç.K., Naccache, D., Paar, C. (eds.) CHES 2001. LNCS, vol. 2162, pp. 175–188. Springer, Heidelberg (2001)
14. Satoh, A., Morioka, S., Takano, K., Munetoh, S.: A compact Rijndael hardware architecture with S-Box optimization. In: Boyd, C. (ed.) ASIACRYPT 2001. LNCS, vol. 2248, pp. 239–254. Springer, Heidelberg (2001)
15. Trichina, E., Korkishko, T.: Secure AES Hardware Module for Resource Constrained Devices. In: Castelluccia, C., Hartenstein, H., Paar, C., Westhoff, D. (eds.) ESAS 2004. LNCS, vol. 3313, pp. 215–229. Springer, Heidelberg (2005)
16. Zhou, Y.B., Feng, D.G.: Side-Channel Attacks: Ten Years After Its Publication and the Impacts on Cryptographic Module Security Testing. Cryptology ePrint Archive, Report 2005/388 (2005), http://eprint.iacr.org/

Boudot's Range-Bounded Commitment Scheme Revisited

Zhengjun Cao[1] and Lihua Liu[2]

[1] Department of Mathematics, Shanghai University, Shanghai, China
caozhj@shu.edu.cn
[2] Department of Information and Computation Sciences, Shanghai Maritime
University, Shanghai, China

Abstract. Checking whether a committed integer lies in a specific interval has many cryptographic applications. In Eurocrypt'98, Chan et
al. proposed an instantiation (CFT Proof). Based on CFT, Boudot presented a popular range-bounded commitment scheme in Eurocrypt'2000.
Both CFT Proof and Boudot Proof are based on the encryption $E(x,r) =
g^x h^r \bmod n$, where n is an RSA modulus whose factorization is *unknown*
by the prover. They did not use a single base as usual. Thus an increase
in cost occurs. In this paper, we show that it suffices to adopt a single
base. The cost of the modified Boudot Proof is about half of that of the
original scheme. Moreover, the key restriction in the original scheme, i.e.,
both the discrete logarithm of g in base h and the discrete logarithm of
h in base g are unknown by the prover, which is a potential menace to
the Boudot Proof, is definitely removed.

Keywords: range-bounded commitment, knowledge of a discrete logarithm, zero-knowledge proof.

1 Introduction

Checking whether a committed integer lies in a specific interval was first developed by Brickell, et al. [2] in Crypto'87. Such kind of proofs have many applications: electronic cash systems [6], group signatures [8], publicly verifiable secret
sharing schemes [16,14,4], and other zero-knowledge protocols [9]. Informally, a
range-bounded commitment is a protocol between a prover, Alice, and a verifier,
Bob, with which Alice commits to a string, x, and proves to Bob that x is within
a predetermined range, H, with accuracy δ.

In the past decade, there are a few schemes investigating range-bounded commitments. Mao [16] proposed a scheme for proof of bit-length based on DLP
(discrete logarithm problem) in PKC'98. In Eurocrypt'98, Chan et al. [6] presented an instantiation (CFT proof for short). It's corrected soon [7] because
the authors did not notice that Alice can cheat Bob if the *order* of the cryptographic group is known by her. Based on CFT proof, Boudot [3] constructed a
popular range-bounded commitment scheme in Eurocrypt'2000 (Boudot proof
for short). The basic idea of the scheme is to decompose a committed number
x as $x = x_1^2 + x_2$. It then uses Fujisaki-Okamoto commitment scheme [13] to

S. Qing, H. Imai, and G. Wang (Eds.): ICICS 2007, LNCS 4861, pp. 230–238, 2007.

show that the committed number x_1^2 is a square. By CFT proof, it proves the committed number x_2 in a proper range.

Both CFT proof and Boudot proof are based on the encryption

$$E(x, r) = g^x h^r \mod n$$

where x is the committed number, r is a random number selected by Alice, n is an RSA modulus whose factorization is unknown to Alice, g is an element of large order in $\mathbb{Z}_n$ and h is an element of the group generated by g such that both the discrete logarithm of g in base h and the discrete logarithm of h in base g are unknown by Alice. We notice that they do not use a single base as usual. Thus an increase in cost occurs.

Why not use a single base instead two bases? The reason, we think, is that they directly followed the structures of Fujisaki-Okamoto commitment [13]. In 2002, the authors [11] explained that a commitment with a single base to s of form $c = g^s \mod n$ does not satisfy the standard hiding property for commitments. For instance, if a prover commits twice to the same value, this is immediately visible. But we notice that they did not consider to permit Alice to update the single base g. Actually, if Alice commits twice to the same value, she can pick a random number θ and update the base g with $\hat{g} = g^\theta \mod n$. Note that g is still permitted to be a system-wide parameter since Alice can update it by herself. But in Fujisaki-Okamoto commitment scheme (with two bases), Alice is not permitted to update the bases. Otherwise, the discrete logarithm of $\hat{g}$ in base $\hat{h}$ or the discrete logarithm of $\hat{h}$ in base $\hat{g}$ will be known to Alice.

In this paper, we show that it suffices to adopt a single base, i.e., $E(x) = g^x \mod n$. The common encryption sufficiently guarantees the security of the modified Boudot commitment scheme. Thus the cost of the modified Boudot proof is about half of that of the original scheme. Its security is immediately reduced to RSA [18] and a variant of Schnorr signature [19] in RSA setting with hidden order. Moreover, the key restriction in the original scheme, both the discrete logarithm of g in base h and the discrete logarithm of h in base g are unknown by the prover, which is a potential menace to the Boudot proof, is definitely removed.

2   Related Work

2.1   CFT Proof

The following description of CFT proof is due to [3].

Let t, l and s be three security parameters. This protocol (due to Chan, Frankel and Tsiounis [6], and corrected in [7], and also due to [14] in another form) proves that a committed number $x \in I$ belongs to J, where the expansion rate $\#J/\#I$ is equal to 2^{t+l+1}. Let n be a large composite number whose factorization is unknown by Alice and Bob, g be an element of large order in $\mathbb{Z}_n^*$ and h be an element of the group generated by g such that both the discrete logarithm of g in base h and the discrete logarithm of h in base g are unknown by Alice. Let H be a hash function which outputs $2t$-bit strings. We denote by $E = E(x, r) = g^x h^r \mod n$ a commitment to $x \in [0, b]$, where r is randomly selected over $[-2^s n + 1, 2^s n - 1]$. This commitment statistically reveals no information about x to Bob.

Protocol. $PK_{[CFT]}(x, r : E = E(x,r) \land x \in [-2^{t+l}b, 2^{t+l}b])$

1. Alice picks $\omega \in_R [0, 2^{t+l}b - 1]$ and $\eta \in_R [-2^{t+l+s}n+1, 2^{t+l+s}n-1]$, and then computes $W = g^{\omega}h^{\eta} \mod n$.
2. Then, she computes $C = H(W)$ and $c = C \mod 2^t$.
3. Finally, she computes $D_1 = \omega + xc$ and $D_2 = \eta + rc$ (in $\mathbb{Z}$). If $D_1 \in [cb, 2^{t+l}b - 1]$, she sends (C, D_1, D_2) to Bob, otherwise she starts again the protocol.
4. Bob checks that $D_1 \in [cb, 2^{t+l}b - 1]$ and that $C = H(g^{D_1}h^{D_2}E^{-c})$. This convinces Bob that $x \in [-2^{t+l}b, 2^{t+l}b]$.

2.2   Proof That Two Commitments Hide the Same Secret

Alice secretly holds $x \in [0, b]$. Let $E = E_1(x, r_1)$ and $F = E_2(x, r_2)$ be two commitments to x. She wants to prove to Bob that she knows x, r_1, r_2 such that $E = E_1(x, r_1)$ and $F = E_2(x, r_2)$, i.e. that E and F hide the same secret x. This protocol is derived from proofs of equality of two discrete logarithms from [10,5,1], combined with a proof of knowledge of a discrete logarithm modulo n [15].

Protocol. $PK(x, r_1, r_2 : E = E_1(x, r_1) \land F = E_2(x, r2))$

1. Alice picks $\omega \in_R [1, 2^{l+t}b - 1], \eta_1 \in_R [1, 2^{l+t+s_1}n - 1], \eta_2 \in_R [1, 2^{l+t+s_2}n - 1]$. Then, she computes $W_1 = g_1^{\omega}h_1^{\eta_1} \mod n$ and $W_2 = g_2^{\omega}h_2^{\eta_2} \mod n$.
2. Alice computes $c = H(W_1 \| W_2)$.
3. She computes $D = \omega + cx, D_1 = \eta_1 + cr_1, D_2 = \eta_2 + cr_2$ (in $\mathbb{Z}$) and sends (c, D, D_1, D_2) to Bob.
4. Bob checks whether $c = H(g_1^D h_1^{D_1} E^{-c} \mod n \| g_2^D h_2^{D_2} F^{-c} \mod n)$.

2.3   Proof That a Committed Number Is a Square

Alice secretly holds $x \in [0, b]$. Let $E = E(x^2, r_1)$ be a commitment to the square of x (in $\mathbb{Z}$). She wants to prove to Bob that she knows x and r_1 such that $E = E(x^2, r_1)$, i.e. that E hides the square x^2. The first proof that a committed number is a square has appeared in [13].

Protocol. $PK(x, r_1 : E = E(x^2, r_1))$

1. Alice picks $r_2 \in_R [-2^s n + 1, 2^s n - 1]$ and computes $F = E(x, r_2)$.
2. Then, Alice computes $r_3 = r_1 - r_2 x$ (in $\mathbb{Z}$). Note that $r_3 \in [-2^s bn+1, 2^s bn - 1]$. Then, $E = F^x h^{r_3} \mod n$.
3. As E is a commitment to x in base (F, h) and F is a commitment to x in base (g, h), Alice can run $PK(x, r_2, r_3 : F = g^x h^{r_2} \mod n \land E = F^x h^{r_3} \mod n)$. By the proof that two commitments hide the same secret described above, she gets (c, D, D_1, D_2).
4. She sends (F, c, D, D_1, D_2) to Bob.
5. Bob checks that $PK(x, r_2, r_3 : F = g^x h^{r_2} \mod n \land E = F^x h^{r_3} \mod n)$ is valid.

2.4   Boudot Proof

Let t, l and s be three security parameters. Let n be a large composite number whose factorization is unknown by Alice and Bob, g be an element of large order in $\mathbb{Z}_n^*$ and h be an element of the group generated by g such that both the discrete logarithm of g in base h and the discrete logarithm of h in base g are unknown by Alice. We denote by $E(x,r) = g^x h^r \bmod n$ a commitment to x in base (g,h) where r is randomly selected over $[-2^s n + 1, 2^s n - 1]$.

Protocol. $PK_{[WithTol]}(x, r : E = E(x,r) \wedge x \in [a - \theta, b + \theta])$

1. [Knowledge of x] Alice executes with Bob: $PK(x, r : E = E(x,r))$
2. [Setting] Both Alice and Bob compute $\widetilde{E} = E/g^a \bmod n$ and $\bar{E} = g^b/E \bmod n$. Alice sets $\widetilde{x} = x - a$ and $\bar{x} = b - x$. Now, Alice must prove to Bob that both $\widetilde{E}$ and $\bar{E}$ hide secrets which are greater than $-\theta$.
3. [Decomposition of $\widetilde{x}$ and $\bar{x}$] Alice computes:

$$\widetilde{x}_1 = \lfloor \sqrt{x - a} \rfloor, \qquad \widetilde{x}_2 = \widetilde{x} - \widetilde{x}_1^2,$$
$$\bar{x}_1 = \lfloor \sqrt{b - x} \rfloor, \qquad \bar{x}_2 = \bar{x} - \bar{x}_1^2$$

Then, $\widetilde{x} = \widetilde{x}_1^2 + \widetilde{x}_2$ and $\bar{x} = \bar{x}_1^2 + \bar{x}_2$, where $0 \le \widetilde{x}_2 \le 2\sqrt{b - a}$ and $0 \le \bar{x}_2 \le 2\sqrt{b - a}$.
4. [Choice of random values for new commitments] Alice randomly selects $\widetilde{r}_1$ and $\widetilde{r}_2$ in $[-2^s n + 1, \cdots, 2^s n - 1]$ such that $\widetilde{r}_1 + \widetilde{r}_2 = r$, and $\bar{r}_1$ and $\bar{r}_2$ such that $\bar{r}_1 + \bar{r}_2 = -r$.
5. [Computation of new commitments] Alice computes:

$$\widetilde{E}_1 = E(\widetilde{x}_1^2, \widetilde{r}_1), \qquad \widetilde{E}_2 = E(\widetilde{x}_2, \widetilde{r}_2)$$
$$\bar{E}_1 = E(\bar{x}_1^2, \bar{r}_1), \qquad \bar{E}_2 = E(\bar{x}_2, \bar{r}_2)$$

6. [Sending of the new commitments] Alice sends $\widetilde{E}_1$ and $\bar{E}_1$ to Bob. Bob computes $\widetilde{E}_2 = \widetilde{E}/\widetilde{E}_1$ and $\bar{E}_2 = \bar{E}/\bar{E}_1$
7. [Validity of the commitments to a square] Alice executes with Bob

$$PK(\widetilde{x}_1^2, \widetilde{r}_1 : \widetilde{E}_1 = E(\widetilde{x}_1^2, \widetilde{r}_1))$$
$$PK(\bar{x}_1^2, \bar{r}_1 : \bar{E}_1 = E(\bar{x}_1^2, \bar{r}_1))$$

which prove that both $\widetilde{E}_1$ and $\bar{E}_1$ hide a square.
8. [Validity of the commitments to a small value] Let $\theta = 2^{t+l+1}\sqrt{b - a}$. Alice executes with Bob the two following CFT proofs:

$$PK_{[CFT]}(\widetilde{x}_2, \widetilde{r}_2 : \widetilde{E}_2 = E(\widetilde{x}_2, \widetilde{r}_2) \wedge \widetilde{x}_2 \in [-\theta, \theta])$$
$$PK_{[CFT]}(\bar{x}_2, \bar{r}_2 : \bar{E}_2 = E(\bar{x}_2, \bar{r}_2) \wedge \bar{x}_2 \in [-\theta, \theta])$$

which prove that both $\widetilde{E}_2$ and $\bar{E}_2$ hide numbers which belong to $[-\theta, \theta]$, where $\theta = 2^{t+l+1}\sqrt{b - a}$, instead of proving that they belong to $[0, 2\sqrt{b - a}]$.

3   It Suffices to Adopt a Single Base

We remark that all above commitment schemes are based on the encryption

$$E(x, r) = g^x h^r \quad \bmod n$$

where x is the committed number, r is a random number selected by Alice, n is an RSA modulus whose factorization is *unknown* by Alice, g is an element of large order in $\mathbb{Z}_n$ and h is an element of the group generated by g such that both the discrete logarithm of g in base h and the discrete logarithm of h in base g are unknown by Alice.

We notice that they do not use a single base as usual. Thus an increase in cost occurs. In the next section, we show that it suffices to adopt a single base, i.e.,

$$E(x) = g^x \mod n$$

The common encryption sufficiently guarantees the securities of those commitment schemes. Thus the cost of the modified Boudot proof is about half of that of the original scheme. Besides, its security is immediately reduced to RSA [18] and a variant of Schnorr signature [19] in RSA setting with hidden order.

4 Modified CFT Proof and Its Security

4.1 Description

Let t, l and s be three security parameters, n be an RSA modulus whose factorization is *unknown* by Alice, g be an element of large order in $\mathbb{Z}_n^*$. Let H be a hash function which outputs $2t$-bit strings. We denote by $E = E(x) = g^x \mod n$ a commitment to $x \in [0, b]$.

Protocol. $PK(x : E = E(x) \wedge x \in [-2^{t+l}b, 2^{t+l}b])$

1. Alice picks $\omega \in_R [0, 2^{t+l}b - 1]$, and computes $W = g^\omega \mod n$.
2. Compute $C = H(W)$ and $c = C \mod 2^t$.
3. Compute $D = \omega + xc$ (in $\mathbb{Z}$). If $D \in [cb, 2^{t+l}b - 1]$, Alice sends (C, D) to Bob, otherwise she starts again the protocol.
4. Bob checks that $D \in [cb, 2^{t+l}b - 1]$ and $C = H(g^D E^{-c} \mod n)$. This convinces Bob that $x \in [-2^{t+l}b, 2^{t+l}b]$.

4.2 Security

It's not difficult to find that the modified scheme is almost as secure as the original scheme. Informally, the security of the modified scheme is just based on the following facts:

(F1) By the security of RSA [18], the single base encryption $E = E(x) = g^x \mod n$ effectively prevents Bob from getting x.

(F2) Alice knows the discrete logarithm of E in base g modulo n. Otherwise, she cannot produce a proper pair (C, D) such that $C = H(g^D E^{-c} \mod n)$, where $c = C \mod 2^t$, t is a public security parameter. Note that the above challenge is just the variant of Schnorr signature [19] in RSA setting. Under the circumstances, Alice cannot cheat Bob even she knows the order of g. We refer to [17].

(F3) D must be of the form $\alpha + xc$, where x is the just discrete logarithm of E in base g, α is selected by Alice before the challenge value C ($\equiv c \bmod 2^t$) is generated. This is immediately derived from the fact (F2).

(F4) The factorization of the modulus n is *unknown* by Alice, which implies that $\alpha + xc$ is just an integer (not a residue class). By checking $D \in [cb, 2^{t+l}b-1]$, it ensures that Bob can be convinced that $x \in [-2^{t+l}b, 2^{t+l}b]$.

Remark 1. The authors [6] gave the original presentation of CFT proof in ElGamal setting [12]. It's corrected soon [7] because Alice can cheat Bob if the *order* of the cryptographic group is *known* by her.

5   Same-Secret Proof with Single Base

Let n be an RSA modulus whose factorization is *unknown* by Alice, g_1 and g_2 be two element of large order in $\mathbb{Z}_n^*$. Let H be a hash function which outputs $2t$-bit strings. Alice secretly holds x. Let $E = E_1(x) = g_1^x \bmod n$ and $F = E_2(x) = g_2^x \bmod n$ be two commitments to x. She wants to prove to Bob that she knows x such that $E = E_1(x)$ and $F = E_2(x)$, i.e. that E and F hide the same secret x.

Protocol. $PK(x : E = E_1(x) \wedge F = E_2(x))$

1. Alice picks $\omega \in_R \mathbb{Z}$ and computes $W_1 = g_1^\omega \bmod n$ and $W_2 = g_2^\omega \bmod n$.
2. She computes $C = H(W_1 \| W_2)$.
3. She computes $D = \omega + cx$ (in $\mathbb{Z}$) and sends (C, D) to Bob.
4. Bob checks whether $C = H(g_1^D E^{-C} \bmod n \| g_2^D F^{-C} \bmod n)$.

Remark 2. One might argue a proof that two commitments hide the same secret in ElGamal setting. Precisely, it only shows that two commitments hide the same secret *residue class* (modulo the *order* of the cryptographic group) instead of the same secret *integer*.

6   Square-Proof with Single Base

Let n be an RSA modulus whose factorization is *unknown* by Alice, g be an element of large order in $\mathbb{Z}_n^*$. Let H be a hash function which outputs $2t$-bit strings. Alice secretly holds x. Let $E = E(x^2) = g^{x^2}$ be a commitment to the square of x (in $\mathbb{Z}$). She wants to prove to Bob that she knows x such that $E = E(x^2)$, i.e. that E hides the square x^2.

Protocol. $PK(x : E = E(x^2))$

1. Alice computes $F = E(x), E = F^x \bmod n$.
2. As E is a commitment to x in base F and F is a commitment to x in base g, Alice can run $PK(x : F = g^x \bmod n \wedge E = F^x \bmod n)$. By the proof that two commitments hide the same secret described above, she gets (C, D).
3. She sends (F, C, D) to Bob.
4. Bob checks that $PK(x : F = g^x \bmod n \wedge E = F^x \bmod n)$ is valid.

7   Boudot's Proof Revisited

7.1   Description

Let t, l and s be three security parameters. Let n be an RSA modulus whose factorization is *unknown* by Alice and Bob, g be an element of large order in $\mathbb{Z}_n^*$. We denote by $E(x) = g^x \bmod n$ a commitment to x in base g.

Protocol. $PK_{[WithTol]}(x : E = E(x) \wedge x \in [a - \theta, b + \theta])$

1. [Knowledge of x] Alice executes with Bob: $PK(x : E = E(x))$
2. [Setting] Both Alice and Bob compute $\widetilde{E} = E/g^a \bmod n$ and $\bar{E} = g^b/E \bmod n$. Alice sets $\widetilde{x} = x - a$ and $\bar{x} = b - x$.
3. [Decomposition of $\widetilde{x}$ and $\bar{x}$] Alice computes:

$$\widetilde{x}_1 = \lfloor \sqrt{x - a} \rfloor, \qquad \widetilde{x}_2 = \widetilde{x} - \widetilde{x}_1^2,$$

$$\bar{x}_1 = \lfloor \sqrt{b - x} \rfloor, \qquad \bar{x}_2 = \bar{x} - \bar{x}_1^2$$

Then, $\widetilde{x} = \widetilde{x}_1^2 + \widetilde{x}_2$ and $\bar{x} = \bar{x}_1^2 + \bar{x}_2$, where $0 \le \widetilde{x}_2 \le 2\sqrt{b - a}$ and $0 \le \bar{x}_2 \le 2\sqrt{b - a}$.

4. [Computation of new commitments] Alice computes:

$$\widetilde{E}_1 = E(\widetilde{x}_1^2), \qquad \widetilde{E}_2 = E(\widetilde{x}_2)$$

$$\bar{E}_1 = E(\bar{x}_1^2), \qquad \bar{E}_2 = E(\bar{x}_2)$$

5. [Sending of the new commitments] Alice sends $\widetilde{E}_1$ and $\bar{E}_1$ to Bob. Bob computes $\widetilde{E}_2 = \widetilde{E}/\widetilde{E}_1$ and $\bar{E}_2 = \bar{E}/\bar{E}_1$
6. [Validity of the commitments to a square] Alice executes with Bob

$$PK(\widetilde{x}_1^2 : \widetilde{E}_1 = E(\widetilde{x}_1^2))$$

$$PK(\bar{x}_1^2 : \bar{E}_1 = E(\bar{x}_1^2))$$

which prove that both $\widetilde{E}_1$ and $\bar{E}_1$ hide a square. (Note that the protocols $PK(x : E = E_1(x) \wedge F = E_2(x))$ and $PK(x : E = E(x^2))$ are called in the step.)

7. [Validity of the commitments to a small value] Let $\theta = 2^{t+l+1}\sqrt{b - a}$. Alice executes with Bob the two following CFT proofs:

$$PK_{[CFT]}(\widetilde{x}_2 : \widetilde{E}_2 = E(\widetilde{x}_2) \wedge \widetilde{x}_2 \in [-\theta, \theta])$$

$$PK_{[CFT]}(\bar{x}_2 : \bar{E}_2 = E(\bar{x}_2) \wedge \bar{x}_2 \in [-\theta, \theta])$$

which prove that both $\widetilde{E}_2$ and $\bar{E}_2$ hide numbers which belong to $[-\theta, \theta]$, where $\theta = 2^{t+l+1}\sqrt{b - a}$.

The correctness arguments for the modified Boudot proof are the same as that of the original scheme. We refer to [3]. But its security is immediately reduced to RSA and a variant of Schnorr signature in RSA setting with hidden order. We refer to §4.2. We remark that the reason of adopting two bases instead of a single base in Boudot proof is that the protocol directly follows the structures of [13].

7.2   Further Discussion

1. Why not use a single base instead two bases. In 2002, the authors [11] explained that:

> A commitment with a single base to s of form $c = g^s \bmod n$ does not satisfy the standard hiding property for commitments. For instance, if a prover commits twice to the same value, this is immediately visible.

Obviously, they did not consider to permit the prover to update the single base.

Now we suggest a solution to this problem. If Alice commits twice to the same value, she can pick a random θ and update the base g with $\hat{g} = g^\theta \bmod n$. Note that g is still permitted to be a system-wide parameter since Alice can update it by herself. But in Fujisaki-Okamoto commitment scheme (with two bases), Alice is not permitted to update the bases. Otherwise, the discrete logarithm of $\hat{g}$ in base $\hat{h}$ or the discrete logarithm of $\hat{h}$ in base $\hat{g}$ will be known to Alice.

2. Efficiency. Roughly speaking, the cost of the commitment with a single base (excluding the cost of updating the base) is about half of that of Damgård-Fujisaki commitment [11]. But the key restriction, both the discrete logarithm of g in base h and the discrete logarithm of h in base g are unknown by Alice, which is a potential menace to Damgård-Fujisaki commitment, is definitely removed. We remark that the updating of g can be completed in the pre-computation.

8   Conclusion

In this paper, we investigate the two range-bounded commitment schemes, i.e., CFT proof and Boudot proof. Based on the latter, we present an efficient range-bounded commitment. The cost of the modified scheme is about half of that of the original scheme because we adopt a single base instead of two bases. Moreover, its security is immediately reduced to RSA and a variant of Schnorr signature in RSA setting with hidden order.

References

1. Bao, F.: An Efficient Verifiable Encryption Scheme for Encryption of Discrete Logarithms. In: Schneier, B., Quisquater, J.-J. (eds.) CARDIS 1998. LNCS, vol. 1820, Springer, Heidelberg (2000)
2. Brickell, E., Chaum, D., Damgård, I., Van de Graaf, J.: Gradual and Verifiable Release of a Secret. In: Pomerance, C. (ed.) CRYPTO 1987. LNCS, vol. 293, pp. 156–166. Springer, Heidelberg (1988)
3. Boudot, F.: Efficient Proofs that a Committed Number Lies in an Interval. In: Preneel, B. (ed.) EUROCRYPT 2000. LNCS, vol. 1807, pp. 431–444. Springer, Heidelberg (2000)
4. Boudot, F., Traoré, J.: Efficient Publicly Verifiable Secret Sharing Schemes with Fast or Delayed Recovery. In: Varadharajan, V., Mu, Y. (eds.) ICICS 1999. LNCS, vol. 1726, pp. 87–102. Springer, Heidelberg (1999)

5. Chaum, D., Evertse, J.-H., Van de Graaf, J.: An Improved Protocol for Demonstrating Possession of Discrete Logarithm and Some Generalizations. In: Price, W.L., Chaum, D. (eds.) EUROCRYPT 1987. LNCS, vol. 304, pp. 127–141. Springer, Heidelberg (1988)
6. Chan, A., Frankel, Y., Tsiounis, Y.: Easy Come Easy Go Divisible Cash. In: Nyberg, K. (ed.) EUROCRYPT 1998. LNCS, vol. 1403, pp. 561–575. Springer, Heidelberg (1998)
7. Chan, A., Frankel, Y., Tsiounis, Y.: Easy Come Easy Go Divisible Cash. Updated version with corrections, GTE Tech. Rep. (1998), available at: http://www.ccs.neu.edu/home/yiannis/
8. Camenisch, J., Michels, M.: Separability and Efficiency for Generic Group Signature Schemes. In: Wiener, M.J. (ed.) CRYPTO 1999. LNCS, vol. 1666, pp. 413–430. Springer, Heidelberg (1999)
9. Camenisch, J., Michels, M.: Proving in Zero-Knowledge that a Number is the Product of Two Safe Primes. In: Stern, J. (ed.) EUROCRYPT 1999. LNCS, vol. 1592, pp. 106–121. Springer, Heidelberg (1999)
10. Chaum, D., Pedersen, T.-P.: Wallet Databases with Observers. In: Brickell, E.F. (ed.) CRYPTO 1992. LNCS, vol. 740, pp. 89–105. Springer, Heidelberg (1993)
11. Damgård, I., Fujisaki, E.: A Statistically-Hiding Integer Commitment Scheme Based on Groups with Hidden Order. In: Zheng, Y. (ed.) ASIACRYPT 2002. LNCS, vol. 2501, pp. 125–142. Springer, Heidelberg (2002)
12. ElGamal, T.: A public-key cryptosystem and a signature scheme based on discrete logarithms. In: Blakely, G.R., Chaum, D. (eds.) CRYPTO 1984. LNCS, vol. 196, pp. 10–18. Springer, Heidelberg (1985)
13. Fujisaki, E., Okamoto, T.: Statistical Zero Knowledge Protocols to Prove Modular Polynomial Relations. In: Kaliski Jr., B.S. (ed.) CRYPTO 1997. LNCS, vol. 1294, pp. 16–30. Springer, Heidelberg (1997)
14. Fujisaki, E., Okamoto, T.: A Practical and Provably Secure Scheme for Publicly Verifiable Secret Sharing and Its Applications. In: Nyberg, K. (ed.) EUROCRYPT 1998. LNCS, vol. 1403, pp. 32–46. Springer, Heidelberg (1998)
15. Girault, M.: Self-Certified Public Keys. In: Davies, D.W. (ed.) EUROCRYPT 1991. LNCS, vol. 547, pp. 490–497. Springer, Heidelberg (1991)
16. Mao, W.: Guaranteed Correct Sharing of Integer Factorization with Off-line Shareholders. Proceedings of Public Key Cryptography 98, 27–42 (1998)
17. Pointcheval, D., Stern, J.: Security proofs for signature schemes. In: Maurer, U.M. (ed.) EUROCRYPT 1996. LNCS, vol. 1070, pp. 387–398. Springer, Heidelberg (1996)
18. Rivest, R., Shamir, A., Adleman, L.M.: A Mehtod for Obtaining Digital Signatures and Public-Key Cryptosystems. Communications of ACM 21(2), 120–126 (1978)
19. Schnorr, C.-P.: Efficient Signature Generation for Smart Cards. Journal of Cryptology, 239–252 (1991)

Toward Practical Anonymous Rerandomizable RCCA Secure Encryptions*

Rui Xue and Dengguo Feng

State Key Laboratory of Information Security,
Institute of Software, Chinese Academy of Sciences
{rxue,feng}@is.iscas.ac.cn

Abstract. Replayable adaptively chosen ciphertext attack (RCCA) security is a relaxation of popular adaptively chosen ciphertext attack (CCA) security for public key encryption system. Unlike CCA security, RCCA security allows modifying a ciphertext into a new ciphertext of the same message. One of the open questions is that if there exists a perfectly rerandomizable RCCA secure encryption [4]. Prabhakaran and Rosulek recently answered this question affirmatively [14]. The scheme they proposed (PR scheme for short) is composed of a double-strands Cramer-Shoup schemes that involves as many as 56 exponents in encryption and 65 exponents in decryption, and 55 exponents operations during rerandomization.

We present a practical perfectly rerandomizable RCCA secure encryption system in this paper. The system constitutes of two layers of encryptions. One layer carries message, the other layer carries a random quantity used to hiding the message in previous layer. This random quantity in the encryption also works as correlation between the two parts of encryption such that they are formed in a prescribed way. The proposed construction dramatically reduces the complexities, compared with PR scheme, to 15 exponents in encryption, 6 exponents decryption as well as 16 exponents operations in rerandomization.

Besides the practical feature, our scheme is also the first *receiver anonymous*, perfectly rerandomizable RCCA secure encryption, which settles an open question in [14]. The scheme is secure under DDH assumption.

1 Introduction

The popular standard for public key encryption security is the security against adaptive chosen ciphertext attack (CCA). Doleve, Dwork and Naor constructed the first scheme secure against CCA based on standard primitive [9]. Cramer and

---

* Supported by National Basic Research Program of China 973 Program Grant 2007CB311202, and supported by the National High Technology Research and Development Program of China (863 program) Grant 2006AA01Z427. The first author is also supported by the China Scholarship Council, and by the Natural Science Foundation of China Grant 60773029.

S. Qing, H. Imai, and G. Wang (Eds.): ICICS 2007, LNCS 4861, pp. 239–253, 2007.

Shoup gave the first practical CCA secure system based on ElGamal cryptosystem [5]. It is then intensively investigated afterwards [15,6,13]. Although CCA security is preferred in most of cryptographic applications, it is, however, also viewed too strong in some scenarios. For example, rerandomizable encryption is used in mixnets [10] with applications to voting anonymization. The nonmalleability of CCA secure system prevents such kind of system being adopted in these applications. A relaxed but strong enough security in this case is desired.

The relaxed security definitions for encryption system appeared in Krawczyk [12], Shoup [16] and An et al. [1]. The notions are called, loose cipher-unforgeability, benign malleability, and generalized CCA security respectively. Later, Canetti et al. [4] systematically developed the relaxed notion about CCA security. All notions mentioned above are proved being equivalent to the notion of publicly detectable RCCA in [4]. Many properties and schemes are setting up or constructed in that paper. One of the open questions remaining solved is the existence of so called "(perfectly) rerandomizable replayable CCA schemes".

The replayable CCA (RCCA in short) security is the same as CCA security, except no guarantees are given against adversaries that just try to modify a ciphertext into a new one with the *same* plaintext. This relaxation allows modifying a ciphertext into a new ciphertext provided that the later is decrypted into the same plaintext as the former. The *(perfectly) rerandomizable* RCCA security augments an encryption system with an algorithm to alter a ciphertext c of a message m into a new ciphertext c' that is computationally indistinguishable from the fresh ciphertext of m.

Groth [11] investigated the rerandomization of RCCA secure cryptosystem. Groth's scheme is proved only to be generic RCCA secure. Prabhakaran and Rosulek [14] constructed the first perfectly rerandomizable replayable CCA secure encryption system (briefly, PR scheme). The PR scheme is an extension of Cramer-Shoup encryption called Double-Strands Cramer-Shoup scheme. One strand of a variant of Cramer-Shoup encryption is used for carrying the message, the other one for helping rerandomization. The two strands of ciphertexts are correlated with shared random masks. In order to prevent the two strands being combined in abnormal ways, some perturbation of the exponents of the message-carrying strand is performed. As a result, the encryption system needs as many as 28 elements for the public key and 30 elements for the private key. The encryption alone involves more than 50 exponentiation operations (see Table1 in Section 3.3 for detailed complexity). The system is secure under the DDH assumption. The notion of key-privacy [3] is modified to denote receiver anonymous property. The PR scheme is not an anonymous rerandomizable RCCA secure scheme. The existence of perfectly rerandomizable RCCA secure encryption is posed as an open question.

Since rerandomizable RCCA security is weaker than CCA security in requirement, it is intuitively plausible and desirable to construct a rerandomizable RCCA scheme that is at least as efficient as CCA secure one (if not more efficient). The main contribution in this paper is a practical receiver anonymous rerandomizable RCCA secure encryption.

The scheme in this paper bears some similarity with PR scheme in that it constitutes of two layers of encryptions. However, ours is not double-strands of Cramer-Shoup like encryptions. One layer is a variant of Cramer-Shoup encryption. But the other is just an ElGamal encryption. The first layer has the functionality of carrying the message like in PR scheme but in a completely different way. The second layer instead is used only to carry a random quantity that is used to hide the message in the other layer. The quantity is also the correlation string between the two layers. The rerandomization of the ciphertext makes use of the rerandomizability of ElGamal encryption. Since two layers in our scheme are both ElGamal type of encryptions, the scheme is also receiver anonymous according to the result by Bellare et al. in [3]. Thus, our construction is not only a practically, perfectly rerandomizable but also receiver anonymous RCCA secure encryption scheme, which settle an open question in [14].

The organization of the paper : After giving out notations and definitions in Section 2, we present a publicly rerandomizable scheme and its secretly rerandomizable version in Section 3. The receiver anonymity and perfectly rerandomization of them are also indicated in Section 3. Section 4 is devoted to the proof of RCCA security of the basic scheme. The last section is our conclusion and future works.

2   Preliminaries

2.1   Some Notations

A function $f(k)$ is a *negligible function* in k if it always holds that $f(k) < 1/k^c$ for any $0 < c \in \mathbb{Z}$ for sufficiently large k. We use $\texttt{negl}(k)$ to denote a negligible function in k, or just $\texttt{negl}$ if k is obvious from contexts. If F is finite set, then the notation "$x \xleftarrow{R} F$" denotes the act of choosing x uniformly from F. Notation "$u \leftarrow f(x)$" denotes the act of assigning the value $f(x)$ to u. The notation $\Pr[x_1 \xleftarrow{R} S_1; x_2 \xleftarrow{R} S_2; \ldots; x_m \xleftarrow{R} S_m : p(x_1, \ldots, x_m)]$ denotes the probability that $p(x_1, \ldots, x_m)$ will be true after the ordered execution of the probabilistic assignments $x_1 \xleftarrow{R} S_1; x_2 \xleftarrow{R} S_2; \ldots; x_m \xleftarrow{R} S_m$.

2.2   Security of Public Key Encryption

We model all algorithms including adversaries as probabilistic polynomial time (PPT) Turing machines. The public-key cryptosystem is defined as usual with three algorithms (K, E, D). Where K is key generation algorithm, E the encryption algorithm, and D the decryption algorithm. The rerandomizable encryption system is a public-key encryption system augmented with an additional rerandomization algorithm *Rand*.

The security of a public key encryption system against CCA and its variants is defined as follows.

Definition 1. *Let (K, E, D) be an encryption system. For any PPT algorithm A if the following probability is negligibly close to $1/2$:*

$$\Pr\left[(pk, sk) \leftarrow K(1^k); (m_0, m_1) \leftarrow A^{\mathcal{O}_1}; b \overset{R}{\leftarrow} \{0, 1\}; c^* \leftarrow E(m_b) : A^{\mathcal{O}_2}(pk, c^*) = b\right].$$

where $\mathcal{O}_1$ runs exactly as decryption algorithm D, and $\mathcal{O}_2$ run exactly as decryption algorithm D except in the following cases:

1. *When a query to $\mathcal{O}_2$ is c^*, $\mathcal{O}_2$ will return $\bot$. Then, the cryptosystem is said secure against chosen ciphertext attack (CCA).*
2. *When a query to $\mathcal{O}_2$ has plaintext in $\{m_0, m_1\}$, $\mathcal{O}_2$ will return test. Then, the cryptosystem is said secure against replayable chosen ciphertext attack (RCCA).*
3. *When a query to $\mathcal{O}_2$ has plaintext in $\{m_0, m_1\}$, $\mathcal{O}_2$ will return $\bot$. Then, the cryptosystem is said secure against weak replayable chosen ciphertext attack (WRCCA).*

2.3   Rerandomizable Encryption

There are two kinds of randomization algorithms defined in [4]: a *public rerandomization algorithm $PRand$* takes a ciphertext c and public key in system as input and turns out a well-formed new ciphertext c' with identical distribution to that of c such that both are decrypted as the same plaintext. A *secret randomization algorithm $Srand$* is the same as public randomization algorithm except taking only a ciphertext as input. A public-key encryption system augmented with a public (secret) randomization algorithm is called a *publicly (secretly) rerandomizable encryption system*. We some times call secretly rerandomizable encryption just as *rerandomizable encryption* as in [14].

For a rerandomizable encryption scheme $(K, E, D, Rand)$, any PPT adversary $\mathcal{A}$, following experiment is called *perfect rerandomization attack* experiment (PRA) in [14].

Stage 1. Pick $(pk, sk) \leftarrow K(1^k)$. The public keys pk is given to $\mathcal{A}$.
Stage 2. Adversary $\mathcal{A}$ gets access to decryption oracle and rerandomization oracle $D_{sk}(\cdot), Rand(\cdot)$.
Stage 3. Adversary submits a message m to encryption oracles. Challenger picks $b \overset{R}{\leftarrow} \{0, 1\}$ at random and
If $b = 0$ **then** pick r_1, r_2 at random, $c_1 \leftarrow E(pk, r_1)$ and $c_2 \leftarrow Rand(c_1, r_2)$
else $c_1 \leftarrow E(pk, r_1)$ and $c_2 \leftarrow E(m, r_2)$
return (c_1, c_2)
Where random strings r_1, r_2 are chosen uniformly from defined ranges in encryption scheme, and $E(m, r_1)$ indicates the ciphertext of m encrypted using random string r_1.
Stage 4. Adversary $\mathcal{A}$ continues to get access to decryption and randomization oracles $D_{sk}(\cdot), Rand(\cdot)$.
Stage 5. Adversary $\mathcal{A}$ outputs a bit b'.

The advantage of adversary $\mathcal{A}$ in PRA experiment is $\Pr[b' = b] - \frac{1}{2}$.

Definition 2 (Perfectly Rerandomizable Encryption). *A rerandomizable encryption system* $(K, E, D, Rand)$ *is said perfectly rerandomizable if for any PPT algorithm* $\mathcal{A}$, *the advantage of any PPT algorithm* $\mathcal{A}$ *in PRA experiment is negligible in security parameter* k.

Loosely speaking, a (perfectly) rerandomizable encryption guarantees the rerandomization to a ciphertext c will return a new ciphertext c' of the same message that is indistinguishable from any fresh encryption of original message.

Let $\mathcal{E} = (K, E, D, Rand)$ be a rerandomizable encryption system. Let R be the range of random strings used in encryption. The following is a direct conclusion from the definition above.

Lemma 1. *If for any* $r_1, r_2 \in R$, *we have* $Rand(E(m, r_1), r_2) = E(m, f(r_1, r_2))$, *where* $f(r_1, r_2)$ *is a random variable in* R. *The cryptosystem* $\mathcal{E}$ *is a perfectly rerandomizable encryption system, if for any two independent strings* r_1, r_2 *chosen uniformly from* R, $f(r_1, r_2)$ *is uniformly distributed on* R.

2.4 Decisional Diffie-Hellman Assumption

The security of scheme in this paper depends on the hardness of Decisional Diffie-Hellman (DDH) problem. For any group G of prime order q, a tuple (g_1, g_2, g_3, g_4) in G^4 is a Diffie-Hellman (DH) tuple if there is a $r \in \mathbb{Z}_q$ such that $(g_1, g_2, g_3, g_4) = (g_1, g_2, g_1^r, g_2^r)$. The *decisional Diffie-Hellman assumption* holds in G if any PPT algorithm cannot tell DH tuples from uniformly chosen tuples from G^4 except with negligible probability. Let Rand is the event that the tuple (g_1, g_2, g_3, g_4) is chosen from distribution of random tuples, and DH the event that the tuple is chosen from distribution of Diffie-Hellman tuples. The advantage $\mathrm{Adv}_{\mathcal{A}}^{DDH}$ of PPT algorithm $\mathcal{A}$ telling the DH tuples from random tuples is

$$\mathrm{Adv}_{\mathcal{A}}^{DDH} = |\Pr[\mathcal{A}(g_1, g_2, g_3, g_4) = 1 \mid \mathrm{DH}] - \Pr[\mathcal{A}(g_1, g_2, g_3, g_4) = 1 \mid \mathrm{Rand}]|$$

The probability is over the coin toss of $\mathcal{A}$ and the randomness of the chosen of (g_1, g_2, g_3, g_4).

As in [14], the scheme in this paper employs two groups $G, \hat{G}$ with special relationship: G is with order q, and $\hat{G}$ order p. Where group $\hat{G}$ is a subgroup in $\mathbb{Z}_q^*$. This is exemplified by the following groups: Let $p, 2p + 1, 4p + 3$ (first kind *Cunningham chain* of length 3 [2]) be a primes chain. Group $\mathcal{QR}_p$ denotes the quadratic residue modulo p. Then $\hat{G} = \mathcal{QR}_{2p+1}$ and $G = \mathcal{QR}_{4p+3}$ are desired groups. It is widely believed that DDH assumption holds in quadratic residue modulo a safe prime. It is conjectured there are infinite many Cunningham chain (see Prabhakaran and Mike Rosulek [14] for details).

3 Rerandomizable Encryption Schemes

We present three randomizable encryption schemes in this section. The first two are publicly randomizable encryption systems, and the last one is a secretly randomizable. The first publicly rerandomizable system is our basic scheme. We will only give out the security proof for the first scheme in next section. The proof for the variants are essentially the same, which are omitted.

3.1 Publicly Rerandomizable Encryption System (PRE)

The publicly rerandomizable encryption system consists of four algorithms $(\mathsf{KeyGen}, \mathsf{Enc}, \mathsf{Dec}, \mathsf{PRand})$:

Key Generation. Taking security parameter k as input, algorithm KeyGen chooses a cyclic group G of prime order q and a subgroup $\hat{G} \subseteq \mathbb{Z}_q^*$ of order p (see the last paragraph of Section 2.4) such that DDH problem is hard in G and $\hat{G}$. Where the length of p is k. It then chooses $g_1, g_2 \leftarrow G$, $\hat{g} \leftarrow \hat{G}$ and $x, y, a, b, a', b' \leftarrow \mathbb{Z}_q, \lambda \leftarrow \mathbb{Z}_p$ at random. To choose a collision resistant Hash function $H : \hat{G} \times G \rightarrow \mathbb{Z}_q$. The public key pk and secret key sk are defined as

$$pk := (\hat{g}, \hat{e} = \hat{g}^\lambda;\ g_1, g_2, h = g_1^x g_2^y, c = g_1^a g_2^b, d = g_1^{a'} g_2^{b'}, H),$$
$$sk := (\lambda;\ x, y, a, b, a', b')$$

Encryption. Given a message $m \in G \backslash \{1_G\}$, the encryption algorithm Enc runs as follows. First it chooses $r, s \leftarrow \mathbb{Z}_q, t \leftarrow \hat{G}, \gamma \leftarrow \mathbb{Z}_p$ at random. It then computes

$$u_0 \leftarrow \hat{g}^\gamma, w_0 \leftarrow \hat{e}^\gamma t, \alpha \leftarrow H(m),$$
$$u_1 \leftarrow g_1^r, v_1 \leftarrow g_2^r, w_1 \leftarrow h^r m^t,$$
$$u_2 \leftarrow g_1^s, v_2 \leftarrow g_2^s, w_2 \leftarrow (c^{\alpha t} d^t)^s.$$

The ciphertext is $C = (u_0, w_0; u_1, v_1, w_1, u_2, v_2, w_2)$.

Decryption. Given a ciphertext $C = (u_0, w_0; u_1, v_1, w_1, u_2, v_2, w_2)$ and sk, the decryption algorithm Dec first computes

$$t \leftarrow w_0/u_0^\lambda, \qquad \overline{m} \leftarrow w_1/(u_1^x v_1^y), \qquad m \leftarrow \overline{m}^{1/t}, \qquad \alpha \leftarrow H(m)$$

To check if $\overline{m} \neq 1_G \wedge w_2 \overset{?}{=} u_2^{(a\alpha + a')t} v_2^{(b\alpha + b')t}$. If it holds, then the algorithm outputs m; otherwise it outputs $\bot$.

Rerandomization. Given ciphertext $C = (u_0, w_0; u_1, v_1, w_1, u_2, v_2, w_2)$ and public key pk. The public rerandomization algorithm PRand selects $r', s', t' \overset{R}{\leftarrow} \mathbb{Z}_q, \gamma' \overset{R}{\leftarrow} \mathbb{Z}_p$ at random and then computes

$$C' = (u_0 \hat{g}^{\gamma'}, w_0 \hat{e}^{\gamma'} t';\ u_1^{t'} g_1^{r'}, v_1^{t'} g_2^{r'}, w_1^{t'} h^{r'}, u_2^{s'}, v_2^{s'}, w_2^{s't'})$$

It outputs C' as replayed ciphertext.

This completes the description of the cryptosystem. We first verify that decryption of honestly constructed ciphertext C will yield correct value. Since $u_1 = g_1^r, v_1 = g_2^r$, we have

$$v_1 = u_1^w,\ u_1^x v_1^y = g_1^{rx} g_2^{ry} = (g_1^x g_2^y)^r = h^r \text{ and } \overline{m} = w_1/h^r = w_1/(u_1^x v_1^y).$$

Similarly, let $t = w_3/u_3^\lambda$, $m = \overline{m}^{1/t}$ and $\alpha = H(m)$,

$$u_2^{(a\alpha+a')t} v_2^{(b\alpha+b')t} = g_1^{(a\alpha+a')ts} g_2^{(b\alpha+b')ts} = (g_1^{a\alpha ts} g_2^{b\alpha ts})(g_1^{a'ts} g_2^{b'ts})$$
$$= c^{ts\alpha} d^{ts} = (c^{\alpha t} d^t)^s = w_2.$$

If $m \neq 1_G$, the decryption test will pass, and the output will be m.
Next, the rerandomized ciphertext is

$$C' = (u_0 \hat{g}^{\gamma'}, w_0 \hat{e}^{\gamma'} t'; u_1^{t'} g_1^{r'}, v_1^{t'} g_2^{r'}, w_1^{t'} h^{r'}, u_2^{s'}, v_2^{s'}, w_2^{s't'})$$
$$= (\hat{g}^{\gamma+\gamma'}, \hat{e}^{\gamma+\gamma'} t t'; g_1^{rt'+r'}, g_2^{rt'+r'}, h^{rt'+r'} m^{tt'}, g_1^{ss'}, g_2^{ss'}, (c^{\alpha t} d^t)^{ss't'})$$
$$= (\hat{g}^{\overline{\gamma}}, \hat{e}^{\overline{\gamma}} \overline{t}; g_1^{\overline{r}}, g_2^{\overline{r}}, h^{\overline{r}} m^{\overline{t}}, g_1^{\overline{s}}, g_2^{\overline{s}}, (c^{\alpha \overline{t}} d^{\overline{t}})^{\overline{s}})$$

Where

$$\overline{\gamma} \equiv \gamma + \gamma' \mod p \qquad\qquad \overline{r} \equiv rt' + r' \mod q \qquad (1)$$
$$\overline{s} \equiv ss' \mod q \qquad\qquad \overline{t} \equiv t t' \mod q$$

It is again a well formed ciphertext for message m that can be decrypted successfully. Here is the right place to indicate the perfect rerandomizability and anonymity of our scheme:

Proposition 1. *The rerandomizable encryption* (KeyGen, Enc, Dec, PRand) *is a perfectly reranzomizable encryption.*

Proof. It is easy to see that for any given γ, random variable $\overline{\gamma} \equiv \gamma + \gamma' \mod p$ is uniformly distributed on $\mathbb{Z}_p$ if γ' is uniformly distributed. Similarly to see from (1) that $\overline{r}, \overline{s}$ and $\overline{t}$ are all uniformly distributed in $\mathbb{Z}_q$, whenever r', t', s' are independently and uniformly chosen from $\mathbb{Z}_q$. This shows the perfect rerandomness according to Lemma 1.   ✦

Since the encryption constructed above is two layers of ElGamal type of encryption, it is a conclusion in [3] that ElGamal encryption is key-privacy and hence receiver anonymity in our sense.

Proposition 2. *The encryption* (KeyGen, Enc, Dec, PRand) *is receiver anonymous.*

3.2   Secretly Rerandomizable Encryption System

Publicly rerandomizable encryption system in last subsection needs public key for randomization algorithm to make a randomization to the purported ciphertext. This is not desired in some applications like universal mixnets [10]. Where each mixing server will permute many ciphertexts from different sources to different receivers. The public keys are either unavailable to mix servers or unintended to mix servers.

We expand the publicly rerandomizable encryption systems in last subsection to obtain a secretly rerandomizable encryption system (briefly SRE) (or rerandomizable RCCA encryption system [14]). SRE system consists of four algorithms (SKeyGen, SEnc, SDec, SRand). The algorithms SKeyGen and SDec behave in the same way respectively as KeyGen and Dec in last subsection. The other two are as follows.

Encryption. Given a message $m \in G$, the encryption algorithm SEnc runs as follows. First it chooses $r, s \leftarrow \mathbb{Z}_q, t \leftarrow \hat{G}, \gamma \leftarrow \mathbb{Z}_p$ at random. It then computes

$$\overline{u}_0 \leftarrow \hat{g}^{\gamma'}, \overline{w}_0 \leftarrow \hat{e}^{\gamma'}, u_0 \leftarrow \hat{g}^{\gamma}, w_0 \leftarrow \hat{e}^{\gamma} t,$$

$$\overline{u}_1 \leftarrow g_1^{r'}, \overline{v}_1 \leftarrow g_2^{r'}, \overline{w}_1 \leftarrow h^{r'}, u_1 \leftarrow g_1^r, v_1 \leftarrow g_2^r, w_1 \leftarrow h^r m^t,$$

$$\alpha \leftarrow H(m), u_2 \leftarrow g_1^s, v_2 \leftarrow g_2^s, w_2 \leftarrow (c^\alpha d)^{ts}.$$

The ciphertext is $C = (\overline{u}_0, \overline{w}_0, u_0, w_0; \overline{u}_1, \overline{v}_1, \overline{w}_1, u_1, v_1, w_1, u_2, v_2, w_2)$.

Rerandomization. Given ciphertext C denoted as above. The secretly rerandomization algorithm SRand selects $r_1, r_1', s_2, t' \leftarrow \mathbb{Z}_q, \gamma_0, \gamma_0' \leftarrow \mathbb{Z}_p$ at random and then computes C' as

$$(\overline{u}_0^{\gamma_0'}, \overline{w}_0^{\gamma_0'}, u_0 \overline{u}_0^{\gamma_0}, w_0 \overline{w}_0^{\gamma_0} t'; \overline{u}_1^{r_1'}, \overline{v}_1^{r_1'}, \overline{w}_1^{r_1'}, u_1^{t'} \overline{u}_1^{r_1}, v_1^{t'} \overline{v}_1^{r_1}, w_1^{t'} \overline{w}_1^{r_1}, u_2^{s_2}, v_2^{s_2}, w_2^{t' s_2})$$

It outputs C' as the replayed ciphertext.

The rerandomization of C does not take public key pk as input, rather, only the information from C is used. This shows that it is indeed a secretly randomizable encryption.

3.3   Complexity

There are two secretly rerandomizable schemes in the literature and they appeared in [11] and [14] respectively. We compare the efficiency of our scheme in Section 3.2 with them in the following:

Groth [11] proposed the first secretly rerandomizable encryption system with *weak* RCCA security. The scheme there used $O(k)$ group elements to encode a k-bit message. The public key and secret key is of length $O(k)$.

The scheme proposed by Prabhakaran and Rosulek in [14] as a first secretly rerandomizable system with RCCA security used 40 elements from $\hat{G}$ and 14 elements from G in their ciphertext. Public key there uses 13 group elements, and secret key uses 20 group elements.

The secretly rerandomizable encryption scheme in this paper uses 4 elements from $\hat{G}$ and 9 elements from G in a ciphertext. The public key here uses 7 group elements, and secret key uses 5 group elements.

The number of operations in the group performed by our scheme is summarized and compared to Groth's scheme and PR's scheme in Table 1. It is easy to see that ours is the most practical scheme and much more efficient in the length of ciphertext and operations needed during encryption and decryption as well as rerandomization.

Table 1. The comparison of the number of group operations performed by our scheme with those by existing RCCA schemes. Where k is the number of bits in plaintext.

Schemes	Functions	Exponentiations	Multiplications
	Enc	$O(k)$	$O(k)$
Groth's Scheme	Dec	$O(k)$	$O(k)$
	Rand	$O(k)$	0
	Enc	56	18
PR's Scheme	Dec	65	62
	Rand	55	47
	Enc	15	4
Our Scheme	Dec	6	4
	Rand	16	6

4   Proof of RCCA Security

In this section we will prove the publicly rerandomizable RCCA security for scheme in Section 3.1. The system is a combination of two cryptosystems: one is an expansion of Cramer-Shoup encryption system, another is ElGamal encryption system with public key $pk_1 = (\hat{g}, \hat{e})$ and secret key $sk_1 = \lambda$. To denote it as Γ. The RCCA attack to the system forms an attack to the ElGamal encryption Γ. This attack is called indirect RCCA attack to Γ. We show that under indirect RCCA attack, ElGamal system Γ remains secure. To be more faithful to the proof of our main theorem, we formalize the following indirect attack game:

Stage 1. Adversary queries a key generation oracle. The key generation oracle computes $pk = (\hat{g}, \hat{e} = \hat{g}^\lambda), sk = \lambda$ and responds with pk.

Stage 2. The adversary makes a sequence of indirect decryption oracle.
For each indirect decryption query, the adversary will submits a pair of messages (m, c). Where $m \in G \backslash \{1_G\}$ and c a cipher encrypted with pk. Here c could be any ill formed ciphertext without using pk. The decryption oracle decrypt c to get $t \in \hat{G}$ and responds with $m^{1/t}$.

Stage 3. The adversary submits a message $m_0 \in G \backslash \{1_G\}$, and the encryption oracle chooses $t_0 \in \hat{G}$ and $\gamma \leftarrow \mathbb{Z}_p$ at random, and responds with $\psi^* = (m_0^{t_0}, (\hat{g}^\gamma, \hat{e}^\gamma t_0))$

Stage 4. The adversary continues to make calls to indirect decryption oracle, subject only to the restriction that the submitted should not the same as the target message ψ^*.

Stage 5. The adversary outputs a value $\hat{t} \in \hat{G}$.

We say the adversary succeeded in indirect attack game if $\hat{t} = t_0$.

Lemma 2. *Under the assumption of DDH problem is hard in G and $\hat{G}$, the encryption system Γ is secure with respect to the indirect attack. Specifically, for any PPT algorithm A, adversary A's has negligible success probability in indirect attack game.*

The proof is followed from definition and omitted due to lack of spaces.

We now show the RCCA security of the scheme.

Theorem 1 (RCCA security). *Under the assumption of DDH problem is hard in the group G and that the hash H is a collision resistant hash function, the system is a rerandomized RCCA secure encryption system.*

Proof. The rerandomization of the system is straightforward to see. The proof for RCCA security share the similarity to that for original Cramer-Shoup cryptosystem [5,7] but with different arguments in details. We reduce the security of system to the security of DDH problem assuming the collision resistance of hash function H.

For any PPT algorithm $\mathcal{A}$ with success probability $\mathrm{Pr}_{\mathcal{A}}[\mathsf{Succ}]$ during RCCA attack to the real cryptosystem, we construct an algorithm $\hat{\mathcal{A}}$ to distinguish DDH tuples from random tuples as follow.

The input for $\hat{\mathcal{A}}$ is a tuple (g_1, g_2, g_3, g_4) that is either a random tuple meaning that each entry g_i is independently chosen from G uniformly, or a DH tuple meaning that there is a random $r \in \mathbb{Z}_q$ such that $g_3 = g_1^r, g_4 = g_2^r$. The algorithm $\hat{\mathcal{A}}$ runs the following experiment

$$\hat{\mathcal{A}}(g_1, g_2, g_3, g_4)$$

$$x, y, a, b, a', b' \leftarrow \mathbb{Z}_q, \hat{g} \leftarrow \hat{G}, \lambda \leftarrow \mathbb{Z}_p$$

$$\hat{e} = \hat{g}^\lambda; h = g_1^x g_2^y, c = g_1^a g_2^b, d = g_1^{a'} g_2^{b'}$$

$$pk = (\hat{g}, \hat{e}; g_1, g_2, h, c, d, H), \quad sk = (\lambda; x, y, a, b, a', b')$$

$$(m_0, m_1, \sigma) \leftarrow \mathcal{A}^{\mathcal{O}_1}(pk), \text{ where } 1_G \neq m_0 \neq m_1 \neq 1_G$$

$$\mathbf{b} \leftarrow \{0,1\}, s \leftarrow \mathbb{Z}_q, t^* \leftarrow \hat{G}, \gamma \leftarrow \mathbb{Z}_p, \alpha^* := H(m_\mathbf{b})$$

$$C^* = (\hat{g}^\gamma, \hat{e}^\gamma t^*; g_3, g_4, g_3^x g_4^y m_\mathbf{b}^{t^*}, g_3^s, g_4^s, (g_3^{a\alpha^*+a'} g_4^{b\alpha^*+b'})^{t^* s})$$

$$\mathbf{b}' \leftarrow \mathcal{A}^{\mathcal{O}_2}(pk, C, \sigma)$$

If $\mathbf{b} = \mathbf{b}'$ then output 1

otherwise output 0

Where H is the collision resistant hash function used in the cryptosystem and the string σ is state information of $\mathcal{A}$ that will be transformed to the second decryption enquiry phase.

The two oracles are decryption oracles. The oracle $\mathcal{O}_1$, whenever recieve a query, behaves exactly the same as in the cryptosystem using knowledge of sk to decrypt the query. The oracle $\mathcal{O}_2$ runs just same as the decryption algorithm except when the query has plaintext in $\{m_0, m_1\}$. When the plain text for the query to oracle $\mathcal{O}_2$ is in $\{m_0, m_1\}$ then oracle $\mathcal{O}_2$ will outputs test.

Firstly, we have the following result:

Lemma 3. *If the adversary $\hat{A}$ gets DH tuple, A's view of the experiment is the same as that in an attack execution to the real encryption scheme.*

Proof of Lemma 3. When the input tuple (g_1, g_2, g_3, g_4) to $\hat{A}$ is random DH tuple, there exists a $r \in \mathbb{Z}_q$ such that $g_2 = g_1^\delta, g_3 = g_1^r, g_4 = g_1^{\delta r} = g_2^r$. The challenging ciphertext in the experiment is

$$C^* = (\hat{g}^\gamma, \hat{e}^\gamma t^*; \ g_3, g_4, g_3^x g_4^y m_b^{t^*}, g_3^s, g_4^s, (g_3^{a\alpha^*+a'} g_4^{b\alpha^*+b'})^{t^*s})$$

$$= (\hat{g}^\gamma, \hat{e}^\gamma t^*; \ g_1^r, g_2^r, (g_1^x g_2^y)^r m_b^t, g_1^{rs}, g_2^{rs}, (g_1^{a\alpha^*+a'} g_2^{b\alpha^*+b'})^{t^*rs}).$$

Where $\alpha^* = H(m_b)$. Which is a well formed ciphertext for message m_b encrypted with public key pk. The oracles in the experiment run exact in the same way as in the real attacking executions. This shows the view of adversary A in this case is the same as that in attacking in the real system. This ends the proof of Lemma.   ✧

Let Rand be the event that the tuple (g_1, g_2, g_3, g_4) is chosen from distribution of random tuples, and DH the event that the tuple is chosen from distribution of Diffie-Hellman tuples.

   Lemma 3 implies that conditioned the input is DH tuples, the success probability $\Pr_A[\mathsf{Succ}]$ of adversary A attacking the encryption system in RCCA game is same as the probability of algorithm $\hat{A}$ outputs 1. That is,

$$\Pr_A[\mathsf{Succ}] = \Pr[\hat{A} = 1 \mid \mathsf{DH}] \tag{2}$$

However, the DDH intractability assumption implies

$$|\Pr[\hat{A} = 1 \mid \mathsf{DH}] - \Pr[\hat{A} \mid \mathsf{Rand}]| = \mathtt{negl}(k) \tag{3}$$

where k is the security parameter. This is the case since algorithm $\hat{A}$ is a PPT algorithm as A is.

   The advantage of adversary attacking real system is, using equation (2) and (3),

$$\left| \Pr_A[\mathsf{Succ}] - \frac{1}{2} \right| = \left| \Pr[\hat{A} = 1 \mid \mathsf{DH}] - \frac{1}{2} \right|$$

$$\leq \left| \Pr[\hat{A} = 1 \mid \mathsf{DH}] - \Pr[\hat{A} = 1 \mid \mathsf{Rand}] \right| + \left| \Pr[\hat{A} = 1 \mid \mathsf{Rand}] - \frac{1}{2} \right|$$

$$= \left| \Pr[\hat{A} = 1 \mid \mathsf{Rand}] - \frac{1}{2} \right| + \mathtt{negl}(k) \tag{4}$$

This, together with the conclusion (5) in following Lemma 4, will show that the advantage of A attacking real system is negligible. Since A is any such adversary, that will complete the proof of the theorem. It remains to prove the following:

Lemma 4. *If algorithm $\hat{A}$ gets random tuple as input, algorithm A has no information about the bit $\mathbf{b}$ chosen by $\hat{A}$ except with negligible probability. That is,* the probability that adversary $\mathcal{A}$ correctly guesses bit $\mathbf{b}$ chosen by $\hat{\mathcal{A}}$ is negligibly close to $1/2$. Hence,

$$\left| \Pr[\hat{\mathcal{A}} = 1 \mid \mathbf{Rand}] - \frac{1}{2} \right| = \mathtt{negl}(k) \tag{5}$$

Proof of Lemma4. For a random tuple $(g_1, g_2, g_3, g_4) \in G^4$, there exists δ, r, γ uniformly in $\mathbb{Z}_q$ such that

$$(g_1, g_2, g_3, g_4) = (g_1, g_1^\delta, g_1^r, g_1^\eta)$$

It is with overwhelming probability that $\eta \neq r\delta \pmod{q}$ and $\delta \neq 0 \pmod{q}$ except with negligible probability. We suppose $\eta \neq r\delta$ in the following proof. Let $r' \in \mathbb{Z}_q$ satisfy $g_4 = g_2^{r'}$, then $r' \neq r$.

We call a ciphertext $C = (u_0, w_0; u_1, v_1, w_1, u_2, v_2, w_2)$ *valid* if and only if $\log_{g_1} u_1 = \log_{g_2} v_1$. The following claim says, adversary $\mathcal{A}$ might be able to get useful information about $\mathbf{b}$ only if $\mathcal{A}$ queries with invalid ciphertext.

Claim 1. *If the oracles $\mathcal{O}_1, \mathcal{O}_2$ reject all the invalid queries by A, then the distribution of $\mathbf{b}$ independent on the view of adversary A during the attack.*

Proof of the Claim 1. We show this by showing that any valid ciphertext query will not be able to give $\mathcal{A}$ further information about (x, y).

Before attack, $\mathcal{A}$'s view about x, y is from pk. To be exactly from h. Even A might solve discrete logarithm, A can only know that

$$\log_{g_1} h = x + \delta y. \tag{6}$$

A linear combination about x, y.

We will see that adversary cannot get any information about x, y from the challenge ciphertext $C^* = (u_0^*, w_0^*; u_1^*, v_1^*, w_1^*, u_2^*, v_2^*, w_2^*)$. From which $\mathcal{A}$ gets

$$\log_{g_1}(w_1^*/m_{\mathbf{b}}^{t^*}) = rx + r'\delta y \tag{7}$$

Where $\delta = \log_{g_1} g_2$, $u_1^* = g_1^r$ and $v_1^* = g_2^{r'}$. By Lemma 2 and randomness of (g_1, g_2, g_3, g_4), $w_1^*/m_{\mathbf{b}}^t$ is uniformly distributed in G in the view of adversary. Equation systems (6) and (7) will give out a uniformly distributed point (x, y) on the line (6). Thus adversary $\mathcal{A}$ cannot obtain any further information about (x, y).

If, however, adversary queries only valid ciphertext $(u_0, w_0; u_1, v_1, w_1, u_2, v_2, w_2)$. Then $\log_{g_1} u_1 = \log_{g_2} v_1 = \bar{r}$, and $u_1^x v_1^y = g_1^{\bar{r}x} g_2^{\bar{r}y} = h^{\bar{r}}$. Hence, $\bar{r} \log h = \bar{r}x + \bar{r}\delta y$. This is a linear dependent relations of equation (6). No further information about x, y can be obtained. This ends the proof of Claim 1.   ✧

Claim 2. *The oracles $\mathcal{O}_1, \mathcal{O}_2$ will output $\perp$ for all invalid queries that is not a rerandomization of challenge meassage C^*, except with negligible probability.*

Proof of the Claim 2. Consider the first invalid query ciphertext

$$C = (u_0, w_0; u_1, v_1, w_1, u_2, v_2, w_2)$$

to oracles. If it comes from the rerandomization of the challenge ciphertext C^*, adversary will get reply test. We will only consider invalid queries that is not a rerandomization of C^* in the following.

Let $\overline{m} = w_1/(u_1^x v_1^y)$, $t = w_0/u_0^\lambda$. As the first invalid query, by the result shown in the proof of last claim, adversary cannot get the value $\overline{m}$ except with negligible possibility. This is because (x, y) is now a random point (on line (6)). This further implies that $\mathcal{A}$ cannot generate correct value α' such that $\alpha' = H(\overline{m}^{1/t})$ except with negligible probability due to the collision resistance property of H. If $\log_{g_1} u_2 = \log_{g_2} v_2 = s'$, the ciphertext C cannot pass the decryption test $w_2^{(ts')^{-1}} = c^{H(\overline{m}^{1/t})} d$ except with negligible probability.

Now we are in the case that adversary queries C with $\hat{r} = \log_{g_1} u_2 \neq \log_{g_2} v_2 = \hat{r}'$. Let $m := \overline{m}^{1/t}$ and $\alpha = H(m)$. Lemma 2 ensures that adversary will choose t such that $m^t \neq m_{\mathbf{b}}^{t^*}$ with overwhelming probability (here comes the restriction of $m_{\mathbf{b}} \neq 1_G$). This shows $\alpha^* = H(m_{\mathbf{b}}) \neq \alpha$ except with negligible probability.

We investigate the probability of C passing the test

$$u_2^{(a\alpha+a')t} v_2^{(b\alpha+b')t} = w_2. \tag{8}$$

We consider the distribution of (a, b, a', b') conditioned the view of adversary $\mathcal{A}$. Before attacking, from public key pk, adversary knows at most (even if $\mathcal{A}$ can solve discrete logarithms) that

$$\log_{g_1} c = a + \delta b \tag{9}$$
$$\log_{g_1} d = a' + \delta b' \tag{10}$$

The further information might be obtained from the challenge ciphertext C^*, where

$$\log_{g_1} w_2^* = r_1(\alpha^* a + a')t^* + r_1' \delta(\alpha^* b + b')t^*. \tag{11}$$

Where $r_1 = rs \pmod{q}$ and $r_1' = r's \pmod{q}$. We have $r_1 \neq r_1'$ since $r \neq r'$.

Adversary queries the invalid ciphertext C and passes the test (8) if and only if it satisfies

$$\log_{g_1} w_2 = \hat{r}(\alpha a + a')t + \hat{r}' \delta(\alpha b + b')t. \tag{12}$$

Recall that we have now $\delta \neq 0$, $\alpha' \neq \alpha^*$, $r_1 \neq r_1'$, and $\hat{r} \neq \hat{r}'$ except with negligible probability. Rewriting of equations (9), (10), (11), and (12) gives

$$\begin{pmatrix} \log_{g_1} c \\ \log_{g_1} d \\ \log_{g_1} w_2^* \\ \log_{g_1} w_2 \end{pmatrix} = \underbrace{\begin{pmatrix} 1 & \delta & 0 & 0 \\ 0 & 0 & 1 & \delta \\ r_1 t^* \alpha^* & r_1' t^* \alpha^* \delta & r_1 t^* & r_1' t^* \delta \\ \hat{r} t \alpha & \hat{r}' t \alpha \delta & \hat{r} t & \hat{r}' t \delta \end{pmatrix}}_{:=M} \begin{pmatrix} a \\ b \\ a' \\ b' \end{pmatrix} \tag{13}$$

The matrix M is with determinant $\det M = t t^* \delta^2 (\alpha - \alpha^*)(r_1 - r_1')(\hat{r} - \hat{r}') \neq 0$ with all but negligible probability. For each guess value of w_2, there will be a unique tuple (a, b, a', b') satisfying the equations. Since w_2 could be any element in group G, the first invalid query that is able to pass decryption test with negligible probability.

The reject of an invalid decryption query will rule out one possibility of tuple (a, b, a', b'). The n'th invalid decryption query will pass the test with probability only at most $1/(q - n - 1)$. Suppose there are totally n many invalid decryption query, one of them will pass the test with probability at most $n/(q - n - 1)$. Since algorithm $\mathcal{A}$ is a PPT algorithm, the number of invalid queries n will be bounded up by a polynomial, while $|q| \geq k$ and q is exponential in k. Therefore, $n/(q - n - 1)$ is negligible in k.

In other words, the decryption oracles will reject all invalid queries except with negligible probability. This accomplishes the proof of Claim 2 and Lemma 4.   ✧

This also finishes the proof of Theorem 1.   □

To combine the conclusions in Proposition 1, Proposition 2, and Theorem 1, we have

Theorem 2. *The encryption system in Section 3.1 is an anonymous, perfectly rerandomizable RCCA secure system. And the encryption system in Section 3.2 is a secretly anonymous, perfectly rerandomizable RCCA secure system.*

5   Conclusion

While the PR scheme is the first perfectly rerandomizable RCCA secure scheme, their construction is not receiver anonymous as stated by its authors in [14]. We present the first receiver anonymous, perfectly rerandomizable RCCA secure encryptions. The constructions inherit the double-strands feature from PR scheme in Prabhakaran and Rosulek [14]. It constitutes of two layers of encryptions: one layer to carry message, the other layer to carry a random quantity to hiding the message in previous layer. New constructions dramatically reduce the complexities compared with PR scheme. They are plausible to be applied in the scenarios like mix-nets [10,8], where the rerandomization of encryption are required and the encryption with weaker re-encryption are not enough.

Our final aim is to construct an efficient perfectly rerandomizable RCCA secure encryption. Though the constructions in this paper are much efficient than PR scheme, they are far from efficient than desired. Some other properties like universal composability of proposed constructions need further investigation and we plan to do it as a part of our future work.

Acknowledgement

Most of this work was done while Rui Xue was at UIUC. He thanks Manoj Prabhakaran for his warm hospitality. We thank Manoj Prabhakaran and Mike Rosulek for discussions about RCCA secure encryption from which this work originated.

References

1. An, J.H., Dodis, Y., Rabin, T.: On the security of joint signature and encryption. In: Knudsen, L.R. (ed.) EUROCRYPT 2002. LNCS, vol. 2332, pp. 83–107. Springer, Heidelberg (2002)
2. Andersen, J.K., Weisstein, E.W.: Cunningham chain. From MathWorld CA Wolfram Web (2005), http://www.cs.umd.edu/jkatz/gradcrypto2/scribes.html
3. Bellare, M., Boldyreva, A., Desai, A., Pointcheval, D.: Key-privacy in public-key encryption. In: Boyd, C. (ed.) ASIACRYPT 2001. LNCS, vol. 2248, pp. 566–582. Springer, Heidelberg (2001)
4. Canetti, R., Krawczyk, H., Nielsen, J.B.: Relaxing chosen-ciphertext security. In: Boneh, D. (ed.) CRYPTO 2003. LNCS, vol. 2729, pp. 565–582. Springer, Heidelberg (2003)
5. Cramer, Shoup.: A practical public key cryptosystem provably secure against adaptive chosen ciphertext attack. In: Krawczyk, H. (ed.) CRYPTO 1998. LNCS, vol. 1462, Springer, Heidelberg (1998)
6. Cramer, R., Shoup, V.: Universal hash proofs and a paradigm for adaptive chosen ciphertext secure public-key encryption. In: Knudsen, L.R. (ed.) EUROCRYPT 2002. LNCS, vol. 2332, pp. 45–64. Springer, Heidelberg (2002)
7. Cramer, R., Shoup, V.: Design and analysis of practical public-key encryption schemes secure against adaptive chosen ciphertext attack. SIAM Journal of Computing 33, 167–226 (2003)
8. Danezis, G.: Breaking four mix-related schemes based on universal re-encryption. In: Katsikas, S.K., Lopez, J., Backes, M., Gritzalis, S., Preneel, B. (eds.) ISC 2006. LNCS, vol. 4176, pp. 46–59. Springer, Heidelberg (2006)
9. Dolev, D., Dwork, C., Naor, M.: Non-malleable cryptography. In: Awerbuch, B. (ed.) Proceedings of the 23rd Annual ACM Symposium on the Theory of Computing, New Orleans, LS, pp. 542–552. ACM Press, New York (1991)
10. Golle, P., Jakobsson, M., Juels, A., Syverson, P.: Universal re-encryption for mixnets. In: Okamoto, T. (ed.) CT-RSA 2004. LNCS, vol. 2964, pp. 163–178. Springer, Heidelberg (2004)
11. Groth, J.: Rerandomizable and replayable adaptive chosen ciphertext attack secure cryptosystems. In: Naor, M. (ed.) TCC 2004. LNCS, vol. 2951, pp. 152–170. Springer, Heidelberg (2004)
12. Krawczyk, H.: The order of encryption and authentication for protecting communications (or: How secure is SSL?). In: Kilian, J. (ed.) CRYPTO 2001. LNCS, vol. 2139, pp. 310–331. Springer, Heidelberg (2001)
13. Lindell, Y.: A simpler construction of CCA2-secure public-key encryption under general assumptions. In: Biham, E. (ed.) EUROCRPYT 2003. LNCS, vol. 2656, pp. 241–254. Springer, Heidelberg (2003)
14. Prabhakaran, M., Rosulek, M.: Rerandomizable RCCA encryption. In: Menezes, A. (ed.) CRYPTO 2007. 27th Annual International Cryptology Conference, Santa Barbara, CA, USA. LNCS, vol. 4622, pp. 517–534. Springer, Heidelberg (2007)
15. Sahai, A.: Non-malleable non-interactive zero knowledge and adaptive chosen-ciphertext security. In: FOCS 1999. 40th Annual Symposium on Foundations of Computer Science, Washington - Brussels - Tokyo, oct 1999, pp. 543–553. IEEE Computer Society Press, Los Alamitos (1999)
16. Shoup, V.: A proposal for an ISO standard for public key encryption (version 2.1) (December 20 2001), http://www.shoup.net/papers/

Secure Multiparty Computation of DNF

Kun Peng

Institute for Infocomm Research

Abstract. Homomorphism based multiparty computation techniques are studied in this paper as they have several advantages over the other multiparty computation schemes. A new homomorphism based multiparty computation technique is proposed to evaluate functions in DNF form. The new technique exploits homomorphism of a certain sealing function to evaluate a function in DNF. The new technique has two advantages over the existing homomorphism based multiparty computation schemes. Firstly, it supports any input format. Secondly, a general method to reduce any function to DNFs is proposed in this paper. With this method, functions like the famous millionaire problem can be reduced to DNFs and efficiently evaluated. Security of the new scheme is formally defined in the static active adversary model and proved in a new simulation model.

1 Introduction

Secure multiparty computation [1, 2, 5, 6, 8, 9, 10, 11, 12, 13, 14, 15, 16, 23, 24, 25, 26, 27, 28] is a technique to evaluate a function without revealing any information about the inputs except the output. The basic technique of multiparty computation is to present the function in a circuit composed of a few logic gates and reduce the computation to evaluation of each gate. The inputs to the function must be sealed and output of each gate must be private so that privacy of the multiparty computation is protected.

Most existing multiparty computation schemes garble the inputs and outputs wires of the gates to achieve privacy and this mechanism has a few drawbacks. Firstly, they do not provide any concrete method to design an evaluation circuit for the evaluated function. Instead they usually assume that the circuit already exists and is ready to be garbled. Without a concrete circuit, the consequent operations and analysis are based on assumptions like "after the circuit is generated by a party..." or "if the number of levels of gates is a logarithm of the length of all the inputs ...". Secondly, they need either a single circuit generator (who knows how each gate is garbled and thus can learn additional information about the inputs by monitoring execution of function evaluation) or a complex and inefficient distributed multiparty circuit generation algorithm. Thirdly, it is complex and inefficient for them to publicly prove and verify correctness of the circuit without compromising its privacy. Fourthly, it is complex and inefficient to match all the input variables to the function with the garbled inputting wires

S. Qing, H. Imai, and G. Wang (Eds.): ICICS 2007, LNCS 4861, pp. 254–268, 2007.

of the circuit, especially when public verifiability of this matching is required. Finally, efficiency is low when appropriate trust sharing, public verifiability and provable security are required.

We are interested in another solution [1, 9, 11, 12, 16, 23, 24, 25, 26, 28], which employs homomorphic sealing function to seal the inputs and exploit homomorphism of the sealing function to implement multiparty computation. Intermediate outputs of all the gate are sealed, so does not reveal any information assuming the sealing function is difficult to break. So the circuit can be public and no gate needs garbling. Therefore the drawbacks of the first solution are overcome. However, this solution has its own drawbacks. Firstly, only several certain kinds of gates are supported and thus the function must be in a special format. [9, 11] require that the function only employs three kinds of gates: "+", "-" and multiplication. [1, 28] only support NOT and OR gates, which [12] only supports XOR and AND gates. [16] requires a very special format for the function: Standard low-degree polynomials over a finite field. Obviously, given a random function it is possible that it cannot be reduced to a polynomial number of gates in a special format. So each scheme in the second solution has its own favourite functions, which can be reduced to a polynomial number of gates in the special format in that scheme and thus can be efficiently evaluated. Moreover, each of them requires that each input variable must be in a special format and they fail if any input variable is invalid. In addition, some schemes [23, 24, 25, 26] are only suitabe to handle some certain functions.

In this paper, a new homomorphism based secure multiparty computation scheme is proposed. Any function in DNF (disjunctive normal form) form[1] can be efficiently evaluated in the new scheme. It has two main advantages over the existing homomorphism based multiparty computation schemes. Firstly, it does not require any special input format. Instead, any input format is supported and an appropriate format can be flexibly chosen for the evaluated function. Secondly, a general method to reduce any function to DNFs is proposed in this paper. With this method, functions like the famous millionaire problem can be reduced to simple DNFs and then efficiently evaluated. The new scheme employs a flexible participant model. Like [10], it does not require all the input providers to take part in the computation. Although there may be many inputs and input providers to a function, a small number of computation performers can be employed, such that communication between them is not a heavy overhead in practice. This participant model is especially suitable for applications like e-auction and e-voting. Static active adversary model is used in the new scheme, which is strong enough for most practical applications. The UC (universal composable) security model [4] is not employed in the new scheme. Correctness and soundness of the new scheme are defined in a straightforward manner while its privacy is defined in a new simulation model detailed in Section 2, which is simpler and more practical than the UC model and other traditional simulation models. Security of the new scheme is formally guaranteed when a majority of the computation performers are honest.

---

[1] Detailed definition of function in DNF will be given in Section 4.

2   Security Model

There are usually three kinds of participants in multiparty computation: IPs (input providers), CPs (computation performers) and result receivers. They respectively provide inputs, carry out the computation and receive the result. Although it is assumed in most multiparty computation schemes that all the participants play all the three roles, that assumption is impractical in many applications like e-auction and e-voting. A typical application is inputs from many IPs are evaluated by several CPs. So in this paper, the participant model in [10] is adopted: the IPs and the CPs are not the same group of participants and the number of CPs is small. However, our participant model is a general model and the three sets of players need not be disjoint. In garbled circuit based secure computation, more participants like circuit generator (called compiler or issuer in some schemes) are often needed. In this paper, we design a homomorphism based secure computation scheme, so only need the three kinds of participants. When we say a CP is corrupted, we mean an adversary obtains its complete secret information (including historical record) and controls it behaviour. In other words, we adopt active adversary model. Moreover, we assume the adversaries are static. Two kinds of synchronous communication channels are used in this paper. A public broadcast channel also called bulletin board is set up for exchange of public information. In addition, there is an authenticated confidential channel from each IP to each CP. The following security properties are required in a multiparty computation protocol.

- Correctness: when given encryption (or commitment) of inputs $x_1, x_2, \ldots, x_n$ and asked to compute function $f()$, if a majority of CPs are not corrupted, the protocol outputs $f(x_1, x_2, \ldots, x_n)$.
- Public verifiability: there is a public verification procedure, by which any one can publicly check whether the protocol outputs $f(x_1, x_2, \ldots, x_n)$ when inputs $x_1, x_2, \ldots, x_n$ are given to function $f()$.
- Soundness: if a majority of CPs pass the public verification procedure, the protocol outputs $f(x_1, x_2, \ldots, x_n)$ when given encryption (or commitment) of input $x_1, x_2, \ldots, x_n$ and $f()$.
- Privacy: if a majority of CPs are not corrupted no information about the input is revealed except what can be deduced from the result of the function.

In the security definition above, the complex UC model [4] is not used. Correctness and soundness are more straightforward defined. However, definition of privacy is still intuitive and informal. So it is more formally defined in a simulation model simpler than the UC model as follows.

Definition 1. *There exists a polynomial algorithm for a party without any knowledge about any input to simulate the transcript of the secure computation protocol such that no polynomial algorithm can distinguish the simulated transcript and the real transcript with a probability non-negligibly larger than 0.5.*

3   Parameters and Primitives

p, q, G, g, h are public parameters. p is a large prime such that $p - 1$ has a large factor q with no small factor. G is the cyclic subgroup of Z_p^* with order q. g and h are generators of G such that $\log_g h$ is unknown. A primitive to be used later, the t-out-of-m secret sharing algorithm in [22], is described as follows.

- To share a secret s among m parties $A_1, A_2, \ldots, A_m$, a dealer builds two polynomials $F(x) = \sum_{l=0}^{t-1} f_l x^l \bmod q$ and $H(x) = \sum_{l=0}^{t-1} h_l x^l \bmod q$ where $f_0 = s$ and f_l for $l = 1, 2, \ldots, t - 1$ and h_l for $l = 0, 1, \ldots, t - 1$ are random integers in Z_q.
- The dealer publishes sharing commitments $E_l = g^{f_l} h^{h_l} \bmod p$ for $l = 0, 1, \ldots, t - 1$ on the bulletin board.
- The dealer sends A_k its share $(s_k, r_k) = (F(k), H(k))$ through the authenticated confidential channel.
- A_k verifies $g^{s_k} h^{r_k} = \prod_{l=0}^{t-1} E_l^{k^l} \bmod p$. If the verification is passed, A_k can be sure that (s_k, r_k) is the kth share of the secret committed in E_0. As m and t are usually small integers, each verification costs 2 exponentiations and $O(t)$ multiplications.
- If at least t correct shares are put together, the secret committed in E_0 can be recovered as $s = \sum_{k \in \Phi} s_k u_k \bmod q$ where $u_k = \prod_{l \in \Phi, l \neq k} \frac{l}{l-k}$ and Φ is a set containing the indexes of t correct shares.

Note that definition of u_k will be used throughout the paper. Pedersen [22] proves that when $\log_g h$ is unknown and discrete logarithm is a hard problem, there is only one polynomial way to open commitment E_0, which is denoted as $s \longleftarrow REC(E_0)$ in this paper. Pedersen also illustrates that his secret sharing scheme is homomorphic. Namely, $REC(E_0) + REC(E_0') = REC(E_0 E_0') \bmod q$ where E_0 and E_0' are the first components in two commitments.

Besides the general secret sharing algorithm described above, a special variant of it is employed in this paper. In the special variant, a public known integer s instead of a secret is shared. Its purpose is not to secretly hide the integer but to publicly distribute it into a sharing format. Implementation of the special secret sharing algorithm is simple: the commitment generation and sharing generation function are the same as in the general secret sharing algorithm except that $F(x) = s$, $H(x) = 0$ and the shares are public. So anyone can calculate commitment $g^s, 1, 1, \ldots, 1$ and each A_k's share is $(s, 0)$. This special variant is called simplified secret sharing, which only costs one exponentiation but has all the properties of the original secret sharing algorithm except privacy of the shared integer.

In this paper, ElGamal encryption is employed. Private key x_k is chosen for A_k from Z_q. A_k's public key y_k is $g^{x_k} \bmod p$. Note that ElGamal encryption is semantically secure. More precisely, given a ciphertext c and two messages m_1 and m_2, such that $c = E(m_i)$ where $i = 1$ or 2, there is no polynomial algorithm to find out i with a probability non-negligibly larger than 0.5 when the private key is unknown. In this paper, $ZP \ [\ x_1, x_2, \ldots, x_\alpha \ | \ R_1, R_2, \ldots, R_\beta \ ]$ denotes a ZK proof of knowledge of $x_1, x_2, \ldots, x_\alpha$ satisfying conditions $R_1, R_2, \ldots, R_\beta$. In this paper, there is a security parameter T such that T is a small integer and 2^T is no larger than the smallest factor of q.

4   Reduction to DNFs and Sealing the Inputs

A function with μ IPs $IP_1, IP_2, \ldots, IP_\mu$ and inputs $m_1, m_2, \ldots, m_\mu$ can be reduced to DNFs as follows where m_ι is the input of IP_ι for $\iota = 1, 2, \ldots, \mu$.

1. Integer L is chosen such that $2^L \geq S$ and $2^{L-1} < S$ where S is the size of the co-domain of the function. Sort all the variables in the co-domain in a certain order and the kth variable is transformed into a new format: the binary representation of k.
2. The function is divided into L sub-functions, each of which receives the input of the function and outputs one bit of the result of the function in the new output format.
3. Each sub-function is transformed into a DNF as follows.
    (a) The truth table mapping $m_1, m_2, \ldots, m_\mu$ through the sub-function to $\{0, 1\}$ is established.
    (b) Every row with an output 1 in the truth table is picked out. Each chosen row is transformed into a clause, which tests whether m_ι equals to the ιth input variable in the row for $\iota = 1, 2, \ldots, \mu$. Each test in the clause is a basic logic computations and they are linked with AND logic.
    (c) Linking all the clauses with OR logic produces a DNF.
    (d) Two methods can be employed to optimisation DNFs. The first method adjusts the length and number of the inputs. A long input is divided into multiple shorter inputs such that the the number of rows in the truth table decreases. The second method is Karnaugh map, which simplifies a DNF into least minterm form (See Pages 104–106 of [20]). Both methods are tried until the simplest DNFs are obtained after multiple trials.
4. Outputs of all the DNFs form a L bit binary string, which can be transformed back into the functions' original co-domain (the bit string representing integer k is transformed to the kth output in the original co-domain).

Note that the algorithm above is not unique. For example, Karnaugh map can be replaced by Quine-McCluskey technique (See Page 99 of [20]). After the simplest DNF circuit is obtained, the function can be efficiently evaluated as described later in this paper. An example will be given in Section 7 to illustrate high efficiency of this method.

To protect privacy of secure multiparty computation, the inputs of any DNF must be sealed when it is processed. The unsealing power is shared among the CPs.In our solution, the secret sharing algorithm in Section 3 is employed to seal the inputs where the CPs $A_1, A_2, \ldots, A_m$ act as the share holders. The inputs to the DNFs of the function are sealed as follows using the t-out-of-m verifiable secret sharing scheme in [22] as described in Section 3 and we require $m+1 = 2t$.

1. For $\iota = 1, 2, \ldots, \mu$ each IP_ι seals m_ι in commitment $E_{\iota,l}$ for $l = 0, 1, \ldots, t - 1$ and shares it among the CPs. The commitments are published on the

bulletin board and share $(s_{\iota,k}, r_{\iota,k})$ is sent to A_k through the authenticated confidential channel for $k = 1, 2, \ldots, m$. Thus all the inputs to all the DNFs are sealed.

2. Every A_k verifies validity of each of his shares: $g^{s_{\iota,k}} h^{r_{\iota,k}} \overset{?}{=} \prod_{l=0}^{t-1} E_{\iota,l}^{k^l} \bmod p$ for $\iota = 1, 2, \ldots, \mu$. If an invalid share is found by a CP, it is published on the bulletin board. As the communication channel used to distribute the shares is authenticated, no IP can deny any invalid share it sends out. Therefore, dishonest IPs can be detected and expelled.

3. All the DNFs are transformed into sealed format (composed of sealed inputs and logic operation on them) one by one. A DNF in the form of (2) is transformed to

$$\vee_{i=1}^n \left(REC(E_{i,1,0}) = a_{i,1} \wedge REC(E_{i,2,0}) = a_{i,2} \wedge \ldots \wedge REC(E_{i,M(i),0}) = a_{i,M(i)} \right) \tag{1}$$

where $E_{i,j,l} = E_{\iota,l}$ for $l = 0, 1, \ldots, t-1$ if $m_{i,j} = m_\iota$. For $k = 1, 2, \ldots, m$ each A_k holds $(s_{\iota,k}, r_{\iota,k})$ as his share of $REC(E_{i,j,0})$ if $m_{i,j} = m_\iota$.

In each DNF, only the inputs to the DNF are sealed while all the equations, all the AND and OR logic relations and the way they are combined and linked are public. So without any proof anyone can publicly and directly check that in our new scheme that each DNF is correctly organised and all the DNFs cooperate to evaluate the target function.

5 Evaluation of DNF

A DNF is in the form of

$$\vee_{i=1}^n \left(m_{i,1} = a_{i,1} \wedge m_{i,2} = a_{i,2} \wedge \ldots \wedge m_{i,M(i)} = a_{i,M(i)} \right) \tag{2}$$

where $M(i)$ is the number of inputs involved in the ith clause in that DNF and $m_{i,j} \in \{m_1, m_2, \ldots, m_\mu\}$. In DNF (1) there are three levels of computation. The bottom level is the equations; the middle level is AND logic and the top level is OR logic. The three levels are computed one by one from the bottom to the top.

5.1 Computation on the Bottom Level

By simply exploiting homomorphism of the employed secret sharing algorithm, (1) is simplified to

$$\vee_{i=1}^n \left(REC(g^{a_{i,1}}/E_{i,1,0}) = 0 \ \wedge \ REC(g^{a_{i,2}}/E_{i,2,0}) = 0 \ \wedge \right.$$
$$\left. \ldots \wedge \ REC(g^{a_{i,M(i)}}/E_{i,M(i),0}) = 0 \right) \tag{3}$$

Every commitment variable and share in the simplified DNF must be adjusted as follows.

1. A set $A = \bigcup_{i=1,j=1}^{i<n,j<M(i)} \{a_{i,j}\}$ is set up to include all the constant integers involved in all the equations in the DNF in the form (1). Suppose A has a size ν and $A = \{a_1, a_2, \ldots, a_\nu\}$.

2. For $\iota = 1, 2, \ldots, \nu$, commitment $\hat{E}_{\iota,l}$ for $l = 0, 1, \ldots, t-1$ and shares $(\hat{s}_{\iota,k}, \hat{r}_{\iota,k})$ for $k = 1, 2, \ldots, m$ are publicly available for a_ι using the simplified secret sharing algorithm in Section 3.
3. For each $a_{i,j}$, if $a_{i,j} = a_\iota$, then $\hat{E}_{i,j,l} = \hat{E}_{\iota,l}$ for $l = 0, 1, \ldots, t-1$ and $\hat{s}_{i,j,k} = \hat{s}_{\iota,k}$, $\hat{r}_{i,j,k} = \hat{r}_{\iota,k}$ for $k = 1, 2, \ldots, m$.
4. (3) is presented in the form

$$\vee_{i=1}^{n} \ (REC(E'_{i,1,0}) = 0 \wedge REC(E'_{i,2,0}) = 0 \wedge \ldots \wedge REC(E'_{i,M(i),0}) = 0) \quad (4)$$

where every commitment variable for (4), $E'_{i,j,l}$, is publicly available as $\hat{E}_{i,j,l}/E_{i,j,l} \bmod p$ for $i = 1, 2, \ldots, n$, $j = 1, 2, \ldots, M(i)$ and $l = 0, 1, \ldots, t-1$. A_k calculates $s'_{i,j,k} = \hat{s}_{i,j,k} - s_{i,j,k} \bmod q$ and $r'_{i,j,k} = \hat{r}_{i,j,k} - r_{i,j,k} \bmod q$ as its share of $REC(E'_{i,j,0})$ for $i = 1, 2, \ldots, n$, $j = 1, 2, \ldots, M(i)$ and $k = 0, 1, \ldots, m$.

5.2 Computation on the Middle Level

Homomorphism of the employed secret sharing algorithm is further exploited to transform (4) into

$$\vee_{i=1}^{n} \ \textstyle\sum_{j=1}^{M(i)} REC(E'_{i,j,0})t_j = 0 \quad (5)$$

where each t_j is a random integer.

1. The CPs cooperate to choose T bit random integers t_j for $j = 1, 2, \ldots, M$ where $M = max(M(1), M(2), \ldots, M(n))$. More precisely, each A_k secretly chooses random integers $t_{j,k}$ from Z_q for $j = 1, 2, \ldots, M$ and publishes $h_{j,k} = h(t_{j,k})$ for $j = 1, 2, \ldots, M$ where $h()$ is a collision resistant one-way function. After each $h_{j,k}$ has been published, the CPs publish $t_{j,k}$ for $j = 1, 2, \ldots, M$ and $k = 1, 2, \ldots, m$. Finally, $h_{j,k} = h(t_{j,k})$ for $j = 1, 2, \ldots, M$ and $k = 1, 2, \ldots, m$ is verified and $t_j = \sum_{k=1}^{m} t_{j,k} \bmod 2^T$ for $j = 1, 2, \ldots, M$ are calculated. For the sake of high efficiency, $h()$ can be a hash function. If there is any concern for collision resistance in hash functions, $h(x)$ can be $g^x \bmod p$.
2. (5) is presented in the form of (6).

$$\vee_{i=1}^{n} \ REC(E'_{i,0}) = 0 \quad (6)$$

where every commitment variable for (6), $E'_{i,l}$, is publicly available as $\prod_{j=1}^{M(i)} E'^{t_j}_{i,j,l} \bmod p$ for $i = 1, 2, \ldots, n$ and $l = 0, 1, \ldots, t-1$. A_k calculates $s'_{i,k} = \sum_{j=1}^{M(i)} s'_{i,j,k} t_j \bmod q$ and $r'_{j,k} = \sum_{j=1}^{M(i)} r'_{i,j,k} t_j \bmod q$ as its share of $REC(E'_{i,0})$ for $i = 1, 2, \ldots, n$ and $k = 0, 1, \ldots, m$.

5.3 Computation on the Top Level

(6) is equivalent to

$$\prod_{i=1}^{n} REC(E'_{i,0}) = 0,$$

which according to homomorphism of the employed secret sharing scheme is equivalent to

$$REC(E'^{\prod_{i=2}^{n} REC(E'_{i,0})}_{1,0}) = 0 \qquad \text{or namely} \qquad REC(E'^{\prod_{i=2}^{n} \sum_{k \in K} s_{i,k} u_k}_{1,0}) = 0,$$

which is equivalent to

$$REC((\prod_{k \in K} E'^{s'_{2,k} u_k}_{1,0})^{\prod_{i=3}^{n} \sum_{k \in K} s'_{i,k} u_k}) = 0, \tag{7}$$

where K is a set containing the indices of t honest CPs and $u_k = \prod_{l \in K, l \neq k} \frac{l}{l-k}$.

$\prod_{k \in K} E'^{s'_{2,k} u_k}_{1,0}$ is denoted as $E''_{1,0}$. To evaluate (7), $E''_{1,0}$ has to be calculated without revealing $s'_{2,k}$ for $k \in K$. Moreover, $E''_{1,l}$ for $l = 1, 2, \ldots, t-1$ have to be calculated to form a complete commitment. In addition, each A_k with k in K should get its share necessary to reconstruct the secret in $E''_{1,0}$. The commitment generation and shares distribution operations are as follows.

1. For $k \in K$ each A_k calculates and publishes $c'_{1,k} = (g^{\gamma_{1,k}} \bmod p, \, y_k^{\gamma_{1,k}} g^{s'_{1,k}}$ $\bmod p)$ and $e'_{1,k} = (g^{\delta_{1,k}} \bmod p, \, y_k^{\delta_{1,k}} h^{r'_{1,k}} \bmod p)$ where $\gamma_{1,k}$ and $\delta_{1,k}$ are randomly chosen from Z_q.

2. For $k' \in K$ each $A_{k'}$ calculates $E''_{1,l,k'} = E'^{s'_{2,k'} u_{k'}}_{1,l} \bmod p$ for $l = 0, 1, \ldots, t-1$ and $c''_{1,k,k'} = c'^{s'_{2,k'} u_{k'}}_{1,k} \bmod p$, $e''_{1,k,k'} = e'^{s'_{2,k'} u_{k'}}_{1,k} \bmod p$ for $k \in K$.

3. $E''_{1,l} = \prod_{k' \in K} E''_{1,l,k'} \bmod p$ for $l = 0, 1, \ldots, t-1$ and $c''_{1,k} = \prod_{k' \in K} c''_{1,k,k'}$ $\bmod p$, $e''_{1,k} = \prod_{k' \in K} e''_{1,k,k'} \bmod p$ for $k \in K$.

Note that in the algorithm above, two integers k' and k are used for the indices of the CPs. The reason is that each CP have two roles: share holder and evaluator. So two integers are needed for each index: A_k stands for the kth CP holding $(s'_{1,k}, r'_{1,k})$ while $A_{k'}$ stands for the k'^{th} CP raising $(c'_{1,k}, e'_{1,k})$ and the commitment variables to the power of its secret $s'_{2,k'} u_{k'}$. Thus $E''_{1,0}$ and its subsidiary commitment variables are generated and each honest CP gets a encrypted share necessary to reconstruct the secret in $E''_{1,0}$. Therefore, (7) is transformed to

$$REC(E''^{\prod_{i=3}^{n} \sum_{k \in K} s'_{i,k} u_k}_{1,0}) = 0 \tag{8}$$

with the corresponding commitment variables and shares publicly available. (8) is equivalent to

$$REC((\prod_{k \in K} E''^{s'_{3,k} u_k}_{1,0})^{\prod_{i=4}^{n} \sum_{k \in K} s'_{i,k} u_k}) = 0 \tag{9}$$

(9) is then transformed to

$$REC((\prod_{k \in K} E''^{s'_{4,k} u_k}_{2,0})^{\prod_{i=5}^{n} \sum_{k \in K} s'_{i,k} u_k}) = 0, \tag{10}$$

where $E''_{2,l} = \prod_{k' \in K} E''^{s'_{3,k'} u_{k'}}_{1,l} \bmod p$ for $l = 0, 1, \ldots, t-1$ and the corresponding encrypted shares are $c''_{2,k} = \prod_{k' \in K} c''^{s'_{3,k'} u_{k'}}_{1,k} \bmod p$, $e''_{2,k} = \prod_{k' \in K} e''^{s'_{3,k'} u_{k'}}_{1,k}$

mod p for $k \in K$. (9) is transformed to (10) in the same way as (7) is transformed to (8). More precisely, each $A_{k'}$ with $k' \in K$ raises the commitment variables and encrypted shares of (9) to the power of his secret $s_{3,k'}u_{k'}$ and then the honest CPs' outputs are combined.

The transform continues until (6) is reduced to

$$REC(\textstyle\prod_{k\in K} E''^{s'_{n,k}u_k}_{n-2,0}) = 0$$

(with supporting commitment variables $E''_{n-2,l}$ for $l = 1, 2, \ldots, t-1$ and corresponding encrypted shares $c''_{n-2,k}$, $e''_{n-2,k}$ for $k \in K$) and finally

$$REC(E''_{n-1,0}) = 0 \tag{11}$$

with supporting commitment variables $E''_{n-1,l}$ for $l = 1, 2, \ldots, t-1$ and corresponding encrypted shares $c''_{n-1,k}$, $e''_{n-1,k}$ for $k \in K$ where $E''_{n-1,l} = \prod_{k'\in K} E''^{s'_{n,k'}u_{k'}}_{n-2,l} \bmod p$ and $c''_{n-1,k} = \prod_{k'\in K} c''^{s'_{n,k'}u_{k'}}_{n-2,k} \bmod p$, $e''_{n-1,k} = \prod_{k'\in K} e'^{s'_{n,k'}u_{k'}}_{n-2,k} \bmod p$ for $k \in K$.

All the operations described intuitively above in this subsection can be described in an abstract manner as follows. For $i = 2, 3, \ldots, n$:

1. for $k' \in K$ each $A_{k'}$ calculates

$$E''_{i-1,l,k'} = E''^{s'_{i,k'}u_{k'}}_{i-2,l} \bmod p \text{ for } l = 0, 1, \ldots, t-1 \tag{12}$$

$$c''_{i-1,k,k'} = c''^{s'_{i,k'}u_{k'}}_{i-2,k} \bmod p \text{ for } k \in K \tag{13}$$

$$e''_{i-1,k,k'} = e''^{s'_{i,k'}u_{k'}}_{i-2,k} \bmod p \text{ for } k \in K \tag{14}$$

2. $E''_{i-1,l} = \prod_{k'\in K} E''_{i-1,l,k'}$ for $l = 0, 1, \ldots, t-1$ and $c''_{i-1,k} = \prod_{k'\in K} c''_{i-1,k,k'}$, $e''_{i-1,k} = \prod_{k'\in K} e''_{i-1,k,k'}$ for $k \in K$

where $E''_{0,l} = E'_{1,l}$ for $l = 0, 1, \ldots, t-1$ and $c''_{0,k} = c'_{1,k}$ for $k \in K$, $e''_{0,k} = e'_{1,k}$ for $k \in K$.

5.4   Secret Reconstruction

(11) is solved as follows.

1. For $k \in K$ each A_k decrypts his encrypted share $e''_{n-1,k}$ using ElGamal decryption function: $r_k = D_k(e''_{n-1,k})$ and publishes r_k.
2. A secret is reconstructed: $r = \prod_{k\in K} r_k^{u_k} \bmod p$.
3. If $r = E''_{n-1,0}$, then the DNF is 1. Otherwise, it is 0.

6   Implementation and Efficiency Optimisation

There is an efficiency concern in the operation in Section 5.1, which needs μ inversions, $\sum_{i=1}^{n} M(i)$ multiplications and ν simplified secret sharing operations.

m and t are small integers like 3 or 4. μ is usually not too large in practical applications. The DNF optimisation mechanism guarantees that n is not large if the function is suitable for DNF solution. So the only efficiency concern is about ν, which may be large in some cases. Although each simplified secret sharing operation only cost 1 exponentiation, a large cost is needed when ν is large. An optimised function is proposed as follows to replace the corresponding commitment and sharing functions in Section 5.1 to commit to and share publicly known integers $a_{i,j}$ for $i = 1, 2, \ldots, n$ and $j = 1, 2, \ldots, M(i)$ in the simplified sharing format when ν is large.

1. A set $A = \bigcup_{i=1, j=1}^{i<n, j<M(i)} \{a_{i,j}\}$ is set up to include all the constant integers involved in all the equations in the DNF in the form (1). Suppose A has a size ν and $A = \{a_1, a_2, \ldots, a_\nu\}$ and the largest integer in A is ρ bits long.
2. For $\tau = 1, 2, \ldots, \rho - 1$, $G_\tau = G_{\tau-1}^2$ are calculated where $G_0 = 1$.
3. For $\iota = 1, 2, \ldots, \nu$, the commitment of a_ι is publicly available as $(\hat{E}_{\iota,0}, \hat{E}_{\iota,1}, \ldots,$
   $\hat{E}_{\iota,t-1}) = (\prod_{\tau=0}^{\rho-1} G_\tau^{b_{\iota,\tau+1}} \bmod p, 1, 1, \ldots, 1)$ and its share for every A_k is publicly available as $(\hat{s}_{\iota,k}, \hat{r}_{\iota,k}) = (a_\iota, 0)$ where $b_{\iota,\tau}$ is the τth bit of a_ι.
4. For each $a_{i,j}$, if $a_{i,j} = a_\iota$, then $\hat{E}_{i,j,l} = \hat{E}_{\iota,l}$ for $l = 0, 1, \ldots, t-1$ and $\hat{s}_{i,j,k} = \hat{s}_{\iota,k}$, $\hat{r}_{i,j,k} = \hat{r}_{\iota,k}$ for $k = 1, 2, \ldots, m$.

After this optimisation, cost for committing to and sharing the constant integers in the function is $2(\rho - 1)$ multiplications. Therefore, evaluation of DNFs is efficient. However, until now public verification has not been taken into account. A cautious method to achieve public verifiability called complete public verification procedure is to publicly verify validity of any secret operation. Thus the following proof and verification computations are needed.

1. Each A_k has to publicly prove that his share of $REC(E'_{1,0})$ is encrypted in $c'_{1,k}$ and $e'_{1,k}$ through ZK proof:

$$ZP\,[\ \gamma_{1,k},\ \delta_{1,k},\ s'_{1,k},\ t'_{1,k}\mid c'_{1,k} = (g^{\gamma_{1,k}} \bmod p,\ y_k^{\gamma_{1,k}} g^{s'_{1,k}} \bmod p),\ (15)$$
$$e'_{1,k} = (g^{\delta_{1,k}} \bmod p,\ y_k^{\delta_{1,k}} h^{r'_{1,k}} \bmod p),\ g^{s'_{1,k}} h^{t'_{1,k}} = \prod_{l=0}^{t-1} E'^{k^l}_{1,l} \bmod p\ ],$$

Proof and verification of (15) for $k \in K$ cost $13t$ full length exponentiations, $t(t+5)$ short exponentiations and $t(t+15)$ multiplications.

2. Computation of (12), (13) and (14) must be publicly proved and verified for $i = 2, 3, \ldots, n$ and $k' \in K$ through ZK proof:

$$ZP\,[\ s'_{i,k'},\ t'_{i,k'}\mid E''_{i-1,l,k'} = E''^{s'_{i,k'}u_{k'}}_{i-2,l} \bmod p \text{ for } l = 0, 1, \ldots, t-1,$$
$$c''_{i-1,k,k'} = c''^{s'_{i,k'}u_{k'}}_{i-2,k} \bmod p \text{ for } k \in K,\ e''_{i-1,k,k'} = e''^{s'_{i,k'}u_{k'}}_{i-2,k} \bmod p \text{ for } k \in K,$$
$$g^{s'_{i,k'}} h^{t'_{i,k'}} = \prod_{l=0}^{t-1} E'^{k'^l}_{i,l} \bmod p\ ],\qquad (16)$$

Proof and verification of (12), (13) and (14) for $i = 2, 3, \ldots, n$ and $k' \in K$ cost $(n-1)t(3t+12)$ full length exponentiations, $(n-1)t(t+5)$ short exponentiations and $(n-1)t(4t+16)$ multiplications.

3. Decryption in Step 1 in Section 5.4 must be publicly proved and verified through ZK proof:

$$ZP \left[\; x_k \; | \; g^{x_k} = y_k, \; a''^{x_k}_{n-1,k} r_k = b''_{n-1,k} \; \right] \tag{17}$$

for $k \in K$. (17) can be publicly proved and verified through ZK proof of equality of logarithms [7], which costs $6t$ exponentiations and $3t$ multiplications.

4. As mentioned in Section 4 sharing of the μ secret inputs must be verified, which costs the CPs totally $2m\mu$ exponentiations and $O(m\mu t)$ multiplications. As illustrated in Section 4 if a CP finds an invalid share from an IP, he can publish it and the IP cannot deny it as the communication channel between them is authenticated.

There is a more efficient method to achieve public verifiability. It does not require to publicly verify validity of every secret operation. Instead, it only publicly proves and verifies that $\prod_{i=1}^{n} \sum_{j=1}^{M(i)} (a_{i,j} - m_{i,j}) t_j$ is correctly committed in $E''_{n-1,0}$ and correctly reconstructed. So only the following proof and verification operations are needed.

1. A'_k publicly proves for $i = 2, 3, \ldots, n$ and $k' \in K$

$$ZP \left[\; s'_{i,k'}, \; t'_{i,k'} \; | \; E''_{i-1,0,k'} = E''^{s'_{i,k'} u_{k'}}_{i-2,0} \bmod p, \right.$$
$$\left. g^{s'_{i,k'}} h^{t'_{i,k'}} = \prod_{l=0}^{t-1} E'^{k'^l}_{i,l} \bmod p \; \right],$$

verification of which guarantees that $E''_{n-1,0}$ is correctly generated. The proof and verification of (18) are implemented in Figure 1.

2. It is publicly proved and verified that correct shares are used to reconstruct the secret committed in $E''_{n-1,0}$ in Section 5.4. More precisely, after each A_k publishes $s_k = D_k(c''_{n-1,k})$ and $r_k = D_k(e''_{n-1,k})$, it is publicly verified

$$s_k r_k = \prod_{l=0}^{t-1} E''^{k^l}_{n-1,l} \bmod p \text{ for } k \in K.$$

This efficient public verification procedure (including proof and verification) only costs 6 full length exponentiations, $t^2 + t + 2$ short exponentiations and $t^2 + t + 6$ multiplications, and thus is much more efficient than the complete verification procedure. If it is passed, it is guaranteed that $g^{\prod_{i=1}^{n} \sum_{j=1}^{M(i)} (a_{i,j} - m_{i,j}) t_j}$ is correctly reconstructed to determine the result of the function. If it fails, the complete verification procedure is run and every secret operation is verified until an invalid secret operation is detected. Then the participant responsible for the invalid secret operation is expelled. If a penalty is given to any detected dishonest participant, the participants will usually be honest and in most cases only the efficient verification procedure is needed. Therefore, the DNFs can be efficiently evaluated while public verifiability is achieved.

Theorem 1, Theorem 2 and Theorem 3 illustrate correctness, soundness and privacy of the new scheme respectively. Privacy of the new secure computation protocol with the complete public verification procedure can be proved as well. Due to space limitation, their proof is left to the readers.

---

1. A'_k publishes $z_{1,i,k'}$ and $z_{2,i,k'}$ where

$$z_{1,i,k'} = (E''^{u_{k'}}_{i-2,0})^{v_{1,i,k'}} \bmod p$$
$$z_{2,i,k'} = g^{v_{1,i,k'}} h^{v_{2,i,k'}} \bmod p$$

and $v_{1,i,k'}$, $v_{2,i,k'}$ are randomly chosen from Z_q.
2. A verifier randomly chooses and publishes a 128 bit integer $u_{i,k'}$.
3. A'_k publishes $w_{1,i,k'}$ and $w_{2,i,k'}$ where

$$w_{1,i,k'} = v_{1,i,k'} - s'_{i,k'} u_{i,k'} \bmod q$$
$$w_{2,i,k'} = v_{2,i,k'} - t'_{i,k'} u_{i,k'} \bmod q$$

Anyone can verify

$$z_{1,i,k'} = (E''^{u_{k'}}_{i-2,0})^{w_{1,i,k'}} E''^{u_{i,k'}}_{i-1,0,k'} \bmod p$$
$$z_{2,i,k'} = g^{w_{1,i,k'}} h^{w_{2,i,k'}} (\textstyle\prod_{l=0}^{t-1} E'^{k'^l}_{i,l})^{u_{i,k'}} \bmod p$$

Fig. 1. ZK proof and verification of (18)

Theorem 1. *The new secure computation protocol is correct.*

Theorem 2. *The new secure computation scheme is sound with the efficient public verification procedure.*

Theorem 3. *The new secure computation protocol is private with the efficient public verification procedure.*

7   A Typical Example and Comparison

Using the DNF generation algorithm in Section 4, the famous millionaire problem (the most popular and typical example in secure computation) is reduced to a simple DNF as follows.

1. m_1 and m_2 are L-bit messages to be compared where $m_1 = (m_{1,1}, m_{1,2}, \ldots, m_{1,L})$, $m_2 = (m_{2,1}, m_{2,2}, \ldots, m_{2,L})$ and $m_{i,j}$ is the jth most important bit of m_i.
2. The DNF to evaluate the function is

$$(m_{1,1} = 1 \wedge m_{2,1} = 0) \vee (m_{1,1} = m_{2,1} \wedge m_{1,2} = 1 \wedge m_{2,2} = 0) \vee$$
$$\ldots \vee (m_{1,1} = m_{2,1} \wedge m_{1,2} = m_{2,2} \wedge \ldots \wedge m_{1,L-1} = m_{2,L-1}$$
$$\wedge m_{1,L} = 1 \wedge m_{2,L} = 0)$$

which is a simple DNF and can be efficiently evaluated.

In Table 1, the new secure computation scheme is compared with the existing general purpose secure computation schemes. Secure computation techniques only dealing with a special function (like [23, 24, 25, 26]) are not included. As

Table 1. Comparison of properties

Scheme	Sound-ness	Privacy	Flexibility in format	Computation	Communi-cation
[21]	No	Yes	No	$\geq 15KLT$ $= 61440000$	$\geq 37LT + 2T$ $= 148080$
[18]	Yes	Yes	No	$\geq 15KLT$ $= 61440000$	$\geq 37LT + 2T$ $= 148080$
[17]	Yes	Yes	No	average $\geq 4665KL$ $= 477696000$	$\geq 1626L$ $= 162600$
[3]	Yes	Yes	No	average $\geq 4039.5KL$ $= 413644800$	$\geq 1543L$ $= 154300$
[28]	No	Incomplete	No	$> L^4$ $= 100000000$	$\geq 343L^3$ $= 343000000$
New	Yes	Yes	Yes	$1.5K(4L + 40n - 18)+$ $6K'(n-1) + 2L + 44n - 41$ $= 1208663$	$10L + 30n$ -20 $= 1280$

pointed out in Section 1 it is very difficult to precisely estimate the cost of secure computation schemes employing an abstract circuit [8, 9, 10, 11, 17, 18, 21]. They only claimed that a certain evaluation circuit is established to evaluate a function while the concrete algorithm to generate the circuit is not provided and the concrete structure of the circuit is unknown. So there is not an instantiated protocol to be analysed in regard to efficiency in these schemes. Fortunately the concrete cost of [17, 18, 21] can be estimated according to [19], whose result is then used in Table 1. Unfortunately, there is no hint available to the concrete cost of [8, 9, 10, 11], which are thus not included in Table 1. The schemes in [9] and [1] are similar to [17] and [28] respectively, so are not separately listed in Table 1.

For fairness of the comparison, the circumstance of the existing schemes is adopted in the new scheme. For the sake of simplicity and generality, t, the sharing threshold, is set to be 2. As the cost of preliminary operations including set-up of distributed system (distribution of private key[2] or input), input encryption, input validity check and all the public verification operations are not counted in computation efficiency analysis of the existing schemes, their cost is not counted in computation of the new protocols as well. In Table 1, n stands for the number of clauses in the DNF; K is the bit length of a full length integer; K' is the length of challenges in ZK proof primitives and T is the cutting factor in cut-and-choose mechanism. The number of full length multiplications is counted in terms of computation while addition, multiplication of small integers and exponentiations with small base are ignored and exponentiations with full length base are converted into multiplications with a rule: an exponentiation with a x bit exponent is equivalent to $1.5x$ multiplications. In Table 1, transportation of integers with significant length (e.g. 1024 bits long) is counted in regard to

---

[2] In some secure computation schemes [1, 28], distributed generation of private key is extremely inefficient.

communication. In the example in Table 1, the evaluated function is the millionaire problem and $K = 1024$, $K' = 128$, $L = 100$, $n = 10$ and $T = 40$. It is clearly illustrated in Table 1 that the new secure computation scheme is secure, flexible and much more efficient than the existing secure computation schemes.

8 Conclusion

A new homomorphism based secure multiparty computation scheme with formal security, strong flexibility and high efficiency is proposed. Compared to the other homomorphism based multiparty computation schemes [1, 9, 11, 12, 16, 28], the new scheme is more suitable for functions which can be reduced to polynomial-size DNFs. The new scheme achieves flexibility in input format and supports any input format. Privacy of the new scheme is formally proved in a novel security model, which has independent value. A typical example of evaluating the millionaire problem is given to clearly illustrate advantage of the new scheme in efficiency. The example also demonstrates practicality and applicability of the new scheme.

References

1. Beaver, D.: Minimal-latency secure function evaluation. In: Preneel, B. (ed.) EUROCRYPT 2000. LNCS, vol. 1807, pp. 335–350. Springer, Heidelberg (2000)
2. Ben-Or, M., Goldwasser, S., Killian, J., Wigderson, A.: Multi-prover interactive proofs: How to remove intractability assumptions. In: STOC 1988, pp. 113–131
3. Cachin, C., Camenisch, J.: Optimistic fair secure computation (extended abstract). In: Bellare, M. (ed.) CRYPTO 2000. LNCS, vol. 1880, pp. 94–112. Springer, Heidelberg (2000)
4. Canetti, R.: Universally composable security: A new paradigm for cryptographic protocols. In: FOCS 2001, pp. 136–145
5. Canetti, R., Fiege, U., Goldreich, O., Naor, M.: Adaptive secure computation. In: ACM STOC 1996, pp. 143–202
6. Chaum, D., Crepeau, C., Damgård, I.: Multiparty unconditionally secure protocols (extended abstract). In: STOC 1988, pp. 11–19
7. Chaum, D., Pedersen, T.: Wallet databases with observers. In: Brickell, E.F. (ed.) CRYPTO 1992. LNCS, vol. 740, pp. 89–105. Springer, Heidelberg (1993)
8. Cramer, R., Damgård, I., Dziembowski, S., Hirt, M., Rabin, T.: Efficient multiparty computations secure against an adaptive adversary. In: Stern, J. (ed.) EUROCRYPT 1999. LNCS, vol. 1592, pp. 311–326. Springer, Heidelberg (1999)
9. Cramer, R., Damgård, I., Nielsen, J.: Multiparty computation from threshold homomorphic encryption. In: Pfitzmann, B. (ed.) EUROCRYPT 2001. LNCS, vol. 2045, pp. 280–299. Springer, Heidelberg (2001)
10. Damgård, I., Ishai, Y.: Constant-round multiparty computation using a black-box pseudorandom generator. In: Shoup, V. (ed.) CRYPTO 2005. LNCS, vol. 3621, pp. 378–394. Springer, Heidelberg (2005)
11. Damgård, I., Nielsen, J.: Universally composable efficient multiparty computation from threshold homomorphic encryption. In: Boneh, D. (ed.) CRYPTO 2003. LNCS, vol. 2729, pp. 247–264. Springer, Heidelberg (2003)

12. Fischlin, M.: A cost-effective pay-per-multiplication comparison method for millionaires. In: Naccache, D. (ed.) CT-RSA 2001. LNCS, vol. 2020, pp. 457–472. Springer, Heidelberg (2001)
13. Gennaro, R., Rabin, M., Rabin, T.: Simplified VSS and fast-track multiparty computations with applications to threshold cryptography. In: PODC 1998, pp. 101–111
14. Goldreich, O., Micali, S., Wigderson, A.: How to play any mental game or a completeness theorem for protocols with honest majority. In: STOC 1987, pp. 218–229.
15. Hirt, M., Maurer, U.: Robustness for free in unconditional multi-party computation. In: Kilian, J. (ed.) CRYPTO 2001. LNCS, vol. 2139, pp. 101–118. Springer, Heidelberg (2001)
16. Ishai, Y., Kushilevitz, E.: Randomizing polynomials: A new representation with applications to round-efficient secure. In: IEEE Symposium on Foundations of Computer Science 2000, pp. 294–304
17. Jakobsson, M., Juels, A.: Mix and match: Secure function evaluation via ciphertexts. In: Okamoto, T. (ed.) ASIACRYPT 2000. LNCS, vol. 1976, pp. 143–161. Springer, Heidelberg (2000)
18. Juels, A., Szydlo, M.: A two-server, sealed-bid auction protocol. In: Blaze, M. (ed.) FC 2002. LNCS, vol. 2357, pp. 72–86. Springer, Heidelberg (2003)
19. Kurosawa, K., Ogata, W.: Bit-slice auction circuit. In: Gollmann, D., Karjoth, G., Waidner, M. (eds.) ESORICS 2002. LNCS, vol. 2502, pp. 24–38. Springer, Heidelberg (2002)
20. McKay, C.: Digital Circuit, a Preparation for Microprocessors. Prentice-Hall, Englewood Cliffs (1978)
21. Naor, M., Pinkas, B., Sumner, R.: Privacy perserving auctions and mechanism design. In: ACM Conference on Electronic Commerce 1999, pp. 129–139
22. Pedersen, T.: Non-interactive and information-theoretic secure verifiable secret sharing. In: Davies, D.W. (ed.) EUROCRYPT 1991. LNCS, vol. 547, pp. 129–140. Springer, Heidelberg (1991)
23. Peng, K., Boyd, C., Dawson, E., Lee, B.: An efficient and verifiable solution to the millionaire problem. In: Park, C.-s., Chee, S. (eds.) ICISC 2004. LNCS, vol. 3506, pp. 315–330. Springer, Heidelberg (2005)
24. Peng, K., Boyd, C., Dawson, E., Lee, B.: Ciphertext comparison, a new solution to the millionaire problem. In: Qing, S., Mao, W., Lopez, J., Wang, G. (eds.) ICICS 2005. LNCS, vol. 3783, pp. 84–96. Springer, Heidelberg (2005)
25. Peng, K., Boyd, C., Dawson, E., Okamoto, E.: A novel range test. In: Batten, L.M., Safavi-Naini, R. (eds.) ACISP 2006. LNCS, vol. 4058, pp. 247–258. Springer, Heidelberg (2006)
26. Peng, K., Dawson, E.: Range test secure in the active adversary model. In: AISW 2007. ACM International Conference Proceeding Series, vol. 249, pp. 159–162
27. Rabin, T., Ben-Or, M.: Verifiable secret sharing and multiparty protocols with honest majority. In: ACM STOC 1989, pp. 73–85
28. Sander, T., Young, A., Yung, M.: Non-interactive cryptocomputing for NC^1. In: FOCS 1999, pp. 554–567

Square Like Attack on Camellia

Lei Duo[1], Chao Li[1], and Keqin Feng[2]

[1] Department of Science, National University of Defense Technology,
Changsha, China
duoduolei@gmail.com
[2] Department of Math, Tsinghua University,
Beijing, China

Abstract. In this paper, a square like attack on Camellia is presented, by which 9-round 128-bit key Camellia without FL/FL^{-1} functions layer and whitening is breakable with complexity of $2^{86.9}$ encryptions and 2^{66} data and 12-round 256-bit key Camellia without FL/FL^{-1} function layer and whitening is breakable with the complexity of $2^{250.8}$ encryptions and 2^{66} data. And we can also apply such method to block cipher having XORing sBoxes in diffusion layer.

Keywords: Camellia, Block Cipher, Square attack.

1 Introduction

Camellia [1] is a symmetric key block cipher developed jointly in 2000 at NTT and Mitsubishi Electric Corporation. It has the modified Feistel structure with irregular rounds, which is called the FL/FL^{-1} functions layers. Camellia has been accepted by ISO/IEC [11] as an international standard. It is also a winner of NESSIE, CRYPTREC project and IETF [11].

Efficient methods analyzing Camellia include linear attack [13], differential attack [13] truncated differential attack [6,8,14], impossible differential attack [16,14], higher order differential attack [4,7], Collision attack [10,15] and square attack [10,5,17]. The best attack on 128-bit key Camellia was linear attack [13], which can attack 10-round Camellia without FL/FL^{-1} functions layer and whitening with complexity of 2^{121}. The best attack against 256-bit key Camellia was impossible differential attack, which can attack 12-round Camellia without FL/FL^{-1} functions layer and whitening with complexity of 2^{181}.

In this paper, we improve the attacking results on Camellia. Our method uses active set [2], which was first introduced in square attack [2,3], to build the attack, however, the balanced byte is not core byte in our attack, special properties on XORing of active sBoxes are applied to build the distinguisher, so we call it square like attack. Such properties are first discovered and are in effect on the ciphers with XORing in diffusion layer.

Brief description of Camellia is presented in section 2. In section 3, active bytes transformations on Camellia are illustrated and some new properties are demonstrated. Our basic attacking method is described in section 4. Section 5

S. Qing, H. Imai, and G. Wang (Eds.): ICICS 2007, LNCS 4861, pp. 269–283, 2007.

is its extension. The paper concludes with our most important results contrast with other known results.

2   Description of the Camellia

Camellia has a 128-bit block size and supports 128-, 192- and 256-bit keys. Camellia with a 128-bit key and 256-bit key is written as 128-Camellia, 256-Camellia. The design of Camellia is based on the Feistel structure and its number of rounds is 18 (128-bit key) or 24 (192-, 256-bit key). The FL/FL^{-1} functions layer is inserted in it every 6 rounds in order to thwart future unknown attacks. Before the first round and after the last round, there are pre- and post-whitening layers.

We refer $x^{(r)}, k^{(r)}$ to the rth round output and rth round subkey, refer $x_L^{(r)}$ and $x_R^{(r)}$ to the left, right half bytes of $x^{(r)}$, which implies $x^{(r)} = x_L^{(r)} \| x_R^{(r)}$. Let $P_L \| P_R$ and $C_L \| C_R$ be the Plaintext and Ciphertext.

Let $x^{(r,i)}$ be the ith byte of $x^{(r)}$. The $x_L^{(r)}$ is a 8-byte sequence, we have $x_L^{(r)} = (x_L^{(r,1)}, \ldots, x_L^{(r,8)})$. F function contains key-addition K-function, sBoxes transformation S-function and diffusion function P-function, these functions are described as follows. The figure illustration of F-function is Fig.1.

The key addition function is

$$K(x_L^{(r)}, k^{(r+1)}) \overset{def}{=} (x_L^{(r,1)} \oplus k^{(r+1,1)}, \ldots, x_L^{(r,8)} \oplus k^{(r+1,8)}).$$

S-function contains 4 types of S-boxes s_1, s_2, s_3, and s_4. s_2, s_3, s_4 are variations of s_1,

$$S(y_1, \ldots, y_8) \overset{def}{=} (s_1(y_1), s_2(y_2), s_3(y_3), s_4(y_4), s_2(y_5), s_3(y_6), s_4(y_7), s_1(y_8)).$$

The relation among the four sBoxes is that

$$s_2(a) = s_1(a) \lll 1, \quad s_3(a) = s_1(a) \ggg 1, \quad s_4(a) = s_1(a \lll 1).$$

Let $P(z_1, \ldots, z_8) \overset{def}{=} (z_1', \ldots, z_8')$. The P-function:$\{0,1\}^{64} \mapsto \{0,1\}^{64}$ maps $(z_1, \ldots, z_8)$ to $(z_1', \ldots, z_8')$. The P-function and its inverse function P^{-1} are

$$
\begin{aligned}
z_1' &= z_1 \oplus z_3 \oplus z_4 \oplus z_6 \oplus z_7 \oplus z_8 \\
z_2' &= z_1 \oplus z_2 \oplus z_4 \oplus z_5 \oplus z_7 \oplus z_8 \\
z_3' &= z_1 \oplus z_2 \oplus z_3 \oplus z_5 \oplus z_6 \oplus z_8 \\
z_4' &= z_2 \oplus z_3 \oplus z_4 \oplus z_5 \oplus z_6 \oplus z_7 \\
z_5' &= z_1 \oplus z_2 \oplus z_6 \oplus z_7 \oplus z_8 \\
z_6' &= z_2 \oplus z_3 \oplus z_5 \oplus z_7 \oplus z_8 \\
z_7' &= z_3 \oplus z_4 \oplus z_5 \oplus z_6 \oplus z_8 \\
z_8' &= z_1 \oplus z_4 \oplus z_5 \oplus z_6 \oplus z_7
\end{aligned}
\qquad,\qquad
\begin{aligned}
z_1 &= z_2' \oplus z_3' \oplus z_4' \oplus z_6' \oplus z_7' \oplus z_8' \\
z_2 &= z_1' \oplus z_3' \oplus z_4' \oplus z_5' \oplus z_7' \oplus z_8' \\
z_3 &= z_1' \oplus z_2' \oplus z_4' \oplus z_5' \oplus z_6' \oplus z_8' \\
z_4 &= z_1' \oplus z_2' \oplus z_3' \oplus z_5' \oplus z_6' \oplus z_7' \\
z_5 &= z_1' \oplus z_2' \oplus z_5' \oplus z_7' \oplus z_8' \\
z_6 &= z_2' \oplus z_3' \oplus z_5' \oplus z_6' \oplus z_8' \\
z_7 &= z_3' \oplus z_4' \oplus z_5' \oplus z_6' \oplus z_7' \\
z_8 &= z_1' \oplus z_4' \oplus z_6' \oplus z_7' \oplus z_8'
\end{aligned}
$$

The R round Camellia without FL/FL^{-1} functions and pre-, post- whitening function is written as follows,

$$
\begin{cases}
x_L^{(0)} \| x_R^{(0)} &= P_L \| P_R \\
x_L^{(r)} &= x_R^{(r-1)} \oplus K(S(P(x_l^{(r-1)}))), \\
x_R^{(r)} &= x_L^{(r-1)}, \\
C_L \| C_R &= x_L^{(R)} \| x_R^{(R)}.
\end{cases}
$$

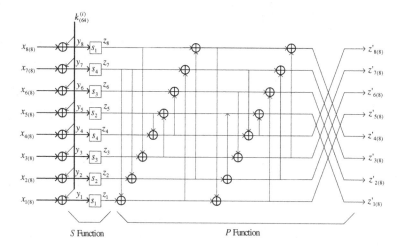

Fig. 1. Round function of Camellia-1

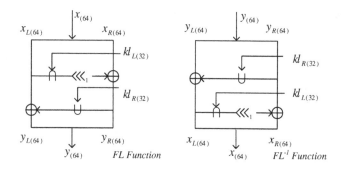

Fig. 2. FL/FL^{-1} functions

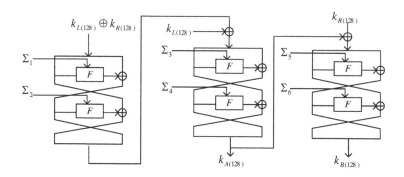

Fig. 3. Key Schedule of Camellia

The P-permutation, which is a linear transformation, can be move into previous round or post round. If pre-, post-whitening and FL/FL^{-1} are not taken

Table 1. Round Keys.(We only give the first 14 rounds key.)

128bit key	subkey	value	192-,256-bit key	subkey	value
Pre-whitening	$kw^{(1)}$	$(k_L \lll_0)_L$	Pre-whitening	$kw^{(1)}$	$(k_L \lll_0)_L$
	$kw^{(2)}$	$(k_L \lll_0)_R$		$kw^{(2)}$	$(k_L \lll_0)_R$
F (Round1)	$k^{(1)}$	$(k_A \lll_0)_L$	F (Round1)	$k^{(1)}$	$(k_B \lll_0)_L$
F (Round2)	$k^{(2)}$	$(k_A \lll_0)_R$	F (Round2)	$k^{(2)}$	$(k_B \lll_0)_R$
F (Round3)	$k^{(3)}$	$(k_L \lll_{15})_L$	F (Round3)	$k^{(3)}$	$(k_R \lll_{15})_L$
F (Round4)	$k^{(4)}$	$(k_L \lll_{15})_R$	F (Round4)	$k^{(4)}$	$(k_R \lll_{15})_R$
F (Round5)	$k^{(5)}$	$(k_A \lll_{15})_L$	F (Round5)	$k^{(5)}$	$(k_A \lll_{15})_L$
F (Round6)	$k^{(6)}$	$(k_A \lll_{15})_R$	F (Round6)	$k^{(6)}$	$(k_A \lll_{15})_R$
FL	$k^{(l1)}$	$(k_A \lll_{30})_L$	FL	$k^{(l1)}$	$(k_R \lll_{30})_L$
FL^{-1}	$k^{(l2)}$	$(k_A \lll_{30})_R$	FL^{-1}	$k^{(l2)}$	$(k_R \lll_{30})_R$
F (Round7)	$k^{(7)}$	$(k_L \lll_{45})_L$	F (Round7)	$k^{(7)}$	$(k_B \lll_{30})_L$
F (Round8)	$k^{(8)}$	$(k_L \lll_{45})_R$	F (Round8)	$k^{(8)}$	$(k_B \lll_{30})_R$
F (Round9)	$k^{(9)}$	$(k_A \lll_{45})_L$	F (Round9)	$k^{(9)}$	$(k_L \lll_{45})_L$
F (Round10)	$k^{(10)}$	$(k_L \lll_{60})_R$	F (Round10)	$k^{(10)}$	$(k_L \lll_{45})_R$
F (Round11)	$k^{(11)}$	$(k_A \lll_{60})_L$	F (Round11)	$k^{(11)}$	$(k_A \lll_{45})_L$
F (Round12)	$k^{(12)}$	$(k_A \lll_{60})_R$	F (Round12)	$k^{(12)}$	$(k_A \lll_{45})_R$
FL	$k^{(l3)}$	$(k_L \lll_{77})_L$	FL	$k^{(l3)}$	$(k_L \lll_{60})_L$
FL^{-1}	$k^{(l4)}$	$(k_L \lll_{77})_R$	FL^{-1}	$k^{(l4)}$	$(k_L \lll_{60})_R$
F (Round13)	$k^{(13)}$	$(k_L \lll_{94})_L$	F (Round13)	$k^{(13)}$	$(k_R \lll_{60})_L$
F (Round14)	$k^{(14)}$	$(k_L \lll_{94})_R$	F (Round14)	$k^{(14)}$	$(k_R \lll_{60})_R$
Round15~Round18			Round15~Round18		
Postwhitening	$kw^{(3)}$	$(k_A \lll_{111})_L$	FL	$kl^{(5)}$	$(k_A \lll_{77})_L$
	$kw^{(4)}$	$(k_A \lll_{111})_R$	FL^{-1}	$kl^{(6)}$	$(k_A \lll_{77})_R$
			Round19~Round24		
			Postwhitening	$kw^{(3)}$	$(k_B \lll_{111})_L$
				$kw^{(4)}$	$(k_B \lll_{111})_R$

into consideration, two equivalence structures of Camellia called Camellia-3 and Camellia-4 [10] are given as follows.

The Camellia-3 is

$$
\begin{cases}
\widetilde{x}_L^{(0)} \| \widetilde{x}_R^{(0)} = P_L \| P^{-1}(P_R) \\
\widetilde{x}_L^{(r)} = \widetilde{x}_R^{(r-1)} \oplus S(\widetilde{x}_l^{(r-1)} \oplus k^{(r)}), \qquad r \text{ is odd} \\
\widetilde{x}_L^{(r)} = P(\widetilde{x}_R^{(r-1)} \oplus S(P(\widetilde{x}_l^{(r-1)}) \oplus k^{(r)})), \qquad r \text{ is even} \\
\widetilde{x}_R^{(r)} = \widetilde{x}_L^{(r-1)}, \\
C_L \| C_R = \widetilde{x}_L^R \| P(\widetilde{x}_R^R).
\end{cases}
$$

The Camellia-4 is

$$
\begin{cases}
\widehat{x}_L^{(0)} \| \widehat{x}_R^{(0)} = P^{-1}(P_L) \| P_R \\
\widehat{x}_L^{(r)} = P(\widehat{x}_R^{(r-1)} \oplus S(P(\widehat{x}_l^{(r-1)}) \oplus k^{(r)})), \qquad r \text{ is odd} \\
\widehat{x}_L^{(r)} = \widehat{x}_R^{(r-1)} \oplus S(\widehat{x}_l^{(r-1)} \oplus k^{(r)}), \qquad r \text{ is even} \\
\widehat{x}_R^{(r)} = \widehat{x}_L^{(r-1)}, \\
C_L \| C_R = P(\widehat{x}_L^R) \| \widehat{x}_R^R.
\end{cases}
$$

The FL/FL^{-1} functions are shown in Fig.2, which are defined as follows: $(\{0,1\}^{64} \times \{0,1\}^{64} \to \{0,1\}^{64})$, $(x_L \| x_R, kl_L \| kl_R) \to y_L \| y_R$. The FL function is

$$y_R = ((x_L \cap kl_L) \lll_1) \oplus x_R,$$
$$y_L = (y_R \cup kl_R) \oplus x_L.$$

Fig.3 shows the key schedule of Camellia. Two 128-bit variables k_L and k_R are defined as follows. For 128-bit keys, the 128-bit key k is used as k_L and k_R is **0**. For 256-bit keys, the left 128-bit of the key k is used as k_L and the right 128-bit of k is used as k_R. Two 128-bit variables k_A and k_B are generated from k_L and k_R as shown in Fig.3, in which $\Sigma_i (i = 1, \ldots, 6)$ are constants used as Key. The round keys are rotation of k_A, k_B, k_L and k_R, which is shown in Table2.

3   Basic Attacks on Camellia

3.1   Preliminaries

The concepts of square attack and Λ-set were introduced by Daemen et. al [2].

Let Γ-set be a 256 collection of state bytes $\alpha^{(i)} = (\alpha^{(i,1)}, \ldots, \alpha^{(i,n)})$, $i \in [0..255]$, where $\alpha^{(i,j)}$ is the jth byte of $\alpha^{(i)}$. If the jth byte of elements in Γ are different from one another,

$$\alpha^{(i,j)} \neq \alpha^{(i',j)}, \forall i, i' \in [0..255], i \neq i'$$

the jth byte is called active byte. The jth byte is called fixed byte, if the jth bytes are unchanged in Γ-set.

$$\alpha^{(i,j)} = \alpha^{(i',j)}, \forall i, i' \in [0..255], i \neq i'$$

And if $\sum_{i \in [0..255]} \alpha^{(i,j)} = 0$, then the jth byte is called balanced byte. To make thing simple, we use λ, θ, δ, and γ to signify a byte and active byte is denoted λ, fixed byte is denoted θ and balanced byte is denoted δ, other is denoted γ. A Γ-set is called Θ-set, if all its bytes are fixed bytes. A Γ-set is called Λ-set, if all its bytes are active bytes or fixed bytes.

The following Theorem 1 is the most important properties of this paper and the attack is based on which. Before that, let give some notions. Let $\Lambda = \{\lambda^{(i)}\}$ be a one byte Λ-set , $\Theta = \{\theta^{(i)}\}$ be one byte Θ-set and $\theta^{(i)} = \theta$. Let $Count_{f(\Lambda,\Theta)}(\gamma) \overset{def}{=} \#\{\gamma | f(\lambda^{(i)}, \theta^{(i)}) = \gamma, \lambda^{(i)} \in \Lambda, \theta^{(i)} \in \Theta, i \in [0..255]\}$. The $Count_{f(\Lambda,\Theta)}(\gamma)$ is the count of γ, when the inputs changes trough the input sets Λ and Θ.

The S-box of Camellia has following properties.

Theorem 1. *Let* $\Lambda = \{\lambda^{(i)}\}$ *be a* Λ*-set and* $\Theta = \{\theta^{(i)}\}$ *be* Θ*-set, in which* $\theta^{(i)} = \theta$ *and* $\lambda^{(i)}, \theta \in \{0,1\}^8$. *S-Boxes of Camellia have following properties*

1. $Count_{s_\iota(\Lambda)}(\gamma) = 1$, $\iota \in \{1,2,3,4\}$, $\gamma \in \{0,1\}^8$;
2. $Count_{s_1(\Lambda) \oplus s_2(\Lambda)}(\gamma) \in \{0,2\}$, $\gamma \in \{0,1\}^8$;
3. $Count_{s_1(\Lambda) \oplus s_3(\Lambda)}(\gamma) \in \{0,2\}$, $\gamma \in \{0,1\}^8$;
4. $Count_{s_2(\Lambda) \oplus s_3(\Lambda)}(\gamma) \in \{0,4\}$, $\gamma \in \{0,1\}^8$;

5. $Count_{s_\iota(\Lambda)\oplus s_\iota(\Lambda\oplus\Theta)}(\gamma) = \{0,2,4\}$, $\iota \in \{1,2,3,4\}$, $\gamma \in \{0,1\}^8$;
6. $Count_{s_\iota(\Lambda)\oplus s_\iota(\Lambda\oplus\Theta_1)\oplus s_\kappa(\Lambda)\oplus s_\kappa(\Lambda\oplus\Theta_2)}(\gamma) = \{0,2,4,6,8,\ldots\}$, $\iota,\kappa \in \{1,2,3,4\}$, $\iota \neq \kappa$ and $\gamma \in \{0,1\}^8$,

where $\Lambda \oplus \Theta \overset{def}{=} \{\lambda^{(i)} \oplus \theta^{(i)}\}$.

The proof is omitted for we can check them directly. The item 1 is based on the sBoxes are permutations and item 2,3,4 are based on the liner relation between sBoxes s_1, s_2 and s_3. Item 5 is ,in fact, the differential table of sBoxes.

3.2 5-Round Distinguishers

In this section, we build a 5-round distinguishers on Camellia-4. Let $\Theta \overset{def}{=} \{\theta^{(i,1)}, \ldots, \theta^{(i,8)}\}$ be a Θ-set. Let $\Lambda_0 \overset{def}{=} \{\lambda_0^{(i,1)}, \theta_0^{(i,2)}, \ldots, \theta_0^{(i,8)}\}$ be a Λ-set, in which the first byte is a active byte. We select the plaintext set as $\{P_L\} = \Theta$ and $\{P_R\} = \Lambda_0$. Let $F(\Theta) \overset{def}{=} \{F(\theta^{(i)})\}$. Let $\Theta_1 = \{\theta_1^{(i,1)}, \ldots, \theta_1^{(i,8)}\} \overset{def}{=} P^{-1}(\Theta)$. Let $\Theta_2 = \{\theta_2^{(i,1)}, \ldots, \theta_2^{(i,8)}\} \overset{def}{=} P(S(K(P(\Theta_1))))$. Then, five round Camellia-4 has following properties.

$$\widehat{x}_R^{(0)} = P_R = (\lambda_0^{(i,1)}, \theta_0^{(i,2)}, \ldots, \theta_0^{(i,8)}),$$
$$\widehat{x}_R^{(1)} = P^{-1}(P_L) = (\theta_1^{(i,1)}, \ldots, \theta_1^{(i,8)}),$$
$$\widehat{x}_R^{(2)} = P(S(K(P(\widehat{x}_R^{(1)})))) \oplus \widehat{x}_R^{(0)} = (\lambda_0^{(i,1)} \oplus \theta_2^{(i,1)}, \theta_0^{(i,2)} \oplus \theta_2^{(i,2)}, \ldots, \theta_0^{(i,8)} \oplus \theta_2^{(i,8)}),$$
$$\widehat{x}_R^{(3)} = S(K(\widehat{x}_R^{(2)})) \oplus \widehat{x}_R^{(1)}$$
$$= (s_1(\lambda_0^{(i,1)} \oplus \theta_2^{(i,1)} \oplus k^{(2,1)}) \oplus \theta_1^{(i,1)}, s_2(\theta_0^{(i,2)} \oplus \theta_2^{(i,2)} \oplus k^{(2,2)}) \oplus \theta_1^{(i,2)}$$
$$, \ldots, s_1(\theta_0^{(i,8)} \oplus \theta_2^{(i,8)} \oplus k^{(2,8)}) \oplus \theta_1^{(i,8)})$$
$$\overset{def}{=} (s_1(\lambda_0^{(i,1)} \oplus \theta_3^{(i,1)}) \oplus \theta_1^{(i,1)}, s_2(\theta_3^{(i,2)}) \oplus \theta_1^{(i,2)}), \ldots, s_1(\theta_3^{(i,8)}) \oplus \theta_1^{(i,8)})$$

Let
$$\widetilde{\lambda}_1^{(i)} \overset{def}{=} s_1(\lambda_0^{(i,1)} \oplus \theta_3^{(i,1)}) \oplus \theta_1^{(i,1)} \oplus (\oplus_{j\in\{3,4,6,7,8\}}(s_1(\theta_3^{(i,j)}) \oplus \theta_1^{(i,j)})) \oplus k^{(4,1)}$$
$$\widetilde{\lambda}_2^{(i)} \overset{def}{=} s_1(\lambda_0^{(i,1)} \oplus \theta_3^{(i,1)}) \oplus \theta_1^{(i,1)} \oplus (\oplus_{j\in\{2,4,5,7,8\}}(s_2(\theta_3^{(i,j)}) \oplus \theta_1^{(i,j)})) \oplus k^{(4,2)}$$
$$\widetilde{\lambda}_3^{(i)} \overset{def}{=} s_1(\lambda_0^{(i,1)} \oplus \theta_3^{(i,1)}) \oplus \theta_1^{(i,1)} \oplus (\oplus_{j\in\{2,3,5,6,8\}}(s_3(\theta_3^{(i,j)}) \oplus \theta_1^{(i,j)})) \oplus k^{(4,3)}$$
$$\widetilde{\theta}_4^{(i)} \overset{def}{=} (\oplus_{j\in\{2,3,4,5,6,7\}}(s_4(\theta_3^{(i,j)}) \oplus \theta_1^{(i,j)})) \oplus k^{(4,4)}$$
$$\widetilde{\lambda}_5^{(i)} \overset{def}{=} s_1(\lambda_0^{(i,1)} \oplus \theta_3^{(i,1)}) \oplus \theta_1^{(i,1)} \oplus (\oplus_{j\in\{2,6,7,8\}}(s_2(\theta_3^{(i,j)}) \oplus \theta_1^{(i,j)})) \oplus k^{(4,5)}$$
$$\widetilde{\theta}_6^{(i)} \overset{def}{=} (\oplus_{j\in\{2,3,5,7,8\}}(s_3(\theta_3^{(i,j)}) \oplus \theta_1^{(i,j)})) \oplus k^{(4,6)}$$
$$\widetilde{\theta}_7^{(i)} \overset{def}{=} (\oplus_{j\in\{3,4,5,6,8\}}(s_4(\theta_3^{(i,j)}) \oplus \theta_1^{(i,j)})) \oplus k^{(4,7)}$$
$$\widetilde{\lambda}_8^{(i)} \overset{def}{=} s_1(\lambda_0^{(i,1)} \oplus \theta_3^{(i,1)}) \oplus \theta_1^{(i,1)} \oplus (\oplus_{j\in\{4,5,6,7\}}(s_1(\theta_3^{(i,j)}) \oplus \theta_1^{(i,j)})) \oplus k^{(4,8)}$$

then,
$$\widehat{x}_R^{(4,1)} = s_1(\widetilde{\lambda}_1) \oplus s_3(\widetilde{\lambda}_3) \oplus s_4(\widetilde{\theta}_4) \oplus s_3(\widetilde{\theta}_6) \oplus s_4(\widetilde{\theta}_7) \oplus s_1(\widetilde{\lambda}_8) \oplus \theta_2^{(i,1)} \oplus \lambda_2^{(i,1)}$$
$$\widehat{x}_R^{(4,2)} = s_1(\widetilde{\lambda}_1) \oplus s_2(\widetilde{\lambda}_2) \oplus s_4(\widetilde{\theta}_4) \oplus s_2(\widetilde{\lambda}_5) \oplus s_4(\widetilde{\theta}_7) \oplus s_1(\widetilde{\lambda}_8) \oplus \theta_2^{(i,2)}$$

$$\widehat{x}_R^{(4,3)} = s_1(\widetilde{\lambda}_1) \oplus s_2(\widetilde{\lambda}_2) \oplus s_3(\widetilde{\lambda}_3) \oplus s_2(\widetilde{\lambda}_5) \oplus s_3(\widetilde{\theta}_6) \oplus s_1(\widetilde{\lambda}_8) \oplus \theta_2^{(i,3)}$$
$$\widehat{x}_R^{(4,4)} = s_2(\widetilde{\lambda}_2) \oplus s_3(\widetilde{\lambda}_3) \oplus s_4(\widetilde{\theta}_4) \oplus s_2(\widetilde{\lambda}_5) \oplus s_3(\widetilde{\theta}_6) \oplus s_4(\widetilde{\theta}_7) \oplus \theta_2^{(i,4)}$$
$$\widehat{x}_R^{(4,5)} = s_1(\widetilde{\lambda}_1) \oplus s_2(\widetilde{\lambda}_2) \oplus s_3(\widetilde{\theta}_6) \oplus s_4(\widetilde{\theta}_7) \oplus s_1(\widetilde{\lambda}_8) \oplus \theta_2^{(i,5)}$$
$$\widehat{x}_R^{(4,6)} = s_2(\widetilde{\lambda}_2) \oplus s_3(\widetilde{\lambda}_3) \oplus s_2(\widetilde{\lambda}_5) \oplus s_4(\widetilde{\theta}_7) \oplus s_1(\widetilde{\lambda}_8) \oplus \theta_2^{(i,6)}$$
$$\widehat{x}_R^{(4,7)} = s_3(\widetilde{\lambda}_3) \oplus s_4(\widetilde{\theta}_4) \oplus s_2(\widetilde{\lambda}_5) \oplus s_3(\widetilde{\theta}_6) \oplus s_1(\widetilde{\lambda}_8) \oplus \theta_2^{(i,7)}$$
$$\widehat{x}_R^{(4,8)} = s_1(\widetilde{\lambda}_1) \oplus s_4(\widetilde{\theta}_4) \oplus s_2(\widetilde{\lambda}_5) \oplus s_3(\widetilde{\theta}_6) \oplus s_4(\widetilde{\theta}_7) \oplus \theta_2^{(i,8)}.$$

Let us consider some properties of $\widehat{x}_R^{(4)}$ and $\widehat{x}_R^{(5)}$.

Since $\widehat{x}_R^{(4,8)} = s_1(\widetilde{\lambda}_1) \oplus s_4(\widetilde{\theta}_4) \oplus s_2(\widetilde{\lambda}_5) \oplus s_3(\widetilde{\theta}_6) \oplus s_4(\widetilde{\theta}_7) \oplus \theta_2^{(2,8)}$ and $\widehat{x}_R^{(5,8)} = s_1(\widehat{x}_R^{(4,8)} \oplus k^{(5,8)})$, we have

$$Count_{\{\widehat{x}_R^{(4,8)}\}}(\gamma) \in \{0,2\}, \text{ if } \widetilde{\lambda}_1 = \widetilde{\lambda}_5, \tag{1}$$

$$Count_{\{\widehat{x}_R^{(5,8)}\}}(\gamma) \in \{0,2\}, \text{ if } \widetilde{\lambda}_1 = \widetilde{\lambda}_5, \tag{2}$$

To make $\widetilde{\lambda}_1 = \widetilde{\lambda}_5$, we have,

$$\widetilde{\lambda}_1 = \widetilde{\lambda}_5$$
$$\Leftrightarrow s_1(\lambda_0^{(i,1)} \oplus \theta_3^{(i,1)}) \oplus \theta_1^{(i,1)} \oplus (\oplus_{j \in \{3,4,6,7,8\}}(s_\iota(\theta_3^{(i,j)}) \oplus \theta_1^{(i,j)})) \oplus k^{(4,1)}$$
$$= s_1(\lambda_0^{(i,1)} \oplus \theta_3^{(i,1)}) \oplus \theta_1^{(i,1)} \oplus (\oplus_{j \in \{2,6,7,8\}}(s_\iota(\theta_3^{(i,j)}) \oplus \theta_1^{(i,j)})) \oplus k^{(4,5)}$$
$$\Leftrightarrow (\oplus_{j \in \{3,4,6,7,8\}}(s_\iota(\theta_3^{(i,j)}) \oplus \theta_1^{(i,j)})) \oplus k^{(4,1)}$$
$$= (\oplus_{j \in \{2,6,7,8\}}(s_\iota(\theta_3^{(i,j)}) \oplus \theta_1^{(i,j)})) \oplus k^{(4,5)}$$
$$\Leftrightarrow (\oplus_{j \in \{3,4\}}(s_\iota(\theta_3^{(i,j)}) \oplus \theta_1^{(i,j)})) \oplus k^{(4,1)} = (\oplus_{j \in \{2\}}(s_\iota(\theta_3^{(i,j)}) \oplus \theta_1^{(i,j)})) \oplus k^{(4,5)}$$

So, $\widetilde{\lambda}_1 = \widetilde{\lambda}_5$ requires,

$$(\oplus_{j \in \{2,3,4\}}(s_\iota(\theta_3^{(i,j)}) \oplus \theta_1^{(i,j)})) \oplus k^{(4,1)} \oplus k^{(4,5)} = 0 \tag{3}$$

Let $\Theta \| \Lambda \overset{def}{=} \{\theta^{(i)} \| \lambda^{(i)}\}$. Let 256 Λ-set be
$$(\Theta \| \Lambda_0)_\iota = (\{\theta^{(i,1)}, \dots, \theta^{(i,8)}, \lambda_0^{(i,1)}, \theta_0^{(i,2)}, \dots, \theta_0^{(i,8)}\})_\iota, \iota \in [0..255]$$
in which, $\lambda_0^{(i,1)}$ is active byte, other bytes are fixed bytes, $\theta_0^{(i,2)}$ (or $\theta_0^{(i,3)}$, $\theta_0^{(i,4)}$) is different for different ι and other bytes are unchanged for all $\iota \in [0..255]$.

In five round Camellia-4, if we select plaintext set as $(\{P_L \| P_R\})_\iota = (\Theta \| \Lambda_0)_\iota$, then existing one ι makes $\widetilde{\lambda}_1 = \widetilde{\lambda}_5$. For, when Θ is unchanged, the left part of Eq.3 is only influenced by $s_\iota(\theta_3^{(i,j)})$, $j \in \{2,3,4\}$. And $s_\iota(\theta_3^{(i,j)})$ is only influenced by $\theta_0^{(i,j)}$, where $j \in \{2,3,4\}$. Then we find a 5-round distinguisher on Camellia-4. There are some more 5-round distinguishers as follows.

For, $\widehat{x}_R^{(4,2)} = s_1(\widetilde{\lambda}_1) \oplus s_2(\widetilde{\lambda}_2) \oplus s_4(\widetilde{\theta}_4) \oplus s_2(\widetilde{\lambda}_5) \oplus s_4(\widetilde{\theta}_7) \oplus s_1(\widetilde{\lambda}_8) \oplus \theta^{(2,2)}$,

$$Count_{\{\widehat{x}_R^{(4,2)}\}}(\gamma) \in \{0,2,4\}, \text{ if } \widetilde{\lambda}_1 = \widetilde{\lambda}_8 \text{ or } \widetilde{\lambda}_2 = \widetilde{\lambda}_5. \tag{4}$$

$$Count_{\{\widehat{x}_R^{(5,2)}\}}(\gamma) \in \{0,2,4\}, \text{ if } \widetilde{\lambda}_1 = \widetilde{\lambda}_8 \text{ or } \widetilde{\lambda}_2 = \widetilde{\lambda}_5. \tag{5}$$

If $\tilde{\lambda}_2 = \tilde{\lambda}_5$, then we have

$$\tilde{\lambda}_2 = \tilde{\lambda}_5 \Leftrightarrow (\oplus_{j \in \{4,5,6\}} (s_\iota(\theta_3^{(i,j)}) \oplus \theta_1^{(i,j)})) \oplus k^{(4,2)} \oplus k^{(4,5)} = 0,$$

For $\tilde{\lambda}_1 = \tilde{\lambda}_8$, we have

$$\tilde{\lambda}_1 = \tilde{\lambda}_8 \Leftrightarrow \bigoplus_{j \in \{3,5,8\}} s_\iota(\theta_2^{(i,j)} \oplus k^{(2,j)}) \oplus \theta_1^{(i,j)}) \oplus k^{(4,1)} \oplus k^{(4,5)} = 0.$$

In five round Camellia-4, if we select plaintext set as $(\{P_L \| P_R\})_\iota = (\Theta \| \Lambda_0)_\iota$, in which if $\theta_0^{(i,4)}$ (or $\theta_0^{(i,5)}$, $\theta_0^{(i,6)}$) is different for different ι, then existing one ι makes $\tilde{\lambda}_2 = \tilde{\lambda}_5$ and if $\theta_0^{(i,3)}$ (or $\theta_0^{(i,5)}$, $\theta_0^{(i,8)}$) is different for different ι, then existing one ι makes $\tilde{\lambda}_1 = \tilde{\lambda}_8$.

Now, let us reconsider,

$$\hat{x}_R^{(4,2)} = s_1(\tilde{\lambda}_1) \oplus s_2(\tilde{\lambda}_2) \oplus s_4(\tilde{\theta}_4) \oplus s_2(\tilde{\lambda}_5) \oplus s_4(\tilde{\theta}_7) \oplus s_1(\tilde{\lambda}_8) \oplus \theta^{(2,2)},$$

If we have $\tilde{\lambda}_1 = \tilde{\lambda}_2 \wedge \tilde{\lambda}_5 = \tilde{\lambda}_8$ or $\tilde{\lambda}_1 = \tilde{\lambda}_5 \wedge \tilde{\lambda}_2 = \tilde{\lambda}_8$, then we have

$$Count_{\{\hat{x}_R^{(4,2)}\}}(\gamma) \in \{0, 2, 4, 6, 8, \ldots\},$$
$$Count_{\{\hat{x}_R^{(5,2)}\}}(\gamma) \in \{0, 2, 4, 6, 8, \ldots\}.$$

Similarly, when the Λ-set Λ_0 is selected as $\{\theta_0^{(0,1)}, \lambda_0^{(0,2)}, \theta_0^{(0,3)}, \ldots, \theta_0^{(0,8)}\}$, $\{\theta_0^{(0,1)}, \theta_0^{(0,2)}, \lambda_0^{(0,3)}, \theta_0^{(0,4)}, \ldots, \theta_0^{(0,8)}\}$ or $\{\theta_0^{(0,1)}, \theta_0^{(0,2)}, \theta_0^{(0,3)}, \lambda_0^{(0,4)}, \theta_0^{(0,5)}, \ldots, \theta_0^{(0,8)}\}$, we can get similar properties, these properties are summarized in Table 2.

4   The Square Like Attack

In this section, we construct the attacks on Camellia without pre-, post- whitening and FL/FL^{-1} functions.

The 6-round Square like attack uses the property of that, in Camellia-4 if the 1st byte of $\{P_R\}$ is active byte and $(\tilde{\lambda}_1 = \tilde{\lambda}_5)$ then, $Count_{\{\hat{x}_R^{(5,8)}\}}(\gamma) \in \{0, 2\}$. This attack can be described by the following steps.

Step1. Select 256 Λ-set $\Lambda_\iota = \{\lambda_\iota^{(i,1)}, \theta_\iota^{(i,2)}, \ldots, \theta_\iota^{(i,8)}\}$, $\iota \in [0..255]$, in which $\lambda_\iota^{(i,1)} = \lambda_{\iota'}^{(i,1)}$, $\theta_\iota^{(i,j)} = \theta_{\iota'}^{(i,j)}$, $j \in \{2,3,5,6,7,8\}$ and $\theta_\iota^{(i,4)} \neq \theta_{\iota'}^{(i,4)}, \forall \iota \neq \iota'$, and a Θ-set Θ. The 256 Plaintext sets are $(\{P_L \| P_R\})_\iota = (\Theta \| \Lambda_\iota)$. Then get the ciphertext sets $(\{C_L \| C_R\})_\iota$ and record them.

Step 2. For each $(\{C_L \| C_R\})_\iota$, Guess $k^{(6,8)}$, then check $Count_{\{x_R^{(5,8)}\}}(\gamma) \in \{0, 2\}$ being satisfied or not by Eq(6).

$$\hat{x}_R^{(5,8)} = s_1(\hat{x}_R^{(6,8)} \oplus k^{(5,8)}) \tag{6}$$

In this 6-round attack, the time that step 1 takes is 2^{16} 6-round encryptions takeing. Since Eq.(6) has 1 additions, 1 substitutions, getting $\hat{x}_R^{(6)}$ from C_R takes 5 addition, and 6-round Camellia has 44×6 additions, 8×6 substitutions, then the time of each guessing key in step 2 takes almost $\frac{1}{48}$ times 6 round encryption.

Table 2. Relation between active byte and special properties on its fifth round outputs, in which $\{P_L\} = \{\theta^{(i,1)}, \ldots, \theta^{(i,8)}\}$

Plaintext $-$ set $\{P_R\}$	Byte	Set	Condition
		$Count_{\{Byte\}}(\gamma) \in$ **Set if (Condition)**	
$\{\lambda^{(i,1)}, \theta^{(i,2)}, \ldots, \theta^{(i,8)}\}$	$\widehat{x}_R^{(5,8)}$	$\{0,2\}$	$\tilde{\lambda}_1 = \tilde{\lambda}_5$
		$\{0,2,4\}$	$\tilde{\lambda}_1 = \tilde{\lambda}_8 \vee \tilde{\lambda}_2 = \tilde{\lambda}_5$
	$\widehat{x}_R^{(5,2)}$	$\{0,2,4,6,\ldots\}$	$(\tilde{\lambda}_1 = \tilde{\lambda}_2 \wedge \tilde{\lambda}_5 = \tilde{\lambda}_8)$ or $(\tilde{\lambda}_1 = \tilde{\lambda}_5 \wedge \tilde{\lambda}_2 = \tilde{\lambda}_8)$
	$\widehat{x}_R^{(5,4)}$	$\{1\}$	$\tilde{\lambda}_2 = \tilde{\lambda}_5$
	$\widehat{x}_R^{(5,5)}$	$\{1\}$	$\tilde{\lambda}_1 = \tilde{\lambda}_8$
$\{\theta^{(i,1)}, \lambda^{(i,2)}, \theta^{(i,3)}, \ldots, \theta^{(i,8)}\}$	$\widehat{x}_R^{(5,5)}$	$\{0,4\}$	$\tilde{\lambda}_2 = \tilde{\lambda}_3$
		$\{0,2,4\}$	$\tilde{\lambda}_2 = \tilde{\lambda}_5 \vee \tilde{\lambda}_3 = \tilde{\lambda}_6$
	$\widehat{x}_R^{(5,2)}$	$\{0,2,4,6,\ldots\}$	$(\tilde{\lambda}_2 = \tilde{\lambda}_3 \wedge \tilde{\lambda}_5 = \tilde{\lambda}_6)$ or $(\tilde{\lambda}_2 = \tilde{\lambda}_6 \wedge \tilde{\lambda}_3 = \tilde{\lambda}_5)$
	$\widehat{x}_R^{(5,1)}$	$\{1\}$	$\tilde{\lambda}_3 = \tilde{\lambda}_6$
	$\widehat{x}_R^{(5,6)}$	$\{1\}$	$\tilde{\lambda}_2 = \tilde{\lambda}_5$
$\{\theta^{(i,1)}, \theta^{(i,2)}, \lambda^{(i,3)}, \theta^{(i,4)}, \ldots, \theta^{(i,8)}\}$		Pseudo Random Function	
		$\{0,2,4\}$	$\tilde{\lambda}_3 = \tilde{\lambda}_6 \vee \tilde{\lambda}_4 = \tilde{\lambda}_7$
	$\widehat{x}_R^{(5,2)}$	$\{0,2,4,6,\ldots\}$	$(\tilde{\lambda}_3 = \tilde{\lambda}_4 \wedge \tilde{\lambda}_6 = \tilde{\lambda}_7)$ or $(\tilde{\lambda}_3 = \tilde{\lambda}_7 \wedge \tilde{\lambda}_4 = \tilde{\lambda}_6)$
	$\widehat{x}_R^{(5,2)}$	$\{1\}$	$\tilde{\lambda}_4 = \tilde{\lambda}_7$
	$\widehat{x}_R^{(5,7)}$	$\{1\}$	$\tilde{\lambda}_3 = \tilde{\lambda}_6$
$\{\theta^{(i,1)}, \ldots, \theta^{(i,3)}, \lambda^{(i,4)}, \theta^{(i,5)}, \ldots, \theta^{(i,8)}\}$		Pseudo Random Function	
		$\{0,2,4\}$	$\tilde{\lambda}_4 = \tilde{\lambda}_7 \vee \tilde{\lambda}_1 = \tilde{\lambda}_8$
	$\widehat{x}_R^{(5,2)}$	$\{0,2,4,6,\ldots\}$	$(\tilde{\lambda}_1 = \tilde{\lambda}_4 \wedge \tilde{\lambda}_7 = \tilde{\lambda}_8)$ or $(\tilde{\lambda}_1 = \tilde{\lambda}_7 \wedge \tilde{\lambda}_4 = \tilde{\lambda}_8)$
	$\widehat{x}_R^{(5,3)}$	$\{1\}$	$\tilde{\lambda}_1 = \tilde{\lambda}_8$
	$\widehat{x}_R^{(5,8)}$	$\{1\}$	$\tilde{\lambda}_4 = \tilde{\lambda}_7$

In step 2, Eq.(6) repeats 2^8 times for 2^8 guessed key. The probability of wrong key passing the checking is $2^8 \times \binom{256}{128} \times \binom{256}{2} \times \binom{254}{2} \times \ldots \times \binom{2}{2} \times (128!)^{-1} \times$
$128! \times 256^{-256} = 2^8 \times \frac{256!256!}{2^{128} 256^{256} 128!128!} \approx \frac{2^8 2\pi 256256^{256} 256^{256} e^{128} e^{128}}{2^{128} 2\pi 128 e^{256} e^{256} 256^{256} 128^{128} 128^{128}} =$
$2^{-119}(\frac{2}{e})^{256}$, so only right key can pass step 2, then the 6-round attack's complexity is $2^{16}(1 + 2^8 \times \frac{1}{48}) \approx 2^{18.4}$. The selected Plaintexts are 2^{16}.

7-round attack adds one round at the beginning, uses the structure of Camellia-3 and selects the input sets to make $(\{\widetilde{x}_L^{(1)} \| \widetilde{x}_R^{(1)}\})_\iota = (\Theta \| \Lambda_\iota)$. The selected 256 plaintext sets are

$$(\{P_L\})_\iota = \Lambda_\iota = \{\lambda_\iota^{(i,1)}, \theta_\iota^{(i,2)}, \ldots, \theta_\iota^{(i,8)}\},$$
$$(\{P_R\})_\iota = \{P^{-1}(s_1(\lambda_\iota^{(i,1)} \oplus k^{(1,1)}), \theta_\iota^{(i,2)}, \theta_\iota^{(i,3)}, s_4(\theta_\iota^{(i,4)} \oplus k^{(1,4)}), \theta_\iota^{(i,5)}, \ldots, \theta_\iota^{(i,8)})\}.$$

We have $\{\widetilde{x}_R^{(0)}\}_i = \{s_1(\lambda_\iota^{(i,1)} \oplus k^{(1,1)}), \theta_\iota^{(i,2)}, \theta_\iota^{(i,3)}, s_4(\theta_\iota^{(i,4)} \oplus k^{(1,4)}), \theta_\iota^{(i,5)}, \ldots,$
$\theta_\iota^{(i,8)}\}_\iota$. Then, $k^{(1,1)}$, $k^{(1,4)}$ and $k^{(7,8)}$ are guessing key bytes.

This 7-round attack selects 2^{32} plaintext and the attacking complexity is $2^{16} \times 2^{16}(1 + 2^8 \times \frac{1}{56}) \approx 2^{34.5}$. The chosen plaintext are 2^{32}.

The 8-round attack is similar to 7-round attack, just adds one round at the end and guesses the 8th round key bytes to get the $\tilde{x}_R^{(7,8)}$. Getting $\tilde{x}_R^{(7,8)}$ from $\tilde{x}_R^{(8)}$ needs five 8th round key bytes $k^{(8,1)}, k^{(8,4)}, k^{(8,5)}, k^{(8,6)}, k^{(8,7)}$ and needs 11 addition and 6 S-box transformation, which equals 1/8 8-round encryption. Then, the complexity of this attack is $2^{32} \times (1 + 2^{40} \times (\frac{1}{8} + 2^8 \times \frac{1}{64})) \approx 2^{74}$. The chosen plaintexts are 2^{32}.

In 9-round attack, we add one round at the beginning and use the structure of Camellia-4, where the selected special plaintexts should satisfy the properties of that $(\{\hat{x}_L^{(2)} \| \hat{x}_R^{(2)}\})_\iota = (\Theta \| \Lambda_\iota)$. So the plaintext are,

$$
\left\{\begin{array}{c} P_L^{(1)} \\ P_L^{(2)} \\ P_L^{(3)} \\ P_L^{(4)} \\ P_L^{(5)} \\ P_L^{(6)} \\ P_L^{(7)} \\ P_L^{(8)} \end{array}\right\}_\iota = \left\{\begin{array}{c} s_1(\lambda_\iota^{(i,1)} \oplus k^{(2,1)}) \oplus s_4(\theta_\iota^{(i,1)} \oplus k^{(2,4)}) \\ s_1(\lambda_\iota^{(i,1)} \oplus k^{(2,1)}) \oplus s_4(\theta_\iota^{(i,1)} \oplus k^{(2,4)}) \\ s_1(\lambda_\iota^{(i,1)} \oplus k^{(2,1)}) \\ s_4(\theta_\iota^{(i,4)} \oplus k^{(2,4)}) \\ s_1(\lambda_\iota^{(i,1)} \oplus k^{(2,1)}) \\ \theta_\iota^{(i,6)} \\ s_4(\theta_\iota^{(i,4)} \oplus k^{(2,4)}) \\ s_1(\lambda_\iota^{(i,1)} \oplus k^{(2,1)}) \oplus s_4(\theta_\iota^{(i,4)} \oplus k^{(2,4)}) \end{array}\right\}_\iota,
$$

$$
\left\{\begin{array}{c} P_R^{(1)} \\ P_R^{(2)} \\ P_R^{(3)} \\ P_R^{(4)} \\ P_R^{(5)} \\ P_R^{(6)} \\ P_R^{(7)} \\ P_R^{(8)} \end{array}\right\}_\iota = \left\{\begin{array}{c} s_1(s_1(\lambda_\iota^{(i,1)} \oplus k^{(2,1)}) \oplus s_4(\theta_\iota^{(i,4)} \oplus k^{(2,4)}) \oplus k^{(1,1)}) \\ s_2(s_1(\lambda_\iota^{(i,1)} \oplus k^{(2,1)}) \oplus s_4(\theta_\iota^{(i,4)} \oplus k^{(2,4)}) \oplus k^{(1,2)}) \\ s_3(s_1(\lambda_\iota^{(i,1)} \oplus k^{(2,1)}) \oplus k^{(1,3)}) \\ s_4(s_4(\theta_\iota^{(i,4)} \oplus k^{(2,4)}) \oplus k^{(1,4)}) \\ s_2(s_1(\lambda_\iota^{(i,1)} \oplus k^{(2,1)}) \oplus k^{(1,5)}) \\ \theta_\iota^{(i,6)} \\ s_4(s_4(\theta_\iota^{(i,4)} \oplus k^{(2,4)}) \oplus k^{(1,7)}) \\ s_1(s_1(\lambda_\iota^{(i,1)} \oplus k^{(2,1)}) \oplus s_4(\theta_\iota^{(i,4)} \oplus k^{(2,4)}) \oplus k^{(1,8)}) \end{array}\right\}_\iota,
$$

The complexity of this attack is $2^{88} \times (1 + 2^{40} \times (\frac{1}{9} + 2^8 \times \frac{1}{72})) \approx 2^{129.8}$.

In 128-Camellia, part of the 9th round key bits are included in $k^{(1)}$ and $k^{(2)}$. Then, in step 2, we check $Count_{\{x_R^{(7,4)}\}}(\gamma) = 1$ being hold or not, the guessing key bytes are $k^{(1,1)}, k^{(1,2)}, k^{(1,3)}, k^{(1,4)}, k^{(1,5)}, k^{(1,7)}, k^{(1,8)}, k^{(2,1)}, k^{(2,4)}, k^{(8,4)}, k^{(9,2)}, k^{(9,3)}, k^{(9,4)}, k^{(9,5)}, k^{(9,6)}, k^{(9,7)}$. The 28 bits of 9th round key are included in first and second rounds guessing. The complexity of this 9-round attack becomes $2^{88} \times (1 + 2^{12}(\frac{1}{8} + 2^8 \times \frac{1}{72})) \approx 2^{102.2}$. The chosen plaintexts are 2^{88}.

In 256-Camellia, the chosen plaintexts are same as attack on 128-Camellia. Since $k^{(7)} \| k^{(8)} = k^{(1)} \| k^{(2)}_{\lll 30}$, the complexity of 7-round attack becomes $2^{32} \times (1 + 1 \times \frac{1}{56}) \approx 2^{32}$, in which the guessing key bytes are $k^{(1,1)}, k^{(1,2)}, k^{(7,8)}$. Key bits of $k^{(7,8)}$ are included in key bits of $k^{(1,1)}$ and $k^{(1,2)}$.

In these basic attacks, we select 256 Λ-set Λ_ι that requires $\theta_\iota^{(i,4)} \neq \theta_{\iota'}^{(i,4)}$ to guarantee the existence of $\tilde{\lambda}_1 = \tilde{\lambda}_5$. However, to guarantee the Θ-set Θ is

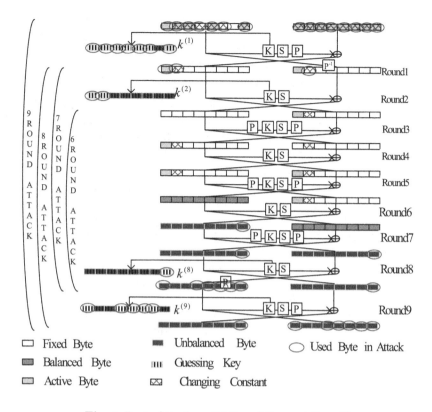

☐ Fixed Byte   ▰ Unbalanced Byte   ○ Used Byte in Attack

▨ Balanced Byte   ▥ Guessing Key

☐ Active Byte   ☒ Changing Constant

Fig. 4. Basic Attack on 6,7,8, and 9 round Camellia

unchanged, 7-round attack requires guessing 1 more key byte and 9-round attack requires guessing 3 more key bytes. In next section, we avert these key guessing.

5   Improvements on the Attack

5.1   Basic Improvement

In 6-round attack, if we select $\{P_L\}_\iota = \Theta_\iota$ and $\{P_R\}_\iota = \Lambda_\iota$, in which the first byte of Λ_ι is active byte and other bytes of Λ_ι and Θ_ι are random selected fixed bytes, then, for each Θ_ι and Λ_ι, the probability of $\widetilde{\lambda}_i = \widetilde{\lambda}_j, i \neq j$ is $\sum_{i=0}^{255} \frac{1}{256}\frac{1}{256} = \frac{1}{256}$. And the probability of non appearance of $\widetilde{\lambda}_i = \widetilde{\lambda}_j$ is $\frac{255}{256}$, for given $i,j \in \{1,\ldots,8\}$. And when the attacker selects t plaintext sets, the non appearance of $\widetilde{\lambda}_i = \widetilde{\lambda}_j$ is $(\frac{255}{256})^t$. We can improve the attack in following way.

Step1. Set $\iota = 1$.

Step2. Select a Λ-set Λ_ι and a Θ-set Θ_ι, in which $\lambda_\iota^{(i,1)}$ is a active byte and other bytes are random selected fixed bytes. Set the Plaintext sets as $\{P_L\|P_R\}_\iota = \Theta_\iota\|\Lambda_\iota$ and get the ciphertext sets as $\{C_L\|C_R\}_\iota$.

Step 3. Guess $k^{(6,8)}$, gets $\widehat{x}_R^{(5,8)}$ by Eq(6), checks $Count_{\{\widehat{x}_R^{(5,8)}\}}(\gamma) \in \{0,2\}$ being satisfied or not. If $Count_{\{\widehat{x}_R^{(5,8)}\}}(\gamma) > 2$ or $\#\{Count_{\{x_R^{(5,8)}\}}(\gamma) = 1\} > 128$, then selects a new key. If the exist a key $k^{(6,8)}$ pass the checking, then it is a correct key. Or else $\iota = \iota + 1$ and goto step 2.

In this 6-round attack, the time that step 2 takes is 2^8 6-round encryptions takeing. For each guessing key step 3 takes almost $\frac{1}{48}$ times 6 round encryption. In step 2, Eq.(6) repeats 2^8 times. The probability of wrong key passing the checking is $2^{-119}(\frac{2}{e})^{256} \approx 2^{-232}$, so only right key can pass step 2. And when $\iota = 2^{10}$, the probability appearance of $\widetilde{\lambda}_1 = \widetilde{\lambda}_5$ is 0.99. Then the 6-round attack's complexity is $2^{18}(1 + 2^8 \times \frac{1}{48}) \approx 2^{20.4}$. The selected Plaintexts are 2^{18}.

The 7,8,9-round 128-bit Camellia attacks use same structure as previous section. In 7-round attack, the guessing key bytes are $k^{(1,1)}$ and $k^{(7,8)}$. In 8-round attack, the guessing key bytes are $k^{(1,1)}$, $k^{(7,8)}$, $k^{(8,1)}$, $k^{(8,4)}$, $k^{(8,5)}$, $k^{(8,6)}$, $k^{(8,7)}$. In 9-round attack, the guessing key bytes are $k^{(1,1)}$, $k^{(1,2)}$, $k^{(1,3)}$, $k^{(1,5)}$, $k^{(1,8)}$, $k^{(2,1)}$, $k^{(8,8)}$, $k^{(9,1)}$, $k^{(9,4)}$, $k^{(9,5)}$, $k^{(9,6)}$, $k^{(9,7)}$, in which the 13 bits of 9th round key is included in 1st guess round key. The chosen plaintexts for 7,8 and 9 rounds are 2^{26}, 2^{26} and 2^{66}, respectively. The complexities are $2^{26} \times (1 + 2^8 \times \frac{1}{56}) = 2^{28.5}$, $2^{26} \times (1 + 2^{40}(\frac{1}{8} + 2^8 \times \frac{1}{64})) \approx 2^{68}$ and $2^{66} \times (1 + 2^{27}(\frac{1}{9} + 2^8 \times \frac{1}{72})) \approx 2^{94.9}$, respectively.

In 9-round attack, if we select the ciphertext similar as previous discussion on plaintext and check the $Count_{\{\widehat{x}_R^{(2,5)}\}}(\gamma) = 1$ being satisfied or not, then the guessing round key bytes are $k^{(9,1)}$, $k^{(9,2)}$, $k^{(9,4)}$, $k^{(9,7)}$, $k^{(9,8)}$, $k^{(8,4)}$, $k^{(2,5)}$, $k^{(1,1)}$, $k^{(1,2)}$, $k^{(1,6)}$, $k^{(1,7)}$, $k^{(1,8)}$. Then, the complexity of attack becomes $2^{66} \times (1 + 2^{21}(\frac{1}{9} + 2^3 \times \frac{1}{72})) \approx 2^{84.8}$.

5.2   Improvement on 256-Bit Camellia

In 7,8,9 and 10-round attacks on 256-Camellia the chosen plaintext are same as above section. However, the 7th round key is same as first round key and 8th round key is same as 2nd round key, then in 7-round attack, the guessing round key bytes are $k^{(1,1)}$ and $k^{(7,5)}$, in which 6 bits of $k^{(7,5)}$ are included in $k^{(1,1)}$. In 8-round attack, the guessing round key bytes are $k^{(1,1)}$, $k^{(7,5)}$, $k^{(8,1)}$, $k^{(8,2)}$, $k^{(8,6)}$, $k^{(8,7)}$, and $k^{(8,8)}$. In 9-round attack, the guessing round key bytes are $k^{(1,1)}$, $k^{(1,2)}$, $k^{(1,3)}$, $k^{(1,5)}$, $k^{(1,8)}$, $k^{(2,1)}$, $k^{(8,5)}$, $k^{(9,1)}$, $k^{(9,2)}$, $k^{(9,6)}$, $k^{(9,7)}$, and $k^{(9,8)}$. In 10-round attack, the guessing round key bytes are $k^{(1,1)}$, $k^{(1,2)}$, $k^{(1,3)}$, $k^{(1,5)}$, $k^{(1,8)}$, $k^{(2,1)}$, $k^{(8,5)}$, $k^{(9,1)}$, $k^{(9,2)}$, $k^{(9,6)}$, $k^{(9,7)}$, $k^{(9,8)}$ and $k^{(10)}$. Since 6 bits of $k^{(8,5)}$ are included in $k^{(2,1)}$, the selected plaintext for 7,8,9 and 10-round attacks are 2^{26}, 2^{26}, 2^{66} and 2^{66}, respectively. The complexities are $2^{26} \times (1 + 2^2 \times \frac{1}{56}) \approx 2^{26}$, $2^{26} \times (1 + 2^{40} \times (\frac{1}{8} + 2^2 \times \frac{1}{64})) \approx 2^{63}$, $2^{66} \times (1 + 2^{40} \times (\frac{1}{9} + 2^2 \times \frac{1}{72})) \approx 2^{103.4}$ and $2^{66} \times (1 + 2^{64} \times (\frac{1}{10} + (2^{40} \times (\frac{1}{10} + 2^2 \times \frac{1}{80})))) \approx 2^{167.3}$, respectively.

In 11-round attack, we add one round at the end of 10-round and check the output $x_R^{(7,8)}$. Then the attacking key bytes are $k^{(1,1)}$, $k^{(1,2)}$, $k^{(1,3)}$, $k^{(1,5)}$, $k^{(1,8)}$, $k^{(2,1)}$, $k^{(8,8)}$, $k^{(9,1)}$, $k^{(9,4)}$, $k^{(9,5)}$, $k^{(9,6)}$, $k^{(9,7)}$, $k^{(10)}$ and $k^{(11)}$.

In key schedule of Camellia, if k_B is given, then $k_A \oplus k_R$ can be gotten by direct computation. So if k_B and $(k_R)_L$ are given, then $(k_A)_L$ is known and if k_B

Table 3. The Summary of known attacks on Camellia

Round	$FL/$ FL^{-1}	Method	Data	Time 128-bit	Time 256-bit	Notes
6	N/Y	SLA	2^{18}	$2^{20.4}$	$2^{20.4}$	This Paper
6	N/Y	SA	$2^{11.7}$	2^{112}	2^{112}	[5]
8	No	TDC	$2^{83.6}$	$2^{55.6}$	2^{63}	[8]
8	No	SLA	2^{26}	2^{68}	2^{63}	This Paper
8	Yes	ISA	2^{48}	2^{98}	2^{82}	[10]
8	Yes	SA	2^{48}	—	2^{116}	[17]
9	No	SLA	2^{66}	$2^{84.8}$	$2^{103.4}$	This Paper
9	No	VSA	2^{88}	2^{90}	2^{122}	[10]
9	No	DC	2^{105}	2^{105}	2^{105}	[13]
9	No	CA	$2^{113.6}$	2^{121}	$2^{175.6}$	[15]
9	Yes	ISA	2^{48}	2^{122}	2^{146}	[10]
9	No	BA	$2^{123.9}$	—	$2^{169.9}$	[10]
9	No	HODC	2^{21}	—	2^{188}	[4]
9	Yes	SA	$2^{60.5}$	—	2^{202}	[17]
10	No	LA	2^{120}	2^{121}	2^{121}	[13]
10	No	DC	2^{105}	—	$2^{165.7}$	[13]
10	No	SLA	2^{66}	—	$2^{167.3}$	This Paper
10	No	ICA	2^{14}	—	$2^{207.4}$	[10]
10	Yes	ISA	2^{48}	—	2^{210}	[10]
10	No	CA	2^{14}	—	$2^{239.9}$	[15]
10	No	RA	$2^{126.5}$	—	$2^{240.9}$	[15]
10	No	HODC	2^{21}	—	$2^{254.7}$	[4]
11	No	LA	2^{120}	—	$2^{181.5}$	[13]
11	No	SLA	2^{66}	—	$2^{211.6}$	This Paper
11	No	DC	2^{105}	—	$2^{231.5}$	[13]
11	No	VSA	2^{88}	—	2^{250}	[10]
11	N/Y	HODC	2^{93}	—	$2^{255.6}$	[4]
12	No	IPDC	2^{120}	—	2^{181}	[16]
12	No	LA	2^{120}	—	$2^{245.4}$	[13]
12	No	SLA	2^{66}	—	$2^{249.6}$	This Paper

Note 1. BA: Boomerang Attack; CA: Collision Attack; DC: Differential Attack; HODC: High Order Differential Attack; ICA: Improved Collision Attack; IPDC: Impossible Differential Attack; LA: Linear Attack; RA: Rectangle Attack; SA: Square Attack; TDC: Truncated Differential Attack; VSA: Variant Square Attack;

and $(k_R)_R$ are given, then $(k_A)_R$ is known. In 192-and 256-Camellia, the third round key is $(k_R)_L$ and the 11th round key is $(k_A)_L$. The first two round keys are $(k_B)_L$ and $(k_B)_R$.

To improve the attack, we use chosen ciphertext attack, in which we select the ciphertext set $\{C_L \| C_R\}_\iota$ same as the plaintext $\{P_L \| P_R\}_\iota$ in 11-round chosen plaintext attack. Then, the attacking key bytes become $k^{(11,1)}$, $k^{(11,2)}$, $k^{(11,3)}$, $k^{(11,5)}$, $k^{(11,8)}$, $k^{(10,1)}$, $k^{(4,8)}$, $k^{(3,1)}$, $k^{(3,4)}$, $k^{(3,5)}$, $k^{(3,6)}$, $k^{(3,7)}$, $k^{(2)}$ and $k^{(1)}$. From $k^{(2)}$, $k^{(1)}$,

$k^{(11)}$ and k^{12}, we can get $k^{(3)}$ and $k^{(4)}$. In fact, 24 bits of $k^{(3,1)}$, $k^{(3,4)}$, $k^{(3,5)}$, $k^{(3,6)}$, $k^{(3,7)}$ can be get from $k^{(2)}$,$k^{(1)}$ and key bytes $k^{(11,1)}$, $k^{(11,2)}$, $k^{(11,3)}$,$k^{(11,5)}$ and $k^{(11,8)}$. Then the chosen ciphertext in 11-round attack is 2^{66} and the complexity is $2^{66} \times (1 + 2^{64} \times (\frac{1}{11} + 2^{64} \times (\frac{1}{11} + 2^{16} \times (\frac{1}{11} + 2^8 \times \frac{1}{88})))) \approx 2^{211.6}$.

12-round attack adds one round at the beginning of 11-round selected plaintext attack and uses select ciphertext attack. So the selected ciphertext is same as 11-round chosen ciphertext attack and the guessing key bytes are $k^{(12,1)}$,$k^{(12,2)}$, $k^{(12,3)}$, $k^{(12,5)}$,$k^{(12,8)}$, $k^{(11,1)}$,$k^{(5,8)}$, $k^{(4,1)}$, $k^{(4,4)}$, $k^{(4,5)}$,$k^{(4,6)}$, $k^{(4,7)}$,$k^{(3)}$, $k^{(2)}$ and $k^{(1)}$. The $k^{(5)}$ is same as part of $k^{(11)}$ and k^{12}. From $k^{(2)}$, $k^{(1)}$, $k^{(12,1)}$,$k^{(12,2)}$, $k^{(12,3)}$, $k^{(12,5)}$,$k^{(12,8)}$ and $k(11,1)$, we can get 46 bits of $k^{(4,1)}$, $k^{(4,4)}$, $k^{(4,5)}$,$k^{(4,6)}$, $k^{(4,7)}$ and $k^{(3)}$. $k^{(5)}$ can be get from $k^{(1)}$,$k^{(2)}$ and $k^{(3)}$. Then, the 12-round attack requires 2^{66} ciphertext and the complexity is $2^{66} \times (1 + 2^{64} \times (\frac{1}{12} + 2^{64} \times (\frac{1}{12} + 2^{43} \times (\frac{1}{12} + 2^{16} \times (\frac{1}{12} + 1 \times \frac{1}{96}))))) \approx 2^{249.6}$.

5.3   The Influences of FL/FL^{-1} Function

If FL/FL^{-1} layer is included, the properties of XORing of sBoxes can not pass the FL/FL^{-1} layer, so the attack is possible only by adding the rounds at the end of 6-round basic attack and guessing more key bytes of FL/FL^{-1} layer. Then the attack is only possible for 7-round 128-Camellia and 9-round 256-Camellia.

6   Conclusions

The Square like attack is possible for the XORing of active Sboxes has some special properties. The rotation of key schedule of Camellia influence the security of Camellia. Table.3 gives a summary of known attacks on Camellia.

Acknowledgments

The work is supported in part by NSFC 60573028 and by NUDT FBR JC07-02-02. We thank the anonymous reviewers for their very helpful comments.

References

1. Aoki, K., Ichikawa, T., Kanda, M., et al.: Camellia: A 128-Bit block cipher suitable for multiple platforms-design and analysis. In: Ito, T., Abadi, M. (eds.) TACS 1997. LNCS, vol. 1281, pp. 39–56. Springer, Heidelberg (1997)
2. Daemen, J., Knudsen, L.R., Rijmen, V.: The block cipher SQUARE. In: Biham, E. (ed.) FSE 1997. LNCS, vol. 1267, pp. 149–165. Springer, Heidelberg (1997)
3. Daemen, J., Rijmen, V.: The Design of Rijndael, AES - The Advanced Encryption Standard. Springer, Heidelberg (2002)
4. Hatano, Y., Sekine, H., Kaneko, T.: Higher order differential attack of Camellia (II). In: Nyberg, K., Heys, H.M. (eds.) SAC 2002. LNCS, vol. 2595, Springer, Heidelberg (2003)

5. He, Y., Qing, S.: Square attack on reduced Camellia cipher. In: Qing, S., Okamoto, T., Zhou, J. (eds.) ICICS 2001. LNCS, vol. 2229, pp. 238–245. Springer, Heidelberg (2001)

6. Kanda, M., Matsumoto, T.: Security of Camellia against truncated differential cryptanalysis. In: Matsui, M. (ed.) FSE 2001. LNCS, vol. 2355, Springer, Heidelberg (2002)

7. Kawabata, T., Kaneko, T.: A study on higher order differential attack of Camellia.: The 2nd open NESSIE workshop (2001)

8. Lee, S., Hong, S., Lee, S., Lim, J., Yoon, S.: Truncated differential cryptanalysis of Camellia. In: Kim, K.-c. (ed.) ICISC 2001. LNCS, vol. 2288, pp. 32–38. Springer, Heidelberg (2002)

9. Ledig, H., Muller, F., Valette, F.: Enhancing collision attacks. In: Joye, M., Quisquater, J.-J. (eds.) CHES 2004. LNCS, vol. 3156, Springer, Heidelberg (2004)

10. Lei, D., Chao, L., Feng, K.: New observation on Camellia. In: Preneel, B., Tavares, S. (eds.) SAC 2005. LNCS, vol. 3897, pp. 51–64. Springer, Heidelberg (2006)

11. NTT Information Sharing Platform Laboratories: Internationally standardized encryption algorithm form Japan "Camellia", avaliable at http://info.isl.ntt.co.jp/crypt/camellia/dl/Camellia20061108v4_eng.pdf

12. Shirai, T., Kanamaru, S., Abe, G.: Improved upper bounds of differential and linear characteristic probability for Camellia. In: Daemen, J., Rijmen, V. (eds.) FSE 2002. LNCS, vol. 2365, Springer, Heidelberg (2002)

13. Shirai, T.: Differential, linear, boomerang and rectangle cryptanalysis of reduced-round Camellia. In: Proceedings of 3rd NESSIE workshop (November 2002)

14. Sugita, M., Kobara, K., Imai, H.: Security of reduced version of the block cipher Camellia against truncated and impossible differential cryptanalysis. In: Boyd, C. (ed.) ASIACRYPT 2001. LNCS, vol. 2248, pp. 193–207. Springer, Heidelberg (2001)

15. Wu, W., Feng, D., Chen, H.: Collision attack and pseudorandomness of reduced-round Camellia. In: Handschuh, H., Hasan, M.A. (eds.) SAC 2004. LNCS, vol. 3357, pp. 256–270. Springer, Heidelberg (2004)

16. Wu, W., Zhang, W., Feng, D.: Impossible differential cryptanalyssi of ARIA and Camellia, JCST

17. Yeom, Y., Park, S., Kim, I.: On the security of Camellia against the Square attack. In: Daemen, J., Rijmen, V. (eds.) FSE 2002. LNCS, vol. 2365, pp. 89–99. Springer, Heidelberg (2002)

Differential Fault Analysis on CLEFIA

Hua Chen, Wenling Wu, and Dengguo Feng

State Key Laboratory of Information Security, Institute of Software,
Chinese Academy of Sciences, Beijing 100080, P.R. China
{chenhua,wwl,feng}@is.iscas.ac.cn

Abstract. CLEFIA is a new 128-bit block cipher proposed by SONY corporation recently. The fundamental structure of CLEFIA is a generalized Feistel structure consisting of 4 data lines. In this paper, the strength of CLEFIA against the differential fault attack is explored. Our attack adopts the byte-oriented model of random faults. Through inducing randomly one byte fault in one round, four bytes of faults can be simultaneously obtained in the next round, which can efficiently reduce the total induce times in the attack. After attacking the last several rounds' encryptions, the original secret key can be recovered based on some analysis of the key schedule. The data complexity analysis and experiments show that only about 18 faulty ciphertexts are needed to recover the entire 128-bit secret key and about 54 faulty ciphertexts for 192/256-bit keys.

Keywords: Block Cipher, Generalized Feistel Structure, Differential Fault Attack.

1 Introduction

The idea of fault attack was first suggested in 1997 by Boneh, DeMillo and Lipton[1], which makes use of the faults during the execution of a cryptographic algorithm. Under the idea, the attack was successfully exploited to break an RSA CRT with both a correct and a faulty signature of the same message. Shortly after, Biham and Shamir proposed an attack on secret key cryptosystems called Differential Fault Analysis (DFA)[2], which combined the ideas of fault attack and differential attack. Since the presentation of DFA, many research papers have been published on using this cryptanalysis technique to successfully attack various cryptosystems, including ECC, 3DES, AES, RC4, and so on[3][4][5][6][7][8][9][10][11].

The block cipher CLEFIA was proposed by SONY corporation recently[12]. It is a 128-bit block cipher which supports 128-bit, 192-bit and 256-bit keys. The fundamental structure of CLEFIA is a generalized Feistel structure consisting of 4 data lines. There are two 32-bit F-functions per one round, which respectively use two different S-boxes and two different diffusion matrices. The key scheduling part shares the generalized Feistel structure with the data processing part.

S. Qing, H. Imai, and G. Wang (Eds.): ICICS 2007, LNCS 4861, pp. 284–295, 2007.

The number of rounds is 18, 22, and 26 for 128-bit, 192-bit, and 256-bit keys, respectively.

In [12], the strength of CLEFIA against some well-known attacks were examined by the designers, including differential cryptanalysis, linear cryptanalysis, impossible differential cryptanalysis, related-key cryptanalysis and so on. However, the differential fault attack was not mentioned.

In this paper, an efficient differential fault attack against CLEFIA is presented. The attack adopts the byte-oriented model of random faults. In the attack, four bytes of faults can be simultaneously obtained in one round by inducing randomly one byte fault in the last round, which can efficiently reduce the total induce times. After obtaining the subkeys in the last several rounds, and through some analysis of the key schedule, the whole secret key can be determined with only 18 faulty ciphertexts on average for 128-bit key and 54 faulty ciphertexts on average for 192 or 256-bit key. The experimental results also verify the facts.

This paper is organized as follows. In Section 2, the basic description of CLEFIA is presented. Then the basic idea of our attack is given in Section 3. Section 4 provides the detailed attacking procedure for different key sizes, the data complexity analysis of our attack and the experimental results through the computer simulation. Finally, the conclusion remarks are presented in section 5.

2   Description of CLEFIA

In this section, the basic description of CLEFIA is presented. Due to the page limitation, only $GFN_{d,r}$, F-functions, encryption function and key scheduling are introduced. The lacking of introducing the other parts of CLEFIA will not affect the description of our attack.

In the following description of CLEFIA, let a_b represent the bit length of a is b, | represent concatenation and $^t a$ represent the transposition of a vector a.

Description of $GFN_{d,r}$. CLEFIA uses a 4-branch and an 8-branch Type-2 generalized Feistel network[13]. Denote d-branch r-round generalized Feistel network as $GFN_{d,r}$. In CLEFIA, $GFN_{d,r}$ employs two different 32-bit F-functions F_0 and F_1 whose input/output are defined as follows.

$$F_0, F_1 = \begin{cases} \{0,1\}^{32}, \{0,1\}^{32} \to \{0,1\}^{32} \\ RK_{(32)}, x_{(32)} \mapsto y_{(32)} \end{cases}$$

For d 32-bit input X_i and output Y_i $(0 \leq i < d)$, and $dr/2$ 32-bit round keys RK_i $(0 \leq i < dr/2)$, $GFN_{d,r}(d = 4, 8)$ are defined as follows.

$$GFN_{4,r} = \begin{cases} \{\{0,1\}^{32}\}^{2r}, \{\{0,1\}^{32}\}^4 \to \{\{0,1\}^{32}\}^4 \\ RK_{0(32)}, ..., RK_{2r-1(32)}, x_{0(32)}, ..., x_{3(32)} \mapsto y_{0(32)}, ..., y_{3(32)} \end{cases}$$

$$GFN_{8,r} = \begin{cases} \{\{0,1\}^{32}\}^{4r}, \{\{0,1\}^{32}\}^8 \to \{\{0,1\}^{32}\}^8 \\ RK_{0(32)}, ..., RK_{4r-1(32)}, x_{0(32)}, ..., x_{7(32)} \mapsto y_{0(32)}, ..., y_{7(32)} \end{cases}$$

The detailed description of $GFN_{4,r}$ is as follows.

Step 1. $T_0|T_1|T_2|T_3 \leftarrow X_0|X_1|X_2|X_3$
Step 2. For $i = 0$ to $r - 1$ do the following:
   Step 2.1 $T_1 = T_1 \oplus F_0(RK_{2i}, T_0)$, $T_3 = T_3 \oplus F_1(RK_{2i+1}, T_2)$
   Step 2.2 $T_0|T_1|T_2|T_3 \leftarrow T_1|T_2|T_3|T_0$
Step 3. $Y_0|Y_1|Y_2|Y_3 \leftarrow T_3|T_0|T_1|T_2$

The description of $GFN_{8,r}$ is similar to $GFN_{4,r}$, and not introduced here.

The inverse function $GFN_{d,r}^{-1}$ are realized by changing the order of RK_i and the direction of word rotation at Step 2.2 and Step 3 of $GFN_{4,r}$.

F-Functions. F-functions $F_0 : (RK_{(32)}, x_{(32)}) \mapsto y_{(32)}$ can be described as follows:

Step 1. $T \leftarrow RK \oplus x$
Step 2. Let $T \leftarrow T_0|T_1|T_2|T_3$, $T_i \in \{0,1\}^8$
   $T_0 = S_0(T_0)$, $T_1 = S_1(T_1)$
   $T_2 = S_0(T_2)$, $T_3 = S_1(T_3)$
Step 3. Let $y \leftarrow y_0|y_1|y_2|y_3$, $y_i \in \{0,1\}^8$
   $^t(y_0, y_1, y_2, y_3) = M_0 \,^t(T_0, T_1, T_2, T_3)$

F_0 uses two different 8×8 S-boxes S_0 and S_1. S_0 is constructed by combining 4×4 small S-boxes. S_1 is constructed with the inverse transform plus affine operation in finite field. The diffusion matrix M_0 is a 4×4 Hadamard-type matrix. Figure 1 depicts the F-function F_0.

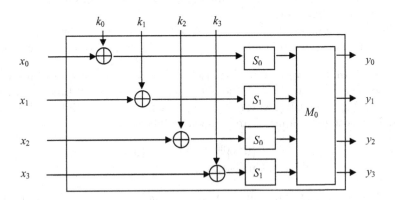

Fig. 1. *F-function F_0*

$F_1 : (RK_{(32)}, x_{(32)}) \rightarrow y_{(32)}$ is similar to F_0 except that, the order of S-boxes is S_1, S_0, S_1, S_0 and M_0 is substituted by M_1. M_1 is also a 4×4 Hadamard-type matrix.

For both M_0 and M_1, the multiplications between matrices and vectors are performed in $GF(2^8)$ defined by the lexicographically first primitive polynomial

$z^8 + z^4 + z^3 + z^2 + 1$. M_0^{-1} and M_1^{-1} respectively represents the inverse matrix of M_0 and M_1.

2.1   Encryption Function

The encryption function of CLEFIA is denoted as ENC_r. Let $P, C \in \{0,1\}^{128}$ be a plaintext and a ciphertext, which can be divided into $P = P_0|P_1|P_2|P_3$ and $C = C_0|C_1|C_2|C_3$, $P_i, C_i \in \{0,1\}^{32}, 0 \le i \le 3$. Let $WK_0, WK_1, WK_2, WK_3 \in \{0,1\}^{32}$ be whitening keys and $RK_i \in \{0,1\}^{32} (0 \le i < 2r)$ be round keys provided by the key scheduling. Then, r round encryption function ENC_r can be described as follows.

$$ENC_r : \begin{cases} \{\{0,1\}^{32}\}^4, \{\{0,1\}^{32}\}^{2r}, \{\{0,1\}^{32}\}^4 \to \{\{0,1\}^{32}\}^4 \\ WK_{0(32)}, ..., WK_{3(32)}, RK_{0(32)}, ..., RK_{2r-1(32)}, P_{0(32)}, ..., P_{3(32)} \\ \mapsto C_{0(32)}, ..., C_{3(32)} \end{cases}$$

The detailed description is as follows.

Step 1. $T_0|T_1|T_2|T_3 \leftarrow P_0|(P_1 \oplus WK_0)|P_2|(P_3 \oplus WK_1)$
Step 2. $T_0|T_1|T_2|T_3 \leftarrow GFN_{4,r}(RK_0, ..., RK_{2r-1}, T_0, ..., T_3)$
Step 3. $C_0|C_1|C_2|C_3 \leftarrow T_0|(T_1 \oplus WK_2)|T_2|(T_3 \oplus WK_3)$

Figure 2 depicts the encryption function ENC_r.

2.2   Key Scheduling

The key scheduling generates whitening keys $WK_i(0 \le i < 4)$, and round keys $RK_j(0 \le j < 2r)$.

Let K be a k-bit key, where k is 128, 192 or 256. The key scheduling is divided into the following two sub-parts.

(1) Generating an intermediate key L from K.
(2) Expanding K and L to generate WK_i and RK_j.

The key scheduling is explained according to the sub-parts.

For the 128-bit key scheduling, the 128-bit intermediate key L is generated by applying $GFN_{4,12}$ which takes twenty-four 32-bit constant values $CON_i^{128}, 0 \le i < 24$ as round keys and $K = K_0|K_1|K_2|K_3$ as an input. Then K and L are used to generate $WK_i(0 \le i < 4)$ and $RK_j(0 \le j < 36)$ in the following steps.

Step 1. $L \leftarrow GFN_{4,12}(CON_0^{(128)}, ..., CON_{23}^{(128)}, K_0, ..., K_3)$
Step 2. $WK_0|WK_1|WK_2|WK_3 \leftarrow K$
Step 3. For $i = 0$ to 8 do the following:
$T \leftarrow L \oplus (CON_{24+4i}^{(128)}|CON_{24+4i+1}^{(128)}|CON_{24+4i+2}^{(128)}|CON_{24+4i+3}^{(128)})$
$L = \Sigma(L)$
if i is odd. $T = T \oplus K$
$RK_{4i}|RK_{4i+1}|RK_{4i+2}|RK_{4i+3} \leftarrow T$

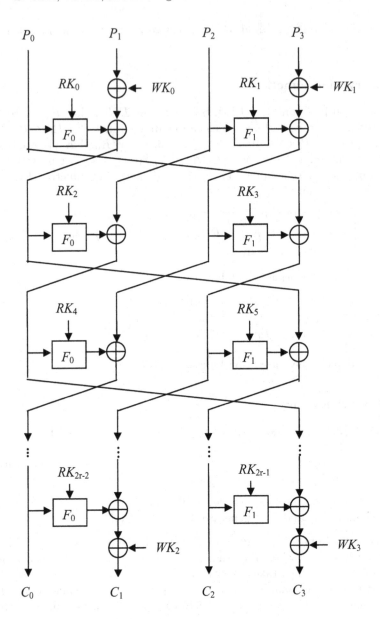

Fig. 2. ENC_r

The *DoubleSwap* function $\sum : \{0,1\}^{128} \rightarrow \{0,1\}^{128}$ is defined as follows:

$X_{128} \mapsto Y_{128}$
$Y = X[7-63]X[121-127]X[0-6]X[64-120]$

Figure 3 depicts the $\sum$ function.

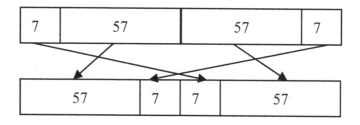

Fig. 3. *Function* $\sum$

The following steps show the 192-bit/256-bit key scheduling and the value of k is respectively set as 192 and 256.

Step 1. Set $k = 192$ or $k = 256$

Step 2. If $k = 192$: $K_L \leftarrow K_0|K_1|K_2|K_3, K_R \leftarrow K_4|K_5|\bar{K}_0|\bar{K}_1$
else if $k = 256$: $K_L \leftarrow K_0|K_1|K_2|K_3, K_R \leftarrow K_4|K_5|K_6|K_7$

Step 3. Let $K_L = K_{L0}|K_{L1}|K_{L2}|K_{L3},\quad K_R = K_{R0}|K_{R1}|K_{R2}|K_{R3}$
$L_L|L_R \leftarrow GFN_{8,10}(CON_0^{(k)}, ..., CON_{39}^{(k)}, K_{L0}, ...K_{L3}, K_{R0}, ..., K_{R3})$

Step 4. $WK_0|WK_1|WK_2|WK_3 \leftarrow K_L \oplus K_R$

Step 5. For $i = 0$ to 10 (if $k = 192$) or 12 (if $k = 256$) do the following:

If $(i \bmod 4) = 0$ or 1:
$T \leftarrow L_L \oplus (CON_{40+4i}^{(k)}|CON_{40+4i+1}^{(k)}|CON_{40+4i+2}^{(k)}|CON_{40+4i+3}^{(k)})$
$L_L = \sum(L_L)$
if i is odd, $T = T \oplus K_R$
else:
$T \leftarrow L_R \oplus (CON_{40+4i}^{(k)}|CON_{40+4i+1}^{(k)}|CON_{40+4i+2}^{(k)}|CON_{40+4i+3}^{(k)})$
$L_R = \sum(L_R)$
if i is odd, $T = T \oplus K_L$
$RK_{4i}|RK_{4i+1}|RK_{4i+2}|RK_{4i+3} \leftarrow T$

3   Basic Idea of Our Attack

3.1   Fault Model and Basic Assumptions

The byte-oriented model of random faults is adopted in our attack and the basic assumptions are as follows.

(1) Only one byte fault can be induced into the register storing the intermediate results. The adversary knows neither the location of the fault nor its concrete value.

(2) For one plaintext, two different ciphertexts under the control of the same secret key are available to the attacker: the right ciphertext and the faulty one.

3.2 Basic Idea of Our Attack

Let r be the round number of CLEFIA algorithm. The basic idea for our differential fault attack on CLEFIA is as follows:

(1) choose randomly a plaintext and obtain the corresponding right ciphertext.

(2) Disturb another encryption of the plaintext until one random byte fault is successfully induced into T_0 of the $(r-1)$-th round, which causes four bytes faults into T_0 of the r-th round, and obtain the corresponding faulty ciphertext. Calculate the candidate values of all the bytes of RK_{2r-2} using differential analysis technique. Repeat the induce procedure until all the bytes of RK_{2r-2} are recovered; Similarly, RK_{2r-1} can be recovered by inducing fault into T_2 of $(r-1)$-th round.

(3) Disturb another encryption of the plaintext until one random byte fault is successfully induced into T_0 of the $(r-2)$-th round, which causes four bytes faults into T_0 of the $(r-1)$-th round, and obtain the corresponding faulty ciphertext. Calculate the candidate values of all the bytes of $RK_{2r-4} \oplus WK_3$ using differential analysis technique. Repeat the induce procedure until all the bytes of $RK_{2r-4} \oplus WK_3$ are recovered; Similarly, $RK_{2r-3} \oplus WK_2$ can be recovered by inducing fault into T_2 of $(r-2)$-th round.

(4) Disturb another encryption of the plaintext until one random byte fault is successfully induced into T_0 of the $(r-3)$-th round, which causes four bytes faults into T_0 of the $(r-2)$-th round, and obtain the corresponding faulty ciphertext. Calculate the candidate values of all the bytes of RK_{2r-6} using differential analysis technique. Repeat the induce procedure until all the bytes of RK_{2r-6} are recovered; Similarly, RK_{2r-5} can be recovered by inducing fault into T_2 of $(r-3)$-th round.

(5) If the key size is 128, jump to step (6); else continue inducing faults according to the similar procedures as step (2)-step (4) until $RK_{2r-8} \oplus WK_2$, $RK_{2r-7} \oplus WK_3$, RK_{2r-10}, RK_{2r-9}, $RK_{2r-12} \oplus WK_3$, $RK_{2r-11} \oplus WK_2$, RK_{2r-14}, RK_{2r-13}, $RK_{2r-16} \oplus WK_2$, $RK_{2r-15} \oplus WK_3$, RK_{2r-18} and RK_{2r-17} are all recovered.

(6) Based on the recovered round keys, analyze the key scheduling of CLEFIA, and deduce the whole secret key K.

4   DFA on CLEFIA

4.1 Notations and Symbols

In order to clearly illustrate the following attacking procedure, some notations and symbols are to be defined.

Firstly, $X_i^j = (x_{i,0}^j, x_{i,1}^j, x_{i,2}^j, x_{i,3}^j)$ and $Y_i^j = (y_{i,0}^j, y_{i,1}^j, y_{i,2}^j, y_{i,3}^j)$, $j \in \{0,1\}$, are respectively defined as the input and output of the S-boxes in F_j of the i-th round. Y_i^j is also the input of M_j of the i-th round. $Z_i^j = (z_{i,0}^j, z_{i,1}^j, z_{i,2}^j, z_{i,3}^j)$, $j \in \{0,1\}$, is defined as the output of M_j of the i-th round.

$\Delta X_i^j = (\Delta x_{i,0}^j, \Delta x_{i,1}^j, \Delta x_{i,2}^j, \Delta x_{i,3}^j)$ and $\Delta Y_i^j = (\Delta y_{i,0}^j, \Delta y_{i,1}^j, \Delta y_{i,2}^j, \Delta y_{i,3}^j)$, $j \in \{0,1\}$, are respectively defined as the input and output differences of the

S-boxes in F_j of the i-th round. $\Delta Z_i^j = (\Delta z_{i,0}^j, \Delta z_{i,1}^j, \Delta z_{i,2}^j, \Delta z_{i,3}^j)$, $j \in \{0,1\}$, is defined as the output difference of M_j of the i-th round.

Then define $IN^j(a,b) = \{x \in GF(2^8) | S_j(x) \oplus S_j(x \oplus a) = b\}$, $a \neq 0, b \in GF(2^8)$, $j \in \{0,1\}$.

For the 128-bit key scheduling, denote $L^i = (L_0^i, L_1^i, L_2^i, L_3^i)$ as the initial value of L and $T^i = (T_0^i, T_1^i, T_2^i, T_3^i)$ as the final value of T in the i-th iteration in Step 3. For the 192/256-bit key scheduling, denote $L_L^i = (L_{L0}^i, L_{L1}^i, L_{L2}^i, L_{L3}^i)$ as the initial value of L_L, $L_R^i = (L_{R0}^i, L_{R1}^i, L_{R2}^i, L_{R3}^i)$ as the initial value of L_R and $T^i = (T_0^i, T_1^i, T_2^i, T_3^i)$ as the final value of T in the i-th iteration in Step 5.

Finally, let $C_{i,j}(0 \leq i, j \leq 3)$ represent the j-th byte of C_i.

4.2 Attacking Procedure with 128-Bit Key

The attacking procedure with 128-bit key is as follows.

(1) Select randomly a plaintext P, and obtain the right ciphertext C under the secret key $K = (K_0, K_1, K_2, K_3)$.

(2) Attack the 18-th round encryption and recover RK_{34} and RK_{35}.

a) Induce one byte random fault into T_0 of the 17-th round and obtain the corresponding faulty ciphertext $C^* = (C_0^*, C_1^*, C_2^*, C_3^*)$. So $\Delta X_{18}^0 = (C_{0,0} \oplus C_{0,0}^*, C_{0,1} \oplus C_{0,1}^*, C_{0,2} \oplus C_{0,2}^*, C_{0,3} \oplus C_{0,3}^*)$, $\Delta Z_{18}^0 = (C_{1,0} \oplus C_{1,0}^*, C_{1,1} \oplus C_{1,1}^*, C_{1,2} \oplus C_{1,2}^*, C_{1,3} \oplus C_{1,3}^*)$, $\Delta Y_{18}^0 = M_0^{-1}(\Delta Z_{18}^0)$.

b) Therefore, $x_{18,i}^0 \in IN^j(\Delta x_{18,i}^0, \Delta y_{18,i}^0), 0 \leq i \leq 3$, $j = i$ mod 2. Because $x_{18,i}^0 = C_{0,i} \oplus RK_{34,i}$, $RK_{34,i} \in (C_{0,i} \oplus IN^j(\Delta x_{18,i}^0, \Delta y_{18,i}^0))$.

c) Repeat the procedure of a) and b) until RK_{34} can be uniquely determined.

d) Through the similar procedure of a)-c), RK_{35} can be recovered by inducing one byte random fault into T_2 of the 17-th round.

(3) Attack the 17-th round encryption and recover $RK_{32} \oplus WK_3$ and $RK_{33} \oplus WK_2$.

a) Induce one byte random fault into T_0 of the 16-th round and obtain the corresponding faulty ciphertext $C^* = (C_0^*, C_1^*, C_2^*, C_3^*)$. It is easy to deduce $\Delta X_{17}^0 = C_3 \oplus C_3^* \oplus \Delta Z_{18}^1 = C_3 \oplus C_3^* \oplus F_1(C_2 \oplus RK_{35}) \oplus F_1(C_2^* \oplus RK_{35})$. $\Delta Z_{17}^0 = (C_{0,0} \oplus C_{0,0}^*, C_{0,1} \oplus C_{0,1}^*, C_{0,2} \oplus C_{0,2}^*, C_{0,3} \oplus C_{0,3}^*)$, $\Delta Y_{17}^0 = M_0^{-1}(\Delta Z_{17}^0)$.

b) Therefore, $x_{17,i}^0 \in IN^j(\Delta x_{17,i}^0, \Delta y_{17,i}^0), 0 \leq i \leq 3$, $j = i$ mod 2. Because $x_{17,i}^0 = C_{3,i} \oplus WK_3 \oplus z_{18,i}^1 \oplus RK_{32,i}$, $RK_{32,i} \oplus WK_{3,i} \in (C_{3,i} \oplus z_{18,i}^1 \oplus IN^j(\Delta x_{17,i}^0, \Delta y_{17,i}^0))$.

c) Repeat the procedure of a) and b) until $RK_{32} \oplus WK_3$ can be uniquely determined.

d) Through the similar procedure of a)- c), $RK_{33} \oplus WK_2$ can be recovered by inducing one byte random fault into T_2 of the 16-th round.

(4) Attack the 16-th round encryption and recover RK_{30} and RK_{31}.

a) Induce one byte random fault into T_0 of the 15-th round and obtain the corresponding faulty ciphertext $C^* = (C_0^*, C_1^*, C_2^*, C_3^*)$.

b) $\Delta X_{16}^0 = C_2 \oplus C_2^* \oplus \Delta Z_{17}^1 = C_2 \oplus C_2^* \oplus F_1(RK_{33}, X_{17}^1 \oplus RK_{33}) \oplus F_1(RK_{33}, X_{17}^1 \oplus RK_{33} \oplus \Delta X_{17}^1)$. To compute $F_1(RK_{33}, X_{17}^1 \oplus RK_{33})$, it is no need to know the value of RK_{33} because $RK_{33} \oplus (X_{17}^1 \oplus RK_{33}) = X_{17}^1$. Since X_{17}^1 has been known in step (3), $F_1(RK_{33}, X_{17}^1 \oplus RK_{33})$ can be calculated out. Similarly, to compute $F_1(RK_{33}, X_{17}^1 \oplus RK_{33} \oplus \Delta X_{17}^1)$, $X_{17}^1 \oplus \Delta X_{17}^1$ should be known. It is easy to deduce $\Delta X_{17}^1 = C_1 \oplus C_1^* \oplus \Delta Z_{18}^0 = C_1 \oplus C_1^* \oplus F_0(RK_{34}, C_0) \oplus F_0(RK_{34}, C_0^*)$, so ΔX_{16}^0 can be calculated out.

c) $\Delta Z_{16}^0 = \Delta X_{17}^0 = C_3 \oplus C_3^* \oplus \Delta Z_{18}^1 = C_3 \oplus C_3^* \oplus F_1(RK_{35}, C_2) \oplus F_1(RK_{35}, C_2^*)$. So $\Delta Y_{16}^0 = M_0^{-1}(\Delta Z_{16}^0)$.

d) Therefore, $x_{16,i}^0 \in IN^j(\Delta x_{16,i}^0, \Delta y_{16,i}^0), 0 \le i \le 3, j = i \bmod 2$. Because $x_{16,i}^0 = C_{2,i} \oplus F_1(RK_{33}, X_{17}^1 \oplus RK_{33}) \oplus RK_{30,i}$, $RK_{30,i} \in (C_{2,i} \oplus F_1(RK_{33}, X_{17}^1 \oplus RK_{33}) \oplus IN^j(\Delta x_{16,i}^0, \Delta y_{16,i}^0))$.

e) Repeat the procedure of a)- d) until RK_{30} can be uniquely determined.

f) Through the similar procedure of a)- e), RK_{31} can be recovered by inducing one byte random fault into T_2 of the 15-th round.

(5) Analyze the 128-bit key scheduling and recover K.

a) In step 3 of the 128-bit key scheduling, $RK_{32}, RK_{33}, RK_{34}$ and RK_{35} are generated when $i = 8$. As RK_{34} and RK_{35} have been recovered, $T_2^8 = RK_{34}$ and $T_3^8 = RK_{35}$ are also known. As i is not odd, $L_2^8 = T_2^8 \oplus CON_{58}^{(128)}$, $L_3^8 = T_3^8 \oplus CON_{59}^{(128)}$.

b) Through the inverse transformation of $\sum$ and L_2^7 can be calculated out. As $i = 7$ is odd, $T_2^7 = L_2^7 \oplus CON_{54}^{(128)} \oplus K_2$. Because $T_2^7 = RK_{30}$ is known, K_2 can also be calculated out. Therefore, $WK_2 = K_2$ is obtained. As $RK_{33} \oplus WK_2$ has been recovered, RK_{33} is also obtained. So $T_1^8 = RK_{33}$ is also recovered.

c) Apply the inverse transformation of $\sum$, L_3^7 can be calculated out. As $T_3^7 = L_3^7 \oplus CON_{55}^{(128)} \oplus K_3$ and $T_3^7 = RK_{31}$ has been known, K_3 can be obtained. Therefore, $WK_3 = K_2$ is obtained. As $RK_{32} \oplus WK_3$ has been recovered, RK_{32} is also obtained. So $T_0^8 = RK_{32}$ is recovered.

d) As all the bytes of T^8 have been obtained, L^8 can be easily calculated out. Repeat the inverse transformation of $\sum$ until L^0 is deduced. So $K = GFN_{4,12}^{-1}(CON_0^{(128)}, ..., CON_{23}^{(128)}, L^0)$ is recovered.

4.3   Attacking Procedure with 192/256-Bit Keys

The attacking procedure with 192-bit key and 256-bit key is very similar. Due to the page limitation, only the attacking procedure with 192-bit key is presented as follows.

(1) Attack respectively the 22-nd, 21-st, 20-th, 19-th, 18-th, 17-th, ..., and 14-th round encryption, recover $RK_{42}, RK_{43}, RK_{40} \oplus WK_3, RK_{41} \oplus WK_2, RK_{38}, RK_{39}, RK_{36} \oplus WK_2, RK_{37} \oplus WK_3, RK_{34}, RK_{35}, RK_{32} \oplus WK_3, RK_{33} \oplus WK_2, RK_{30}, RK_{31}, RK_{28} \oplus WK_2, RK_{29} \oplus WK_3, RK_{26}$ and RK_{27}. Here, the similar methods in the 128-bit attacking procedure are adopted to recover the above subkey values.

(2) Analyze the 192-bit key scheduling and recover K.

a) In step 5 of the 192-bit key scheduling, RK_{26} and RK_{27} are generated when $i = 6$. As RK_{26} and RK_{27} have been recovered, $T_2^6 = RK_{26}$ and $T_3^6 = RK_{27}$ are also known. As i is not odd, $L_{R2}^6 = T_2^6 \oplus CON_{66}^{(192)}$, $L_{R3}^6 = T_3^6 \oplus CON_{67}^{(192)}$.

b)Through the transformation of $\sum$, L_{R3}^7 can be calculated out. As $i = 7$ is odd, $T_3^7 = L_{R3}^7 \oplus CON_{71}^{(192)} \oplus K_{L3}$. Because $T_3^7 = RK_{31}$ is recovered, K_{L3} can be calculated out.

c) RK_{34} and RK_{35} are generated when $i = 8$. Since RK_{34} and RK_{35} have been recovered, $T_2^8 = RK_{34}$ and $T_3^8 = RK_{35}$ are also known. As i is not odd, $L_{L2}^8 = T_2^8 \oplus CON_{74}^{(192)}$, $L_{L3}^8 = T_3^8 \oplus CON_{75}^{(192)}$.

d) Through the transformation of $\sum$, L_{L3}^9 can be calculated out. As $i = 9$ is odd, $T_3^9 = L_{L3}^9 \oplus CON_{79}^{(192)} \oplus K_{R3}$. Because $T_3^9 = RK_{39}$ has been recovered, K_{R3} can be calculated out. As $WK_3 = K_{L3} \oplus K_{R3}$, WK_3 is recovered. Since $RK_{40} \oplus WK_3$, $RK_{37} \oplus WK_3$, $RK_{32} \oplus WK_3$ and $RK_{29} \oplus WK_3$ have been recovered, RK_{40}, RK_{37}, RK_{32} and RK_{29} can be obtained.

e) RK_{42} and RK_{43} are generated when $i = 10$. As RK_{42} and RK_{43} have been recovered, $T_2^{10} = RK_{42}$ and $T_3^{10} = RK_{43}$ are also known. $L_{R2}^{10} = T_2^{10} \oplus CON_{82}^{(192)}$, $L_{R3}^{10} = T_3^{10} \oplus CON_{83}^{(192)}$. Through the inverse transformation of $\sum$, L_{R2}^7 can be calculated out. $T_2^7 = L_{R2}^7 \oplus CON_{70}^{(192)} \oplus K_{L2}$. As $T_2^7 = RK_{30}$ has been recovered, K_{L2} can be calculated out.

f) As RK_{32} is known, $T_0^8 = RK_{32}$ is also obtained. $L_{L0}^8 = T_0^8 \oplus CON_{72}^{(192)}$. Through the transformation of $\sum$, L_{L2}^9 can be calculated out. $T_2^9 = L_{L2}^9 \oplus CON_{78}^{(192)} \oplus K_{R2}$. Because $T_2^9 = RK_{38}$ is recovered, K_{R2} can be calculated out.

g) As $WK_2 = K_{L2} \oplus K_{R2}$, WK_2 is recovered. Since $RK_{41} \oplus WK_2$, $RK_{36} \oplus WK_2$, $RK_{33} \oplus WK_2$ and $RK_{28} \oplus WK_2$ have been obtained, RK_{41}, RK_{36}, RK_{33} and RK_{28} can be recovered. Thus

$$L_R^{10} = (RK_{40}|RK_{41}|RK_{42}|RK_{43}) \oplus (CON_{80}^{(192)}|CON_{81}^{(192)}|CON_{82}^{(192)}|CON_{83}^{(192)}),$$

$$L_L^8 = (RK_{32}|RK_{33}|RK_{34}|RK_{35}) \oplus (CON_{72}^{(192)}|CON_{73}^{(192)}|CON_{74}^{(192)}|CON_{75}^{(192)})$$

can be obtained.

h) Repeat the inverse transformation of $\sum$ until L_L^0 and L_R^0 are deduced. So $K_L|K_R = GFN_{8,10}^{-1}(CON_0^{(192)}, ..., CON_{39}^{(192)}, L_L^0|L_R^0)$ is recovered.

4.4   Data Complexity Analysis

In CLEFIA, two different S-boxes S_0 and S_1 are adopted. S_0 is generated by combining 4×4 small S-boxes. S_1 is constructed with the inverse operation plus affine transform in finite field. For the non-empty $IN^0(a,b)(a \neq 0, b \in GF(2^8))$ of S_0, the propagation of (a,b)s satisfying $|IN^0(a,b)| \leq 4$ is 96.2%. For the case of $|IN^0(a,b)| = 2$, 2 faulty ciphertexts should be generated to recover the input of S_0. For the case of $|IN^0(a,b)| = 4$, about 4 faulty ciphertexts should be generated to recover the input of S_0. So about 3 faulty ciphertexts on average are needed to recover the input of S_0. For the non-empty $IN^1(a,b)(a \neq 0, b \in GF(2^8))$ of S_1, the propagation of (a,b)s satisfying $|IN^1(a,b)| = 2$ is 99.2%. So about 2 faulty ciphertexts on average are needed to recover the input of S_1.

In the attacking procedure in section 4.2 and 4.3, if the i-th round is to be attacked, the $(i-1)$-th round will be randomly induced one byte fault, which can cause four bytes faults to simultaneously happen in the i-th round. So in order to recover a subkey or the sum of a subkey and a post-whitening subkey, only about 3 faulty ciphertexts on average are needed. As one round encryption is composed of two F function and two subkeys are used, about 6 faulty ciphertexts on average should be obtained. For 128-bit key, three round encryptions are to be attacked, so about 18 faulty ciphertexts on average are required. For 192/256-bit keys, nine round encryptions are to be attacked, so about 54 faulty ciphertexts on average are required.

4.5   Computer Simulation

Our attack method has been successfully implemented through the computer simulation. The programming language is Visual C++ 6.0 and the operation system is Windows XP. The attack experiments are repeated ten times on CLE-FIA with 128-bit, 192-bit and 256-bit key respectively.

Table 1 gives the induce number of DFA on CLEFIA. Apparently, in most cases, the induce number is 18 for 128-bit key and 54 for 192/256-bit keys, which verify the former data complexity analysis results.

Table 1. Experimental Results of DFA on CLEFIA

the i-th experiment	128-bit	192-bit	256-bit
1	19	54	54
2	19	54	55
3	18	54	54
4	18	54	54
5	18	55	54
6	20	54	54
7	18	54	54
8	18	55	54
9	18	54	55
10	18	54	55

5   Conclusion

In this paper, the differential fault analysis on CLEFIA is explored. The byte-oriented model of random faults is adopted in our attack. Four bytes of faults can be simultaneously obtained in one round by inducing randomly one byte fault in the last round, which can efficiently reduce the total induce times in the attack. After obtaining the subkeys in the last several rounds, and through some analysis of the key schedule, only 18 faulty ciphertexts on average are needed to recover the whole value of secret key for 128-bit key and 54 faulty ciphertexts on average for 192/256-bit keys. The experimental results through the computer simulation also verify the theoretical complexity analysis results.

Acknowledgment

The authors would like to thank the anonymous reviewers for many helpful comments and suggestions. The research presented in this paper was supported by National Natural Science Foundation of China(Grant No. 60603013, 60503014 and 90604036) and 863 Project (Grant No. 2007AA01Z470).

References

1. Boneh, D., DeMillo, R.A., Lipton, R.J.: On the importance of checking cryptographic protocols for faults. In: Fumy, W. (ed.) EUROCRYPT 1997. LNCS, vol. 1233, pp. 37–51. Springer, Heidelberg (1997)
2. Biham, E., Shamir, A.: Differential fault analysis of secret key cryptosystem. In: Kaliski Jr., B.S. (ed.) CRYPTO 1997. LNCS, vol. 1294, pp. 513–525. Springer, Heidelberg (1997)
3. Biehl, I., Meyer, B., Muller, V.: Differential fault analysis on elliptic curve cryptosystems. In: Bellare, M. (ed.) CRYPTO 2000. LNCS, vol. 1880, pp. 131–146. Springer, Heidelberg (2000)
4. Hemme, L.: A differential fault attack against early rounds of (Triple-) DES. In: Joye, M., Quisquater, J.-J. (eds.) CHES 2004. LNCS, vol. 3156, pp. 254–267. Springer, Heidelberg (2004)
5. Dusart, P., Letourneux, G., Vivolo, O.: Differential fault analysis on AES. In: Zhou, J., Yung, M., Han, Y. (eds.) ACNS 2003. LNCS, vol. 2846, pp. 293–306. Springer, Heidelberg (2003)
6. Blomer, J., Seifert, J.P.: Fault based cryptanalysis of the Advanced Encryption Standard (AES). In: Wright, R.N. (ed.) FC 2003. LNCS, vol. 2742, pp. 162–181. Springer, Heidelberg (2003)
7. Chen, C.N., Yen, S.M.: Differential fault analysis on AES key schedule and some countermeasures. In: Safavi-Naini, R., Seberry, J. (eds.) ACISP 2003. LNCS, vol. 2727, pp. 118–129. Springer, Heidelberg (2003)
8. Giraud, C.: DFA on AES. In: Dobbertin, H., Rijmen, V., Sowa, A. (eds.) AES 2004. LNCS, vol. 3373, pp. 27–41. Springer, Heidelberg (2005)
9. Piret, G., Quisquater, J.J.: A differential fault attack technique against SPN structures, with application to the AES and KHAZAD. In: Walter, C.D., Koç, Ç.K., Paar, C. (eds.) CHES 2003. LNCS, vol. 2779, pp. 77–88. Springer, Heidelberg (2003)
10. Hoch, J.J., Shamir, A.: Fault analysis of stream ciphers. In: Joye, M., Quisquater, J.-J. (eds.) CHES 2004. LNCS, vol. 3156, pp. 240–253. Springer, Heidelberg (2004)
11. Biham, E., Granboulan, L., Nguyn, P.Q.: Impossible fault analysis of RC4 and differential fault analysis of RC4. In: Gilbert, H., Handschuh, H. (eds.) FSE 2005. LNCS, vol. 3557, pp. 359–367. Springer, Heidelberg (2005)
12. Shirai, T., Shibutani, K., Akishita, T., Moriai, S., Iwata, T.: The 128-bit Blockcipher CLEFIA. In: Biryukov, A. (ed.) FSE 2007, vol. 4593, pp. 181–195. Springer, Heidelberg (2007)
13. Zheng, Y., Matsumoto, T., Imai, H.: On the construction of block ciphers provably secure and not relying on any unproved hypotheses. In: Brassard, G. (ed.) CRYPTO 1989. LNCS, vol. 435, pp. 461–480. Springer, Heidelberg (1990)

Extending FORK-256 Attack to the Full Hash Function

Scott Contini, Krystian Matusiewicz, and Josef Pieprzyk

Centre for Advanced Computing, Algorithms and Cryptography,
Department of Computing, Macquarie University
{scontini,kmatus,josef}@ics.mq.edu.au

Abstract. In a paper published in FSE 2007, a way of obtaining near-collisions and in theory also collisions for the FORK-256 hash function was presented [8]. The paper contained examples of near-collisions for the compression function, but in practice the attack could not be extended to the full function due to large memory requirements and computation time. In this paper we improve the attack and show that it is possible to find near-collisions in practice for any given value of IV. In particular, this means that the full hash function with the prespecified IV is vulnerable in practice, not just in theory. We exhibit an example near-collision for the complete hash function.

1 Introduction

Recent spectacular attacks on many established hash functions endangered most commonly used dedicated hash functions and cast some doubts on the remaining ones. This rekindled the interest in designing more secure yet still efficient alternatives. While most of the dedicated hash functions used source-heavy unbalanced Feistel networks [11], some alternatives were proposed that utilise the other option, target-heavy UFNs. One of the examples is the hash function Tiger [1] and a recent design FORK-256, proposed by Hong et al. [5,6].

Soon after FORK-256 was presented, works [9,7] showed that the step transformation has a particular weakness that may threaten the function. Indeed, soon after those ideas were refined and the attack on the full compression function was presented [8], including example near-collisions [3]. Section 8 of the paper [8] briefly mentions how to extend the result to the full compression function, but there is a mistake in the description (see Section 3 of this paper). Additionally, a cost based analysis [2] was never considered and from this viewpoint the attack suffers due to the large memory requirements. In fact, the combination of large memory and long running time preclude the idea from being implemented to find near-collisions in practice.

This paper. In this paper we correct our mistake from [8] and give an improved method for finding near-collisions (and full collisions) for any given IV. Our method modifies the algorithm from [8] in order to keep the memory usage low and improve the efficiency of one phase of the attack. Consequently, we are

S. Qing, H. Imai, and G. Wang (Eds.): ICICS 2007, LNCS 4861, pp. 296–305, 2007.

able to actually implement the algorithm to produce near-collisions for the full FORK-256 with the real IV. We give an example near-collision.

In Section 2 we define some notations and give a brief description of FORK-256. In Section 3, we briefly recall the original attack from [8]. Section 4 contains our main contribution in which we explain the new version of the algorithm including a detailed analysis. Finally, we present an example of a near-collision with the IV specified by the designers and then we conclude our work.

2   Brief Description of FORK-256

FORK-256 is a dedicated hash function based on the classical Merkle-Damgård iterative construction with the compression function that maps 256 bits of state and 512 bits of message to 256 bits of a new state. Here we give a concise description – more details can be found in [5].

The compression function consists of four parallel branches BRANCH_j, $j = 1, 2, 3, 4$, each one of them using a different permutation σ_j of 16 message words M_i, $i = 0, \ldots, 15$.

The same set of eight chaining variables

$$\text{CV}_\ell = (A_0, B_0, C_0, D_0, E_0, F_0, G_0, H_0)$$

is input to the four branches. After computing outputs of parallel branches

$$h_j = \text{BRANCH}_j(\text{CV}_\ell, M), \quad j = 1, \ldots, 4,$$

the compression function updates the set of chaining variables according to the formula

$$\text{CV}_{\ell+1} := \text{CV}_\ell + [(h_1 + h_2) \oplus (h_3 + h_4)] \ ,$$

where modular and XOR additions are performed word-wise. Before the first application of the compression function registers $\text{CV}_0 = (A_0, \ldots, H_0)$ are initialised by appropriate constants presented in Table 3.

Each branch function BRANCH_j, $j = 1, 2, 3, 4$ consists of eight steps. In each step $k = 1, \ldots, 8$ the branch function updates its own copy of eight chaining variables using the step transformation depicted in Fig. 1.

We will denote the value of register R in j-th branch after step i as $R_i^{(j)}$.

Before the computation of j-th branch, all $A_0^{(j)}, \ldots, H_0^{(j)}$ are initialised with corresponding values of eight chaining variables.

Note that the crucial role in the step transformation play two so-called Q-structures, marked in the picture with grey.

Functions f and g mapping 32-bit words to 32-bit words are defined as

$$f(x) = x + \left(ROL^7(x) \oplus ROL^{22}(x)\right) \ ,$$
$$g(x) = x \oplus \left(ROL^{13}(x) + ROL^{27}(x)\right) \ .$$

Constants $\delta_0, \ldots, \delta_{15}$ used in each step are defined as the first 32 bits of fractional parts of binary expansions of cube roots of the first 16 primes and are presented in Table 4. Finally, permutations σ_j of message words and permutations π_j of constants are shown in Table 1.

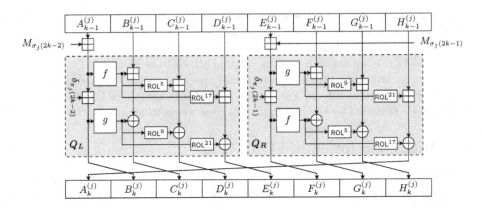

Fig. 1. Step transformation of a single branch of FORK-256. Q-structures are greyed out.

Table 1. Message and constant permutations used in four branches $j = 1, \ldots, 4$ of FORK-256

j	message permutation σ_j	permutation of constants, π_j
1	0 1 2 3 4 5 6 7 8 9 10 11 12 13 14 15	0 1 2 3 4 5 6 7 8 9 10 11 12 13 14 15
2	14 15 11 9 8 10 3 4 2 13 0 5 6 7 12 1	15 14 13 12 11 10 9 8 7 6 5 4 3 2 1 0
3	7 6 10 14 13 2 9 12 11 4 1 5 8 5 0 1 3	1 0 3 2 5 4 7 6 9 8 11 10 13 12 15 14
4	5 12 1 8 15 0 13 11 3 10 9 2 7 14 4 6	14 15 12 13 10 11 8 9 6 7 4 5 2 3 0 1

3   Attack on the Compression Function of FORK-256

In this section we recall the main points of the attack on the compression function of FORK-256 presented in [8] that our attack builds on.

The first essential fact is that it is possible to relatively easily find situations when non-zero differences in registers A and E do not spread to other registers during the step transformation. In other words, it is possible to obtain characteristics of the form $(\Delta A, 0, 0, 0, 0, 0, 0, 0) \to (0, \Delta B, 0, 0, 0, 0, 0, 0)$ and $(0, 0, 0, 0, \Delta E, 0, 0, 0) \to (0, 0, 0, 0, 0, \Delta F, 0, 0)$ without resorting to cancelling the difference by appropriate message word difference (cf. Fig. 1). Such characteristics are called micro-collisions and they are possible if the right difference is fed to the register A (or E) and appropriate corresponding "constants" B, C and D (F, G, H correspondingly) are set. Details on how those differences and constants can be found are presented in [8].

The second important ingredient is the possibility of using micro-collisions to find differential paths spanning the whole function that can be used to obtain collisions for the complete compression function. One such path, used in the original FORK-256 attack utilises difference in message word M_{12} only and is presented in Fig. 2.

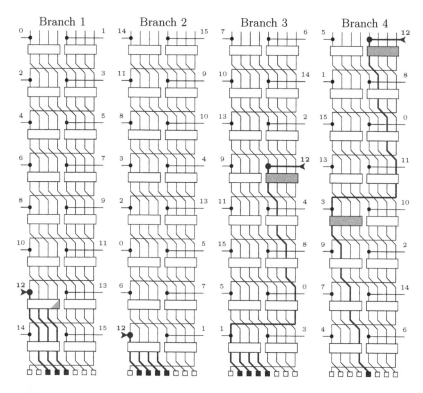

Fig. 2. High-level path used to find near-collisions in FORK-256. Thick lines show the propagation of differences. Indices of the message words that are fed into each step transformation are given in the left and right columns of each branch. Q-structures for which micro-collisions have to be found are greyed out.

The original attack from [8] first shows how to find chosen-IV near-collisions (or full collisions) and then briefly suggests a way of extending it to an attack on the full FORK-256. For now, we only focus on the low-memory version of the attack: The reason for this will be evident later.

The idea is to first choose an appropriate difference for M_{12}, then make branches 3 and 4 work (see Fig. 2) and then use free message words to get branch 1 and 2 to work. Initially all message words can be anything. To get branch 4 to work, one manipulates the values of registers F_0, G_0, H_0 and message words M_5, M_1, M_8, M_{15}, M_0, M_{13}, M_{11} in order to get the micro-collisions in the two Q-structures. Then to get branch 3 to work, message words M_6, M_{10}, M_{14}, and M_2 are manipulated along with register B_0. The change in B_0 upsets the branch 4, but by manipulating M_{11} again, the characteristic through both branches holds.

For the remaining part of the characteristic (branches 1 and 2), the main observation is that message words M_9 and M_4 can be freely changed without upsetting branches 3 and 4. This gives 2^{64} possibilities for satisfying the full characteristic. In fact, there are no requirements for branch 2, and only a single microcollision needs to happen for branch 1 at $D_6^{(1)} \to E_7^{(1)}$ (step 7). Satisfying this microcollision can be left to chance. With a precomputation trick and a good choice of difference in M_{12}, [8] finds pairs of outputs that differ in at most 108-bits (differences in registers C, D, F and part of B only) in time equivalent to $2^{18.6}$ FORK-256 operations. Such outputs can be called near-collisions. For $2^{108} \cdot 2^{18.6} = 2^{126.6}$ work, full collisions are expected. The result is faster than birthday attack.

However, it must be emphasised that these are *chosen-IV* near-collisions and collisions. It requires choosing values for B_0, F_0, G_0, and H_0. In Section 7.2 of the paper, a way to eliminate the need to choose B_0 is suggested, though it uses large precomputation tables – on the order of 2^{73} words of memory. Assuming the choice of B_0 can be eliminated, [8] argues in Section 8 that real collisions can be found by prepending a message block that yields the right values of F_0, G_0, and H_0 when that message block is sent through the compression function with the real IV defined in FORK-256. But it claims that finding this message block can be done *after* the execution of the algorithm that finds the chosen-IV collision. This is not correct. The characteristic depends upon *all* chaining variable regsisters. In other words, it is not only F_0, G_0, and H_0 that have to match the inputs to the chosen-IV collision, but also A_0 through E_0. This is easy to see: if one has a near-collision such as any one given from [8], you cannot change an input register value and still have the same near-collision because the difference propagates rapidly.

There is a simple fix for the error in Section 8. The requirements for F_0, G_0 and H_0 are dictated by the predetermined difference in M_{12}. Thus, one can process the prepended message block first: simply try random first messages blocks until allowable values for F_0, G_0, and H_0 are found. Then, one can execute the search algorithm to determine a second message block that yields a partial collision/full collision for the chaining variables determined from the prepended block. More details are in Section 4.2.

It would be nice to implement the attack to show that it works and can at least produce near-collisions, thus showing that there are real problems with FORK-256 (as opposed to attacks that are of theoretical interest only). Note that the low-memory version cannot be implemented because of the requirement on B_0, which would amplify the running time significantly (beyond what can be done in on a typical PC using a reasonable amount of CPU time). Neither can the large memory version since computers with 2^{73} of memory do not yet exist. Moreover it is claimed in [8] that finding the right values of F_0, G_0, and H_0 takes 2^{96} steps.

Our new contribution is to present a simplified and improved near-collision (and collision) search algorithm which does not use large memory and can be ran on a typical PC to produce near-collisions on the full FORK-256 with specified IV within a few days of run time. The simplified algorithm is a modification of the low-memory attack from [8]. We ran our new algorithm and found several near-collisions on the full FORK-256 with the real IV.

4   Improving the Attack

The obstacle for extending the low-memory attack from [8] to the full hash function is the requirement for particular values of four chaining values, B_0 required by branch 3 and F_0, G_0, H_0 required by branch 4. Nothing can be done about constants necessary to achieve micro-collision in the first step of branch 4. However, by careful modification of some steps of the procedure we can eliminate the need for choosing the value of the constant B_0.

4.1   The Algorithm

Instead of solving for branch 4, then branch 3, and later making a small adjustment to branch 4 again, the idea is to go through the first step of branch 4 only, then switch to branch 3, and finally return to solve for the rest of branch 4.

Let d denote the modular difference used in M_{12}. Recall that an allowable value x is a value fed to register A (or E) such that there exist constants B, C, D (or F, G, H) that cause simultaneous micro-collisions to happen in all three lines when $x, x + d$ are the values of register A (or E). The modified algorithm first precomputes for difference d all allowable values for step 5 of the left Q-structure of branch 4. Then, the steps are as follows:

Branch 4, step 1. We find x_1 such that $x_1, x_1 + d$ give simultaneous g-δ_{15}-f micro-collisions for step 1 of branch 4, compute corresponding constants τ_1, τ_2, τ_3 and assign $F_0 := \tau_1$, $G_0 := \tau_2$, $H_0 := \tau_3$. Set M_{12} to $x_1 - E_0$ and M'_{12} to $x_1 - E_0 + d$.

Branch 3. We choose values of M_7, M_6, M_{10}, M_{14}, M_{13} and M_2 appearing in the first three steps of branch 3 randomly and compute the function up to the beginning of step 4. We check if the value $E_4^{(3)} + M_{12}$ is an allowable value for the g-δ_6-f micro-collision in step 4, i.e. we test if there exist constants μ_0, μ_1, μ_2 such that the pair $E_4^{(3)} + M_{12}$, $E_4^{(3)} + M_{12} + d$ yields micro-collisions when those constants are set in registers $F_3^{(3)}$, $G_3^{(3)}$, $H_3^{(3)}$. If it is not, we pick fresh values of the message words and repeat the process. Once we get the right values (this needs around 2^{23} trials using the difference from [8]) we modify values of M_6, M_{10}, M_{14}, M_{13} and M_2 to adjust the values of $F_3^{(3)}$, $G_3^{(3)}$, $H_3^{(3)}$ to appropriate constants μ_0, μ_1, μ_2. This modification is similar to the original except here we are required to modify M_{13}, whereas the original algorithm avoided it because it was set in branch 4 (instead the original algorithm modified B_0). Now branch 3 is ready.

Branch 4, steps 2–4. We start with choosing random values for M_5, M_1, and M_{15}. Then values of M_8, M_0, and M_{11} are chosen to preserve the subtraction difference d through the first 4 steps of the characteristic. This is easy to do, for example, by setting the message blocks so that the input to the f function is zero (the output of the f function is the only thing that can change the subtraction difference). Then we compute up to the beginning of step 5. Next, we use our precomputed table to loop through all choices of M_3 that lead to allowable values and we test each one to see if any of them does not cause a difference propagation to $C_5^{(4)}$ for the current value of $B_4^{(4)}$ that is there. In other words, we are looking for a value of M_3 that actually induces a single micro-collision in line B and has the potential to cause simultaneous micro-collisions in the other two lines. This is illustrated in Fig. 3. If no solution is found, then we go back to solve for branch 3 again with new random values.[1]

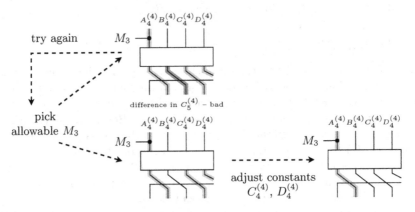

Fig. 3. Illustration of the procedure used in step 5 of branch 3. We want to get micro-collisions in all three lines without the need for modifying the value of $B_4^{(4)}$.

Once such a solution is found, we have to set the values of $C_4^{(4)}$ and $D_4^{(4)}$ to appropriate constants so that we obtain simultaneous micro-collisions for all three lines. We do this by adjusting the values of M_1, and M_{15} and appropriately compensating for these changes by adjusting M_0 and M_{11}. After this is done, branches 3 and 4 are ready.

Branches 1 and 2. The part of the algorithm that deals with branches 1 and 2 is identical to the one presented in [8] and it does not require any further explanations.

In the original attack [8], the search complexity for a near-collision is dominated by branches 1 and 2. The search through branches 1 and 2 involved 2^{64} potential characteristics for the cost of 2^{58} FORK-256 operations. Provided that the cost of our modified algorithm for branches 3 and 4 is less than this, the overall complexity is unchanged.

With the difference of $d =$ 0x22f80000 the probability of passing step 4 of branch 3 is about 2^{-24} and the probability of passing step 5 in branch 4 is about 2^{-19}. The cost of a single check is about eight steps of FORK-256, so 2^{-3} full FORK-256 evaluations. Thus, passing branches 3 and 4 in our modified algorithm requires about 2^{40} FORK-256 evaluations. Hence, it does not influence the final complexity of the attack.

---

[1] We cannot repeat Branch 4 again since we will always end up with the same value for $B_4^{(4)}$.

4.2   Fixing Appropriate Chaining Values

So far we have removed the need for the fourth initial chaining value to be fixed. This leaves us with three 32-bit words, each one to be set to one of the possible constants required by simultaneous micro-collisions in step 1 of branch 4. This means that by prepending a random message block and computing the digest that in turn becomes the chaining value for the main part of the attack we have the probability of getting the right values of those registers at least 2^{-96}, less than $2^{126.6}$ required for the second phase. However, we can do much better when we use the fact that *any* of the possible constants will suffice in each of the three initial registers.

Let $\mathcal{A}$ be the set of allowable values for g-δ_{15}-f micro-collision in step 1 of branch 4 for a given difference d. For each allowable value $a \in \mathcal{A}$ we can compute sets $\mathcal{F}_a, \mathcal{G}_a, \mathcal{H}_a$ of constants that yield a micro-collision in the corresponding line. Then, the probability that a randomly selected triple constitute good constants for some allowable value a is

$$P = 1 - \prod_{a \in \mathcal{A}} \left(1 - \frac{|\mathcal{F}_a| \cdot |\mathcal{G}_a| \cdot |\mathcal{H}_a|}{2^{96}} \right)$$

This probability depends on the choice of the difference d. For both differences $d = $ 0xdd080000 and $d = $ 0x22f80000 used in [8] it is equal to $P = 2^{-64.8}$, but there are other differences with much higher values of P. Of course those differences may give worse performance in the main part of the attack because they are not tuned to yield optimal chance of passing requirements of branch 1. What really matters though is that original differences are suitable for the improved attack.

4.3   Experimental Results

We implemented this modified strategy and tested it. As an example, we present in Table 2 a pair of messages that give a near-collision of weight 42 of the full hash function FORK-256. Here we used difference $d = $0x3f6bf009 since it has $P = 2^{-21.7}$ for the first phase of the attack.

Table 2. Example of a near-collision of weight 42 for the complete hash function FORK-256. The first block is used to obtain the desired values of chaining registers that enable the attack on the compression function.

M	2d4458a4	57976f57	3e44cfd9	1ab54cb2	7ec11870	173f6573	6141c261	7db20d3e
	2feeb74d	5fac87a6	61a73fa1	3454b23d	451d389b	78f061ec	7c32fb06	57ef1928
	79dcd071	39dc97f0	3a1bff42	031d364c	fef000e6	40873ef5	d0741256	649430cf
	97ef5538	3eab6a7e	b4f9cf72	9eba8257	<u>4e84d457</u>	5a6c49b6	ad1d9711	0f69afa2
M'	2d4458a4	57976f57	3e44cfd9	1ab54cb2	7ec11870	173f6573	6141c261	7db20d3e
	2feeb74d	5fac87a6	61a73fa1	3454b23d	451d389b	78f061ec	7c32fb06	57ef1928
	79dcd071	39dc97f0	3a1bff42	031d364c	fef000e6	40873ef5	d0741256	649430cf
	97ef5538	3eab6a7e	b4f9cf72	9eba8257	<u>8df0c460</u>	5a6c49b6	ad1d9711	0f69afa2
diff	00000000	83480012	32b4070c	681a1279	648600ad	00000000	00000000	00000000

5   Conclusions

In this paper we presented an attack that can find near-collisions and even collisions for the full hash function of FORK-256. We improved on previous results that used large memory and were too inefficient to implement in practice. This in a sense completes the attack and adds another result relevant to the analysis of FORK-256 and possibly also similar designs.

We remark that the authors of FORK-256 recently proposed a patched version of their function [4], largely due to [8]. Because of a change in functions f and g and a modified structure of the step transformation, the new FORK does not allow for finding micro-collisions. Despite this, Saarinen found an attack on the new FORK [10] faster than birthday paradox but requiring large memory. It would be interesting to see if either the time or memory requirements can be improved.

Acknowledgements. The authors were supported by Australian Research Council grant DP0663452.

References

1. Anderson, R., Biham, E.: Tiger: A fast new hash function. In: Gollmann, D. (ed.) Fast Software Encryption. LNCS, vol. 1039, pp. 121–144. Springer, Heidelberg (1996)
2. Bernstein, D.J.: What output size resists collisions in a xor of independent expansions? In: ECRYPT Hash Workshop (May 2007)
3. Contini, S., Matusiewicz, K., Pieprzyk, J.: Cryptanalysis of FORK-256. web page (2007), http://www.ics.mq.edu.au/~kmatus/FORK/
4. Hong, D., Chang, D., Sung, J., Lee, S., Hong, S., Lee, J., Moon, D., Chee, S.: New FORK-256. Cryptology ePrint Archive, Report, 2007/185 (2007), http://eprint.iacr.org/2007/185
5. Hong, D., Sung, J., Hong, S., Lee, S., Moon, D.: A new dedicated 256-bit hash function: FORK-256. In: First NIST Workshop on Hash Functions (2005)
6. Hong, D., Sung, J., Lee, S., Moon, D., Chee, S.: A new dedicated 256-bit hash function. In: Robshaw, M. (ed.) FSE 2006. LNCS, vol. 4047, Springer, Heidelberg (2006)
7. Matusiewicz, K., Contini, S., Pieprzyk, J.: Weaknesses of the FORK-256 compression function. IACR Cryptology e-print Archive, Report 2006/317 (2006), http://eprint.iacr.org/2006/317
8. Matusiewicz, K., Peyrin, T., Billet, O., Contini, S., Pieprzyk, J.: Cryptanalysis of FORK-256. In: FSE 2007. LNCS, vol. 4593, pp. 19–38. Springer, Heidelberg (2007)
9. Mendel, F., Lano, J., Preneel, B.: Cryptanalysis of reduced variants of the FORK-256 hash function. In: Abe, M. (ed.) CT-RSA 2007. LNCS, vol. 4377, pp. 85–100. Springer, Heidelberg (2006)
10. Saarinen, M.-J.O.: A meet-in-the-middle collision attack against the new FORK-256. In: Proceedings of Indocrypt 2007. LNCS, Springer, Heidelberg (2007)
11. Schneier, B., Kesley, J.: Unbalanced Feistel networks and block cipher design. In: Gollmann, D. (ed.) FSE 1996. LNCS, vol. 1039, pp. 121–144. Springer, Heidelberg (1996)

A   Constants

Table 3. Constants used to initialise chaining variables of FORK-256

A_0	B_0	C_0	D_0	E_0	F_0	G_0	H_0
6a09e667	bb67ae85	3c6ef372x	a54ff53a	510e527f	9b05688c	1f83d9ab	5be0cd19

Table 4. Step constants $\delta_0, \ldots, \delta_{15}$ used in FORK-256

δ	0	1	2	3	4	5	6	7
0	428a2f98	71374491	b5c0fbcf	e9b5dba5	3956c25b	59f111f1	923f82a4	ab1c5ed5
8	d807aa98	12835b01	243185be	550c7dc3	72be5d74	80deb1fe	9bdc06a7	c19bf174

Attacking Reduced-Round Versions of the SMS4 Block Cipher in the Chinese WAPI Standard*

Jiqiang Lu

Information Security Group, Royal Holloway, University of London
Egham, Surrey TW20 0EX, UK
lvjiqiang@hotmail.com

Abstract. SMS4 is a 32-round block cipher with a 128-bit block size and a 128-bit user key. It is used in WAPI, the Chinese WLAN national standard. In this paper, we present a rectangle attack on 14-round SMS4, and an impossible differential attack on 16-round SMS4. These are better than any previously known cryptanalytic results on SMS4 in terms of the numbers of attacked rounds.

Keywords: Block cipher, SMS4, Impossible differential cryptanalysis, Rectangle attack.

1 Introduction

The Chinese national standard for Wireless Local Area Networks (WLANs), WLAN Authentication and Privacy Infrastructure (WAPI), has been the subject of extensive international debate, especially between China and USA, since over the last four years it has been a rival for IEEE 802.11i [6] for adoption as an ISO (International Organization for Standardization) international standard. WAPI and IEEE 802.11i have both been proposed as security amendments to the ISO/IEC 8802-11 WLAN standard [7]. The two schemes use two different block ciphers for encryption of data: IEEE 802.11i uses the AES [14] cipher, while WAPI uses the SMS4 [1] cipher. In March 2006, IEEE 802.11i was approved as the standard, and WAPI was rejected, partially because of uncertainties regarding the security of the undisclosed SMS4 cipher. However, because it is a Chinese national standard, WAPI continues to be used in the Chinese WLAN industry, and many international corporations, such as SONY, support WAPI in relevant products.

The SMS4 cipher was released in a Chinese version only, in January 2006 [1]; it has a 128-bit block size, a 128-bit user key, and a total of 32 rounds. To the best of our knowledge, the only previously published cryptanalytic result on the SMS4 algorithm is an integral attack [9] on 13-round SMS4, presented recently in [10]; moreover, a differential fault analysis on the SMS4 implementation was presented in [16].

In this paper, we exploit certain 12-round rectangle distinguishers with probability $2^{-237.64}$, which can be used to mount a rectangle attack on SMS4 reduced

---

* This work as well as the author was supported by a British Chevening / Royal Holloway Scholarship and the European Commission under contract IST-2002-507932 (ECRYPT).

S. Qing, H. Imai, and G. Wang (Eds.): ICICS 2007, LNCS 4861, pp. 306–318, 2007.

to 14 rounds. We also exploit certain 12-round impossible differentials, which enables us to mount an impossible differential attack on SMS4 reduced to 16 rounds. The attacks use the early abort technique described in [11,12,13].

The rest of this paper is organised as follows. In the next section, we describe the notation used throughout this paper and the SMS4 cipher. In Section 3, we introduce a number of properties of SMS4 and give some necessary definitions. In Sections 4 and 5, we present our cryptanalytic results. Section 6 concludes this paper.

2   Preliminaries

2.1   Notation

We use the following notation throughout this paper.

- $\oplus$: bitwise logical exclusive OR (XOR)
- $\lll i$: left rotation by i bits
- e_j : a 32-bit word with zeros in all positions but bit j, $(0 \leq j \leq 31)$
- $e_{i_1, \cdots, i_j}$: $e_{i_1} \oplus \cdots \oplus e_{i_j}$, $(0 \leq i_1, \cdots, i_j \leq 31)$
- ? : an arbitrary 32-bit word, where two words represented by the ? symbol may be different

The notion of difference used throughout this paper is with respect to the $\oplus$ operation. It is assumed that the least significant bit of a 32-bit word is referred as the 0-th bit and the most significant bit is referred as the 31st bit.

2.2   The SMS4 Cipher

The SMS4 [1] block cipher takes as an input a 128-bit plaintext P, represented as four 32-bit words $P = (P_0, P_1, P_2, P_3)$, and has a total of 32 rounds. Let $X^{i+1} = (X_{i+1,0}, X_{i+1,1}, X_{i+1,2}, X_{i+1,3})$ denote the four-word output of the i-th round, $(0 \leq i \leq 31)$[1]. Then, the encryption procedure of SMS4 is as follows:

1. Set $X^0 = (X_{0,0}, X_{0,1}, X_{0,2}, X_{0,3}) = (P_0, P_1, P_2, P_3)$.
2. For $i = 0$ to 31:
    - $X_{i+1,0} = X_{i,1}$,
    - $X_{i+1,1} = X_{i,2}$,
    - $X_{i+1,2} = X_{i,3}$,
    - $X_{i+1,3} = X_{i,0} \oplus \mathrm{L}(\mathrm{S}(X_{i,1} \oplus X_{i,2} \oplus X_{i,3} \oplus RK_i))$,
3. The ciphertext is $X^{32} = (X_{32,0}, X_{32,1}, X_{32,2}, X_{32,3})$,

where RK_i is the 32-bit round subkey for the i-th round, the transformation L is defined as $\mathrm{L}(x) = x \oplus (x \lll 2) \oplus (x \lll 10) \oplus (x \lll 18) \oplus (x \lll 24)$, for $x \in Z_2^{32}$, and the transformation S applies the same 8×8 bijective S-Box (see Table 1) four times in parallel to an input, and it is defined as follows.

$$input : A = (a_0, a_1, a_2, a_3) \in (Z_2^8)^4, \ output : B = (b_0, b_1, b_2, b_3) \in (Z_2^8)^4$$

$$substitution : B = \mathrm{S}(A) \Leftrightarrow b_j = \text{S-Box}(a_j), \ for \ j = 0, 1, 2, 3.$$

---

[1] Note that the first round is referred as Round 0.

Table 1. The S-Box table of SMS4

	0x0	0x1	0x2	0x3	0x4	0x5	0x6	0x7	0x8	0x9	0xa	0xb	0xc	0xd	0xe	0xf
0x0	d6	90	e9	fe	cc	e1	3d	b7	16	b6	14	c2	28	fb	2c	05
0x1	2b	67	9a	76	2a	be	04	c3	aa	44	13	26	49	86	06	99
0x2	9c	42	50	f4	91	ef	98	7a	33	54	0b	43	ed	cf	ac	62
0x3	e4	b3	1c	a9	c9	08	e8	95	80	df	94	fa	75	8f	3f	a6
0x4	47	07	a7	fc	f3	73	17	ba	83	59	3c	19	e6	85	4f	a8
0x5	68	6b	81	b2	71	64	da	8b	f8	eb	0f	4b	70	56	9d	35
0x6	1e	24	0e	5e	63	58	d1	a2	25	22	7c	3b	01	21	78	87
0x7	d4	00	46	57	9f	d3	27	52	4c	36	02	e7	a0	c4	c8	9e
0x8	ea	bf	8a	d2	40	c7	38	b5	a3	f7	f2	ce	f9	61	15	a1
0x9	e0	ae	5d	a4	9b	34	1a	55	ad	93	32	30	f5	8c	b1	e3
0xa	1d	f6	e2	2e	82	66	ca	60	c0	29	23	ab	0d	53	4e	6f
0xb	d5	db	37	45	de	fd	8e	2f	03	ff	6a	72	6d	6c	5b	51
0xc	8d	1b	af	92	bb	dd	bc	7f	11	d9	5c	41	1f	10	5a	d8
0xd	0a	c1	31	88	a5	cd	7b	bd	2d	74	d0	12	b8	e5	b4	b0
0xe	89	69	97	4a	0c	96	77	7e	65	b9	f1	09	c5	6e	c6	84
0xf	18	f0	7d	ec	3a	dc	4d	20	79	ee	5f	3e	d7	cb	39	48

The composed transformation L ∘ S is called T in the specification document [1]. Fig. 1 depicts one encryption round of SMS4. Decryption is identical to encryption, except that the round keys are used in the reverse order.

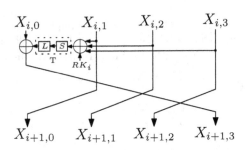

Fig. 1. The i-th encryption round of SMS4

The key schedule of SMS4 accepts a 128-bit user key MK, represented as four 32-bit words (MK_0, MK_1, MK_2, MK_3). The j-th round subkey RK_j $(0 \leq j \leq 31)$ is generated as follows.

- Compute $(K_0, K_1, K_2, K_3) = (MK_0 \oplus FK_0, MK_1 \oplus FK_1, MK_2 \oplus FK_2, MK_3 \oplus FK_3)$, where $FK_0 = 0xa3b1bac6$, $FK_1 = 0x56aa3350$, $FK_2 = 0x677d9197$, and $FK_3 = 0xb27022dc$.
- Compute $RK_j = K_{j+4} = K_j \oplus L'(S(K_{j+1} \oplus K_{j+2} \oplus K_{j+3} \oplus CK_j))$, where the transformation L' is defined as $L'(x) = x \oplus (x \lll 13) \oplus (x \lll 23)$, for $x \in Z_2^{32}$, and the constant $CK_j = (ck_{j,0}, ck_{j,1}, ck_{j,2}, ck_{j,3}) \in (Z_2^8)^4$, with $ck_{j,k} = 28j + 7k \bmod 256$ $(k = 0, 1, 2, 3)$. The composed transformation L' ∘ S is called T' in the specification document.

3   Properties of SMS4 and Definitions

We first introduce three properties of SMS4, which are important to our attacks.

Property 1. *For the nonlinear transformation S, $\mathrm{S}(\Delta x) = 0$ if, and only if, $x = 0$ ($x \in Z_2^{32}$).*

Property 2. *For the linear transformation L, $\mathrm{L}(x) = 0$ if, and only if, $x = 0$ ($x \in Z_2^{32}$).*

Property 3. *For the S-Box, there exist 127 possible output differences for any nonzero input difference, of which 1 output difference occurs with probability 2^{-6}, and each of the other 126 output differences occurs with probability 2^{-7}.*

Property 1 is obvious; Properties 2 and 3 can be verified by two simple computer programs.

We next give two definitions.

Definition 1. *Let Λ be an arbitrary but nonempty subset of any of the four sets $\{0, 1, \cdots, 7\}$, $\{8, 9, \cdots, 15\}$, $\{16, 17, \cdots, 23\}$ and $\{24, 25, \cdots, 31\}$, then we define the set $\Omega(e_\Lambda)$ as follows:*

$$\Omega(e_\Lambda) = \{x | x = \mathrm{L}(y), \mathrm{Pr}(\mathrm{S}(\Delta e_\Lambda) \to \Delta y) = 2^{-6}, x, y \in Z_2^{32}\}.$$

Note that $|\Omega(e_\Lambda)| = 1$ holds for any nonempty Λ by Property 3.

Definition 2. *Let Λ be an arbitrary but nonempty subset of the set $\{0, 1, \cdots, 31\}$; then we define the three sets $\Theta(e_\Lambda)$, $\Upsilon(e_\Lambda, m \in \Theta(e_\Lambda))$ and $\Pi(e_\Lambda, m \in \Theta(e_\Lambda), n \in \Upsilon(e_\Lambda, m))$ as follows:*

- $\Theta(e_\Lambda) = \{x | x = \mathrm{L}(y), \mathrm{Pr}(\mathrm{S}(\Delta e_\Lambda) \to \Delta y) > 0, x, y \in Z_2^{32}\}$.
- $\Upsilon(e_\Lambda, m \in \Theta(e_\Lambda)) = \{x | x = \mathrm{L}(y) \oplus e_\Lambda, y \in \{z | \mathrm{Pr}(\mathrm{S}(\Delta m) \to \Delta z) > 0, z \in Z_2^{32}\}, x, y \in Z_2^{32}\}$.
- $\Pi(e_\Lambda, m \in \Theta(e_\Lambda), n \in \Upsilon(e_\Lambda, m)) = \{x | x = \mathrm{L}(y) \oplus e_\Lambda, y \in \{z | \mathrm{Pr}(\mathrm{S}(\Delta(e_\Lambda \oplus m \oplus n)) \to \Delta z) > 0, z \in Z_2^{32}\}, x, y \in Z_2^{32}\}$.

4   Rectangle Attack on 14-Round SMS4

Being a variant of the boomerang attack [15] and an improvement of the amplified boomerang attack [8], the rectangle attack [4] shares the same basic idea of using two short differentials with larger probabilities instead of a long differential with a smaller probability. A rectangle attack is based on a rectangle distinguisher, which treats a block cipher $E : \{0, 1\}^n \times \{0, 1\}^k \to \{0, 1\}^n$ as a cascade of two sub-ciphers $E = E^1 \circ E^0$.

In this section, we exploit certain 12-round rectangle distinguishers with probability $2^{-237.64}$, such that we can conduct a rectangle attack on SMS4 reduced to that operates 14 rounds.

4.1   12-Round Rectangle Distinguishers with Probability $2^{-237.64}$

Let E^0 denote Rounds 0 to 7 of SMS4, and E^1 denote Rounds 8 to 11 of SMS4. The differentials for the 12-round distinguishers are as follows.

- The following 8-round differentials $\alpha \rightarrow \beta'$ are used for E^0: $(e_{\Psi_1}, e_\Psi, e_\Psi, e_\Psi) \rightarrow (e_{\Psi_2}, e_{\Psi_3}, e_{\Psi_4}, e_{\Psi_5})$, where Ψ is an arbitrary but nonempty subset of any of the four sets $\{0, 1, \cdots, 7\}$, $\{8, 9, \cdots, 15\}$, $\{16, 17, \cdots, 23\}$ and $\{24, 25, \cdots, 31\}$, $e_{\Psi_1} \in \Omega(e_\Psi)$, $e_{\Psi_2} \in \Theta(e_\Psi)$, $e_{\Psi_3} \in \Upsilon(e_\Psi, e_{\Psi_2})$, $e_{\Psi_4} \in \Pi(e_\Psi, e_{\Psi_2}, e_{\Psi_3})$, and $e_{\Psi_5} \in \{x | x = \mathrm{L}(y) \oplus e_\Lambda, y \in \{z | Prob.(\mathrm{S}(\Delta(e_{\Psi_2} \oplus e_{\Psi_3} \oplus e_{\Psi_4})) \rightarrow \Delta z) > 0, z \in Z_2^{32}\}, x, y \in Z_2^{32}\}$.
- The following 4-round differentials $\gamma \rightarrow \delta'$ are used for E^1: $(e_\Phi, e_\Phi, e_\Phi, 0) \rightarrow (e_\Phi, e_\Phi, e_\Phi, e_{\Phi_2})$, where Φ is an arbitrary but nonempty subset of any of the four sets $\{0, 1, \cdots, 7\}$, $\{8, 9, \cdots, 15\}$, $\{16, 17, \cdots, 23\}$ and $\{24, 25, \cdots, 31\}$, $e_{\Phi_2} \in \Theta(e_\Phi)$.

See Table 2 for the details of these two groups of differentials, where the difference in a round is the input difference to this round. The same meaning is used with the differentials in the next section. Note that different Ψ and/or Φ correspond to different rectangle distinguishers. In the following, we assume Ψ and Φ are fixed.

Table 2. The two groups of differentials in the 12-round rectangle distinguisher, where † means that the probability is addressed later

Round(i)	$\Delta X_{i,0}$	$\Delta X_{i,1}$	$\Delta X_{i,2}$	$\Delta X_{i,3}$	Prob.	Round(i)	$\Delta X_{i,0}$	$\Delta X_{i,1}$	$\Delta X_{i,2}$	$\Delta X_{i,3}$	Prob.
0	e_{Ψ_1}	e_Ψ	e_Ψ	e_Ψ	2^{-6}	7	e_Ψ	e_{Ψ_2}	e_{Ψ_3}	e_{Ψ_4}	†
1	e_Ψ	e_Ψ	e_Ψ	0	1	output	e_{Ψ_2}	e_{Ψ_3}	e_{Ψ_4}	e_{Ψ_5}	/
2	e_Ψ	e_Ψ	0	e_Ψ	1	8	e_Φ	e_Φ	e_Φ	0	1
3	e_Ψ	0	e_Ψ	e_Ψ	1	9	e_Φ	e_Φ	0	e_Φ	1
4	0	e_Ψ	e_Ψ	e_Ψ		10	e_Φ	0	e_Φ	e_Φ	1
5	e_Ψ	e_Ψ	e_Ψ	e_{Ψ_2}	†	11	0	e_Φ	e_Φ	e_Φ	†
6	e_Ψ	e_Ψ	e_{Ψ_2}	e_{Ψ_3}		output	e_Φ	e_Φ	e_Φ	e_{Φ_2}	/

In the following, we need to sum the square of the probabilities of all the possible differentials $\alpha \rightarrow \beta'$. As there exist many more differential characteristics than we can count, it is infeasible to compute the exact square sum; however, we can compute a lower bound for it. By the Property 3 in Section 3, we can learn that for a fixed Ψ, there exists one e_{Ψ_2} such that the probability that $\mathrm{L}(\mathrm{S}(\Delta e_\Psi)) \rightarrow \Delta e_{\Psi_2}$ is 2^{-6}, and exist 126 e_{Ψ_2} such that the probability that $\mathrm{L}(\mathrm{S}(\Delta e_\Psi)) \rightarrow \Delta e_{\Psi_2}$ is 2^{-7}. Due to the L transformation, the four 32-bit words in any e_Ψ are all nonzero. Thus, for any e_{Ψ_2}, if we define the *Event* A: $(\mathrm{L}(\mathrm{S}(\Delta e_{\Psi_2})) \oplus e_\Psi) \rightarrow \Delta e_{\Psi_3}$, then we can learn that there exists one possible e_{Ψ_3} with probability 2^{-24}, and exist $\binom{4}{3} \cdot 126$ possible e_{Ψ_3} with probability 2^{-25}, $\binom{4}{2} \cdot 126^2$ possible e_{Ψ_3} with probability 2^{-26}, $\binom{4}{1} \cdot 126^3$ possible e_{Ψ_3} with probability 2^{-27} and 126^4 possible e_{Ψ_3} with probability 2^{-28}. Consequently, for any e_{Ψ_2} and e_{Ψ_3}, if we define the *Event* B: $(L(S(\Delta(e_\Psi \oplus e_{\Psi_2} \oplus e_{\Psi_3}))) \oplus e_\Psi) \rightarrow \Delta e_{\Psi_4}$, then there exists one possible e_{Ψ_4} with probability 2^{-24}, and exist $\binom{4}{3} \cdot 126$ possible e_{Ψ_4} with probability 2^{-25}, $\binom{4}{2} \cdot 126^2$ possible e_{Ψ_4} with probability 2^{-26}, $\binom{4}{1} \cdot 126^3$ possible e_{Ψ_4} with probability 2^{-27} and 126^4 possible e_{Ψ_4} with probability 2^{-28}. Therefore, we can compute a square sum of at least $(2^{-6})^2 \cdot [(2^{-6})^2 + 126 \cdot (2^{-7})^2] \cdot [1 \cdot (2^{-24})^2 + \binom{4}{3} \cdot 126 \cdot (2^{-25})^2 + \binom{4}{2} \cdot 126^2 \cdot (2^{-26})^2 + \binom{4}{1} \cdot 126^3 \cdot (2^{-27})^2 + 126^4 \cdot (2^{-28})^2]^3 \approx 2^{-109.64}$.

For the 4-round differentials $\gamma \rightarrow \delta'$, as mentioned earlier, there are 127 possible e_{Φ_2}, 1 possibility with probability 2^{-6} and each of the other 126 possibilities with probability 2^{-7}, thus, this 12-round rectangle distinguisher has a probability of at least $2^{-109.64} \cdot [(1 \cdot 2^{-6} + 126 \cdot 2^{-7})]^2 \cdot 2^{-128} \approx 2^{-237.64}$ for the correct key, while it has a probability of $(2^{-128} \cdot 127)^2 \approx 2^{-242.02}$ for a wrong key.

The 12-round distinguisher can be used to mount a rectangle attack on 14-round SMS4. Without loss of generality, we assume the attacked 14 rounds are the first 14 rounds from Rounds 0 to 13. Given the 127 input differences $(e_\Phi, e_\Phi, e_\Phi, e_{\Phi_2})$ to Round 12, there are at most 127^5 possible output differences $\{(e_\Phi, e_\Phi, e_{\Phi_2}, e_{\Phi_3}) | e_{\Phi_3} \in \Upsilon(e_\Phi, e_{\Phi_2})\}$ just after Round 12, and at most 127^9 possible output differences $\{(e_\Phi, e_{\Phi_2}, e_{\Phi_3}, e_{\Phi_4}) | e_{\Phi_3} \in \Upsilon(e_\Phi, e_{\Phi_2}), e_{\Phi_4} \in \Pi(e_\Phi, e_{\Phi_2}, e_{\Phi_3})\}$ just after Round 13.

As mentioned in the Introduction, our rectangle attack, as well as the impossible differential attack in the next section, uses the early abort technique introduced in [11,12,13]; the main idea of the early abort technique is to partially determine whether or not a candidate quartet in a rectangle attack (or a candidate pair in an impossible differential attack) is valid earlier than usual, by guessing only a small fraction of subkeys required; if not, we can discard it immediately, which results in less computations in the left steps and may allow us to break more rounds by guessing the subkeys involved, depending on how many candidates are remaining.

The attack procedure is as follows.

4.2   Attack Procedure

1. Choose $2^{120.82}$ pairs of plaintexts $(P_i, \widetilde{P}_i)$ with difference $(e_{\Psi_1}, e_\Psi, e_\Psi, e_\Psi)$, $i = 1, 2, \cdots, 2^{120.82}$. In a chosen-plaintext attack scenario, obtain their corresponding ciphertext pairs; we denote them by $(C_i, \widetilde{C}_i)$, respectively. These ciphertext pairs generate about $2^{120.82 \times 2}/2 = 2^{240.64}$ candidate quartets $((C_{i_1}, \widetilde{C}_{i_1}), (C_{i_2}, \widetilde{C}_{i_2}))$, for $1 \leq i_1 \leq i_2 \leq 2^{120.82}$. We only choose those such that both $C_{i_1} \oplus C_{i_2}$ and $\widetilde{C}_{i_1} \oplus \widetilde{C}_{i_2}$ belong to $\{(e_\Phi, e_{\Phi_2}, e_{\Phi_3}, e_{\Phi_4}) | e_{\Phi_3} \in \Upsilon(e_\Phi, e_{\Phi_2}), e_{\Phi_4} \in \Pi(e_\Phi, e_{\Phi_2}, e_{\Phi_3})\}$.
2. For all the remaining quartets $((C_{i_1}, \widetilde{C}_{i_1}), (C_{i_2}, \widetilde{C}_{i_2}))$, do as follows.
   (a) For (C_{i_1}, C_{i_2}), compute the four-byte difference of their intermediate values just before the L transformation in Round 13; we denote them by $(\Delta^{13}_{i_1,i_2,0}, \Delta^{13}_{i_1,i_2,1}, \Delta^{13}_{i_1,i_2,2}, \Delta^{13}_{i_1,i_2,3})$, respectively. For $(\widetilde{C}_{i_1}, \widetilde{C}_{i_2})$, compute the four-byte difference of their intermediate values just before the L transformation in Round 13; we denote them by $(\widetilde{\Delta}^{13}_{i_1,i_2,0}, \widetilde{\Delta}^{13}_{i_1,i_2,1}, \widetilde{\Delta}^{13}_{i_1,i_2,2}, \widetilde{\Delta}^{13}_{i_1,i_2,3})$, respectively.

(b) For $j = 0$ to 3: Guess the j-th byte $RK_{13,j}$ of the subkey RK_{13} in Round 13, and partially decrypt every remaining quartet $((C_{i_1}, C_{i_2}), (\widetilde{C}_{i_1}, \widetilde{C}_{i_2}))$ with $RK_{13,j}$ to get the j-th bytes of their intermediate values just after the S transformation in Round 13; we denote them by $((T_{i_1,j}, T_{i_2,j}),$ $(\widetilde{T}_{i_1,j}, \widetilde{T}_{i_2,j}))$, respectively. Finally, check if $T_{i_1,j} \oplus T_{i_2,j} = \Delta^{13}_{i_1,i_2,j}$ and $\widetilde{T}_{i_1,j} \oplus \widetilde{T}_{i_2,j} = \widetilde{\Delta}^{13}_{i_1,i_2,j}$. If 6 or more quartets pass this test, execute next with them, (otherwise, repeat this iteration with another key guess). Finally, for every remaining $((C_{i_1}, \widetilde{C}_{i_1}), (C_{i_2}, \widetilde{C}_{i_2}))$ we get their intermediate values just after Round 12; we denote them by $((T_{i_1}, \widetilde{T}_{i_1}), (T_{i_2}, \widetilde{T}_{i_2}))$, respectively.

3. For all the quartets $((T_{i_1}, \widetilde{T}_{i_1}), (T_{i_2}, \widetilde{T}_{i_2}))$, do as follows.

   (a) For (T_{i_1}, T_{i_2}), compute the four-byte difference of their intermediate values just before the L transformation in Round 12; we denote them by $(\Delta^{12}_{i_1,i_2,0}, \Delta^{12}_{i_1,i_2,1}, \Delta^{12}_{i_1,i_2,2}, \Delta^{12}_{i_1,i_2,3})$, respectively. For $(\widetilde{T}_{i_1}, \widetilde{T}_{i_2})$, compute the four-byte difference of their intermediate values just before the L transformation in Round 12; we denote them by $(\widetilde{\Delta}^{12}_{i_1,i_2,0}, \widetilde{\Delta}^{12}_{i_1,i_2,1}, \widetilde{\Delta}^{12}_{i_1,i_2,2}, \widetilde{\Delta}^{12}_{i_1,i_2,3})$, respectively.

   (b) For $j = 0$ to 3: Guess the j-th byte $RK_{12,j}$ of the subkey RK_{12} in Round 12, partially decrypt every quartet $((T_{i_1}, T_{i_2}), (\widetilde{T}_{i_1}, \widetilde{T}_{i_2}))$ with $RK_{12,j}$ to get the j-th bytes of their intermediate values just after the S transformation in Round 12; we denote them by $((Q_{i_1,j}, Q_{i_2,j}), (\widetilde{Q}_{i_1,j}, \widetilde{Q}_{i_2,j}))$, respectively. Finally, check if $Q_{i_1,j} \oplus Q_{i_2,j} = \Delta^{12}_{i_1,i_2,j}$ and $\widetilde{Q}_{i_1,j} \oplus \widetilde{Q}_{i_2,j} = \widetilde{\Delta}^{12}_{i_1,i_2,j}$. If 6 or more quartets pass this test, execute next with them, (otherwise, repeat this iteration with another key guess).

4. For every (RK_{12}, RK_{13}) passing Step 3, we can deduce that there are at most 2^{64} possible 128-bit user keys from these two 32-bit subkeys. Then, we do a trial encryption with one known pair of plaintext and ciphertext. If a 128-bit key is suggested, output it as the user key of the 14-round SMS4; otherwise, go to Step 2-(b).

To produce a difference $(e_\Phi, e_\Phi, e_\Phi, e_{\Phi_2})$ just before Round 12, the two ciphertext pairs in a right quartet must have differences belonging to the set $\{(e_\Phi, e_{\Phi_2}, e_{\Phi_3}, e_{\Phi_4}) | e_{\Phi_3} \in \Upsilon(e_\Phi, e_{\Phi_2}), e_{\Phi_4} \in \Pi(e_\Phi, e_{\Phi_2}, e_{\Phi_3})\}$, so a candidate quartet that does not meet this filtering condition is an incorrect quartet. As a result, only about $2^{240.64} \cdot (\frac{127^9}{2^{128}})^2 \approx 2^{110.46}$ candidate quartets are chosen in Step 1.

In Steps 2-(b) and 3-(b), a candidate quartet passes every test with a probability of $(\frac{1}{127})^2 \approx 2^{-13.98}$, and the number of the pairs passing every step has a binomial distribution, so it is expected that almost all the 2^{56} guesses of $(RK_{12,0}, RK_{12,1}, RK_{12,2}, RK_{13,0}, RK_{13,1}, RK_{13,2}, RK_{13,3})$ will pass the test with $j = 2$ in Step 3-(b), and for every guess about $2^{110.46} \cdot 2^{-13.98 \times 7} = 2^{12.6}$ candidate quartets are expected to remain after the test with $j = 2$ in Step 3-(b). In the test with $j = 3$ in Step 3-(b), the probability that 6 or more quartets pass the tests for a wrong guess is approximately $\sum_{i=6}^{2^{12.6}} [\binom{2^{12.6}}{i} \cdot (2^{-13.98})^i \cdot (1 - 2^{-13.98})^{2^{12.6}-i}] \approx 2^{-17.77}$, thus it is expected that about $2^{64} \cdot 2^{-17.77} = 2^{46.23}$

Table 3. The two 6-round differentials in the 12-round impossible differentials, where $x_i \in \Theta(e_\Gamma), y_i \in \Upsilon(e_\Gamma, x_i), z_i \in \Pi(e_\Gamma, x_i, y_i), (i = 1, 2)$

Round(i) ↓	$\Delta X_{i,0}$	$\Delta X_{i,1}$	$\Delta X_{i,2}$	$\Delta X_{i,3}$	Round(i) ↑	$\Delta X_{i,0}$	$\Delta X_{i,1}$	$\Delta X_{i,2}$	$\Delta X_{i,3}$
0	e_Γ	e_Γ	e_Γ	0	6	z_2	y_2	x_2	e_Γ
1	e_Γ	e_Γ	0	e_Γ	7	y_2	x_2	e_Γ	e_Γ
2	e_Γ	0	e_Γ	e_Γ	8	x_2	e_Γ	e_Γ	e_Γ
3	0	e_Γ	e_Γ	e_Γ	9	e_Γ	e_Γ	e_Γ	0
4	e_Γ	e_Γ	e_Γ	x_1	10	e_Γ	e_Γ	0	e_Γ
5	e_Γ	e_Γ	x_1	y_1	11	e_Γ	0	e_Γ	e_Γ
output	e_Γ	x_1	y_1	z_1	output	0	e_Γ	e_Γ	e_Γ

guesses of (RK_{12}, RK_{13}) are suggested after the test with $j = 3$ in Step 3-(b). In Step 4, the expected number of wrong 128-bit keys is about $2^{-128} \cdot 2^{46.23+64} = 2^{-17.77}$, which is very low.

The attack requires $2^{121.82}$ chosen plaintexts. The required memory space is dominated by the ciphertexts, which is about $2^{121.82} \cdot 16 = 2^{125.82}$ memory bytes. The time complexity of Steps 2–4 is dominated by the partial decryptions for $j = 0$ in Step 2-(b), which is about $4 \cdot 2^8 \cdot 2^{110.46} \cdot \frac{1}{14} \approx 2^{116.66}$ 14-round SMS4 computations.

As the probability of the distinguisher is $2^{-237.64}$, it is expect there are $8(= 2^{240.64} \cdot 2^{-237.64})$ right quartets for the correct key in Step 3-(c). The probability that 6 or more quartets pass the test in Step 3-(c) for the correct subkeys is approximately $\sum_{i=6}^{2^{240.64}} [\binom{2^{240.64}}{i} \cdot (2^{-237.64})^i \cdot (1 - 2^{-237.64})^{2^{240.64}-i}] \approx 0.8$, therefore, with a success probability of 80%, this related-key rectangle attack can break 14-round SMS4, faster than an exhaustive key search.

5   Impossible Differential Attack on 16-Round SMS4

An impossible differential [2] is a differential [5] with a zero probability; that is, it would never happen under any situation.

In this section, we exploit certain 12-round impossible differentials in SMS4. Finally, we show that impossible differential cryptanalysis can break SMS4 reduced to 16 rounds.

5.1   12-Round Impossible Differentials

The 12-round impossible differentials are $(e_\Gamma, e_\Gamma, e_\Gamma, 0) \nrightarrow (0, e_\Gamma, e_\Gamma, e_\Gamma)$, where Γ is defined as an arbitrary but nonempty subset of the set $\{0, 1, \cdots, 15\}$. These 12-round impossible differentials are built in a miss-in-the-middle manner [3]: a 6-round differential with probability 1 is concatenated with another 6-round differential with probability 1, but the intermediate differences of these two differentials contradict one another. See Table 3.

The first 6-round differential with probability 1 is $(e_\Gamma, e_\Gamma, e_\Gamma, 0) \rightarrow (e_\Gamma, ?, ?, ?)$. The input difference $(e_\Gamma, e_\Gamma, e_\Gamma, 0)$ to Round 0 propagates with probability 1 to the difference $(e_\Gamma, e_\Gamma, 0, e_\Gamma)$ after one round, which then propagates with a 1 probability to the difference $(0, e_\Gamma, e_\Gamma, e_\Gamma)$ after the following two rounds. Then, the difference $(0, e_\Gamma, e_\Gamma, e_\Gamma)$ definitely propagates to a difference belonging to the set $\{(e_\Gamma, e_\Gamma, e_\Gamma, x_1) | x_1 \in \Theta(e_\Gamma)\}$ after Round 3, which finally propagates with probability 1 to a difference belonging to $\{(e_\Gamma, x_1, y_1, z_1) | x_1 \in \Theta(e_\Gamma), y_1 \in \Upsilon(e_\Gamma, x_1), z_1 \in \Pi(e_\Gamma, x_1, y_1)\}$ after Rounds 4 and 5. On the other hand, when we roll back the output difference $(0, e_\Gamma, e_\Gamma, e_\Gamma)$ of the second 6-round differential through the three consecutive rounds from Rounds 9 to 11 in the reverse direction, we will get the difference $(e_\Gamma, e_\Gamma, e_\Gamma, 0)$ just before Round 9 with probability 1. Then, when we roll back the difference $(e_\Gamma, e_\Gamma, e_\Gamma, 0)$ through Round 8, we will definitely get a difference belonging to the set $\{(x_2, e_\Gamma, e_\Gamma, e_\Gamma) | x_2 \in \Theta(e_\Gamma)\}$. Finally, when we continue to go back for two more rounds, we can definitely get a difference belonging to the set $\{(z_2, y_2, x_2, e_\Gamma) | x_2 \in \Theta(e_\Gamma), y_2 \in \Upsilon(e_\Gamma, x_2), z_2 \in \Pi(e_\Gamma, x_2, y_2)\}$ just before Round 6. Now, a contradiction occurs, for we never get the one-round output difference $\{(y_2, x_2, e_\Gamma, e_\Gamma) | x_2 \in \Theta(e_\Gamma), y_2 \in \Upsilon(e_\Gamma, x_2)\}$ given an input difference belonging to $\{(e_\Gamma, x_1, y_1, z_1) | x_1 \in \Theta(e_\Gamma), y_1 \in \Upsilon(e_\Gamma, x_1), z_1 \in \Pi(e_\Gamma, x_1, y_1)\}$. More specifically, to get a one-round output difference belonging to $\{(y_2, x_2, e_\Gamma, e_\Gamma) | x_2 \in \Theta(e_\Gamma), y_2 \in \Upsilon(e_\Gamma, x_2)\}$, the input difference of the second 6-round differential should belong to the set $\{(z_2, y_2, x_2, e_\Gamma) | x_2 \in \Theta(e_\Gamma), y_2 \in \Upsilon(e_\Gamma, x_2), z_2 \in \Pi(e_\Gamma, x_2, y_2)\}$, however, note that the output difference of the first 6-round differential is $\{(e_\Gamma, x_1, y_1, z_1) | x_1 \in \Theta(e_\Gamma), y_1 \in \Upsilon(e_\Gamma, x_1), z_1 \in \Pi(e_\Gamma, x_1, y_1)\}$, so it is a necessary that the following five conditions should hold for some sextuple $(x_1, y_1, z_1, x_2, y_2, z_2)$, where $x_1, x_2 \in \Theta(e_\Gamma)$, $y_1 \in \Upsilon(e_\Gamma, x_1)$, $y_2 \in \Upsilon(e_\Gamma, x_2)$, $z_1 \in \Pi(e_\Gamma, x_1, y_1)$ and $z_2 \in \Pi(e_\Gamma, x_2, y_2)$:

$$x_2 = y_1, \tag{1}$$

$$y_2 = x_1, \tag{2}$$

$$z_1 = e_\Gamma, \tag{3}$$

$$z_2 = e_\Gamma, \tag{4}$$

$$L(S(x_1 \oplus y_1 \oplus e_\Gamma)) \oplus e_\Gamma = e_\Gamma. \tag{5}$$

By Properties 1 and 2 in Section 3, we can learn that Eq. (5) is equivalent to the following equation:

$$x_1 \oplus y_1 \oplus e_\Gamma = 0. \tag{6}$$

We perform a computer search over all the possibilities that may satisfy Eqs. (1)–(4) and (6), but find that there does not exist such a qualified sextuple $(x_1, y_1, z_1, x_2, y_2, z_2)$ for any nonempty subset Γ of the set $\{0, 1, \cdots, 15\}$. Thus, these 12-round impossible differentials are impossible.

Before further proceeding, we would like to give the following two remarks: i) We did not check whether there also exist similar 12-round impossible differentials if Γ is defined as an arbitrary but nonempty subset of the set $\{0, 1, \cdots, 31\}$ (excluding those described above), for this is much more time-consuming due to a sharp increase on the number of the possible differences. It is reasonably thought that there also exist similar 12-round impossible differentials for them. ii) We did not check whether one or more of the 12-round impossible differentials can be extended to 13-round impossible differentials by appending one-round differential $(e_\Gamma, x_1, y_1, z_1) \to (x_1, y_1, z_1, ?)$ after the first 6-round differential or one-round differential $(?, z_2, y_2, x_2) \to (z_2, y_2, x_2, e_\Gamma)$ before the second 6-round differential; as there are so many possibilities (some may be identical) for any Γ that we do not have an enough powerful computer/workstation on our hands to check these possibilities with a bearable running time.

We can use a 12-round impossible differential to conduct an impossible differential attack on SMS4 reduced to 16 rounds, by taking advantage of the early abort technique introduced in [13]. We assume the attacked 16 rounds are from Rounds 0 to 15. To reduce the data and time complexities of the attack, we choose $\Gamma = \{0, 1, \cdots, 15\}$. We use the 12-round impossible differential from Rounds 2 to 13. Given the output difference $(e_{0,1,\cdots,15}, e_{0,1,\cdots,15}, e_{0,1,\cdots,15}, 0)$ of Round 1, there are 127^2 possible input differences to Round 1, and at most 127^6 possible input differences to Round 0; we denote them by the set Σ_1. Given the input difference $(0, e_{0,1,\cdots,15}, e_{0,1,\cdots,15}, e_{0,1,\cdots,15})$ to Round 14, there are at most 127^2 possible output differences just after Round 14, and at most 127^6 possible output differences just after Round 15; we denote them by the set Σ_2. The attack procedure is as follows.

5.2   Attack Procedure

1. Select 2^9 structures of 2^{96} plaintexts each, where the most significant 16 bits of the rightmost two words of the plaintexts in a structure are fixed to certain values, and all the other 96 bit positions take all the possible values. Each structure generates $(2^{96}/2)^2 = 2^{190}$ plaintext pairs (P_i, P_j) with difference $(?, ?, e_{0,1,\cdots,15}, e_{0,1,\cdots,15})$; thus, the 2^9 structures propose 2^{199} plaintext pairs with difference $(?, ?, e_{0,1,\cdots,15}, e_{0,1,\cdots,15})$. In a chosen-plaintext attack scenario, obtain all the ciphertexts of P_i and P_j; we denote them by C_i and C_j, respectively. Choose only the ciphertext pairs (C_i, C_j) such that $P_i \oplus P_j \in \Sigma_1$ and $C_i \oplus C_j \in \Sigma_2$.

2. For all the remaining pairs (C_i, C_j), compute the four-byte difference of their intermediate values just before the L transformation in Round 15; we denote them by $(\Delta_{i,j,0}^{15}, \Delta_{i,j,1}^{15}, \Delta_{i,j,2}^{15}, \Delta_{i,j,3}^{15})$, respectively. Do as follows.

   (a) For $l = 0$ to 3: Guess the l-th byte $RK_{15,l}$ of the subkey RK_{15} in Round 15, partially decrypt (C_i, C_j) with $RK_{15,l}$ to get the l-th bytes of their intermediate values just after the S transformation in Round 15; we denote them by $(T_{i,l}, T_{j,l})$, respectively, and keep the pairs such that $T_{i,l} \oplus T_{j,l} = \Delta_{i,j,l}^{15}$.

   Finally, for every remaining (C_i, C_j) we can get their intermediate values just after Round 14 under the guess for RK_{15}; we denote them by (T_i, T_j), respectively.

(b) For all the remaining pairs (T_i, T_j), compute the four-byte difference of their intermediate values just before the L transformation in Round 14; we denote the first two bytes by $(\Delta_{i,j,0}^{14}, \Delta_{i,j,1}^{14})$, respectively.

(c) For $l = 0$ to 1: Guess the l-th byte $RK_{14,l}$ of the subkey RK_{14} in Round 14, partially decrypt (T_i, T_j) with $RK_{14,l}$ to get the l-th bytes of their intermediate values just after the S transformation in Round 14; we denote them by $(Q_{i,l}, Q_{j,l})$, respectively, and keep only the pairs such that $Q_{i,l} \oplus Q_{j,l} = \Delta_{i,j,l}^{14}$.

3. For all the plaintext pairs (P_i, P_j) corresponding to the remaining ciphertext pairs (C_i, C_j) after Step 2-(c), compute the four-byte difference of their intermediate values just before the L transformation in Round 0; we denote them by $(\Delta_{i,j,0}^0, \Delta_{i,j,1}^0, \Delta_{i,j,2}^0, \Delta_{i,j,3}^0)$, respectively. Do as follows.

(a) For $l = 0$ to 3: Guess the l-th byte $RK_{0,l}$ of the subkey RK_0 in Round 0, partially decrypt (P_i, P_j) with $RK_{0,l}$ to get the l-th bytes of their intermediate values just after the S transformation in Round 0; we denote them by $(R_{i,l}, R_{j,l})$, respectively, and keep only the pairs such that $R_{i,l} \oplus R_{j,l} = \Delta_{i,j,l}^0$.

Finally, for every remaining (P_i, P_j) we can get their intermediate values just after Round 0 under the guess for RK_0; we denote them by (R_i, R_j), respectively.

(b) For all the remaining pairs (R_i, R_j), compute the four-byte difference of their intermediate values just before the L transformation in Round 1; we denote the first two bytes by $(\Delta_{i,j,0}^1, \Delta_{i,j,1}^1)$, respectively.

(c) Guess the first byte $RK_{1,0}$ of the subkey RK_1 in Round 1, and partially decrypt (R_i, R_j) with $RK_{1,0}$ to get the first bytes of their intermediate values just after the S transformation in Round 1; we denote them by $(S_{i,0}, S_{j,0})$, respectively. Keep only the pairs such that $S_{i,0} \oplus S_{j,0} = \Delta_{i,j,0}^1$.

(d) Guess the second byte $RK_{1,1}$ of the subkey RK_1 in Round 1, partially decrypt (R_i, R_j) with $RK_{1,1}$ to get the second bytes of their intermediate values just after the S transformation in Round 1; we denote them by $(S_{i,1}, S_{j,1})$, respectively, and check if $S_{i,1} \oplus S_{j,1} = \Delta_{i,j,1}^1$. If there exists a qualified pair, then discard the guess of the 96 subkey bits, and try another; otherwise, record it, and execute Step 4.

4. For a recorded guess of the 96 subkey bits, we can deduce that there are at most 2^{96} possible 128-bit user keys from these two 32-bit subkeys. Then, we do a trial encryption with one known pair of plaintext and ciphertext. If a 128-bit key is suggested, output it as the user key of the 16-round SMS4; otherwise, go to Step 2-(a).

To get the difference $(0, e_{0,1,\cdots,15}, e_{0,1,\cdots,15}, e_{0,1,\cdots,15})$ just before Round 14 a ciphertext pair must have a difference belonging to Σ_2, and its corresponding plaintext pair must have a difference belonging to Σ_1 to get the difference $(e_{0,1,\cdots,15}, e_{0,1,\cdots,15}, e_{0,1,\cdots,15}, 0)$ just before Round 2, which poses a filtering condition of $\frac{127^6}{2^{64}} \cdot \frac{127^6}{2^{128}} \approx 2^{-108.12}$ over all the ciphertext pairs. There is a filtering condition of $\frac{1}{127}$ in every test of Steps 2-(a), 2-(c), 3-(a) and 3-(c). Therefore, it is expected that only $2^{13.99}$ pairs pass Step 3-(c) for every guess of

$(RK_0, RK_{1,0}, RK_{14,0}, RK_{14,1}, RK_{15})$, and all these remaining pairs have the difference $(0, e_{0,1,\cdots,15}, e_{0,1,\cdots,15}, e_{0,1,\cdots,15})$ just before Round 14. In Step 3-(d), a remaining pair propagates with a probability of $\frac{1}{127}$ to a pair of intermediate values with difference $(e_{0,1,\cdots,15}, e_{0,1,\cdots,15}, e_{0,1,\cdots,15}, 0)$ just after Round 1, thus, we expect with a probability of $\frac{1}{127}$ to get a pair $(S_{i,1}, S_{j,1})$ such that $S_{i,1} \oplus S_{j,1} = \Delta_{i,j,1}^1$, which means the pair has a difference $(e_{0,1,\cdots,15}, e_{0,1,\cdots,15}, e_{0,1,\cdots,15}, 0)$ just after Round 1; however, a subkey guess for which there exists such a pair is impossible. Hence, after analysing all the $2^{13.99}$ remaining ciphertext pairs, only $2^{96} \cdot (1 - 2^{-6.99})^{2^{13.99}} \approx 2^{-88.32}$ possible guesses of the 96 subkey bits pass Step 3-(d). As a result, the expected number of wrong 128-bit keys in Step 4 is about $2^{-128} \cdot 2^{96} = 2^{-32}$, which is extremely low, so we can find the correct 128-bit user key.

The attack requires 2^{105} chosen plaintexts. The time complexity of Steps 2–4 is dominated by the partial encryptions/decryptions in Steps 2-(a), 2-(c), 3-(a), 3-(c) and 3-(d), which is approximately $\sum_{l=1}^{11}(2 \cdot 2^{90.88} \cdot 2^{8 \cdot l} \cdot \frac{1}{127^{l-1}} \cdot \frac{1}{16}) + 2 \cdot 2^{96} \cdot [1 + (1 - 2^{-6.99}) + \cdots + (1 - 2^{-6.99})^{2^{13.99}}] \cdot \frac{1}{16} \approx 2^{107}$ 16-round SMS4 computations.

6 Concluding Remarks

In this paper, we analyse the security of the SMS4 block cipher used in WAPI, a Chinese national standard. We present a rectangle attack on SMS4 reduced to 14 rounds and an impossible differential attack on SMS4 reduced to 16 rounds. These are better than any previously known cryptanalytic results on SMS4 in terms of the numbers of attacked rounds.

Like most cryptanalytic results on block ciphers, our attacks are theoretical in the sense of the assumptions of differential cryptanalysis. We stress that our cryptanalytic attacks do not endanger the full 32 round version of SMS4; the 32 rounds provide a sufficient safety margin against our attacks.

Acknowledgments

The author is very grateful to his supervisor Prof. Chris Mitchell and an anonymous referee for their editorial comments.

References

1. Office of State Commercial Cryptography Administration.: P.R. China, The SMS4 Block Cipher (in Chinese), Archive available at:
   `http://www.oscca.gov.cn/UpFile/200621016423197990.pdf`
2. Biham, E., Biryukov, A., Shamir, A.: Cryptanalysis of Skipjack reduced to 31 rounds using impossible differentials. In: Stern, J. (ed.) EUROCRYPT 1999. LNCS, vol. 1592, pp. 12–23. Springer, Heidelberg (1999)
3. Biham, E., Biryukov, A., Shamir, A.: Miss in the middle attacks on IDEA and Khufu. In: Knudsen, L.R. (ed.) FSE 1999. LNCS, vol. 1636, pp. 124–138. Springer, Heidelberg (1999)

4. Biham, E., Dunkelman, O., Keller, N.: The rectangle attack — rectangling the Serpent. In: Pfitzmann, B. (ed.) EUROCRYPT 2001. LNCS, vol. 2045, pp. 340–357. Springer, Heidelberg (2001)

5. Biham, E., Shamir, A.: Differential cryptanalysis of the Data Encryption Standard. Springer, Heidelberg (1993)

6. The Institute of Electrical and Electronics Engineers (IEEE), http://grouper.ieee.org/groups/802/11

7. International Standardization of Organization (ISO).: International Standard–ISO/IEC 8802-11: Wireless LAN Medium Access Control (MAC) and Physical Layer (PHY) specifications, http://www.iso.org/iso/en/CatalogueDetailPage.CatalogueDetail?CSNUMBER=39777

8. Kelsey, J., Kohno, T., Schneier, B.: Amplified boomerang attacks against reduced-round MARS and Serpent. In: Schneier, B. (ed.) FSE 2000. LNCS, vol. 1978, pp. 75–93. Springer, Heidelberg (2001)

9. Knudsen, L.R., Wagner, D.: Integral cryptanalysis. In: Daemen, J., Rijmen, V. (eds.) FSE 2002. LNCS, vol. 2365, pp. 112–127. Springer, Heidelberg (2002)

10. Liu, F., Ji, W., Hu, L., Ding, J., Lv, S., Pyshkin, A., Weinmann, R.P.: Analysis of the SMS4 block cipher. In: Pieprzyk, J., Ghodosi, H., Dawson, E. (eds.) ACISP 2007. LNCS, vol. 4586, pp. 158–170. Springer, Heidelberg (2007)

11. Lu, J., Kim, J., Keller, N., Dunkelman, O.: Related-key rectangle attack on 42-round SHACAL-2. In: Katsikas, S.K., Lopez, J., Backes, M., Gritzalis, S., Preneel, B. (eds.) ISC 2006. LNCS, vol. 4176, pp. 85–100. Springer, Heidelberg (2006)

12. Lu, J., Kim, J., Keller, N., Dunkelman, O.: Differential and rectangle attacks on reduced-round SHACAL-1. In: Barua, R., Lange, T. (eds.) INDOCRYPT 2006. LNCS, vol. 4329, pp. 17–31. Springer, Heidelberg (2006)

13. Lu, J., Kim, J., Keller, N., Dunkelman, O.: Improving the efficiency of impossible differential cryptanalysis of reduced Camellia and MISTY1, Archive available at: http://jiqiang.googlepages.com

14. National Institute of Standards and Technology.: U.S.A., Advanced Encryption Standard (AES) FIPS-197 (2001)

15. Wagner, D.: The boomerang attack. In: Knudsen, L.R. (ed.) FSE 1999. LNCS, vol. 1636, pp. 156–170. Springer, Heidelberg (1999)

16. Zhang, L., Wu, W.: Differential fault attack on SMS4 (in Chinese). Chinese Journal of Computers 29(9) (2006)

A Framework for Game-Based Security Proofs

David Nowak

Research Center for Information Security, AIST, Tokyo

Abstract. To be accepted, a cryptographic scheme must come with a proof that it satisfies some standard security properties. However, because cryptographic schemes are based on non-trivial mathematics, proofs are error-prone and difficult to check. The main contributions of this paper are a refinement of the game-based approach to security proofs, and its implementation on top of the proof assistant Coq. The proof assistant checks that the proof is correct and deals with the mundane part of the proof. An interesting feature of our framework is that our proofs are formal enough to be mechanically checked, but still readable enough to be humanly checked. We illustrate the use of our framework by proving in a systematic way the so-called semantic security of the encryption scheme Elgamal and its hashed version.

Keywords: formal verification, game, proof assistant, security.

1 Introduction

Information security is nowadays an important issue. Its essential ingredient is cryptography. To be accepted, a cryptographic scheme must come with a proof that it satisfies some standard security properties. However, because cryptographic schemes are based on non-trivial mathematics such as number theory, group theory or probability theory, this makes the proofs error-prone and difficult to check. Bellare and Rogaway even claim that "many proofs in cryptography have become essentially unverifiable" [5]. In particular, proofs often rely on assumptions that are not clearly stated. This is why they advocate the usage of sequences of games (a.k.a. game-playing technique or game-hopping technique).

This methodology is explicitly presented in [5] and [20] but has been used in various styles before in the literature. It is a way to structure proofs so as to make them less error-prone, more easily verifiable, and, ideally, machine-checkable. A proof starts with the initial game which comes from the definition of the security property to be proved. This can be seen as a challenge involving the attacker and oracles. Attacker and oracles are efficient probabilistic algorithms (usually modeled as probabilistic polynomial-time algorithms). Oracles model services provided by the environment. For example an oracle might provide signed messages in order to model the spying of signed messages circulating on a network. A testing oracle checks whether an attack is successful of not. There are also encryption and decryption oracles. From the initial game, one builds a sequence of games such that the last one is simple enough to reason on directly. The result

S. Qing, H. Imai, and G. Wang (Eds.): ICICS 2007, LNCS 4861, pp. 319–333, 2007.

is then backtracked to the initial game. This is possible because transformations result either in an equivalent game or introduce small enough and quantified changes.

Our contributions. Recently, Halevi [15] has advocated the need for a software which can deal with the mundane part of writing and checking game-based proofs. In order to aim at such goal, we present a refinement of the game-based approach to security proofs, and its implementation[1] on top of the proof assistant Coq[2]. A proof assistant can indeed check that a proof is correct and deal with its mundane part. Of course, human interaction is still needed in order to deal with the creative part of the proof. But, when using a proof assistant, two things are necessary. First, all the intermediate lemmas must be explicited; some of those lemmas are not stated by cryptographers in their proofs because they are considered too obvious in the context of security proofs. Second, a precise mathematical meaning must be given to games; in papers, this is usually either left implicit or informally explained in English. This is why we need to refine the game-based approach. We base our formalization on [20] where games are seen as probability distributions. Our aim is to have a framework in which proofs are formal enough to be mechanically checked, and readable enough to be humanly checked.

The approach to game-based proofs by Shoup [20] differs from the one by Bellare and Rogaway [5]: In the latter, games are seen as syntactic objects. An interest in founding our formalization on this latter approach would be the possibility for more automation because game transformations would be syntactic. But each syntactic transformation should then be proved correct with respect to a precise semantics in terms of probability distributions. However in [5] the semantics is left implicit. They provide arguments for their syntactic transformations, but they cannot be directly formalized in a proof assistant due to the lack of semantics.

We illustrate the use of our framework by proving in a systematic way the so-called semantic security of the encryption scheme ElGamal and its hashed version [12]. It is a widely-used asymmetric key encryption algorithm. It is notably used by GNU Privacy Guard software, recent versions of PGP and other cryptographic software. Under the so-called Decisional Diffie-Hellman (DDH) assumption [10], it can be proved *semantically secure* [21]. To the best of our knowledge, this is the first time a cryptographic scheme is fully machine-checked. This is not the case in related work (see Section 2).

Outline. We start with related work in Section 2. In Section 3, we introduce our mathematical framework. In Section 4, we formalize some security notions. In Section 5, we show how to prove semantic security for the encryption scheme ElGamal and its hashed version. Implementation issues in Coq are addressed in Section 6.

---

[1] A link to the source code is provided on Cryptology ePrint Archive together with the full version of this paper [18].

[2] See http://coq.inria.fr/

2   Related Work

A lot of work has been done in direction of automatic discovery of proofs. It is essentially based on the Dolev-Yao model [11] which requires a high-level of abstraction, and is thus far from the view usually adopted by cryptographers. In this paper, we are not considering automatic discovery of proofs, but instead we want to facilitate the writing and checking of actual proofs by cryptographers.

The so-called generic model and random oracle model have been formalized in Coq and applied to ElGamal [3]. In contrast to our approach, it is not based on sequences of games which had not yet been popularized by [5] and [20].

CryptoVerif is a software for automated security proofs with sequences of games [6]. It is in particular illustrated with a proof of the Full-Domain Hash (FDH) signature scheme [4]. However this proof relies on certain equivalences that have to be introduced by the user. Those non-trivial equivalences are proved manually in Appendix B of [7]. These are difficult parts of the proof that cannot be handled by CryptoVerif. Moreover this tool consists of 14800 lines of non-certified O'Caml codes. On the other hand, our tool is certified: all our game transformations have been proved correct in the proof assistant Coq.

A probabilistic Hoare-style logic has been proposed (but not implemented) in [9] to formalize game-based proofs. This logic allows for rigorous proofs but those proofs differ from game-based proofs by cryptographers. Indeed, because their language allows for while loops and state variables, they are led to use a Hoare-style logic. They illustrate their logic by proving semantic security of the non-hashed version of ElGamal. In our approach, logical reasoning is closer to the one used by cryptographers: we avoid while loops and state variables, and thus do not have to use a Hoare-style logic. It is possible because the variables used in [20] are mathematical variables in the sense that they are defined once and only once whereas the value of a state variable can change in the course of execution. By the way, the property that a variable is defined once and only once is also enforced in CryptoVerif. Moreover, while loops, if used, would have to be restricted because their unrestricted use might break the hypothesis that the attacker and the oracles are efficient algorithms. Our games are probability distributions which are easily defined in our framework. In the case of ElGamal, we finally obtain a more natural proof of semantic security than the one in [9].

In [16] a process calculus is defined (but not implemented) which allows to reason about cryptographic protocols using bisimulation techniques. Contrary to our approach it is not game-based and differs from usual proofs by cryptographers. It is illustrated by a proof of semantic security for ElGamal.

An encoding of game-based proofs in a proof assistant has been proposed very recently in [1]. It is dedicated for proofs in the random oracle model while our work focuses on the standard model. Up to now the implementation by [1] has only been used to prove the PRP/PRF switching lemma, but not yet a full-fledged cryptographic scheme. Compared to them, we have been very careful in making our design choices such that our implementation remains light. This is an important design issue in formal verification because formal proofs grow quickly in size when one tackles real-world use-cases. For illustration, one can compare the size of our implementation with theirs: their complete implementation consists of 7032 lines of code (compare with our 3381 lines) and their proof of the switching lemma consists of 535 lines (compare with our 160 lines for proving both correctness and semantic security of ElGamal).

3   Mathematical Framework

In this section we recall a few mathematical bases on which rely security proofs: probabilities, cyclic groups and properties relating them. We formulate them in a way suitable for formalization in the proof assistant Coq. In particular, we use the elegant notion of monad stemming from category theory [17] and functional programming [22][3].

3.1   Probabilities

Oracles and games are probabilistic algorithms. We model them as functions returning finite probability distributions. A probabilistic choice is a side effect. A standard way to model side effects is with a monad [17,22]. And indeed probability distributions have a monadic structure [2,19]. In our case we only need to consider the simpler case of finite probability distributions. In their definition we use the notion of multiset (sometimes also called a bag) which is a set where an element may have more than one occurrence. For example, the multisets $\{1, 2, 2\}$ and $\{1, 2\}$ are different; and the union of $\{1, 2, 2, 3\}$ and $\{1, 4, 4\}$ is equal to $\{1, 1, 2, 2, 3, 4, 4\}$.

Definition 3.1 (Finite probability distribution). *A finite probability distribution δ over a set A is a finite multiset of ordered pairs from $A \times \mathbb{R}$ such that $\sum_{(a,p)\in\delta} p = 1$. We write Δ_A for the set of finite probability distributions over a set A.*

From now on, we will use the word *distribution* as an abbreviation for *finite probability distribution*. Games and oracles are distributions defined by using three primitive operations: $[a]$ is the distribution consisting of only one value a with probability 1; let $x \Leftarrow \delta$ in $\varphi(x)$ consists of selecting randomly one value x from the distribution δ and passes it to the function φ; and $\bigoplus\{a_1, \ldots, a_n\}$ is the uniform distribution of the values $a_1, \ldots, a_n$. Before giving their formal meaning in the definition below, we need to define the ponderation of a distribution by a real number p:

$$p \cdot \{(a_1, p_1), \ldots, (a_n, p_n)\} =_{\text{def}} \{(a_1, p \cdot p_1), \ldots, (a_n, p \cdot p_n)\}$$

Definition 3.2 (Operations)

$$[a] \quad =_{def} \quad \{(a, 1)\} \tag{1}$$

$$\text{let } x \Leftarrow \delta \text{ in } \varphi(x) \quad =_{def} \quad \bigcup_{(a,p)\in\delta} p \cdot \varphi(a) \tag{2}$$

---

[3] No knowledge of category theory or functional programming is assumed.

$$\bigoplus \{a_1, \ldots, a_n\} \quad =_{def} \quad \{(a_1, \frac{1}{n}), \ldots, (a_n, \frac{1}{n})\} \tag{3}$$

It is easily seen that those three operations above produce well-defined distributions.

In the rest of this paper, we use the following abbreviations:

(i) let $x \leftarrow a$ in $\varphi(x)$ for   let $x \Leftarrow [a]$ in $\varphi(x)$, and
(ii) let $x \xleftarrow{R} A$ in $\varphi(x)$ for   let $x \Leftarrow \bigoplus A$ in $\varphi(x)$.

In (i) we choose ramdomly a value from a distribution with only one value: it is a deterministic assignment. (ii) is a notation for choosing a uniformly random value from a list of values.

It might seem surprising that our distributions are multisets instead of sets. If we were to take sets, our definition of let would be more tricky as it would involve a phase of normalization. Let us see why on an example. Consider the distribution defined by let $x \xleftarrow{R} \{1, 2\}$ in $[x \overset{?}{=} x]$ where $\overset{?}{=}$ is the function that returns the boolean true if its two arguments are equal, or false otherwise. The above defined distribution is equal to the multiset $\{(\text{true}, \frac{1}{2}), (\text{true}, \frac{1}{2})\}$. If distributions were sets, we would have to define let in such a way that it returns what might be called the normal form $\{(\text{true}, 1)\}$.

The following theorem states that we have indeed defined a (strong) monad.

Theorem 3.3 (Monad laws)

$$\text{let } x \leftarrow a \text{ in } \varphi(x) \quad = \quad \varphi(a) \tag{4}$$
$$\text{let } x \Leftarrow \delta \text{ in } [x] \quad = \quad \delta \tag{5}$$
$$\text{let } y \Leftarrow (\text{let } x \Leftarrow \delta \text{ in } \varphi(x)) \text{ in } \psi(y) \quad = \quad \text{let } x \Leftarrow \delta \text{ in let } y \Leftarrow \varphi(x) \text{ in } \psi(y) \tag{6}$$

In order to ease notations we assume that the operator let ... in is right-associative: this means that, for example, the right-hand side expression of Equation (6) above should be understood as

let $x \Leftarrow \delta$ in (let $y \Leftarrow \varphi(x)$ in $\psi(y)$).

Equation (4) allows for propagating constants. Equation (6) states associativity which allows for getting rid of nested let.

Based on our notion of distribution, we can now define the probability that an element chosen randomly from a distribution satisfies a certain predicate.

Definition 3.4 (Probability). *The probability* $\mathbf{Pr}\left(P(\delta)\right)$ *that an element chosen randomly in a distribution δ satisfies a predicate P is given by:*

$$\mathbf{Pr}\left(P(\delta)\right) \quad =_{def} \sum_{(a,p) \in \delta \text{ s.t. } P(a)} p$$

We write $\mathbf{Pr}_{\text{true}}\left(\delta\right)$ for $\mathbf{Pr}\left((x \mapsto x = \text{true})(\delta)\right)$ where $x \mapsto x = \text{true}$ is the predicate that holds iff its argument x is equal to the boolean value true.

The following proposition tells us how to compute the probability for a distribution defined by a let.

Proposition 3.5. *For all P, δ and φ,*

$$\mathbf{Pr}\left(P\left(\text{let } x \Leftarrow \delta \text{ in } \varphi(x)\right)\right) \;=\; \sum_{(a,p)\in\delta} p \cdot \mathbf{Pr}\left(P\left(\varphi(a)\right)\right)$$

The following corollary shows how to compute the probability of a successful equality test between a random value and a constant.

Corollary 3.6. *For any finite set A, for any $a \in A$,*

$$\mathbf{Pr}_{\text{true}}\left(\begin{array}{c} \text{let } x \xleftarrow{R} A \text{ in} \\ [x \overset{?}{=} a] \end{array}\right) \;=\; \frac{1}{|A|}$$

The following corollary allows for rewriting under a let.

Corollary 3.7. *For all sets A and B, for any distribution $\delta \in \Delta_A$, for all functions φ and ψ from A to Δ_B, if $\quad \forall a \in A \cdot \mathbf{Pr}\left(P\left(\varphi(a)\right)\right) = \mathbf{Pr}\left(P\left(\psi(a)\right)\right)$*

then $\quad \mathbf{Pr}\left(P\left(\text{let } x \Leftarrow \delta \text{ in } \varphi(x)\right)\right) \;=\; \mathbf{Pr}\left(P\left(\text{let } x \Leftarrow \delta \text{ in } \psi(x)\right)\right)$

As another corollary, we obtain a mean to replace a randomly uniform choice in a goal by a universal quantifier[4].

Corollary 3.8. *For all P, A, φ and p,*

$$\left(\forall x \in A \cdot \mathbf{Pr}\left(P\left(\varphi(x)\right)\right) = p\right) \;\Rightarrow\; \mathbf{Pr}\left(P\left(\text{let } x \xleftarrow{R} A \text{ in } \varphi(x)\right)\right) = p$$

The reverse implication is not true. We can see that on a counterexample: if the reverse implication was true, from Corollary 3.6 we would deduce that $\forall x \in A \cdot \mathbf{Pr}_{\text{true}}\left([x \overset{?}{=} a]\right) = \frac{1}{|A|}$. This is not true. Here x is either equal or not to a: in case of equality the probability is 1; in case of non-equality the probability is 0. It shows us a fundamental difference between universal quantification and random choice.

The following proposition allows for moving around independent random choices in the definitions of games. In the proposition below, *independent* means that the variable x is not used in the expression δ_2 and the variable y is not used in the expression δ_1.

Proposition 3.9. *For all finite sets A, B and C, for any $\delta_1 \in \Delta_A$, for any $\delta_2 \in \Delta_B$, for any $\varphi : A \times B \to \Delta_C$, if δ_1 and δ_2 are independent, then:*

$$\mathbf{Pr}\left[P\left(\begin{array}{l} \text{let } x \Leftarrow \delta_1 \text{ in} \\ \text{let } y \Leftarrow \delta_2 \text{ in} \\ \varphi(x,y) \end{array}\right)\right] \;=\; \mathbf{Pr}\left[P\left(\begin{array}{l} \text{let } y \Leftarrow \delta_2 \text{ in} \\ \text{let } x \Leftarrow \delta_1 \text{ in} \\ \varphi(x,y) \end{array}\right)\right]$$

---

[4] We assume here a backward reasoning as in the proof assistant Coq where we start from the goal and go backward to the hypothesis. For example, if our goal is Q and we have a theorem stating that $P \Rightarrow Q$, applying this theorem leaves us with P as a new goal.

3.2   Cyclic Groups

A group $(G, *)$ consists in a set G with an associative operation $*$ satisfying certain axioms. We write a^{-1} for the inverse of a. We write a^i for $\underbrace{a * \cdots * a}_{i \text{ times}}$. A group $(G, *)$ is finite if the set G is finite. In a finite group G, the number of elements is called the order of G. A group is cyclic if there is an element $\gamma \in G$ such that for each $a \in G$ there is an integer i with $a = \gamma^i$. Such γ is called a generator of G. The following permutation properties of cyclic groups will allow us below to connect probabilities with cyclic groups. Let G be a finite cyclic group.

Proposition 3.10. *If the order of G is q, then $\{\gamma^i \mid 0 \le i < q\} = G$*

Proposition 3.11. *For any $b \in G$, $\{a * b \mid a \in G\} = G$*

The set of bit strings of length l equipped the the bitwise exclusive disjunction $\oplus$ forms a commutative group (not cyclic) where the following proposition holds:

Proposition 3.12. *For any $s' \in \{0,1\}^l$, $\{s \oplus s' \mid s \in \{0,1\}^l\} = \{0,1\}^l$*

3.3   Probabilities over Cyclic Groups

The following theorem and its corollaries make explicit a fundamental relation between probabilities and cyclic groups. They are important properties used implicitly by cryptographers but never explicitly stated because they are considered too obvious in the context of security proofs. However it is necessary to explicit them when using a proof assistant.

Let G be a finite cyclic group of order q and $\gamma \in G$ be a generator. We write $\mathbb{Z}_q$ for the set of integers $\{0, \ldots, q-1\}$.

Theorem 3.13. *for all sets A, B and C, for any bijective function $f : A \to B$, for any function $g : B \to C$, for any predicate P on C,*

$$\mathbf{Pr}\left[P\left(\begin{array}{l}\text{let } x \xleftarrow{R} A \text{ in}\\ \left[g(f(x))\right]\end{array}\right)\right] = \mathbf{Pr}\left[P\left(\begin{array}{l}\text{let } y \xleftarrow{R} B \text{ in}\\ \left[g(y)\right]\end{array}\right)\right]$$

Corollary 3.14. *for any set A, for any function f from G to A, for any predicate P on A,*

$$\mathbf{Pr}\left[P\left(\begin{array}{l}\text{let } x \xleftarrow{R} \mathbb{Z}_q \text{ in}\\ \left[f(\gamma^x)\right]\end{array}\right)\right] = \mathbf{Pr}\left[P\left(\begin{array}{l}\text{let } m \xleftarrow{R} G \text{ in}\\ \left[f(m)\right]\end{array}\right)\right]$$

Proof. By Proposition 3.10 and Theorem 3.13.   □

Corollary 3.15. *for any set A, for any function f from G to A, for any predicate P on A, for any $m' \in G$,*

$$\mathbf{Pr}\left[P\left(\begin{array}{l}\text{let } m \xleftarrow{R} G \text{ in}\\ \left[f(m * m')\right]\end{array}\right)\right] = \mathbf{Pr}\left[P\left(\begin{array}{l}\text{let } m \xleftarrow{R} G \text{ in}\\ \left[f(m)\right]\end{array}\right)\right]$$

Proof. By Proposition 3.11 and Theorem 3.13.   □

Corollary 3.16. *for any set A, for any function f from $\{0,1\}^l$ to A, for any predicate P on A, for any $s' \in \{0,1\}^l$,*

$$\mathbf{Pr}\left(P\left(\begin{matrix} \text{let } s \xleftarrow{R} \{0,1\}^l \text{ in} \\ [f(s \oplus s')] \end{matrix} \right) \right) = \mathbf{Pr}\left(P\left(\begin{matrix} \text{let } s \xleftarrow{R} \{0,1\}^l \text{ in} \\ [f(s)] \end{matrix} \right) \right)$$

Proof. By Proposition 3.12 and Theorem 3.13.   □

In Section 3.3 of [20] the proof of semantic security for the encryption scheme ElGamal uses implicitly such corollaries. Shoup writes: *"by independence, the conditional distribution of δ is the uniform distribution on G, and hence from this, one sees that the conditional distribution of $\zeta = \delta \cdot m_b$ is the uniform distribution on G"*. The *"by independence"* part corresponds to our corollary 3.14, while the *"one sees that"* part corresponds to our corollary 3.15. It is perfectly legitimate not to state precisely things that are anyway obvious to the reader. But for our implementation on top of the proof assistant Coq it was necessary to state such theorems explicitly and formally.

4   Formal Security

In this section we formalize in our framework some security notions which are fundamental in cryptography: the Decisional Diffie-Hellman assumption (DDH), entropy smoothing and semantic security.

4.1   The Decisional Diffie-Hellman Assumption

Let G be a finite cyclic group of order q and $\gamma \in G$ be a generator[5].

The DDH assumption [10] for G states that, roughly speaking, no efficient algorithm can distinguish between triples of the form $(\gamma^x, \gamma^y, \gamma^{xy})$ and $(\gamma^x, \gamma^y, \gamma^z)$ where x, y and z are chosen randomly in the set $\mathbb{Z}_q$. More formally, there exists a negligible upper-bound ϵ_{DDH} such that for any efficient algorithm φ from $G \times G \times G$ to $\Delta_{\{\text{false, true}\}}$:

$$\left| \mathbf{Pr}_{\text{true}}\left(\begin{matrix} \text{let } x \xleftarrow{R} \mathbb{Z}_q \text{ in} \\ \text{let } y \xleftarrow{R} \mathbb{Z}_q \text{ in} \\ \varphi(\gamma^x, \gamma^y, \gamma^{xy}) \end{matrix} \right) - \mathbf{Pr}_{\text{true}}\left(\begin{matrix} \text{let } x \xleftarrow{R} \mathbb{Z}_q \text{ in} \\ \text{let } y \xleftarrow{R} \mathbb{Z}_q \text{ in} \\ \text{let } z \xleftarrow{R} \mathbb{Z}_q \text{ in} \\ \varphi(\gamma^x, \gamma^y, \gamma^z) \end{matrix} \right) \right| \leq \epsilon_{\text{DDH}}$$

As will be seen in Section 5, security proofs in our framework mainly consist in game transformations. Thus, as in [9], we do not need to define precisely the

---

[5] We do not assume that q is prime. However most groups in which DDH is believed to be true have prime order [8].

terms *efficient* and *negligible*. However they can be given precise definitions in terms of polynomials.

4.2   Entropy Smoothing

A family $(H_k)_{k \in K}$, where each H_k is a hash function from G to $\{0,1\}^l$, is entropy smoothing iff there exists a negligible upper-bound ϵ_{ES} such that for any efficient algorithm φ from $K \times \{0,1\}^l$ to $\Delta_{\{false, true\}}$:

$$\left| \mathbf{Pr}_{true} \left(\begin{array}{l} \text{let } k \xleftarrow{R} K \text{ in} \\ \text{let } m \xleftarrow{R} G \text{ in} \\ \varphi(k, H_k(m)) \end{array} \right) - \mathbf{Pr}_{true} \left(\begin{array}{l} \text{let } k \xleftarrow{R} K \text{ in} \\ \text{let } h \xleftarrow{R} \{0,1\}^l \text{ in} \\ \varphi(k, h) \end{array} \right) \right| \leq \epsilon_{ES}$$

Roughly speaking, it means that no efficient algorithm can distinguish between $(k, H_k(m))$ and (k, h) where k, m and h are chosen randomly.

4.3   Semantic Security

The notion of semantic security was introduced by Goldwasser and Micali [13]. They later showed that it is equivalent to indistinguishability under Chosen Plaintext Attack (IND-CPA) [14]. We use this latter formulation which is nowadays the most commonly used.

We assume two oracles: a key generation oracle keygen which generates a pair of public and private keys; and an encryption oracle encrypt which encrypts a given plaintext with a given public key. Because oracles are probabilistic algorithms, they are modeled as functions returning distributions. The attacker is modeled as two deterministic efficient algorithms A_1 and A_2 that take among other input a random seed r taken for some non-empty set R.

The semantic security game $SSG(\text{keygen}, \text{encrypt}, A_1, A_2)$ consists in calling the oracle keygen, then passing the generated public key and a random seed to A_1 which returns a pair of messages m_1 and m_2. One of the messages is chosen randomly and encrypted by the oracle encrypt which returns the corresponding ciphertext. This ciphertext is passed to A_2 which tries to guess which of the two messages was encrypted. In our framework, it is defined by:

$$\begin{array}{l} \text{let } (kp, ks) \Leftarrow \text{keygen}() \text{ in} \\ \text{let } r \xleftarrow{R} R \text{ in let } (m_1, m_2) \leftarrow A_1(r, kp) \text{ in} \\ \text{let } b \xleftarrow{R} \{1, 2\} \text{ in let } c \Leftarrow \text{encrypt}(kp, m_b) \text{ in} \\ \text{let } \hat{b} \leftarrow A_2(r, kp, c) \text{ in} \\ [\hat{b} \stackrel{?}{=} b] \end{array}$$

Definition 4.1 (Semantic security). *An encryption scheme with key generation algorithm* keygen *and encryption algoritm* encrypt *is semantically secure iff for all deterministic efficient algorithms A_1 and A_2,*

$$\left| \mathbf{Pr}_{true} \left(SSG(\text{keygen}, \text{encrypt}, A_1, A_2) \right) - \frac{1}{2} \right| \text{ is negligible.}$$

5   Application to the ElGamal Encryption Scheme

In our implementation, we illustrate the use of our framework by proving in a systematic way the so-called semantic security of the encryption scheme ElGamal [12] and its hashed version. In this paper, due to lack of space, we only show the hashed version.

The simplest version of ElGamal does not use hash functions. However, in practice, it is more convenient to consider messages which are bit strings (say of length l) instead of elements of a cyclic group. The hashed version of the ElGamal encryption scheme allows for this. We assume that we are given an entropy-smoothing family of hash functions $(H_k)_{k \in K}$, each H_k being a function from G to $\{0,1\}^l$. The ElGamal encryption scheme consists in the following probabilistic algorithms:

- The key generation algorithm keygen():
  let $x \xleftarrow{R} \mathbb{Z}_q$ in let $k \xleftarrow{R} K$ in $[((\gamma^x, k), (x, k))]$
- The encryption algorithm encrypt$((\alpha, k), m)$:
  let $y \xleftarrow{R} \mathbb{Z}_q$ in $[(\gamma^y, H_k(\alpha^y) \oplus m)]$
- The decryption algorithm decrypt$((x, k), c)$:
  $[H_k(\pi_1(c)^x) \oplus \pi_2(c)]$
  where π_1 and π_2 denote the first and second projections of an ordered pair.

Messages are elements of $\{0,1\}^l$; public keys are elements of $G \times K$; secret keys are elements of $\mathbb{Z}_q \times K$; ciphertexts are elements of $G \times \{0,1\}^l$.

Theorem 5.1. *The hashed ElGamal encryption scheme is semantically secure.*

Proof. In this proof we implicitly apply Corollaries 3.7 and 3.8, and Proposition 3.9. In particular the reader will notice that the order of variable definitions varies along the game transformations as allowed by Proposition 3.9.

Let us fix A_1 and A_2. We proceed by successive game transformations.

G0. By definition of semantic security, we must prove that:

$$\left| \mathbf{Pr}_{\text{true}} \left(\begin{array}{l} \text{let } (kp, ks) \Leftarrow \text{keygen}() \text{ in} \\ \text{let } r \xleftarrow{R} R \text{ in let } (m_1, m_2) \leftarrow A_1(r, kp) \text{ in} \\ \text{let } b \xleftarrow{R} \{1, 2\} \text{ in let } c \Leftarrow \text{encrypt}(kp, m_b) \text{ in} \\ \text{let } \hat{b} \leftarrow A_2(r, kp, c) \text{ in} \\ [\hat{b} \stackrel{?}{=} b] \end{array} \right) - \frac{1}{2} \right| \text{ is negligible}$$

G1. Knowing that ϵ_{DDH} and ϵ_{ES} are negligible, we are led to prove that:

$$\left| \mathbf{Pr}_{\text{true}} \left(\begin{array}{l} \text{let } (kp, ks) \Leftarrow \text{keygen}() \text{ in} \\ \text{let } r \xleftarrow{R} R \text{ in let } (m_1, m_2) \leftarrow A_1(r, kp) \text{ in} \\ \text{let } b \xleftarrow{R} \{1, 2\} \text{ in let } c \Leftarrow \text{encrypt}(kp, m_b) \text{ in} \\ \text{let } \hat{b} \leftarrow A_2(r, kp, c) \text{ in} \\ [\hat{b} \stackrel{?}{=} b] \end{array} \right) - \frac{1}{2} \right| \leq \epsilon_{\text{DDH}} + \epsilon_{\text{ES}}$$

G2. We unfold definitions of oracles and apply associativity of let (by Theorem 3.3 (6)).

$$
\left| \mathbf{Pr_{true}} \left|
\begin{array}{l}
\text{let } x \stackrel{R}{\leftarrow} \mathbb{Z}_q \text{ in} \\
\text{let } k \stackrel{R}{\leftarrow} K \text{ in} \\
\text{let}(kp, ks) \leftarrow ((\gamma^x, k), (x, k)) \text{ in} \\
\text{let } r \stackrel{R}{\leftarrow} R \text{ in} \\
\text{let } (m_1, m_2) \leftarrow A_1(r, kp) \\
\text{let } b \stackrel{R}{\leftarrow} \{1, 2\} \text{ in} \\
\text{let } y \stackrel{R}{\leftarrow} \mathbb{Z}_q \text{ in} \\
\text{let } c \leftarrow (\gamma^y, H_{\pi_2(kp)}(\pi_1(kp)^y) \oplus m_b) \text{ in} \\
\text{let } \hat{b} \leftarrow A_2(r, kp, c) \text{ in} \\
[\hat{b} \stackrel{?}{=} b]
\end{array}
\right. - \frac{1}{2} \right| \leq \; \epsilon_{\text{DDH}} + \epsilon_{\text{ES}}
$$

G3. We propagate definitions of kp, ks, m_1, m_2, c and $\hat{b}$ (by Theorem 3.3 (4)).

$$
\left| \mathbf{Pr_{true}} \left|
\begin{array}{l}
\text{let } x \stackrel{R}{\leftarrow} \mathbb{Z}_q \text{ in} \\
\text{let } y \stackrel{R}{\leftarrow} \mathbb{Z}_q \text{ in} \\
\text{let } k \stackrel{R}{\leftarrow} K \text{ in} \\
\text{let } r \stackrel{R}{\leftarrow} R \text{ in} \\
\text{let } b \stackrel{R}{\leftarrow} \{1, 2\} \text{ in} \\
[A_2(r, (\gamma^x, k), (\gamma^y, H_k(\gamma^{xy}) \oplus \pi_b(A_1(r, (\gamma^x, k))))) \stackrel{?}{=} b]
\end{array}
\right. - \frac{1}{2} \right| \leq \epsilon_{\text{DDH}} + \epsilon_{\text{ES}}
$$

G4. According to DDH assumption, we have that:

$$
\left| \mathbf{Pr_{true}} \left|
\begin{array}{l}
\text{let } x \stackrel{R}{\leftarrow} \mathbb{Z}_q \text{ in} \\
\text{let } y \stackrel{R}{\leftarrow} \mathbb{Z}_q \text{ in} \\
\text{let } k \stackrel{R}{\leftarrow} K \text{ in} \\
\text{let } r \stackrel{R}{\leftarrow} R \text{ in} \\
\text{let } b \stackrel{R}{\leftarrow} \{1, 2\} \text{ in} \\
[A_2(r, (\gamma^x, k), (\gamma^y, \\
\quad H_k(\gamma^{xy}) \oplus \\
\quad \pi_b(A_1(r, (\gamma^x, k))))) \stackrel{?}{=} b]
\end{array}
\right. - \mathbf{Pr_{true}} \left|
\begin{array}{l}
\text{let } x \stackrel{R}{\leftarrow} \mathbb{Z}_q \text{ in} \\
\text{let } y \stackrel{R}{\leftarrow} \mathbb{Z}_q \text{ in} \\
\text{let } z \stackrel{R}{\leftarrow} \mathbb{Z}_q \text{ in} \\
\text{let } k \stackrel{R}{\leftarrow} K \text{ in} \\
\text{let } r \stackrel{R}{\leftarrow} R \text{ in} \\
\text{let } b \stackrel{R}{\leftarrow} \{1, 2\} \text{ in} \\
[A_2(r, (\gamma^x, k), (\gamma^y, \\
\quad H_k(\gamma^z) \oplus \\
\quad \pi_b(A_1(r, (\gamma^x, k))))) \stackrel{?}{=} b]
\end{array}
\right| \leq \epsilon_{\text{DDH}}
$$

where the left-hand side game is the one from **G3**. We are thus left to prove that[6]:

$$
\left| \mathbf{Pr_{true}} \left|
\begin{array}{l}
\text{let } x \stackrel{R}{\leftarrow} \mathbb{Z}_q \text{ in} \\
\text{let } y \stackrel{R}{\leftarrow} \mathbb{Z}_q \text{ in} \\
\text{let } k \stackrel{R}{\leftarrow} K \text{ in} \\
\text{let } r \stackrel{R}{\leftarrow} R \text{ in} \\
\text{let } b \stackrel{R}{\leftarrow} \{1, 2\} \text{ in} \\
\text{let } z \stackrel{R}{\leftarrow} \mathbb{Z}_q \text{ in} \\
[A_2(r, (\gamma^x, k), (\gamma^y, H_k(\gamma^z) \oplus \pi_b(A_1(r, (\gamma^x, k))))) \stackrel{?}{=} b]
\end{array}
\right. - \frac{1}{2} \right| \leq \epsilon_{\text{ES}}
$$

---

[6] Indeed, for all r_1, r_2, r_3, $r_{1,2}$, $r_{2,3}$, in order to prove that $|r_1 - r_3| \leq r_{1,2} + r_{2,3}$, it is sufficient to prove that $|r_1 - r_2| \leq r_{1,2}$ and $|r_2 - r_3| \leq r_{2,3}$.

G5. We replace the randomly uniform choice of z and the computation γ^z with a random choice of an element of G (by Corollary 3.14).

$$\left| \mathbf{Pr}_{\text{true}} \left[\begin{array}{l} \text{let } k \overset{R}{\leftarrow} K \text{ in} \\ \text{let } m_z \overset{R}{\leftarrow} G \text{ in} \\ \text{let } x \overset{R}{\leftarrow} \mathbb{Z}_q \text{ in} \\ \text{let } y \overset{R}{\leftarrow} \mathbb{Z}_q \text{ in} \\ \text{let } r \overset{R}{\leftarrow} R \text{ in} \\ \text{let } b \overset{R}{\leftarrow} \{1,2\} \text{ in} \\ {[}A_2(r,(\gamma^x,k),(\gamma^y,H_k(m_z) \oplus \pi_b(A_1(r,(\gamma^x,k))))) \overset{?}{=} b{]} \end{array} \right] - \frac{1}{2} \right| \leq \epsilon_{\text{ES}}$$

G6. According to the entropy-smoothing assumption, we have that:

$$\left| \mathbf{Pr}_{\text{true}} \left[\begin{array}{l} \text{let } k \overset{R}{\leftarrow} K \text{ in} \\ \text{let } m_z \overset{R}{\leftarrow} G \text{ in} \\ \text{let } x \overset{R}{\leftarrow} \mathbb{Z}_q \text{ in} \\ \text{let } y \overset{R}{\leftarrow} \mathbb{Z}_q \text{ in} \\ \text{let } r \overset{R}{\leftarrow} R \text{ in} \\ \text{let } b \overset{R}{\leftarrow} \{1,2\} \text{ in} \\ {[}A_2(r,(\gamma^x,k),(\gamma^y, \\ \quad H_k(m_z)\oplus \\ \quad \pi_b(A_1(r,(\gamma^x,k))))) \overset{?}{=} b{]} \end{array} \right] - \mathbf{Pr}_{\text{true}} \left[\begin{array}{l} \text{let } k \overset{R}{\leftarrow} K \text{ in} \\ \text{let } h \overset{R}{\leftarrow} \{0,1\}^l \text{ in} \\ \text{let } x \overset{R}{\leftarrow} \mathbb{Z}_q \text{ in} \\ \text{let } y \overset{R}{\leftarrow} \mathbb{Z}_q \text{ in} \\ \text{let } r \overset{R}{\leftarrow} R \text{ in} \\ \text{let } b \overset{R}{\leftarrow} \{1,2\} \text{ in} \\ {[}A_2(r,(\gamma^x,k),(\gamma^y, \\ \quad h\oplus \\ \quad \pi_b(A_1(r,(\gamma^x,k))))) \overset{?}{=} b{]} \end{array} \right] \right| \leq \epsilon_{\text{ES}}$$

which is **G5** except that $\frac{1}{2}$ is replaced by the probability of another game.

We are thus left to prove that this probability is equal to $\frac{1}{2}$:

$$\mathbf{Pr}_{\text{true}} \left[\begin{array}{l} \text{let } k \overset{R}{\leftarrow} K \text{ in} \\ \text{let } x \overset{R}{\leftarrow} \mathbb{Z}_q \text{ in} \\ \text{let } y \overset{R}{\leftarrow} \mathbb{Z}_q \text{ in} \\ \text{let } r \overset{R}{\leftarrow} R \text{ in} \\ \text{let } b \overset{R}{\leftarrow} \{1,2\} \text{ in} \\ \text{let } h \overset{R}{\leftarrow} \{0,1\}^l \text{ in} \\ {[}A_2(r,(\gamma^x,k),\gamma^y,h \oplus \pi_b(A_1(r,(\gamma^x,k)))) \overset{?}{=} b{]} \end{array} \right] = \frac{1}{2}$$

G7. We delete the right operand of $\oplus$ (by Corollary 3.16):

$$\mathbf{Pr}_{\text{true}} \left[\begin{array}{l} \text{let } k \overset{R}{\leftarrow} K \text{ in} \\ \text{let } x \overset{R}{\leftarrow} \mathbb{Z}_q \text{ in} \\ \text{let } y \overset{R}{\leftarrow} \mathbb{Z}_q \text{ in} \\ \text{let } r \overset{R}{\leftarrow} R \text{ in} \\ \text{let } h \overset{R}{\leftarrow} \{0,1\}^l \text{ in} \\ \text{let } b \overset{R}{\leftarrow} \{1,2\} \text{ in} \\ {[}A_2(r,(\gamma^x,k),\gamma^y,h) \overset{?}{=} b{]} \end{array} \right] = \frac{1}{2}$$

This is true by Corollary 3.6. □

6   Implementation in the Proof Assistant Coq

The proof assistant Coq. Coq is a goal-directed proof assistant. This means that if we are trying to prove that a formula Q (the goal) is true, and we have a theorem stating that P_1 & P_2 implies Q, then we can apply this theorem. Coq will replace the goal Q by two subgoals P_1 and P_2. We proceed this way until we finally reach goals that are either axioms or are true by definition. On the way, Coq builds a so-called proof term. The critical part of Coq is its kernel which takes a proof term as an input and checks whether it is correct or not. On top of that there is a script language which allows users to state theorems and build their proofs interactively. This script language includes predefined tactics to prove automatically some mathematical statements such as tautologies, Presburger arithmetic statements, linear inequations over real numbers... Users can also define their own tactics.

Our framework in Coq. Our current implementation consists of the following Coq files:

CoqLib.v addendum to the Coq standard library
Distrib.v distributions, probabilities and necessity
Equiv.v equivalence modulo a negligible probability
DistribAuto.v automatically generated properties of distributions
Group.v basic group theory, cyclic groups
GroupProba.v probabilities over cyclic groups
BitString.v bit strings
Challenge.v correctness and security games
DDH.v the DDH assumption
Hash.v hash functions, entropy smoothing
Tactic.v support for automation
CryptoGames.v the main file including the full library
ElGamal.v correctness and semantic security for ElGamal
HashedElGamal.v correctness and semantic security for hashed ElGamal

Our library consists of 3381 lines of Coq and O'Caml code. The O'Caml part is a program which generates automatically 5923 other lines of Coq code. By using our library, the proofs of correctness and semantic security for ElGamal and hashed ElGamal consists respectively of only 160 lines and 209 lines of Coq code. This shows that our framework, while allowing for fully formal and readable security proofs, is scalable. Therefore, we believe that it can be further extended and applied to much more involved security proofs.

We write games as Coq functions and reason on them using the full logic of Coq: this is a so-called shallow embedding. We use Coq notations which allow for games and formulas to be written in a syntax close to the one used in this paper. For example, the game **G1** in the proof of Theorem 5.1 appears in Coq as:

```
mlet k <~ keygen in
mlet r <$ seed in
mlet mm <- A1 r (fst k) in
mlet b <$ [true; false] in
mlet c <~ encrypt (fst k) (if b then fst mm else snd mm) in
mlet b' <- A2 r (fst k) c in
[[eqb b' b]]
```

Probabilistic choices occurring in games are modeled with a monad. A similar encoding of randomized algorithms was given in [2]. However our encoding is much simpler due to the fact that it is enough for our purpose to consider distributions which are finite.

We provide automated tactics which can move deterministic assignments, random choices and calls to oracles from one place to another inside the game, and prove automatically that this transformation leads to an equivalent game. Those tactics are defined in the file **Tactic.v**. In the file **Distrib.v** we also define a tactic which automatically reduces the correctness of a cryptographic scheme into an equation which is then trivially proved. For example, in the case of ElGamal, it generates the following equation: $m = \gamma^{xy} * m * (\gamma^{yx})^{-1}$. For hashed ElGamal, we get $m = H_k(\gamma^{xy}) \oplus (H_k(\gamma^{yx}) \oplus m)$.

Acknowledgements. We would like to thank Reynald Affeldt for having directed us to this research area in the first place, and for helpful discussions. We are also grateful to Yang Cui, Nicolas Marti, Kirill Morozov, Miki Tanaka and Rui Zhang for fruitful discussions.

References

1. Affeldt, R., Tanaka, M., Marti, N.: Formal proof of provable security by game-playing in a proof assistant. In: ProvSec 2007. LNCS, vol. 4784, pp. 151–168. Springer, Heidelberg (2007)
2. Audebaud, P., Paulin-Mohring, C.: Proofs of randomized algorithms in Coq. In: Uustalu, T. (ed.) MPC 2006. LNCS, vol. 4014, pp. 49–68. Springer, Heidelberg (2006)
3. Barthe, G., Tarento, S.: A machine-checked formalization of the random oracle model. In: Filliâtre, J.-C., Paulin-Mohring, C., Werner, B. (eds.) TYPES 2004. LNCS, vol. 3839, pp. 33–49. Springer, Heidelberg (2006)
4. Bellare, M., Rogaway, P.: The exact security of digital signatures - how to sign with RSA and Rabin. In: Maurer, U.M. (ed.) EUROCRYPT 1996. LNCS, vol. 1070, pp. 399–416. Springer, Heidelberg (1996)
5. Bellare, M., Rogaway, P.: Code-based game-playing proofs and the security of triple encryption. Cryptology ePrint Archive, Report 2004/331 (2004), http://eprint.iacr.org/
6. Blanchet, B., Pointcheval, D.: Automated security proofs with sequences of games. In: Dwork, C. (ed.) CRYPTO 2006. LNCS, vol. 4117, pp. 537–554. Springer, Heidelberg (2006)
7. Blanchet, B., Pointcheval, D.: Automated security proofs with sequences of games. Cryptology ePrint Archive, Report 2006/069 (2006), http://eprint.iacr.org/

8. Boneh, D.: The Decision Diffie-Hellman problem. In: Buhler, J.P. (ed.) Algorithmic Number Theory. LNCS, vol. 1423, pp. 48–63. Springer, Heidelberg (1998)
9. Corin, R., denHartog, J.: A probabilistic Hoare-style logic for game-based cryptographic proofs. In: Bugliesi, M., Preneel, B., Sassone, V., Wegener, I. (eds.) ICALP 2006. LNCS, vol. 4052, pp. 252–263. Springer, Heidelberg (2006)
10. Diffie, W., Hellman, M.E.: New directions in cryptography. IEEE Transactions on Information Theory IT-22(6), 644–654 (1976)
11. Dolev, D., Yao, A.C.-C.: On the security of public key protocols (extended abstract). In: FOCS, pp. 350–357. IEEE Computer Society Press, Los Alamitos (1981)
12. Elgamal, T.: A public key cryptosystem and a signature scheme based on discrete logarithms. IEEE Transactions on Information Theory 31(4), 469–472 (1985)
13. Goldwasser, S., Micali, S.: Probabilistic encryption and how to play mental poker keeping secret all partial information. In: STOC, pp. 365–377. ACM Press, New York (1982)
14. Goldwasser, S., Micali, S.: Probabilistic encryption. J. Comput. Syst. Sci. 28(2), 270–299 (1984)
15. Halevi, S.: A plausible approach to computer-aided cryptographic proofs. Cryptology ePrint Archive, Report 2005/181 (2005), http://eprint.iacr.org/
16. Mitchell, J.C., Ramanathan, A., Scedrov, A., Teague, V.: A probabilistic polynomial-time process calculus for the analysis of cryptographic protocols. Theor. Comput. Sci. 353(1-3), 118–164 (2006)
17. Moggi, E.: Notions of computation and monads. Information and Computation 93(1), 55–92 (1991)
18. Nowak, D.: A framework for game-based security proofs. Cryptology ePrint Archive, Report 2007/199 (2007), http://eprint.iacr.org/
19. Ramsey, N., Pfeffer, A.: Stochastic lambda calculus and monads of probability distributions. In: POPL, pp. 154–165 (2002)
20. Shoup, V.: Sequences of games: a tool for taming complexity in security proofs. Cryptology ePrint Archive, Report 2004/332 (2004), http://eprint.iacr.org/
21. Tsiounis, Y., Yung, M.: On the security of ElGamal based encryption. In: Imai, H., Zheng, Y. (eds.) PKC 1998. LNCS, vol. 1431, pp. 117–134. Springer, Heidelberg (1998)
22. Wadler, P.: Comprehending monads. In: LISP and Functional Programming, pp. 61–78 (1990)

What Semantic Equivalences Are Suitable for Non-interference Properties in Computer Security[*]

Xiaowei Huang[1], Li Jiao[2], and Weiming Lu[1]

[1] Academy of Mathematics and System Science,
Chinese Academy of Sciences, P.R. China
xwhuang@amss.ac.cn
[2] State Key Laboratory of Computer Science,
Institute of Software, Chinese Academy of Sciences, P.R. China

Abstract. Non-interference properties are an important class of security properties. Many different non-interference properties have been presented based on different underlying models including the process algebraic languages. Usually, in specifying the non-interference properties using process algebraic languages, a specific semantic equivalence is introduced. Though weak bisimulation based non-interference properties have been studied extensively, it is not always satisfactory. This paper considers the topic on pursuing a probably more suitable semantic equivalence for specifying the non-interference properties. We find several alternatives, e.g., should testing equivalence, impossible future equivalence and possible future equivalence, etc. As another topic in the paper, based on the structural operational semantics, we suggest a compositional rule format, the SISNNI format, for an impossible future equivalence based non-interference property, i.e., the SISNNI property. We show that the SISNNI property is compositional in any SISNNI languages, i.e., languages in the SISNNI format.

Keywords: semantic equivalences, rule format, non-interference, computer security.

1 Introduction

To verify whether a system satisfies certain information flow property [1], a formal description of this property is necessary. Non-interference is proposed as a formal description of the information flow property. Though practical systems are usually designed to be with multi-level security [9], they may be simply represented as two-level systems [1,11]. Based on two level systems, the non-interference properties guarantee that a high level user should not interfere with the low level user.

Practical systems are modeled with various mathematical models, and thus non-interference properties should have totally different representations [8]. Besides, even in a given mathematical model, several information flow properties are always available. In this paper, we will focus on those properties based on process algebraic languages. We suppose three specific operators, i.e., the hiding operator of CSP and the parallel

[*] This research was financially supported by the National Natural Science Foundation of China (No. 60421001).

S. Qing, H. Imai, and G. Wang (Eds.): ICICS 2007, LNCS 4861, pp. 334–349, 2007.

composition operator and restriction operator of CCS, since they have been used in the formal characterizations of some information flow properties.

In [1] and [7], many information flow properties have been proposed based on the variants of CCS and CSP, respectively. We only concern those properties in [1]. On one hand, NNI (Non-determinism Non Interference) is proposed as a direct translation of the Non Interference, which requires that for each trace σ of the given system p, there exists another trace δ with the same subsequence of low level actions and without high inputs [1]. However, it is not satisfactory when synchronous communications are considered, and therefore lead to another property, named SNNI (Strong NNI). On the other hand, NDC (Non-Deducibility on Compositions) says that a low level user sees of the system is not modified by composing any high level process to the system.

As an extension to these properties, two strengthened properties are proposed to make the above properties suitable for the dynamic context. P-NDC (Persistent NDC) requires that each reachable state should satisfy the NDC property, and likewise, SSNNI (Strong SNNI) requires that each reachable state should satisfy the SNNI property.

Furthermore, observing that the above properties are all based on weak trace equivalence, they may be further promoted by other finer weak equivalences, such as the testing equivalence and the weak bisimulation. Therefore, several weak bisimulation based properties, e.g., BNNI (Bisimulation NNI), BSNNI (Bisimulation SNNI), SB-SNNI (Strong BSNNI), BNDC (Bisimulation NDC) and P-BNDC (Persistent BNDC), have been proposed in [1].

We will show in the paper that, weak bisimulation is not always satisfactory, because it requires that two related processes have the same branching structures, which is not needed for the non-interference. In fact, a counterexample will be put forward to illustrate that a trivially secure process will be deemed to be insecure if weak bisimulation based non-interference properties are applied.

Based on this observation, we suggest a criterion to make clear what semantic equivalences are suitable for the non-interference properties. Then, several semantic equivalences are suggested to be more suitable than weak bisimulation, e.g., should testing equivalence [2], impossible future equivalence [26,25] and possible future equivalence [3].

As an example, we will take impossible future equivalence into consideration, and propose the non-interference properties based on it. These properties include INNI (Impossible-future NNI), ISNNI (Impossible-future SNNI), SISNNI (Strong ISNNI), INDC (Impossible-future NDC) and P-INDC (Persistent INDC).

After that, we will show the compositional results of the SISNNI property by proposing a rule format for it. Any languages observing the rule format will be compositional for the SISNNI property, i.e., if all subprocesses hold the SISNNI property, then the composite process will also hold the SISNNI property.

Rule format is a concept coming from the structural operational semantics (SOS). SOS [12] have been widely used in defining the meanings of the operators in various process algebraic language, such as CCS [13] and ACP [19]. Transition System Specifications (TSSs) [16], which borrowed from logic programming, form a theoretical basis for SOS. By imposing some syntactic restrictions on TSS, one can retrieve so-called rule formats. From a specified rule format, one may deduce some interesting properties, within which two properties are concerned in the paper.

On one hand, rule format guarantees the congruence of some equivalence. As stated in [20], equivalence relation $\sim$ is congruent on some TSS, if $\sim$ satisfies the compatibility property, which states that, for any n-ary function symbol f in the TSS and processes p_i, q_i, if $p_i \sim q_i$ for $1 \leq i \leq n$ then $f(p_1, ..., p_n) \sim f(q_1, ..., q_n)$. On the other hand, rule format guarantees the compositionality of some property. A property φ is compositional on some TSS if $f(p_1, ..., p_n)$ satisfies property φ when f is any n-ary function symbol in the TSS and processes p_i satisfies property φ for $1 \leq i \leq n$. We will use language as an alias of the TSS.

Up to now, some rule formats have been presented to be congruence format for semantic equivalences, for examples, GSOS format [21] and ntyft/nxyft format [17] have been proved to be congruent on the strong bisimulation, de Simone [18] format was proved to be congruent on the failure equivalence, and so on. On the other hand, Tini [11] have proposed rule formats, e.g., rooted SBSNNI format and P-BNDC format, to be compositional formats for the SBSNNI property and P-BNDC property, respectively. The readers are referred to Mousavi, Reniers and Groote [14] for a latest review on the rule formats.

The authors have proposed a rule format, i.e., the weak ω-failure format, to be a congruence format for the impossible future equivalence [6]. In this paper, we will prove that, if we make a clear cut on the observable actions into high level actions and low level actions, and restrict that the high level actions (resp. the low level actions) cannot interplay with the low level actions (resp. the high level actions) in any transition rule, then the weak ω-failure format is also a compositional format for the SISNNI property.

The structure of this paper is as follows. The next section will provide some preliminaries on the process algebraic languages and the SOS, and make a division on the observable actions into high level actions and low level actions. Section 3 will make a review on several non-interference properties. In Section 4, we will make a discussion on what make an weak equivalence suitable for the non-interference properties and then present several alternatives for the weak bisimulation. Section 5 will discuss along the canonical way the properties based on impossible future equivalence, which is proved to be one of the suitable alternative weak equivalences. Then, in Section 6, we will propose the SISNNI format and prove that it is a compositional format for the SISNNI property. Finally, we will conclude the paper in Section 7.

2   Preliminaries on Process Algebraic Languages

Let *Act* denote a set of names which will be used to label on events and Act^* be the set of all action sequences. We usually use $a, b, ...$ to range over the actions in *Act*, and use $A, B, ...$ to range over the sets of actions in *Act*. τ is generally used to denote the internal actions which can not be observed by the outer world, and we use $\alpha, \beta, ...$ to range over the actions in $Act \cup \{\tau\}$. $\delta, \mu, \sigma, ...$ is to range over the sequences of actions. Φ is to range over the sets of sequences. $p, q, ...$ will be used to represent processes. Besides, $\varepsilon = \tau^*$. $\mathbb{N}$ is the set of natural numbers and ω is the cardinality of $\mathbb{N}$.

Basically, presenting a set of syntactic constructions is the first step to define a process algebraic languages, e.g., CCS, CSP and ACP.

Definition 2.1 [15]. Let $V = \{x_1, x_2, ...\}$ be a set of variables. A signature Σ is a collection of function symbols $f \notin V$ equipped with a function $ar : \Sigma \to N$. The set $\mathbb{T}(\Sigma)$ of terms over a signature Σ is defined recursively by: 1) $V \subseteq \mathbb{T}(\Sigma)$; 2) if $f \in \Sigma$ and $t_1, ..., t_{ar(f)} \in \mathbb{T}(\Sigma)$, then $f(t_1, ..., t_{ar(f)}) \in \mathbb{T}(\Sigma)$.

A term $c()$ is abbreviated as c. For $t \in \mathbb{T}(\Sigma)$, $var(t)$ denotes the set of variables that occur in t. $\mathbb{T}(\Sigma)$ is the set of closed terms over Σ, i.e., the terms $p \in \mathbb{T}(\Sigma)$ with $var(p) = \emptyset$. A term is an open term if it is not a closed term. A Σ substitution ζ is a mapping from V to $\mathbb{T}(\Sigma)$.

In the paper, we will use $p, q, ...$ to range over the closed terms, and call them processes.

As stated in the introduction, we require that three previously-defined operators, i.e., the hiding operator of CSP, the restriction operators and parallel composition operator of CCS, are in the language, because they have been used in [1] to characterize some non-interference properties which will be discussed in the paper. Therefore, the syntax of a language may be:

$p ::= p\backslash A \mid p/A \mid p|p \mid ...$, where $A \subseteq Act$ is a set of observable actions.

SOS has been widely accepted as a tool to define operational semantics of processes. TSSs are a formalization of SOS [12]. The readers are referred to Aceto, Fokkink and Verhoef [15] for a comprehensive review on SOS.

Definition 2.2. A positive Σ-literal is an expression $t \xrightarrow{\alpha} t'$ and a negative Σ-literal is an expression $t \not\xrightarrow{\alpha}$ with $t, t' \in \mathbb{T}(\Sigma)$ and $\alpha \in Act \cup \{\tau\}$. A transition rule over Σ is an expression of the form $\frac{H}{C}$ with H a set of Σ literals (the premises of the rule) and C a positive Σ-literal (the conclusion). The left- and right-hand side of C are called the source and the target of the rule, respectively. Moreover, if $r = \frac{H}{C}$ then let $ante(r) = H$ and $cons(r) = C$.

A TSS, written as (Σ, Ψ), consists of a signature Σ and a set Ψ of transition rules over Σ. A TSS is positive if the premises of its rules are positive. In the paper, we often use language as an alias of the TSS.

Here, as an example, the rules for the restriction operator, the hiding operator and the parallel composition operator are as follows.

$$p/A : \frac{p \xrightarrow{\alpha} p'}{p/A \xrightarrow{\alpha} p'/A} \alpha \notin A \qquad \frac{p \xrightarrow{a} p'}{p/A \xrightarrow{\tau} p'/A} a \in A$$

$$p\backslash A : \frac{p \xrightarrow{\alpha} p'}{p\backslash A \xrightarrow{\alpha} p'\backslash A} \alpha \notin A$$

$$p|q : \frac{p \xrightarrow{\alpha} p'}{p|q \xrightarrow{\alpha} p'|q} \quad \frac{q \xrightarrow{\alpha} q'}{p|q \xrightarrow{\alpha} p|q'} \quad \frac{p \xrightarrow{a} p', q \xrightarrow{b} q'}{p|q \xrightarrow{\tau} p'|q'} (a, b) \in f$$

where $(a, b) \in f$ means that actions a and b may communicate synchronously.

Following it, the labeled transition systems (LTSs) are to be defined. LTSs are standard semantic models for the various process algebraic languages, and in fact, each process has an equivalent LTS by the help of the transition rules.

Definition 2.3. Let Σ be a signature. A transition relation over Σ is a relation $\text{Tr} \subseteq T(\Sigma) \times Act \cup \{\tau\} \times T(\Sigma)$. Element (p, α, p') of a transition relation is written as $p \xrightarrow{\alpha} p'$.

Thus a transition relation over Σ can be regarded as a set of closed positive Σ-literals (transitions).

Definition 2.4. A labeled transition system (LTS) is a triple $(T, \text{Tr}, Act \cup \{\tau\})$, where T is the set of processes, i.e., the set of closed terms, and Tr is the transition relation defined as above.

After assigning the processes their corresponding LTSs by SOS, a natural topic is to decide whether two processes with different syntactic expressions are equivalent. Certainly, two processes with isomorphic LTSs should be deemed to be equivalent, which forms the so-called tree equivalence. However, tree equivalence may be too strong for practical uses. Therefore, various semantic equivalences weaker than tree equivalence are presented for different aims. The readers are referred to Glabbeek [3,4] for comprehensive reviews on semantic equivalences.

A common characterization of the equivalences is that, any semantics of some process p can be characterized denotationally by a function $O(p)$, which constitute the observable behaviors of p [3]. Therefore, the equivalence $\sim_O$ can be defined by $p \sim_O q \Longleftrightarrow O(p) = O(q)$.

Here, as an example, we present the definition of weak trace equivalence. Other equivalences used in the paper will be introduced whenever they are mentioned.

For an action sequence $\delta = \alpha_1...\alpha_n$, if there exists $p_1, ..., p_n \in T(\Sigma)$ such that $p \xrightarrow{\alpha_1} p_1 \xrightarrow{\alpha_2} ... \xrightarrow{\alpha_n} p_n$, then we call δ a trace of p, denoted as $p \xrightarrow{\delta}$ or $p \xrightarrow{\alpha_1} ... \xrightarrow{\alpha_n}$.

In weak semantics, the weak transition relations and the weak traces also need to be defined. Let p be a process, we write $p \xRightarrow{a}$ iff $p \xrightarrow{\tau^*} \xrightarrow{a} \xrightarrow{\tau^*}$, where τ^* denotes any number of internal transitions. Hence, for an observable action sequence $\delta = a_1...a_n$, $p \xRightarrow{\delta}$ iff $p \xRightarrow{a_1} ... \xRightarrow{a_n}$.

Definition 2.5. Let p, q be two processes and set $\mathcal{T}(p) = \{\delta \in Act_H^* | p \xRightarrow{\delta}\}$ be the set of all trace of p. Then, p and q are weak trace equivalent, denoted as $p \sim_t q$, iff $\mathcal{T}(p) = \mathcal{T}(q)$.

For a given equivalence, one of the most frequently-asked problems is whether or not it can be preserved under some frequently-used operators, such as prefixing, choice, parallel composition, etc., in classical process algebraic languages like CCS [13], CSP [27] and ACP [19]. Generally, there exist two ways to deal with this problem: the first one is to prove the congruence properties of these operators one by one. It is a straightforward and intuitive way, but may be somewhat clumsy. The second one is to pursue a rule format for this specified equivalence. And the given equivalence can be preserved under any operator in this format.

Definition 2.6. Let Σ be a signature. A context $C(x_1, ..., x_n)$ of n holes over Σ is simply a term in $\mathbb{T}(\Sigma)$ in which n variables occur, each variable only once. If $t_1, ..., t_n$ are terms over Σ, then $C(t_1, ..., t_n)$ denotes the term obtained by substituting t_1 for the first variable occurring in C, t_2 for the second variable occurring in C, etc. If $x_1, ..., x_n$ are all different variables, then $C(x_1, ..., x_n)$ denotes a context of n holes in which x_i is the ith occurring variable.

In the following, we give the definition on the congruence of an equivalence in a language.

Definition 2.7. Let $\mathcal{L} = (\Sigma, \Psi)$ be a language. An equivalence relation $\sim$ is congruent in language $\mathcal{L}$ iff $\forall i \in \{1, ..., n\} : p_i \sim q_i \Longrightarrow C(p_1, ..., p_n) \sim C(q_1, ..., q_n)$ for any context $C(x_1, ..., x_n)$ of n holes in language $\mathcal{L}$, where p_i and q_i are closed terms, i.e., processes, over Σ.

In fact, a congruence format is to make restrictions on the syntax and rules to guarantee that, in a given language satisfying this format, the given equivalence will be congruent.

Likewise, we can define the compositionality of some property in a language.

Definition 2.8. Let $\mathcal{L} = (\Sigma, \Psi)$ be a language. A property φ is compositional in language $\mathcal{L}$ iff $\forall i \in \{1, ..., n\} : p_i \in \varphi \Longrightarrow C(p_1, ..., p_n) \in \varphi$, for any context $C(x_1, ..., x_n)$ of n holes in language $\mathcal{L}$, where $p_i \in \varphi$ means that p_i satisfies the property φ.

A compositional format is to make restrictions on the syntax and rules to guarantee that, in a given language satisfying this format, the given property will be compositional.

For the application of the above process algebraic theory in specifying the non-interference properties, two kinds of partitions on the observable actions are necessary:

1) Set Act is to be separated into two disjoint sets Act_H and Act_L in order to divide clearly the observable actions into two levels. And, we have $Act = Act_H \cup Act_L$. This division comes from an idea that the users will be classified into two classes, High and Low.

2) Set Act is to be separated into two disjoint sets O and I in order to divide clearly the functions of each action into a output action or an input action. Similarly, we need $Act = O \cup I$.

Finally, function $purge_L(\delta)$ takes a trace δ and returns an action sequence with all Low actions removed.

3   Several Related Non-interference Properties

In this section, we will simply review several non-interference properties presented in the seminal paper of Focardi and Gorrieri [1].

Definition 3.1 [1]. Let p be a process.

1) $p \in$ NNI $\Longleftrightarrow (p\backslash_I Act_H)/Act_H \sim_t p/Act_H$, where $p\backslash_I Act_H$ is defined as $p\backslash (Act_H \cap I)$.
2) $p \in$ SNNI (Strong NNI) $\Longleftrightarrow p/Act_H \sim_t p\backslash Act_H$.
3) $p \in$ NDC $\Longleftrightarrow \forall q \in T_H : p/Act_H \sim_t (p|q)\backslash Act_H$.

Proposition 3.2 [1]. SNNI $\subset$ NNI, NDC = SNNI.

The above three properties are based on the weak trace equivalence. And if substituting the weak trace equivalence with other weak equivalences, we may have three corresponding non-interference properties. But, the relations between them maybe will not be akin to Proposition 3.2 yet. For example, the properties based on the weak bisimulation BNNI, BSNNI and BNDC will be in the following relation.

Proposition 3.3 [1]. BNDC $\subset$ BNNI, BNDC $\subset$ BSNNI, BNNI $\not\subseteq$ BSNNI and BSNNI $\not\subseteq$ BNNI.

However, these properties may not be used in the dynamic contexts [10]. Therefore, one more promotion can be made on them.

Definition 3.4 [10,28]. Let p be a process.

1) $p \in$ SBSNNI iff, for all $\sigma, p' : p \overset{\sigma}{\Longrightarrow} p'$, we have $p' \in$ BSNNI.
2) $p \in$ P-BNDC iff, for all $\sigma, p' : p \overset{\sigma}{\Longrightarrow} p'$, we have $p' \in$ BNDC.

4   What Semantic Equivalences Are Suitable

In this section, we will make a discussion on one of the main topics in the paper, i.e., what semantic equivalences are suitable for the non-interference properties. The first two subsections come from the works of Focardi and Gorrieri [1] which interpret the reason why weak bisimulation is chosen as the specific weak equivalence for non-interference properties in their works. Then, in the third subsection, we will give a counterexample to show that the weak bisimulation is not always satisfactory. This situation makes us consider the actual requirements for a given weak equivalence to be suitable and therefore propose a criterion in the fourth subsection. Then, in the following several subsections, we will seek for several suitable weak equivalences.

4.1   Weak Trace Equivalence vs. Testing Equivalence

Focardi and Gorrieri [1] have discussed the different performances of these two equivalences when defining the non-interference properties, and claimed that, compared with the weak trace equivalence, testing equivalence is more suitable for non-interference due to its ability in detecting the high level deadlocks. They presented an example to show that, if there exist high level deadlocks, low level user may deduce information from the high level user and make the information flow insecure.

Weak trace equivalence has been defined in Section 2 and, to ease the following discussion, we will also give the definition of the testing equivalence.

Testing equivalence is a combination of the may testing equivalence and the must testing equivalence, which are two important testing-theoretical equivalences in the testing theory firstly proposed by Nicola and Hennessy [5]. Tests are processes with a special action $\sqrt{}$ to denote the successful termination. The way testing a process p is to synchronize p with a test t on all observable actions except for $\sqrt{}$, denoted as $p|t$ in the CCS terms or $p\|_{Act}t$ in the CSP terms. Then, various testing theoretical equivalences are defined based on the necessity of the presence of the successful termination in $p|t$.

In defining the must testing equivalence, a notion named maximal run needs to be introduced beforehand. A maximal run of a transition system is a sequence of states $(p_i|t_i)_{0 \le i \le n}$ for $n \in \mathbb{N} \cup \{\omega\}$ such that $p_i|t_i \xrightarrow{\alpha_{i+1}} p_{i+1}|t_{i+1}$ for all $0 \le i \le n-1$ and if $n \ne \omega$ then $\not\exists \alpha \in Act \cup \{\tau\} : (p_n|t_n) \xrightarrow{\alpha}$.

Definition 4.1.1 [2]. Let p, q be two processes and t be a test.

1) p may t iff $\exists \delta \in Act^* : p|t \xrightarrow{\delta \sqrt{}}$.

2) p must t iff, for all maximal runs $(p_i|t_i)_{i<n} : (p|t = p_0|t_0)$ implies $\exists i < n : p_i|t_i \xrightarrow{\sqrt{}}$.

Moreover, p and q are may (resp. must) testing equivalence, denoted as $p \sim_{may} q$ (resp. $p \sim_{must} q$), iff, for all tests t, p may (resp. must) t implies q may (resp. must) t, and vice versa. And p and q are testing equivalence, denoted as $p \sim_{test} q$, iff they are both may testing equivalence and must testing equivalence, i.e., $p \sim_{test} q \equiv p \sim_{may} q \wedge p \sim_{must} q$.

4.2 Testing Equivalence vs. Weak Bisimulation

The defect of testing equivalence has also been pointed out that it may falsely deem all systems with high level loops insecure. This defect forms one of the main attacks made by Focardi and Gorrieri, and then they turn to the weak bisimulation. The other reason is that the weak bisimulation may be checked in polynomial time with respect to the number of the states in the LTSs, but for the testing equivalence, it may be PSPACE complete.

Definition 4.2.1. A relation $R \subseteq T \times T$ is a weak bisimulation if $(p, q) \in R$ implies, for all $\alpha \in Act \cup \{\tau\}$,

1) if $p \xrightarrow{\alpha} p'$, then there exists q' such that $q \overset{\hat{\alpha}}{\Longrightarrow} q'$ and $(p', q') \in R$, and

2) if $q \xrightarrow{\alpha} q'$, then there exists p' such that $p \overset{\hat{\alpha}}{\Longrightarrow} p'$ and $(p', q') \in R$,

where $q \overset{\hat{\alpha}}{\Longrightarrow} q'$ stands for $q \overset{\alpha}{\Longrightarrow} q'$ if $\alpha \in Act$ and $q \xrightarrow{\tau^*} q'$ if $\alpha = \tau$.

4.3 Weak Bisimulation Is Not Always Satisfactory

However, though the weak-bisimulation-based non-interference properties, such as BNNI, BSNNI and BNDC, etc., have better performance than those based on trace equivalence and testing equivalence, they are not always satisfactory. The reason is that if two processes are weak bisimulated then their corresponding LTSs have the same branching structures. But on the other hand, non-interference cares little on the branching structures of processes, because a low level user cannot deduce anything from the branching structure of a give LTS. Therefore, the requirement on the branching structures may make the weak bisimulation too strong for specifying the non-interference properties.

In fact, we may construct a system to be secure by intuitiveness but may be falsely deemed to be insecure by the weak simulation based non-interference properties. It can

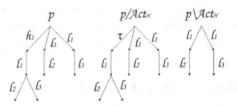

Fig. 1. Weak bisimulation may be too strong in characterizing the non-interference properties

be verified that the process p in Figure 1 does not satisfy the BSNNI, BNDC, SBSNNI properties, because $p/Act_H \nsim_{ws} p\backslash Act_H$. However, it is secure if the only high level action h_1 is just a high level output action.

On the other hand, p will satisfy the corresponding non-interference properties based on impossible future equivalence, should testing equivalence or possible future equivalence, which care less branching structures than the weak bisimulation. We will introduce them in the following subsections. In fact, in Figure 1, $\forall p', \delta : p \overset{\delta}{\Longrightarrow} p'$, we have $p'/Act_H \sim_{shd} p'\backslash Act_H$, $p'/Act_H \sim_{if} p'\backslash Act_H$ and $p'/Act_H \sim_{pf} p'\backslash Act_H$.

4.4 Criterions

Based on the above observations, we may have a general criterion in seeking a suitable semantic equivalence as the underlying equivalence for characterizing non-interference properties. In fact, this equivalence is expected to

1) deal with high level deadlocks as the testing equivalence does,

2) deal with high level loops in a fair way as the weak bisimulation,

3) be decidable in polynomial time in case that the LTSs have only finite states and labels, and

4) be compositional on the hiding operator, the restriction operator and the parallel composition operator.

It is trivial that the weak bisimulation meets these criterions, but as we have argued in the preceding subsection, it may be too strong in some cases. Therefore, we want to find several alternatives.

4.5 From Testing Equivalence to Acceptance Testing

Leveling with the above criterions, we may find that the testing equivalence can only satisfy the first clause. The fact that it does not satisfy the second clause has been stated in Section 4.2, the fact that it does not satisfy the third clause has been pointed out in [1], and the fact that it does not satisfy the fourth clause has been shown by several papers including the authors [2,24,6].

In fact, the reason that the testing equivalence does not satisfy the second and the third clause exists in the maximal run of must testing equivalence. It is the maximal run that makes the internal loops catastrophic [2].

Definition 4.5.1. Let p, q be two processes and t be a test. p acc t iff, for all $\sigma \in Act^*$ and for all $p'|t'$ with $p|t \overset{\sigma}{\Longrightarrow} p'|t'$, there must exist $a \in Act \cup \{\sqrt{}\}$ such that $p'|t' \overset{a}{\Longrightarrow}$.

Moreover, p and q are acceptance testing equivalence, denoted as $p \sim_{acc} q$, iff, for all tests t, p acc t implies q acc t, and vice versa.

In fact, from the above definition, we find that, after excluding the concept of maximal runs from its definition, acceptance testing equivalence can deal with the internal loops in a fair way that the internal transitions may be executed an arbitrary but only finite number of times.

4.6 From Acceptance Testing to Should Testing

We have observed that the acceptance testing equivalence, or failure equivalence, may not be invariant under the hiding operator of CSP, which makes them not be the equivalence what we are seeking for. In [2], Rensink and Vogler have proposed the should testing equivalence to amend the defect of the acceptance testing equivalence.

Definition 4.6.1. Let p, q be two processes and t be a test. p shd t iff, for all $\sigma \in Act^*$ and for all $p'|t'$ with $p|t \overset{\sigma}{\Longrightarrow} p'|t'$, there must exist $\delta \in Act^*$ such that $p'|t' \overset{\delta\sqrt{}}{\Longrightarrow}$.

Moreover, p and q are should testing equivalent, denoted as $p \sim_{shd} q$, iff, for all tests t, p shd t implies q shd t, and vice versa.

4.7 Several Other Alternatives

Two other possible alternatives will be presented in this subsection. We will show their relationships with the should testing equivalence and the weak bisimulation.

Definition 4.7.1. $(\sigma, \Phi) \in Act^* \times \mathcal{P}(Act^+)$ is a weak impossible future pair of process p iff there exists some p' such that $p \overset{\sigma}{\Longrightarrow} p'$ and $\Phi \cap \mathcal{T}(p') = \emptyset$. The set of all weak impossible future pairs of process p is called the weak impossible future of p, denoted by $\mathcal{IF}(p)$.

For any two processes p and q, they are weak impossible future equivalent, denoted as $p \sim_{if} q$, iff $\mathcal{IF}(p) = \mathcal{IF}(q)$.

Definition 4.7.2 $(\sigma, \Phi) \in Act^* \times \mathcal{P}(Act^+)$ is a weak possible future pair of process p iff there exists some p' such that $p \overset{\sigma}{\Longrightarrow} p' \wedge \Phi = \mathcal{T}(p')$. The set of all weak possible future pairs of process p is called the weak possible future of p, denoted as $\mathcal{PF}(p)$.

Moreover, for any two processes p and q, they are weak possible future equivalent, denoted as $p \sim_{pf} q$, iff $\mathcal{PF}(p) = \mathcal{PF}(q)$.

Proposition 4.7.3. Let p and q be two processes. $p \sim_{wb} q \Longrightarrow p \sim_{pf} q \Longrightarrow p \sim_{if} q \Longrightarrow p \sim_{shd} q$.

4.8 Semantic Lattice

The left graph in Figure 2 shows a semantic lattice of the equivalences mentioned above. The arrows denote the 'coarser than' relations between two related semantic equivalences.

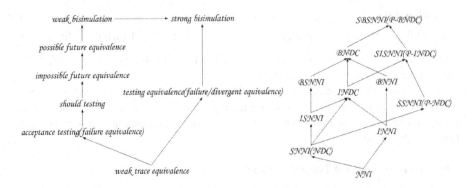

Fig. 2. Lattices for semantic equivalences and non-interference properties

5   Properties Based on Impossible Future Equivalence

In this section, we will present the non-interference properties based on impossible future equivalence. The reason why we choose impossible future equivalence is that it has a simpler denotational characterization than should testing equivalence, and it is coarser than possible future equivalence. The properties based on other equivalences may be defined and analyzed similarly.

Definition 5.1 (Impossible Future NNI, SNNI, NDC)

(1) $p \in$ INNI $\iff p/Act_H \sim_{if} (p\backslash_I Act_H)/Act_H$;

(2) $E \in$ ISNNI $\iff E/Act_H \sim_{if} E\backslash Act_H$;

(3) $E \in$ INDC $\iff \forall F \in \mathcal{P}_H : E/Act_H \sim_{if} (E|F)\backslash Act_H$.

Proposition 5.2. (1) BNNI $\subset$ INNI $\subset$ NNI; (2) BSNNI $\subset$ ISNNI $\subset$ SNNI. (3) BNDC $\subset$ INDC $\subset$ NDC.

Proof. Immediately from the fact $\sim_{wb}$ is finer than $\sim_{if}$, and $\sim_{if}$ is finer than $\sim_t$.   □

Definition 5.3. (1) $E \in$ SISNNI $\iff E' \in$ ISNNI for all E' with $E \Longrightarrow E'$;

(2) $E \in$ P-INDC $\iff$ for all E' with $E \Longrightarrow E'$, we have $E' \in$ INDC.

Proposition 5.4. SISNNI $\subset$ INDC $\subset$ ISNNI.

Proof. To show that SISNNI $\subset$ INDC, it is enough to prove that if $p \in$ SISNNI, then $p\backslash Act_H \sim_{if} (p|q)\backslash Act_H$ for all $q \in Process_H$, because $p \in$ SISNNI implies $p\backslash Act_H \sim_{if} p/Act_H$. Then, by the distributive law of $\backslash Act_H$ over parallel composition operator, which will be prove in Proposition 6.3.3, $(p|q)\backslash Act_H \sim_{if} p\backslash Act_H|q\backslash Act_H$. Then $p\backslash Act_H|q\backslash Act_H \sim_{if} p\backslash Act_H$ since $p\backslash Act_H$ is an empty process. Finally, we obtain $(p|q)\backslash Act_H \sim_{if} p\backslash Act_H|q\backslash Act_H \sim_{if} p\backslash Act_H$.

INDC $\subset$ ISNNI is trivial from their definitions.   □

Proposition 5.5. SISNNI = P-INDC.

The right graph in Figure 2 shows a lattice of the non-interference properties mentioned in the paper. The arrows denote the 'weaker than' relations between two related properties.

6 Compositional Format for the SISNNI Property

6.1 Definition of the SISNNI Format

In this section, a compositional format for the SISNNI property will be proposed. Firstly, we need to define a class of special rules, i.e., patience rules.

Definition 6.1.1 [15,14]. A rule of the form $\dfrac{x_i \xrightarrow{\tau} x_i'}{f(x_1, ..., x_i, ..., x_n) \xrightarrow{\tau} f(x_1, ..., x_i', ..., x_n)}$ with $1 \leq i \leq n$ is called a patience rule of the ith argument of f.

Definition 6.1.2 [29]. An argument $i \in N$ of an operator f is active if f has a rule in which x_i appears as left-hand side of a premise. A variable x occurring in a term t is receiving in t if t is the target of a rule in which x is the right-hand side of a premise. An argument $i \in N$ of an operator f is receiving if a variable x is receiving in a term t that has a subterm $f(t_1, ..., t_n)$ with x occurring in t_i.

Definition 6.1.3 [6]. A de Simone language $\mathcal{L}$ is in weak ω-failure format if

1) patience rules are the only rules with τ-premises, and
2) patience rules for active arguments and receiving arguments are necessary.

Definition 6.1.4. A weak ω-failure language $\mathcal{L}$ is in SISNNI format if

1) labels in a rule are either all in set $Act_H \cup \{\tau\}$ or all in set $Act_L \cup \{\tau\}$. It means that a rule is in the form of $\dfrac{\{x_i \xrightarrow{h_i} x_i'\}_{i \in I}}{f(x_1, ..., x_n) \xrightarrow{h} g(x_1', ..., x_n')}$ or $\dfrac{\{x_i \xrightarrow{l_i} x_i'\}_{i \in I}}{f(x_1, ..., x_n) \xrightarrow{l} g(x_1', ..., x_n')}$ such that $I \subseteq \{1, ..., n\}$, h_i and h are all in set $Act_H \cup \{\tau\}$, l_i and l are all in set $Act_L \cup \{\tau\}$, and
2) No rules in the form $\dfrac{}{f(x_1, ..., x_n) \xrightarrow{h} g(x_1', ..., x_n')}$ with $h \in Act_H \cup \{\tau\}$ are allowed.

The first clause of Definition 6.1.4 restricts that high level actions and low level actions should not occur at the same time in a rule, which is a standard restriction of the CCS language. In CCS, only the parallel composition operator allows the presence of the two positive premises, and it also needs that the actions of these two premises are corresponding, i.e., if one is action a then the other is action $\bar{a}$.

The second clause of Definition 6.1.4 excludes the high level prefixing operator from the SISNNI format, which is consistent with the fact that high level prefixing operator is not compositional on the SISNNI property.

Moreover, the nondeterministic choice operator of CCS and SPA is also not in SISNNI format. In fact, the nondeterministic choice operator is not invariant under the impossible future equivalence.

Fortunately, as argued in the ACP [19] language, the prefixing operator may be substituted with a sequential composition operator. And the nondeterministic choice operator may be substituted with several operators in CSP [27], including internal choice and external choice. These operators satisfy the SISNNI format.

6.2 Ruloids and Ruloid Theorem

Ruloids and the ruloid theorem originated from the works of Bloom [22,23] for the GSOS format.

For a language $\mathcal{L} = (\Sigma, \Psi)$ in the SISNNI format, the ruloids $\mathcal{R}(C, \alpha)$, for a context $C(x_1, ..., x_n)$ of n holes and an action α, are a set of expressions like the transition rules:

$$\frac{\{x_i \xrightarrow{\alpha_i} x_i'\}_{i \in I}}{C(x_1, ..., x_n) \xrightarrow{\alpha} D(y_1, ..., y_n)} \tag{1}$$

such that D is another context, $y_i = x_i'$ for $i \in I$ and $y_i = x_i$ for $i \notin I$, where $I \subseteq \{1, 2, ..., n\}$. These expressions characterize all possible behaviors of the context $C(x_1, ..., x_n)$ in the language. Moreover, we define $\mathcal{R}(C) = \bigcup_{\alpha \in Act \cup \{\tau\}} \mathcal{R}(C, \alpha)$.

It should be noted that the context D does not need to have exactly n holes. In fact, after leaving out the copying and the lookahead in the de Simone format (the SISNNI format is a subformat of the de Simone format), the number of the holes of D should be less than or equivalent to n. But for convenience, in form (1), we still write it as $D(y_1, ..., y_n)$.

Furthermore, two properties need to be imposed on $\mathcal{R}(C, \alpha)$, we call them soundness property and completeness property, by a little abusing the terminologies.

Definition 6.2.1. Let $\mathcal{L} = (\Sigma, \Psi)$ be a language in the SISNNI format, and $C(x_1, ..., x_n)$ be any context of n holes in $\mathcal{L}$. A set $\mathcal{R}(C, \alpha)$ of ruloids of form (1) are ruloids of context C and action α, with $\alpha \in Act \cup \{\tau\}$, iff

1) Soundness. Let $r \in \mathcal{R}(C, \alpha)$ be a ruloid of form (1). If ζ is a closed Σ substitution such that $\zeta(x_i) \xrightarrow{\alpha_i} \zeta(x_i')$ for all $i \in I$, then there must exist a context D such that $\zeta(C(x_1, ..., x_n)) \xrightarrow{\alpha} \zeta(D(y_1, ..., y_n))$.

2) Completeness. Let ζ be any closed Σ substitution. If $\zeta(C(x_1, ..., x_n)) \xrightarrow{\alpha}$, then there must exist a ruloid r of form (1) in ruloids $\mathcal{R}(C, \alpha)$, and $\zeta(x_i) \xrightarrow{\alpha_i}$ for all $i \in I$.

Here, a strategy to obtain the ruloids for some context C of n holes is possible, and it can be proved that the ruloids obtained by the strategy will satisfy the soundness and completeness properties of Definition 6.2.1, which forms the ruloid theorem.

As a corollary to the ruloids and the ruloid theorem, we may have the following proposition which will be used in the next subsection. This proposition states that each trace of the composite process can be decomposed into traces of its subprocesses.

Proposition 6.2.2. Let $\mathcal{L} = (\Sigma, \Psi)$ be a SISNNI language, and $C(x_1, ..., x_n)$ be any context of n holes. Suppose that ζ is any closed Σ substitution mapping x_i into p_i. If σ is a trace in $\mathcal{T}(C(p_1, ..., p_n))$, then, for all $1 \leq i \leq n$, there should be a trace σ_i in $\mathcal{T}(p_i, \omega)$ such that, when $C(p_1, ..., p_n) \xRightarrow{\sigma} C'(p_1', ..., p_n')$, we have $p_i \xRightarrow{\sigma_i} p_i'$.

6.3 The Proof of the Compositional Theorem

To ease to proving of following propositions, an alternative characterization on the impossible future equivalence is needed.

Proposition 6.3.1. Let p, q be two processes. For $1 \leq i \leq \omega$, $p \sim_{if} q$ iff

1) for any $\sigma \in \mathcal{T}(p)$ and p' with $p \overset{\sigma}{\Longrightarrow} p'$, there exists q' such that $q \overset{\sigma}{\Longrightarrow} q'$ and $\mathcal{T}(q') \subseteq \mathcal{T}(p')$, and

2) for any $\sigma \in \mathcal{T}(q)$ and q' with $q \overset{\sigma}{\Longrightarrow} q'$, there exists p' such that $p \overset{\sigma}{\Longrightarrow} p'$ and $\mathcal{T}(p') \subseteq \mathcal{T}(q')$.

The following two propositions say that, in any SISNNI language, operators $/Act_H$ and $\backslash Act_H$ are both distributive on any context of n holes.

Proposition 6.3.2. Let $\mathcal{L}$ be an SISNNI language, and C be any context of n holes. If $p_1, ..., p_n$ are any processes, then $C(p_1, ..., p_n)/Act_H \sim_{if} C(p_1/Act_H, ..., p_n/Act_H)$.

Proof. The only problem may exist when a ruloid like $\dfrac{\{x_i \overset{h_i}{\to} x_i'\}_{i \in I}}{C'(x_1, ..., x_n) \overset{\tau}{\to} D(y_1, ..., y_m)}$

is applied, where $I \subseteq \{1, ..., n\}$, $|I| > 1$ and $\forall i \in I : h_i \in Act_H$. Therefore, when $C(p_1, ..., p_n)/Act_H \Longrightarrow C'(p_1', ..., p_n')/Act_H \overset{\tau}{\to} C''(p_1'', ..., p_n'')/Act_H$, it is possible that $C(p_1/Act_H, ..., p_n/Act_H) \Longrightarrow C'(p_1'/Act_H, ..., p_n'/Act_H)$
$\overset{\tau}{\to} C_1'(p_{11}'/Act_H, ..., p_{n1}'/Act_H) \overset{\tau}{\to} C_2'(p_{12}'/Act_H, ..., p_{n2}'/Act_H) \overset{\tau}{\to} ... \overset{\tau}{\to}$
$C_k'(p_{1k}'/Act_H, ..., p_{nk}'/Act_H) \equiv D(p_1''/Act_H, ..., p_n''/Act_H)$ occurs in $C(p_1/Act_H, ..., p_n/Act_H)$ with $k = |I|$.

However, observe that all $\mathcal{T}(C_m'(p_{1m}'/Act_H, ..., p_{nm}'/Act_H))$ with $1 \leq m \leq k$ are equivalent. Therefore, each impossible future pair of $C(p_1/Act_H, ..., p_n/Act_H)$ has corresponding impossible future pair of $C(p_1, ..., p_n)/Act_H$, and vice versa. □

Proposition 6.3.3. If $p_1, ..., p_n$ are any processes satisfying the SISNNI property, then $C(p_1, ..., p_n)\backslash Act_H \sim_{if} C(p_1\backslash Act_H, ..., p_n\backslash Act_H)$.

Theorem 6.3.4 [6]. Weak ω-failure format is a congruence format for the impossible future equivalence.

Theorem 6.3.5. SISNNI format is a compositional format for the SISNNI property.

Proof. It is enough to prove that $C(p_1, ..., p_n)/Act_H \sim_{if} C(p_1, ..., p_n)\backslash Act_H$ if $p_i/Act_H \sim_{if} p_i\backslash Act_H$ for all $1 \leq i \leq n$. By Proposition 6.3.2, $C(p_1, ..., p_n)/Act_H \sim_{if} C(p_1/Act_H, ..., p_n/Act_H)$. By Proposition 6.3.3, $C(p_1, ..., p_n)\backslash Act_H \sim_{if} C(p_1\backslash Act_H, ..., p_n\backslash Act_H)$. Now, $C(p_1/Act_H, ..., p_n/Act_H) \sim_{if} C(p_1\backslash Act_H, ..., p_n\backslash Act_H)$ can be guaranteed by Theorem 6.3.4 and $p_i/Act_H \sim_{if} p_i\backslash Act_H$. Finally, we will obtain the conclusion by the transitivity of the impossible future equivalence, because it is an equivalence relation. □

7 Conclusions

We have observed in the paper that, for characterizing the non-interference-like information flow properties, the weak bisimulation may not be the only suitable semantic equivalence, and even may falsely deem some systems insecure though they are actually secure. Then, we present several alternative semantic equivalences and argue that they can play the same role with the weak bisimulation in verifying whether a system holds some information flow security. Moreover, they will not lead to the faults caused by the weak bisimulation, or at least make less faults than weak bisimulation does.

As the second topic, we propose a rule format to guarantee the compositionality of the SISNNI property, which is an impossible future equivalence based non-interference property. This rule format make little modifications on the congruence format for the impossible future equivalence proposed by the authors. If a language is in this format, then impossible future equivalence is a congruence and SISNNI property is compositional.

References

1. Focardi, R., Gorrieri, R.: Classification of Security Properties(Part I: Information Flow). In: Focardi, R., Gorrieri, R. (eds.) Foundations of Security Analysis and Design. LNCS, vol. 2171, pp. 331–396. Springer, Heidelberg (2001)
2. Rensink, A., Vogler, W.: Fair Testing. Information and Computation 205(2), 125–198 (2007)
3. van Glabbeek, R.J.: The Linear Time - Branching Time Spectrum I: The Semantics of Concrete, Sequential Processes. In: Bergstra, J.A., Ponse, A., Smolka, S.A. (eds.) Handbook of Process Algebra, ch. 1, pp. 3–100. Elsevier, Amsterdam (2001)
4. van Glabbeek, R.J.: The Linear Time - Branching Time Spectrum II: The semantics of sequential systems with silent moves. In: Best, E. (ed.) CONCUR 1993. LNCS, vol. 715, pp. 66–81. Springer, Heidelberg (1993)
5. De Nicola, R., Hennessy, M.: Testing Equivalences for Processes. Theoretical Computer Science 34, 83–133 (1984)
6. Huang, X., Jiao, L., Lu, W.: Rule Formats for Weak Parametric Failure Equivalences (submitted)
7. Ryan, P.Y.A.: Mathematical Models of Computer Security. In: Focardi, R., Gorrieri, R. (eds.) Foundations of Security Analysis and Design. LNCS, vol. 2171, pp. 1–62. Springer, Heidelberg (2001)
8. van der Meyden, R., Zhang, C.: A Comparison of Semantic Models for Noninterference. In: Dimitrakos, T., Martinelli, F., Ryan, P.Y.A, Schneider, S. (eds.) FAST 2006. LNCS, vol. 4691, Springer, Heidelberg (2006)
9. Bell, D.E., Padula, L.J.L.: Secure Computer Systems: Unified Exposition and Multics Interpretation. ESD-TR-75-306, MITRE MTR-2997 (March 1976)
10. Focardi, R., Rossi, S.: Information Flow Security in Dynamic Contexts. In: Proceeding of the IEEE Computer Security Foundations Workshop, pp. 307–319. IEEE Computer Society Press, Los Alamitos (2002)
11. Tini, S.: Rule Formats for Compositional Non-Interference Properties. Journal of Logic and Algebraic Progamming 60, 353–400 (2004)
12. Plotkin, G.D.: A Structural Approach to Operational Semantics. The Journal of Logic and Algebraic Programming, 60–61,17–139 (2004)
13. Milner, R.: Communication and Concurrency. Prentice-Hall, Englewood Cliffs (1989)
14. Mousavi, M.R., Reniers, M.A., Groote, J.F.: SOS formats and meta-theory: 20 years after. Theoretical Computer Science 373, 238–272 (2007)
15. Aceto, L., Fokkink, W.J., Verhoef, C.: Structural Operational Semantics. In: Bergstra, J.A., Ponse, A., Smolka, S.A. (eds.) Handbook of Process Algebra, Ch. 3, pp. 197–292. Elsevier, Amsterdam (2001)
16. Groote, J.F., Waandrager, F.W.: Structural Operational Semantics and Bisimulation as a Congruence. Information and Computation 100(2), 202–260 (1992)
17. Groote, J.F.: Transition System Specifications with Negative Premises. Theoretical Computer Science 118, 263–299 (1993)

18. Simone, R.D.: Higher-level synchronising devices in Meiji-SCCS. Theoretical Computer Science 37, 245–267 (1985)
19. Baeten, J.C.M., Weijiland, W.P.: Process Algebra. Cambridge Tracts in Theoretical Computer Science. Cambridge University Press, Cambridge (1990)
20. Burris, S., Sankappanavar, H.P.: A Course in Universal Algebra. Graduate Texts in Mathematics, vol. 78. Springer, Berlin (1981)
21. Bloom, B., Istrail, S., Meyer, A.R.: Bisimualtion can't be Traced. Journal of the ACM 42(1), 232–268 (1995)
22. Bloom, B.: Structural Operational Semantics for Weak Bisimulations. Theoretical Computer Science 146, 27–68 (1995)
23. Bloom, B.: Ready Simulation, Bisimulation, and the Semantics of CCS-Like Languages. PhD thesis, MIT (1990)
24. Ulidowski, I.: Finite Axiom Systems for Testing Preorder and De Simone Process Languages. Theoretical computer Science 239(1), 97–139 (2000)
25. van Glabbeek, R.J., Voorhoeve, M.: Liveness, Fairness and Impossible Futures. In: Baier, C., Hermanns, H. (eds.) CONCUR 2006. LNCS, vol. 4137, pp. 126–141. Springer, Heidelberg (2006)
26. Voorhoeve, I., Mauw, S.: Impossible Futures and Determinism. Information Processing Letters 80(1), 51–58 (2001)
27. Hoare, C.A.R.: Communicating Sequential Processes. Prentice-Hall, Englewood Cliffs (1985)
28. Bossi, A., Focardi, R., Piazza, C., Rossi, S.: Unwinding in Information Flow Security. Electronic Notes of Theoretical Computer Science 99, 127–154 (2004)
29. van Glabbeek, R.J.: On Cool Congruence Formats for Weak Bisimulations. In: Van Hung, D., Wirsing, M. (eds.) ICTAC 2005. LNCS, vol. 3722, pp. 331–346. Springer, Heidelberg (2005)

Modeling Agreement Problems in the Universal Composability Framework

Masayuki Terada[1,2], Kazuki Yoneyama[2], Sadayuki Hongo[1], and Kazuo Ohta[2]

[1] NTT DoCoMo, Inc.,
3–5 Hikari-no-oka, Yokosuka, Kanagawa, Japan
[2] University of Electro-Communications,
1–5 Chofu-ga-oka, Chofu, Tokyo, Japan

Abstract. Agreement problems are one of the keys to distributed computing. In this paper, we propose a construction of the ideal-model functionality of one of the most important agreement problems, non-blocking atomic commitment (NBAC), in the universally-composability (UC) framework. NBAC is not only important in realizing dependable transactions in distributed computing environments but also useful in constructing security protocols that require the fairness property, such as fair exchange protocols. Our construction of NBAC functionality (namely $\mathcal{F}_{\mathrm{NBAC}}$) is exactly equivalent to the NBAC definition; it is formally proved that a protocol UC-securely realizes $\mathcal{F}_{\mathrm{NBAC}}$ *if and only if* the protocol is an NBAC protocol. The proposed functionality and its proof of equivalence to NBAC enables the NBAC protocols to be used as a provably secure building block, and thus makes it much easier to feasibly and securely create higher-level protocols.

1 Introduction

Motivation. Agreement problems, which represent consistent decision making processes among independent subjects interacting with each other, are the most essential problem in the distributed computing literature. Their resolution is indispensable to realize trustworthy electronic commerce; e.g., consistent money transfer among banks is guaranteed by transaction processing systems that solve one type of agreement problem, namely the atomic commitment problem[1].

Protocols that can solve agreement problems, namely agreement protocols, are not only useful in themselves but also needed as fundamental building-blocks for realizing security protocols since multi-party protocols that require fairness explicitly or implicitly must include a process to resolve agreement problems. For example, broadcast channels, commonly used in multi-party protocols[2], are realized by solving the Byzantine agreement problem[3]. Another example is fair exchange[4,5], which is known to be unconditionally reducible into non-blocking atomic commitment (NBAC)[6] among trusted processes.[7,8]

Since the agreement problems are well-studied and a number of agreement protocols for diverse environments and assumptions have been developed so far[6,3,9,8], modeling agreement problems as *securely composable* functionalities enables us to dispense with reinventing the wheel when creating multi-party

S. Qing, H. Imai, and G. Wang (Eds.): ICICS 2007, LNCS 4861, pp. 350–361, 2007.

protocols and makes it easier to implement those protocols by introducing the concept of reusability, which is quite common in software programming, to security protocol design.

To realize this scenario, it is important to design functionalities that are "exactly equivalent" to the agreement protocols; a too strong functionality may lack protocols that realize it, while a too weak functionality may make it difficult to prove the security of the protocols that uses the functionality. The aim of this paper is to introduce functionalities that are provably equivalent to the agreement protocols so that we can use them as securely composable and substitutable building-blocks and so permit the design of high-level and complex security protocols.

Contributions. In this paper, we propose a construction of the functionality of NBAC, which is a fundamental agreement problem[6,10,11] known to be capable of becoming a building block in the construction of fair exchange protocols[7,8], in the universal composability (UC) framework[12]. To ensure that the functionality, namely $\mathcal{F}_{NBAC}$, captures the NBAC properties exactly, we introduce an oracle called *failure detection oracle* ($\mathcal{O}^{FD}$), which detects if any failure has occurred during protocol execution. This oracle is a sort of *failure detector*[13] commonly used to abstract the error detection abilities of distributed processes (e.g. timeout detection) in the distributed computing literature[14]. To be exact, the introduced oracle has abilities equivalent to those of the *anonymous perfect failure detector* (usually denoted as $?\mathcal{P}$)[11], which can correctly detect any failure but does not provide any information about where the failure has occurred.

A proof of the exactness of the proposed functionality $\mathcal{F}_{NBAC}$ is also provided in this paper. Designing a functionality that exactly represents the properties of the agreement protocols is, however, not be so straightforward that everyone can intuitively understand its correctness; it must be proved that the designed functionality exactly satisfies the properties in order to utilize the functionality as a securely composable building block. We provide proofs that the proposed functionality $\mathcal{F}_{NBAC}$ is exactly equivalent to NBAC; i.e., some protocol π securely realizes $\mathcal{F}_{NBAC}$ *if and only if* π holds all of the NBAC properties.

Related works. The concept of universal protocol composition has been attracted much attention, however, few studies have focused upon the agreement properties of protocols.

Lindell et al.[15] focus upon composability of the Byzantine agreement (or generals) problem[3], which are known to be reducible from the problem to establish a broadcast channel in a point-to-point network. Their notable impossibility results show that a Byzantine agreement protocol requires more than $2/3$ honest parties to be secure under parallel composition even if the messages are authenticated, although it was originally believed that the Byzantine agreement with authenticated messages (authenticated Byzantine agreement) could be solved under any number of dishonest (corrupted) parties.[3]

Garay et al.[16] specified a composable ideal functionality that gives the *resource-fair* property, which states that if one party learns the output of the protocol, then so can all other parties, as long as they expend roughly the same amount of resources. The functionality is defined in a similar way to the UC framework, but works in the framework where the environment compensate the additional resources for honest parties prematurely aborted by the adversary. This functionality and framework provide the notion of fairness (which is a similar notion to agreement) as a composable building block in secure multi-party computation protocols, however, this model assumes synchronous channels and the functionality is constructed upon a fair delivery mechanism that provides *complete fairness*[2], where if one party receives the output, all parties receive the output; these assumptions are too ideal and hard to realize in real systems.

In the distributed computing literature, on the other hand, NBAC[6] is considered to be a fundamental agreement problem to ensure the atomicity of a distributed transaction, and its characteristics including solvability have been well-studied[10,1,17,11,9,14,8].

NBAC can be solved in the asynchronous model if (a certain class of) failure detectors can be assumed. For example, every following protocol solves NBAC in certain environment: the 3-phase commitment (3PC) protocol[6], the 2-phase commitment (2PC) protocol[1][1] and the optimistic NBAC protocol[8]. A different application or situation would need a different NBAC protocol since every protocol has its own strengths and weaknesses; e.g., the 3PC protocol is the most versatile but is extremely complicated[9], 2PC is easy to implement but requires special assumptions on a process (i.e. coordinator), and the optimistic NBAC is simple and efficient but applicable only to the 2-party setting where each party has a trusted module such as a smartcard.

The functionality proposed in this paper makes all protocols that correctly hold the NBAC properties under parallel composition usable as securely composable building blocks in the UC framework.

2   Preliminaries

2.1   Non-Blocking Atomic Commitment (NBAC)

An NBAC agreement guarantees that the participating processes, each of which votes yes or no, eventually agree upon a common outcome, commit or abort. In this agreement, commit can be decided only if all participants vote yes[2]. If any process votes no, abort must be decided. Every correct process is guaranteed to receive the decided value.

Precisely, the NBAC problem is defined as follows.[6,17]

---

[1] The 2PC protocol is usually known to solve the atomic commitment problem, which is similar to NBAC but does not guarantee the Termination property, but it solves NBAC if no misbehavior (including crash) of the coordinator process and resilient channels between the coordinator and the other processes can be assumed.

[2] Note that "if" direction is not guaranteed.

Definition 1 (NBAC). *The NBAC problem consists of a set of independent processes that reach a unanimous decision,* commit *or* abort, *according to initial votes of the processes,* yes *or* no, *such that the following properties[3] are satisfied:*

Agreement. *No two processes decide differently;*

Termination. *Every correct process eventually decides;*

Commit-Validity (C-Validity). *If all processes propose* yes *and there is no failure, then the decision value must be* commit; *and*

Abort-Validity (A-Validity). *If at least one process proposes* no, *then the decision value must be* abort.

While NBAC is an essential problem in the distributed computing literature, it is also valuable in constructing fair exchange protocols as mentioned in Sect. 1. Fair exchange is reducible into NBAC between trusted processes by the following reduction algorithm[7]:

FairExchange(item i, description d) {
  ⟨send i to exchange partners over secure channel⟩
  timed wait for ⟨expected item i_e from exchange partners⟩
    ⟨check d on i_e⟩
  if (check succeeds and no timeout)
    then $vote :=$ yes **else** $vote :=$ no **endif**
  $result := \mathrm{NBAC}(vote)$
  if $(result =$ commit$)$
    then return i_e **else return** ⟨abort⟩ **endif**
}

The fair exchange protocol based on this algorithm enables parties to fairly exchange arbitrary items. When using the optimistic NBAC protocol[8] as the NBAC part of this algorithm, this exchange realizes optimistic (strong) fair exchange of arbitrary items while other known optimistic protocols can guarantee strong fairness only when at least one exchanged item has a special property called strong generatability[5][4].

2.2   UC Framework

In the following, we briefly introduce the concept of the UC framework; its comprehensive and rigorous definition is described in [12].

The UC framework is a sort of simulation-based security framework, where the "formal specification" of the security requirements of a task is represented as a set of instructions of a trusted process, namely ideal-model functionality.

---

[3] C-Validity and A-Validity are often called "non-triviality" and "uniform-validity", respectively.

[4] However, note that fair exchange by this method requires both parties to run trusted processes; i.e., each party has to have access to a trusted device such as a smartcard. This requirement would be easily satisfied by recent mobile phones (equipped with (U)SIM cards), but might be rather difficult in other environments.

A protocol is said to *UC-realize* the functionality (for the task) if running the protocol "emulates" the functionality, in sense that observable outputs from the parties and an adversary running the protocol and those from the parties and an ideal adversary (i.e. a simulator) interacting with the functionality cannot be distinguished by the *environment* machine with non-negligible probability. The environment machine is a probabilistic interactive Turing machine (PITM) that can hand arbitrary inputs to the parties and the adversary and can collect (observe) outputs from them.

The characteristic merit of this framework is to guarantee secure *universal composition* of the protocol (i.e. universal composition theorem); when a protocol UC-realize a functionality, the functionality that is "called" within another protocol (like a subroutine) can be securely substituted by an execution of the protocol UC-realizing the functionality[5].

This merit makes security protocols modular as building-blocks and makes it much easier to design and analyze complicated security protocols, however, the other side of the coin is the difficulty of designing functionalities. Since universal composability is founded upon tight simulatability between a protocol and a functionality, a functionality that is either stronger or weaker than the desired properties of the task obstructs secure composition of the protocol; a too strong functionality often lacks protocols that realize it, while a too weak functionality often makes it impossible to prove the security of the hybrid protocol that use the functionality even if the protocol is actually secure.

Designing an adequate functionality exactly equivalent to the desired properties of a task, therefore, is quite important in realizing modularized designs and simplified implementation of security protocols in the UC framework.

3   Ideal Functionality of NBAC

The ideal functionality in the UC framework is represented as a trusted party that captures the desired specification of the task by way of specifying a set of instructions.

Since the desired specification of NBAC is defined as the four NBAC properties (i.e., Agreement, Termination, C-Validity and A-Validity), designing the ideal functionality of NBAC is, accordingly, basically similar to finding a constraint satisfaction algorithm that *exactly* satisfies these properties.

As mentioned in Sect. 2, it is important to be careful not to make the functionality "too ideal" — it should exactly satisfy the properties to make the functionality useful as a secure building block. For example, a functionality, which outputs commit if all input values are yes or outputs abort otherwise, obviously satisfies all NBAC properties, but is almost useless as the ideal functionality of NBAC. This functionality is too ideal to be securely realized by any practical

---

[5] To be more exact, provided that protocol ρ UC-realizes some functionality $\mathcal{F}$ and protocol π in which parties make calls to $\mathcal{F}$ UC-realizes some functionality $\mathcal{G}$, protocol π^ρ in which parties run ρ instead of calling $\mathcal{F}$ also UC-realizes $\mathcal{G}$.

NBAC protocol in the real world, so any hybrid protocol constructed with this functionality would also be unrealizable.

In order for the functionality to exactly capture the desired properties, the functionality interacts with a party called *simulator*, which simulates attacks by an adversary in the real-world model. Most agreement protocols including NBAC, however, have a property that cannot be represented even by interacting with the simulator; i.e., the condition "there is no failure" in the C-Validity properties. A simulator naturally knows whether a failure occurs internally, but there is no means for a functionality to *rightly* know that from the simulator; even if the simulator sends a message that indicates that a failure has occurred, the functionality may not trust it because the UC framework does not guarantee that the simulator sends a message based on its internal states correctly . Accordingly, another means by which the functionality can accurately know whether a failure has occured is needed for the functionality to correctly represent the C-Validity property.

3.1   Failure Detection Oracle

To adequately represent the C-Validity property, we introduce the failure detection oracle, denoted by $\mathcal{O}^{FD}$. This oracle is an ideal failure detector that detects if any failure (including network failure, prematurely abortion or any other misbehaviors by corrupted party) is caused by the adversary.

Definition 2 (Failure detection oracle). *Failure detection oracle $\mathcal{O}^{FD}$ is an oracle that outputs $f \leftarrow \{0,1\}$ upon receiving sid, where f takes the following value according to failure events in the protocol execution identified by sid:*

$$f = \begin{cases} 1 & (\textit{if no failure occurs in the protocol}), or \\ 0 & (\textit{otherwise}). \end{cases} \tag{1}$$

No failure *in the above definition means that every participant behaved correctly and every message is transfered as expected by the protocol definition.*

Since $\mathcal{O}^{FD}$ is a virtual function to define a functionality in the ideal model, protocols realizing a functionality with this oracle do not have to assume the existence of $\mathcal{O}^{FD}$ in the real-world model. However, interestingly, this oracle has equivalent abilities to the *anonymous perfect failure detector* $(?\mathcal{P})$, which can detect any failure *completely* (i.e. any failure is detected within some time) and *accurately* (i.e. no failure is detected unless a failure occurs) but does not provide any information about where the failure happened; this failure detector is known to be sufficient to transform *Consensus*[6] into NBAC.[18]

---

[6] The Consensus problem is another agreement problem where the following *validity* property holds instead of C-Validity and A-Validity properties in NBAC: *a value decided must be a value proposed by some process.*

3.2 Definition of $\mathcal{F}_{\text{NBAC}}$

The ideal functionality of NBAC, namely $\mathcal{F}_{\text{NBAC}}$, is defined as follows:

Definition 3 (Ideal functionality of NBAC ($\mathcal{F}_{\text{NBAC}}$)). *This functionality proceeds as follows, running with participants* $\mathbf{P} = \{P_1, P_2, ..., P_n\}$, *simulator $\mathcal{S}$, and failure detection oracle* $\mathcal{O}^{FD}$:

1. *Upon receiving a vote* $(\text{Vote}, sid, \mathbf{P}, vote_i)$ *from* P_i, *where* $vote_i \leftarrow \{0, 1\}$ *is the proposal value of P_i (yes: 1, no: 0), check if a vote from P_i is recorded. If it is already recorded, ignore the received vote. If not, record the vote.*
2. *When all votes from* $\mathbf{P}$ *are recorded, send* $(\text{Exec}, sid, \mathbf{P})$ *to $\mathcal{S}$.*
3. *Upon receiving* $(\text{Notice}, sid, \phi, \chi)$ *from $\mathcal{S}$, where $\phi \leftarrow \{0, 1\}$ indicates if abort was forcibly caused by the adversary (forcibly aborted: 1, otherwise: 0) and* $\chi = \chi_1 || \chi_2 || ... || \chi_n \leftarrow \{0, 1\}^n$ *indicates if termination of a participant P_i was interrupted by corrupt acts of the adversary (P_i can terminate: $\chi_i = 1$, P_i is corrupted and cannot terminate: $\chi_i = 0$), send sid to* $\mathcal{O}^{FD}$.
4. *Upon receiving f from* $\mathcal{O}^{FD}$, *send* $(\text{Result}, sid, result_i)$ *to P_i, where $result_i$ takes the following value:*

$$result_i = \begin{cases} \perp & (\text{if } \chi_i = 0 \text{ and } P_i \text{ is corrupted}), \\ \prod_{j=1}^{n} vote_j & (\text{else if } f = 1), \\ \prod_{j=1}^{n} vote_j \cdot \phi & (\text{otherwise}). \end{cases} \qquad (2)$$

$result_i$ is the decision value that participant P_i receives. 0 and 1 represent abort *and* commit, *respectively.* $\perp$ *indicates that P_i cannot decide (i.e., does not terminate).*

4   Proving the Equivalence of $\mathcal{F}_{\text{NBAC}}$ to NBAC

In this section, we prove that $\mathcal{F}_{\text{NBAC}}$ defined in Sect. 3 is the equivalent functionality of NBAC; i.e., a protocol is an NBAC protocol if and only if it UC-securely realizes $\mathcal{F}_{\text{NBAC}}$.

Before proving it, we firstly provide a formal definition of an NBAC protocol, namely π_{NBAC}, by using symbolic logic in order to rigorously discuss the equivalence of the functionality to NBAC. Next, we prove two lemmas: 1) π_{NBAC} UC-realizes $\mathcal{F}_{\text{NBAC}}$ (i.e., $\mathcal{F}_{\text{NBAC}}$ is not stronger than π_{NBAC}), and 2) any protocol realizing $\mathcal{F}_{\text{NBAC}}$ is π_{NBAC} (i.e., $\mathcal{F}_{\text{NBAC}}$ is not weaker than π_{NBAC}). The equivalence can be stated as a corollary of these two lemmas.

4.1   Formal Definition of NBAC

Although the definition of NBAC in Sect. 2 (1) is commonly used and easy to understand, it isn't rigorous enough to discuss the equivalence of $\mathcal{F}_{\text{NBAC}}$ to NBAC. An NBAC protocol can be formally defined by using symbolic logic as follows:

Definition 4 (NBAC protocol). *A protocol running with a set of independent processes* $\mathbf{P} = \{P_1, P_2, ..., P_n\}$ *is an NBAC protocol π_{NBAC} if it satisfies the* *following, where P_i inputs a vote value $v_i (\in \{0, 1\};$ yes : 1, no : 0) and receives a decision value $r_i (\in \{0, 1, \bot\};$ commit : 1, abort : 0, no decision $:\bot), \mathbf{P}_C (\subseteq \mathbf{P})$ is a set of corrupted (incorrect) processes, and f is a value defined as Eqn. 1:*

Agreement. *The requirement of Agreement property, No two processes decide differently, means that the results of any two different processes (r_i and $r_j (i \neq j)$) are equal if both processes receive the result ($r_i \neq \bot \cap r_j \neq \bot$). Hence, this property can be formalized as follows:*

$$\forall ((r_i, r_j) | r_i \neq \bot, r_j \neq \bot) r_i = r_j. \tag{3}$$

(Termination). *This property requires that any honest process ($P_i (\notin \mathbf{P}_C)$) can terminate and get a result ($r_i \neq \bot$). Hence,*

$$\forall (r_i | P_i \notin \mathbf{P}_C) r_i \neq \bot. \tag{4}$$

(C-Validity). *This property requires that the result of any process is commit ($\forall (r_i) r_i = 1$) if all votes are yes (($\forall (v_j) v_j = 1$)) and there is no failure (i.e., the failure detection oracle $\mathcal{O}^{FD}$ outputs $f = 1$). Hence,*

$$\forall (r_i) r_i = 1 \text{ if } (\forall (v_j) v_j = 1) \cap (f = 1). \tag{5}$$

(A-Validity). *This property requires that the result of any terminated process is abort ($\forall (r_i | r_i \neq \bot) r_i = 0$) if at least one vote is no ($\exists (v_j) v_j = 0$). Hence,*

$$\forall (r_i | r_i \neq \bot) r_i = 0 \text{ if } \exists (v_j) v_j = 0. \tag{6}$$

4.2   Proving That π_{NBAC} UC-Realizes $\mathcal{F}_{\text{NBAC}}$

Lemma 1. *An NBAC protocol (π_{NBAC}) UC-securely realizes $\mathcal{F}_{\text{NBAC}}$.*

Proof. To prove this lemma, it suffices to show that there exists a simulator $\mathcal{S}$ that can simulate any adversary by internal execution of π_{NBAC}.

Suppose simulator $\mathcal{S}$ runs as follows:

1. Upon receiving message (Exec, sid, $\mathbf{P}$), internally run π_{NBAC} with vote values $v_i = vote_i$ and obtain decision values r_i ($i = 1, ..., n$).
2. Equate ϕ and χ_i as follows:

$$\phi = \begin{cases} 0 & (\exists (r_i | r_i \neq \bot) r_i = 0), \\ 1 & (\text{otherwise}); \end{cases} \tag{7}$$

$$\chi_i = \begin{cases} 0 & (r_i = \bot), \\ 1 & (\text{otherwise}). \end{cases} \tag{8}$$

3. Send (Notice, sid, ϕ, χ) to the functionality in terms of the above ϕ and χ_i.

In the following, we prove that such a simulator can simulate any adversary so that environment $\mathcal{Z}$ cannot distinguish $\mathcal{F}_{\text{NBAC}}$ and π_{NBAC}; i.e., the observable output of $\mathcal{F}_{\text{NBAC}}$ ($result_i$) and that of π_{NBAC} (r_i) are always consistent ($result_i = r_i$).

The proof is divided into the following two cases: P_i is not corrupted (case 1) and P_i is corrupted (case 2).

Case 1: P_i is not corrupted. If P_i is assumed not to be corrupted (P_i is correct), i.e., $P_i \notin \mathbf{P}_C$, it holds $r_i \neq \bot$ according to Termination property and $\chi_i = 1$ is given by Eqn. (8).

Under this assumption, r_i must have the following values: $r_i = 1$ if $(\forall(v_j)v_j = 1) \cap (f = 1)$ according to C-Validity property, $r_i = 0$ if $\exists(v_j)v_j = 0$ according to A-Validity property; r_i is undefined in other cases, i.e., if $(\forall(v_j)v_j = 1) \cap (f = 0)$, however, it must be 0 or 1 according to the assumption (cf. Termination property).

Consequently, r_i holds the following value in terms of $v_j(j = 1, ..., n)$ and f.

$$r_i = \begin{cases} 1 & (\forall(v_j)v_j = 1 \cap f = 1), \\ 0 \text{ or } 1 & (\forall(v_j)v_j = 1 \cap f = 0), \\ 0 & (\exists(v_j)v_j = 0). \end{cases} \qquad (9)$$

In the first case, $result_i$ has the following value according to Eqn. (2):

$$result_i = \prod_{j=1}^{n} vote_j = 1. \qquad (10)$$

It holds $result_i = r_i$.

In the second case, Agreement property requires that $\forall(r_j | r_j \neq \bot)r_j = r_i$. Eqn. (7) gives $\phi = 0$ if $\exists(r_j)r_j = 0$, or $\phi = 1$ otherwise. Hence, it holds that $r_i = \phi$. Since $\forall(j)vote_j = v_j = 1$, $result_i$ becomes:

$$result_i = \prod_{j=1}^{n} vote_j \cdot \phi = 1 \cdot \phi = \phi. \qquad (11)$$

It also holds that $result_i = r_i$ in this case.

In the last case, it obviously holds that $result_i = 0(= r_i)$ since $\prod_{j=1}^{n} vote_j = 0$. Therefore, it always holds that $result_i = r_i$ if P_i is not corrupted.

Case 2: P_i is corrupted. If P_i is assumed to be corrupted, Termination property does not restrict r_i not to become $\bot$ (no decision) so that r_i may take any value of $\{0, 1, \bot\}$.

If $r_i \neq \bot$, it holds that $result_i = r_i$ as shown in case 1. If $r_i = \bot$, Eqn. (8) gives $\chi_i = 0$. Since $\chi_i = 0$ and P_i is corrupted in this case, it becomes $result_i = \bot$ according to Eqn. (2); it holds that $result_i = r_i(= \bot)$.

Hence, simulator $\mathcal{S}$ can simulate any adversary so that environment $\mathcal{Z}$ cannot distinguish $\mathcal{F}_{\text{NBAC}}$ and π_{NBAC}, and therefore π_{NBAC} UC-securely realizes $\mathcal{F}_{\text{NBAC}}$. $\qquad\square$

4.3   Proving That Any Protocol UC-Realizing $\mathcal{F}_{\text{NBAC}}$ Is π_{NBAC}

Next, we prove that any protocol that UC-realizes $\mathcal{F}_{\text{NBAC}}$ is π_{NBAC} by proving the following contrapositive lemma.

Lemma 2. *A protocol that is not π_{NBAC} cannot UC-realize $\mathcal{F}_{\text{NBAC}}$.*

Proof. In the following, we show that no simulator can simulate adversaries such that the environment cannot distinguish $\mathcal{F}_{\text{NBAC}}$ and protocol π that does not hold at least one of the NBAC properties.

If π does not hold Agreement property. Assume that π does not hold Agreement property and thus outputs decision values r_i, r_j where $r_i \neq r_j (r_i \neq\perp, r_j \neq\perp)$.

In order that π UC-securely realize $\mathcal{F}_{\text{NBAC}}$, there must exist a simulator such that $\mathcal{F}_{\text{NBAC}}$ outputs $result_i, result_j$ where $result_i \neq result_j (i \neq j)$.

However, $\mathcal{F}_{\text{NBAC}}$ always outputs $result_i$ and $result_j$ such that $result_i = result_j$ for any pair of i and j when $result_i \neq\perp$ and $result_j \neq\perp$, regardless to the behavior of the simulator; i.e., $\mathcal{F}_{\text{NBAC}}$ outputs either $result_i = result_j = \prod_{k=1}^{n} vote_k$ or $result_i = result_j = \prod_{k=1}^{n} vote_k \cdot \phi$. Hence, under this assumption, the outcome of π and $\mathcal{F}_{\text{NBAC}}$ become inconsistent so the environment can easily distinguish them.

If π does not hold Termination property. Assume that π does not hold Termination property and thus outputs $r_i =\perp$ to $P_i(\notin \mathbf{P}_C)$.

$\mathcal{F}_{\text{NBAC}}$ always gives $result_i \neq\perp$ according to Eqn. (2) to P_i if P_i is not corrupted. $result_i$ and r_i contradict each other and are thus distinguishable.

If π does not hold C-Validity property. Assume that π does not hold C-Validity property and thus outputs $r_i = 0$ to P_i despite $\forall(v_j)v_j = 1$ and $f = 1$.

Under this assumption, $\mathcal{F}_{\text{NBAC}}$ outputs $result_i = \prod_{j=1}^{n} vote_j = 1$ to P_i, according to Eqn. (2); it becomes $result_i \neq r_i$.

If π does not hold A-Validity property. Assume that π does not hold A-Validity property and thus outputs $r_i = 1$ despite $\exists(v_j)v_j = 0$.

According to Eqn. (2), $\mathcal{F}_{\text{NBAC}}$ outputs $result_i = \prod_{j=1}^{n} vote_j = 0$ when $\exists(v_j)v_j = 0$ and therefore $result_i \neq r_i$ under this assumption.

Consequently, an execution of π, which does not hold at least one of the NBAC properties, is inevitably distinguishable from $\mathcal{F}_{\text{NBAC}}$ running with any simulator; a protocol that is not π_{NBAC} cannot UC-securely realize $\mathcal{F}_{\text{NBAC}}$ and therefore any protocol that can UC-securely realize $\mathcal{F}_{\text{NBAC}}$ is π_{NBAC}. □

4.4 Equivalence of $\mathcal{F}_{\text{NBAC}}$ to NBAC

As a corollary of Lemma 1 and Lemma 2, the following theorem can be stated:

Theorem 1. *Some protocol π realizes $\mathcal{F}_{\text{NBAC}}$ if and only if π is an NBAC protocol (π_{NBAC}).*

The equivalence of $\mathcal{F}_{\text{NBAC}}$ to NBAC is thus proved. □

5 Conclusion

We proposed a construction of ideal functionality of the non-blocking atomic commitment, namely $\mathcal{F}_{\text{NBAC}}$, in the universal composability framework. To exactly capture the NBAC properties by the functionality, we introduced a failure detection oracle $\mathcal{O}^{FD}$, which is an ideal failure detector notifying the functionality of the occurrence of failures caused by the adversary during protocol execution. We also confirmed that the proposed functionality is a proper functionality of NBAC by proving the equivalence of the $\mathcal{F}_{\mathrm{NBAC}}$ and the formalized NBAC protocol π_{NBAC}; i.e., a protocol UC-realizes $\mathcal{F}_{\mathrm{NBAC}}$ if and only if the protocol is π_{NBAC}.

Our construction of NBAC can be easily applied to design another agreement problems. For example, the atomic commitment (AC) problem, the most frequently-examined agreement problem in the distributed computing field, is equivalent to NBAC without the Termination property; the equivalent functionality can be defined as follows:

Definition 5 (Ideal functionality of AC ($\mathcal{F}_{\mathrm{AC}}$)). *This functionality proceeds as follows, running with participants* $\mathbf{P} = \{P_1, P_2, ..., P_n\}$*, simulator* $\mathcal{S}$*, and failure detection oracle* $\mathcal{O}^{FD}$*:*

1. *(Same as Step 1 $\sim$ 3 of $\mathcal{F}_{\mathrm{NBAC}}$, see Def. 3)*
2. *Upon receiving f from $\mathcal{O}^{FD}$, send* (Result, sid, $result_i$) *to P_i, where $result_i$ takes the following value:*

$$result_i = \begin{cases} \perp & (if \ \chi_i = 0), \\ \prod_{j=1}^{n} vote_j & (else \ if \ f = 1), \\ \prod_{j=1}^{n} vote_j \cdot \phi & (otherwise). \end{cases} \tag{12}$$

$result_i$ is the decision value that participant P_i receives. 0 and 1 represent abort *and* commit*, respectively. $\perp$ indicates that P_i cannot decide (i.e., does not terminate).*

The only difference of $\mathcal{F}_{\mathrm{AC}}$ from $\mathcal{F}_{\mathrm{NBAC}}$ is the condition that $result_i$ becomes $\perp$; this difference reflects the fact that only corrupted processes can become unable to terminate in NBAC but any process can become unable to terminate in AC. The proof of equivalence between an AC protocol and $\mathcal{F}_{\mathrm{AC}}$ is also similar to that of NBAC and is thus trivial.

As mentioned in Sect. 1, these agreement protocols are useful in constructing other higher-level (and more complicated) protocols such as fair exchange protocols. The proposed functionality $\mathcal{F}_{\mathrm{NBAC}}$ and other functionalities derivable from our $\mathcal{F}_{\mathrm{NBAC}}$ construction (e.g. $\mathcal{F}_{\mathrm{AC}}$) will be beneficial in designing such complicated protocols and in making it easier to formally prove their security, without sacrificing any feasibility or realizability of the protocols in the real world.

References

1. Gray, J., Reuter, A.: Transaction Processing: Concepts and Techniques. Morgan Kaufmann, San Francisco (1992)
2. Goldwasser, S., Lindell, Y.: Secure computation without agreement. In: Malkhi, D. (ed.) DISC 2002. LNCS, vol. 2508, pp. 17–32. Springer, Heidelberg (2002)
3. Lamport, L., Shostak, R., Pease, M.: The byzantine generals problem. ACM Trans. Programming Language and Systems 4, 382–401 (1982)
4. Asokan, N.: Fairness in Electronic Commerce. PhD thesis, University of Waterloo (1998)

5. Pagnia, H., Vogt, H., Gärtner, F.C.: Fair exchange. The Computer Journal 46, 55–75 (2003)
6. Skeen, D.: Nonblocking commit protocols. In: Proc. 1981 ACM SIGMOD Intl. Conf. Management of Data, pp. 133–142 (1981)
7. Avoine, G., Gärtner, F.C., Guerraoui, R., Kursawe, K., Vaudenay, S., Vukolic, M.: Reducing fair exchange to atomic commit. Technical Report 200411, Swiss Federal Institute of Technology (EPFL), School of Computer and Communication Sciences, Lausanne, Switzerland (2004)
8. Terada, M., Mori, K., Hongo, S.: An optimistic NBAC-based fair exchange method for arbitrary items. In: Domingo-Ferrer, J., Posegga, J., Schreckling, D. (eds.) CARDIS 2006. LNCS, vol. 3928, pp. 105–118. Springer, Heidelberg (2006)
9. Gray, J., Lamport, L.: Consensus on transaction commit. Technical Report MSR-TR-2003-96, Microsoft Research (2004)
10. Gray, J.: A comparison of byzantine agreement problem and the transaction commit problem. In: Simons, B., Spector, A. (eds.) Fault-Tolerant Distributed Computing. LNCS, vol. 448, pp. 10–17. Springer, Heidelberg (1990)
11. Guerraoui, R., Kouznetsov, P.: On the weakest failure detector for non-blocking atomic commit. In: Proc. 2nd IFIP Intl. Conf. Theoretical Computer Science (TCS). IFIP Conference Proceedings, vol. 223, pp. 461–473. Kluwer, Dordrecht (2002)
12. Canetti, R.: Universally composable security: A new paradigm for cryptographic protocols. In: Proc. 42nd Symp. Foundations of Computer Science (FOCS) Full version at Cryptology ePrint Archive 2000/067, pp. 136–145 (2001)
13. Chandra, T.D., Toueg, S.: The weakest failure detector for solving consensus. J. ACM 43, 225–267 (1996)
14. Freiling, F.C., Guerraoui, R., Kouznetsov, P.: The failure detector abstraction. Technical Report 2006-003, Faculty of Mathematics and Computer Science, University of Mannheim (2006)
15. Lindell, Y., Lysyanskaya, A., Rabin, T.: On the composition of authenticated byzantine agreement. In: Proc. 34th Annual ACM Symp. Theory of Computing (STOC), pp. 514–523 (2002)
16. Garay, J.A., MacKenzie, P.D., Prabhakaran, M., Yang, K.: Resource fairness and composability of cryptographic protocols. In: Halevi, S., Rabin, T. (eds.) TCC 2006. LNCS, vol. 3876, pp. 404–428. Springer, Heidelberg (2006)
17. Guerraoui, R.: Revisiting the relationship between non-blocking atomic commitment and consensus. In: Helary, J.-M., Raynal, M. (eds.) WDAG 1995. LNCS, vol. 972, pp. 87–100. Springer, Heidelberg (1995)
18. Guerraoui, R.: Non-blocking atomic commit in asynchronous distributed systems with failure detector. Distributed Computing 15, 17–25 (2002)

A System Architecture for History-Based Access Control for XML Documents

Patrick Röder*, Omid Tafreschi**, Fredrik Mellgren, and Claudia Eckert

Darmstadt University of Technology,
Department of Computer Science,
D-64289 Darmstadt, Germany
{roeder,tafreschi,mellgren,eckert}@sec.informatik.tu-darmstadt.de

Abstract. In this paper, we present a history-based model which considers not only the content of an XML document to define access, but also how this content was created. The last aspect is an important factor for access control. Within the proposed model, the creation of documents is stored in histories, which also contain the source and destination of copied document parts. This enables us to define access depending on the origin of document parts. Applying this model in an environment where multiple users can edit documents concurrently is a challenging task, since access decisions depend on other documents, which are possibly edited at the same time. For this purpose, we present a system architecture which supports an efficient workflow and reduces the overhead for determining access rights of documents depending on other documents.

Keywords: Access Control, Document Security, XML, XPath.

1   Introduction

In the modern business world, many IT systems use XML as a standard for information storage and exchange. In such systems, security is crucial, since unauthorized access and information theft are responsible for a major part of damages caused by computer crime [9]. Access control (AC) is a central security mechanism to reduce that kind of loss. Although much work on AC in the areas of file systems or relational databases has already been done, defining access to XML documents is a different issue as stated in [7].

Consequently, a large number of models for AC for XML documents were proposed [2,5,6,8,13]. These approaches consider the content of a document to define access to its parts. This leads to a flexible way of defining policies independently of concrete instances. However, theses approaches do not regard how the content of an XML document was created. But this is important for AC, e.g., if the source of a copied part of a document is a top secret document, access to

---

* The author is supported by the PhD program *Enabling Technologies for Electronic Commerce* of the German Research Foundation (DFG).
** The author is supported by the German Federal Ministry of Education and Research under grant 01AK706C, project *Premium*.

S. Qing, H. Imai, and G. Wang (Eds.): ICICS 2007, LNCS 4861, pp. 362–374, 2007.

that part has to be restricted, too. A similar situation arises when a document part is copied to a top secret document, e.g., a patent application. In this case, it is desirable to deny access to the document parts located in the source document to avoid information disclosure. Additionally, it is important to know who has modified a document. Consider the following example: A researcher can change the title of a section, e.g., to make a suggestion, until the title is changed by a senior researcher, who has the authority to declare a title as final. Moreover, to enable Chinese Wall policies [3], which are important in the financial domain, the knowledge about previously performed operations is required.

Since in some cases XML elements contain a large amount of data, the granularity of AC on the level of XML elements is too coarse. An XML element can be composed of text parts from different sources. In this case, the AC system must be able to consider these parts individually to increase both flexibility and usability.

For these reasons, we introduced a model in [14] that is capable of defining access based on the content of the current document, the recorded histories and the content of dependent documents. These are documents between which documents parts have been copied to or from the current document. The histories contain information about the operations that led to the current document state. Moreover, these histories also include the source and destination of copied document parts. We use this information to define access.

Applying our model in a scenario where multiple users concurrently edit multiple documents introduces four challenges. First, since access rights of one document depend on other documents, we need a method for accessing these distributed documents when calculating access rights. Second, changes to one document require the recalculation of the views of all dependent documents, which are currently viewed. The straight forward approach for this is to recalculate the views of all dependent documents after a document has been changed. However, this results in a much higher number of view recalculations compared to models which only define access depending on the current edited document. For example, editing 20 depending documents concurrently, leads to a 20 times higher number of view recalculations with the straight forward approach. Therefore, we need a method which reduces the number of these view recalculations. Third, the changes of one user to a document can revoke the access rights of other users which are currently editing dependent documents. As a consequence, access rights can be revoked during an editing process, which can lead to conflicts regarding the content of the document and the access rights. Consequently, we need a method for handling these conflicts. Fourth, aforementioned the straight forward approach causes intermediate editing steps to become relevant for access decisions of other users, which is not desired. For example, a user can change a policy relevant element of a document by first deleting it and then replacing it with an updated version afterwards. In this example, the first step can revoke the access rights of another user, whereas the second step might restore these access rights.

The remainder of this paper is organized as follows: We summarize our model for AC for XML documents in Section 2. In Section 3, we present a system architecture that solves the four challenges mentioned above. Section 4 presents related work. We conclude and discuss future work in Section 5.

2   Model

In this section, we give an overview of our model and its components, which are explained in the following sections. We start with a description of the histories, continue with the operations defined in our model and finally present the syntax of our access rules.

2.1   Histories

We use histories to keep track of changes caused by the operations `create`, `copy`, `delete`, and `change attribute`. The operation `view` is also logged in the histories. These operations are described in detail in Section 2.2. We keep one history for every element itself including its attributes and one history for its text content. The latter history uses markup elements to divide the text into text blocks with a block ID. This mechanism enables us to keep track of sub-elements of arbitrary size. The markup elements are defined by `ac:block` elements, where `ac` is the prefix for the namespace of the access control system. We use the block IDs to reference individual text blocks in the history for the text content. If a view is created for a user, the `ac:block` elements are omitted. Keeping track of such implicitly defined sub-elements allows us to manage protection units smaller than an XML element. Technically, we use XML elements to define those sub-elements, but from a user's point of view, these sub-elements are not visible.

A new text block is created in two cases. First, we create a new text block as a result of copy operations, at both the source and the destination element. Second, we create a new text block whenever text is added to an element.

In addition to the histories, we maintain a unique element ID for each element to reference it independently of its current position within the document. Moreover, each document has a unique document ID. We use these IDs to keep track of copy operations by maintaining an *is-copy-of* relation among the elements and text blocks. Two objects are in is-copy-of relation with each other if one object is a copy of the other.

A history entry consists of an action element, which contains details on the operation and a context description. In addition to the operation, an action element can have up to two arguments that describe the action. For the actions related to attributes, we store the name of the corresponding attribute. The `change attribute` and `create attribute` operations additionally store the new value of the attribute. The `create text` and `delete text` operations store the block ID of the corresponding text block.

2.2   Operations

In this section, we describe the details of the operations supported by our model. These are `view`, `create`, `delete`, `change attribute` and `copy`. Most of the operations can be applied to elements, text and attributes. Each operation, except for `view`, has an effect on the document itself as well as on the histories. The `view` operation creates a history entry only. The `create` operation is divided into creating elements, creating attributes and creating text.

The `create element` operation creates an element without any attributes or text. In addition to the element itself, the history of the element is created. The first entry of the history for the element describes its creation. The attributes of an element are created with the `create attribute` operation, which is also logged with an entry in the history of the enclosing element. It can be required that elements have mandatory attributes. This requirement should be checked on the application level and not within the access control system. This also applies to the deletion of mandatory attributes.

The `create text` operation is used to add new text to an element. This operation has an argument that specifies the position of the new text. If this position is within an existing block, this block is split at the position where the new content should be placed and the new content is placed in-between the split blocks. The split blocks keep their original histories, whereas the new content gets a new history with one entry describing its creation. The boundaries of the split content pieces are denoted by the `ac:block` elements, as described in Section 2.1.

The `delete` operation is used to delete elements, attributes, text or parts of the text. Since elements and their attributes are checked in rules, we need to keep them after deletion. For that purpose, the context of a delete operation is captured in the element history with a delete action entry. A context is a tuple of `Date`, `Subject` and `Role`, where `Date` refers to a date including time and `Role` is the role of the `Subject` that performs the corresponding operation.

The `copy` operation is used for elements, text or parts of the text. In all cases, we apply the corresponding `create` operation to create a new instance at the destination as a copy from the source, which is registered in the destination element. Additionally, the is-copy-of relation of the elements is updated.

The `view` operation displays elements which have not been deleted. When a user wants to view a document, the `view` operation is invoked for every element of the document itself, but also for its attributes and text. In contrast to the read operation of some other systems, e.g., [1,3], the view operation does not imply a data transfer.

The `change attribute` operation allows users to change the value of a specific attribute. Since former values of an attribute can be checked by rules, we record the change with an entry in the element history.

2.3   Rules

In this section, we define a syntax for AC rules, which can express policies that depend on the content of the current document, the recorded history information and the content of dependent documents. Generally speaking, a rule has the typical structure of subject, operation, object and mode. The `mode` field of a rule defines whether it is positive (allow) or negative (deny). The default semantics of our model is deny: if the access to the object is neither allowed nor denied by a rule, then the object is not accessible. If conflicts occur, we take the rule with the superior role and finally apply "deny takes precedence over allow". We use roles [15] to model the subjects to gain a higher level of abstraction and therefore more flexibility compared to directly listing individual subjects.

Instead of listing individual objects in rules in an ACL-like manner [10], we describe objects by their properties, e.g., location within a document or attribute values. For this purpose, we use XPath patterns [4] to describe the objects for which a rule is applicable. We use XPath, since its clearly defined semantics makes the interpretation of the resulting rules unambiguous. Moreover, XPath has a predefined set of mechanisms that can be used for our purpose, which simplifies the implementation of our model.

We define two types of rules. The first type of rule defines permissions for the unary operations `create`, `view`, `delete` and `change attribute`. The objects of an AC rule are defined by an XPath pattern. The second type of rule defines permissions for the binary `copy` operation, which requires the specification of a source and a destination object. We use two XPath patterns for this. The syntax of both types of rules is listed in Figure 1.

Unary rule		Copy rule	
Element	Description	Element	Description
Role	Role	Role	Role
Operation	Operation	Operation	"Copy"
Object	XPath	Object	XPath
		Destination	XPath
Mode	allow | deny	Mode	allow | deny

Fig. 1. Syntax of AC rules

2.4   Accessing History Information with XPath

We use XPath patterns in rules to define access depending on histories. As a consequence, we need a mechanism to access the histories within an XPath pattern. Therefore, we extend the function library of XPath by a set of functions, which we collect in the following six groups. The namespace of our functions is indicated by the prefix 'ac:'. In the context of XPath, we speak of a node instead of an object.

Getting Copies of a Node. This group of functions is related to the is-copy-of relation of nodes among each other. It is required to express rules that define access depending on the source of an object or on the locations to where an object was copied.

The function `ac:copies` returns all nodes that are in is-copy-of relation with the current node, whereas the function `ac:predecessors` returns all nodes of which the current node is a copy. Finally, the function `ac:successors` returns all nodes that are copies of the current node. All three functions also return nodes that are in indirect is-copy-of relation to the current node, e.g., `ac:successors` also returns the copies of the copies of the current node.

Getting Attribute Values. The function `ac:attribute-values` returns a chronologically sorted list of tuples of an attribute value and the context corresponding to the change of the attribute value. It is required to define rules, which inspect former values of an attribute. For example, the rule {`researcherB`, `View`, `deny`, `/Report[count(ac:attribute-values('funded-by')[value='Company A']) > 0]/*`} states that subjects in the role `researcherB` are not allowed to view reports that were funded by `'Company A'` in the past or at present.

Getting Related Nodes Depending on Time. This group of functions retrieves nodes addressed relatively to the context node that existed within a specified time interval. In the XPath terminology, the element to be checked against the pattern is called the *context node*. XPath offers functions to retrieve nodes addressed relatively to the context node, but without the specification of a time interval, since XPath only considers the current state of a document. This time interval is required to select related nodes depending on time, since nodes can be deleted. Therefore, each of these functions can have a time interval as parameter, e.g., `ac:children-at(t1, t2)` returns all nodes that were children of the context node in the time interval between `t1` and `t2`. To inspect a single point in time, `t2` can be omitted. The functions of this group are `ac:parent-at`, `ac:following-at`, `ac:preceding-sibling-at`, `ac:preceding-at`, `ac:following-sibling-at`, `ac:children-at`, `ac:descendant-at`, `ac:root-at` and `ac:-self-at`.

Getting the Context of a History Entry. This group of functions offers access to the context of a specific history entry. Each function returns an element consisting of subject, role and time. These functions are `ac:creation-context` and `ac:deletion-context`.

Getting Accessed Nodes. This group of functions is used to get all nodes which have been accessed by a specified user or by a user in a certain role. For example, these functions are required to express Chinese Wall policies [3]. The functions are `ac:created`, `ac:viewed`, `ac:changed-attribute` and `ac:-deleted`. Each function refers to a specific operation, e.g., `ac:viewed` returns viewed nodes. In addition, the function `ac:accessed` returns all accessed nodes independently of the operation. All functions have two parameters that define conditions on the returned nodes. The first parameter `user` specifies to return only nodes that have been accessed by the specified user. Analogously, we define the parameter `role`. Both parameters can be set to `any` to indicate to return nodes accessed by any user or in any role. Optionally, each parameter can be set to `current`. In this case, the current user or his current role is used for the check. For example, `created(any, current)` returns all nodes which have been created by users who were active in the same role as the one in which the current user is active in.

Getting Specific Nodes of Current Rule. We define three functions for accessing specific nodes within an XPath pattern. The function `ac:current--node` returns the node in question for which the XPath pattern is evaluated. This function is required when the pattern's context changes to a document that is different from the document for which the pattern was initiated. The function `ac:src-node` retrieves the source node in question when checking a copy rule. In a similar fashion, the function `ac:dest-node` returns the destination node of a copy rule. The last two functions are necessary to define copy rules which compare the source and destination objects with each other.

3   System Architecture

In this section, we present a system architecture for applying history-based AC in an environment where multiple users can edit documents concurrently. Its components are explained in the following sections. Additionally, we describe the algorithms and protocols that are required for the interaction between the components.

3.1   Architecture Overview

Our system architecture and its components are depicted in Figure 2. Our system uses four databases. The document database (Doc DB) contains all documents of the system. The rule database (Rule DB) contains the AC rules, which specify allowed or denied accesses to the documents and their parts. The copy database (Copy DB) stores the is-copy-of relation of the objects. Since the is-copy-of relation can be depicted by a graph, we speak of an edge when we refer to a single is-copy-of relation between two objects. Finally, the user database (User DB) stores the credentials of the users of the system as well as the corresponding roles including their hierarchy.

The user interface (UI) presents documents to the user and offers operations that can be performed on the documents. If the user invokes such an operation, the corresponding request is sent to the document processor (DP), which

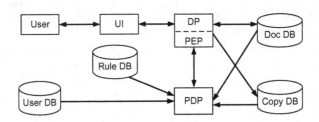

Fig. 2. System architecture

performs the requested operation if it is permitted. Inside the DP, the policy enforcement point (PEP) intercepts each operation and asks the policy decision point (PDP) whether the requested operation is allowed. The PDP uses the four databases to decide whether to allow or deny the requested operation. This architecture allows us to access distributed documents when a rule is evaluated and therefore it represents a solution for the first challenge mentioned in the introduction and. In the following, we explain the workflow for editing a document to illustrate the processes within our architecture.

3.2   Workflow

A document must be opened before it can be viewed or edited. Therefore, the UI offers a command to open a document. This command is sent to the DP, which loads a copy of the document from the document database. We refer to this process as *check-out*, since it has semantics similar to the check-out command of a version control system [16]. After the check-out, the user can edit the document by applying the operations of our model. The changed content of an opened document including the corresponding histories becomes relevant for access decisions of other documents after it is checked-in. Up to then, the content of the opened document is only relevant for access decisions concerning that document itself. The document and the corresponding histories are kept as a local copy in the DP. To *check-in* a document, the user must invoke the corresponding command of the UI. Then, the DP stores the copy of the document back to the document database.

The check-in and check-out concept is more efficient and offers a higher usability compared to directly working on the policy-relevant version of a document. The first concept is more efficient, because changed content must be propagated less often, i.e., only when a document is checked-in compared with immediately after each change. This also reduces the overhead for recalculating permissions. The usability is also higher, because of the transaction semantics of the approach. With this concept a user can decide when the changing of a document is done, instead of having potentially unwanted intermediate states to get relevant for access decisions. With this concept we give a solution for the second and fourth challenge mentioned in the introduction.

Check-Out. When a user invokes the command to check-out a document, the DP first loads a copy of that document from the Doc DB. The Doc DB maintains a list for each document that denotes by which users the corresponding document is currently opened to support concurrent access to documents. The PDP executes Algorithm 1 to create a view. This algorithm removes nodes from the document for which the user in question has no view permission and deleted nodes. For that purpose, the algorithm adds a marker to each node which is set initially to "default", where a node can either be an element, an attribute or a text block. Next, we sort all rules by their role and their mode. More special roles are priorized over less special roles and deny rules are placed before allow rules.

Then, we remove inapplicable rules. For each of the remaining rules, the corresponding XPath pattern is evaluated. The result of this step is a set of nodes that match with the current XPath pattern, which defines the applicable objects of the rule. For each of these nodes, the marker is set according to the mode field of the current rule. If all nodes have a marker different from "default" we stop inspecting rules. Finally, we remove every node with a marker set to "default", every node with a marker set to "deny" and deleted nodes. After that, the PDP sends the view to the DP, which creates history entries for the view operation and forwards the view to the UI.

Algorithm 1. Create View

    Input : rules_{all}, role_{curr}, role_hierarchy, doc
    Output: doc
1 add marker to every node of doc
2 set marker of every node of doc to "default"
3 sort rules_{all} by role (special first) and mode (deny first)
4 **for** *each* rule_i *of* rules_{all} **do**
5   if *operation of* rule_i *is not* "view" *or role of* rule_i *is not inferior or equal to* role_{curr} **then**
6   continue with next iteration of loop
7     $\text{nodes}_{result} \leftarrow$ evaluate XPath of rule_i for doc
8   **for** *each* node_j *of* nodes_{result} **do**
9   if *marker of* node_j *is* "default" **then**
10   set marker of node_j to mode of rule_i
11   if *all markers of* doc *are different from* "default" **then**
12   exit loop
13 **for** *each* node_j *of* doc **do**
14   if *marker of* node_j *is* "default" *or* "deny" *or the node is deleted* **then**
15   remove node_j and subtree below from doc
16 **return** doc

Editing. To edit a document, the user first selects an operation offered by the UI. This operation is sent to the DP, where the PEP intercepts the operation to check whether it is allowed. For this purpose, the PEP sends the requested operation together with the current document to the PDP, which evaluates the rules to answer the request of the PEP. For this purpose, the PDP performs the Algorithm 2.

The algorithm for rule evaluation sorts all rules like the previous algorithm. Then, it checks the applicability of each rule by inspecting its role and its operation. For each rule, the XPath pattern is evaluated to check whether it matches with the object in question. In case of a copy operation, the XPath pattern for the destination is evaluated, too. If the rule is applicable, its mode is returned. After evaluating all rules, the algorithms returns "deny", if none of the rules was applicable. The PDP sends the result of this algorithm back to the DP. If the result is deny, the DP does not perform the requested operation and informs the user via the UI. If the result is allow, the DP performs the requested operation.

Algorithm 2. Evaluate Rules

    Input   : $rules_{all}$, $role_{curr}$, role_hierarchy, op, doc, obj, doc_{dest}, obj_{dest}
    Output: deny | allow
1 sort $rules_{all}$ by role (special first) and mode (deny first)
2 **for** *each* $rule_i$ *of* $rules_{all}$ **do**
3   **if** *operation of* $rule_i$ *is not* op **or** *role of* $rule_i$ *is not inferior or equal to*
      $role_{curr}$ **then**
4   continue with next iteration of loop
5   **if** op *is* *"copy"* **then**
6         $nodes_{result}$ ← evaluate XPath for source of $rule_i$ for doc
7   **else**
8         $nodes_{result}$ ← evaluate XPath of $rule_i$ for doc
9   **if** obj *is not contained in* $nodes_{result}$ **then**
10   continue with next iteration of loop
11   **if** op *is* *"copy"* **then**
12       $nodes_{result}$ ← evaluate XPath for destination of $rule_i$ for doc_{dest}
13   **if** obj_{dest} *is not contained in* $nodes_{result}$ **then**
14   continue with next iteration of loop
15   **return** mode of $rule_i$
16 **return** "deny"

Check-In. A user can invoke the check-in command of the UI to save his changes to an opened document doc_a, which is currently stored only within the DP, to the Doc DB. As a result of this, the checked-in version of the document becomes relevant for the access decisions of other documents, which also includes concurrently opened versions of doc_a. For these documents the permissions must be recalculated, which possibly revokes permissions of currently edited documents. The concurrent editing of a document can also lead to conflicts, where the editing of one user to doc_a is incompatible to the editing of another user, who also has edited doc_a. For these reasons, we have to perform two steps when a document is checked-in. In step one, we have to solve conflicts between the concurrent versions of a document. In step two, we must update the permissions of other affected documents whose permissions depend on the saved document.

To perform step one, we first retrieve the list of concurrently edited versions of doc_a, which is maintained by the Doc DB for each opened document. Next, we must merge all concurrently edited versions of doc_a to one consistent version. We apply a conflict resolution strategy to solve conflicts between concurrently edited documents. It depends on the scenario to define a specific strategy. One possible strategy is to resolve conflicts manually. An automatic strategy can accept or reject changes depending on the role of the subject that performed the changes or depending on the time the changes were performed, since this information is available in the corresponding histories. After the conflicts are solved, the temporarily stored edges, which correspond to the accepted operations, are saved to the Copy DB.

To perform step two, we first inspect the Copy DB to retrieve the opened documents that might depend on doc_a. These documents have at least one node, that is in is-copy-of relation with a node of doc_a. Then, we recalculate the permissions of these documents for their current users. In some cases, permissions of edited nodes are revoked. In these cases, the UI asks the user whether he wants to reject the current changes or keep them and accept being unable to make further changes. These two steps provide a solution for the third challenge mentioned in the introduction.

3.3 Implementation

We have implemented all components of our system architecture in Java version 1.5. We have extended the XPath function library of the Saxon XSLT and XQuery processor[1] version 8.8 with the functions defined in Section 2.4. The implementation supports all operations defined in Section 2.2. In addition, it is able to evaluate and enforce our AC rules defined in Section 2.3. We have verified the feasibility of our model by evaluating the performance of our implementation. For example, the calculation of a view for a document with 2000 nodes takes less than a second. This performance is sufficiently fast, since our check-in and check-out concept avoids additional view recalculations after every operation on depending documents. Instead, we must update views only when a depending document is checked-in. More details about the implementation and performance evaluation can be found in [12].

4   Related Work

The model proposed in [2] supports selective authorizations to parts of documents based on the semantic structure of XML documents. Authorizations can be defined for different nodes together with propagation options. Regarding these aspects, the model is very similar to our work. However, the supported operations and their semantics are different, since our approach is able to differentiate between objects with different histories. The support of copying data differs from our work, since the model proposed in [2] supports only a push of different views of a document to different sets of users, whereas our model allows us to define which elements of one document may be reused in other documents. Similar approaches can be found in [5,6,8,13], where [8,13] consider access control rules for the read operation only. All these approaches consider the XML element as the smallest unit of protection, in contrast to our approach, which is capable of handling parts of the text.

Iwaihara et al. allow to define access based on the version relationship of documents and elements among each other [11]. They define six operations including *copy*, which is similar to our copy operation, but can only be applied to elements or subtrees and not to text content or parts of the text content. In contrast to our model, the modification of the text content of an element is modeled by the operation *update* only, which describes that the entire content of a node is

---

[1] See http://saxon.sourceforge.net/

replaced with a new content. Concerning AC, Iwaihara et al. only consider read and write operations and do not define a copy operation as part of their privileges. Consequently, they can not express which transfers among documents are permitted or denied. Moreover, they do not have the concept of splitting copied elements to have different history information for parts from different sources.

5   Conclusions and Future Work

In this paper, we have summarized our model for defining access control for XML documents and presented a system architecture that enables us to apply the model in a scenario where multiple users concurrently edit documents in an efficient way. The proposed system architecture maintains the rules, the documents and the history, so that this information is accessible for access decisions of the PDP. We introduced the check-in and check-out approach, which reduces the overhead of recalculating permissions for dependent documents. We specified the workflow for editing a document by explaining the algorithm for the calculation of permissions and the algorithm for the creation of views. We are currently using the implementation of our model to study its usability in different application scenarios.

References

1. Bell, D., LaPadula, L.: Secure Computer Systems: Mathematical Foundations and Model. Technical Report M74-244, MITRE Corp, Bedfort, MA (1973)
2. Bertino, E., Ferrari, E.: Secure and Selective Dissemination of XML Documents. ACM Transactions on Information and System Security 5(3), 290–331 (2002)
3. Brewer, F.D., Nash, J.M.: The Chinese Wall Security Policy. In: IEEE Symposium on Security and Privacy, IEEE Computer Society Press, Los Alamitos (1989)
4. Clark, J., DeRose, S.: XML Path Language (XPath) Version 1.0. W3C recommendation, W3C (1999), http://www.w3.org/TR/1999/REC-xpath-19991116
5. Damiani, E., Capitani, S.D., Paraboschi, S., Samarati, P.: Securing XML Documents. In: Zaniolo, C., Grust, T., Scholl, M.H., Lockemann, P.C. (eds.) EDBT 2000. LNCS, vol. 1777, pp. 121–135. Springer, Heidelberg (2000)
6. Damiani, E., di Vimercati, S.D.C., Paraboschi, S., Samarati, P.: A Fine-Grained Access Control System for XML Documents. TISSEC 5(2), 169–202 (2002)
7. Fundulaki, I., Marx, M.: Specifying Access Control Policies for XML Documents with XPath. In: SACMAT 2004. Proceedings of the ninth ACM Symposium on Access Control Models and Technologies, ACM Press, New York (2004)
8. Gabillon, A., Bruno, E.: Regulating Access to XML Documents. In: Working Conference on Database and Application Security, pp. 299–314. Kluwer Academic Publishers, Dordrecht (2002)
9. Gordon, L.A., Loeb, M.P., Lucyshyn, W., Richardson, R.: 2006 CSI/FBI Computer Crime and Security Survey. Technical report, CSI (2006)
10. Graham, G.S., Denning, P.J.: Protection - Principles and Practice. In: Spring Joint Computer Reference, vol. 40, pp. 417–429 (1972)

11. Iwaihara, M., Chatvichienchai, S., Anutariya, C., Wuwongse, V.: Relevancy Based Access Control of Versioned XML Documents. In: SACMAT 2005. Proceedings of the tenth ACM Symposium on Access Control Models and Technologies, Stockholm, Sweden, pp. 85–94. ACM Press, New York (2005)
12. Mellgren, F.: History-Based Access Control for XML Documents. Master's thesis, Technische Universität Darmstadt (June 2007)
13. Murata, M., Tozawa, A., Kudo, M.: XML Access Control using Static Analysis. In: ACM Conference on Computer and Communications Security, ACM Press, New York (2003)
14. Röder, P., Tafreschi, O., Eckert, C.: History-Based Access Control for XML Documents. In: ASIACCS 2007. Proceedings of the ACM Symposium on Information, Computer and Communications Security, ACM Press, New York (2007)
15. Sandhu, R.S., Coyne, E.J., Feinstein, H.L., Youman, C.E.: Role-Based Access Control Models. IEEE Computer 29(2), 38–47 (1996)
16. Tichy, W.F.: RCS - A System for Version Control. Softw. - Practice and Experience 15(7), 637–654 (1985)

Power Efficient Hardware Architecture of SHA-1 Algorithm for Trusted Mobile Computing

Mooseop Kim[1] and Jaecheol Ryou[2]

[1] Electronics and Telecommunications Research Institute (ETRI)
161 Gajeong-dong, Yuseong-gu, Daejeon, 305-700, South Korea
gomskim@etri.re.kr
[2] Division of Electrical and Computer Engineering, Chungnam National University
220 Gung-dong, Yuseong-gu, Daejeon, 305-764, South Korea
jcryou@home.cnu.ac.kr

Abstract. The Trusted Mobile Platform (TMP) is developed and promoted by the Trusted Computing Group (TCG), which is an industry standard body to enhance the security of the mobile computing environment. The built-in SHA-1 engine in TMP is one of the most important circuit blocks and contributes the performance of the whole platform because it is used as key primitives supporting platform integrity and command authentication. Mobile platforms have very stringent limitations with respect to available power, physical circuit area, and cost. Therefore special architecture and design methods for low power SHA-1 circuit are required. In this paper, we present a novel and efficient hardware architecture of low power SHA-1 design for TMP. Our low power SHA-1 hardware can compute 512-bit data block using less than 7,000 gates and has a power consumption about 1.1 mA on a 0.25μm CMOS process.

1 Introduction

The Trusted Computing Group(TCG) is an organization that develops and produces open specifications, with regard to security-based solutions for various computing systems. They published a group of related specifications that define secure procedures as they relate to the boot-up, configuration management, and application execution for personal computing platforms. The core component of the TCG is the Trusted Platform Module(TPM) that acts as a monitoring and reporting component.

TPM is a small chip capable of securely storing cryptographic keys and other cryptographic functions like asymmetric encryption, signature schemes, and hash functions. Using these functionalities user can attest the initial configuration of a platform and seal or bind data to a specific platform configuration. To ensure that the platform behaves correctly, TPM checks all software and applications each time the underlying platform starts. In practice several vendors[16, 17, 18] already deploy laptop computers that are equipped with a TPM chip placed on the main board of the underlying platform. However most of these TPM chips feature high performance usages.

S. Qing, H. Imai, and G. Wang (Eds.): ICICS 2007, LNCS 4861, pp. 375–385, 2007.

As the mobility of the computing platform increases, device theft and loss has always been an issue for mobile devices. Data stored on mobile devices is often at greater risk than data communicated over the air, due to the ease with which those devices can be lost. With the inclusion of sensitive personal information such as address books, as well as high value premium a service on the devices, the risk from loss is increasing. In addition, as mobile devices become smarter and support more data functions, the industry is facing many of the same threats as personal computers from malicious software and attacks. Thus, the need to protect user data and secrets of mobile device is underscored in a mobile computing environment.

For these reasons, TCG is now extending the security realizations into mobile technology and other embedded system platforms. It aims at adapting existing IT security standard, especially the TCG specifications, to mobile device platforms to achieve a trusted mobile platform. A set of Trusted Mobile Platform(TMP) specifications defining security features for mobile devices has been released for public review by the authors and promoters from IBM, Intel, and NTT DoCoMo. In these specifications, TCG recommend to use a hash algorithm to compute and verify the integrity measurement value of underlying platforms.

Contrary to personal computers, mobile devices have strict environment in power consumption, in battery life and in available circuit area. Among these limitations, the power consumption is the major issue in the design of cryptographic circuits for mobile platforms. Therefore, design methodologies at different abstraction levels, such as systems, architectures, logic design, basic cells, as well as layout, must take into account to design the SHA-1 circuit for trusted mobile platform.

In this paper, we introduce an efficient hardware architecture of low power SHA-1 algorithm for trusted mobile platforms. As a result, a compact and low power SHA-1 hardware implementation capable of supporting the integrity check and command authentication of trusted mobile platforms was developed and evaluated.

This paper is constructed as follows. Section 2 describes some related works for low power design of SHA-1 algorithm. Section 3 describes SHA-1 algorithm reviews and architecture of our low power SHA-1 circuits. Section 4 describes synthesis and implementation results. Finally, in section 5, we conclude this work.

2   Previous Works

The Secure Hash Algorithm (SHA) was developed by the National Institute of Standards and Technology (NIST) and published as a federal information processing standard (FIPS PUB 180) in 1993, a revised version was issued as FIPS PUB 180-1 [5] in 1995 and is generally referred to as SHA-1. Numerous FPGA [8-14] and ASIC [6, 7] implementations of SHA-1 algorithm were previously proposed and evaluated. Most of these implementations feature high speeds and high costs suitable for high-performance usages such as WTLS, IPSec and so on.

Early SHA-1 design were mostly straightforward implementations of various loop rolling architectures with limited number of architectural optimization. S.Dominikus [7] used loop rolling technique in order to reduce area requirement. He proposed an architecture uses only 4 operation blocks, one for each round. Using a temporal register and a counter, each operation block is reused for 20 iterations. G.Selimis [10] applied the reuse technique of [7] to the non-linear function of SHA-1 algorithm. He modified the operation block to include the four non-linear functions. Another architecture of the SHA-1 implementation is based on the use of four pipeline stages [14]. This method exploits the characteristics of the SHA-1 algorithm that requires a different non-linear function for each round.

Unfortunately, most of these implementations have been designed aiming only at large message and high speed operation, with no power consumption taken into considerations. As the security of mobile and embedded devices is becoming more important, recent researches focus on efficient low power hash hardware implementation [13], [15].

3   Low Power Hardware Architecture of SHA-1

SHA-1 hash function has been developed by NIST in order to be used in the Digital Signature Standard. For a message of length less than 2^{64}, the SHA-1 computes a 160-bit message digest. SHA-1 algorithm sequentially processes 512-bit data block when computing message digest. So data padding is performed to make the total length of padded data a multiple of 512-bit.

For our SHA-1 implementation, we assume that one 512-bit data block of preprocessed by microprocessor is stored in memory and available to our SHA-1 circuit for reading and writing. The operation of our SHA-1 circuit is broken into three steps. The initial step comprises data reading and conversion to 32-bit data. Here, the interface block reads four 8-bit data and convert them to 32-bit data using for M_t. After data converting, data padding is followed. The next step is round operation which ends with the 80 round. During this step, message expansion block computes W_t and message compression is performed. The final step is needed to compute the final hash values from the intermediate values.

3.1   Architecture of the Compact Implementation

We began the design of our low power SHA-1 hardware architecture by analyzing the basic architecture of SHA-1 algorithm [5]. For each 512-bit message block, the round operation is processed 80 times. As shown in figure 1, each round operation performs several predefined processing, which involves four additions, two circular right shift operations, and logical function f_t operating on three 32-bit values and produces a 32-bit data as output. It seems rather straightforward. However, in order to compute the values of each round, the values from previous round are required. This data dependency imposes a sequential processing, preventing parallel computation between round operations.

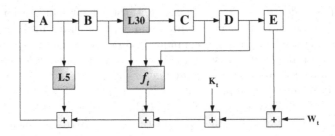

Fig. 1. Round function of SHA-1 algorithm

The first step for our low power circuit design was to find a minimal architecture. A set of key components thus obtained. Components of SHA-1 circuit then designed and applied several low power technologies to each component. Figure 2 shows main components and interactions of our SHA-1 design: interface block, data expansion, controller and message compression.

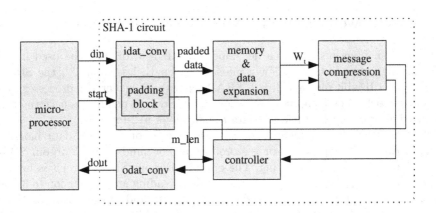

Fig. 2. Outline of SHA-1 circuit block

The microprocessor controls all of the internal operation on the trusted mobile module. It performs functions such as managing the interface to the mobile platform, controlling operation of the TMP crypto engines, processing TMP commands received from the mobile system, and performing security check on the trusted mobile platform. Simple micro-controllers are used for trusted platform module because of cost and power issues.

Interface block is responsible for converting 8-bit data applied to an input into 32-bit ones and vice versa when it outputs the result. It also performs padding operation about the transformed data to generate the padded 512-bit block required by the algorithm. We use 32-bit data bus for efficient design of our SHA-1 circuit. It is not a good idea to make the bus width smaller than 32-bits, because all operation of SHA-1 algorithm and variables need 32 bits of data at

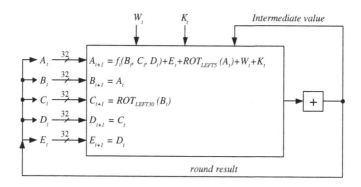

Fig. 3. Functional block diagram of data compression

one time. A smaller bus may requires less registers, but it uses more data selectors and resource sharing is hindered, resulting in an inefficient implementation.

The controller logic block is used to generate signal sequences to check an input signal sequence or to control datapath parts. The basic structure of controller is state register and two logic blocks. The input logic block computes the next state as a function of current state and of the new sets of input signals. The output logic block generates the control signals for datapath using the function signals of the current states. The power can be consumed in the logic blocks or in the clock distribution to the flip-flops of the state register.

The efficiency of a low power SHA-1 hardware in terms of circuit area, power consumption and throughput is mainly determined by the data path structure of data expansion and message compression block. The message compression block performs actual hashing. In each step, it processes a new word generated by the message expansion block. The functional block diagram of message compression is presented in figure 3.

Figure 3 shows that SHA-1 algorithm uses five 32-bit variables (A, B, C, D, and E) to store new values in each round operation. It can be easily seen from [5] that four out of the five values are shifted by one position down in each round and only determining the new value for A requires computation. Therefore, we use a five stage 32-bit shift registers for these variables.

As shown in figure 3, the computation for A requires two circular right shifting and four operand addition modulo 2^{32} where the operands depend on all input values, the round constant K_t, and current message value W_t. For compact and low power SHA-1 circuit design, we use only one 32-bit adder to perform four additions and use register E to store temporary addition values. Therefore, four clock cycles are required to compute a round operation. Equation 1 shows the functional steps for this operation.

$$
\begin{aligned}
t_1 &: E_{t_1} = E_{t_0} + K_t \\
t_2 &: E_{t_2} = E_{t_1} + ROT_{LEFT5}(A_t) \\
t_3 &: E_{t_3} = E_{t_2} + W_t \\
t_4 &: A_t = E_{t_3} + F(B, C, D)
\end{aligned}
\qquad (1)
$$

All aforementioned optimizations lead to the schematic of the compact architecture of the data compression. Dashed line in figure 4 shows the detailed structure of data compression block for our low power SHA-1 design. At first, all registers are initialized and multiplexors choose path zero to load initialization constant $H_0 \sim H_4$ stored in KH. Five clock cycles are required to load initial vector to each register. For optimized power consumption, we applied gated clock to all registers in data compression.

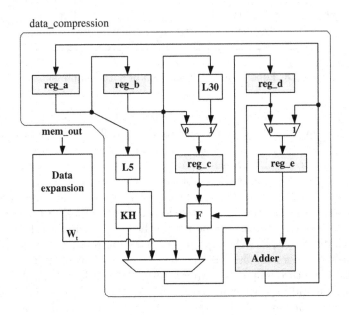

Fig. 4. Detailed architecture of data compression

The F-function in figure 4 is a sequence of logical functions. For each round t, F-function operates on three 32-bit data (B, C, and D) and produces a 32-bit output word. The operation of F-function is shown in equation 2.

$$F(B,C,D) = \begin{cases} (B \wedge C) \oplus (\bar{B} \wedge D) & 0 \leq t \leq 19 \\ B \oplus C \oplus D & 20 \leq t \leq 39 \\ (B \wedge C) \oplus (B \wedge D) \oplus (C \wedge D) & 40 \leq t \leq 59 \\ B \oplus C \oplus D & 60 \leq t \leq 79 \end{cases} \quad (2)$$

During the final round operation, the values of the working variables have to be added to the digest of the previous message block, or specific initial values for the first message block. This can be done very efficiently with additional multiplexer and the five stage shift registers for working variables.

KH in figure 4 stores initial values H_i and constant values K_t. It also stores updated H_i values, which is used as the initial values for next 512-bit data block computing. Computing the final hash value for one input message block takes five clock cycles.

Another important part of SHA-1 data path is data expansion. This block generates message dependant words, W_t, for each step of the data compression. As shown in figure 5, most implementations of data expansion in previous works use 16 stage 32-bit shift register for 512-bit data block processing. This methods are inefficient to use in mobile platforms because they require a significant amount of circuit area and power consumptions.

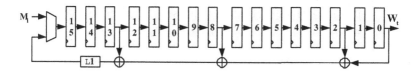

Fig. 5. General data expansion of SHA-1 algorithm

We use only one 32-bit register to store temporary values during computation of the new W_t. Our message expansion block performs the function of the equation 3, where $\oplus$ means bitwise XOR and $M_t^{(i)}$ denotes the first sixteen 32-bit data of i-th data block.

$$
W_t = \begin{cases} M_t^{(i)} & 0 \leq t \leq 15 \\ ROTL^1(W_{t-3} \oplus W_{t-8} \oplus W_{t-14} \oplus W_{t-16}) & 16 \leq t \leq 79 \end{cases} \tag{3}
$$

Four values of memory data have to be read and the result written back to memory in each round. This job takes 4 clock cycles, therefore, each round of SHA-1 takes 4 clock cycles. Dedicated hard wired logic is used for computation of necessary address. The detailed architecture of our data expansion module is shown in figure 6.

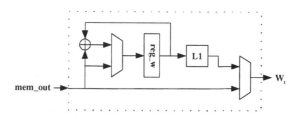

Fig. 6. Compact data expansion of SHA-1 algorithm

The memory used in our circuit is register based and single port 512-bit memory using standard logic cells. In order to minimize the power consumption, the internal registers of memory are disabled when they are not being used, thus reducing the amount of unwanted switching activity. Additional multiplexer is used to select input data between initial input data and intermediate compression data.

3.2   Consideration of Low Power Design

Our SHA-1 design not only result to a higher throughput but it also leads to a more efficient implementation as long as power dissipation is concerned. In order to optimize our low power SHA-1 circuit, resource sharing in the data path is fully employed. We also used some low power circuit design technologies.

First of all, we try to optimize the data path of data compression and data expansion block at the architectural level. At the gate level, gated clock is used to reduce switching activities of latches and sequential logics. The gated clock technique is extensively used in the design of low-power circuits. It consists to gate the clock of sub-circuits that are in idle mode or that have just to keep their data as such. Actually, some logic synthesize tools introduce gated clocks automatically. However, these tools could also gate clocks that have to be always active, which is useless. Therefore, it is preferable to describe in very high speed hardware description language (VHDL) the necessary code to gate a clock and to introduce it only if it is useful.

Although clock gating saves power dissipation in the clocked or sequential logics of the design, power savings in the combinational logic parts are impossible. So, we used an operand isolations, which prevents the activity in the combinational logic by not allowing the input data to toggle in clock cycles when they do not perform any useful computation.

The main goal of these low power circuit design methods are to reduce dynamic power consumption by preventing unwanted switching activities.

4   Implementation Results and Comparison

All hardware architectures of our design were first described in VHDL, and their operation verified through functional simulation using Active HDL, from Aldec Inc. In order to evaluate our low power SHA-1 design, we used Synopsys synthesize flows for the targeted technology. For the target technology, we used $0.25 \mu m$ CMOS standard cell library from Samsung Electronics. The applied voltage was 2.5V and the operating frequency was 25 MHz.

Although the maximum operating frequency obtained using timing analysis is 114 MHz, we use 25 MHz as the operating frequency for evaluating our circuit because the system clock of most mobile phones is about 20 MHz.

The design was fully verified using a large set of test vectors. After synthesis, Synopsys PowerCompiler was used to calculate the overall power dissipation of our design. The activity of the netlist was estimated for various test messages so that the netlist activity could be considered as reasonable values. We would like to emphasize that our design is on the algorithmic and architectural level. Implementing our designs using an low power ASIC library or a full custom design will enable higher energy and power savings.

Table 1 shows the synthesis and power estimation results of our design based on the logic blocks, circuit area and power consumption. Our SHA-1 design consumes an area of 6,812 gates and needs 450 clock cycles to compute the hash of 512 bits of data. The total power consumption at 25 MHz is about 1.1 mA.

Table 1. Logic blocks, complexity, and power consumptions from Samsung 0.25 μm CMOS process

Logic Block	Circuit area		Power consumption	
	gates	percentage	mW@25MHz	percentage
Interface	468	6.8	0.054	1.8
memory	3,434	50.4	0.895	30.2
data expansion	314	4.6	0.17	5.7
controller	350	5.1	0.228	7.7
reg_a~e	876	12.9	0.336	11.3
adder	200	3.0	0.514	17.4
data compression	1,170	17.2	0.764	25.9
Total	6,812	100%	2.961	100%

Table 2. Comparison with previous works of SHA-1 ASIC implementation based on circuit area

SHA-1 computation	Tech.(μm)	Freq.(MHz)	Circuit area
This work	0.25	114	6,812
Y.Ming-yan [6]	0.25	143	20,536
S.Dominikus [7]	0.6	59	10,900

In table 2, we present the comparison of our design with some previous works for SHA-1 ASIC designs. At this point, there are relatively few works available for comparison of consuming power. It can easily be seen from table 2 that our implementation uses 29% less hardware resources than the design of [7].

Table 3. Comparison with commercial TPM chips based on SHA-1 computations

	Freq.(MHz)	SHA-1 performance
This work	25	<18 μs/64-byte
AT97SC3203 [16]	33	<50 μs/64-byte
SSX35A [18]	33	<258 ms/1M-bit

There exist several commercial TPM chips implementing SHA-1 algorithm [16], [17], [18]. In table 3, we present the comparision of our design with the most representative TPM chips with the same functionality. Although the operating frequency of the proposed implementation is lower than that of [16] and [18], the achieved throughput exceeds SHA-1 circuits of some commercial TPM chips designed for desktop computers.

5   Conclusions

In this work, we proposed a compact yet high-speed architecture for a low power SHA-1 cryptographic circuit and evaluated through simulation and synthesis for

ASIC implementation. Our architecture provides a compact and high performance SHA-1 cryptographic hardware for low power trusted mobile computing. The SHA-1 implementation has a chip area of 6,812 gates and has a current consumption of $1.1mA$ at a frequency of 25MHz. Our design requires less than 450 clock cycles to compute the hash of 512 bits of data.

To our best knowledge, the proposed design is at least 270% faster than any commercial TPM chips supporting SHA-1 circuit, while using lower operating frequency and achieving a reduction of the required hardware. The results of power consumption, throughput, and functionality make our low power SHA-1 cryptographic hardware suitable for trusted mobile computing and other low-end embedded systems that urge for high-performance and small-sized solutions. However, the major design advantage of our design is the low power dissipation that is required to calculate the hash value of any given messages.

Acknowledgements

This work was supported by the IT R&D program of MIC/IITA. [2006-S-041-02, "Development of a common security core module for supporting secure and trusted service in the next generation mobile terminals"].

The second author of this research was supported by the MIC (Ministry of Information and Communication), Korea, under the ITRC (Information Technology Research Center) support program supervised by the IITA (Institute of Information Technology Assessment) (IITA-2005-(C1090-0502-0020)).

References

1. Trusted Mobile Platform NTT DoCoMo.: IBM, Intel, Trusted Mobile Platform: Hardware Architecture Description Rev1.0, Trusted Computing Group (2004)
2. Pearson, S., et al.: Trusted Computing Platforms: TCPA Technology in context. Prentice Hall, Englewood Cliffs (2003)
3. Mitchell, C.: Trusted Computing, MPG books (2005)
4. Kinney, S.: Trusted Platform Module Basics: Using TPM in Embedded Systems. Elsevier, Amsterdam (2006)
5. NIST: Secure Hash Standard FIPS-Pub 180-1, National Institute of Standard and Technology (1995)
6. Ming-yan, Y., Tong, Z., Jin-xiang, W., Yi-zheng, Y.: An Efficient ASIC Implementation of SHA-1 Engine for TPM. In: IEEE Asian-Pacific Conference on Circuits and Systems, pp. 873–876 (2004)
7. Dominikus, S.: A Hardware Implementation of MD4-Family Hash Algorithms. IEEE international Conference on Electronic Circuits and Systems 3, 1143–1146 (2002)
8. Zibin, D., Ning, Z.: FPGA Implementation of SHA-1 Algorithm. In: 5th IEEE International conference on ASIC, pp. 1321–1324 (2003)
9. Michail, M.K., Kakarountas, A.P., Milidonis, A., Goutis, C.E.: Efficient Implementation of the Keyed-Hash Message Authentication Code (HMAC) using the SHA-1 Hash Function. In: 11th IEEE International Conference on Electronics, Circuits and Systems, pp. 567–570 (2004)

10. Selimis, G., Sklavos, N., Koufopavlou, O.: VLSI Implementation of the Keyed-HASH Message Authentication Code for the Wireless Application Protocol. In: 10th IEEE International Conference on Electronics, Circuits and Systems, pp. 24–27 (2003)
11. Diez, J.M., et al.: HASH Algorithms for Cryptographic Protocols: FPGA Implementations. In: 10th Telecommunication Forum (TELEFOR 2002) (2002)
12. Kang, Y.-k., et al.: An Efficient Implementation of Hash Function processor for IPSec. In: IEEE Asia-Pacific Conference on ASIC, pp. 93–96 (2002)
13. Michail, H.E., Kakarountas, A.P., Selimis, G.N., Goutis, C.E.: Optimiizing SHA-1 Hash Function for High Throughput with a Partial Unrolling Study. In: Paliouras, V., Vounckx, J., Verkest, D. (eds.) PATMOS 2005. LNCS, vol. 3728, pp. 591–600. Springer, Heidelberg (2005)
14. Sklavos, N., Dimitroulakos, G., Koufopavlou, O.: An Ultra High Speed Architecture for VLSI Implementation of Hash Functions. In: Proc. Of ICECS, pp. 990–993 (2003)
15. Huang, A.L., Penzhorn, W.T.: Cryptographic Hash Functions and Low-Power Techniques for Embedded Hardware. In: IEEE ISIE 2005, pp. 1789–1794 (2005)
16. AT97SC3203 Advance Information Summary, Atmel corp. (2005), available at: http://www.atmel.com/dyn/products/product_card.asp?part_id=3736
17. SLB 9635 TT1.2, Infineon (2005) available at: http://www.infineon.com/cgi-bin/ifx/portal/ep/channelView.do?channelId=-84648channelPage=2Fep
18. SSX35A.: Sinosun (2005), available at https://www.trustedcomputinggroup.org/ShowcaseApp/sh_catalog_files//SSX35%20Mar.05.pdf#search=%22SSX35A
19. Stallings, W.: Cryptography and Network Security: Principles and Practices, 3rd edn., pp. 265–271. Prentice Hall, Englewood Cliffs (2002)
20. Wonjong, K., Seungchul, K., Younghwan, B., Sungik, J., Youngsoo, P., Hanjin, C.: A Platform-Based SoC Design of a 32-bit Smart Card. ETRI Journal 25(6), 510–516 (2003)

Auth-SL - A System for the Specification and Enforcement of Quality-Based Authentication Policies

Anna C. Squicciarini, Abhilasha Bhargav-Spantzel,
Elisa Bertino, and Alexei B. Czeksis

Department of Computer Science, Purdue University
{asquicci,bhargav,bertino,aczeskis}@purdue.edu

Abstract. This paper develops a language and a reference architecture supporting the management and enforcement of authentication policies. Such language directly supports multi-factor authentication and the high level specification of authentication factors, in terms of conditions against the features of the various authentication mechanisms and modules. In addition the language supports a rich set of constraints; by using these constraints, one can specify for example that a subject must be authenticated by two credentials issued by different authorities. The paper presents a logical definition of the language and its corresponding XML encoding. It also reports an implementation of the proposed authentication system in the context of the FreeBSD Unix operating system (OS). Critical issues in the implementation are discussed and performance results are reported. These results show that the implementation is very efficient.

1 Introduction

Authentication is the process by which systems verify the identity claims of their users. It determines *who* the user is and if his claim to a particular identity is true; authenticated identities are then the basis for applying other security mechanisms, such as access control. Generally speaking, a user can be authenticated on the basis of something he holds, he is, or he knows. *Something you know* is typically implemented through mechanisms such as password, or challenge-response protocols. The *something you hold* approach is implemented through token-based mechanisms, smartcards, or a PIN that the user possesses and must present in order to be authenticated. Finally, the *who you are* paradigm is based on biometrics and includes techniques such as fingerprint scans, retina scans, voiceprint analysis, and others.

A same system may have resources with different requirements concerning authentication strengths for the users wishing to access them. A straightforward solution to authentication for resources with such heterogeneous requirements is based on a conservative approach that maximizes authentication checks each time a user connects to the system. However, such a solution may result in

S. Qing, H. Imai, and G. Wang (Eds.): ICICS 2007, LNCS 4861, pp. 386–397, 2007.

computationally consuming authentication tasks and may also be very expensive and complex to deploy. For example, adopting one-time passwords [12] for all users of an organization, independently from the tasks they have to perform and the resources they have to access, may be very expensive; ideally one would like to require such authentication measures only for users who need to access sensitive resources and use conventional passwords for the other users. Additionally, such an approach does not avoid the risk of session hijacking.

We believe that authentication should be based on a variety of mechanisms targeted to the resource security requirements and be easily configurable. Identity of users should always be known and certain during the whole duration of a user session within the system, especially as the user browses multiple resources. *Continuous authentication* [3] has been proposed to tackle issues related to fake authentication from attackers. Most approaches to continuous authentication are based on biometric techniques, like keyboard typing recognition or face recognition through trusted cameras [7]. However these approaches require costly machinery and tools and in addition are based on the assumption that the one method of authentication is to be accepted for every possible resource the user connects to.

Logic based authentication approaches [1, 15] have been proposed to support a weak form of continuous authentication through the association of multiple principals with each user. However, these approaches have mostly focused on abstract representation of roles, groups, and delegation. Mechanically generated proofs have resulted to be impractical to compute. As we discuss in more detail in the related work section, such approaches are not expressive enough to support fine-grained authentication policies. We thus believe that more articulated solutions are needed based on the use of multiple authentication mechanisms combined through *authentication policies* and on the association of authentication requirements with the protected resources. The goal of our work is to develop such a solution.

We propose an authentication framework based on an expressive *authentication policy language*. By using such language, one can specify how many authentication factors are required and of which type, for accessing specified resources, or impose constraints on the authorities by which credentials used for authentication have to be provided, thus providing a *quality-based* authentication. Flexibility in specifying the various factors for authentication is important as typical two-factor authentication mechanisms may not be sufficient to satisfy the security requirements of a given system [16]. It is important to notice that the SAML (Security Assertion Markup Language) standard [11] supports the encoding of authentication statements for exchange among sites in a distributed system. The goals of our authentication policy language are different from the goals of SAML. SAML is a standard for encoding authentication statements; such a statement typically asserts that a given subject has been authenticated under a certain modality by a given entity at a given time. *SAML thus does not deal with taking authentication decisions*; it only deals with encoding and transmitting such decisions. *The goal of our language is exactly to specify policies driving authentication decisions*; as such policies expressed in our language may also take into account previous authentication decisions, taken for example by other sites in a distributed system, together with other information in order to reach an authentication decision.In what follows we refer to our framework as *authentication service language*, abbreviated as *Auth − SL*. Our goal is to develop a comprehensive set of functions for specifying, managing, enforcing, and inspecting authentication policies that can be used by parties and applications in a system.

The contributions of our work are as follows: (1) The development of a reference architecture for a novel authentication service. (2) The specification of a language to express authentication policies. The proposed language supports the specification of the number of authentication factors required for accessing a resource and the qualification of the authentication factors in terms of a large variety of conditions. (3) An implementation of the proposed authentication service and the policy language in the context of the FreeBSD Unix OS, which allows continuous authentication. That is, the user can fluidly re-authenticate users throughout sessions. Authentication policies can be associated with the protected resources, in addition to being used when the user initially connects to the system; our implementation thus supports the notion of continuous authentication. Auth-SL, as our experiments show, is also very efficient; it improves the functionality of the OS without impacting its performance.

We would like to emphasize that our approach departs from the conventional security "pipeline" according to which, during a user session with a system, authentication is executed only once at the beginning of the session, and then access control is applied multiple times during the session. Our approach proposes a different paradigm under which the activities of authentication and access control can be interleaved in a session, depending on the specific security requirements of the resources accessed during the session. It is important to notice that the conventional pipeline can be supported as a special case of our approach.

The rest of the paper is organized as follows. In Section 2 we present the reference architecture for our authentication service. We then present the formal definition of authentication language and discuss the implementation in FreeBSD Unix. Finally we outline future work.

2   Reference Architecture for an Authentication Service

We begin with a reference architecture of our authentication service, to clarify the main logical components. Auth-SL consists of two major subsystems, namely the *authoring subsystem* and the *enforcement subsystem*.

Authoring subsystem. This system supports the specification and the management of the authentication policies. One of its key features is that it supports the specification of which mechanism to use through the specification of conditions against the features of the available mechanisms. Such specification relies on two components: a *library of authentication modules*, very much like a set of PAM modules [8]; and a specialized *UDDI Registry* recording all features of the authentication modules that are relevant for the specification of the authentication policies. Each module in the library supports a specific type of authentication.

Such modules can then be dynamically invoked to enforce the specific authentication policies. The information required about the authentication modules that are needed for authoring authentication policies is as follows: (1) *Module's authentication characteristics*. These data describe the settings for the specific mechanism. For example, in a password based authentication, a characteristic is the maximum number of tries allowed, or the minimum length of the password. For token-based authentication, a characteristic is the authentication method (e.g. SSO, Basic-Auth credentials), NTLM credentials (username, password, domain), and X.509 client certificates, and the software used (e.g. IBM Tivoli Client RSA). (2) *Implementation data*. These parameters qualify the specific implementation of a mechanism and can refer to the storage of the secret token, the cryptographic technique used to transmit it, the audit trails and so forth.

The authentication policies that can be expressed thus depend on the authentication modules available, and the characteristics of these modules. Such data are to be considered part of the knowledge needed to specify adequate authentication policies. For example, if a system administrator knows that a given authentication module is weak, due to implementation limits or module vulnerabilities, he can apply stronger authentication policies. Authored authentication policies are stored into a repository referred to as *Authentication Policy Base* providing query capabilities to properly authorized users, such as system administrators and auditors.

Enforcement subsystem. Upon an authentication request, such system is in charge of evaluating an authentication policy and make an *authentication decision*. The evaluation is executed by the *Authentication Enforcement Point*, which first retrieves a proper authentication policy. Policy evaluation may also take into account previous *authentication events* concerning the subject being authenticated. To express fine grained constraints over past authentications we collect information on the past authentication in two different logs, serving different purposes: (i) track subjects actions related to authentication and (ii) record the conditions under which a successful authentication is executed. In the first log, referred to as *Authentication event log*, we record authentication events (*event* for short) related to the subjects. An authentication event is basically an authentication executed against a subject. Such log tracks in a chronological order all events related with authentication of the users performed during each session. Once the policy is evaluated, a new event is generated and stored in the log in order to keep track of this authentication step. Each record can refer to either an authentication attempt using a specific factor, the verification and/or the failure of the verification of a given factor. A successful authentication implies successful authentication of multiple factors traced in the event log.

The *context data log* instead tracks specific data related to previous authentication. The information stored by such log is used to evaluate whether previously executed authentication can be leveraged for satisfying an authentication policy An instance of the context data log is created when the user begins a session and it is maintained only for the session duration. Each log record stores context data related to the specific authentication performed, and the settings of the module used. In the current Auth-SL system, each entry in a context data log collects: the type of mechanism used, the time of the authentication execution, the number of failed attempts, the party that originally generated the authentication token used, storage information (remote versus local token storage)and the storage mode (encrypted versus clear text token). Note that Auth-SL does not mandate the specific set of data to be tracked. Additional data may be saved, according to the specific system modules and system security requirements.

The output of the enforcement subsystem is an authentication assertion, which can be returned either to the user or transmitted to some other system or application. Since policies are associated with resources, in most cases the authentication service will interact with the access control system. Typically when subject requires access to a resource, the access control system will will require the authentication service to determine if there are authentication policies associated with the resource and, if this is the case, to evaluate such policies.

3   The Policy Language

In this section we discuss the language for the specification of authentication policies. We begin introducing some notation and symbols to be used for the policy specification and then illustrate the syntax of the language.

3.1   Constant Symbols

The constant symbols used in our language are described as follows.

Objects ($\mathcal{O}$) denotes the set of objects available in the system. Each object has an associated set of operations according to which the object can be accessed. We denote the possible set of operations for object o in $\mathcal{O}$ as OP_o[1].

Authentications Modules ($\mathcal{AM}$) is a set of authentication modules available in the system library. We assume that modules are described in terms of parameters collected in a set *ModP*. Each module $m \in \mathcal{AM}$ has an associated profile, defined by a subset $\{var_1^m, \ldots, var_k^m\}$ of elements in *ModP*. In particular, each profile always includes a mechanism type name (denoted as *MechType*), specifying the type of mechanism supported by the module. Some mechanisms are also qualified in terms of the algorithm used for authentication, as for instance the cryptographic algorithm or the algorithm used for biometric authentication.

Policy constraints ($\mathcal{P}$) is a set of policies used to establish authentication requirements for elements in $\mathcal{O}$. We assume that for each $o \in \mathcal{O}$ there is at most a policy $p \in \mathcal{P}$. Policies are defined as combination of *authentication factors* ($\mathcal{F}$), to qualify the authentication to be executed.

Time ($\mathbb{T}$) is the discrete time in the system.

3.2   Formal Definitions

Authentication policies are the key elements to drive authentication decisions. The specification of authentication policies relies on the notion of *Authentication*

---

[1] The set of resources contains at least the object corresponding to the user login.

Factor. Authentication factors define the features of a specific authentication, using one specific mechanism in $\mathcal{AM}$, and are described in terms of **descriptors**. Each descriptor has at least one parameter, which is the *alias* -or unique identifier- of the authentication factor.

Definition 1 (Descriptor). *A descriptor* d *is a predicate of the form* $p(x, \mathbf{t})$, *in which* x *is a variable, and* $\mathbf{t}$ *is a vector of one or more terms²*.

Descriptors can be classified into four different categories, according to the specific property they capture.

- † *Authentication Verifier descriptors.* These descriptors state properties of the verifier of the authentication token. This could be related to the trusted third party that originated the secret token, or to the module that at the time of verification of the identity token checks its integrity.
- † *Module Characteristics.* These properties describe the characteristics of the module used for the authentication and the configuration used to run authentication.
- † *Context Information.* These properties refer to external conditions that may arise during a specific authentication.
- † *Space and time.* These descriptors attest properties of the authentication factors with respect to space and time constraints.

Properties of a specific authentication could potentially be described in various ways. In Auth-SL, we chose to represent them through a finite set of descriptors to enable specification of fine grained authentication policies. Relevant descriptors necessary to express articulated policy conditions are provided in [17]. Authentication factors are specified through a Boolean conjunction of descriptors.

Definition 2 (Authentication factor). *An authentication factor is a Boolean conjunction of descriptors* $d_1, \ldots, d_k$, *each of the form* $d = p(x, \mathbf{t})$, *such that: (1) The same factor variable* x *appears in every descriptor* $d_m = p(x, \mathbf{t})$ $\forall m \in [1, k]$ *(2)* $\exists d_j, j \in [1, k]$ *such that* $p_j(x, a) = Mechanism(x, a), a \in MechType$.

We describe a factor in terms of the descriptors $\{d_1, \ldots, d_k\}$ composing it, when the exact arguments of the descriptors are not needed. As from Definition 2, authentication factors can be defined using any possible combination of descriptors. The only mandatory descriptor is the one specifying the mechanism to use.

Example 1. Examples of authentication factors are the following:

1) $Mechanism(z_2, Biometric) \wedge Algorithm(z_2, VeriFinger) \wedge TimeBefore(z_2, t'')$,
2) $Mechanism(z_1, Kerberos) \wedge TimeBefore(z_1, t)$

The authentication factors, as defined, are stand alone in that the specification of one single factor is not related to any other factor. However, this is not adequate for the specification of complex and multi-factor authentication policies.

---

² Recall that a term is either a variable like *cid* or it is a compound term $f(t_1, \ldots, t_k)$ where f is a function symbol of arity k and $t_1, \ldots, t_k$ are smaller terms.

To correlate different factors and their characteristics specific constraints can be specified. Factor constraints are specified as logic formulae in which the occurring variables are the factor identifiers. We assume the existential and universal formula be specified always over attributes having a finite domain. The domain of constraints supported belongs to the class of *order and inequality constraint domain* [10]. This domain include binary predicates as defined in our comparison assertions set presented in Section 3.1.

Definition 3 (Factor Constraints). *Let $d_1, \ldots, d_k$ be authentication descriptors specified according to Definition 1. A factor constraint ϕ for descriptors $d_1, \ldots, d_k$ is a first order logic formula defined expressing conditions against variables appearing in $\{d_1, \ldots, d_k\}$.*

Example 2. Let d_1, d_2 be two different authentication descriptors. An example of constraints are:

$$\phi_1 = \exists(TrustedParty(x_1, value_1) \wedge TrustedParty(x_2, value_2)) \wedge value_1 \neq value_2$$
$$\phi_2 = \exists(TimeBefore(z_1, t'')) \wedge TimeBefore(z_2, t')) \wedge t' > t''$$

The first constraint requires that the two factors be issued by different trusted parties. This is useful to impose authentication to be proved trough credentials issued by different authorities. The second constraint implies an ordering in the execution of the factors and requires factor d_1 to be executed after d_2.

We are now in the position to formalize the notion of authentication policy.

Definition 4 (Authentication Policy). *An authentication policy p is a tuple of the form $\langle obj, op, [d_1, \ldots, d_k], Ts, \Phi \rangle, k \geq 1$, where:*

- *$obj \in \mathcal{O}$ is the object target of the policy;*
- *$op \in OP_{obj}$ denotes a non-empty set $\{op_1, \ldots, op_k\}$ of operations according to which obj is to be accessed.*
- *$[d_1, \ldots, d_k]$ is a list of authentication factors, such that $d_j \neq d_m$ if $j \neq m$;*
- *Ts denotes the number of mandatory authentication factors to be verified, thus $1 \leq Ts \leq k$;*
- *Φ is a set of factor constraints $\{\phi_1, \ldots, \phi_k\}$; each ϕ_i, $i \in [1, k]$, is specified in terms of descriptors appearing in $d_1, \ldots, d_k$.*

An authentication policy is by definition specified by a combination of factors to be evaluated. The execution of all the factors may or may not all be mandatory, as specified by threshold value, denoted by Ts. The specification of Ts enhances the flexibility of authentication by establishing the sufficient demands needed to authenticate the user. The listed factors are to be evaluated accordingly.

Example 3. The following is an example of authentication policy:

$p = \langle file1, \{open\}, [f_1, f_2], 2, \phi_2 \rangle$ states that to be authenticated for opening $file1$ the user identity should be checked by executing both factors f_1 and f_2. Here, f_1 and f_2 correspond to the factors in Example 1 and ϕ_2 denotes the constraint of Example 2.

To avoid specification of policies which cannot be processed by the policy enforcement point, authentication policies should be *well-formed*.

Definition 5 (Well-formed policy). *Let* obj *be a object,* op *be the associated operation and let* $p=\langle obj, op, [d_1, \ldots, d_k], j, \Phi \rangle$, $k \geq 1$, *be an authentication policy.* p *is a well-formed policy for* obj *if the following condition holds:* $Ts = j, j \leq k$ *and a set of* j *factors* $d_{m1}, \ldots, d_{mj}$ *exists in* $[d_1, \ldots, d_k]$ *such that each* $\phi \in \Phi$ *that involves factor variables in* $d_{k1}, \ldots, d_{kj}$ *is satisfiable.*

By definition, satisfiability of the constraints needs to be guaranteed. Also constraints expressed in terms of factor variables referring to factors that are not part of the subset need to be satisfiable. That is, if they refer to factors that are not part of the list, the policy is not well formed. We clarify this concept with a simple example.

Example 4. Consider a policy that specifies $[f_1, f_2, f_3]$ and requires at least 2 out of 3 factors to be verified. If among the constraints in Φ there is a constraint ϕ_1 that compares qualities of the factor f_1 with qualities of factor f_2 and there is a second constraint ϕ_2 that compares qualities of f_2 with qualities of f_3, then the policy is not well-formed. The constraints can only be evaluated if all the 3 factors are verified, and this contradicts the threshold value.

Verifying whether a policy is well-formed or not is a decidable and deterministic problem, as a consequence of the fact that the set of factors and constraints is always finite and of the adopted constraint language.

4   Implementation of the Authentication Service in FreeBSD Unix

As part of our work, we have developed a prototype of the authentication service in the context of the FreeBSD Unix OS[9]. The main components identified in the framework reported in Section 2 have been translated into modified modules/operations for implementation in FreeBSD. A sketch of the resulting prototype architecture is presented in Figure 1. The core of the system, which is represented by the authentication enforcement point, has been implemented trough a set of APIs, for policy access and context access. We elaborate on those components as well as on the above issues in what follows and we also report some performance results.

Policy Encoding. Each object in the OS is associated with one authentication policy, composed by one or more authentication factors. In order to support an efficient processing of policies, we provide an internal representation of policies expressed according to the C language. Auth-SL policies are encoded using XML and then parsed into C functions by an authoring tool. Each policy function is associated with a unique ID. Policy functions are parameterized with actual constraint values that appear in the policy factors. The C functions, which evaluate the logic of a particular policy, take as input parameters the context data log and the parameter values that qualify the arguments of the descriptors for factor.

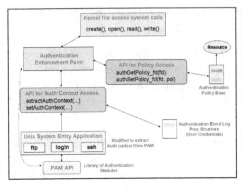
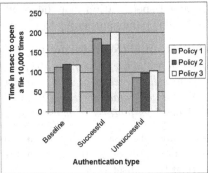

Fig. 1. Prototype architecture   **Fig. 2.** Auth-SL authentication services

Policy Storage and Binding. The storage strategy adopted for the policies
is a key element for ensuring good performance and effective management of
the policies. We exploit the extended attributes stored in the `Extended file`
`Attributes` (EA) of the `inode` for policy storage. As shown in Figure 1, the
`inode` is connected with the resource and the set of API used for policy access. EAs are included as part of the UNIX File System Version 2 (UFS2) for
FreeBSD. The extended file attributes provide a mechanism for supporting the
association of various metadata with files and directories; such metadata are
not directly used by the file system (unlike other attributes such as the *owner,*
permissions, size, and *creation/modification times*) [14]; rather they are meant
to be used by programs for associating attributes with files. However, due to the
limited amount of space available in EA, the whole policy structure cannot be
stored. Moreover, policy functions cannot be stored along with the objects, as
no executable code can be stored at the inodes. Thus, we store the policies in
a central repository and refer them from the EA through a unique id, referred
to as `policyID`. We also use the EA to store the constraints for evaluating the
policy identified by `policyID`.

PAM module extension. PAM presents a common solution for organizing
multiple authentication mechanisms into a single, high-level API for authentication programs. These programs, which are usually system entry applications,
like login or sshd, can use the PAM API to authenticate a user while hiding the
details of the underlying authentication mechanism used. The PAM library consists of several modules, each implementing a particular authentication scheme.
A system administrator uses a set of configuration files in /etc/pam.d/ to associate each system entry application with one or more PAM [9]. Although well
designed, PAM modules cannot be used as they are in the Auth-SL system.
This follows from the fact that our system relies on controlling not only which
authentication mechanism is to be used, but also its parameters. We thus created an `authentication_context` object storing: *type of mechanism, time of*
authentication, number of authentication tries, threshold, TTP, storage location
(local or remote), and storage mode (encrypted, plain text, etc.). We extended

pam_unix module by adding code to store the authentication_context object. Thus we are able to retrieve, control, and record module-specific data during every authentication attempt. The problem of continuous authentication is addressed by creating a set of configuration files, each of which specifies the PAM module that provides a particular type of authentication service. The name of each configuration file reflects the underlying authentication mechanism.

Policy enforcement and continuous authentication. Enforcement of an authentication policy is a multi-step activity, illustrated in Figure 1. As shown, the *authentication enforcement point* is invoked by *kernel file access calls*, which have been connected with the *Unix system entry applications* through a library of APIs for context access. Specifically, policy enforcement is as follows. The authentication activity is initiated when a user initially logs in as a subject (actually a process) and then attempts to perform an operation, such as open, read, write, on an object o, such as a file, device, process, or socket. The operation as part of its execution requires the Authentication Enforcement Point (AEP) to perform an authentication enforcement operation. The AEP gathers the authentication context c (from the context log stored in the ucred struct) of the subject and the policy identifier along with the parameter values stored within the extended file attributes associated with the object o being requested. This is achieved by calling the function *authGetPolicy_fd()*, which returns the policy identifier, by function *authGetPolicy_Const()* which returns the constraints to be passed for the policy evaluation and by the *extractAuthCotext()* function. Once these data are gathered, the function *ContextSatisfies()*, which is the core of the enforcement activity, attempts to match the authentication context logged with the authentication factors required by the authentication policy. The policy identifier is passed as input to the function to select the policy to be enforced.

Performance evaluation. We have conducted several experiments to evaluate the performance of our solution. The tests were carried out on a Intel(R) Xeon(TM) 2.80GHz CPU with 1 GB of RAM. The performance of the prototype has been measured in terms of CPU time (in milliseconds). We present the results of the evaluation of the policies. Due to lack of space we report only some of the experimental results. Our testing consisted of timing the execution of policy functions to determine whether the factors have been verified or not, by looking into the context data log. For the experiments, we considered three simple policies: the first with one a single factor; the second with two factors and zero constraints; and the third with two factors and one constraint binding the two factors. Each policy is composed of two factor assertions, and refers to a password authentication mechanism. The results show that our implementation does not introduce significant latency (as by Figure 2). When policies are not satisfied, the time needed for the open command to complete is significantly reduced. This follows from the fact that the authentication check is performed prior to the application of any access control. If the required authentication factors are not satisfied, the open process terminates quickly. Hence, it is clear that the evaluation of our authentication policies do not significantly burden the system.

5   Related Work

Quality of authentication has been explored as authentication confidence by Ganger et al. [6]. In this approach the system remembers its confidence in each authenticated principals identity. Authorization decisions explicitly consider both the "authenticated" identity and the system confidence in that authentication. The categorization of the authentication type is based on either the possession of secrets or tokens, e.g. passwords or smartcards, or on user specific characteristics like biometrics. Such an approach however does not support a fine granular quality of authentication. We instead provide an expressive policy language supporting quality of authentication. We also provide a reference architecture for authentication services and have implemented a version of it. Our approach is thus more comprehensive and provides a fine granularity control over authentication.

Authentication policies have also been implemented in WebSphere [13] as a part of a flexible set of authentication protocols. These authentication protocols are required to determine the level of security and the type of authentication, which occur between any given client and server for each request. Compared to Websphere policies, our authentication policies are more expressive and have more efficient evaluation as they are enforced at the kernel level.

Our work has some relationship with existing work on authentication logics [1, 2, 15]. For lack of space we limit our discussion to the seminal paper by Abadi et, al. [15], which has goals close to ours. The authors propose a logic based authentication language which has been implemented in the Taos OS. A key notion is such approach is the notion of identity that includes simple principals, credentials and secure channels. The authentication system allows a weak form of continuous authentication through the "speaks-for" notion, that in practice represents subsumption among principals, and the use of authentication cache. By contrast Auth-SL supports the specification of fine-grained authentication requirements that are independent from principals. Besides simple subsumption of principals, Auth-SL supports true multi-factor authentication, enforced through a combination of authentication factors. In addition Auth-SL supports the specification of freshness requirements. Expressing our authentication mechanism in terms of authentication logics could yield to a limited characterization of Auth-SL, which would exclude interesting features such as fine grained conditions against factors and support of temporal constraints. We will further investigate possible extensions of Auth-SL with ideas from the work on authentication logics.

Operating systems define various policies for access control. In particular Security Enhanced Linux [5] (also known as SELinux) provides an expressive policy language which can be used for defining authentication policies. Differently from SELinux, provide a simple syntax which is expressive to describe the various types of authentications and the requirements. Our policies are translated to C functions which are executed at the time of the authentication check. Thus, as compared to SELinux policies, our policies are much simpler to define. Moreover, since our policies are finally encoded as C functions which are pointed to by file objects, we do not require a centralized policy enforcement as in SELinux.

6 Future Work

We plan to extend this work in various directions. The first direction concerns the specification of when the authentication has to be executed; such as when specific events occur, or at periodic time intervals. A second direction concerns the possibility of specifying different authentication policies for different users of the system; this extension would also require an additional component for the policy language and mechanisms for associating policies with users. Finally we plan to implement an authentication service for use by applications and federated digital identity management systems.

References

1. Abadi, M., Burrows, M., Lampson, B.W., Plotkin, G.D.: A calculus for access control in distributed systems. ACM Trans. Program. Lang. Syst. 15(4), 706–734 (1993)
2. Abadi, M., Thau Loo, B.: Towards a declarative language and system for secure networking. In: NetDB 2007. Proceedings of the Third International Workshop on Networking Meets Databases, Cambridge, MA, USA (2007)
3. de Alfaro, L., Manna, Z.: Continuous verification by discrete reasoning. Technical Report CS-TR-94-1524 (1994)
4. v. 1.0 Extensible Markup Language (XML). W3c recommendation, 2006, http://www.w3.org/XML/
5. SELinux for Distributions, http://selinux.sourceforge.net/
6. Ganger, G.R.: Authentication confidences, pp. 169–169 (2001)
7. Klosterman, A., Ganger, G.: Secure continuous biometric-enhanced authentication (2000)
8. Pluggable Authentication Modules, www.sun.com/software/solaris/pam/
9. FreeBSD Project. Freebsd home page, http://www.freebsd.org
10. Revesz, P.Z.: Constraint databases: A survey. In: Semantics in Databases, pp. 209–246 (1995)
11. SAML. v. 1.0 specification set (2002), http://www.oasis-open.org/committees/security/#documents
12. RSA SecureId, http://www.rsasecurity.com/node.asp?id=1156
13. IBM WebSphere Software, www-306.ibm.com/software/websphere/
14. Watson, R.N.M.: Trustedbsd adding trusted operating system features to freebsd. In: USENIX Annual Technical Conference (2001), http://www.usenix.org
15. Wobber, E., Abadi, M., Burrows, M., Lampson, B.: Authentication in the taos operating system. ACM Trans. Comput. Syst. 12(1), 3–32 (1994)
16. Yang, G., Wong, D.S., Wang, H., Deng, X.: Formal analysis and systematic construction of two-factor authentication scheme (short paper). In: Ning, P., Qing, S., Li, N. (eds.) ICICS 2006. LNCS, vol. 4307, Springer, Heidelberg (2006)
17. Bertino, E., Bhargav-Spantzel, A., Squicciarini, A.C.: Policy languages for digital identity management in federation systems. In: POLICY 2006. Proceedings of Workshop on Policies for Distributed Systems and Networks, pp. 54–66 (2006)

A Novel Approach for Untrusted Code Execution

Yan Wen[1], Jinjing Zhao[2], and Huaimin Wang[1]

[1] School of Computer, National University of Defense Technology,
Changsha, China, 410073
wenyan@nudt.edu.cn, whm_w@163.com
[2] Beijing Institute of System Engineering,
Beijing, China, 100101
misszhaojinjing@sina.com.cn

Abstract. In this paper, we present a new approach called Secure Virtual Execution Environment (SVEE) which enables users to "try out" untrusted software without the fear of damaging the system in any manner. A key feature of SVEE is that it implements the OS isolation by executing untrusted code in a hosted virtual machine. Another key feature is that SVEE faithfully reproduces the behavior of applications, as if they were running natively on the underlying host OS. SVEE also provides a convenient way to compare the changes within SVEE and host OS. Referring to these comparison results, users can make a decision to commit these changes or not. With these powerful characteristics, SVEE supports a wide range of tasks, including the study of malicious code, controlled execution of untrusted software and so on. This paper focuses on the execution model of SVEE and the security evaluation for this model.

Keywords: Virtual execution environment, isolated execution, execution model, virtual machine.

1 Introduction

On PC platforms, users often download and execute freeware/shareware. To benefit from the rich software resource on the Internet, most of the PC users seem to be willing to take the risk of being compromised by untrusted code.

To enhance the host security, some host-based security mechanisms have been deployed, such as access control, virus detection and so on. But the access control mechanism will be easily bypassed by authorized but malicious code. The virus detection technology has been introduced to prevent the computer system from the widely prevalent malware, yet such technology does not work well for the unknown malware. A more promising approach for defending against unknown malicious code is based on sandboxing. However, the policies which the commodity sandboxing tools incorporate trend to be too restrictive to execute most useful applications. Consequently, the PC users, often not a computer expert, will prefer functionality to security. Thus, isolation execution, an intrusion-tolerant mechanism, has been applied to allow untrusted programs to run while shields the rest of the system from their effects. But on PC platforms, existing isolation solutions fail to achieve both the OS isolation and the execution environment reproduction (reproducing the execution

S. Qing, H. Imai, and G. Wang (Eds.): ICICS 2007, LNCS 4861, pp. 398–411, 2007.

environment of the trusted environment in the untrusted environment), i.e., they cannot provide security against potential privileged malware without negating the functionality benefits of benign programs.

In this paper, we propose a new execution model called *Secure Virtual Execution Environment* (SVEE) for executing untrusted code. In this execution model, all the untrusted code should be executed within a hosted virtual machine (SVEE VM) while other programs run in host OS. This feature guarantees the OS isolation and provides security against the privileged malicious code. The most desirable feature of SVEE VM is that it boots not from a newly installed OS image but just from the underlying host OS, so the execution environment reproduction is achieved. This is significantly different from the existing VM-based security approaches. In this local-booted OS, no privileged operations will be restricted. Thus, the behavior of untrusted code is reproduced accurately. To retain the acceptable execution results within SVEE VM, SVEE also provides an approach for users to track and compare the changes within SVEE VM and host OS. Using these comparison results for reference, users can make a choice between committing these execution effects and discarding them.

The rest of the paper is organized as follows. Section 2 covers the execution model details of SVEE and discusses its implementation architecture. Section 3 proposes a qualitative security evaluation for SVEE. Section 4 shows the current implementation status and provides an evaluation of the functionality as well as the performance of our approach, then presents our plans for future work. In Section 5, we review previous works on isolated execution technology. Section 6 concludes this paper.

2 Execution Model of SVEE

As discussed in the previous section, the goal of SVEE is to accomplish three capabilities: *OS isolation*, *execution environment reproduction* and *execution effects committing*. The capability of OS isolation is a prerequisite to make the trusted environment be resistant to the attacks from kernel-mode malicious code. Execution environment reproduction is necessary to reproduce the behavior of untrusted code because the behavior of an application is usually determined by the execution environment, especially the contents of the file system. Besides, the execution environment reproduction should not be implemented via duplicating the complete resource of trusted environment, viz. reinstalling the OS and software in the untrusted environment. This is because few PC users can afford such deployment overhead from the usability's standpoint. From the security pointer of view, the resource to be reproduced must be *configurable* for users to avoid uncovering the security-sensitive or privacy-sensitive files. In addition, for many of the applications running within untrusted environment, a user would like to retain the results of activities that are acceptable. So the execution mode of SVEE should provide an approach to track and commit the execution results of the isolated programs.

To achieve OS isolation, the execution model of SVEE must introduce the virtual machine monitor as the software layer to close off the trusted environment and the untrusted ones. According to the definition of Goldberg [1], a virtual machine monitor (VMM) is software for a computer system that creates efficient, isolated programming environments that are "duplicates", which provide users with the appearance of direct access to the real machine environment. These duplicates are referred to as virtual machines. There are two different types of VMMs that can serve as a virtualization environment: Type I VMM and Type II VMM. A Type I VMM just runs above a bare computer hardware platform. It tends to be implemented as a lightweight OS with the virtualization capabilities. A Type II VMM is executed as an application. The OS that manages the real computer hardware is called the "host OS". Every OS that runs in the Type II virtual machine is called a "guest OS ". In a Type II VMM, the host OS provides resource allocation and a standard execution environment to each guest OS.

Considering the performance of the trusted environment, Type II VMM wins an advantage over Type I VMM [1]. For Type I VMM, all OSes run above the virtual machine. So every OS, including the one serving as the trusted environment, cannot but suffer the performance penalties due to virtualization [2]. But for Type II VMM, the trusted environment, viz. the host OS, suffers no performance overhead. In addition, unlike mainframes that are configured and managed by experienced system administrators, desktop and workstation PC's are often preinstalled with a standard OS and managed by the end-user. Ignoring the difficulty of proposing a practical and seamless migration approach for PC platforms, it will maybe take several years to migrate all of them to the Type I VMM. It also might be unacceptable for a PC user to completely replace an existing OS with a Type I VMM. In contrast, Type II VMM allows co-existing with the preinstalled host OS and programs.

Thus, taking into account that PC platform is the prime concern for SVEE, as well as the significant predominance of Type II VMM on PC platforms, we select Type II VMM over Type I VMM.

The execution model is illustrated in Fig. 1. If users wish to execute any untrusted program, they should firstly configure which resource will be reproduced and then boot the local-booted virtual machine (SVEE VM) created by SVEE VMM. From then on, these two OSes, the host OS above the bare computer hardware and the local-booted OS above SVEE VM, will run concurrently. SVEE VMM catches the sensitive instruction traps and emulates their semantics to implement a Type II VMM. In this execution model, The SVEE VM serves as the untrusted execution environment wherein all untrusted programs are bounded. The local-booted OS above this virtual machine just is the virtualized instance of the underling host OS. In the local-booted OS, the behavior of untrusted programs is reproduced accurately while isolating their effects from the host OS which is the execution environment of the trusted applications.

After SVEE ending, the user may make a choice among discarding the modification effects within SVEE, reserving them and committing them. In the first case, the contents of SVEE VM will be destroyed, which means that we simply delete all the reproduced resource and leave the contents of the file system in host OS "as is". In the second case, we reserve all the reproduced resource, so we can start SVEE VM using them next time or access them at any time. And in the third case, the contents of the reproduced resource need to be merged into the host OS.

When merging the reproduced resource and the native file system of host OS, conflicting changes may have taken place within and outside the SVEE VM. For example, the same file may have been modified both in host OS and in SVEE VM. In such cases, it is unclear what the desired merging result should be. Thus, firstly we

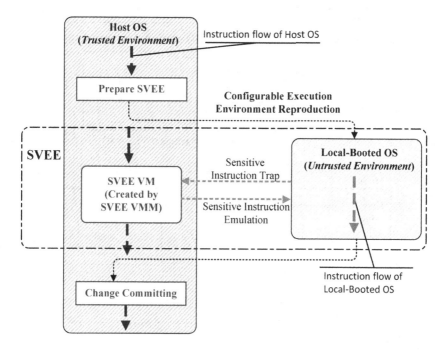

Fig. 1. Execution Model of SVEE

must identify *commit criteria* that ensure the consistency of the file systems in host OS when implementing the commit operation. We use the commit criteria described in [3]. If the commit criteria are not satisfied, then manual reconciliation of conflicting actions that took place inside the SVEE VM and outside will be needed. On this condition, SVEE will provide the user the details about such conflict. Referring to this information, the user can make a choice among optional operation:

Abort, just discards the results of SVEE VM execution.

Retry, that means discarding the results of SVEE VM execution, restarting a new SVEE VM, redoing the actions that were just performed, and then trying to commit again. Usually it often has a high probability to solve the conflicts.

Resolve conflicts, in this case, it is the user's duty to commit the contents manually.

To achieve the capabilities discussed previously, we introduce the local-booted technology implement SVEE. As shown in Fig. 2, SVEE is composed of three key components: *SVEE Virtual Machine Monitor* (SVEE VM), *Virtual Simple Disk* and *Tracking Manager*.

SVEE Virtual Machine Monitor (SVEE VMM): it's a novel local-booted virtual machine monitor which creates the local-booted virtual machine (SVEE VM). The local-booted OS, wherein untrusted programs run, just boots within this virtual machine. With the strong isolation capability of this system virtual machine, we achieve the features of **OS Isolation** and **OS & Application Transparency** effectively. With the local-booting technology, SVEE implements partial one-way isolation [4]. One-way isolation makes the host environment visible within the SVEE

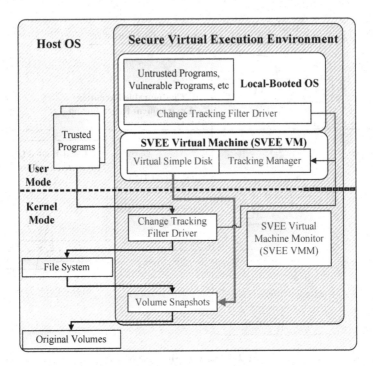

Fig. 2. SVEE Architecture

VM. Our partial one-way isolation means the environment visible within SVEE VM is a branch of host OS, and this branch was created just at the time SVEE VM started. In this sense, execution environment *reproduction* is achieved.

Virtual Simple Disk Based on Volume Snapshot. The key challenge to implement the local-booting technology is how to reuse the system volume, wherein OS is installed. While SVEE VM is running, the host OS is also modifying the same system volume. However, the local-booted OS cannot be aware of these modifications and vice versa. So they will crash because of the content inconsistency between the memory and the disks. SVEE resolves these conflicts by introducing the *virtual simple disk* based on *volume snapshot*. Volume snapshot introduces Copy-on-Write mechanism to shield the modification effects of host O from SVEE VM and vice versa. Virtual simple disk acts as the virtual storage device to export the volume snapshots to SVEE VM. Before exporting volume snapshots, the user can remove the files or folders he does not want to make visible inside SVEE VM. This characteristic makes our *execution environment reproduction* more *configurable*, i.e., the processes in SVEE VM are given access to only the volumes and files exported to SVEE VM, but not the whole file system.

From the perspective of implementation, the snapshot of an entire disk device is more intuitive than a volume snapshot. However for SVEE, such a virtual simple disk has more benefits listed as follows:

Can configure the volumes to export. If SVEE uses the disk snapshots directly, all the volumes in this disk will be visible inside SVEE VM (this is usually not the users' desire). While in our approach, only the volumes the users want to expose will be accessible within SVEE VM.

Volume format transparent. There are several types of volumes in host OS, including single partition volume and multi-partition volumes, e.g., mirrors, stripes and RAID-5. So if the disk to export contains any multi-partition volume, we must export all other disk which this volume depends on. But our approach avoids this trouble.

Convenient to manipulate the data in snapshots. A volume is the basic unit to mount for the file system. Via mounting volume snapshots, we can expediently access their files in the host OS.

Tracking Manager. To support monitoring and committing changes, *change tracking filter drivers* are deployed within both local-booted OS and host OS. The *tracking manger* is responsible for collecting the results and comparing them to generate committing references for users.

As a summary, the key component of SVEE is the SVEE VM, a system virtual machine, whose effects are to be shielded from the host OS. Any untrusted code or the programs that trend to be attacked will be bounded inside SVEE, and share the same consistent OS. One or more such SVEE VMs can be active on the same host OS. Moreover, SVEE also provides a convenient way for users to compare the changes within local-booted OS and host OS. Using these comparison results for reference, users can make a decision to commit these changes or not.

3 Security Evaluation of SVEE

Section 2 has covered the execution model details of SVEE and its advantages under PC platforms. In this section, we evaluate the security of SVEE qualitatively. Thus, the correlative definitions are listed as follows:

$\mathbf{S} = \{ p \mid p$ is a program$\}$

$\mathbf{S^U} = \{ p \mid p \in \mathbf{S}$ is an untrusted program$\}$, $\mathbf{S^T} = \{ p \mid p \in \mathbf{S}$ is a trusted program$\} = \mathbf{S} - \mathbf{S^T}$

$\mathbf{S^M} = \{ p \mid p \in \mathbf{S^U}$ and contains malicious code$\}$, $\mathbf{S^I} = \mathbf{S^U} - \mathbf{S^M}$

$\mathbf{S^V} = \{ p \mid p \in \mathbf{S^T}$ and contains vulnerable code$\}$, $\mathbf{S^S} = \mathbf{S^T} - \mathbf{S^V}$

VMM and OSes are two types of special programs, for they are programs as well as execution environments.

$\mathbf{S}_{env} = \{ p \mid p \in \mathbf{S}$ and runs within $env\}$, $env \in \mathbf{ENV} = \{OS, local\text{-}booted\ OS, host\ OS\}$, OS refers to a conventional multiprogramming OS, *local-booted OS* and *host OS* are illustrated in Fig. 2.

$\mathbf{P}$ (p), $p \in \mathbf{S}_{env.}$: The probability that p will cause a security violation within *env* to occur.

$\mathbf{P_M}$ (p), $p \in \mathbf{S}_{env.}$: The probability that program p within *env* contains malicious code.

$\mathbf{P_V}$ (p), $p \in \mathbf{S}_{env.}$: The probability that a given program p contains vulnerable code which will cause a security violation to occur.

Size (p): the number of lines of a program p in source code, this is a measurement for a software scale.

Based on these definitions, we would get the following conclusions:

$$\mathbf{S} = \mathbf{S^T} \cup \mathbf{S^U} = (\mathbf{S^V} \cup \mathbf{S^S}) \cup (\mathbf{S^M} \cup \mathbf{S^I}) \tag{1}$$

$$\mathbf{P}(p) = \mathbf{P_M}(p) + \mathbf{P_V}(p), \text{ and } \sum_{p \in S_{env}} \mathbf{P}(p) = \sum_{p \in S_{env}} \mathbf{P_M}(p) + \sum_{p \in S_{env}} \mathbf{P_V}(p) \le 1 \tag{2}$$

$$P(S'_{env}) = \sum_{p \in S'_{env}} P(p) < P(S''_{env}) = \sum_{p \in S''_{env}} P(p) \qquad \text{for } S'_{env} \subset S''_{env} \tag{3}$$

As showed in formula (3), the probability of system failure tends to increase with the load on the *env* (i.e., the number of different requests issued, the variety of functions provided, the frequency of requests, etc.).

Noted "secure coder" Wietse Venema estimates that there is roughly one security bug per 1000 lines in software source code. This conclusion assumed the complexities of all the programs to be analyzed are approximately same. So we can deduce that the vulnerability of a program p is proportion to **Size**(*p*). Thus, $\mathbf{P_V}(p)$ can be calculated as:

$$\mathbf{P_V}(p) = \alpha \times \frac{\mathbf{Size}(p)}{\sum_{p_i \in S_{env}} \mathbf{Size}(p_i)}, p \in \mathbf{S}_{env}, \alpha \text{ is a constant.} \tag{4}$$

For a conventional multiprogramming *OS*, we can calculate $\mathbf{P}(\mathbf{S_{OS}})$ by:

$$\mathbf{P}(\mathbf{S_{os}}) = \mathbf{P}(\mathbf{S_{os}^T} \cup \mathbf{S_{os}^U}) = \mathbf{P}(\mathbf{S_{os}^T}) + \mathbf{P}(\mathbf{S_{os}^U}) = \mathbf{P}(\mathbf{S_{os}^V}) + \mathbf{P}(\mathbf{S_{os}^S}) + \mathbf{P}(\mathbf{S_{os}^M}) + \mathbf{P}(\mathbf{S_{os}^I})$$
$$= \mathbf{P}(\mathbf{S_{os}^V}) + \mathbf{P}(\mathbf{S_{os}^M}) + \mathbf{P}(\mathbf{S_{os}^I}) \tag{5}$$

In formula (5), $\mathbf{P}(\mathbf{S^S_{os}})$ is ignored because the programs in $\mathbf{S^S_{os}}$ are trusted and without any vulnerability. Then, with these basic conclusions, we can evaluate the security of the isolation mechanism for hosted SVEE architecture as follows.

For the local-booted OS within SVEE and underlying host OS:

$$\mathbf{P}(\mathbf{S_{Local\text{-}Booted\,OS}}) = \mathbf{P}(\mathbf{S_{Local\text{-}Booted\,OS}^U}) = \mathbf{P}(\mathbf{S_{Local\text{-}Booted\,OS}^M}) + \mathbf{P}(\mathbf{S_{Local\text{-}Booted\,OS}^I}) \tag{6}$$

$$\mathbf{P}(\mathbf{S_{Host\,OS}}) = \mathbf{P}(\mathbf{S_{Host\,OS}^T}) = \mathbf{P}(\mathbf{S_{Host\,OS}^V}) + \mathbf{P}(\mathbf{S_{Host\,OS}^S}) = \mathbf{P}(\mathbf{S_{Host\,OS}^V}) \tag{7}$$

Considering that within host OS, only the *SVEE VMM*, network adapter driver and network protocol components of OS will exchange data with other environments, we can deduce the following formula:

$$\mathbf{S_{Host\,OS}^V} \cong \{SVEE\ VMM, Network\ Components\}, \mathbf{S_{Host\,OS}^T} \subset \mathbf{S_{os}} \text{ and } |\mathbf{S_{Host\,OS}^T}| \ll |\mathbf{S_{os}}|$$
$$\mathbf{Size}(SVEE\ VMM) + \mathbf{Size}(Network\ Components) \ll Size(OS) \tag{8}$$

Based on formula (3), (4), (7) and (8), inequality (9) is reached:

$$\mathbf{P}(\mathbf{S_{Host\,OS}}) \cong \mathbf{P}(SVEE\ VMM) + P(Network\ Components) \ll \mathbf{P}(\mathbf{S_{os}}) \tag{9}$$

Since *SVEE VMM*, a Type II VMM, tends to be shorter, simpler, and easier to debug than conventional multiprogramming OSes, even when $S_{SVEE\ VMM} = S_{OS}$, the VMM is less error-prone. For example, since the VMM is defined by the hardware specifications of the real machine, the field engineer's hardware diagnostic software can be used to checkout the correctness of the VMM.

For all untrusted programs run within SVEE VM, and SVEE is particularly concerned about the host OS security, we can define the probability of a program *p* on one SVEE VM violating the security of another concurrent program on host OS as:

$$P(S_{Local\text{-}Booted\ OS} \mid VMM \mid Host\ OS) + P(S_{Host\ OS}) =$$
$$P(S_{Local\text{-}Booted\ OS}) \times P(VMM) \times P(Host\ OS) + P(S_{Host\ OS}) \tag{10}$$

P ($S_{local\text{-}booted\ OS}$ |*VMM* | *host OS*) is the probability of the simultaneous security failure of local-booted OS, VMM and host OS. If a single OS's security fails, the VMM isolates this failure from the other virtual machines. If the VMM'S security fails, the malicious code will have to break the protection of host OS. But, if functioning correctly, malicious code within local-booted OS will not take advantage of the security breach. This assumes that the designers of the individual OSes are not in collusion with malicious users. This seems to be a reasonable hypothesis.

Based on the formulas of (3), (9) and |{*VMM*}|=|{*host OS*}|=1 << |S_{OS}|, we arrive at the following conclusion:

$$P(S_{Local\text{-}Booted\ OS} \mid VMM \mid Host\ OS) + P(S_{Host\ OS}) =$$
$$P(S_{Local\text{-}Booted\ OS}) \times P(VMM) \times P(Host\ OS) + P(S_{Host\ OS}) << P(S_{OS}) \tag{11}$$

As a summary, based on the inequality (11), the conclusion that the isolation architecture of SVEE improves the security of host OS observably can be reached.

4   Status and Future Work

SVEE has been firstly implemented on Windows with Intel x86 processors because of the prevalence of Windows and Intel processors under PC platforms. A detailed description of SVEE implementation is beyond the scope of this paper. Instead, the framework of the three key components in SVEE is outlined in this section.

It's well-known that Intel x86 processor is not virtualizable [5]. Ignoring the legacy "real" and "virtual 8086" modes of x86, even the more recently architected 32- and 64-bit protected modes are not classically virtualizable for its visibility of privileged state and lack of traps when privileged instructions run at user-level. To address this problem, we have come up with a set of unique techniques that we call *ISDT* (*Instruction Scan and Dynamic Translation*) technology, which is composed of two components: *Code Scanner* (*CS*) and *Code Patcher* (*CP*). Before executing any ring 0 code, *CS* scans it recursively to discover problematic instructions. *CP* then performs in-situ patching, i.e. replace the instruction with a jump to hypervisor memory where an integrated code generator has placed a more suitable implementation. In reality, this is a very complex task as there are lots of odd situations to be discovered and handled correctly.

We implement the volume snapshot using the Windows volume filter driver. This driver creates two types of device objects, one is a *volume filter device object* just located above the original volume to filter all I/O Request Package (IRP) sent to it and execute the *COW* operations, and the other is a *volume snapshot device object* which exports all general volume interfaces to provide a way to access volume snapshots.

To support change committing, we must track all the modification made within SVEE VM and host OS. For Windows, besides file changes, the registry changes are also pivotal. Our approach accomplishes file change tracking as a file system filter driver, and adopts a Native API interceptor to monitor the registry modification. On termination of SVEE, tracking manager collects the change results generated by *change tracking filter driver* and *registry monitor*, and compares them to provider committing reference for uses.

Fig. 3. Screenshot of a Running SVEE

Fig. 3 is a screenshot of a running SVEE VM showed in the window with a title of *Secure Virtual Execution Environment*. The resolution of the local-booted Windows within SVEE VM is 1024x768 while the resolution of host Windows is 800x600, so the icon arrangement within its desktop differs from that of host Windows. As showed in Fig. 3, the programs of *Explorer* and *MediaPlayer* are running in this local-booted Windows. Compared the file system volumes showed in the Explorer programs running within local-booted Windows and outside, we can find that only the volumes C: and D: are exported to it. This just brings forth the SVEE's capability of *configurable execution environment reproduction*: the resource to be reproduced to SVEE VM can be configurable for users. In the Explorer of host Windows, volume K: and L: are the relevant snapshots of C: and D:. When local-booted Windows is running, no programs except SVEE VMM on host Windows can access these snapshots which compose the virtual simple disk of SVEE VM. After local-booted Windows ends, SVEE will help users to access its file system contents for *execution effects committing*.

We have tested the basic functions of SVEE VMM, including instruction set and hardware virtualization. Instruction set virtualization is verified by the QEMU's test-i386 tool, which we have ported to Windows. This tool tests all the x86 user-mode instructions, including SSE, MMX and VM86 instructions. The results show that the execution results of all the instructions are equivalent with those in Host Windows. In addition, we ran PassMark on local-booted Windows. All the virtual hardware devices works perfectly well, including IDE disk, CD-ROM, network card, display adapter and so forth.

For a desktop-oriented workload, we ran Everest Ultimate 2006 both natively and in a local-booted Windows. Everest Ultimate is a synthetic suite of microbenchmarks intended to isolate various aspects of workstation performance. Since user-level computation is almost not taxing for VMMs, we expect local-booted Windows runs to score close to native. Fig. 4 confirms this expectation, showing a slowdown over native of 0.41-4.18%, with a 1.75% average slowdown for SVEE VMM.

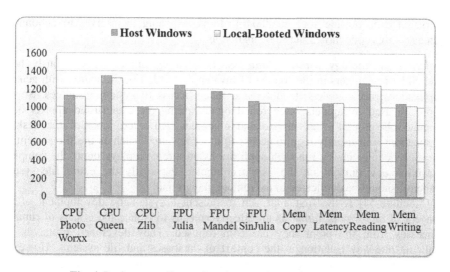

Fig. 4. Performance Comparison between host OS and SVEE VM

To improve the usability and performance of SVEE, we are currently improving the memory management mechanism of SVEE VMM to share the memory pages between SVEE VM and host OS. Multiprocessor virtualization capability is also to be added to SVEE VMM to support Multiprocessor-Specialized host OS version. In addition, we are integrating some intrusion detection mechanisms into SVEE at the virtual hardware layer. To make SVEE VM support the multimedia programs such as 3D games, we plan to reimplement the graphic virtualization mechanism referring to the approach proposed by H. Andres Lagar-Cavilla, et al [6]. Finally, we will investigate the automated change committing technology for SVEE.

5   Related Work

Sandbox. A sandbox is an environment in which the actions of a process are restricted according to a security policy. Sandboxing based approaches involve observing a program's behavior and blocking actions that may compromise the system's security. Janus [7] and Chakravyuha [8] implement sandboxing using kernel interposition mechanism. MAPbox [9] introduces a sandboxing mechanism with the aim at making the sandbox more configurable and usable via providing a template for sandbox policies based on a classification of application behaviors. Safe Virtual Execution (SVE) [10] implements sandboxing using *software dynamic translation*, a technology for modifying binaries at runtime. Systrace [11] proposes a sandboxing system that notifies the user about all the system calls that an program tries to invoke and then generates a policy for the program according to the response from the user.

However, use of sandboxing approaches in practice has been hampered by the difficulty of policy selection: determining resource access rights that would allow the code to execute successfully without compromising system security. Sandboxing tools often adopt highly restrictive policies that preclude execution of most useful applications. So users usually choose functionality over security, i.e., executing untrusted code outside such sandboxing tools, exposing themselves to unbounded damage if this code turned out to be malicious.

Isolation Technology within Mono-OS. Isolated execution has previously been studied by researchers in the context of Java applets [12, 13]. Compared with general applications, such applets do not make much access to system resources. So the approach used by applets often relied on executing these untrusted applets on a "remote playground", i.e., an isolated computer. However, most of the desktop applications will usually require access to more resources such as the file system on the user's computer. To run such applications on a remote playground, the complete execution environment on the user's computer, especially the entire file system contents, should be duplicated to the remote playground.

Literature [4] is the first approach to present a systematic development of the concept of *one-way isolation* as an effective means to isolate the effects of running processes from the point they are compromised. They developed protocols for realizing one-way isolation in the context of databases and file systems. However, they did not present an implementation of their approach. As a result, they do not consider the research challenges that arise due to the nature of COTS applications and commodity OSes.

Alcatraz [14] and its improved version [3], *Security Execution Environment (SEE)*, proposes its improved version with the name of. A key property of SEE is that it reproduces the behavior of applications, as if they were running natively on the underlying host OS. But this approach does not achieve OS isolation, so such protection mechanism can be bypassed by kernel-mode malicious code. And in SEE, a number of privileged operations, such as mounting file systems, and loading/unloading modules are not permitted.

All these approaches suffer from the same problem: they can be turned off if intruders compromise the operating system and gain system privileges [15]. The file protection they provide is thus less effective in a compromised environment.

Isolation Based on Virtual Machine. Covirt [16] proposes that most of applications may be run inside virtual machine instead of host machines. User-mode VMs have been proposed for the Linux OS [17]. All the above approaches suffer from the difficulty of environment reproduction.

Denali [18, 19] is another virtual machine based approach that runs untrusted distributed server applications. Denali focuses on supporting lightweight VMs, relying on modifications to the virtual instruction set exposed to the guest OS and thus requiring modifications to the guest OS. In contrast, we are focusing on heavier weight VMs and make no OS modifications.

VMWare ESX Server provides an isolation approach for server platform with a similar objective to ours. XEN [20] and L4-based virtual machine [21] also implement isolated virtual execution environments. But all of these three environments are just located above computer hardware in form of Type I VMM. So as discussed in section 2, they are not fit for PC platforms because of their drawbacks caused by Type I VMM architecture.

The COW/COW2 mechanism of QEMU [22], an open source emulator, can only isolate the Guest OS's modifications to file system from host OS. But modifications made by host OS will cause the conflicts between the disk and file system content in Guest OS and crash it. Thus QEMU failed to achieve the environment reproduction. Besides, its poor performance prevents it from server as an effective virtual environment. KVM [23], a Kernel-based Virtual Machine based on QEMU, significantly improves the performance. But it also cannot provide the capability of environment reproduction. Besides, it must modify the host OS and rely on the hardware virtualization technology, such as Intel VT and AMD-V.

6   Conclusions

In this paper, we proposed a new execution model called SVEE for executing untrusted code safely and shown the security evaluation for this model. SVEE is versatile enough to coexist with the existing OS and programs. The most considerable benefit of SVEE is that it provides the capability of OS isolation while accomplishing the configurable execution environment reproduction. SVEE also provides a convenient way for users to track the changes made within the SVEE VM, viz. the untrusted execution environment. These changes can be discarded if the user does not accept them. Otherwise, the changes can be committed so as to become visible within host OS.

SVEE accomplishes all the capabilities discussed in section 2: *OS isolation, configurable execution environment reproduction* and *execution effects committing.*

Consequently, SVEE provides security against potential malicious code without negating the functionality benefits provided by benign programs. With these capabilities, SVEE supports a wide range of tasks, including the study of malicious code, controlled execution of untrusted software, experimentation with software configuration changes, testing of software patches and so on.

Acknowledgements

This research is supported by National Basic Research Program of China (Grant No. 2005CB321801), National Natural Science Foundation of China (Grant No. 60673169), and National Science Fund for Outstanding Youths under Grant No. 60625203.

References

1. Goldberg, R.P.: Architectural Principles for Virtual Computer Systems, Ph.D. Thesis. Harvard University, Cambridge, MA (1972)
2. Adams, K., Agesen, O.: A Comparison of Software and Hardware Techniques for x86 Virtualization. In: Proceedings of The 12th International Conference on Architectural Support for Programming Languages and Operating Systems (ASPLOS 2006), pp. 2–13 (2006)
3. Sun, W., Liang, Z., Sekar, R., Venkatakrishnany, V.N.: One-way Isolation: An Effective Approach for Realizing Safe Execution Environments. ISOC Network and Distributed System Security (NDSS 2005) (2005)
4. Liu, P., Jajodia, S., McCollum, C.D.: Intrusion confinement by isolation in information systems. Journal of Computer Security 8, 243–279 (2000)
5. ScottRobin, J.: Analyzing the Intel Pentium's Capability to Support a Secure Virtual Machine Monitor, Master's Thesis. Naval Postgraduate School, Monterey, CA, 133 (1999)
6. Lagar-Cavilla, H.A.e., Tolia, N., Satyanarayanan, M., Lara, E.d.: VMM-Independent Graphics Acceleration. In: Proceedings of the Third International ACM SIGPLAN/SIGOPS Conference on Virtual Execution Environments (VEE 2007), San Diego, CA (2007)
7. Goldberg, I., Wagner, D., Thomas, R., Brewer, E.: A Secure Environment for Untrusted Helper Applications (Confining the Wily Hacker). In: Proceedings of the Sixth USENIX UNIX Security Symposium, San Jose, California (1996)
8. Dan, A., Mohindra, A., Ramaswami, R., Sitaram, D.: ChakraVyuha(CV): A Sandbox Operating System Environment for Controlled Execution of Alien Code. IBM T.J. Watson research center (1997)
9. Acharya, A., Raje, M.: Mapbox: Using Parameterized Behavior Classes to Confine Applications. In: Proceedings of the 9th USENIX Security Symposium (2000)
10. Scott, K., Davidson, J.: Safe Virtual Execution using Software Dynamic Translation. In: Computer Security Applications Conference, pp. 209–218 (2002)
11. Provos, N.: Improving Host Security with System Call Policies. In: Proceedings of the 12th USENIX Security Symposium, Washington, D.C., USA (2003)
12. Chiueh, T.-c., Sankaran, H., Neogi, A.: Spout: A Transparent Distributed Execution Engine for Java Applets. In: Proceedings of the 20th International Conference on Distributed Computing Systems, vol. 394 (2000)
13. Malkhi, D., Reiter, M.K.: Secure Execution of Java Applets using A Remote Playground. IEEE Transactions on Software Engineering 26, 1197–1209 (2000)
14. Liang, Z., Venkatakrishnan, V.N., Sekar, R.: Isolated Program Execution: An Application Transparent Approach for Executing Untrusted Programs. In: Omondi, A.R., Sedukhin, S. (eds.) ACSAC 2003. LNCS, vol. 2823, Springer, Heidelberg (2003)
15. Kernel brk() vulnerability, http://seclists.org/lists/bugtraq/2003/Dec/0064.html
16. Chen, P.M., Noble, B.D.: When Virtual is Better Than Real. In: 8th Workshop on Hot Topics in Operating Systems (2001)

17. Dike, J.: A User-mode Port of the Linux Kernel. In: Proceedings of the 4th Annual Linux Showcase & Conference, Atlanta, Georgia, USA (2000)
18. Whitaker, A., Shaw, M., Gribble, S.D.: Denali: A Scalable Isolation Kernel. In: Proceedings of the Tenth ACM SIGOPS European Workshop, Saint-Emilion, France (2002)
19. Whitaker, A., Shaw, M., Gribble, S.D.: Denali: Lightweight Virtual Machines for Distributed and Networked Applications. In: Proceedings of the 2002 USENIX Technical Conference (2002)
20. Barham, P., Dragovic, B., Fraser, K., Hand, S., Harris, T., Ho, A., Neugebauery, R., Pratt, I., Warfield, A.: Xen and the Art of Virtualization. In: Proceedings of the 19th ACM Symposium on Operating Systems Principles (SOSP 2003), pp. 164–177. ACM Press, New York (2003)
21. Biemueller, S., Dannowski, U.: L4-Based Real Virtual Machines - An API Proposal. In: Proceedings of the MIKES 2007: First International Workshop on MicroKernels for Embedded Systems, Sydney, Australia, pp. 36–42 (2007)
22. Bellard, F.: QEMU, a Fast and Portable Dynamic Translator. In: USENIX Association Technical Conference (2005)
23. Qumranet: KVM: Kernel-based Virtualization Driver (2006)

Detection and Diagnosis of Control Interception

Chang-Hsien Tsai and Shih-Kun Huang

Department of Computer Science, National Chiao Tung University, Taiwan
{chsien,skhuang}@cs.nctu.edu.tw

Abstract. Crash implies that a software is unstable and possibly vulnerable. Stack overflow is one of many causes of crashes. This kind of bug is often hard to debug because of the corrupted stack, so that debuggers cannot trace the control flow of the programs. A control-type crash caused by stack overflow is easy to be developed as a control interception attack. We develop a method to locate this attack and implement it as a plug-in of Valgrind [1]. This tool can be used in the honeypot to detect and diagnose zero-day exploits. We use it to detect several vulnerabilities and automatically locate the bugs.

1 Introduction

According to a recent report [2] developed by the IBM Internet Security Systems, there were 7247 new vulnerabilities in 2006. This number increases nearly 40 percent than the previous year. Over 88 percent of vulnerabilities could be exploited remotely, and over 50 percent allowed attackers to gain access to a machine after exploitation. This serves as a good reason for us to develop a tool to detect attacks and diagnose the vulnerabilities in software.

For better performance, majority of internet servers are implemented in C and C++ programming language. These languages provide low-level operations such as pointer access. While powerful, these operations are the source of common programming errors, one of which is buffer overflow in the stack.

If buffer overflow occurs, the contiguous data are overwritten. This would result in one of three consequences:

1. The program works *normally* like nothing has happened. For example, some data are overwritten, but they will not be used later on. This kind of bug is harmless and may be ignored for a long time.
2. The program works *abnormally*, but most functionalities are as usual. The program may display the extraordinary string or number, because these data are overwritten. This kind of bug is usually easy to identify. With the help of a debugger, the programmer can set *watchpoints* on these suspect variables; the debugger can pause the program as soon as the values of these variables change. There are many researches working on recovering or rollbacking from the abnormal state. Periodic check-points of the system state can be used as replay debugging [3].
3. The program becomes *uncontrollable* because control-sensitive data are corrupted, thereby causing the program to crash.

S. Qing, H. Imai, and G. Wang (Eds.): ICICS 2007, LNCS 4861, pp. 412–426, 2007.

If the flaws can be triggered by user inputs, it is easy for attackers to exploit the bug by intercepting the control flow with carefully crafted input. Even worse, conventional debuggers are handicapped by corrupted stacks . We call this *control interception attack* and develop a tool to detect and diagnose it.

Typical control interception attacks contain *code injection* and *control interception*. Attackers inject malicious code into vulnerable programs. This code is known as shellcode, since the traditional injected code creates a new shell. Through efforts of the hackers [4], new shellcode can even execute as a VNC server.

The second part of the control interception attack is to intercept the control flow of a program. By exploiting the vulnerability of the program, an attacker can overwrite a control-sensitive data to divert the program into the injected code.

1.1   Avoidance of Execution of Injected Code

To mitigate the attacks, many researches attempt to render the injected code harmless. Since the injected code is usually located in the stack or heap, making these areas non-executable [5] would prevent the execution of injected code. However, this technique would cause problems for some software, such as the JIT compiler. Linn et al. [6] observe that successful exploits must invoke system calls. They record the program counter of every invocation of system calls in the executable. The kernel can use the information to differentiate user code from injected code at runtime. Instruction Set Randomization [7][8] *encrypts* trusted binary code with a random key during loading and *decrypts* them during instruction fetching. Injected malicious code becomes garbage and leads to a crash.

Another way is to hinder attackers to predict where the injected code is. Address space layout randomization (ASLR) [5] moves the code segment, stack segment and other segments to different address at each run. PointGuard [9] encrypts all pointers while they reside in memory and decrypts them only before they are loaded to a CPU register. Without knowing where the injected code is, attackers cannot divert the vulnerable program into these code.

1.2   Detection of Control Corruption

Attackers must corrupt the control-sensitive data to intercept the control flow of the vulnerable program. During every function call in C, there are at least two control-sensitive data in the stack: return address and saved frame pointer.

In this work, we present a method to locate the control-type crash with which conventional debuggers are hard to help. We can report where the control state are corrupted and how the program goes there. The algorithm has been implemented as a plug-in of *Valgrind*[1], called Beagle. We use it to evaluate several vulnerabilities and correctly pinpoint these bugs.

The tool can complement the Valgrind in stack overflow detection. The established *memcheck* plug-in of the Valgrind works perfectly in detecting heap overflow. However, Valgrind still lacks the capability to detect stack overflow. In the recent Valgrind user survey [10], the stack overflow detection is the most wanted feature. Valgrind developers answer this request in the FAQ 5.2 with

> "Unfortunately, Memcheck doesn't do bounds checking on static or stack arrays. We'd like to, but it's just not possible to do in a reasonable way that fits with how Memcheck works. Sorry."

If the control-sensitive data in the stack are overwritten, our tool can report where the bug is. With this ability, this tool can be a good honeypot to detect zero-day exploit. Because it can detect the attack immediately and does not need to replay the attack. After detecting an attack, it can diagnose the vulnerable code. This tool can also be used with fuzzers (random input generation tools) to find new vulnerabilities.

The remainder of this paper is organized as follows. In Sect. 2, we cover the control-type crash and why it is hard to debug. In Sect. 3, we propose a scheme to point out the bug. In Sect. 4, we detail the implementation of our tool in Valgrind. In Sect. 5, we evaluate our tool with case studies. Finally, in Sect. 6, we present our conclusions.

2   Background

As stated in Sect. 1, uncontrollable programs often lead to crash. Crash implies that there is either an inherent *bug* (programmed by mistake) or a *vulnerability* (triggered by unexpected input). Programs may run out of control and crash due to the corruption of branch control state. Branch control state determines the branch flow of the next instruction for execution, corresponding to three types of branch instructions: function call, function return, and jump. If the branch targets of these instructions are dynamic addresses, they may be corrupted with an invalid address range. For example, dynamic call target can refer to an offset of a virtual table in C++ implementation, or a function pointer in C language. Function returns are usually dynamic. Jump target can also be dynamic. If these targets are corrupted (either unintentionally, or maliciously), the program may fail to meet specifications. Such programs with corrupted control states may also be exploited and thus become vulnerable. It is difficult to reconstruct system failures after a program has crashed due to a corrupted control state and the propagated distance between crash sites and corrupt sites. To cope with this difficulty, we try to monitor running behavior during programs execution. We aim to design a tool that analyzes the program running behavior and determine where the bug is.

First of all, we must clarify that not all crashes are exploitable. We roughly classify two types of crashes: data-type crash and control-type crash. The data-type crash is caused by accessing an illegal memory address; the control-type crash is caused by transferring control to an illegal address. Control-type crash is usually exploitable, while the other one is usually non-exploitable. Secondly, there are two pieces of information that are very helpful in the debugging process:

where the program crashes and how it goes there. Programmers find out the bug more easily with these clues. Normally, it is harder to debug a control-type crash than other crashes, because these clues are missing after a control-type crash.

2.1 Data-Type Crash

Programs often crash resulting from access to illegal memory, which is either an unmapped address or a privileged address. In the Unix environment, programs crash with a message "segmentation fault." To debug a crash, experienced programmers would trace the code from the crash statement rather than the entry point or any other statement, since the bug is usually the crash statement or its preceding statements. Tracing backwards from the crash statement is easier for debugging. If the bug is not in the current function, programmers continue to trace the caller. In this way, it relies on programmer's expertise to find the bug.

It is not easy to identify the crash statement in a big project, if the program does not indicate any message before the crash. A debugger can easily identify the crash statement by reproducing the crash case. For example, the program crash.c in Fig. 1 ends with a crash.

```
#include <stdio.h>

void foo(char *p){
    *p = 'x';
}

int main(void){
    char *p;
    p = NULL;
    foo(p);
}
```

Fig. 1. crash.c: sample program with a NULL pointer dereference bug

After running the program in gdb, we get the following messages:

```
Program received signal SIGSEGV, Segmentation fault.
0x0804835e in foo (p=0x0) at crash.c:4
4                   *p = 'x';
```

In this case, the program crashes in the function foo at the line 4 of crash.c, which dereferences a NULL pointer p. From the crash statement, we need to trace backwards. The debugger provides a *backtrace*, by which we can follow to trace the caller. We use the command bt to print the backtrace as following:

```
(gdb) bt
#0  0x0804835e in foo (p=0x0) at crash.c:4
#1  0x0804838e in main () at crash.c:10
```

This shows that `main()` calls `foo()` ,and the program crashes within `foo()` at line 4. We can search for the bug from the crash statement and then the caller, `main()`, and so on. After finding out the bug, we can easily fix this bug by initializing the pointer p with a right value.

Debugging is a backward search; however, conventional debuggers only support forward execution. Programmers need to set breakpoints in the right place and observe the values of variables. If the program crashes before reaching any breakpoint, programmers need to set an earlier breakpoint and restart the process. Thus, programmers must set breakpoints carefully or they will miss the bug. To overcome the difficulty, *Bidirectional debuggers* [11] allow programmers to trace programs forwards as well as backwards.

From this debugging example, we demonstrate that *corrupt statement* is much closer to the real bug than the crash statement. The corrupt statement is where important data are corrupted, thereby causing the crash later on. The corrupt statement is usually the bug itself. If we fix the corrupt statement, the program will not crash. In the aforementioned `crash.c` program, there is a NULL pointer dereference crash. The corrupt statement is 'p = NULL;' and it is also the bug. To automatically inference from the crash statement to the corrupt statement, Manevich et al. [12] use the static analysis approach.

2.2   Control-Type Crash

After reviewing the debugging process for a data-type crash, we study the control-type crash. The control-type crash is caused by corrupting control-sensitive data, such as the return address in the stack. These control-sensitive data manage the control flow of the program. If one of them get corrupted, the program is out of control when using the corrupted value. The most common corruption is because of the buffer overflow in the stack.

```
void foo(void){
    char buf[8];
    bar(buf);
} /*crash statement*/

void bar(char *buf){
    strcpy(buf, "this is a long string");    /*bug*/
    ...
}
```

Fig. 2. The crash statement and the bug

If a program writes data to a buffer beyond its boundary, other data subsequent to the buffer would be overwritten. The C standard library has many unsafe functions, such as `strcpy()`, `strcat()` and etc. For performance issue, these functions copy data without boundary checking. The buffer is in the stack or heap, and the overflow is referred as stack overflow or heap overflow respectively. In this paper, we focus on detecting stack overflow. Figure 2 is a sample program with stack overflow vulnerability. The `strcpy()` function writes a long string into the buffer, `buf`, and then the program crashes. As usual, we use gdb to find out the crash statement, but get the following message:

```
Program received signal SIGSEGV, Segmentation fault.
0x7320676e in ?? ()
```

The buggy program crashes, but the gdb cannot report the crash statement in this case. The command `bt` shows no clue as well:

```
(gdb) bt
#0  0x7320676e in ?? ()
#1  0x6e697274 in ?? ()
#2  0xb7fd0067 in ?? () from /lib/tls/libc.so.6
#3  0x080494c4 in ?? ()
#4  0xb7fd7ff4 in ?? () from /lib/tls/libc.so.6
#5  0x00000000 in ?? ()
#6  0xb8000ca0 in ?? () from /lib/ld-linux.so.2
#7  0xbffff358 in ?? ()
#8  0xb7ec6e4b in __libc_start_main() from /lib/tls/libc.so.6
Previous frame inner to this frame (corrupt stack?)
```

We redo the experiment in Microsoft Visual Studio 2003 .NET and get the similar result. Conventional debuggers lose track of the program after the control-type crash, because the control-sensitive data in the stack are corrupted. In this case, programmers must carefully set breakpoints in the debugger before the corruption happens and localize the crash statement in a binary search fashion.

The distinction between the crash statement and the corrupt statement in a control-type crash is essential. The crash statement is obviously where the program crashes, whereas the corrupt statement is where control-sensitive data are corrupted. For example, in Fig. 2, the function *foo* passes its local buffer *buf* to the function *bar*. After calling `strcpy()`, the program's stack is corrupted. However, the program does not crash until the function *foo* returns (in line 4). This example also supports our claim that the corrupt statement is much closer to the bug (the corrupt statement is also the bug).

If attackers overflow the stack with carefully designed values, they can intercept the program. Many kinds of attacks aim to overwrite the control-sensitive data. These attacks contain either a *discrete corruption* or a *continuous corruption*. A discrete corruption is defined as an directly overwrite of control-sensitive data. The typical example of discrete corruption is to overflow via a pointer or a format-string function. A continuous corruption is defined as multiple consecutive writes that overflow the control-sensitive data. The typical example of continuous corruption is the buffer overflow caused by using functions in the C standard library. Attackers can inject any code to execute in the vulnerable program.

3   Detection and Diagnosis of Control Corruption

In this section, we first review several detection methods on control corruption and why they are not precise. Then, we detail our detection method.

3.1   Detection of Library Misuse

Software wrapper is a effective approach to monitor dangerous library call. However it detects only vulnerabilities due to use of library functions. *libsafe* [13] wraps dangerous functions (such as `strcpy()`, `strcat()` and etc.) to enforce boundary checking. Wrapped functions compute the size between the buffer's address and saved frame pointer. If the input data is larger than the size, libsafe halts the program to avoid overwriting the saved frame pointer and the return address. Robertson et al. [14] wrap heap-related functions to detects heap overflow. By wrapping `malloc()`, it inserts canary and padding in front of each memory chunk. By wrapping `free()`, it checksums the chunk to ensure the canary unchanged.

STOBO [15] wraps user functions to detect buffer overflow. It keeps track of lengths of memory buffers and issues warnings when buffer overflows may occur. STOBO finds vulnerabilities in programs even when the test data do not cause overflow, thus sometime issuing false positive.

3.2   Detection of Stack Control Corruption

There are many researches about detecting stack overflow. When they detect corruption in the control-sensitive data, they will terminate the process to avoid executing malicious code. There are two approaches to detect corruption: *canary* and *backup*.

Canary approach is used by StackGuard [16]. A canary is a special value inserted before the saved return address when a new stack frame is allocated. Any attempt to overwrite the saved return address will also overwrite the canary. Just before the function returns, the canary will be checked. If the canary changes, StackGuard detects a stack overflow and terminates the process. The StackGuard aims to protect the saved return address, but it leaves another control-sensitive data, the save framed pointer, under attack. *SSP* [17] and Microsoft Visual Studio /GS option [18] enhance the method by inserting the canary between the saved frame pointer and local variables. The canary approach works fine for continuous corruption. Nevertheless, it may not detect the discrete corruption since the canary can be bypassed.

Backup approach is used by StackShield [19]. It backs up the return address of the current function in another global variable when a new stack frame is allocated. When the function returns, it compares the return address with the stored one. If the value changes, StackShield detects a stack overflow and terminates the process. The same approach is implemented in Win32 PE binary programs [20] as well as DLL [21]. VtPath [22] extracts return addresses from the call stack in a training phase and uses them to detect exploits in runtime.

These approaches all neglect the saved frame pointer. Our tool takes the backup approach since it is better than the canary approach, and we back up both the saved return address and the saved frame pointer.

Other than the aforementioned shortcomings, these methods are designed to detect attacks and kill itself to avoid executing the injected code. Hence, they can not find the corrupt site. The first reason is that they check at the epilog of every function. Therefore, any corruption occurred in a function is not detected until the epilog of the function. The larger the function is, the more imprecise the method is. Programmers must waste much time in finding the corrupt statement backwards in the function. Due to this reason, our method's detection granularity is a basic block. If the corrupt statement is in the library, the bug is usually in the line of function invocation, because most faults occur in misuse of the library, not the implementation of the library itself, for example, the use of strcpy().

After enhancing the detection timing, there is still another problem. If one function corrupts its caller's control-sensitive data via the pointer, the corruption is not detected until returning to the caller. For example in Fig. 2, the function foo passes a pointer of its local variable buf to the function bar, which calls strcpy() to overwrite foo's local variable and return address. The program's control-sensitive data are corrupt, but the program has not yet crashed until the function foo returns[1]. To detect this corruption as soon as possible, we need to check every control-sensitive data in the stack, rather than those of current function only. In this way, we can detect the function foo's control-sensitive data are corrupted after the function strcpy is called.

3.3   Localization of the Corrupt Statement

We first instrument a *Backup* function in every function's prolog and instrument a *Verify* function in the end of every basic block. If the Verify function find a mismatch, it will report the corrupt statement and the stack trace. It also reports which stack frame is corrupt (victim frame). With this detection mechanism we have to ensure that these functions will not disturb the program's normal execution. The jobs of these functions are:

Backup saves the current frame's saved frame pointer and return address. The Backup function also needs to track which frame we are executing. We will cover this in the next section.

Verify compares current frame's saved frame pointer and return address with backups. Then it compares the previous frame's frame pointer and return address with corresponding backups and so on until the main function. If one of these does not match the backup values, the *Report* function will be called.

Report will report the victim stack frame and the backtrace. The currently executing statement is the corrupt statement, and the first unmatched frame

---

[1] Function foo's return address and saved frame pointer are corrupt, but function bar's are normal.

is the victim frame[2]. It is easy to reconstruct the backtrace since we have all the return addresses before corruption. We can infer the calling addresses from these return addresses.

4   Implementation in Valgrind

We implement this method as a plug-in of Valgrind, which is a JIT-based emulator for linux. At runtime, each basic block in the binary is translated into a RISC-like assembly language, called UCode, and the instruments it with Backup and Verify function. The instrumented block is then translated back into the native code to execute.

In Bealge plug-in, we first find the base address of **main**'s stack frame. The data whose address is beyond the base address are used by the startup code of libc, and it is not our concern. The base address will be used as the boundary in the Verify function. When a new basic block comes to the plug-in, we map the code address to a symbol name by using VG_(get_fnname_if_entry) function. If the symbol name is "main", we are instrumenting the **main** function. We save the frame pointer of this function as main_ebp, which is the boundary.

After recoding the main_ebp, we need to instrument Backup function in the prolog of every function. Normally, a function prolog is like:

```
pushl %ebp
movl %esp, %ebp
```

The movl %esp, %ebp is translated to UCode as:

```
GETL %ESP, t6
PUTL t6, %EBP
INCEIPo $2
```

We check each instruction in a basic block. If the opcode is "PUT" and the value is EBP, the program is modifying the EBP register. This usually indicates that a new stack frame is allocated. We instrument the Backup function after such instruction.

We instrument the Verify function before the last instruction of every basic block. In this way, we can make sure the corrupt statement is in this block, if there is a mismatch found in the Verify function. If so, we collect all the return addresses as an array for the parameter of VG_(mini_stack_dump), which prints the stack trace.

A simple implementation of the Verify function is a stack walk algorithm. Figure 3(a) shows the normal stack where every saved frame pointer points to the

---

[2] In the most cases, if the frame pointer in the victim frame does not match the backup, this indicates a continuous corruption. The victim buffer is allocated as this function's local variable. If the return address does not match the backup, but the frame pointer matches the backup, it indicates a discrete corruption on the return address.

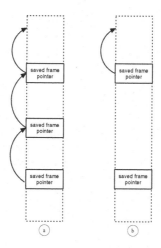

Fig. 3. (a) The normal stack frame (b) Frame pointer omission

previous saved frame pointer. In the algorithm, the saved frame pointer is first compared with the backup. If the values match, it is used as the address to find the saved frame pointer of the parent function. The saved frame pointer of the parent function is then compared with the corresponding backup. The stack walk algorithm goes on until reaching the `main` function (comparing with the `main_ebp`).

4.1   Frame Pointer Omission

The simple stack walk implementation works fine for normal case; however, a compiler optimization technique, called *Frame Pointer Omission* (FPO), may complicate the task. As there are only *seven* general registers in the x86 CPU it is undesirable to dedicate one of them, the `EBP` register, for addressing local variables. Contemporary compilers can generate code that addresses local variables via the `ESP` register instead of the `EBP` register. In gcc, the FPO feature is enabled by the `-fomit-frame-pointer` option, which is implied by several optimization levels.

With FPO, some functions may have no formal stack frame. The `EBP` registers during these functions serve for general purpose rather than pointing to the saved frame pointer. As shown in Fig. 3(b), the static link used by the saved frame pointer is "broken" in these functions. Considering the FPO, we must not only store the value of the save frame pointer but also the value of the `EBP` register.

In the implementation, an array `ebp` stores all the previous seen values of the EBP register. An array `savefp` stores all the previous saved frame pointers. An array `retaddr` stores all the return addresses. The index variable `nframe` is tracking which frame we are executing. In the Backup function, there are several cases:

*EBP == ebp[nframe] This is a new stack frame, and the variable `nframe` is increased by one. The saved frame pointer, the value of the EBP register and the return address are backed up.

EBP == ebp[nframe-1] We returns to the parent function, and the variable nframe is decreased by one.

*EBP == savefp[nframe] We are in the same function.

4.2 setjmp and longjmp Functions

The C standard library provides two functions, setjmp and longjmp, to transfer control directly from one function to another currently executing function (one of the parent functions) without going through the normal return sequence. The setjmp function saves the current stack context for later use by longjmp. There may be several longjmp calls, each of which represents one case of exception. After the longjmp is called, the control will directly transfer to the recently called setjmp with different return values to distinguish the exceptions.

In the implementation of Verify function, we must consider the presence of the longjmp call. In the normal case, the value of the EBP register will be the last used element of the ebp array (indexed by nframe). However, after the longjmp, the EBP register will point to the previous frame where the setjmp is called. The Verify function must first find the matched value of the EBP register in the ebp array before starting matching the retaddr and savefp array.

5 Evaluations

To validate the correctness of our tool, we need to verify that our tool does point out real bugs. In this section, we check several vulnerabilities in open source projects.

5.1 Picasm Error Handling Stack Overflow Vulnerability

Picasm is a Microchip PIC16Cxx assembler, designed to run on most UNIX-like operating systems. When generating error and warning messages, picasm copies strings into fixed length buffers without bounds checking. Below is one of the vulnerable functions.

```
152 void
153 error(int lskip, char *fmt, ...)
154 {
155   va_list args;
156   char outbuf[128];
157
158   err_line_ref();
159   strcpy(outbuf, "Error: ");
160   va_start(args, fmt);
161   vsprintf(outbuf+7, fmt, args);
```

We run the crash case under Beagle and get the following report:

```
corrupted in frame[1]
==10941==    at 0x3AA00D6C: mempcpy (mempcpy.S:58)
==10941==    by 0x3A9D2AD8: vfprintf (vfprintf.c:1535)
==10941==    by 0x3A9EBD2A: vsprintf (iovsprintf.c:46)
==10941==    by 0x8048FBD: error (picasm.c:161)
==10941==    by 0x8049F3A: main (picasm.c:887)
```

The first line indicates the victim frame is the first frame, function `error`, because its local variable `outbuf` is overflow. The next lines indicate the backtrace at the corrupt statement. The "==10941==" is the process id of the process. The corrupt statement is the `vsprintf` in line 161 of `picasm.c`, which copies the error message into the `outbuf` without boundary checking.

5.2 Buffer Overflow in Elm (Expires Header)

Elm is a popular mail user agent for Unix. There is a stack overflow in processing mail header disclosed in Aug 2005. Attackers can craft the following mail with overlong `Expires` header to crash the elm:

```
From: attacker@localhost
To: user@victim.com
Subject: Elm buffer overflow
Expires: UUUUUUUUUUUUUUUUUUUUUUUUUUUUUUUUUUUUUUUUUUUUUUUUUUUUUUUUUU
```

The vulnerability exists in `expires.c:process_expiration_date` that processes the `Expires` header:

```
41 process_expiration_date(date, message_status)
42 char *date;
43 int *message_status;
44 {
   ....
72     items = sscanf(date, "%s %s %s %s %s",
73                 word1, word2, word3, word4, word5);
```

The sscanf() in line 72 reads the string into local variable `word1`, `word2`, `word3`, `word4` and `word5`. The size of these variable is 20 bytes. It enough for date, but is far less than arbitrary string as the crafted email. We use Bealge to get the following result:

```
corrupted in frame[3]
==13073== at 0x3AA3794B: _IO_sputbackc (in /lib/tls/libc-2.3.4.so)
==13073== by 0x3AA214F7: _IO_vfscanf (in /lib/tls/libc-2.3.4.so)
==13073== by 0x3AA2D5A8: vsscanf (in /lib/tls/libc-2.3.4.so)
==13073== by 0x3AA2884A: sscanf (in /lib/tls/libc-2.3.4.so)
```

```
==13073== by 0x8058BAC: process_expiration_date (expires.c:72)
==13073== by 0x8068B07: read_headers (newmbox.c:705)
==13073== by 0x806796C: newmbox (newmbox.c:184)
==13073== by 0x8055B2D: main (elm.c:108)
```

The Elm starts from `main` and then `newmbox`, and so on. The third frame, `process_expiration_date`, is corrupted by the `sscanf` in line 72 of the file `expires.c`.

5.3   Berlios GPSd gpsd_report() Format String Vulnerability

Berlios GPSd is a daemon that monitors GPSes attached to a computer and makes all data available at a TCP socket. In GPSd versions 1.9.0 through 2.7, there is a format string vulnerability that the file `gpsd_report` calls `syslog` with an input from user.

```
112            syslog((errlevel == 0) ? LOG_ERR : LOG_NOTICE, buf);
```

We attack this server with the exploit from Metasploit [4] and find out the bug as following.

```
==15277== Process terminating with default action of signal 11 (SIGSEGV)
==15277==  Access not within mapped region at address 0x3A746E65
==15277==    at 0x3A9E2032: vfprintf (in /lib/i686/libc-2.4.so)
==15277==    by 0x3AA6AAF5: __vsyslog_chk (in /lib/i686/libc-2.4.so)
==15277==    by 0x3AA6ACE9: syslog (in /lib/i686/libc-2.4.so)
==15277==    by 0x8049077: gpsd_report (gpsd.c:112)
==15277==    by 0x804A633: main (gpsd.c:620)
```

5.4   Comparison with CRED

In our survey, CRED [23] is the most related work to ours and its source code is available, so we compare it with our work. From the standpoint of program language, any pointer access out of its storage is a bug. However, there is no size information in a pointer in C language. Jones and Kelly [24] store pointer address and size information for run-time checks in a splay tree. CRED is an extension of Jones and Kelly's work to allow OOB access.

Both as dynamic analysis, CRED is designed to detect buffer overflow, whereas Beagle is designed to detect control corruption. CRED can detect buffer overflow in the stack, but we can not detect some cases if the quasi-invariant is not violated. Nevertheless, CRED can not detect the three vulnerabilities presented in this section, because it does not handle the format-string functions. In addition, CRED can not detect the overflow caused by system call, such as `read()`. Valgrind can not instrument the system call as well, but it will detect the corruption after the system call. This is another advantage to use our method.

As shown in Table 5.4, we conduct several experiments to compare the performance on a 3.4Ghz Intel Pentium 4, Linux system using gcc 4.0.2. Gzip and bzip2

Table 1. Performance of Analysis (seconds)

	gzip-1.3.12	ccrypt-1.7	bzip2-1.0.4
gcc	0.02	0.01	0.02
CRED	0.20	0.79	0.24
beagle	0.30	0.25	0.30

are used to decompress their tarball, and ccrypt is used to encrypt a file. Both CRED and beagle suffer from great performance loss compared with original program. Generally speaking, Beagle runs slower than CRED. However, CRED has worst performance in ccrypt, which has many pointer operations.

6   Conclusion

Unreliable software with inherent bugs may be exploited to violate security specifications, meant to be security faults. We design and implement a tool to backtrack the control-type crash. We can detect control corruption caused by stack overflow, format-string attacks or directly overwrites. It can be an effective tool to diagnose the control-type crash. It is also a good tool to detect and analyze security attacks.

Acknowledgement

This work was sponsored in part by NSC project NSC96-3114-P-001-002-Y, NSC95-2221-E-009-068-MY2, NSC 96-2221-E-001-026, and TWISC@NCTU.

References

1. Nethercote, N., Seward, J.: Valgrind: A program supervision framework. In: Sokolsky, O., Viswanathan, M. (eds.) Electronic Notes in Theoretical Computer Science, vol. 89, Elsevier, Amsterdam (2003)
2. IBM Internet Security Systems: Ibm report: Software security vulnerabilities will continue to rise in 2007,(2007)
   http://www.iss.net/about/press_center/releases/us_ibm_report.html
3. Srinivasan, S.M., Kandula, S., Andrews, C.R., Zhou, Y.: Flashback: A lightweight extension for rollback and deterministic replay for software debugging. In: USENIX Annual Technical Conference, General Track, pp. 29–44 (2004)
4. Metasploit Team: Metasploit project, http://www.metasploit.com/
5. PaX Team: Documentation for the pax project,
   http://pax.grsecurity.net/docs/index.html
6. Linn, C.M., Rajagopalan, M., Baker, S., Collberg, C., Hartman, J.H.: Protecting against unexpected system calls. In: Proceedings of the 2005 USENIX Security Symposium, pp. 239–254 (2005)

7. Barrantes, E.G., Ackley, D.H., Palmer, T.S., Stefanovic, D., Zovi, D.D.: Randomized instruction set emulation to disrupt binary code injection attacks. In: CCS 2003: Proceedings of the 10th ACM conference on Computer and communications security, pp. 281–289. ACM Press, New York (2003)
8. Sovarel, A.N., Evans, D., Paul, N.: Where's the feeb?: The effectiveness of instruction set randomization. In: Proceedings of 14th USENIX Security Symposium (2005)
9. Cowan, C., Beattie, S., Johansen, J., Wagle, P.: PointGuard^{TM}: Protecting pointers from buffer overflow vulnerabilities. In: Proceedings of the 12th USENIX Security Symposium, USENIX, pp. 91–104 (2003)
10. Valgrind Team: 2nd official valgrind survey (2005), http://valgrind.org/gallery/survey_05/summary.txt
11. Biswas, B., Mall, R.: Reverse execution of programs. ACM SIGPLAN Notices 34(4), 61–69 (1999)
12. Manevich, R., Sridharan, M., Adams, S., Das, M., Yang, Z.: Pse: explaining program failures via postmortem static analysis. In: SIGSOFT 2004/FSE-12: Proceedings of the 12th ACM SIGSOFT twelfth international symposium on Foundations of software engineering, pp. 63–72. ACM Press, New York (2004)
13. Baratloo, A., Tsai, T., Singh, N.: Libsafe: Protecting critical elements of stacks. White paper, Bell Labs, Lucent Technologies (1999)
14. Robertson, W., Kruegel, C., Mutz, D., Valeur, F.: Run-time detection of heap-based overflows. In: proceedings of 17th USENIX Large Installation Systems Administration (LISA) Conference (2003)
15. Haugh, E., Bishop, M.: Testing c programs for buffer overflow vulnerabilities. In: Proceedings of the 2003 Symposium on Networked and Distributed System Security (2003)
16. Cowan, C., Pu, C., Maier, D., Walpole, J., Bakke, P., Beattie, S., Grier, A., Wagle, P., Zhang, Q., Hinton, H.: StackGuard: Automatic adaptive detection and prevention of buffer-overflow attacks. In: Proc. 7th USENIX Security Conference, San Antonio, Texas, pp. 63–78 (1998)
17. Etoh, H.: Gcc extension for protecting applications from stack-smashing attacks, http://www.trl.ibm.com/projects/security/ssp/
18. Bray, B.: Compiler security checks in depth. Technical report, Microsoft Corporation (2002)
19. Vendicator: Stack shield: a "stack smashing" technique protection tool for linux,(2000) http://www.angelfire.com/sk/stackshield/
20. Prasad, M., cker Chiueh, T.: A binary rewriting defense against stack based overflow attacks. In: Proceedings of the USENIX Annual Technical Conference, pp. 211–224 (2003)
21. Nebenzahl, D., Sagiv, M.: Install-time vaccination of windows executables to defend against stack smashing attacks. IEEE Trans. Dependable Secur. Comput. 3(1), 78 (2006) (Senior Member-Avishai Wool)
22. Feng, H.H., Kolesnikov, O.M., Fogla, P., Lee, W., Gong, W.: Anomaly detection using call stack information. In: Proceedings of the 2003 Symposium on Security and Privacy, pp. 62–77. IEEE Computer Society Press, Los Alamitos (2003)
23. Ruwase, O., Lam, M.S.: A practical dynamic buffer overflow detector. In: Proceedings of the 11th Annual Network and Distributed System Security Symposium (2004)
24. Jones, R.W.M., Kelly, P.H.J.: Backwards-compatible bounds checking for arrays and pointers in C programs. In: AADEBUG, pp. 13–26 (1997)

BIOS Security Analysis and a Kind of Trusted BIOS

ZhenLiu Zhou and RongSheng Xu

Network Security Laboratory of High Energy Physics, CAS, China
{zhouzl,xurs}@ihep.ac.cn

Abstract. The BIOS's security threats to computer system are analyzed and security requirements for firmware BIOS are summarized in this paper. Through discussion about TCG's trust transitivity, a new approach about CRTM implementation based on BIOS is developed. In this paper, we also put forward a new trusted BIOS architecture-UTBIOS which is built on Intel Framework for EFI/UEFI. The trustworthiness of UTBIOS is based on trusted hardware TPM. In UTBIOS, trust encapsulation and trust measurement are used to construct pre-OS trust chain. Performance of trust measurement is also analyzed in the end.

Keywords: Trusted Computing, Trust Measurement, BIOS, UEFI, TPM.

1 Introduction

The traditional information security mechanisms which are built on the level of operating system can not meet the requirements of the developing information security. The security of computer system requires protection to extend to the firmware level even the hardware level. The firmware BIOS is the software that the computer processor carried out at the earliest stage, so its security will affect directly the security of the whole computer system. The traditional design of BIOS does not consider the security problem, it exists many hidden risks. In 1997, William A. Arbaugh put forward a kind of computer security bootstrap architecture AEGIS [1]. AEGIS is based on the traditional BIOS of IBM PC, it ensures the integrity of the code of the firmware BIOS and improves the security of code at BIOS bootstrap process by using authentication. But AEGIS lacks hardware protection and trusted root of hardware. As a firmware, AEGIS also can't provide extent protection for operating system. Dexter Kozen put forward a language-based approach which checks the security of control flow safety, memory safety and stack safety during compiling process to improve the code security, and using this way to inspect malicious code for open firmware [2] [3]. But the language-based method is so complex that it works poor in practice.

Without a trusted bootstrap process or trusted BIOS the operating system and application cannot be trusted since it is invoked by an un-trusted process. This paper researches how to build a new trusted firmware BIOS.

1.1 UEFI

The Extensible Firmware Interface [9], or EFI, is the layer between the Operating System and platform firmware. EFI is the new model for the interface between

S. Qing, H. Imai, and G. Wang (Eds.): ICICS 2007, LNCS 4861, pp. 427–437, 2007.

operating systems and the platform firmware running them. EFI is the data tables (containing platform specific information), boot and runtime service calls available to the operating system and its loader. The end result of EFI is a standards compliant environment for running pre-boot applications and for booting the operating system.

The EFI specification was primarily intended for the next generation of IA architecture-based computers, and is an outgrowth of the "Intel® Boot Initiative" (IBI) program that began in 1998. In 2005 the Unified EFI Forum was formed. Using the EFI 1.10 specification as the starting point, this industry group is now responsible for developing, managing and promoting the ongoing evolution of the UEFI specification [6][10].

1.2 The Intel Platform Innovation Framework for EFI

The Intel Platform Innovation Framework for EFI (referred to as "the Framework for EFI/UEFI") is a product-strength implementation of EFI and UEFI. The Framework is a set of robust architectural interfaces, implemented in C that has been designed to enable the BIOS industry to accelerate the evolution of innovative, differentiated, platform designs. The Framework is Intel's recommended implementation of the EFI Specification for platforms based on all members of the Intel® Architecture (IA) family [7].

Unlike the EFI Specification, which focuses only on programmatic interfaces for the interactions between the operating system and system firmware, the Framework is an all-new firmware implementation that has been designed to perform the full range of operations that are required to initialize the platform from power on through transfer of control to the operating system.

Figure 1 shows the phases that a platform with Framework-based firmware goes through on a cold boot.

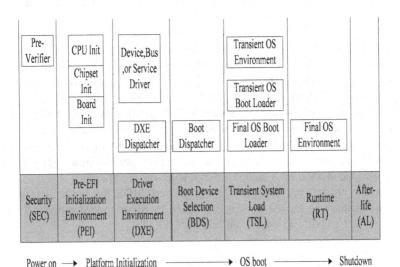

Fig. 1. Framework Firmware Phases

The SEC phase is defined as CRTM in Intel Platform Innovation Framework for EFI [7], but Intel gave an empty implementation of CRTM in Intel's EFI BIOS product. Furthermore, the smallest set of functions for CRTM is not discussed yet in Intel Platform Innovation Framework [7], and it is not sufficient to exclude PEI phase out of the CRTM. Section 4 of this paper discusses about this.

1.3 Trusted Computing

Trusted computing environment requires every component from hardware level to software level in whole system is trusted and excludes any component from system that can not be proved as trusted, such as malicious-codes, viruses, and Trojans etc. This computing and network environment is named as trusted computing ecological environment. For building this trusted computing environment, we should enhance the lower layers security of computer terminal such as hardware and firmware. In 2003, IBM, Intel, and Microsoft established international trusted computing organization TCG (Trusted Computing Group). The TCG is a not-for-profit organization formed to develop, define, and promote open standards for hardware-enabled trusted computing and security technologies, including hardware building blocks and software interfaces, across multiple platforms, peripherals, and devices.

2 Transitive Trust

The trustworthiness of trusted computing of TCG is based on the trusted hardware. The chain of trust is constructed through transitive trust between hardware and software [8] [13]. Any entities must be authenticated and validated about its integrity before be loaded and run. The process of trust transiting that is defined by TCG is illustrated in Figure 2.

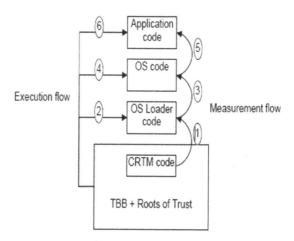

Fig. 2. Transitive Trust

TBB (Trusted Building Blocks) is the basic component of trusted computing platform. The core trusted root of TBB is the Trusted Platform Module (TPM). TPM [12] is a microcontroller chip affixed to the motherboard of computer that stores keys, digital certificates and trust measuring event logs. TPM also has computing capabilities such as digital signature, key exchange, encryption and decryption etc. Although these functions can be realized using pure software, TPM usually adopts independence hardware chips for satisfying sealed store requirement.

Core Root of Trust for Measurement (CRTM) is a trusted component which include the first instruction CPU picks up when power on. CRTM should be trusted non-conditionally.

Ideally, the CRTM is contained in TPM [13], which is illustrated as Figure 3.A. This demands CPU reset vector points to TPM, i.e., the first instruction which CPU picks and executes should be located in TPM after power on. This requires the existing computer architecture to be changed. Implementation decision of this paper is putting CRTM into BIOS firmware illustrated as Figure 3.B. Following the existing computer architecture, the first instruction picked and executed by CPU after Power on is located at address 0xFFFFFFF0 (32bit CPU) in BIOS firmware, so this implementation is more realizable. For this implementation, additional software and hardware protection should be taken to enhance the reliability and security of CRTM.

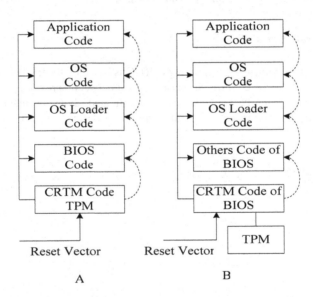

Fig. 3. Different Implementation of CRTM

3 Security Threats Against BIOS

Security threats against BIOS should be analyzed firstly to list security requirements of trusted BIOS.

For requirements of patching and updating BIOS product online, more and more mainboard manufacturers use FLASH ROM to store BIOS firmware. Using of flash ROM makes BIOS code can be read and flashed just by means of pure software without any assistant hardware device under operating system environment. So the third spiteful party can implant malicious codes such as virus and Trojan into BIOS [4]. And the increasing capacity of Flash chip also provides storage space for malicious codes.

Framework for EFI/UEFI even admits user load and execute EFI drivers or EFI applications under EFI Shell [7]. These EFI drivers or applications may come from other devices, such as USB disk or hard disk, than the Flash chip that contains the BIOS code. This causes increasing chances for malicious code being loaded and executed by BIOS.

Intruders can also juggle some bytes to destroy the integrity of BIOS code. This is a kind of denial-of-service attack that will make the computer system can not boot normally. The representative of this kind of attack is CIH virus and its variation.

4 Trusted BIOS

4.1 Security Requirements of Trusted BIOS

Trusted computing requires every step of execution can transit trust and build chain of trust based on trusted hardware from system lower-level to upper-level. These requirements emphasize the integrity protection of entity which is similar with the integrity model of Clark-Wilson [5]. Trust transitivity is implemented by trust measurement. Trust measurement is the process to verify integrity and authenticity of entities.

Trust measurement can prevent execution of illegal and malicious Option ROMs, EFI drivers and EFI applications which come from external to ensure bootstrap process only executes the code from trusted BIOS manufactures, devices driver manufactures, or trusted users. Although malicious code can be embedded into BIOS or BIOS code may be juggled, the trust measurement can prevent the execution of these illegal or malicious codes.

Trusted BIOS need to measure the following three kinds of code. One is BIOS own code of trusted BIOS except CRTM code. The second include option ROM code, EFI driver and EFI application loaded by trusted BIOS from external. The third is OS Loader Code.

When the integrity of BIOS code or data is juggled by unpredictable failure or attack, the trusted BIOS system must support the safe and reliable failure self-recovery mechanism to deal with denial-of-service attack. In order to ensure the trusted self-recovery mechanism may not be destroyed, the BIOS codes that used to implement the failure self-recovery mechanism must be protected by hardware. During the process of recovery, the recovery contents integrity must be measured too. This process is called trusted self-recovery.

4.2 Security Requirements of CRTM

As starting point of the chain of trust measurement, CRTM should be trusted unconditionally. To guarantee the source of trust transiting can be trusted, CRTM should content with four preconditions: 1) CRTM should be protected physically from writing or flashing by means of pure software; 2) CRTM should have capability of trust measuring for the next step executive code; 3) CRTM should have trusted self-recovery mechanism when others component of trusted BIOS is juggled; 4) The code of CRTM should be the minimum set which can fulfill the functions of precondition 2 and 3, including other essential initial codes for CPU, chipset and platform.

5 UTBIOS Architecture and Boot Process

UTBIOS is a trusted bios building on Intel Platform Innovation Framework for EFI/UEFI. The SEC phase is defined as CRTM by Intel in [7], but Intel gave an empty implementation of CRTM in Intel's EFI BIOS product. Furthermore, it is not sufficient to fulfill CRTM functions if PEI phase defined by Intel is excluded out of the CRTM.

Requirements of CRTM are discussed in section 4.2. Based on these requirements, this paper reconstructs the SEC and PEI phase of Intel Framework for EFI, and adds other essential functions in. In UTBIOS, Intel's phase SEC and PEI are combined together to form CRTM. To fulfill trust measuring, hash computing code and TPM driver are embraced in CRTM. Here TPM must be driven as much as early to satisfy the demands of integrity verification and event logging. USB driver is immigrating from DXE phase into CRTM so that when self-recovery code is invoked, the USB storage device can be accessed. So CRTM of UTBIOS is constructed from following five parts: initial code for CPU, chipset, memory and stack; TPM Driver code; hash computing code; self-recovery code including USB driver; PEI Core Code. In UTBIOS, CRTM is

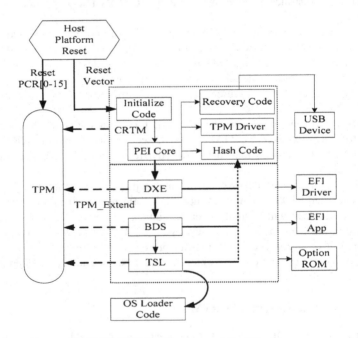

Fig. 4. UTBIOS Architecture and Boot Process

stored at the highest 64KB block of the flash ROM, and is protected physically to avoid being rewritten or flashed using pure software.

Figure 4 shows UTBIOS architecture and boot process.

The boot process is as following: 1) Initialize CPU, chipset, memory and Stack, build the environment of executing language C code; 2) Enter into PEI core, initialize TPM, install TPM protocol, self-recovery protocol including USB driver and Hash Protocol; 3) PEI core measures trust of DXE core, saves trust measuring event log [14][15]. If successful, loads and executes DXE core, else enters into trusted self-recovery mode; 4) According to the requirements of executing environment, DXE core loads internal or external EFI Drivers, EFI Applications, or Option ROM of other devices. During this procedure, DXE core measures trust of those loaded code and saves trust measuring event logs. If successful, loads and executes code, else enters into trusted self-recovery mode; 5) DXE core measures trust of BDS code and saves trust measuring event log. If successful, loads and executes BDS core, else enters into trusted self-recovery mode; 6) According to the requirements of executing environment, BDS core loads Option ROM of boot device, measures trust of the code and saves trust measuring event log. If successful, loads and executes the code, else enters into trusted self-recovery mode; 7) BDS core measures trust of TSL code, saves trust measuring event log. If successful, loads and executes TSL code, else enters into trust self-recovery mode; 8) TSL core measures trust of OS Loader code, saves trust measuring event log. If successful, loads and executes OS Loader code, else enters into trusted self-recovery mode.

When finishing OS loader trust measurement, the UTBIOS transfers system control to OS Loader and the trust measurement of OS Kernel will be measured by OS Loader. As so far, the pre-OS chain of trust is constructed successfully.

After enter into trusted self-recovery mode, the self-recovery protocol that installed in CRTM should be executed and with responsibility for reading trusted BIOS image except CRTM from USB device and writing it back to flash ROM. During the process of trusted self-recovery, the loaded BIOS image need to be trust measured.

6   UTBIOS Trust Encapsulation and Trust Measurement

6.1   Principle of Trust Encapsulation and Trust Measurement

UTBIOS uses digital signature and message digest for trust measurement of various entities. In the process of producing the UTBIOS, vendors are required to bind each component together with the digital signature of message digest of the component. This procedure is called trust encapsulation. All components except CRTM are required to be encapsulated. Trust measurement is the reversed procedure of trust encapsulation. In trust measuring procedure, digital signature is decrypted to get the message digest being signed, and then message digest of the entity being measured is calculated again and compared with the decrypting result to verify the integrity of the entity. The public and private keys used in this procedure are corresponding unique, so it is feasible to judge whether the entity is come from trusted owner or not, and whether the entity is juggled or not. The principle of trust encapsulation and trust measurement is illustrated in Figure 5 and Figure 6.

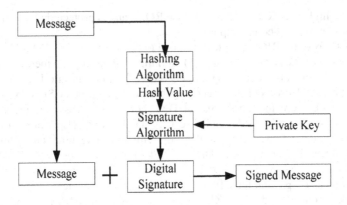

Fig. 5. Trust Encapsulation

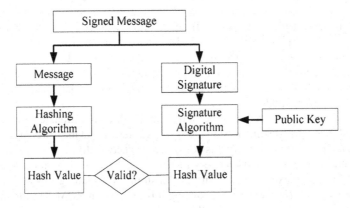

Fig. 6. Trust Measurement

Think about a kind of attack, attackers sign malicious code using their own private key, and replace the trusted BIOS verification public key with their own public key. Then when the malicious code is trust measured, the measuring result would be successful. In this situation, the attackers can embed malicious code into BIOS and run them successfully. In order to prevent this kind of attack, the public key, which is used for trust measurement, can not be stored at the same place with measured module, and should be stored sealed. The best way to prevent this attack occurring is storing public key in TPM. In the trust measurement process, the encapsulated signature of the measured entity is taken apart and sent to TPM, and the verification computing is finished in TPM.

6.2 Trust Initialization

Legacy Option ROM and OS Loader Code maybe not be encapsulated and signed when the system executed at the first time the computer is used by user, so there need a trust initialization procedure when the system run firstly. Following is the way of UTBIOS trust initialization. UTBIOS would self-create a couple of keys automatically when the system runs at first. UTBIOS computes the hash value of exterior entity and uses the private key to sign the hash value of the entity, and discards the private key after the signature. The public key would be sealed and protected by TPM, and the digital signatures of the external entities are preserved in BIOS Flash's NVRAM data area. Once the trust initialization finished, subsequent bootstrap process after that can use the initializing result (including the public key in TPM and the digital signatures in NVRAM) to measure the trust of exterior entities such as unsigned Option ROM and OS Loader.

On the platform in which all exterior entities are signed, there is no need for using trust initialization.

7 Performance

Comparing UTBIOS with Legacy BIOS, the performance of bootstrap speed is affected mainly by trust measurement. The main operations of trust measurement include hash value computing and signature verification. The SHA-1 hash algorithm and RSA Verification whose key length is 2048bits are used in UTBIOS. Signing a message takes much longer than verifying the signature does, but in the process of bootstrap of UTBIOS, there is only verification operation, no signing operation.

We can compute the estimated increased extra time consumed by trust measurement in UTBIOS using following equation:

$$T = T(L1) + T(L2)$$

$$T(L1) = \sum_{i=1}^{n} t(m_i) = \sum_{i=1}^{n} (t(H(i)) + t(V(i)))$$

$$T(L2) = t(H(L2)) + t(V(L2))$$

T (L1) is the total time that consumed by UTBIOS to load the EFI Driver, EFI Application and Option ROM for internal and external entities. T (L2) is the time consumed by trusted BIOS to measure OS Loader Code. t (mi) is the time to measuring the ith entity. t (H()) means the time to compute SHA-1 digest for the ith entity, t (V()) means signature verification time of the ith entity.

On the machine with 1GHz Pentium CPU, creating SHA-1 digest for 1Mbytes message needs 13ms. Table 1 is the time used for SHA-1 algorithm and public keys with different length to check 1500000 Bytes data for one time [17].

Table 1. Digital signature verification times

Hash function	Public key sizes(bits)	Verification time(seconds)
SHA-1	512	0.093
SHA-1	768	0.093
SHA-1	1024	0.094
SHA-1	2048	0.098

SINOSUN SSX3B TPM is used in the implementation, the verification time for 2048 bit of SSX3B TPM is less than 40ms [16].

For the ith entity with 1Mbytes length:

t (H(i))=0.013 seconds
t (V(i))=0.040 seconds

This means the Trust Measurement of measuring 1Mbytes entity costs 0.053 seconds. In UTBIOS, the sum of entity is less than 100 and the size of entity is less than 0.5 Mbytes. So T (L1) is estimated to be 2.7 seconds. The size of OS Loader Code is always less than 10MBytes, the time required to verify OS Loader is about:

t (H(L2))=0.13 seconds
t (V(L2))=0.40 seconds

And T (L2) is estimated to be 0.53 seconds. The T is estimated to be 3.23 seconds. Actually, the sum of entities and it size that needed to be measured by UTBIOS are far less than the maximum number used to be estimated; thereby the actual increase extra time is less than this estimated time.

Experiment results show that the time of UTBIOS boot without Trust Measurement is 11 seconds and the time of UTBIOS boot with Trust Measurement is 16 seconds. Because of device accessed and data exchanged, the actual Trust Measurement extra time is about 4 seconds, which is longer than computed estimated time 3.23 seconds.

8   Conclusions

Without changing the current computer architecture, BIOS should become the Core Root of Trusted Measurement and the root of transitive trust. Based on this idea, this paper proposed a trusted BIOS architecture, implemented a trusted BIOS-UTBIOS which is build on Intel Innovation framework for EFI/UEFI. UTBIOS can not only defend against effectively the security threats faced by firmware, but also can construct pre-OS trust chain successfully. To build a trusted computing terminal and trusted network connection, there have two problems to be solved next: one is to establish practicable trust management mode, the other is to construct post-OS chain of trust.

References

1. Arbaugh, W.A., Farber, D.J., Smith, J.M.: A Secure and Reliable Bootstrap Architecture. In: Procedings, 1997 IEEE Symposium on Security and Privacy (4-7 May 1997) pp. 65–71 (1997)
2. Kozen, D.: Efficient Code Certification. Technical Report98-1661,Computer Science Department, Cornell University (January 1998)
3. Adelstein, F., Stillerman, M., Kozen, D.: Malicious Code Detection for Open Firmware. In: Computer Security Applications Conference. Proceedings 18th Annual (9-13 Decembr 2002) pp. 403–412 (2002)
4. Heasman, J.: Implementing and Detecting an ACPI BIOS Rootkit, http://www.ngssoftware.com/jh_bhf2006.pdf

5. Clark, D.D., Wilson, D.R., Comparison, A.: A Comparison of Commercial and Military Computer Security Policies. In: Proceedings of the 1987 IEEE Symposium on Security and Privacy, IEEE Computer Society Press, Los Alamitos (1987)
6. The Unified, E.F.I.: Forum. Unified Extensible Firmware Interface Specification Version 2.0 (January 31, 2006), http://www.uefi.org
7. Intel Corporation. Intel Platform Innovation Framework for EFI Architecture Specification Version 0.9 (September 16, 2003)
8. TCG. TCG Infrastructure Architecture Version 1.0.
   https://www.trustedcomputinggroup.org/specs/
9. TianoCore, https://www.tianocore.org/
10. UEFI, https://www.uefi.org/
11. Intel Corporation. Intel Platform Innovation Framework for EFI Firmware File System Specification Version 0.9 (September 16, 2003),
    http://www.intel.com/technology/framework/
12. TCG. TPM Main Specification Part 1,2,3 Version 1.2 (March 29, 2006)
    https://www.trustedcomputinggroup.org/specs/
13. TCG. TCG Specification Architecture Overview, https://www.trustedcomputinggroup.org
14. TCG.TCG EFI Platform Version 1.0 Final Revision 1.00,
    https://www.trustedcomputinggroup.org
15. TCG.TCG EFI Protocol Version 1.0 Final Revision 1.00,
    https://www.trustedcomputinggroup.org
16. Sinosun. SSX35, T.P.M.: Datasheet Version 1.2
17. Menasce, D.A.: Security Performance[J]. IEEE Internet Computing 7(3), 84–87 (2003)

Collecting Autonomous Spreading Malware Using High-Interaction Honeypots

Jianwei Zhuge[1], Thorsten Holz[2], Xinhui Han[1], Chengyu Song[1], and Wei Zou[1]

[1] Institute of Computer Science and Technology,
Peking University, China
{zhugejianwei|hanxinhui|songchengyu|zouwei}@icst.pku.edu.cn
[2] Laboratory for Dependable Distributed Systems,
University of Mannheim, Germany
holz@informatik.uni-mannheim.de

Abstract. Autonomous spreading malware in the form of worms or bots has become a severe threat in today's Internet. Collecting the sample as early as possible is a necessary precondition for the further treatment of the spreading malware, e.g., to develop antivirus signatures. In this paper, we present an integrated toolkit called *HoneyBow*, which is able to collect autonomous spreading malware in an automated manner using *high-interaction honeypots*. Compared to low-interaction honeypots, HoneyBow has several advantages due to a wider range of captured samples and the capability of collecting malware which propagates by exploiting new vulnerabilities. We validate the properties of HoneyBow with experimental data collected during a period of about nine months, in which we collected thousands of malware binaries. Furthermore, we demonstrate the capability of collecting new malware via a case study of a certain bot.

Keywords: Honeypots, Intrusion Detection Systems, Malware.

1 Introduction

Since the outbreak of the Code Red worm in 2001, malware has become one of the severest threats to the Internet. Especially autonomous spreading malware in the form of worms or bots that propagates over the Internet and infects thousands of computers all over the world in days or even minutes is a problem. In the form of *botnets*, the comprised computers can even be organized into networks that can be remotely controlled by an attacker, and cause lots of harms following the attackers' purposes [14].

In order to deal effectively and efficiently with the threat associated with malware, CERTs, antivirus vendors, and security researchers need to obtain a sample of the actual malware as quickly as possible in the early stage of propagation. This sample can then be analyzed deeply, e.g., to study the propagation and infection mechanism, in order to develop accurate detection signatures or an appropriate treatment strategy. Conventional sample collection approaches include extraction of the binary from an infected machine, reports from customers, exchange between AV vendors, and similar ways. These conventional approaches generally need human interaction. With the increasing

S. Qing, H. Imai, and G. Wang (Eds.): ICICS 2007, LNCS 4861, pp. 438–451, 2007.

birth rate of new malware and the speeding up of the malware propagation, e.g., in the case of the Slammer worm [6], these malware collection approaches with human interaction are always too late for timely incident response. Therefore, we need a completely automated malware collection scheme to catch these trends.

As a new active attack-decoying technology, *honeypots* have been used in the domain of Internet security threats measurement. A honeypot is defined as an information system resource whose value lies in unauthorized or illicit use of that resource [13]. A honeypot has no production usage, therefore, every access launched by the attackers – including automated malware – can be captured and studied in detail. In general, honeypots can be distinguished into two different types: *low-interaction* and *high-interaction* honeypots. Low-interaction honeypots offer limited interaction level to the attackers, commonly through simulation (or emulation) of network services or operation systems. Therefore, they can often only lure automated attacks, and can be identified by a human attackers easily. A popular example of this kind of honeypots is *honeyd* [8]. High-interaction honeypots, on the other hand, use *real* systems for attackers to interact with. This type of honeypots is commonly more complex, furthermore deployment and maintenance often takes more time. In addition, more risks are involved when deploying high-interaction honeypots since an attacker can get complete control of the honeypot and abuse it, e.g., to attack other systems on the Internet. Thus it is necessary to introduce and implement *data control* mechanisms to prevent the abuse of honeypots. The most common used setup for high-interaction honeypots are GenIII honeynets [2].

In this paper, we introduce the *HoneyBow* toolkit, an automated malware collection system based on the high-interaction honeypot principle. The HoneyBow toolkit integrates three malware collection tools called *MwWatcher*, *MwFetcher*, and *MwHunter*. All of them use different techniques and strategies to detect and collect malware samples, in order to achieve a comprehensive collection efficiency. HoneyBow inherits the high degree expressiveness of high-interaction honeypots: it can be constructed upon various customized honeynet deployments, using the true vulnerable services as victims to lure malware infections, but not emulated vulnerable services. Thus HoneyBow is capable of collecting zero-day malware even if the vulnerability exploited during the propagation phase is unknown to the community before the malware outburst. Furthermore, we do not need to investigate the details of the vulnerabilities and implement an emulated version of the vulnerable services, which is commonly required for low-interaction honeypots. Thus the deployment of the HoneyBow toolkit is more flexible and easy. On the other hand, HoneyBow has its limitation in the scalability compared to low-interaction honeypots. Therefore, we combine HoneyBow and the low-interaction honeypot *Nepenthes* [1] to build an integrated malware collection system.

This paper is organized as follows: Section 2 describes the related work in the area of honeypot and automated malware collection research. Section 3 introduces the HoneyBow toolkit in details, discusses the advantages and limitations of our approach, and shows how to integrate Nepenthes, HoneyBow and the GenIII Honeynet to achieve a fully-automated and efficient distributed malware collection solution. Section 4 compares the malware collection efficiency between Nepenthes and HoneyBow. Finally, we conclude the paper and give the further research directions in Section 5.

2 Related Work

Researchers have developed several methods and tools for malware sample collection based on honeypot techniques, among them the Nepenthes platform [1]. Nepenthes uses the principle of low-interaction honeypots: it *emulates* the vulnerable parts of network services to lure and collect malware samples which attempt to infect the host by exploiting these vulnerable services. As the comparable reference to our HoneyBow toolkit, we compare the advantages, limitations, and the practical effects between them throughout the paper. Using high-interaction honeypots, Levine et al. collected and analyzed rootkits manually [5]. This paper is the first to introduce an automatic malware collection schemes based on high-interaction honeypot principle. Furthermore, we are interested in collecting all types of autonomous spreading malware, i.e., worms, bots, and other kinds of malware, in an automated manner.

Antivirus vendors such as Symantec Inc. developed malware collection tools based on the honeypot technology, and present their measurement status reports on the prevalent malware [12]. However, the actual methods and implementations used for these projects are usually not open to the community due to the commercial benefits.

The Honeynet Project develops the GenIII honeynet [2], which composes the foundation of our deployment. We use a GenIII honeynet as a building block of our system. Portokalidis et al. introduce *Argos* [7], a containment high-interaction honeypot environment to study malware as well as human-generated attacks. Argos is built upon the Qemu x86-emulator and is capable of detecting exploitation with the help of a technique called *taint tracing*. In addition, the tool generates intrusion detection signatures for a detected attack. Argos has not implemented special mechanisms for malware sample collection yet, but the principles behind the HoneyBow toolkit can be integrated into Argos. The Potemkin virtual honeyfarm by Vrable et al. exploits virtual machines, aggressive memory sharing, and late binding of resources to emulate more than 64,000 high-interaction honeypots using ten physical servers [16]. Although the implementation of Potemkin is not publicly available, and there are only preliminary results for the scalability available, it shows a promising approach for improving the scalability limitation of high-interaction honeypots deployment, which can be used by the HoneyBow toolkit to overcome its limitations in the area of scalability.

A study similar to ours own was conducted by Goebel et. al [3]. They collected 2,034 valid, unique malware binaries using Nepenthes listening on about 16,000 IPs within a university environment for a period of eight weeks, and present the measurement and analysis results of autonomous spreading malware. We collect two orders of magnitude more malware binaries by combining Nepenthes and HoneyBow. Furthermore, our study lasts for nine months, thus we can study long-term effects and the temporal changes of malware.

Rajab et al. also use Nepenthes to collect spreading bot instances and focus their work on botnets [10]. To support distributed deployment on the PlanetLab testbed, they deploy a modified version of the Nepenthes platform. We propose a standalone structure integrating Nepenthes, HoneyBow and the GenIII Honeynet for distributed honeynet deployment, and have constructed a widely distributed honeynet on the public Internet of China, which contains up to 50 high-interaction honeypots located at 17 nodes now. The presented results are based on the data collected by such an infrastructure.

3   The HoneyBow Toolkit

In this section, we introduce the HoneyBow toolkit in detail. We present the individual building blocks HoneyBow is based on, and show how the high-interaction honeypot principle can be used to construct an automated malware collection approach, especially for collecting malware samples that use unknown or new vulnerabilities.

A high-interaction honeypot is a conventional computer system, deployed to be probed, attacked, and compromised [13]. Such a system has no production usage in the network and no regularly active users. Thus it should neither have any unusual activities on the system nor generate any network traffic. These assumptions aid in attack detection: every interaction with the honeypot is suspicious by definition. HoneyBow uses this idea and is an approach to collect malware with high-interaction honeypots. Compared to Nepenthes, this has the advantage that we do not need to emulate any vulnerable services: we can use a conventional machine, patch it to an arbitrary patch-level, deploy the honeypot, and wait for successful compromises. The key concept is that a malware binary usually propagates itself through the network and installs a copy of itself into the victim's file system after a successful compromise. If we thus monitor the network flow stream and the changes to the file system, we can detect an infection attempt and also obtain a binary copy of the malware sample.

3.1   Architecture of the HoneyBow Toolkit

The HoneyBow toolkit uses similar concept as the GenIII honeynet architecture, the most common setup for high-interaction honeypots used nowadays. In the honeynet research area, there are two well-known methods to deploy high-interaction honeynets: the first is called *physical honeynets* and the second one is called *virtual honeynets* [9]. Physical honeynets use normal machines for deploying high-interaction honeypots, and use an actual networking device to link them together into a honeynet. In contrast to this, virtual honeynets use virtual machines (VMs) like VMware or Virtual PC to set up virtual honeypots. Obviously, virtual honeypots have advantages due to lower deployment costs and easier management compared to physical honeynet. On the other hand, this kind of honeypots also has several disadvantages, e.g., in the area of performance degradation, single point of failure, and higher risk of fingerprinting.

The HoneyBow toolkit supports both methods of high-interaction honeynet deployment. As depicted in Figure 1, the HoneyBow toolkit consists of three malware collection tools: *MwWatcher*, *MwFetcher*, and *MwHunter*, all of which implement different malware collection strategies. Additionally, two tool called *MwSubmitter* and *MwCollector* support distributed deployment and malware collection.

The individual building blocks of HoneyBow perform the following tasks:

- MwWatcher is one of the three malware collection tools implemented in the Honey-Bow toolkit. It is based on the essential feature of honeypot – no production activity – and watches the file system for suspicious activity caused by malware infections in real time. The tool is executed on a high-interaction honeypot and exploits a characteristic feature of propagating malware: when some malware successfully exploits a vulnerable service and infects the honeypot, the malware sample will

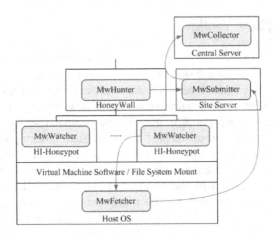

Fig. 1. Schematic Overview of the HoneyBow architecture

commonly transfer a copy of itself to the victim and stored it in the file system. MwWatcher will then detect this change of the filesystem and catch a binary copy of the malware sample. This sample is moved to a hidden directory and waits for further collection by another tool called MwFetcher.

- MwFetcher is the second malware collection tool in the toolkit. This tool runs periodically on the host OS, issues a command to shutdown the honeypot OS, and generates a listing of all files from the hard disk image of the honeypot system. Then this listing is compared to a file list generated formerly from the clean system, and all added or modified files are extracted since they could be artifacts of successful infections. The samples collected by MwWatcher are also extracted and aggregated with the MwFetcher results. After sample extracting, MwFetcher will activate a restore procedure which reverts the honeypot OS to a clean state.
- MwHunter is the third malware collection tool in the toolkit and it is based on the PE Hunter [18] tool. MwHunter is implemented as a dynamic preprocessor plugin for *Snort*, an open source network intrusion detection system, and can be integrated into the Snort instance running at inline mode on the Honeywall of a standard GenIII honeynet [15]. MwHunter relies on the `stream4` and `stream_reassembly` preprocessor build in the Snort daemon: it extracts Windows executables in PE format from the reassembled network stream and dumps them to the disk. The tool tries to find a PE header based on the DOS header magic `MZ` and PE header magic `PE|00|`, and then uses a simple heuristic to calculate the file length. Starting at the position of the header, the resulting number of bytes is then dumped to a file. When an executable has been successfully identified, MwHunter will treat the captured binary as a malware sample due to the properties of the honeynet environment. MwHunter generates an alert including the five tuple *(source IP, source port, IP protocol, destination IP, destination port)* of the network stream, timestamp, and MD5sum of the captured sample.

In a virtual honeynet deployment, apparently, the host OS refers to the operation system where the virtual machine software is installed, and the restore procedure can be easily implemented using the revert functionality that almost all of the virtual machines such as VMware support. But in a physical honeypot deployment, generally, we need to manually reinstall the operation system or restore the file system using system management software such as Norton Ghost. To achieve automated malware collection and honeypot operation, we introduce a full-automatic system restore procedure for physical honeypots based on the *IPMI* (Intelligent Platform Management Interface[1]) and *PXE* (Preboot Execution Environment [4]) protocol. A schematic overview of the system is given in Figure 2. In a physical honeynet deployment, the host OS refers to the little customized Linux kernel which is downloaded and activated via the PXE protocol. MwFetcher operates after step 4 (load base OS) and before step 5 (download the backup honeypot OS image).

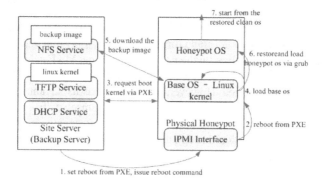

Fig. 2. Full-automatic system restore procedure for physical honeypots

MwSubmitter and MwCollector support a distributed deployment: multiple Mw-Fetcher instances can be deployed in a distributed honeynet and each instance sends the collected information to MwSubmitter. This tool monitors the capture logs of the different malware collection tools and the collected binaries, and submits new collected samples to MwCollector. MwCollector is a network daemon at a central malware collection server, accepting MwSubmitter's sample submissions, and storing all collected information and samples in a central database.

Because malware for the Windows operating system constitutes the vast majority of malware in the wild, we implemented the HoneyBow toolkit for now only for Windows. For other platforms such as Linux or FreeBSD, the mechanism of real-time file system monitoring behind MwWatcher, and executables identification and extraction behind MwHunter, can also be implemented. The implementation details differ, but the principle remains the same.

3.2 Comparison of Advantages and Limitations

The HoneyBow toolkit integrates three malware collection tools using different malware identification and collection techniques: MwWatcher runs on the honeypot and

---

[1] www.intel.com/design/servers/ipmi/

adopts real-time file system monitoring to detect and collect the changed files as malware samples. MwFetcher is executed periodically on the host OS and uses cross-view file system list comparing technique to extract added/modified files. MwHunter is intended to sit inline at the network level in front of high-interaction honeypots, and it can identify and extract Windows executables from the network stream. Due to the nature of honeynet environments, the resulting files collected by these three tools can be treated as malware samples with a low false negative rate.

Although these three tools achieve the same objective, each has their own advantages and limitations when comparing them with one another. We summarize and list the comparison results in Table 1. MwWatcher can be easily detected and bypassed if the malware implements some evading detection mechanisms. In contrast, MwFetcher and MwHunter operate outside the honeypot box and are thus hard to detect by malware. As MwWatcher and MwHunter monitor the file system and the network, respectively, in real time, they can both deal with temporary files which delete themselves after execution. MwHunter can even capture some forms of memory-only malware samples which do not store a copy of themselves on the permanent storage. MwFetcher can not collect temporary files because they have been already eliminated when MwFetcher compares the listing after a certain period. However, MwFetcher has its advantages on detecting concealed malware, including rootkits, which protect themselves from exposing to the application level APIs and tools. MwHunter relies on the signatures of Windows executables during the transmission through the network: if the executable is compressed, encrypted, or encoded, then they can not be detected by MwHunter.

Table 1. Comparison of advantages and limitations among the three different HoneyBow tools

	Collection technique	Advantages	Limitations
MwWatcher	Real-time file system monitoring	Can deal with temporary files	Can be easily detected by malware
MwFetcher	Cross-view file system list comparing	Can deal with concealed malware, such as rootkits; Hard to be detected by malware	Can not collect temporary files; Loss of exact time and attacker information
MwHunter	Identification and extraction from network streams	Can deal with temporary files and some memory-only samples; Passive, hard to be detected by malware	Can not deal with some specially crafted binaries, e.g., self-extracting archives

Since these three tools have their unique advantages and limitations, we integrate them into the HoneyBow toolkit, and hope to achieve better coverage of collecting autonomous spreading malware.

Compared with the Nepenthes platform based on the low-interaction honeypot principle, the HoneyBow toolkit has several advantages. First, HoneyBow is capable of collecting zero-day malware samples which exploit unknown vulnerabilities. This feature is significant for CERTs and AV vendors, since they can then obtain a malware sample in the early stage of their propagation. For example, we could capture samples of bots that use new attack vectors (e.g., MocBot which uses MS06-040 for propagation [11], see Section 4.2) which were not caught by Nepenthes. Second, the high-interaction approach taken by HoneyBow does not need any signature of the malware, including no detailed information about the exploited vulnerability. Thus we do not need to investigate the specific vulnerability and implement an emulated version of the vulnerable service. The deployment and maintenance of the HoneyBow toolkit is quite easy. Third, we can customize the patch level, installed network services, and existing vulnerabilities of the deployed high-interaction honeypots, to satisfy the different requirements of malware collection. Such a customization does not need to modify or re-configure the HoneyBow toolkit and demonstrates the flexibility and easy-of-use of the tool. Fourth, HoneyBow has the capability of collecting the second-stage samples (and possibly even more stages) downloaded by the initial malware.

On the other hand, HoneyBow has several limitations: First, the scalability of HoneyBow is limited. Although we can assign several IP addresses to a high-interaction honeypot to enlarge the measurement scope and improve the malware collection effect, HoneyBow lacks a large scalability compared with Nepenthes, which can emulate more than 16,000 different IP addresses on a single physical machine. With techniques similar to the ones used by Potemkin [16], this could be addressed in the future. Second, HoneyBow relies on special hardware conditions (IPMI-enabled motherboard) when deployed in the physical honeynet mode, and the cost of such a hardware is relative high. When deployed in the virtual honeynet mode, the malware sample can detect the virtual environment (e.g. VMware) and the presence of MwWatcher in order to evade the collection and analysis. Third, HoneyBow can only collect malware samples that remotely exploit security vulnerabilities and infect the honeypot successfully by sending a binary to the victim. Malware that propagates via e-mail or via drive-by downloads can not be captured with such an approach.

Since both malware collection tools have their own advantages and limitations, we should combine these two different malware collection methods adequately, exploiting their advantages while restraining their limitations, to achieve the best malware collection efficiency and coverage.

3.3 Integration of HoneyBow, Nepenthes, and the GenIII Honeynet

To measure security threats on the Internet, we have constructed a distributed honeynet based on the architecture shown in Figure 3. One of the most important objectives of the distributed honeynet is to collect autonomous spreading malware samples in the early stage of their propagation. Furthermore, we want to measure the prevalence of specific malware samples. To achieve these objectives, we integrate HoneyBow, Nepenthes, and the GenIII Honeynet into one architecture. Each honeynet site contains two physical machines: one is used to deploy a standard GenIII virtual honeynet setup based on VMware, and the other takes the role of a *Site Server*. This machine is responsible for the storage, upload, and analysis of the collected samples and attack data.

The HoneyBow tools are installed at different components of the honeynet site: MwWatcher runs on the honeypot guest OS. We use both Windows 2000 and Windows XP as guest OS, in order to cover the two common OS installed on end-user machines. MwFetcher is executed on the host machine of the virtual honeynet, and MwHunter is placed on the Honeywall in front of the honeypots. In order to integrate

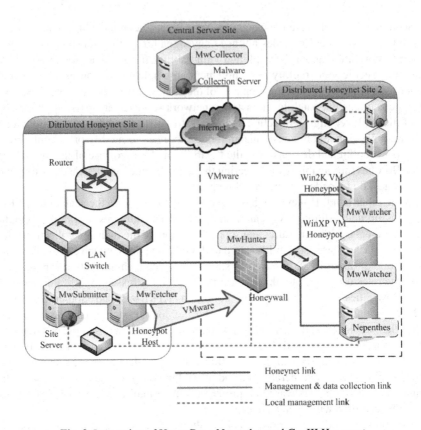

Fig. 3. Integration of HoneyBow, Nepenthes and GenIII Honeynet

malware collection methods based on the low-interaction honeypot principle, we install
Nepenthes in a Linux VM and place it behind the Honeywall. All of the malware samples collected by MwWatcher, MwFetcher, MwHunter, and Nepenthes are aggregated
to an NFS-mounted directory on the Site Server. From there, all samples are submitted
by MwSubmitter to the MwCollector located at a central server site.

4   Collection Results of Autonomous Spreading Malware

In this section, we present the results of collecting and analyzing autonomous spreading
malware with the help of a widely distributed honeynet deployment containing 17 sites
and up to 50 honeypots around the public Internet of China. Each site is constructed
based on the topological structure shown in Figure 3, except the MwHunter tool because
it was integrated in the architecture just recently. Our collection and analysis results are
based on nine months in-the-wild measurements, which took place during October 2006
and June 2007.

4.1   Statistical Results

With the help of the distributed honeynet setup integrating Nepenthes, HoneyBow and
GenIII Honeynet, we had a *hit count* of about 800,000. The hit count specifies the
total number of downloaded samples, i.e., how often we successfully captured a binary,
disregarding multiple copies of the same binary. As a metric for uniqueness we use
the MD5sum. While this has same problems, e.g., small changes in a binary result in a
completely different MD5sum, it allows us to quickly determine whether or not we have
seen a particular binary before. Using this metric, we collected nearly 100,000 unique
sample binaries during the measurement period of nine months.

This means that we have on average about 2,800 collected and 360 new unique binaries per day. The large amount of collected binaries is to some degree due to our weak
measurement of uniqueness: by using MD5 hash values, even slight differences in two
binaries cause a completely different hash value. This implies that if we capture a polymorphic worm, we can not efficiently differentiate different versions of the same binary.
As part of our future work, we plan to develop better metrics to differentiate between
malware binaries.

All collected binaries were analyzed with *MwScanner*, a tool that combines nine
common antivirus (AV) engines, to identify the known malware variations and families, and to examine the detection rates of these AV engines. Using MwScanner, each
collected sample is scheduled to be scanned several times: immediately after collection,
after 1 day, after 3 days, after 2 weeks, and finally after 1 month. These results allow us
to study the response rates of common AV engines to the threat brought by autonomous
spreading malware. In general, the detection rates are rather low. The detection rates
vary between 50.4% and 92.8% for the nine engines in the first scan. Even the best
engine in our test detected only 93.7% of the samples in the last scan one whole month
after the samples was collected.

Table 2 summarizes the comparison of collected malware samples for both Nepenthes and HoneyBow. On average, Nepenthes collects 1,539 samples per day and
HoneyBow 1,359, thus Nepenthes captures slightly more samples per day. Nepenthes
has predominance on the number of captures because of their capacity to capture unsuccessful infections and some forms of exclusive samples. However, the situation changes
when comparing the number of unique samples per day: We collect about 63.7 unique
samples with Nepenthes and 296 unique samples with HoneyBow per day. HoneyBow
thus yields a higher number of unique malware samples than Nepenthes, mainly because it does not rely on known vulnerabilities. With the help of MwScanner, we are
able to compare the numbers of collected malware variations and families between Nepenthes and HoneyBow: We use the output of an AV-engine to assign a given malware
sample to a malware family and malware variant. For example, if binary *A* has the AV-
label *Trojan.Delf-1470* and binary *B* the label *Trojan.Delf-142*, both belong to the same
family, but are different variants. As shown in Table 2, during the measurement period,
Nepenthes collected 467 different malware variations of 64 families, but HoneyBow
achieved 1,011 variations of 171 families.

In Figure 4, we illustrate the temporal distribution of hit counts and number of unique
samples captured over the period of nine months. The hit count in Figure 4(a) shows
that both tools collect a comparable amount of binary samples per day, disregarding

Table 2. Comparison of total / average number of collected malware samples for number of captures, binaries, variants, and families between Nepenthes and HoneyBow

	Captures (hit count)	Binaries	Variants	Families
Nepenthes (Total)	427,829	17,722	467	64
HoneyBow (Total)	376,456	82,137	1,011	171
Nepenthes (Average per day)	1,539	63.7	15.0	8.2
HoneyBow (Average per day)	1,359	296.0	17.8	10.6

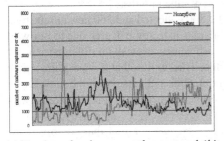 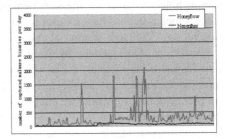

(a) Number of malware samples captured (*hit count*) per day

(b) Number of unique malware binaries captured per day

Fig. 4. Comparison of malware collection effects between Nepenthes and HoneyBow

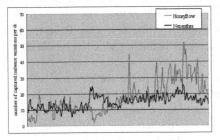 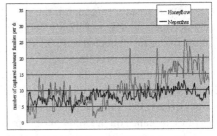

(a) Number of different malware variants captured per day

(b) Number of different malware families captured per day

Fig. 5. Comparison of malware collection effects between Nepenthes and HoneyBow

duplicate copies. Figure 4(b) shows clearly the advantages of HoneyBow for collecting unique binaries: on almost all days, we collect more unique binaries with HoneyBow than with Nepenthes.

The spikes in Figure 4(b) (and also Figure 4(a)) are mainly caused by polymorphic worms: in each iteration, such a worm changes certain parts of itself and thus the MD5 hash value is different. Due to our metric of uniqueness, a polymorphic worm thus generates many hits and a large amount of unique binaries. In the wild, we commonly see polymorphic worms like *All.Aple* which cause such spikes.

In Figure 5, we illustrate the temporal distribution of number of different malware variants and families captured over the period of nine months. In both areas, HoneyBow usually outperform Nepenthes. This is mainly due to the fact that Nepenthes relies on static signatures of how to respond to an incoming attack. If a malware binary uses a vulnerability that Nepenthes does not know how to emulate (or sometimes even a slight variation of a known vulnerability), the tool can not capture a copy of this particular binary. On the other hand, HoneyBow follows the high-interaction principle and uses a real system, thus the actual system replies to an incoming attack and we do not need to emulate a vulnerability.

4.2 MocBot Case

With the help of an anecdotal report, we want to show how HoneyBow is also able to capture malware samples that use an unknown or recent vulnerability.

During the MocBot outbreak in August 2006 [11], our distributed honeynet deployment and the HoneyBow toolkit played an important role. In the early stages of the MocBot outbreak, our HoneyBow system captured the sample for the first time at 03:54 pm of August 13 (Beijing time - CST). After the MocBot sample was downloaded and executed on the high-interaction honeypot, it connected to an IRC-based botnet. The Command and Control (C&C) server used the domain bniu.househot.com, and the bot joined an obfuscated channel to accept the botherder's commands. After several hours, the MocBot sample received an obfuscated command which could be decoded as e http://media.pixpond.com/[removed].jpg. The bot was thus instructed to download and execute a file from a remote location. This command installed a second-stage infection Trojan named *Ranky*. As shown in Table 3, HoneyBow collected both samples in a very early time. MwScanner was executed by schedule at 04:10 am with latest signature base: none of the AV engines was able to identify the MocBot sample.

Table 3. MocBot samples captured by the HoneyBow toolkit in its early stages of propagation

Sample MD5	Family	Timestamp (CST)	Honeypot
9928a1e6601cf00d0b7826d13fb556f0	IRCBot	2006-08-13 03:54	vmpot.2k
4e618ca11b22732f412bafdac9028b19	Ranky	2006-08-13 11:14	vmpot.2k

Since the exploited vulnerability (MS06-040) was not implemented in Nepenthes (and is not implemented as of today), this tool can not deal with malware that exploits this particular vulnerability. After a deep analysis of the captured sample binary, CNCERT/CC took appropriate strategies, announced the situation and treatment mechanisms to the public. With the help of this information, the botnet constructed by MocBot was then taken down and its propagation was restrained.

5 Conclusion and Future Work

In this paper, we presented an integrated toolkit called HoneyBow to collect samples of autonomous spreading malware. HoneyBow is based on the high-interaction honeypot principle and can collect malware in an automated manner. The HoneyBow toolkit contains MwWatcher, MwFetcher, and MwHunter, each of them using a different malware collection strategy. Compared with the Nepenthes platform based on the low-interaction honeypot principle, HoneyBow has its advantages due to a larger range of captured samples and the capability of collecting malware samples that use new vulnerabilities. The toolkit has its limitation mainly in the area of scalability. Thus we introduced a topological structure which integrates Nepenthes, HoneyBow, and GenIII honeynets, to achieve an even better malware collection coverage. Measurement results of a nine-month period and the MocBot case validated that HoneyBow has better collection coverage compared to Nepenthes and that it is capable of capturing unknown malware samples.

Nepenthes and HoneyBow are both only intended for malware sample collection: they ignore some valuable information about malware propagation including information about the attackers, targeted services, and exploited vulnerabilities. As an improvement, we extend these tools to support the collection of more detailed information. Even with the combination of Nepenthes and HoneyBow, we can not collect malware that uses other propagation vectors like e-mails or exploitation of browsers. We plan to extend our system with client-side honeypots [17] which can be used to fill this gap.

Acknowledgments

This work was supported in part by the 863 High-Tech Research and Development Program of China under Grant No. 2006AA01Z445, Chinese Information Security Research Plan under Grant No. 2006A30, and the Electronic Development Fund of Ministry of Information Industry of China under Grant No. [2006]634. The first author Jianwei Zhuge was supported by a IBM Ph. D. Fellowship Plan.

We would like to thank the anonymous reviewers for valuable comments on a previous version of this paper.

Availability

The HoneyBow toolkit is released under the GNU General Public License (GPL). The software is available for download at `http://honeybow.mwcollect.org/`.

References

1. Baecher, P., Koetter, M., Holz, T., Dornseif, M., Freiling, F.C.: The nepenthes platform: An efficient approach to collect malware. In: Zamboni, D., Kruegel, C. (eds.) RAID 2006. LNCS, vol. 4219, pp. 165–184. Springer, Heidelberg (2006)
2. Balas, E., Viecco, C.: Towards a Third Generation Data Capture Architecture for Honeynets. In: Proceeedings of the 6th IEEE Information Assurance Workshop, IEEE Computer Society Press, Los Alamitos (2005)
3. Goebel, J., Holz, T., Willems, C.: Measurement and Analysis of Autonomous Spreading Malware in a University Environment. In: Proceeding of 4th Conference on Detection of Intrusions & Malware, and Vulnerability Assessment (DIMVA 2007) (2007)

4. Intel Corporation and SystemSoft. The preboot execution environment specification v2.1 (September 1999), http://www.pix.net/software/pxeboot/archive/pxespec.pdf

5. Levine, J., Grizzard, J., Owen, H.: Application of a methodology to characterize rootkits retrieved from honeynets. In: Proceedings of the 5th Information Assurance Workshop, pp. 15–21 (2004)

6. Moore, D., Paxson, V., Savage, S., Shannon, C., Staniford, S., Weaver, N.: Inside the slammer worm. IEEE Security and Privacy 1(4), 33–39 (2003)

7. Portokalidis, G., Slowinska, A., Bos, H.: Argos: an emulator for fingerprinting zero-day attacks for advertised honeypots with automatic signature generation. SIGOPS Oper. Syst. Rev. 40(4), 15–27 (2006)

8. Provos, N.: A virtual honeypot framework. In: Proceedings of the 13th USENIX Security Symposium (August 2004)

9. Provos, N., Holz, T.: Virtual Honeypots: From Botnet Tracking to Intrusion Detection. Addison-Wesley Professional, Reading (2007)

10. Rajab, M.A., Zarfoss, J., Monrose, F., Terzis, A.: A multifaceted approach to understanding the botnet phenomenon. In: Proceedings of the 6th ACM SIGCOMM Conference on Internet Measurement, pp. 41–52. ACM Press, New York (2006)

11. Stewart, J.: Mocbot/MS06-040 IRC bot analysis, (August 2006), http://www.secureworks.com/research/threats/mocbot-ms06040/

12. Symantec Inc. Symantec Internet security threat report: Trends for January - June 2007, (2007), http://www.symantec.com/business/theme.jsp?themeid=threatreport

13. The Honeynet Project. Know Your Enemy, http://honeynet.org/

14. The Honeynet Project. Know Your Enemy: Tracking Botnets (March 2005), http://www.honeynet.org/papers/bots/

15. The Honeynet Project. Honeywall CDROM, (March 2007), http://honeynet.org/tools/cdrom/

16. Vrable, M., Ma, J., Chen, J., Moore, D., Vandekieft, E., Snoeren, A.C., Voelker, G.M., Savage, S.: Scalability, fidelity, and containment in the potemkin virtual honeyfarm. SIGOPS Oper. Syst. Rev. 39(5), 148–162 (2005)

17. Wang, Y.-M., Beck, D., Jiang, X., Roussev, R., Verbowski, C., Chen, S., King, S.T.: Automated web patrol with strider honeymonkeys: Finding web sites that exploit browser vulnerabilities. In: NDSS (2006)

18. Werner, T.: honeytrap: Ein Meta-Honeypot zur Identifikation und Analyse neuer Angriffstechniken. In: Proceedings of the 14th DFN-CERT Workshop Sicherheit in vernetzten Systemen (2007), http://honeytrap.mwcollect.org

DDoS Attack Detection Algorithms Based on Entropy Computing

Liying Li[1], Jianying Zhou[2], and Ning Xiao[3]

[1] National University of Singapore, Singapore
liliying@alumni.nus.edu.sg
[2] Institute for Infocomm Research, Singapore
jyzhou@i2r.a-star.edu.sg
[3] Symantec Software Dev. (Chengdu) Co. Ltd, China
ning_xiao@symantec.com

Abstract. Distributed Denial of Service (DDoS) attack poses a severe threat to the Internet. It is difficult to find the exact signature of attacking. Moreover, it is hard to distinguish the difference of an unusual high volume of traffic which is caused by the attack or occurs when a huge number of users occasionally access the target machine at the same time. The entropy detection method is an effective method to detect the DDoS attack. It is mainly used to calculate the distribution randomness of some attributes in the network packets' headers. In this paper, we focus on the detection technology of DDoS attack. We improve the previous entropy detection algorithm, and propose two enhanced detection methods based on cumulative entropy and time, respectively. Experiment results show that these methods could lead to more accurate and effective DDoS detection.

Keywords: DDoS detection, entropy computing, network security.

1 Introduction

The traditional *Denial of Service* (DoS) attack is usually a point-to-point attack. The attacker makes use of proper service requests to occupy excessive service resources to force the server crash, or to make other legal users unable to attain timely service responses. When the host under attack has limited computing, memory and network bandwidth, the consequence of DoS attacks could be fairly serious. However, along the development of computer and network technology, the impact of DoS attacks has been significantly mitigated.

Distributed Denial of Service. (DDoS) attack is an extension of the traditional DoS attack. DDoS attack is a kind of distributed, cooperative large-scale attack. It has the same working principles as DoS, but compared with the traditional DoS whose attack is originated from a single attacker point, the realization of DDoS comes from hundreds or even thousands of PC attackers which have been installed Daemon, and it is a group-based attack behavior. The targets of DDoS are usually high-volume websites, search engines, or government departments.

S. Qing, H. Imai, and G. Wang (Eds.): ICICS 2007, LNCS 4861, pp. 452–466, 2007.

Compared with the traditional DoS attack, DDoS attacks possess more attacking resources and have more destroying power, and thus they are more difficult to be detected and defended. DDoS attacks have brought tremendous threat to the security of Internet, and also gain much research attention in the area of network security [4, 20].

Now, the DDoS attacks tend to become more distributed and automated, and the destruction is more serious. The attacks have some technical trends: (1) make use of clusters of controlled PCs to start intensive attacks; (2) produce randomly distributed source IP addresses to conceal the track; (3) change the structure of attack packets randomly; (4) explore the bugs and weaknesses of both network protocols and operating systems; (5) send packets faster with no apparent attack characteristics. Hybrid attacks make the defense even harder.

Once the DDoS attacks have been carried forward, the attack packets will flood to the targeted victim and submerge those legal users' packets, making those legal users unable to access the server's resources. Only by timely detection of DDoS attacks, the system could make proper response to escape big loss. Research conducted by other organizations shows that statistical measurements and processing is an effective approach to DDoS problem [12]. The EMERALD project at SRI International uses intrusion detection signatures with Bayesian inference to detect distributed attacks [14]. A destination address monitoring scheme was proposed in [17]. Using only a few observation points, the authors proposed a method to monitor the macroscopic effect of DDoS flooding attacks [7]. In [2], the authors detect flooding attacks at the edge and classify them as incoming or outgoing attacks with an *Artificial Neural Network* (ANN).

In this paper, we put forward two new DDoS detection methods based on the traditional entropy detection method [1, 8]. One uses computing cumulative entropy, which monitors the network for a period of time instead of making judgment soon after detecting abnormal network condition. The other method makes use of the concept of time to judge the network condition without setting a threshold of traffic volume, but observing whether the abnormal network condition persistently lasts for a certain period. We conduct experiments for the traditional entropy detection and the cumulative entropy detection methods, respectively. The test results demonstrate that our improved methods have better detection capability than before.

The rest of this paper is organized as follows. We briefly introduce the background of DDoS attack detection in Section 2, then propose two new approaches based on cumulative entropy and time, respectively in Section 3. Section 4 describes our implementation, and Section 5 shows the experiment results. Finally, we conclude the paper in Section 6.

2 Previous Work

In this section, we first introduce the background of DDoS attack detection, and then focus on the entropy detection algorithms which would be the premise of our improved algorithms shown in Section 3.

2.1 DDoS Detection Background

In the past years, it was discovered that DDoS attack methods and tools are becoming more sophisticated, effective, and also more difficult to trace to the real attackers. On the defense side, current technologies are still unable to withstand large-scale attacks [3].

Defending the DDoS attacks involves three phases: before the attack, during the attack and after the attack. The first one is precaution, which needs a process or long time to deploy the network to guard against the attack. The last one is the second line of defense. Therefore, a practical way to defend the DDoS attack is to prevent the attack flow reach the target and to ensure its availability. Protection using history-based IP filtering is a method when facing the attack [18]. But the premise of defense is to detect the attack timely and exactly.

The main DDoS detection methods comprise two categories: *signature-based detection* and *anomaly detection*. Our research is focused on the anomaly detection.

Signature-Based Detection. Suppose that the intruder's activity could be expressed by a pattern that gives an accurate description of some known attack or intrusion manners. The purpose of this method is to detect whether the object's activity matches these patterns or not. This method could detect the known intrusions, but could do nothing for the new intrusions. The difficulty is how to derive the pattern that could present the phenomenon of intrusion and will not cover other normal behaviors at the same time.

This method has high accuracy for the attack detection, but it is not useful for those intrusions or attacks without experience knowledge. The updating of detection rules is always slower than the emergence of new attacks. At present, after a new bug is published on the Internet, we might find the attack method and codes for this bug next day, but the relative detection rules will come out after several days. The time gap between the new attack and the update of user's rules will give the intruders enough time to launch attacks. In addition, many published attack detection rules still have high error rate, and more and more hackers tend to not publicize the bugs they have found. Therefore, it is difficult to summarize the characteristics of those attacks. In [9], the authors propose to discover the DDoS attacking signature by analyzing the TCP/IP packet header against the well defined rules and conditions, and distinguish the difference between normal and abnormal traffic. A general feature space modeling methodology was presented to identify DDoS attacks. It changes the non-separable attacks to separable cases, and it also allows the unknown attacks potentially being identified by their own features [15].

Anomaly Detection. This method pre-defines the normal and abnormal system activities, and thus to identify the abnormal behaviors among all normal system activities. When the anomaly occurs, it should be detected and responded by alerting or prevention. Some anomaly detection system could allow users to define a threshold or baseline for a normal behavior. This baseline could be constructed by sample statistics, or neural network. Then the detection system works. When finding the behavior exceeds this baseline, the system gives an alarm. More specifically, it compares the detection record of the network communication condition with the normal record. When the difference is large, we say some anomaly occurs and the detection system will warn the intrusion in time.

In [13], the authors use energy function variance based on wavelet analysis to detect DDoS attack traffic. A covariance model was proposed to effectively differentiate between normal and attack traffic, and to some extents verifies the effectiveness of multivariate correlation analysis for DDoS detection [16].

The objects used in the anomaly detection include: attack flow speed, packet size and port distribution, distribution of the packet arrival time, concurrent traffic flow number, advanced protocol characteristics, in/out data rate, and so on.

2.2 Entropy Detection

In information theory, the Shannon entropy or information entropy is a measure of the uncertainty associated with a random variable. It can be interpreted as the average shortest message length, in bits, that can be sent to communicate the true value of the random variable to a recipient. This represents a fundamental mathematical limit on the best possible lossless data compression of any communication: the shortest average number of bits that can be sent to communicate one message out of all the possibilities is the Shannon entropy. This concept was introduced by Claude E. Shannon in his 1948 paper "*A Mathematical Theory of Communication*".

This entropy detection method is mainly used to calculate the distribution randomness of some attributes in the network packets' headers. These attributes could be the packet's source IP address, TTL value, or some other values indicating the packet's properties. For example, the detector captures 1000 continuous data packets at a peak point, and calculates the frequency of each distinct IP address among these 1000 packets. By further calculation of this distribution, we could measure the randomness of these packets [8].

After analyzing the phenomenon of DDoS attack, we could know that, when the attack comes out, there will be large number of data packets, high volume of traffic flow, and many incomplete connection requests. The attackers always fabricate a lot of data packets, and the IP addresses of these packets are generally different and randomly distributed. The analysis of these characteristics could help us to detect the DDoS attack better.

Entropy could be calculated by computing a series of continuous packets. The entropy value gives a description about the corresponding random distribution of these source IP addresses. The bigger the entropy, more random the source IP is. The smaller the entropy, the narrower the distribution range of packets' source addresses is, and some addresses have quite high emergence probability. Under normal network condition, the entropy of network packets always fluctuates to some extent. But when the attacks come out, the entropy value will have perceptible changes. We could detect the change of the source IP distribution through monitoring the entropy change, and thus provide reasons for keeping or discarding those packets.

Next, we discuss the detection methods by analyzing the distribution of packet's source IP. This is also the entropy computing model used as the basis for our improved detection algorithms. The formula of entropy calculation is as follows [1]:

$$H = -\sum_{i=1}^{n} p_i \log_2 p_i \tag{1}$$

where p_i is the emergence probability of each distinct source IP address, n is the total number of packets being analyzed, and H is the entropy.

In [8], the authors proposed an improvement of this entropy detection computing. In the implementation of their algorithm, the authors use a fixed-size sliding window to simplify the computation complexity of the entropy. The window size is W, the probability p_i here equals to emergence probability of each distinct source IP address, that is the counts of one address divided by the total packet number. Therefore, we do not need to calculate all the packets' entropy value for our detection, but just compute W packets' entropy value for our judgments.

A proficient attacker usually tries to defeat the detection algorithm by secretly producing flooding attack and simulating the monitors' expected normal data flow. After knowing some packet attributes' entropy values, these attackers could use the attack tools to produce some flooding with adjustable entropy values. By guess, test and summary, these attackers could probably know the normal entropy range in the monitors, and adjust their own flooding to match it, although it is not easy to realize.

3   Improved Entropy Detection Methods

In this section, we propose two improved DDoS detection methods based on entropy computing. One uses computing cumulative entropy, and the other is time-based.

3.1   Cumulative Entropy Detection

Cumulative Sum (CUSUM) is an algorithm from statistical process control that could detect the mean variation of a statistical process. CUSUM is based on the fact that if there is some change happened, the probability distribution of the random sequence will also be changed [10, 11].

Here we further improve the previous entropy detection algorithm by incorporating the idea of cumulative sum and variation detection [10, 11] to our own entropy approach and try to cumulate the entropy according to some rules, thus it will have more accurate DDoS attack detection rate.

In our DDoS attack method, suppose X_n is the entropy value calculated by using sliding window[8] at each time interval of Δ_n, and the random sequence $\{X_n\}$ is extracted as network service random model. In the normal occasion, this sequence is independent and distributed. Assume the variation parameter is the average value of sequence $\{X_n\}$. Before change, this value $E(X_n) = \alpha$ is very small, and always positive. Before attack, when the network is normal, the distribution of IP addresses should be stable, and have little randomness, thus the entropy value should be small. But when DDoS attack happens, this average value will increase suddenly, $E(X_n)$ will become far bigger than α, and becomes a constant or dynamic value.

CUSUM algorithm[10, 11] has an assumption that in the normal case, the average value of the random sequence should be negative, and it becomes positive after change. Therefore, without losing any statistics properties, we transfer the sequence $\{X_n\}$ into another random sequence $\{Z_n\}$ with negative average value. Let $Z_n = X_n - \beta$, where $\alpha = \alpha - \beta$. In a given network environment, the parameter β is a constant, used for producing a negative random sequence $\{Z_n\}$, and thus the entire negative value of $\{Z_n\}$ will not be cumulated along the time. In our detection algorithm, we define that $\beta = 2\alpha$. Assume that when the network entropy value becomes two times as the normal network entropy, we say that the network is abnormal, and then we start to cumulate. When the attack happens, Z_n will suddenly become very large and positive. The detection threshold is the limit for the positive, which is the cumulative value of Z_n.

We use this recursive formula for cumulative sum:

$$\begin{cases} y_n = (y_{n-1} + Z_n)^+ \\ y_0 = 0 \end{cases} \tag{2}$$

where $x^+ = \begin{cases} 0, & x \leq 0 \\ x, & x > 0 \end{cases}$, y_n and represents the cumulative positive value of Z_n.

The bigger y_n is, the stronger the attack is. For the variation in time period τ_N (when $y_{\tau_n} \geq N$), the judgment function could be:

$$d_N(y_n) = \begin{cases} 0, & (y_n \leq N) \\ 1, & (y_n > N) \end{cases} \tag{3}$$

where $d_N(y_n)$ is the judgment at time n, the value 1 shows that attack happens, while 0 shows the normal case. N is the detection threshold.

The advantage of this improved algorithm lies in that it comprises implicitly a concept of process cumulating. In the previous entropy detection algorithms, we always judge the network condition according to a threshold. For example, when the network entropy is bigger than a value, we say the network is abnormal or some attack happens. But this judgment may not be suitable in some occasions. For example, the traffic flow in the network suddenly increases, but the flow is actually from some legal users. The function of cumulating process is to avoid the false alarm when the network has something abnormal just at a time point. We need to cumulate the total entropy during a time period, and judge this value whether exceeds the limit or not, and the results in this way should be more accurate. From the equation $y_n = (y_{n-1} + Z_n)^+$, we know when Z_n is fluctuating among negative and positive values, the cumulative value y_n might finally be 0, or just very small positive value. In this case, the network may only suddenly become abnormal, or not stable, but it is not attacked, and our detection will not give false alarm.

In the non-parameter CUSUM algorithm [10, 11], the idea of sequential variation is first proposed. But its approach is to analyze the ratio between the new arrival IP number in a time unit and the total IP number, and thus construct a random sequence. To implement that algorithm, we need to create a database containing a large amount of legal IP address, and each time we should compare and calculate the number of all new IP in each time unit. The calculation is complicated and has low efficiency. In our improvement, we use the entropy statistics based on sliding window [8]. Because the nature of entropy, it could clearly show the distribution of source IP's randomness. By controlling the sliding window size, we could enhance the detection accuracy. For example, when the host has large traffic flow in normal work, and the IP is very distributed, we could properly increase the window size to have better detection.

The implementation and test results of this cumulative entropy detection algorithm will be shown in Sections 4 and 5.

3.2   Time-Based Entropy Detection

In the anomaly detection, we usually have to set a threshold value. When the statistics exceed this threshold, we say that the system is facing attacks. In the previous entropy detection algorithms, when a single value is beyond the range or a cumulative value exceeds a value, the system will give an alarm. The setting of this threshold is usually through experience, to some extent. For some systems' design, they could also get a proper threshold value by using neural network to study the normal network. Here, we do not consider neural network, but try to use some simple method to complete timely and accurate attack detection.

Based on the cumulative entropy detection described before, we make some improvement. Here, we give up the threshold value N and do not cumulate the entropy. Instead, we propose a time-based entropy detection method. The main concept is to use time to judge the network condition, not according to a threshold value to judge the attack condition.

We calculate the network entropy V using a fixed rate and time unit t. Suppose X_n is the entropy value computed by sliding window in each time interval $\triangle_n$. By the formula $Z_n = X_n - \beta$, set $\beta = 2\alpha$ (here β could be other values according to the environment), so we get a random sequence $\{Z_n\}$ with negative average value. (The computation of Z_n is the same as described in cumulative entropy method.) Let $V_j = Z_n$. Construct a vector X, with initial value $X_0^T = [-1 - 1 \cdots - 1 - 1]$. Vector X has n elements, and the initial value for each element is -1.

$$x_j^{new} = \Phi(v_j) = \begin{cases} +1, & v_j > 0 \\ -1, & v_j < 0 \quad (1 <= j <= n) \\ x_j^{old}, & v_j = 0 \end{cases} \tag{4}$$

Using the above update rule, we could update each X_j according to the relative V_j. When the vector $X^T = [+1 + 1 \cdots + 1 + 1]$, or say all the elements of X

becomes +1, it shows that there is some attack in the network, and the alarm is triggered. The update of each X_j is cyclic, and the value of j is from 1 to n, then 1 to n again. The advantage of this algorithm is that we could control the total attack detection time by setting those two parameters: t and n, where t is the data collection interval, and n is the element number of vector X. For example, when $t = 2s$, $n = 15$, and the system will give an alarm only when the network abnormal entropy persists over 30s. A sudden traffic increase in a short time might still be a normal traffic, and we allow it. But if the network's anomaly lasts for more than 30s, or even longer, we could believe that, the system might be abnormal, and some attacks might happen.

The threshold-based approach is widely applicable, and it may lead to a more real-time and timely attack detection. But for the time-based approach, we tend to emphasize the time tolerance. In some allowable range, we could ignore the network anomalies. But only when exceeding our tolerable limit, defined by a time period, we regard the network is abnormal or attack happens. These two approaches may have their own advantages under different environments. In some cases, the DDoS detection that combines threshold-based and time-based approaches may be more efficient, and have fewer false alarms.

4 Implementation

In this system, we need to start two threads for handling. The first thread (statisticThread) is mainly responsible for capturing packets and buffering them. The second thread (analysisThread) is used to analyze the packets' properties, and is controlled by a timer.

4.1 statisticThread Analysis

Our statistic thread is designed mainly based on the modification of Winpcap [6]. Winpcap is a system for capturing and analyzing packets under the platform

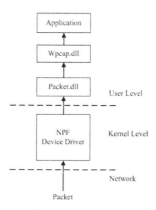

Fig. 1. Winpcap Processing

of Win32. It includes a kernel-level packet filter, a basic DLL (packet.dll) and
an advanced DLL (Wpcap.dll) independent of the system as shown in Figure 1.

Based on the sliding window mode, we could buffer those packet contents we
are interested in, and ensure the space utilization and computation convenience
at the same time.

```
statistic_Info statisticWin[WINDOW_SIZE_RECORD];
```

Before the system runs, we need to create the database containing all legal IP
address according to the system's history record. In order to hasten the system's
running, we design a hash mechanism shown in Figure 2. First build a hash lookup
table according to the IP address database, and realize the fast query for IP.

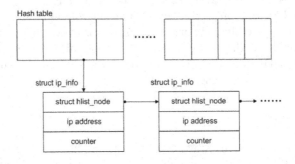

Fig. 2. Hash Table Structure

After invoking the function *pcap_next_ex*() to get the original packets from
Winpcap, we enter the processing function. According to the current winPos, we
calculate the saving address, and then save the information, and modify winPos.

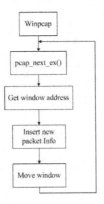

Fig. 3. statisticThread Processing

```
statistic_Info * pShannon = & statisticWin [winPos];
memcpy((u_char*)&pShannon->header, &pkt_data[26], sizeof(UINT32)*3);
pShannon->header.protocol = pkt_data[23];
winPos = (winPos + 1) % WINDOW_SIZE_RECORD;
```

The statisticThread Processing is shown in Figure 3.

4.2   analysisThread Analysis

The main function of the thread analysisThread is to save the data characteristics in the window. Set a timer that starts every 1s. Calculate the average value of the sequence $\{X_n\}$, and according to $Z_n = X_n - \beta$ and $y_n = (y_{n-1} + Z_n)^+$ to calculate the relative data. Plot the fluctuation graph, and judge whether the attack exists.

In the practical implementation, we start the detection analysis on those packets having the same IP address. The analysis thread starts every 1s, and we analyze the relative packets' characteristics during this 1s period, and conduct cumulating. When the cumulative value reaches a certain limit, the system will give an alarm.

5   Experiment Results

In this section, we show the experiment results and analyze the traditional entropy detection method and our two improved methods: cumulative entropy detection method and time-based detection method. In this test, our sliding window size is set to 1000, and the total test time is 300s.

5.1   General Entropy Statistics

Test method: we start two attacks [5]. The first one is between the time 40s and 80s, and the second one is from 180s to 230s. The effect of this entropy detection method is quite good, and the entropy value changes quickly, and increases to around 10. Here we only calculate every 1000 packets' entropy value. When the attack comes, the number of packets increases a lot, and a large number of random IP addresses come out. The extreme condition is that for every 1000 packets, each packet has a different IP address. In this case, the extreme and maximum value of entropy should be:

$$H = -\sum_{i=1}^{1000} p_i \log_2 p_i = -1000 \times 0.001 \times \log_2 0.001 \approx 9.966 \tag{5}$$

The test result is shown in Figure 4 below.

This experiment result is shown in the condition of one PC attacks another PC, and the CPU utilization of the attacked computer is reaching to 100% immediately. Note the configuration of the attacked computer has one CPU of Intel core 2 duo T5600, and its memory capacity is 512M. When we use two attackers to simulate the test, the attacked PC is directly shut down. Therefore, we could see the powerful destruction of TCP-SYN-Flood.

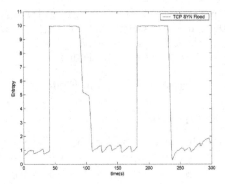

Fig. 4. Entropy Statistics under TCP-SYN-Flood

5.2   Cumulative Entropy Detection

We calculate the current packets' entropy every 1 second. From Figure 5, we could see that the normal entropy value is fluctuating around 2 bits in our network environment.

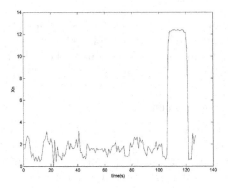

Fig. 5. Entropy Statistics X_n in Network

We set $\beta = 2\alpha = 4$ bits, and then $Z_n = X_n - \beta$. In the normal condition, the sequence of $\{Z_n\}$ should be negative, sometimes Z_n may be bigger than 0. But when the attack happens, Z_n will rapidly increase a lot. As shown in Figure 6, the entropy becomes 10 bits, which is much bigger than 0.

By the formulas $y_n = (y_{n-1} + Z_n)^+$, $y_0 = 0$, we could cumulate the positive value of Z_n. As shown in Figure 7, in the normal case, y_n should be 0 or a small positive value close to 0. When the attack happens, this cumulative value y_n increases quickly. By setting the threshold N, when $y_n > N$, the system will give an alarm.

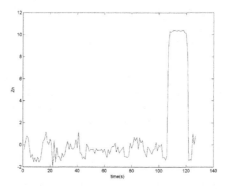

Fig. 6. Offset Entropy Statistics Z_n

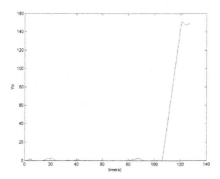

Fig. 7. Cumulative Entropy Y_n

5.3 Time-Based Entropy Detection

In this test, we choose $t = 1s$, $n = 10$, which means that every 1s we compute
the entropy value, and judge whether it is the two times of the normal value. If

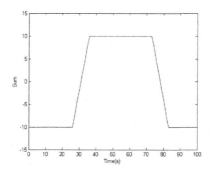

Fig. 8. Time-based Entropy Detection

so, we believe that something abnormal happened in this network. If the vector's
n elements are all changed to +1, which means that the abnormal persisted over
$t \times n = 10s$, and we believe that the network is attacked. The test result is shown
in Figure 8.

Because here $n = 10$, when the vector becomes $[+1 + 1 \cdots + 1]$, and there are
total ten +1, we compute the sum equals to 10 in the graph. When the network
is completely good, nothing abnormal exists, and the sum then is -10. Of course,
the values of n and t depend on the practical environment.

5.4   Discussions

From the graphs shown previously, we could see that, for the statistics of entropy,
when the attack occurs, there will be a rapid increase for the statistics, and it
then reaches a very big value. If the network administrator sets such a value,
when exceeding this value, the system will regard it as attack coming. For the
cumulative entropy detection approach, we make use of a process to cumulating
entropy. We emphasize that the anomaly lasts for a time period, not just happens
at a time point. When the attack comes, the system does not immediately give
an alarm like the traditional entropy detection method, but the system needs to
cumulate a time-period's attack condition, and then gives the judgment. When
the network just has some abnormal flow in a normal network environment,
our cumulative entropy may not give an alarm. This approach reduces the false
alarm rate.

As we use sliding window method to complete the calculation of entropy,
the entropy we compute is not all network packets' entropy in a time unit, but
just the window size's entropy. Thus we could use another way to judge the
anomaly. Set the window size $W = 1000$. From the previous test results, the
normal entropy value should be around 2 bits, and the maximum entropy value
should be 9.96, when every packet has different IP address. Because we set a
small window value, when the attack comes, large number of random IP packets
will lead to the rapid increase of entropy, close to 10. During the attack, this
value is quite stable. See from the graph, it is approximately a line. In normal
traffic case, the entropy always fluctuates, without a stable value. According to
this point, we might use a small window size W, calculate its maximum entropy
E_{max}, and when $(E - E_{max}) \rightarrow 0$, we say that network is abnormal.

6   Conclusions

In this paper, we studied the DDoS detection algorithms based on entropy monitoring, and proposed two improved entropy detection approaches: cumulative
entropy and time-based methods. We also conducted experiments for the traditional entropy detection method and the cumulative entropy detection method,
respectively. From the test results, we could see that our cumulative entropy
detection method has good detection capability. For different network environments, how to configure the threshold value is a key point, which influences the

detection efficiency. In the time-based entropy detection method, we introduced a new concept of time cumulating. By setting a system's tolerable detection time, DDoS detection can be carried out without giving a typical threshold value.

References

1. Shannon, C.E., Weaver, W.: The Mathematical Theory of Communication. University of Illinois Press (1963)
2. Siaterlis, C., Maglaris, V.: Detecting Incoming and Outgoing DDoS Attacks at the Edge using a Single set of Network Characteristics. In: 10th IEEE Symposium on Computers and Communications (ISCC 2005), pp. 469–475 (2005)
3. Chang, R.K.C.: Defending against Flooding-based Distributed Denial-of-Service Attacks: a Tutorial. IEEE Communications Magazine 40(10), 42–51 (2002)
4. Cao, Y., Li, H., Lv, D.: DDoS-based TCP SYN Flood and Defense. Electrical Technology (2004)
5. Dittrich, D.: The Stacheldraht' Distributed Denial of Service Attack Tool (1999), http://staff.washington.edu/dittrich/misc/stacheldraht.analysis
6. Risso, F., Delgioanni, L., Varenni, G., Viano, P., Pai, N.: WinPcap: The Windows Packet Capture Library, http://www.winpcap.org/
7. Yuan, J., Mills, K.: Monitoring the Macroscopic Effect of DDoS Flooding Attacks. IEEE Transactions on Dependable and Secure Computing 2(4) (2005)
8. Feinstein, L., Schnackenberg, D.: Statistical Approaches to DDoS Attack Detection and Response. In: 2003 DARPA Information Survivability Conference and Exposition (DISCEX 2003), pp. 303–314 (2003)
9. Limwiwatkul, L., Rungsawangr, A.: Distributed Denial of Service Detection using TCP/IP Header and Traffic Measurement Analysis. In: 2004 International Symposium on Communications and Information Technologies (ISCIT 2004), Sapporo, Japan (2004)
10. Lu, J., Yin, C., Zhuang, X., Lu, K., Li, O.: DDoS Attack Detection based on Non-parameter CUSUM. In: Computer and Network (2004)
11. Lin, B., Li, O., Liu, Q.: DDoS Attacks Detection Based On Sequential Change Detection. Computer Engineering 31(9) (2005)
12. Li, Q., Chang, E.-C., Chan, M.C.: On the Effectiveness of DDoS Attacks on Statistical Filtering. IEEE INFOCOM 2005, 1373–1383 (2005)
13. Li, L., Lee, G.: DDoS Attack Detection and Wavelets. In: 12th International Conference on Computer Communications and Networks (ICCCN 2003), pp. 421–427 (2003)
14. Porras, P.A., Neumann, P.G.: EMERALD: Event Monitoring Enabling Responses to Anomalous Live Disturbances. In: 1997 National Information Systems Security Conference (NISSC 1997), pp. 353–365 (1997)
15. Jin, S.Y., Yeung, D.S.: DDOS Detection Based on Feature Space Modeling. In: 3rd International Conference on Machine Learning and Cybernetics, Shanghai, pp. 4210–4215 (2004)
16. Jin, S.Y., Yeung, D.S.: A Covariance Analysis Model for DDoS Attack Detection. In: 2004 IEEE International Conference on Communications (ICC 2004), pp. 1882–1886 (2004)
17. Shim, S.-H., Yoo, K.-M., Han, K.-E., Kang, C.-K., So, W.-H., Song, J.-T., Kim, Y.-C.: Destination Address Monitoring Scheme for Detecting DDoS Attack in Centralized Control Network. In: 2006 Asia-Pacific Conference on Communications, pp. 1–5 (2006)

18. Peng, T., Leckie, C., Ramamohanarao, K.: Protection from Distributed Denial of Service Attacks using History-based IP Filtering. In: 2003 IEEE International Conference on Communications (ICC 2003), pp. 482–486 (2003)
19. Lu, W., Traore, I.: An Unsupervised Approach·for Detecting DDoS Attacks based on Traffic-based Metrics. In: 2005 IEEE Pacific Rim Conference on Communications, Computers and Signal Processing (PACRIM 2005), pp. 462–465 (2005)
20. Xu, K., Xu, M., Wu, J.: Research on Distributed Denial-of-service Attacks: a Survey. Mini-micro Systems 25(3) (2004)

Firewall for Dynamic IP Address in Mobile IPv6

Ying Qiu, Feng Bao, and Jianying Zhou

Institute for Infocomm Research
21 Heng Mui Keng Terrace, Singapore 119613
{qiuying,baofeng,jyzhou}@i2r.a-star.edu.sg

Abstract. Mobile communication is becoming the mainstream with the rapid growth of mobile devices penetrating our daily life. More and more mobile devices such as mobile phones, personal digital assistants, notebooks etc, are capable of Internet access. Mobile devices frequently change their communication IP addresses in mobile IPv6 network following its current attached domain. This raises a big challenge for building firewall for mobile devices. The conventional firewalls are primarily based on IPv4 networks where the security criteria are specified only to the fixed IP addresses or subnets, which apparently do not apply to mobile IPv6. In this paper we propose three solutions for mobile IPv6 firewall. Our approaches make the firewall adaptive to dynamic IP addresses in mobile IPv6 network. They have different expense and weight corresponding to different degree of universality. The paper focuses the study more from practical aspect.

Keywords: Firewall, Mobile IP6.

1 Introduction

Firewalls are frequently used to prevent unauthorized Internet users from accessing private networks connected to the Internet, such as intranets. All messages entering or leaving the intranet need to pass through the firewall, which examines each message and blocks those that do not meet the specified security criteria. In the traditional firewall, the security criteria are specified only for fixed IP addresses or subnets.

Along with the increasing number of 3G networks and WiFi hotspots, people can now easily gain access to the Internet anywhere using their mobile devices, such as mobile phones, personal digital assistants (PDA) and laptop computers etc. Mobile IPv6 [1] enables IP mobility for IPv6 nodes. It allows a mobile IPv6 node to be reachable via its home IPv6 address irrespective of the link and the domain that the mobile attaches to. The Route Optimization is also supported in the mobile IPv6 specification. The Route Optimization technology enables optimized routing of packets between a mobile node and its correspondent nodes.

To build up firewall for mobile devices, we are facing the challenge: the firewalls need a series of fixed IP addresses or subnets to specify the security criteria, meanwhile the roaming mobile nodes need variable IP addresses to indicate their current location so that the mobile nodes can be reached seamlessly. In this paper we analyze the mobile IPv6 specification and firewall technology, and then present in detail of building a dynamic firewall in mobile IPv6 environment. For Ethernet devices, we suggested to

S. Qing, H. Imai, and G. Wang (Eds.): ICICS 2007, LNCS 4861, pp. 467–479, 2007.

employ the feature of MAC address filter. For the mobile nodes with traceable addresses, masking the low 64-bits of source address is a simple and efficient solution. For general mobile nodes, we introduced an extended firewall and the improved Return Routability protocol.

The rest of this paper is organized as follows. Section 2 reviews the basic operation of Mobile IPv6 and firewalls. Section 3 presents our solution for configuring the firewall rules in mobile IPv6 networks. Section 4 describes an analysis of security and performance of our approaches. Section 5 concludes the paper.

2   Mobile IPv6 and Firewall

2.1   Mobility Support in IPv6

In the current IETF Mobile IPv6 specifications [1], every mobile node (*MN*) has a home address (*HoA*), an IP address assigned to a mobile node within its home subnet. A *MN* is always addressable by its home address, whether it is currently attached to its home subnet or is away from home.

While a mobile node roams and attaches to some foreign subnet, it is also addressable by one or more care-of addresses (*CoAs*), in addition to its home address. A care-of address is an IP address associated with a mobile node while visiting a particular foreign subnet. The subnet prefix of the mobile node's care-of address is the subnet prefix of the foreign subnet being visited by the node. A mobile node typically acquires its *CoA* through stateless [3] or stateful (eg., DHCPv6 [4]) address autoconfiguration.

After getting a new *CoA* on the foreign subnet, a mobile node informs its current *CoA* to its home agent (*HA*) [1,5] by sending a Home Binding Update (*BU_HA*) message to the home agent:

$$BU_{HA} = \{Src=CoA, Dst=HA, Opt=HoA, ... \}$$

As the paper deals with the problem how a MIPv6 packet goes through firewalls, we just discuss and analyze the IP address in the header of a traffic packet and ignore its payload.

The home binding update message creates an association between *HoA* and *CoA* for the mobile node with the specified lifetime at the home agent. *HA* thereafter uses proxy Neighbor Discovery [6] to intercept any IPv6 packets addressed to *MN*'s *HoA* on the home subnet, and tunnels each intercepted packet to *MN*'s *CoA* [1]. To tunnel intercepted packets, *HA* encapsulates the packets using IPv6 encapsulation, with the outer IPv6 header addressed to *MN*'s *CoA*.

The mobile node may also initiates *route optimization* operation with its correspondent node (*CN*) to inform its current *CoA* by sending a Correspondent Binding Update (*BU_CN*) message to the correspondent nodes. Figure 1 shows the procedure:

When *MN* wants to perform route optimization, it sends

$$HoTI = \{Src=HoA, Dst=CN, ...\}$$

and

$$CoTI = \{Src=CoA, Dst=CN, ...\}$$

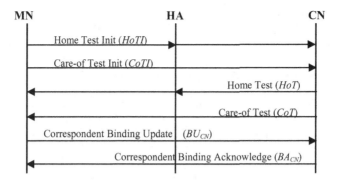

Fig. 1. The procedure of Correspondent Binding Update

to *CN*. *HoTI* tells *MN*'s home address *HoA* to *CN*. It is reverse tunneled through the home agent *HA*, while *CoTI* informs *MN*'s care-of address *CoA* and is sent directly to *CN*.

When *CN* receives *HoTI*, it takes the source IP address of *HoTI* as input and generates a *home cookie* and replies *MN* with *home cookie*

$$HoT = \{Src=CN, Dst=HoA, ...\}.$$

Similarly, when *CN* receives *CoTI*, it takes the source IP address of *CoTI* as input and generates a *care-of cookie* and sends it

$$CoT = \{Src=CN, Dst=CoA, ...\}$$

to *MN*. Note that *HoT* is sent via *MN*'s home agent *HA* while *CoT* is delivered directly to *MN*.

When *MN* receives both *HoT* and *CoT*, it hashes together the two cookies to form a session key which is then used to authenticate the correspondent binding update message to *CN*:

$$BU_{CN} = \{Src=CoA, Dst=CN, HoA, ...\}.$$

Note that *CN* is stateless until it receives BU_{CN} and verifies the authentication MAC_{BU}. If MAC_{BU} is verified positive, *CN* may reply with a binding acknowledgement (BA_{CN}) message

$$BA_{CN} = \{Src=CN, Dst=CoA, HoA, ...\}.$$

CN then creates a binding cache entry for the mobile node *MN*. The binding cache entry binds *HoA* with *CoA* which allows future packets to *MN* be sent to *CoA* directly.

When sending a packet to the *MN*, the *CN* checks its cached bindings for an entry for the packet's destination address. If a cached binding for this destination address is found, the node uses an IPv6 Routing Header [7] to route the packet to the *MN* by way of the *CoA* indicated in this binding. If, instead, the *CN* has no cached binding for this destination address, the node sends the packet normally (i.e., to the *MN*'s *HoA* with no routing header), and the packet is subsequently intercepted and tunneled to the *MN* by its *HA* as described above. Therefore, route optimization allows a *CN* to communicate directly with the *MN*, avoiding delivering traffic via the *MN*'s *HA*.

From the above brief review, we observed that the source/ destination addresses in the packets from/to *MN*s are not fixed. It would occur the transmit problem through firewalls.

2.2 Problem Statement of Mobile IPv6 and Firewall

Firewalls usually decide whether to allow or to drop packets based on source IP address and destination address as well as protocol type and port numbers. RFC4487 [2] analyzed various scenarios involving MIP6 and firewalls. It classified three scenarios of firewall networks:

1) When the correspondent node is within a network protected by firewall(s), the major issue is how the firewall accepts the packets from/to the address *CoA*, which has no associated rule with the diverse *CoA* in the firewall. Requiring the firewalls to update the connection state upon detecting Binding Update messages from a node outside the network protected by the firewall does not appear feasible or desirable, because changing the firewall states without verifying the validity of the Binding Update messages could lead to denial of service attacks.

2) When the *HA* is within a network protected by a firewall, the firewall(s) may drop connection setup requests from *CN*s and packets from *MN*s' *CoA*s if the firewall(s) protecting the *HA* block unsolicited incoming traffic (e.g., as stateful inspection packet filters do).

3) When a mobile node is within or moves from outside into a network protected by firewall(s), the firewall blocks the traffic to the *MN* due to the its new *CoA*.

2.3 IPv6 Address Generation

An interface which uses IPv6 usually gets link-local address and global address allocated at least. Link-local address is used for control functions, while global address is used for usual data communications.

In mobile IPv6, IP address is usually generated by the following three methods: Stateless Address Autoconfiguration, Stateful Address Autoconfiguration & Manual Configuration.

Stateless Address Autoconfiguration [3]
Address autoconfiguration in IPv6 usually means that a node can configure its own IP address, using information on the network.

In IPv6, the 128 bit IP address is separated to two parts: i) network prefix (64 bits), which identifies network; and ii) interface ID (64 bits), which identifies a node (interface). Interface ID is configured by the node on its own (usually derived from the MAC address), and the prefix is advertised by the network (usually router). These two parts are combined to form an IPv6 address.

Stateful Address Autoconfiguration
Stateful Address Autoconfiguration uses a server, such as DHCPv6 [4], to manage and allocate address to nodes.

With DHCPv6, DHCP servers are placed on the network to allocate addresses to a network interface.

Note that the DHCP server manages address information and maintains which address is allocated to whom. In address allocation with DHCP, a node can use only one DHCP server (although there may be multiple DHCP servers on the same network).

Manual Configuration
It means to set IP address to an interface manually. This includes setting a pre-configured address based on a configuration file at the boot.

3   Deploying Firewall in Mobile IPv6

3.1   Traceable IP Address and Untraceable IP Address

From the brief description in subsection 2.3, we know the IP address generated by the method of stateless address autoconfiguration is traceable, because its low 64 bits is fixed even though its prefix depends on the router. In contrast, the IP address obtained by the method of stateful address auto-configuration is untraceable because there is no association between the previous and subsequent addresses of an interface if it attaches different routers.

We can define the following two types of addresses.

Traceable Address: If the series of IP addresses for an interface are derived from certain data (e.g. MAC address), no matter it is generated by manual configuration or stateless autoconfiguration, we call the IP addresses are traceable.

Untraceable Address: If the series of IP addresses for an interface are not derived from certain data, no matter it is generated by manual configuration or stateful auto-configuration or other stateless autoconfiguration [8, 9], we call the IP addresses are untraceable.

In the following subsections, we will discuss how to configure and deploy the firewall in a variety of scenarios. We will focus on how to manage the variation of *MN*'s IP address. Other firewall filtering issues, such as protocol type, port number, etc., will be ignored because they are not changed along with the locations of mobile nodes and can be set in advance.

3.2   Scenario of the CN Protected by Firewall(s)

Figure 2 presents the scenario that the correspondent node of a mobile node is protected by firewall.

Firewall Configuration if *MN*'s *CoA* is Traceable Address
The disadvantage of IPv4 is that its address is only 32 bits meanwhile the MAC address is 48 bits. Therefore the IPv4 address is not able to include the MAC address information. If a mobile node roams to foreign networks, its new IPv4 address is totally

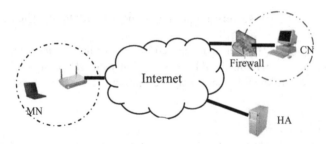

Fig. 2. CN is protected by a firewall

different from its previous IPv4 address and we are not able to trace back any information of its previous address from its new address.

In IPv6, the stateless address autoconfiguration is wildly deployed due to efficiency and lightweight. If a *MN*'s IPv6 address is generated by the stateless address autoconfiguration, the IPv6 address always contains the interface identity (derived from the unique MAC address). Hence, if two IPv6 addresses share the same 64-bit interface identity, we consider them to be the same device.

Therefore, the firewall rules for a mobile node could mask the low 64-bits of the IPv6 address. For example, if a mobile node's home address (*HoA*) is *y:y:y:y:xxxx:xxff :fexx:xxxx*. Its care-of address in the network A would be *a:a:a:a:xxxx:xxff:fexx:xxxx* and its IPv6 address in network B would *be b:b:b:b:xxxx:xxff:fexx:xxxx*, we could set the firewall rules with following pattern for the mobile node:

> *TARGET   INPUT*
> *--source   y:y:y:y:xxxx:xxff:fexx:xxxx*
>   *--source mask   0::ffff:ffff:ffff:ffff*
>   *--destination   address_of_CN*
>   *--protocol   135*

and

> *TARGET   OUTPUT*
> *-- destination   y:y:y:y:xxxx:xxff:fexx:xxxx*
>   *-- destination mask   0::ffff:ffff:ffff:ffff*
>   *--source   address_of_CN*
>   *--protocol   135*

where protocol 135 specifies the protocol of Mobility Header.

After filtering by mask *0::ffff:ffff:ffff:ffff*, all of the source addresses from/to *MN* are the same *xxxx:xxff:fexx:xxxx* and match the firewall rules. However, only messages *HoTI, HoT, CoTI, CoT, BU$_{CN}$* and *BA$_{CN}$* can go through the firewall because they are with the mobile protocol type 135.

From above analysis, we could summarize that the firewall, which protects the correspond node of mobile node, does not block the communication between the mobile node with traceable address and the correspondent nodes. However, the traceable addresses are not always available. The next subsection will discuss solution for mobile nodes with untraceable addresses.

Firewall Configuration if *MN*'s *CoA* is UntraceableAddress

If the mobile device is an Ethernet device, we could use the MAC feature in firewall to filter it. The rule pattern is:

> *TARGET INPUT*
> * --mac-source   xx:xx:xx:xx:xx:xx*
> * --destination   address_of_CN*

where, *xx:xx:xx:xx:xx:xx* is the MAC address of the *MN*.

The filter feature for MAC source addresses only makes sense for packets coming from an Ethernet device. It is not suitable for the mobile devices that do not support Ethernet, such as mobile phone. Hence, we have to come back IP layer.

From the perspective of the correspondent node, the care-of address of mobile node is an untraceable address. It is not able to set up firewall rules based on the kind of addresses. Mobile IPv6 specification [1] introduces a new herder "Type 2 Routing Header" which carries the home address of the mobile node. The new routing header uses a different type to that defined for "regular" IPv6 source routing, enabling firewalls to apply different rules to source routed packets than to Mobile IPv6. Therefore, we suggest that the current firewalls extend a feature to filter the field of Home Address Option in the mobility header as well as the field Type 2 Routing Header. With the new feature, we use 3 firewall rule patterns for the mobile node, which home address is *y:y:y:y:xxxx:xxff:fexx:xxxx* and its current care-of address is *a:a:a:a:xxxx:xxff:fexx:xxxx*:

> *TARGET INPUT*
> * --source   y:y:y:y:xxxx:xxff:fexx:xxxx*
> * --destination   address_of_CN*

> *TARGET OUTPUT*
> * --destination   y:y:y:y:xxxx:xxff:fexx:xxxx*
> * --source   address_of_CN*

and

> *TARGET INPUT &OUTPUT*
> * --home-address y:y:y:y:xxxx:xxff:fexx:xxxx*
> * --protocol 135*

where --protocol 135 specifies the protocol of Mobility Header.

Accordingly, we proposed an improved Return Routability (RR) procedure [10] in which the message of *HoTI*, *HoT*, *CoTI* and *CoT* bundles *HoA* and *CoA* together instead of *HoA* or *CoA* alone in the original RR procedure. (The analysis in [10] indicated that binding *HoA* and *CoA* together makes the original RR protocol much stronger.)

Now let's look every message in the improved RR procedure:

The *HoTI* message: its source address is *y:y:y:y:x:xxxx: xxff:fexx:xxxx* and destination address is *address_of_CN*. The *HoTI* message meets the firewall rules and then passes the firewall.

The *HoT* message: its destination address is *y:y:y:y:xxxx: xxff:fexx:xxxx* and source address is *address_of_CN*. The *HoT* message meets the firewall rules and then passes the firewall.

The *CoTI* message: the message with source address *a:a:a:a:xxxx:xxff:fexx:xxxx*, destination address *address_of_CN*, home address *y:y:y:y:xxxx:xxff:fexx:xxxx* and mobility header protocol 135. The *CoTI* message meets the extended firewall rule and is also able to pass the firewall.

The *CoT* message: the message with destination address *a:a:a:a:xxxx:xxff:fexx:xxxx*, source address *address_of_CN*, home address *y:y:y:y:x:xxff:fexx:xxxx* and mobility header protocol 135. The *CoT* message meets the extended firewall rule and is also able to pass the firewall.

The BU_{CN} message: the message with source address *a:a:a:a:xxxx:xxff:fexx:xxxx* and destination address *address_of_CN,* home address *y:y:y:y:x:xxff:fexx:xxxx* and mobility header protocol 135. The BU_{CN} message meets the extended firewall rule and can pass the firewall.

The BA_{CN} message: the message with destination address *a:a:a:a:xxxx:xxff:fexx:xxxx*, source address *address_of_CN,* home address *y:y:y:y:x:xxff:fexx:xxxx* and mobility header protocol 135. The BA_{CN} message meets the extended firewall rule and can pass the firewall.

Upon receiving the BU_{CN} message, the correspondent node opens a dynamic pinhole for the address *a:a:a:a:xxxx:xxff:fexx:xxxx* so that following traffic packets from this address with any protocols can reach the correspondent node.

After this modification, the firewall, which protects the correspondent node of mobile node, will not block any more the communication between the mobile node with untraceable address and the correspondent nodes.

Of course, the application of the solution is more general. It is certainly suitable for the mobile nodes with traceable addresses.

Based on the same mechanism, the description of other scenarios is simple in the following subsections.

3.3 Scenario of the HA Protected by Firewall(s)

Figure 3 displays the scenario that the home agent of a mobile node is protected by firewall. In the specification of mobile IPv6 [1, 5], the following messages from the mobile node will send to/through its home agent: Home Binding Update BU_{HA}, Home Test Init *HoTI* and Home Test *HoT*.

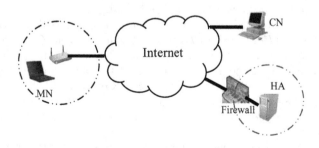

Fig. 3. HA is protected by a firewall

Firewall Configuration if *MN*'s *CoA* is Traceable Address

Similar to the usage described in above section, we set the below firewall rules in the firewalls that protect the *HA*.

> *TARGET INPUT*
> *--source y:y:y:y:xxxx:xxff:fexx:xxxx*
> *--source-mask 0::ffff:ffff:ffff:ffff*
> *--destination address_of_HA*
> *--protocol 135*

and

> *TARGET OUTPUT*
> *--destination y:y:y:y:xxxx:xxff:fexx:xxxx*
> *--destination-mask 0::ffff:ffff:ffff:ffff*
> *--source address_of_HA*
> *--protocol 135*

After masking by *0::ffff:ffff:ffff:ffff*, all of the addresses from/to *MN* become the same *xxxx:xxff:fexx:xxxx* and match the firewall rules. But, only the messages BU_{HA} and BA_{HA} can go through the firewall because they are with the mobile protocol type 135.

According to RFC 3776 [5], the *HoTI/HoT* message is encapsulated by ESP tunneling mode in the MN-HA path, so the headers do not contain the mobile protocol type 135. However, upon receiving the BU_{HA} message, the home agent opens a dynamic pinhole and sets up a security tunnel for *MN*'s *CoA* so that following traffic packets from this address with any protocols can reach the home agent. Thereafter, the encapsulated *HoTI* and *HoT* can pass through the firewall.

From above analysis, we summarize that the firewall, which protects the home agent of mobile node, does not block the communication between the mobile node with traceable address and the home agent.

Firewall Configuration if *MN*'s *CoA* is UntraceableAddress

If the mobile device is an Ethernet device, we could also use the MAC feature in firewall to filter it:

> *TARGET INPUT*
> *--mac-source xx:xx:xx:xx:xx:xx*
> *--destination address_of_HA*

For general purpose, we propose a firewall configuration based on the improved RR protocol and add 3 firewall patterns for the mobile node:

> *TARGET INPUT*
> *--source y:y:y:y:xxxx:xxff:fexx:xxxx*
> *--destination address_of_HA*

> *TARGET OUTPUT*
> *-- destination y:y:y:y:xxxx:xxff:fexx:xxxx*
> *--source address_of_HA*

and

> TARGET   INPUT&OUTPUT
> *--home-address   y:y:y:y:xxxx:xxff:fexx:xxxx*
> *--protocol   135 -j ACCEPT*

where --protocol 135 specifies the protocol of Mobility Header.

Now let's look at every message in the improved RR procedure in which the *HoA* and *CoA* are bundled together:

The BU_{HA} message: the message with source address *a:a:a:a:xxxx:xxff:fexx:xxxx* and destination address *address_of_HA*, home address *y:y:y:y:x:xxff:fexx:xxxx* and mobility header protocol 135. The BU_{HA} message meets the extended firewall rule and can pass the firewall.

The BA_{HA} message: the message with destination address *a:a:a:a:xxxx:xxff:fexx:xxxx*, source address *address_of_HA*, home address *y:y:y:y:x:xxff:fexx:xxxx* and mobility header protocol 135. The BA_{HA} message meets the extended firewall rule and can pass the firewall.

Upon receiving the BU_{HA} message, the home agent opens a dynamic pinhole and sets up a security tunnel for the address *a:a:a:a:xxxx:xxff:fexx:xxxx* so that following traffic packets from this address with any protocols can reach the home agent. Thereafter, the encapsulated *HoTI* and *HoT* can pass through the firewall.

3.4   Scenario of the MN Protected by Firewall(s)

Figure 4 indicates the scenario where the *MN* is within a network protected by firewall. In the specification of mobile IPv6 [1, 5], the *MN* will send/receive following messages: BU_{HA}, BA_{HA}, *HoTI*, *HoT*, *CoTI*, *CoT*, BU_{CN} and BA_{CN}.

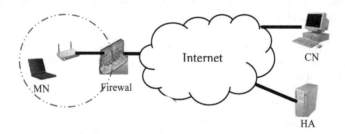

Fig. 4. MN within a network protected by a firewall

No matter if a *MN* is roaming into a visiting network or already stays in the visiting network and need to update its *CoA*, after allocated or authorized a new *CoA*, it informs its *HA* and *CN* of its current *CoA*. Since the *MN* is always the initiator, it is able to apply the pinholes from the firewall for the communications with other parties.

The procedure of the home binding update is:

1) the mobile node gets current care-of address;
2) the mobile node solicits a firewall pinhole for the communications between the care-of address and its home agent (a fixed address) with the protocol number 50 (ESP) and 135 (Mobility Header);

3) the mobile node sends the home binding update message BU_{HA} to its home agent through the pinhole;

4) the home agent sends back a acknowledgement BA_{HA} through the pinholes and set up security tunnel between the home agent and its home agent;

5) thereafter every packet between the mobile node and its home agent goes through the security tunnel.

The procedure of the correspondent binding update is:

1) the mobile node sends the *HoTI* message to its home agent through the security tunnel;

2) after receiving the *HoT* message from the correspondent node, the home agent forwards the *HoT* message to the mobile node through the security tunnel, too;

3) the mobile node solicits a firewall pinhole with protocol number 135 for the communications between the care-of address and the correspondent node;

4) the mobile node sends the *CoTI* message to its correspondent node through the pinhole;

5) the correspondent node sends back the *CoT* message through the pinhole;

6) the mobile send the binding update message BU_{CN} to its correspondent node through the pinhole;

7) the correspondent node sends back a acknowledgement BA_{CN} through the pinholes;

8) the mobile node requires to open more ports for the pinhole;

9) thereafter every packet between the mobile node and its correspondent node goes through the pinhole.

4   Analysis of Security and Performance

The purpose of the paper is to provide some schemes to make conventional firewalls suitable for mobile IPv6 network, and should not bring new threats. The paper proposed three methods: filtering MAC address, masking low 64 bits of source address and extending the firewall functions. Below we discuss and analyze the security and performance of these approaches.

1) Method of filtering MAC address: Since the method just employs the feature of the ordinary firewalls, it does not bring any further security issue. However, its application scope is limited due to the restriction of Ethernet devices.

2) Method of masking low 64 bits: As the method ignores the address prefix, it fails to detect the source location of the packets. This brings the threat of address spoofing because the firewall is opened to all nodes if they have the same interface identity, no matter where these nodes are. In order to reduce the risk, the protocol option is switch on to filter the mobility header (135). As the messages with mobility header are very small in term of size and need a little processing, it would not bring a serious threat.

The method does not introduce any new fields and operations. Hence its performance is the same as the ordinary firewall.

The application scope is also restricted due to the requirement of traceable addresses.

3) Method of extending the firewall function: In mobile IPv6 network, the *CoA* in the source address field of binding update message is no sense to the firewall rules, an identity field is required so that the firewall recognizes the packets' owner. The method extends the ordinary ip6tables' features to filter the home address in the home address option header or in typing 2 routing header.

The improved RR protocol [10] is also needed as the *CoTI/CoT* messages in original RR protocol do not contain the home address information.

The improved RR protocol provides much stronger security than the original RR protocol. It can prevent three redirect attacks: Session Hijacking Attacks, movement Halting Attacks and Traffic Permutation Attacks. This protocol just bundles *HoA* and *CoA* together in the messages of *HoTI*, *HoT*, *CoTI* and *CoT*, and does not change the original RR's architecture.

If the firewalls deployed in IPv6 networks support the 3rd addresses (Routing Header, Home Address Option or Destination Options Header), the concern of performance by the modification is minor because the architecture and operation are the similar as the original one. After all, either Routing Header or Home Address Option is an inner address and not always next to the IPv6 Header, the firewall performance will suffer and hardware implementations become difficult in this solution comparing with traditional firewalls that just check the most outside IP addresses.

5 Conclusions

We first reviewed the mechanism of mobile IPv6 networking and analyzed the exchanging messages among the mobile nodes, home agents and correspondent nodes. Then we proposed three potential solutions to make the firewall friendly in mobile IPv6 network.

For Ethernet devices, we suggested to employ the feature of MAC address filter. For the mobile nodes with traceable addresses, masking the low 64-bits of source address is a simple and efficient solution. For general mobile nodes, we introduced an extended firewall and the improved Return Routability protocol. The extended firewall could always monitor the home addresses of mobile nodes as well as the care-of addresses. It also improved the security capability of the original RR protocol without changing its architecture

References

1. Johnson, D., Perkins, C., Arkko, J.: Mobility Support in IPv6., IETF RFC 3775 (June 2004)
2. Le, F., Faccin, S., Patil, B., Tschofenig, H.: Mobile IPv6 and Firewalls: Problem Statement. IETF RFC 4487 (May 2006)
3. Thomson, S., Narten, T.: IPv6 Stateless Address Autoconfiguration. IETF RFC 2462 (December 1998)
4. Droms, R., et al.: Dynamic Host Configuration Protocol for IPv6 (DHCPv6). IETF RFC 3315 (July 2003)
5. Arkko, J., Devarapalli, V., Dupont, F.: Using IPsec to Protect Mobile IPv6 Signaling Between Mobile Nodes and Home Agents. IETF RFC 3776 (June 2004)

6. Narten, T., Nordmark, E., Simpson, W.: Neighbor Discovery for IP Version 6. IETF RFC 2461 (December 1998)
7. Deering, S., Hinden, R.: Internet Protocol, Version 6 (IPv6) Specification. IETF RFC 2460 (December 1998)
8. Narten, T., Draves, R.: Privacy Extensions for Stateless Address Autoconfiguration in IPv6. IETF RFC 3041 (January 2001)
9. Aura, T.: Cryptographically Generated Addresses (CGA). IETF RFC 3972 (March 2005)
10. Qiu, Y., Zhou, J.Y., Deng, R.: Security Analysis and Improvement of Return Routability Protocol. In: Burmester, M., Yasinsac, A. (eds.) MADNES 2005. LNCS, vol. 4074, pp. 174–181. Springer, Heidelberg (2006)
11. Linux HOWTO: ip6tables

Application of the PageRank Algorithm to Alarm Graphs

(Extended Abstract)

James J. Treinen[1,2] and Ramakrishna Thurimella[2]

[1] IBM Corporation, Boulder, CO 80301, USA
jamestr@us.ibm.com
[2] University of Denver, Denver, CO 80208, USA
ramki@cs.du.edu

Abstract. The task of separating genuine attacks from false alarms in large intrusion detection infrastructures is extremely difficult. The number of alarms received in such environments can easily enter into the millions of alerts per day. The overwhelming noise created by these alarms can cause genuine attacks to go unnoticed. As means of highlighting these attacks, we introduce a host ranking technique utilizing *Alarm Graphs*. Rather than enumerate all potential attack paths as in *Attack Graphs*, we build and analyze graphs based on the alarms generated by the intrusion detection sensors installed on a network. Given that the alarms are predominantly false positives, the challenge is to identify, separate, and ideally predict future attacks. In this paper, we propose a novel approach to tackle this problem based on the PageRank algorithm. By elevating the rank of known attackers and victims we are able to observe the effect that these hosts have on the other nodes in the Alarm Graph. Using this information we are able to discover previously overlooked attacks, as well as defend against future intrusions.

Keywords: Intrusion Detection,Security Visualization, Watch Lists, Alarm Graphs, PageRank.

1 Introduction

Managing the high volume of alarms generated by large intrusion detection environments can be very challenging. A major problem faced by those who deploy current intrusion detection technology is the large number of false alarms generated by Intrusion Detection Sensors (IDSs), which can be well over 90 percent [13,14].

Since their introduction, Attack Graphs have received considerable attention as a way to model the vulnerabilities of a network. These graphs model the paths that an attacker could take in order to successfully compromise a target. Naïve representations typically result in models that grow exponentially in the number of possible states. Because the resulting graphs are unwieldy even for small networks, recent research has focused on reducing their visual complexity and making them tractable for computational purposes [11,25].

S. Qing, H. Imai, and G. Wang (Eds.): ICICS 2007, LNCS 4861, pp. 480–494, 2007.

In this paper, we propose *Alarm Graphs*, an alternative to Attack Graphs, that are built from the alarms produced by the monitoring infrastructure. We establish that several useful insights about intrusions can be gained when these graphs are augmented with knowledge of known attacks, and are analyzed using the PageRank algorithm.

Specifically, our contributions support the following goals:

- **Risk Assessment.** When faced with the task of monitoring large networks, it is easy for human analysts to develop tunnel vision, narrowing their attention to a subset of hosts such as web servers which are commonly known to be involved in attacks. In comparison, our technique allows analysts to algorithmically assess the risk of all nodes and not lose sight of the "big picture" by considering how known attacks affect their neighbors.
- **Systematic Identification of Missed Attacks.** Our technique provides a methodical analysis of the network, and reports the full extent of damage due to an attack. This data is invaluable for forensics and intrusion prevention. When our algorithm was run against historic intrusion data, it identified compromised nodes that were missed by security personnel using manual evaluation techniques.
- **Automated Watch List Generation.** The output generated by our algorithm is a list of those hosts which have higher probability of being involved in future attacks. During our experiments, our algorithm predicted a surprisingly high number of attacks when run against historic intrusion data. For exact numbers, see Section 5.4.
- **Sensor Tuning.** During the course of our analysis, we found that hosts which generated high volumes of false alarms often repeatedly earned a high rank, despite not being involved in a genuine attack. This information provides a means to create filters to remove the false alarms, thus decreasing the overall cost associated with running the monitoring infrastructure, while increasing the overall fidelity of the alarm stream.
- **Visualization.** Alarm Graphs can be visualized using tools such as GraphViz [9]. Because the alarms are reduced to a single link between distinct hosts, as opposed to full enumeration of the alarm log, visualizations produced are compact and easily digestible by a human analyst.

The remainder of this paper is organized as follows. Related work is reviewed in Section 2. An overview of the experimental environment and a discussion of representing alarms as directed graphs is provided in Section 3. The PageRank algorithm is discussed in Section 4. We present our results in Section 5, and provide examples of attacks which were discovered using our technique. Section 6 presents concluding remarks.

2   Related Work

Prior research in the area of analyzing intrusion detection alarms has focused mainly on the classification of alarms as either false or true attacks. Julisch proposes a classification system using cluster analysis to identify the root causes of alarms in order to remove false positives from the system in [13,14]. A technique employing machine learning in conjunction with cluster analysis to identify genuine attacks based on previously labeled attacks is described by Pietraszek in [28].

Our research draws inspiration from the field of Attack Graph generation. Attack Graphs are used to model the set of possible actions that could result in a compromised network. As described by Lippmann and Ingols in [17], research on Attack Graphs has focused on three areas. The first is the modeling of network connectivity and known vulnerability findings as a means of enumerating the options available to an attacker to successfully compromise a target host [1,2,11,12,20,21,22,29]. The second is the definition of formal languages used to describe these graphs, as well as the conditions under which state transitions within them are allowed [5,30]. The third thrust of research has focused on grouping large numbers of intrusion detection alerts by compiling end-to-end attack scenarios or strategies based on Attack Graph analysis as discussed by Ning, et al. in [21,22,23].

Although various works [25,29] have discussed methods for the use of probabilistic processes to analyze Attack Graphs, they generally make the assumption that the values which describe the probability of a state transition are predefined. This is addressed by Mehta, et al. in [19], who provide a method for ranking Attack Graphs using link analysis techniques to find the values algorithmically. After the ranking values are computed for an Attack Graph, the nodes with the highest ranks are highlighted as those which have the greatest probability of being involved in an attack. Starting with these marked nodes, an analyst can then focus their attention on the most important portions of the Attack Graph, and use the information contained therein to develop mitigation strategies. It is this concept that we extend in our work by applying a similar analysis technique. Our approach differs from previous work in that rather than use Attack Graphs, we construct an Alarm Graph using the set of intrusion detection alarms triggered for a specified time period. A second key difference between our approach and the previous work is that we augment this graph with data on known attacks, and use link analysis techniques to gain deeper understanding as to how the known attacks influence other nodes in the graph.

3 Preliminaries

3.1 Data Collection

The alarms used in our analysis are generated by a set of intrusion detection sensors (IDSs) representing all major vendors. As such, our technique is technology neutral. The alarms are collected at a central Enterprise Security Manager (ESM) which consolidates them for display in a Security Operations Center (SOC). The ESM has the ability to maintain hot lists of suspicious IP addresses. If an alert is received for an address on this list, the alert is marked for higher priority review by SOC personnel. The ESM performs other automated analysis that is out of the scope of this paper.

Alarms are stored temporarily in a database on the ESM, and are periodically extracted and stored in a permanent data warehouse. The data warehouse was custom built to facilitate off-line analysis. We automatically retrieve the set of alarms used during our analysis via a query to the data warehouse, eliminating any need for manual intervention.

3.2   Modeling Alarms as Directed Graphs

Definition 1. *The set of all intrusion detection alarms A is a set of 5-tuples* $a = < t, s, d, g, n >$ *which capture the information contained in an IDS alarm.*

Each $a \in A$ is comprised of the sensor type t, either host based or network based; the source IP address of the attack s; the destination, or target IP of the attack d; the alarm signature g which describes the perceived malicious activity; and a count n describing the number of times this combination repeats. This information is stored as a table in a data warehouse, and is easily retrievable.

Table 1. Typical intrusion detection alarms

Sensor Type	Source IP	Target IP	Signature	Count
Network	10.1.1.1	10.1.1.3	Share Enumeration	500
Network	10.1.1.1	10.1.1.3	Buffer Overflow	300
Network	10.1.1.2	10.1.1.3	Buffer Overflow	300
Network	10.1.1.3	10.1.1.4	Share Enumeration	100
Host	10.1.1.4	10.1.1.4	Brute Force Login	10

Definition 2. *An* Alarm Graph *models the set of alarms A as a directed graph* $G = (V, E)$. *The set of vertices represents the IP space of A, and the set of edges models the set of detected alarms between the various IP addresses.*

Using the set of alarms A, we generate a directed graph $G = (V, E)$. We define S as the set of distinct source IP addresses, and D as the set of distinct destination IP addresses. The set of vertices $V = S \cup D$, such that each $v \in V$ represents an IP address from the set of alarms A. It is important to note that S and D are not disjoint, and in fact $S \cap D$ can make up a large percentage of the overall IP space. A directed edge $e \in E = (s, d)$ is drawn corresponding with the direction of the perceived attack. We deduce the direction of each alarm from the source IP to the destination IP address. The directed graph $G = (V, E)$ is then generated such that each IP address in the alarm set is represented as a vertex in the graph, and each edge represents the detection of one or more detected alarms between the two vertices. Alarms which are triggered by Host Intrusion Detection Sensors (HIDS), where the sensor resides on the machine being attacked, are denoted as self-loops, as the source IP address is not captured by this type of sensor.

For the purposes of our analysis, the raw alarm data shown in Table 1 is summarized by the adjacency function $f_G : S \times D \to \{0, 1\}$. We define the adjacency function f_G such that if for any $s \in S, d \in D$ an alarm is triggered by the IDS, a corresponding entry exists $f_G(s, d) = 1$, representing the directed edge $e = s \to d \in E$. Or,

$$f_G(s, d) = \begin{cases} 1 \text{ if an alarm is triggered from s to d;} \\ 0 \text{ otherwise.} \end{cases}$$

The alarms are summarized such that independent of how many alarms are triggered between distinct pairs of hosts, only one edge is drawn. The rationale behind this approach is that given the high volume of false alarms, the structure that describes the alarm flow is more important than the actual volume. This sentiment echoes Chakrabarti, et al. [4] who note during their analysis of web graphs that the link structure of the web implies underlying social networks. We extend this concept to the social structures implied by the connections present in Alarm Graphs. Understanding this link structure provides an effective means of discovering attacks that would have otherwise gone unnoticed. The results are such that the IDS alarms which are shown in Table 1 are modeled as the directed graph shown in Figure 1.

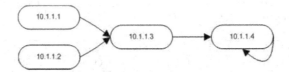

Fig. 1. Intrusion detection alarms from Table 1 as a directed graph

4   The Ranking Algorithm

We employ Page and Brin's PageRank algorithm [3,27] to analyze our Alarm Graphs. The page rank algorithm was originally designed to rank the relative importance of a web page among the set of all pages in the World Wide Web. PageRank utilizes the link structure provided via hyperlinks between web pages to gauge this importance. Each hyperlink from a page to a target page is considered a vote, or endorsement of a page's value by the page which links to it. PageRank is computed recursively, and as such, any page that is linked to from a page that has high rank will itself receive a higher rank due to the fact that an important page has linked to it. A random surfer model is assumed, in which a user selects a random starting point and navigates the web via random clicks to other pages. If a surfer lands on a page with no outbound links, known as a dangling state, they are assumed to start the process again from a new random location. It is also assumed that at any point, a surfer can randomly jump to a new starting point. This random re-entry is captured via a damping factor γ, which is divided by the number of nodes in the graph, and added to all other nodes equally. This model yields Eq. 1.

$$PR(v_i) = \frac{(1 - \gamma)}{N} + \gamma \sum_{v_j \in IN(v_i)} \frac{PR(v_j)}{|OUT(v_j)|} \qquad (1)$$

The first term of this equation represents the probability of a node being reached via a random entry into the graph, either through a bookmark or the surfer typing a known URL into the browser. The second term is the summation of the probabilities given to a state from all nodes that link into the node. As such, $\{v_1, v_2, v_3...v_n\} \in V$ are the vertices in the web graph, $IN(v_i)$ is the set of pages that link in to v_i, $|OUT(v_j)|$ is the number of links out of v_j, and N represents $|V|$ [3,27].

The output of the PageRank function is given by the vector $PR = (pr_1, pr_2, ...,$ $pr_n)$ where pr_i represents the rank of vertex v_i. The values of PR correspond to the entries of the dominant eigenvector of the normalized adjacency matrix of G. This eigenvector is defined as:

$$PR = \begin{pmatrix} pr_1 \\ pr_2 \\ \vdots \\ pr_n \end{pmatrix}$$

where PR is the solution to:

$$PR = \begin{pmatrix} \frac{1-\gamma}{N} \\ \frac{1-\gamma}{N} \\ \vdots \\ \frac{1-\gamma}{N} \end{pmatrix} + \gamma \begin{pmatrix} \alpha(v_1, v_1) & \cdots & \alpha(v_1, v_N) \\ \alpha(v_2, v_1) & \ddots & \vdots \\ \alpha(v_N, v_1) & \cdots & \alpha(v_N, v_N) \end{pmatrix} PR$$

using the adjacency function:

$$\alpha(v_i, v_j) = \begin{cases} \frac{1}{|OUT(v_j)|} & \text{if an edge exists from } v_i \text{ to } v_j; \\ 0 & \text{otherwise.} \end{cases}$$

This algorithm models the probability that a user who is randomly surfing the Internet will land on a given page [3,19,27].

4.1   Extending PageRank to Alarm Graphs

We extend the concept of ranking web graphs to ranking Alarm Graphs in the following manner. Each alarm in the alarm set has the potential to represent a genuine attack. For the purposes of our analysis, we think of an attack as a state transition from the node representing the attacker to a successful compromise of the target IP of the alarm. Following this logic, each path in the Alarm Graph represents a potential path of compromise by an attacker through the monitored network.

Using Alarm Graphs, we model the potential paths that an attacker could take through the network, as detected by the intrusion detection sensors, in lieu of the web graph which is proposed in the original PageRank discussion. Using this model, we can then analyze which nodes in the graph have the highest probability of being visited by an attacker, given random entry into the Alarm Graph.

The use of the PageRank algorithm requires that we model the IDS alarms as an ergodic Markov model. Simply put, ergodicity of a Markov model means that every state in the graph is reachable from every other state, given sufficient time. Ergodicity also guarantees that the model will converge to a stable state given sufficient time [8]. The model generated using IDS alarms is not ergodic without some modification. We remedy this in the same manner as is proposed in the original PageRank paper [27], by creating a link from all dangling states to all other nodes in the graph, where a dangling state is defined as a state in the graph from which no outbound links originate. The intuition here is that if an attacker reaches a dangling state, or the end of a potential attack path as detected by the IDS, that they can begin a new attack by jumping randomly to another portion of the graph. The PageRank algorithm captures the effect of this random re-entry into the graph via the damping factor, as described in Equation 1.

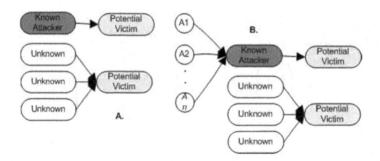

Fig. 2. Ideal coloring of an Alarm Graph

Ideally, when using this approach we would produce rankings in which nodes undergoing genuine attacks receive the highest ranks, and as the level of risk for a host decreases, so does its corresponding rank. Using these ranks, we would like to produce visualizations that highlight nodes of highest risk as shown in Figure 2a. However, in order to accomplish this consistently, we must incorporate additional information into the graph prior to executing the ranking algorithm.

4.2   Incorporation of Known Attacks

The results of data analysis are known to improve if the analysts (or algorithm) are able to include additional up front knowledge of the data set [7]. The data warehouse that stores our intrusion detection alarms also contains a labeled data set of known attacks that have been identified by the SOC during the course of monitoring the network. We will refer to this data as the set of known security incidents. Prior to ranking the Alarm Graph G, we augment the graph with this data in a manner that improves the quality of the ranking output.

The graph augmentation occurs as follows. In the same manner that a link from one web page to another can be considered a vote or endorsement for the target page, the existence of an edge to a given node in the Alarm Graph can be considered a vote that the targeted node is involved in an attack. Extending this notion, if we know for certain that a given node is involved in an attack, we would like to observe how this fact influences the other vertices in the graph. We accomplish this by annotating the graph with a set of n auxiliary nodes, each of which casts a vote for a single known attacker or victim. The size of n is variable based on the size of the Alarm Graph as a whole. For the purposes of our experiments we uniformly set $n = 50$. Our primary goal is to evaluate the risk that other nodes are extensions of known attacks. Our analysis does not evaluate physical network connectivity, rather we examine the existence of traffic between pairs of hosts that has been perceived as malicious by the IDS. It is important to note that no edges are drawn toward auxiliary nodes, which ensures that no auxiliary vertex will appear as a highly ranked host. We illustrate this technique in Figure 2b.

Given this annotated Alarm Graph we can now calculate the influence of known attackers and victims on the remaining vertices in the graph using the PageRank algorithm. PageRank is computed recursively, and once the model converges, we are able to observe the influence of these high ranking nodes on the network. The results provide us with a realistic representation of those nodes that have the highest risk of being extensions of known attacks.

5   Results

To test the efficacy of our approach, we conducted a series of experiments using intrusion detection data from a production network. The results show that our technique can be used to conduct a more complete analysis of the data produced by the intrusion detection infrastructure. The data consisted of all alarms produced within a 24-hour period. Our experiments were conducted over a 30-day period using data produced by 125 intrusion detection sensors. On average we observed 1,800 distinct source IP addresses and 1,000 target IP addresses per day. Note that for all examples, the true IP addresses have been obfuscated to protect the confidentiality of the subject network. The total number of alarms received at the SOC averaged 10,000 network IDS (NID) alarms, and 40,000 host IDS (HID) alarms per day. On average, computation of the ranks took between 2 to 5 minutes on a 1 CPU machine with 1Ghz processor and 2 Gbyte RAM, depending on the alarm volume for that day.

5.1   Emergence of Unseen Hosts and Forensic Analysis

During the course of our experiments we discovered that the vast majority of incidents were attributed to a small subset of the overall IP space. This has the adverse effect of causing the analysts to subconsciously focus on this familiar subset of IP addresses, and potentially overlook attacks occurring on other hosts. By using our algorithm, we were able to highlight newly emerging hosts for analysis. As the structure of the underlying Alarm Graph changed over time, new IP addresses moved to the top of the IP ranking automatically. Newly appearing hosts increased in rank and importance if they had a direct connection from an IP address that had been identified as a known attacker or target. This happened as a result of the new host inheriting a portion of the high rank associated with the known attacker or victim. A new host's rank also rose if it was the victim of a coordinated attack wherein it was targeted by multiple attackers. In either of these scenarios, our algorithm consistently marked these hosts as high risk.

5.2   Anomalous Alarm Pattern Recognition

By algorithmically identifying anomalous link patterns in the Alarm Graphs, we are able to highlight sets of alarms which have a higher probability of being genuine attacks. For example, the cluster of alerts shown in Figure 3 is an uncommon structure in the graph and represents the emergence of a Denial of Service (DoS) Attack.

5.3   Identification of Missed Attacks

Figure 4 demonstrates the ability of our algorithm to discover attacks which were missed by the SOC. The darker nodes in the graph are those hosts for which a known incident had occurred. The ranks of these vertices were artificially inflated using the previously described technique. The lighter color nodes represent hosts which inherited these high ranks, and were marked for inspection by our algorithm, but had not been discovered by the SOC. This example

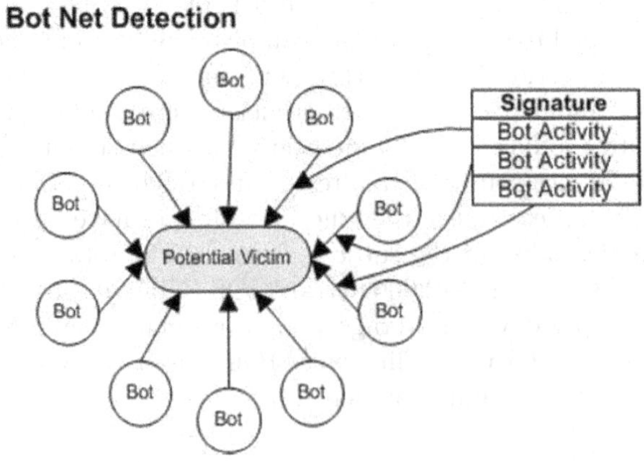

Fig. 3. Probable denial of service attack

shows a brute force dictionary attack against an FTP service running on multiple servers. The SOC detected a portion of this attack, and opened an incident record. However, the analyst only identified half of the victims of the attack. The upper half of Figure 4 illustrates those hosts which were marked as targets, while the lower left portion shows those which were missed. By elevating the rank of the attacking node, our algorithm highlighted the additional three hosts. Upon inspection, these were found to be victims of the same attack. We have included packet capture data from the alarms to further illustrate the attack.

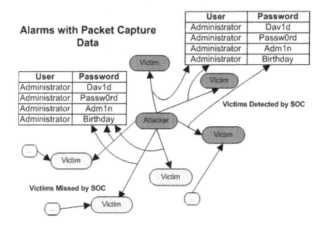

Fig. 4. Detection of partially identified dictionary attack

5.4   Automated Watch List Generation

Watch lists of suspicious IP addresses are maintained by the ESM and are used to monitor the alarm stream for any alerts generated by these hosts. Currently, these watch lists are populated manually. By using the results generated by our algorithm, it is now possible to build these watch lists automatically. By using the ranked output, we can successfully predict those IP addresses which have the highest probability of being involved in an attack during the subsequent day. Evaluation of our watch lists showed that on average we were able to successfully predict 83% of the security incidents that were manually flagged in a 30-day sample of historic alarm data. This evaluation was conducted using a watch list comprised of the 100 highest ranked IP addresses, or 3% of the roughly 3,000 unique IP addresses that triggered an alarm in the SOC on a given day.

We define successful prediction of an incident as the inclusion of either the source or destination IP address of the alarms comprising that incident on a watch list produced by our algorithm. Using our algorithm, we were able to produce a list of those IP addresses which were suspicious based on the number distinct attackers, or because they were close to hosts which held high rank in the Alarm Graph and inherited a portion of this high ranking based on the recursive calculation of the PageRank algorithm. Figure 5 illustrates the performance of the watch lists generated via the ranking algorithm over a 30-day period. For purposes of completeness, it should be noted that a diminishing return on investment is observed in watch list size. On average, when the size of the watch list was reduced to 50, the success rate fell only by 5%. If the size was increased above 100, the results improved only slightly.

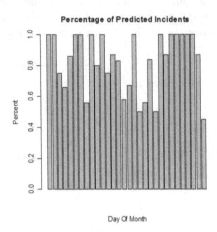

Fig. 5. 30-day trend of incident prediction using a watch list size of 100

5.5   Facilitation of Sensor Tuning

The ranking algorithm sometimes repeatedly identified hosts that received a high rank, but were not involved in genuine attacks. When this behavior was observed over a period of time, we were able to use the patterns identified by the algorithm to filter the alarms that were causing the fictitious spikes. This type of filtering improves the overall effectiveness of the IDS infrastructure as it reduces the load on the ESM and the analysts, and improves the overall quality of the incoming alarms, resulting in a higher number of genuine attacks being detected.

5.6   Visualization

Figure 6 shows a subgraph of an Alarm Graph generated from production IDS data. The full Alarm Graph is too large to display in a readable manner in print. This figure illustrates two known attacks. The nodes are colored so that the darker the color of the vertex, the higher its rank. The darkest vertices in the graph are those hosts which are known to be involved in attacks, and are shown with the corresponding auxiliary nodes added. Those vertices which are a lighter shade of gray have inherited high rankings, and will appear on the watch list generated at the end of the ranking routine. Additional gray nodes exist in the form of hosts which have received IDS alarms from multiple sources. These atypical patterns are caught by our ranking algorithm, and these hosts will appear on the watch list as well.

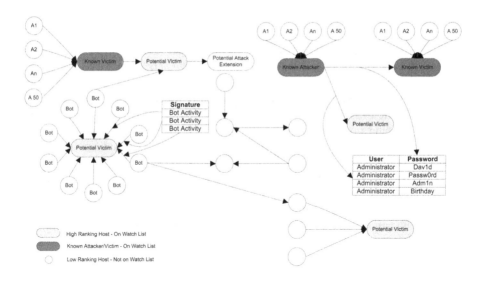

Fig. 6. Colored Alarm Graph from production network, including auxiliary nodes and attack signatures

The visual representation of the colored Alarm Graphs provides a compact model that can be used by a human analyst to quickly triage the monitored network, providing visual cues as to which systems require immediate attention. Because the alarms are summarized into a single edge per pair of hosts for which an alarm was raised, the graphs grow slowly as compared to the overall alarm volume, and are easily understood for realistic networks.

5.7   Limitations

Certain type of attacks cannot be detected using our technique. These can be classified into the following categories.

1. **Atomic Attacks.** Attacks which are comprised of a single action are very difficult to detect using our technique. However, rules generally exist in the ESM to automatically detect this type of attack. Once they are labeled in the data warehouse the ranking algorithm will detect any propagation of these attacks to other nodes.
2. **New Hosts.** In this situation, a new IP address appears in the alarm logs that has not been previously observed. Because the host was not previously in the alarm logs, it will not be included in any watch lists. This type of host can be detected using our technique for off-line analysis if one of two conditions is true. First, if the host is a descendant of a node in the Alarm Graph which is known to be involved in an incident it will inherent a portion of the high rank and appear in the watch list. Secondly, the host will be flagged if it is linked to by a sufficient number of distinct attackers.

6   Conclusion

The PageRank algorithm, when applied to annotated Alarm Graphs, is a useful tool for efficiently and methodically analyzing large sets of intrusion detection alarms. Our technique provides an effective means of performing forensic analysis to uncover attacks which were overlooked during real-time monitoring. Additionally, we are able to generate watch lists of IP addresses which are known to have high risk of being involved in an attack. The watch lists are comprised of hosts that are in close proximity to a known attacker or victim, or that are a member of an anomalous structure in the Alarm Graph.

The incorporation of known attacks into our analysis allows us to drastically improve the quality of our results. Prior to annotating the Alarm Graphs with the incident data, the rankings produced were of minimal value, as the distributions reflected the random nature of the underlying graph. However, by including the attack data we are now able to highlight those hosts that deserve a higher rank. By forcing these high ranks, we are able to observe the ripple effect of malicious hosts throughout the network. This provides an effective means of decreasing the likelihood that an attack will be lost in the noise of the false alarms.

The algorithm is being improved in the following ways:

1. Removal of Auxiliary Nodes: The main drawback of the addition of auxiliary nodes is that the size of the graph increases with each incident. By adjusting the probabilities of the incoming edges of a victim, auxiliary nodes will no longer be required.
2. Parallel Edges: Parallel edges will be drawn for distinct alarm signatures and severities which will allow us to assign more weight to nodes which trigger multiple discrete alarm signatures, or for those hosts which trigger high severity alerts.

Acknowledgment

The authors would like to thank the anonymous referees for their valuable feedback.

References

1. Ammann, P., Wijesekera, D., Kaushik, S.: Scalable, Graph-Based Network Vulnerability Analysis. In: Proceedings of the 9th ACM Conference On Computer and Communications Security, pp. 217–224. ACM Press, New York (2002)
2. Artz, M.: NETSpa: A Network Security Planning Architecture. Master's Thesis. Massachusetts Institute of Technology. (2002)
3. Brin, S., Page, L.: The Anatomy of a Large-Scale Hypertextual Web Search Engine. Computer Networks 30(1-7), 107–117 (1998)
4. Chakrabarti, S., Dom, B., Gibsony, D., Kleinberg, J., Kumar, R., Raghavan, P., Rajagopalan, S., Tomkins, A.: Mining the Link Structure of the World Wide Web. IEEE Computer 32(8) (1999)

5. Cuppens, F., Ortalo, R.: LAMBDA A Language to Model a Database for Detection of Attacks. In: Proceedings of the 3rd Annual International Symposium On Recent Advances in Intrusion Detection, Berlin, Germany (2000)
6. Cuppens, F., Miege, A.: Alert Correlation in a Cooperative Intrusion Detection Framework. In: Proceedings of the 2002 IEEE Symposium on Security and Privacy, IEEE Computer Society Press, Los Alamitos (2002)
7. Fayyad, U., Piatetsky-Shapiro, G., Smyth, P.: The KDD Process for Extracting Useful Knowledge From Volumes of Data. In: Communications of the ACM, pp. 27–34. ACM Press, New York (1996)
8. Grimmet, G., Stirzaker, D.: Probability and Random Processes. Clarendon Press, Oxford (1992)
9. GraphViz., http://www.graphviz.org
10. Honig, A., Howard, A., Eskin, E., Stolfo, S.: Adaptive Model Generation: An Architecture for the Deployment of Data Mining-based Intrusion Detection Systems. In: Barbara, D., Sushil, J. (eds.) Applications of Data Mining in Computer Security, pp. 153–194. Kluwer Academic Publishers, Boston (2002)
11. Ingols, K., Lippmann, R., Piwowarski, K.: Practical Attack Generation for Network Defense. In: Proceedings of the 22nd Annual Computer Security Applications Conference, Miami Beach, FL (2006)
12. Jajodia, S., Noel, S., O'Berry, B.: Topological Analysis of Network Attack Vulnerability. In: Kumar, V., Srivastava, J., Lazarevic, A. (eds.) Managing Cyber Threats: Issues, Approaches and Challenges, Kluwer Academic Publisher, Dodrecht, Netherlands (2003)
13. Julisch, K., Dacier, M.: Mining Intrusion Detection Alarms for Actionable Knowledge. In: Proceedings of the Eighth ACM SIGKDD International Conference on Knowledge Discovery and Data Mining, pp. 366–375. ACM Press, New York (2002)
14. Julisch, K.: Clustering Intrusion Detection Alarms to Support Root Cause Analysis. ACM Transactions on Information and System Security 6(4), 443–471 (2003)
15. Lee, W., Stolfo, S.: Data Mining Approaches for Intrusion Detection. In: Proceedings of the 7th USENIX Security Symposium, pp. 79–94 (1998)
16. Lee, W., Stolfo, S., Chan, P., Eskin, E., Fan, W., Miller, M., Hershkop, S., Zhang, J.: Real Time Data Mining-based Intrusion Detection. In: Proceedings of the 2nd DARPA Information Survivability Conference and Exposition (2001)
17. Lippmann, R., Ingols, K.: An Annotated Review of Past papers on Attack Graphs. MIT Lincoln Laboratory Technical Report (ESC-TR-2005-054) (2005)
18. Mauw, S., Oostdijk, M.: Foundations of Attack Trees. In: The 8th Annual Conference on Information Security and Cryptology, Seoul, Korea, pp. 186–198 (2005)
19. Mehta, V., Bartzis, C., Zhu, H., Clarke, E., Wing, J.: Ranking Attack Graphs. In: Proceedings of the 9th Annual International Symposium On Recent Advances in Intrusion Detection, Hamburg, Germany, pp. 127–144 (2006)
20. Moore, A., Ellison, R., Linger, R.: Attack Modeling for Information Security and Survivability. In: Software Engineering Institute, Technical Note CMU/SEI-2001-TN-01 (2001)
21. Ning, P., Cui, Y., Reeves, D.: Constructing Attack Scenarios Through Correlation of Intrusion Alerts. In: Proceedings of the 9th ACM Conference on Computer and Communications Security, ACM Press, New York (2002)
22. Ning, P., Xu, D.: Learning Attack Strategies From Intrusion Alerts. In: Proceedings of the 10th ACM Conference on Computer and Communications Security, pp. 200–209. ACM Press, New York (2003)
23. Ning, P., Cui, Y., Reeves, D., Xu, D.: Techniques and Tools for Analyzing Intrusion Alerts. ACM Transaction on Information and System Security 7(2), 274–318 (2004)

24. Noel, S., Wijesekera, D., Youman, C.: Modern Intrusion Detection, Data Mining, and Degrees of Attack Guilt. In: Barbara, D., Sushil, J. (eds.) Applications of Data Mining in Computer Security, pp. 1–31. Kluwer Academic Publishers, Boston (2002)
25. Noel, S., Jajodia, S.: Managing Attack Graph Complexity Through Visual Hierarchical Aggregation. In: IEEE Workshop on Visualization for Computer Security, IEEE Computer Society Press, Los Alamitos (2004)
26. Noel, S., Robertson, E., Jajodia, S.: Correlating Intrusion Events and Building Attack Scenarios Through Attack Graph Distances. In: Proceedings of the 20th Annual Computer Security Applications Conference (2004)
27. Page, L., Brin, S., Motwani, R., Winograd, T.: The PageRank Citation Ranking: Bringing Order to the Web (1999), http://dbpubs.stanford.edu/pub/1999-66
28. Pietraszek, T.: Using Adaptive Alert Classification to Reduce False Positives in Intrusion Detection. In: Proceedings of the 7th Annual International Symposium On Recent Advances in Intrusion Detection, Sophia Antipolis, France, pp. 102–124 (2004)
29. Sheyner, O., Haines, J., Jha, S., Lippmann, R., Wing, J.: Automated Generation and Analysis of Attack Graphs. In: IEEE Symposium on Security and Privacy, IEEE Computer Society Press, Los Alamitos (2002)
30. Templeton, S., Levitt, K.: A Requires/Provides Model for Computer Attacks. In: Proceedings of New Security Paradigms Workshop, pp. 30–38 (2000)

Drive-By Pharming

Sid Stamm[1], Zulfikar Ramzan[2], and Markus Jakobsson[1]

[1] Indiana University, Bloomington IN, USA
[2] Symantec Corporation, Mountain View CA, USA

Abstract. This paper describes an attack concept termed Drive-by Pharming where an attacker sets up a web page that, when simply viewed by the victim (on a JavaScript-enabled browser), attempts to change the DNS server settings on the victim's home broadband router. As a result, future DNS queries are resolved by a DNS server of the attacker's choice. The attacker can direct the victim's Internet traffic and point the victim to the attacker's own web sites regardless of what domain the victim thinks he is actually going to, potentially leading to the compromise of the victim's credentials. The same attack methodology can be used to make other changes to the router, like replacing its firmware. Routers could then host malicious web pages or engage in click fraud. Since the attack is mounted through viewing a web page, it does not require the attacker to have any physical proximity to the victim nor does it require the explicit download of traditional malicious software. The attack works under the reasonable assumption that the victim has not changed the default management password on their broadband router.

1 Introduction

Home Networks & Drive-by Pharming. Home broadband routers are becoming more popular as people wish to share broadband Internet access with, or provide wireless access to, all computers in their homes. These routers typically run a web server, and configuration of the router is done through a web-management interface. People assume that this internal network is safe from outside attackers since home routers are usually configured by default to reject all incoming connection requests.

However, we show that it's possible to construct a web page that, when simply viewed, can manipulate its visitors' home routers, changing its settings. The attacker can then selectively siphon off the victim's internet traffic to an attacker-controlled server, leading to the theft of sensitive credentials and identity information. The attack, which we call *Drive-by Pharming* can also enable spread of malware, target phishing attacks, or starve the visitor from critical security updates. The attacks do not require the attacker to have any physical proximity to the victim's machine. Also, the attack methodology applies equally to wired and wireless routers. The attack only assumes that the victim is running a JavaScript-enabled browser and that the default management password on the router has not been changed. Moreover, many standard protection mechanisms

S. Qing, H. Imai, and G. Wang (Eds.): ICICS 2007, LNCS 4861, pp. 495–506, 2007.

for wireless networks (e.g., encrypting the traffic through WPA), do nothing to stop these attacks.

In more detail, the paper describes a web-based automated method to detect routers on a victim's internal network and then change the router settings using JavaScript-generated host scans and a cross-site request forgery (using HTTP requests). We then describe attacks stemming from this internal network scanning, delving into the effects of changing the DNS values on home routers and how this can be used by attackers to perform more successful and difficult to detect phishing scams. We also present ways for this attack to become self-sustaining and spread in a viral fashion between routers using human users as a trigger for its spread.

Combining the results of an informal survey that found that 50% of home users use a broadband router with default or no password [11] and a formal study that shows 95% of home users allow JavaScript in their browsers [13], we estimate that 47.5% of all home users (hundreds of millions of users [8]), are potentially susceptible to the attacks we describe.

1.1 Phishing and Pharming

Phishing is a prevalent scam in which attackers masquerade as an authority in an attempt to obtain identity credentials from victims. It is a significant industry, but Gartner estimates that approximately 3% of a phishing attack's targets will fall victim [15]. Violino explains how scammers can dramatically increase their yield by spoofing DNS records for a victim domain [12]. When DNS records are spoofed, instead of going to the "correct" web site corresponding to a web site such as bank.com), victims will navigate to a fraudulent site that appears to be legitimate. The browser will even display bank.com in its address bar. The scammer can stealthily usurp all web traffic directed at the victim domain. These DNS spoof attacks, or Pharming attacks, are harder to detect than ordinary fraudulent web sites since the address bar on the browser displays the domain of the spoofed site. There is no need to lure victims to a phishing site when they will find a pharmed site on their own—removing the possibility that someone will catch an attack based on the lure. Pharming can easily be accomplished when an attacker can change settings on home routers. Traditional techniques for pharming include directly compromising a DNS server, poisoning its cache, or even compromising the HOSTS file on an end-user's PC. This paper demonstrates a different way to engage in pharming—namely, by compromising the DNS settings on the end-user's home broadband router. The paper further shows a relatively easy-to-carry-out mechanism for achieving this aim through the use of a specially crafted web page.

1.2 Attacking a Home Router

Most end users create a small internal network at home by purchasing a consumer router (such as a Linksys, Belkin, Netgear, D-Link, to name a few). For the entirety of this paper, we will discuss attacks on consumer or home routers—those purchased for use in homes and small businesses, not commercial-grade routers. Any reference in this paper to a "router" indicates the consumer routers and not commercial grade ones.

Assumptions can be made about the internal IP address of a deployed consumer router; alternatively, one can guess the visitor's internal IP address range (or detect it using a simple Java Applet [6]) and initiate a JavaScript-based host scan via the victim's browser to detect consumer routers with HTTP-based administration. Once a router is identified, the malicious (external) web site can use the victim's browser as a conduit to take control over the router on the victim's (internal) network. This leads to many attack scenarios, like modifying the router's DNS settings or changing its firmware, which we propose and describe in detail. More details and proposed countermeasures are discussed in our related Technical Report [5].

Overview. Section 2 describes related work. In Section 3, we describe how an internal network is identified, and what types of attacks emerge from control over a home router. We continue by discussing how attempts to attack a router from inside an internal network can be accomplished quickly and quietly. Section 4 describes the technology and techniques used to discover and attack an internal home router from an external web site, describing some of the JavaScript code utilized. In Section 5 we discuss the different types of attacks that can be mounted by controlling a home router and how these may spread in a socio-viral fashion.

2 Related Work

Internal Net Discovery. Kindermann has written a Java Applet that discovers a host's internal (i.e., NAT'ed) IP address [6]. Simply because this detection is accomplished via a Java Applet, and 94% of people on the Internet leave Java enabled [13], his method of internal IP discovery can be considered quite reliable. He also describes ways to prevent sites from using his technique to determine a host's internal IP: disable ActiveX, Java, and all other plug-ins.

Grossman [3] shows that once an internal IP is obtained, host scanning using JavaScript is easy by attempting to load images or scripts from a host on various ports. Likewise, scanning for web-serving hosts on a network is simple, and a list of web-serving IPs can be quickly identified. SPI Labs [17] show that existing image names and dimensions combined with the default password used to access the router can provide a "fingerprint" giving away the type of router. We use this technique combined with knowledge of default router passwords and default router DHCP schemes to quickly identify routers on internal networks — then reconfigure them. Tsow et al .[11] show how router firmware can be changed by accessing its configuration web page.

Building on these works, we illustrate stealthy attacks on internal networks that manipulate a router's settings or completely takes control by replacing the router's firmware. The attacks are both difficult for service providers and victimized consumers to detect, and also exhibit high success rates.

Bad Security Assumptions. According to Microsoft, 3.5 million Windows computers are infected with back-door trojans [1,16]; many infections are caused by web pages that automatically trigger a download of an executable or ActiveX control which the targeted user must authorize by clicking "run" when prompted. People blindly authorize these drive-by, possibly malicious executables because of repeated prompts (authorizing is the only way to stop them) or because they are unaware what the prompt means.

Drive-by virus infections are amplified when internal networks are not secured. Oppliger [9] suggested that many people who employ firewalls as a security measure might gain a false sense of complete security on the internal network. He claims they assume it will keep all bad traffic out of the internal network, thus eliminating the need for internal network protections. We show this is not the case, since an external web site set up by the attacker can attack the victim's internal network, using the browser as a conduit; the intrusion is accomplished through HTTP originating from inside the internal network — access allowed by nearly all firewall configurations. We stress that our proposed attacks do not deal with drive by personal computer infections; instead, the infection is targeted at the home routers and uses standard Web technologies (which have legitimate uses).

JavaScript Malware. It has been proposed that distributed denial of service (DDoS) attacks can be mounted from a set of clients visiting an attacker's site [7]. Using JavaScript (or similar technologies) a web site can send instructions to all of its visitors to create traffic at a victim's web site. We extend this DDoS idea by using compromised routers (which are more likely to remain in an attacker's control) as well as corrupt DNS records to create a large amount of unwanted traffic to a victim's site.

3   Intuition

Figure 1 shows how an internal network can be discovered and attacked, changing the configuration of a home router. Related work has exposed steps 1–4 of the attack shown in Figure 1. This paper explains how to accomplish step 5 (changing settings on a router) and what types of attacks this enables.

3.1   Attack Scenarios

Access to a home router from the inside can lead to its complete compromise, making it a zombie performing actions at an attacker's will. This threat is significant since most zombified hosts are personal computers, which may be restarted or removed from a network frequently in the case of notebook computers. A

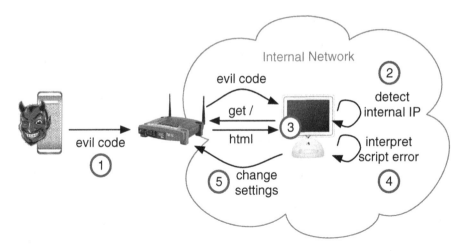

Fig. 1. How a home network's routers are attacked with Internal Net Discovery. (1) A client loads requests a page from the attacking server through the home router. The page is rendered and (2) the client's internal IP address range is either guessed or an Applet is run to detect the client's internal IP. (3) JavaScript requests resources from hosts on the network, which (4) throws JavaScript errors which the client-run page interprets to discover and fingerprint the victim's router. (5) The script attempts to change the discovered router's settings.

home router is sedentary, and often left powered on, or unattended, for months at a time, resulting in a zombie with a persistent Internet connection that more reliably responds to its controller. Additionally, home router compromise can lead to subversive DNS spoofing where DNS records are compromised on victims' local networks causing them to visit malicious sites though they attempt to navigate to legitimate ones such as http://www.securebank.com.

Security Patch DoS. An attacker could redirect requests for Windows updates or antivirus updates through his own server, which can starve affected clients from some critical patches: this leaves victims vulnerable to security flaws even after the are patched.

High-Yield Phishing. An attacker can redirect victims to his own copies of web sites that seem hosted at legit domains (like bank.com) with intent to harvest their passwords; the victims will most likely be oblivious of such a change.

High-Yield Malware. Using DNS spoofing through the compromised router, an attacker can pose as an authority (such as an antivirus website) suggesting that victims install malware that is advertised as critical software. To identify especially vulnerable targets, the attacker can record IP addresses of routers he compromises using Drive-By Pharming, and share this list with other people who have nefarious plans.

3.2   Internal Net Discovery

Since it is assumed that a network behind a firewall is safe from intruders [9], most commercial home network routers (including wireless routers used for sharing a broadband connection) are pre-configured out of the box to *disallow* administration features over the Internet, or Wide-Area Network (WAN) interface but allow administration over the internal network or Local Area Network (LAN) interfaces.

But as we describe, an attacker can still access the LAN-side configuration page from the WAN port due to the methods employed by many home users to make their single broadband connection accessible to their whole family. Most often, people purchase an inexpensive personal router/switch device to provide WiFi access to the Internet or to share a single broadband Internet connection with multiple computers. These devices usually include a NAT firewall and a DHCP server so connected computers do not have to be manually configured. Thus IP addresses are distributed to computers on the LAN from a reserved private IP space of 10.*.*.* or 192.168.*.*. Internet traffic is then routed to and from the proper computers on the LAN using a Network Address Translation (NAT) technique. Because of the employment of NAT, an attacker cannot simply connect at will to a specific computer behind the router — the router's forwarding policy must be set by the network's administrator in anticipation of this connection, thus preventing malware from entering the network in an unsolicited fashion. If a piece of malware were able to run on one of the computers behind the router, it would more easily be able to compromise devices — especially if it knows the IP addresses of other devices on the network. This is possible because it is often wrongly assumed that the router (or its firewall) will keep all the "bad stuff" out, so there is no dire need for strict security measures inside a home network.

3.3   Identifying/Configuring Routers

Once the internal IP of a victim has been identified, assumptions about the addressing scheme of the internal network can be made. For example, if Alice's internal IP is 192.168.0.10, one can assume that all of the computers on the internal network have an IP starting with 192.168.0. This knowledge can be used to scan the network for other devices, such as the router (steps 3, 4, 5 in Figure 1).

Using JavaScript (or similar logic developed with HTML and CSS), a malicious web page can "ping" hosts on the internal network to see which IP addresses host a live web-based configuration system.[1] More JavaScript can be used to load

---

[1] Most off-the-shelf routers are pre-configured to be the lowest address in the range they serve. For example, if Alice has internal IP 192.168.0.10 an attacker can comfortably assume the router has internal IP 192.168.0.1. This *greatly reduces* the number of addresses that need to be checked before attempting to compromise a router; though it is not always accurate, this assumption should be acceptable in most cases.

images from these servers — images that will be unique to each model of router, giving the malicious software a hint about how to re-configure the host.

When a router's model is known, the malicious scripts can attempt to access configuration screens using known default username/password combinations for that specific router model. By transmitting requests in the form of a query string, the router's settings can easily be changed. The preferred DNS servers, among other settings, can be manipulated easily if the router is not protected by a password or if it uses a default password.

Owners of these routers are not required to set a password! Since administration via the WAN port (the Internet) is turned off by default, some manufacturers assume no administration password is needed. Membership of a router's internal network is not sufficient to determine that a person is attempting to change the settings of a router: it could instead be JavaScript malware as described.

4   Attacking a Network

An attacker who can detect a victim's internal network has the ability to attack the router controlling the network, and thus control any data going through the compromised router. To take control, first an attacker must discover the internal IP address of the victim's router. Next, the attacker must determine the make or model of the router in an effort to understand its configuration scheme, and then eventually accesses the router and manipulates its settings from the victim's computer. All of this can be done in an automated fashion, swiftly in most cases—when routers are configured with default passwords.

4.1   Router Discovery

Many home routers have a standard internal IP address (e.g., 192.168.1.100). In other cases, the malicious web-site can deploy a very simple Java Applet [6] to detect the *internal* IP. Given the internal IP address of a host (e.g., 192.168.0.10), other IP addresses that are likely to be on the internal network are enumerated (e.g., 192.168.0.1, 192.168.0.2, ..., 192.168.0.254). Some JavaScript code then executes to append off-site <script> tags to the document resembling the following:

<**script** src="http://192.168.0.1"></**script**>

These tags tell the browser to load a script from a given URL and are commonly used to load off-site scripts with many purposes. One example of commonplace use of this is advertisement tracking: a web site embeds a script from http://adsformoney.com in order to display advertisements specified by the adsformoney.com web service. The script must be loaded from the advertisement company's site and not the publisher's site so that the advertisement company can verify the integrity of the script that is served. The effect of using script tags in this way is that a web-based request can be sent to an arbitrary server (or router) from a client's browser. Requests can thus be sent to another host on a victim's internal network through that victim's browser.

It is expected that all of these <script> elements will fail to load and generate a JavaScript error — the key is that they will fail in different ways. If the specified URL is a valid web server, the browser will fetch the root HTML page from that server and fail since the root HTML page is not valid JavaScript. If the specified URL is *not* serving web pages, the request will time out.

Leveraging error information, one can also determine the router's make and model. In particular, the router has a web server which might host an image (e.g., the manufacturer's logo). Using an <IMG> tag with onload() or onerror() handlers, one can detect the presence or absence of an image to determine which router is used.

4.2   Manipulating Routers

Routers with web-based configuration rely on HTML forms to obtain configuration data from a user. While most utilize the HTTP POST method to send data from the web browser to the router, many routers will still accept equivalent form submissions via HTTP GET. This means that form data can be submitted in the URL or query string requested from the router.

For example, the D-Link DI-524 allows configuration of the DMZ host through a web form. A DMZ or demilitarized zone host is a host on the internal network that is sent all incoming connection requests from the WAN. The form contains the input variables dmzEnable and dmzIP4. When sent the query string "/adv_dmz.cgi?dmzEnable=1&dmzIP4=10", the DI-524 enables DMZ and sets the host to 192.168.0.10. Similar query strings can be constructed for other configuration forms.

Swift Attack Scenario. Additionally, it is important to note that all of these seemingly sequential attack stages can be accomplished in one step. Consider a web site whose only aim is to set the DMZ host to 192.168.0.10 on all networks using DI-524 routers with default passwords (the DI-524 has a null administrator password by default). The author of the site could embed this script tag in his HTML to attempt this attack:

<script src = "http://<ip>/adv_dmz.cgi?dmzEnable=1&dmzIP4=10"></script>

This attack will only fail if the owner of the victim network has set a password or is not using a DI-524. Following is another plausible example that specifies a default username and password for a router:

<script src = "http://root:pwd@<ip>/apply.cgi?DNS_serv=p.com"></script>

5   New Attacks

We have shown how routers' IP addresses can be discovered and their configurations can be changed using JavaScript. This leaves networks that are vulnerable to Internal Network Detection open to DNS spoofing, or Pharming, as well as complete router control or zombification. Additionally, compromise of home routers has the potential to spread in a viral fashion, by turning routers into sources of the exploit, then advertising their existence.

5.1   Pharming

We implemented a DNS-configuration change by compromising a D-Link DI-524. By accessing a website with simple Java and JavaScript (as documented in Section 3.2) to detect our internal network we found the router's IP address. Additionally, the JavaScript was able to identify our router model by successfully loading an image. *We stress that this image was available from the router without authenticating. Only web page requests required authentication on this model.* Once the router model was identified (by IP address and image loaded), a request to change the DNS server settings was sent to the router:

<**script src** = "http://192.168.0.1/h_wan_dhcp.cgi?dns1=w.x.y.z"></**script**>

This changed the DNS server address distributed by the router to w.x.y.z, one *other* than the one specified by our service provider. We set up a test (rogue) DNS server at this location, and included fraudulent DNS records for some popular web sites. When we attempted to access these web sites, the DNS requests were directed to the *new* DNS server specified by our exploit, and IP address to which the requests were resolved directed us to a fake page. We developed similar proof of concepts for the Linksys WRT54GS and NetGear WGR614 routers. We remark that when DNS server settings change, the browser will do a fresh look-up for each domain, so measures like DNS pinning [4] will fail to provide protection.

5.2   Growing Zombies

The DNS-server address-changing attack relies on the attacker controlling a DNS server. Another method of attack would be to modify the router's software to contain persistent false records [11]. The malicious firmware can be pre-configured to serve bad DNS data itself. Alternatively, the firmware can "phone home" to an attacker's server and identify itself as a compromised "zombie." This can be done much in the fashion that malware currently "zombifies" computers. These zombies can be configured to perform DDoS attacks or to allow the attacker to change the set of spoofed DNS records at any time.

A victim, who visits the attacker's web site, becomes vulnerable to internal network discovery, and thus router is compromised. Next, the malicious web page tells the router to enable "WAN port administration" so that an arbitrary Internet host can configure it. The victim's browser then contacts the attacking server to begin "updating" the router's firmware. The attacker's server, easily detecting the *external IP* of the router (which is the same as the external IP of the victim's computer) then accesses the router over the WAN port. The server uploads new firmware to the router, which is then configured to behave in any way the attacker desires. If desired, the attacker can ensure the router will behave as it did before compromise, but with subtle modifications such as remote control. The victim's router is now a zombie under the control of the attacker.

Proof of Concept. We implemented this router firmware modification by compromising a D-Link DI-524 as described. A client within the DI-524's internal network accessed our malicious web page. The web page targeted the DI-524, which was configured with default settings (no password). The web page caused the router's WAN port configuration to become enabled. Next, the web page sent a request-based message back to its' host server which used the remote IP of the request (the victim's and his router's external IP) to access the router with the default password (blank). Finally, the malicious server transmitted new firmware to the router, changing the version of the firmware on the router.

5.3   Viral Spread

Zombifying routers by replacing firmware can be deployed through a web page executing JavaScript on one of the router's internal network hosts. A router compromised in this fashion is open to a staggeringly large variety of purposes. There is nothing to say that the new firmware may contain web serving software and content *including the malicious scripts themselves*. Effectively, a compromised router could be transmogrified into a router that also serves the virus that compromised it.

An infected router could be instructed to use search engines to locate web-based bulletin boards, and post its address to lure readers into viewing its content. This mechanism would draw unwitting victims to infect their own networks—resulting in a spread from router to router via human-initiated transmission. This socio-viral spread, much like the social spread of other malware [10], will depend on the content of the viral site to spread itself.

This viral spread mechanism is hard to "shut down" since there are presumably many infected routers. In other words, there is no single source that can be turned off. In contrast, if a single web site hosts malicious code, then the site's owner can potentially be contacted for a takedown.

6   Conclusions

This paper described a new attack concept, termed *Drive-by Pharming*, that provides an alternate (and in our opinion easy-to-carry-out) method by which a pharming attack can be mounted. The attacker creates a web page, that simply when viewed by the victim, changes the DNS settings on the victim's home broadband router. From then on, when the victim navigates to his usual web sites, his data can be siphoned off to an attacker. The victim will likely be unaware that this change has taken place since even the address bar on his browser will indicate that he is viewing a legitimate web page. The attack requires that the victim run a JavaScript-enabled browser and use the default password on their home broadband router – both of which happen reasonably often enough to make the attack's implications widespread.

We developed proof-of-concept code to demonstrate the Drive-by Pharming attack on three popular home broadband routers. We also explained how this drive-by modification of router settings can be used to help ease the spread of viruses by denying automated security upgrades and patches to victims.

The attacks demonstrate that even with well-defined security policies, extensive firewall and IPS rules, as well as the growing enforcement of the same-origin policies on web browsers, attacks based on Internal Network Detection are still very much possible. These attacks use the victim's browser as a conduit to their internal network. As the complexity of both the web and web browsing environment grow, we expect that many similar attack concepts will be discovered in the future.

Acknowledgments

We thank Alex Tsow for insight on how common home routers behave.

References

1. Braverman, M.: Windows Malicious Software Removal Tool: Progress Made, Trends Observed, Microsoft Antimalware Team Whitepaper (November 10, 2006)
2. Gandhi, M., Jakobsson, M., Ratkiewicz, J.: Badvertisements: Stealthy Click-Fraud with Unwitting Accessories. Anti-Phishing and Online Fraud, Part I Journal of Digital Forensic Practice 1(2) (November 2006)
3. Grossman, J., Niedzialkowski, T.C.: Hacking Intranet Websites from the Outside: JavaScript malware just got a lot more dangerous. Black Hat Briefings, Las Vegas, NV USA (2006)
4. Haque, M.A.: DNS: Spoofing and Pinning,
   http://viper.haque.net/~timeless/blog/11/
5. Stamm, S., Ramzan, Z., Jakobsson, M.: Drive-By Pharming, Indiana University Computer Science Technical Report 641 (December 13, 2006)
6. MyAddress Applet by Lars Kindermann (2003) (Page accessed) (October 17, 2006),
   http://reglos.de/myaddress/MyAddress.html
7. Lam, V.T., Antonatos, S., Akritidis, P., Anagnostakis, K.G.: Puppetnets: misusing web browsers as a distributed attack infrastructure. In: Proceedings of the 13th ACM Conference on Computer and Communications Security (CCS 2006), ACM Press, New York (2006)
8. Madden, M.: Internet Penetration and Impact. Pew Internet and American Life Project Memo (April 26, 2006),
   http://www.pewinternet.org/PPF/r/182/report_display.asp
9. Oppliger, R.: Internet security: firewalls and beyond. Communications of the ACM 40(5), 92–102 (1997)
10. Stamm, S., Jakobsson, M., Gandhi, M.: Social Propogation of Malware,
    http://www.indiana.edu/~phishing/verybigad/
11. Tsow, A., Jakobsson, M., Yang, L., Wetzel, S.: Warkitting: the Drive-by Subversion of Wireless Home Routers. The Journal of Digital Forensic Practice (2006)

12. Violino, B.: After Phishing? Pharming! CSO Magazine (October 2005),
    http://www.csoonline.com/read/100105/pharm.html
13. TheCounter.com Statistics, Jupitermedia Corporation (April 2007),
    http://www.thecounter.com/stats
14. Survey Reveals the Majority of U.S. Adult Computer Users Are Unprotected from
    Malware, ESET software press release (July 17, 2006),
    http://eset.com/company/article.php?contentID=1553
15. Gartner Says Number of Phishing E-Mails Sent to U.S. Adults Nearly Doubles in
    Just Two Years, Gartner, Inc. Press Release (November 9, 2006),
    http://www.gartner.com/it/page.jsp?id=498245‾
16. Microsoft says Half of Windows Computers Have Trojans, Internet News (October
    26, 2006), http://www.internetnews.com/security/article.php/3640216
17. Detecting, Analyzing, and Exploiting Intranet Applications using JavaScript, SPI
    Labs Research Brief (accessed October 17, 2006), http://www.spidynamics.com/
    spilabs/education/articles/JS-portscan.html
18. The Symantec Internet Security Threat Report, Symantec Corporation. vol. 10
    (September 2006),
    http://www.symantec.com/enterprise/threatreport/index.jsp

Author Index

Lecture Notes in Computer Science

Sublibrary 4: Security and Cryptology

Vol. 4284: X. Lai, K. Chen (Eds.), Advances in Cryptology – ASIACRYPT 2006. XIV, 468 pages. 2006.

Vol. 4283: Y.Q. Shi, B. Jeon (Eds.), Digital Watermarking. XII, 474 pages. 2006.

Vol. 4266: H. Yoshiura, K. Sakurai, K. Rannenberg, Y. Murayama, S.-i. Kawamura (Eds.), Advances in Information and Computer Security. XIII, 438 pages. 2006.

Vol. 4258: G. Danezis, P. Golle (Eds.), Privacy Enhancing Technologies. VIII, 431 pages. 2006.

Vol. 4249: L. Goubin, M. Matsui (Eds.), Cryptographic Hardware and Embedded Systems - CHES 2006. XII, 462 pages. 2006.

Vol. 4237: H. Leitold, E.P. Markatos (Eds.), Communications and Multimedia Security. XII, 253 pages. 2006.

Vol. 4236: L. Breveglieri, I. Koren, D. Naccache, J.-P. Seifert (Eds.), Fault Diagnosis and Tolerance in Cryptography. XIII, 253 pages. 2006.

Vol. 4219: D. Zamboni, C. Krügel (Eds.), Recent Advances in Intrusion Detection. XII, 331 pages. 2006.

Vol. 4189: D. Gollmann, J. Meier, A. Sabelfeld (Eds.), Computer Security – ESORICS 2006. XI, 548 pages. 2006.

Vol. 4176: S.K. Katsikas, J. López, M. Backes, S. Gritzalis, B. Preneel (Eds.), Information Security. XIV, 548 pages. 2006.

Vol. 4117: C. Dwork (Ed.), Advances in Cryptology - CRYPTO 2006. XIII, 621 pages. 2006.

Vol. 4116: R. De Prisco, M. Yung (Eds.), Security and Cryptography for Networks. XI, 366 pages. 2006.

Vol. 4107: G. Di Crescenzo, A. Rubin (Eds.), Financial Cryptography and Data Security. XI, 327 pages. 2006.

Vol. 4083: S. Fischer-Hübner, S. Furnell, C. Lambrinoudakis (Eds.), Trust and Privacy in Digital Business. XIII, 243 pages. 2006.

Vol. 4064: R. Büschkes, P. Laskov (Eds.), Detection of Intrusions and Malware & Vulnerability Assessment. X, 195 pages. 2006.

Vol. 4058: L.M. Batten, R. Safavi-Naini (Eds.), Information Security and Privacy. XII, 446 pages. 2006.

Vol. 4047: M.J.B. Robshaw (Ed.), Fast Software Encryption. XI, 434 pages. 2006.

Vol. 4043: A.S. Atzeni, A. Lioy (Eds.), Public Key Infrastructure. XI, 261 pages. 2006.

Vol. 4004: S. Vaudenay (Ed.), Advances in Cryptology - EUROCRYPT 2006. XIV, 613 pages. 2006.

Vol. 3995: G. Müller (Ed.), Emerging Trends in Information and Communication Security. XX, 524 pages. 2006.

Vol. 3989: J. Zhou, M. Yung, F. Bao (Eds.), Applied Cryptography and Network Security. XIV, 488 pages. 2006.

Vol. 3969: Ø. Ytrehus (Ed.), Coding and Cryptography. XI, 443 pages. 2006.

Vol. 3958: M. Yung, Y. Dodis, A. Kiayias, T.G. Malkin (Eds.), Public Key Cryptography - PKC 2006. XIV, 543 pages. 2006.

Vol. 3957: B. Christianson, B. Crispo, J.A. Malcolm, M. Roe (Eds.), Security Protocols. IX, 325 pages. 2006.

Vol. 3956: G. Barthe, B. Grégoire, M. Huisman, J.-L. Lanet (Eds.), Construction and Analysis of Safe, Secure, and Interoperable Smart Devices. IX, 175 pages. 2006.

Vol. 3935: D.H. Won, S. Kim (Eds.), Information Security and Cryptology - ICISC 2005. XIV, 458 pages. 2006.

Vol. 3934: J.A. Clark, R.F. Paige, F.A.C. Polack, P.J. Brooke (Eds.), Security in Pervasive Computing. X, 243 pages. 2006.

Vol. 3928: J. Domingo-Ferrer, J. Posegga, D. Schreckling (Eds.), Smart Card Research and Advanced Applications. XI, 359 pages. 2006.

Vol. 3919: R. Safavi-Naini, M. Yung (Eds.), Digital Rights Management. XI, 357 pages. 2006.

Vol. 3903: K. Chen, R. Deng, X. Lai, J. Zhou (Eds.), Information Security Practice and Experience. XIV, 392 pages. 2006.

Vol. 3897: B. Preneel, S. Tavares (Eds.), Selected Areas in Cryptography. XI, 371 pages. 2006.

Vol. 3876: S. Halevi, T. Rabin (Eds.), Theory of Cryptography. XI, 617 pages. 2006.

Vol. 3866: T. Dimitrakos, F. Martinelli, P.Y.A. Ryan, S. Schneider (Eds.), Formal Aspects in Security and Trust. X, 259 pages. 2006.

Vol. 3860: D. Pointcheval (Ed.), Topics in Cryptology – CT-RSA 2006. XI, 365 pages. 2006.

Vol. 3858: A. Valdes, D. Zamboni (Eds.), Recent Advances in Intrusion Detection. X, 351 pages. 2006.

Vol. 3856: G. Danezis, D. Martin (Eds.), Privacy Enhancing Technologies. VIII, 273 pages. 2006.

Vol. 3786: J.-S. Song, T. Kwon, M. Yung (Eds.), Information Security Applications. XI, 378 pages. 2006.

Vol. 3108: H. Wang, J. Pieprzyk, V. Varadharajan (Eds.), Information Security and Privacy. XII, 494 pages. 2004.

Vol. 2951: M. Naor (Ed.), Theory of Cryptography. XI, 523 pages. 2004.

Vol. 2742: R.N. Wright (Ed.), Financial Cryptography. VIII, 321 pages. 2003.